Warman's Jewelry

CHRISTIE ROMERO

Wallace-Homestead Book Company
Radnor, Pennsylvania

Volumes in the
Encyclopedia of Antiques and Collectibles
Harry L. Rinker, Series Editor

Warman's Americana & Collectibles, 6th Edition,
edited by Harry L. Rinker

Warman's American Pottery & Porcelain,
by Susan and Al Bagdade

Warman's Country Antiques & Collectibles, 2nd Edition,
by Dana Gehman Morykan and Harry L. Rinker

Warman's English & Continental Pottery & Porcelain, 2nd Edition,
by Susan and Al Bagdade

Warman's Furniture,
edited by Harry L. Rinker

Warman's Glass,
by Ellen Tischbein Schroy

Warman's Jewelry,
by Christie Romero

Warman's Oriental Antiques,
by Gloria and Robert Mascarelli

Warman's Paper,
by Norman E. Martinus and Harry L. Rinker

Copyright © 1995 by Christie Romero
All Rights Reserved

Published in Radnor, Pennsylvania 19089, by Wallace-Homestead,
a division of Chilton Book Company

Author photo by Jimmie Romero

Manufactured in the United States of America

Library of Congress Cataloging in Publication Data

Romero, Christie.
   Warman's jewelry / Christie Romero.
      p.   cm.—(Encyclopedia of antiques and collectibles)
   Includes bibliographical references and index.
   ISBN 0-87069-696-3
   1. Jewelry—History—19th century—Catalogs. 2. Jewelry—
History—20th century—Catalogs. 3. Jewelry—Collectors and
collecting—Catalogs. I. Title. II. Series.
NK7309.8.R66   1995
739'.27'09034075—dc20   94-25278
                                      CIP

2 3 4 5 6 7 8 9 0   4 3 2 1 0 9 8 7 6

CONTENTS

Part III   Twentieth-Century Jewelry

Part IV   Special Collectible Jewelry

ACKNOWLEDGMENTS

This is the "credit where credit is due" department. The list is long. Trite though it may seem to say, it is also true that this book would not have been possible without the help, support, and encouragement of a great many people, including all of my dealer and collector friends and colleagues who lent jewelry and gave information, and my insatiably curious, ever-inquisitive students, past, present, and future—especially the "lifers" and "repeat offenders" (you know who you are)—for whom this book was written.

A special note of appreciation for some special people: To Sherry Shatz, friend, assistant, and proofreader, my undying gratitude for her unflagging, indispensable help, for becoming "computer literate" in order to enter data for me, for compiling words for the glossary, and for telling me when my sentences didn't read right. To my pal Liz Cook, deepest thanks for her gemological and descriptive expertise, and for taking time out of her busy schedule to lend me a hand (and jewelry) whenever I needed it. To my esteemed colleague Janet Zapata, heartfelt appreciation for her advice, knowledge, empathy (or should I say commiseration?), and encouragement. I am also indebted to Sam Gassman, a Renaissance man, for generosity beyond measure with his time, expertise, and jewelry. To Joyce Albers, Milly Combs, Mary Lou Diebold, Gail Gerretsen, Ellen Hoffs, Leigh Leshner, Cheri Mulligan, Terrance O'Halloran, Kirsten Olson, Connie Parente, Chuck Pinkham, and Victoria Taylor, who willingly entrusted me with *tons* of jewelry from their inventories and collections, I am especially grateful. Thanks, too, to Julie Robinson for her sharing of painstaking research, correspondence and hours of phone conversations, and to Tom Paradise for his scholarly contributions and hours of phone conversations. My telephone interviews with studio artists Claire Falkenstein, Florence Resnikoff, Merry Renk, and Richard Gompf yielded important firsthand information. I thank dealer/collector/writer Ellen Hoffs for introducing me to them, for lending me her reference material, and for her professional critique. Historian Toni Greenbaum and gallery owner Steven Cabella also generously shared their extensive knowledge.

Credit is due in particular to my consulting editor, Harry L. Rinker, whose idea this was in the first place. Little did I know then what I was in for when I agreed to add a volume on jewelry to the *Warman's Encyclopedia of Antiques and Collectibles*. It has been an elucidating experience. Thanks Harry, for your guidance and sage counsel. Thanks too, to your staff at Rinker Enterprises and the Institute for the Study of Antiques and Collectibles: Ellen T. Schroy, for *her* invaluable experience and advice; Terese, Dana, and Nancy for their assistance, and Harry, Jr. for his artistic contributions. To my editor at Chilton, Troy Vozzella, appreciation for his patience, forbearance, and willingness to listen to all my concerns.

Several auction house personnel deserve mention for their assistance: Peter Shemonsky at Grogan's (for his verbal skills as well as for photos and information on items in his sales), Mary Borchert at Butterfield's Los Angeles, Sharon Dunning at Dunning's, Gloria Lieberman and Virginia Salem at Skinner's, and Carol Elkins at Sotheby's West. In the research department, the staff at the G.I.A. Library—Elise Misiorowski, Dona Dirlam, and Jo Ellen Cole—gave invaluable aid. Thanks too, to Sandy Rosenbaum in the Costume and Textile Dept. at the L.A. County Museum of Art for the use of the library, research librarians at the Library of

Congress, L.A. and Long Beach Public Libraries, and my stepsister, researcher Lauren Dines. To Bob McIntosh and his staff at Black & White Photo Company, Karen and Cindy, thanks for making my photographic efforts look good. To photographer Frank Cooper and wife Suzanne, thanks for advice and a great cover photo. My appreciation goes to Gail Dremel for her computer literacy and for her assistance in getting me organized during the beginning stages.

For their support and words of encouragement, thanks to authors Lillian Baker and Dr. Joe Sataloff, and to my longtime friends (and frequent contributors to my collection), dealers Frankie Church (my earliest mentor), Gilly Phipps, Judy Hafdahl, and Leah Weis. To my mother and stepfather, Peggy and Norm Levine, my father Sam Schultz, my brother and "coach" Ron Schultz (and his jewelry-loving wife and daughters, Laura, Johana, and Emily)—writers all—gratitude for my "good training" and for having faith in me.

And finally, to my dear, ever-supportive husband, Jimmie, the Mr. Wiz who kept my computer working, put up with all my trials and tribulations, and did housework, too!: I dedicate this book to you, with love.

Christie S. Romero

INTRODUCTION

Warman's Jewelry is a "field guide" to styles and types of antique, period, and vintage collectible jewelry currently on the market in the United States. It is for anyone who owns old jewelry, whether it is a collector's collection, a dealer's inventory, an heir's inheritance, a packrat's accumulation, or a garage-saler's find. No matter how they've acquired it, most people want to know the same basic things about a piece: how old it is, where and how it was made, who made it, what it is made of, and the ubiquitous bottom line, what it is worth. Jewelry has always been kept and worn for many different reasons, but only within the last ten to fifteen years has conscientious collecting (by style or period, material, country of origin, etc.) become a major reason to buy. As greater numbers of collectors have entered the field, there has been a growing need for more information about the many varieties of collectible jewelry being bought and sold today. *Warman's Jewelry* was written in response to that need.

The focus of this book is American: what was made here, and what is now available here. Americans tend to have an "inferiority complex" when it comes to competing with what was produced in Europe. This attitude is beginning to change with the burgeoning recognition and appreciation of American talents and ingenuity. Several categories are included which have not received a great deal of attention in other price guides: American Arts & Crafts, post-war modernist American studio artists, '50s and '60s fine jewelry, and a Special Collectibles section which covers Native American jewelry and the product of two regions which are closely tied to the U.S.: Mexican and Scandinavian jewelry.

Jewelry is the only art form where the "intrinsic" value of the materials from which it is made can have greater value than the work itself. Many beautiful and historically significant pieces have been destroyed for their stones and metal, particularly after a certain style becomes "outdated" or "old-fashioned." This usually happens before there is retrospective appreciation for the style, before it becomes "collectible."

Stones and metal are paint and canvas. Rare and beautiful stones can be used to great effect to enhance a jewel. However, supply and demand and the public's perceptions can alter value. For example, aluminum was once a rare and valuable metal, and platinum was looked upon as "unripe gold." While our culture has consistently placed a higher value on gold and precious gemstones (diamonds, rubies, sapphires, and emeralds), other factors, such as craftsmanship, design and designer, and provenance, as well as rarity and desirability, can outweigh intrinsic value. The following table of seven criteria (3 **C**s, 2 **D**s, 2 **S**s), with questions to ask when evaluating a piece of jewelry, can be a useful aid:

Craftsmanship—Is it well made, with attention to details and finish?

Condition—Are there any cracks, chips, dents, missing parts, metal corrosion, or other damage? Are all parts original? Has it been repaired? Is there evidence of lead solder on precious metal?

Color—Especially important in costume jewelry. Is/are the color(s) currently fashionable, popular? In gemstones, is the color desirable for its kind?

Design—Can the style be attributed to the period in which it was made? Can it be attributed to a particular maker? Is the piece balanced and proportioned? Does it have "eye appeal"? (this is a subjective evaluation)

Demand—Is the piece highly sought after, currently in vogue?

Scarcity—Is this a rare item, or is it commonly available?

Size—Is it a large or small piece? Is the size appropriate for the style? (Large size is usually more desirable, but style and the wearer's proportions should also be taken into consideration)

Note that age alone does not make a piece valuable. A badly made and poorly designed 150-year-old piece is worth no more today than it was when it was first produced. If it is in poor condition, it is probably worth less! A loupe or magnifier is an essential tool for examining a piece of jewelry. Ten power (10×) is the standard magnification. In addition to detecting alterations and repairs, a loupe is necessary to read hallmarks and maker's marks, to evaluate condition, and to analyze materials (stones, metal, enamel, etc.) and construction. It is important to scrutinize a piece thoroughly, both front *and* back, in order to detect the clues that will tell you what you need to know before you buy.

A word of caution is in order when buying gemstone-set jewelry. The public has been conditioned to believe that the intrinsic value of all gemstones is high and that jewelry set with them is expensive. To some extent this is true, but the range of gemstone values is wide and variables are many. Unless you have some gemological knowledge and have studied the complexities of the market carefully, you can easily get burned. Your best defense against ripoff is your *own* knowledge, but when in doubt, consult a gemologist (G.G., F.G.A., or C.G.A.) for gemstone identification, a qualified gemstone appraiser (who should also be a gemologist) for values. Another caveat: Appraisers are not licensed or regulated by law, but some of them are credentialed by recognized national appraisal organizations. Make sure the appraiser you choose has had the proper training and experience.

In order to truly understand old jewelry, you must see and handle a *lot* of it. Readers are encouraged to avail themselves of every opportunity to do so, including attending shows, flea markets, museum exhibitions, and seminars, conferences, and classes on antique jewelry. A unique opportunity to enhance one's knowledge with lectures and hands-on experience takes place annually in July at the University of Maine in Orono, the Antique & Period Jewelry and Gemstones Course known colloquially as "Jewelry Camp," directed by Joyce Jonas.

The Gemological Institute of America and three national appraisal organizations (American Society of Appraisers, International Society of Appraisers, National Association of Jewelry Appraisers) respectively provide specialized instruction in gemology and gems and jewelry valuation theory and techniques. A correspondence course in jewelry appraisal, The Master Valuer Program, is also available.

My own classes in antique, period and vintage jewelry are held in Southern California at various locations throughout the year, and annually at the Institute for the Study of Antiques and Collectibles in Emmaus, Pennsylvania.

Another opportunity to see, handle and closely examine antique and period jewelry is the auction preview. Christie's and Sotheby's in New York City hold "important" and "magnificent" jewelry sales at which historically and gemologically significant pieces are offered. If in-person inspection is not possible, the color catalogs for these sales, which include biographical and other pertinent information, are excellent reference resources. These and the other auction houses whose names and addresses appear on page xx, also offer a wide range of antique, period, and contemporary jewelry, and were the sources for much of the fine jewelry pictured and listed in this book. All of them hold previews of upcoming sales which are well worth attending. Their catalogs, with prices realized, provide up-to-date market information.

ORGANIZATION OF THE BOOK

Warman's Jewelry is divided into four main sections: Victorian Jewelry, Turn of the Century Jewelry, Twentieth Century Jewelry, and Special Collectible Jewelry. Within each section, the listings are arranged by category in the manner most appropriate and conducive to locating a particular type of piece. Within each category, the listings are alphabetical by type of piece (Bracelet, Brooch/Pin, etc.). A timeline precedes and a glossary follows the main body of the book. The index is cross-referenced by type of piece (e.g., all earrings listings), name of maker/designer (e.g., all pieces made by Eisenberg), material (e.g., all pieces made of jet), and motif (e.g., animals).

Timeline: One of the unique features of *Warman's Jewelry* is the timeline. Its purpose is to aid in circa-dating and to put jewelry in context with other relevant historical events, discoveries and inventions. It also summarizes some of the information included in the text of each section. The dates can be used to set the earliest and/or latest possible circa date for a piece. For example, demantoid garnets were discovered in the Urals in 1868. Therefore a piece set with demantoids cannot logically date before 1870, and is more likely to be circa 1880 or 1890.

Construction methods, materials and findings, if unaltered, can also be helpful circa-dating clues. For example, the safety catch for brooches was introduced around the turn of the century (several different versions were patented at about the same time). An original safety catch on a brooch, then, is a telltale sign of twentieth century manufacture. Care must be taken, however, to ascertain that the finding is in fact original. Alterations on old pieces are common.

Patents are another useful circa-dating tool, when used as a clue to a piece's age in addition to other factors, such as style and manufacturer's dates of operation. In the listings, patent numbers found on the back of a piece are given along with the corresponding year in which the patent was issued. (Prior to the 1930s, the patent's actual date of issue is more often stamped on a piece, rather than the number.) This is not necessarily the year in which the piece was made, as patents are valid for seventeen years (design patents for fourteen). The piece could have been made later, but it certainly could not have been made *earlier* than the year the patent was issued.

Clothing styles have often dictated or at least influenced types and styles of jewelry, so it is helpful to have some knowledge of fashion history when researching and dating a piece. Significant events related to fashion are listed in the timeline, but space did not permit the inclusion of every stylistic change in clothing and jewelry fashion. Some of this information can be found in the text of each section, and, for further information, books on fashion history are included in the references.

The dates given in the timeline are as accurate as could be ascertained. I attempted to confirm each date in two or more sources, using original sources or notations whenever possible. Research is never complete, however. New information continues to be discovered which sometimes contradicts previously published "facts." Different dates are often given in various sources for the same event. Sometimes there is a span of a number of years between date of first invention and dates of patenting, perfecting, publishing results, commercialization, and common use. One source may cite, for example, the date a new manufacturing process was *patented*, but another may give the date it was *invented*, perhaps five years earlier. Or it may have taken its inventor five years to perfect, and may not have been available to the public for another five. The difficult task for historians is to decide which date is the most accurate, significant and helpful. We don't always agree. Analysis of history is often a matter of subjective interpretation.

History: Jewelry does not exist in a vacuum. Fashion and history have a cause-and-effect relationship to jewelry designs. Events, discoveries, inventions, social trends and fads play important roles in jewelry history. Each category of this book is prefaced by an encapsulated history, so that readers will understand why a particular piece of jewelry was made and worn during a given period. Design elements that identify a particular style or period, and well-known designers and manufacturers are also included.

It is not always possible to pinpoint the age of a piece exactly. A dated publication can help to circa-date a piece, but relying on only one piece of evidence can also be misleading. Some "models" (manufacturers' name for designs) continued to be made for many years, even decades, as long as they were popular and sold well. There is a "bell curve" to every style or trend—an ascension, peak, and tapering off in popularity. Styles evolve, coexist, and overlap. This is better understood when history is viewed as a continuum of *simultaneous* events, rather than as a linear succession of events. Improved methods of communication have hastened the rate of influence and change over the past century and a half; today, trends come and go at breakneck speed. Historians used to record changes in fashion by the decade; now changes occur annually. Today's pieces should be easier for future historians to circa-date.

References: For further information, a number of books and other references that relate to specific jewelry topics are listed within each section and category. Those that cover several topics are listed under each relevant category. Because of growing interest and the constant need for updated information, new titles and new editions appear every year. At press time, the following books of a general nature were in print. Some of these and some out-of-print and specialized publications may only be available through book dealers who specialize in books on antiques and/or gems and jewelry. Many of them publish catalogs of their inventory, run ads in antiques trade papers, or sell at shows. Ask to be put on their mailing lists. Listed are author, title, most recent edition, publisher (if self-published, listed as "published by author"), and date of publication.

Lillian Baker, *100 Years of Collectible Jewelry, 1850-1950*, Collector Books, 1978, 1993 value update; Vivienne Becker, *Antique & Twentieth Century Jewellery*, 2nd ed., N.A.G. Press, 1987; Howard L. Bell, Jr., *Cuff Jewelry*, published by author, 1994; Jeanene Bell, *Answers to Questions About Old Jewelry, 1840-1950*, 3rd ed., Books Americana, 1992; David Bennett & Daniela Mascetti, *Understanding Jewellery*, 2nd ed., Antique Collectors' Club, 1994; Roseann Ettinger, *Popular Jewelry, 1840-1940*, Schiffer Publishing, 1990; Duncan James, *Old Jewellery*, Shire Publications Ltd, Buckinghamshire, UK, 1989; Arthur Guy Kaplan, *The Official Price Guide to Antique Jewelry*, 6th ed., House of Collectibles, 1990, 1994 Reprint; Karen Lorene, *Buying Antique Jewelry: Skipping the Mistakes*, Lorene Publications, 1987; Donald S. McNeil, *Jewelers' Dictionary*, 3rd ed., Chilton Book Co., 1979; Anna M. Miller, *Buyer's Guide to Affordable Antique Jewelry*, Carol Publishing Group, 1993; Harold Newman, *An Illustrated Dictionary of Jewelry*, Thames & Hudson, 1987; Dorothy T. Rainwater, *American Jewelry Manufacturers*, Schiffer Publishing, 1988; Sheryl Gross Shatz, *What's It Made Of? A Jewelry Materials Identification Guide*, 2nd ed., published by author, 1994; Oppi Untracht, *Jewelry Concepts and Technology*, Doubleday, 1985.

Numerous books on diamonds and colored gemstones have been published, some of them consumer-oriented and non-technical. The catalog of the G.I.A. (Gemological Institute of America) Bookstore, 1660 Stewart St., Santa Monica, CA 90404, (800) 421-7250, Ext. 702, lists the ones in print, which can be ordered by mail.

The video cassette is a new medium for disseminating information in the antiques field. My video, *Hidden Treasures, A Collector's Guide to Antique and Vintage Jewelry of the 19th and 20th Centuries*, produced by Venture Entertainment Group, is the first of its kind on the subject.

Periodicals: Specialized periodicals are listed in the appropriate categories. Two that cover a broad range of jewelry topics are:

Gems & Gemology, the quarterly journal of the Gemological Institute of America (see address on page x). Includes articles on period jewelry.

Jewelers' Circular-Keystone/Heritage, One Chilton Way, Radnor, PA 19089. Monthly trade publication of the retail jewelry industry and semiannual report on antique and period jewelry and watches.

Collectors' Clubs: Perhaps as an indication of the newness, and/or the diversity, of the field, there is no national organization with local chapters of jewelry collectors in general. However, a number of specialized jewelry-related clubs and societies exist in the United States. Most of these can be found listed under the appropriate category. A few for which there is no category, or which span several categories, are listed here:

American Hatpin Society, Beverly Churchfield, president, 2101 Via Aguila, San Clemente, CA 92672 (714) 498-1792.

Bead Societies are located in a number of U.S. cities. A comprehensive listing can be found in Peter Francis, Jr.'s *Beads of the World*, Schiffer Publishing, 1994.

International Club for Collectors of Hatpins and Hatpin Holders, Lillian Baker, founder, 15237 Chanera Ave., Gardena, CA 90249.

National Antique Comb Collectors Club (and newsletter), Belva Green, editor, 3748 Sunray Dr., Holiday FL 34691.

National Cuff Link Society (newsletter "The Link"), Eugene Klompus, president, P.O. Box 346, Prospect Heights, IL 60070 (708) 632-0561.

The Society of Jewelry Historians, c/o Joyce Jonas, Director, 215 E. 80th St., New York, N.Y. 10021.

Museums: As of yet, the U.S. does not have a museum with an extensive *permanent* collection of jewelry on display comparable to museums in Great Britain and Europe. Specialized collections can be found listed under the appropriate category. A few other museums with unique collections are: The Bead Museum, Prescott, Arizona; Miller Comb Museum, Homer, Alaska; Providence Jewelry Museum, Providence, Rhode Island (old jewelry-making equipment and other items related to the area's costume jewelry manufacturing industry).

Reproductions: Fakes, reproductions, and stylistic copycats are rampant in jewelry. Whenever a particular style or type of jewelry becomes popular, knockoffs proliferate. This has long been a common practice. Repros become especially problematic when they enter the secondary market after a number of years, with signs of wear making them difficult to distinguish from an original of the period. Notations on reproductions are included in the listings categories when applicable.

Marks: Rather than list maker's marks separately in an appendix, they are illustrated within their related categories. Marks that are names or initials which are easily read are described but not illustrated. Marks that would be otherwise difficult to identify are shown in drawings by Harry L. Rinker, Jr.

Attribution of unsigned pieces must rely on provenance or documentation, such as company catalogs or archives, and fashion magazines or trade publications which picture the item in question along with its maker's name. Most old jewelry is unmarked and un-attributable and must be evaluated solely on its own merits. Ideally, the same should be true of "signed" pieces, but the fact is that an "important" name on a piece scores points with collectors and adds value. Nevertheless, the name itself should not be the only or even the first thing taken into consideration when evaluating a signed piece. Marks and attributions are "the frosting on the cake," and are therefore listed at the end of the listings descriptions.

Listings: The variety of jewelry is so great that it would be impossible to include examples of every kind. Unlike some other collectibles, with jewelry there is less likelihood of finding pieces identical to those shown or listed. In certain categories, such as mass-produced costume jewelry of the mid-twentieth century, multiples of the same design can still be found. What you will find more often are comparable pieces—from the same period, of the same style, made from the same materials. The prices listed are for specific pieces of specific quality and condition. It is important to make sure you are comparing "apples to apples." Although they may be beyond most budgets, "high-end" pieces are listed as a basis for comparison and as sought-after examples. They set standards by which other pieces of their genre can be measured. However, the pieces in this book are not all necessarily the very best examples of their kind; rather they are representative of what is on the market today.

Watches are not included in the listings. Although a watch can often be a jewel as well as a timepiece, the factors that determine value and collectiblity are too complex and special-ized to fit within the scope of this book. Watch collectors already have a number of fine references at their disposal. However, watch accessories, such as chains, fobs, and pins, are included. Of necessity, some other categories were also omitted: most "generic" (undatable or otherwise unidentifiable) jewelry, ethnic jewelry (indigenous Middle Eastern, Oriental, African, etc.), and late twentieth-century jewelry. Several other jewelry books include pieces from the seventies through the nineties. While it is important to stay abreast of recent developments, it is often difficult to determine what tomorrow's collectibles will be from today's vantage point. Thirty years is considered a sufficient span of time for a clear perspective on what has "staying power" for jewelry collectors. Therefore, *Warman's Jewelry* covers the twentieth century up to 1965.

Most of the pieces pictured and listed in this book were for sale, or sold at auction, in 1993 and 1994. Those that are from private collections were usually acquired at antiques shows, shops and malls, auctions, flea markets, and yard sales over the past several years, but are valued at current levels. Prices listed are *average retail,* the median of prices noted in various parts of the U.S., except for auction results, designated by **(A)**, which are actual, rounded to the nearest dollar and including the 10% to 15% buyer's premium charged by the auction house. Regional retail prices may be higher or lower than average retail, and often depend upon the individual dealer. Auction prices are subject to a number of variables, and are not considered retail or wholesale. They represent the price that one person—a dealer *or* private party—paid at the time and place the piece was offered for sale.

Every effort was made to be consistent in the listings descriptions. However, it was not always possible to examine the jewelry firsthand, and information provided in catalogs was not always complete (e.g., weights, numbers and cuts of stones). The most detailed informa-tion on pieces sold at auction came from *Jewelry Price Report,* now defunct; however, its co-publisher, Gail Levine, has recently launched a similar semiannual report, *Auction Market Resource for Gems and Jewelry,* a comprehensive compilation of recent auction results from a dozen different houses.

Measurements are in inches, rounded to the nearest eighth. Width or diameter is at the widest point; total length includes any findings. Rings are measured shoulder to shoulder and top to bottom. Necklace and flexible bracelet lengths are clasp to clasp. Width of brooches, clips, earrings, and pendants is side to side, length is top to bottom as the piece is worn. Stone measurements are usually given in millimeters, weights in carats. Total weight for the entire piece, metal and gemstones if any, is in pennyweights.

Photographs: Unless otherwise credited, photographs were taken by the author. The captions for the photographed pieces in *Warman's Jewelry* are as detailed as the listings for pieces not pictured. The reasoning behind this is threefold. First, the reader will more clearly understand the terms used to describe a piece when they can be correlated to the photo, and thus understand the descriptions of pieces *not* pictured. Second, because we often look but don't see, the captions will call the reader's attention to details that might otherwise be missed, as well as to details not visible in the photos, such as findings, marks, and cuts of stones. Third, these descriptions are given in hopes that they will help to further a common usage of terms whenever we attempt to describe an unseen piece. Terms that may be unfamiliar to the reader are further explained in the glossary.

Glossary: Jewelry has its own lexicon. Many jewelry terms are derived from the French, which became the language of choice when jewelry-making terminology was adopted internationally in the eighteenth century. This glossary lists terms used in *Warman's Jewelry* and is necessarily incomplete. The general references list several jewelry dictionaries that the reader can use as supplements. Often there is more than one word that can be used to describe a piece of jewelry. For example, the word used to describe a piece of jewelry fastened to clothing by means of a pinning device is either *brooch* or *pin*. Some say that size determines which word is used, but no one has determined at exactly what size a brooch becomes a pin. Others say that *brooch* is the only correct term and *pin* is the word for the mechanism itself, the hinge or joint, pinstem, and catch. In this book, whenever more than one word can be used for a jewelry form, both are included in the listings, e.g., "Brooch/Pin."

PRICE NOTES: BUYER'S GUIDE, NOT SELLER'S GUIDE

The marketplace where a piece is sold affects price as much as other criteria, i.e., design, craftsmanship, condition, demand and scarcity, and intrinsic value of metals and stones in fine jewelry. In most cases, the prices in this book are those a buyer should expect to pay for a piece in excellent to very good condition. Pieces with flaws that affect value are so noted in the descriptions. Except for auction results, prices are *average* retail, which means that some collectors would consider the price a bargain and others would say it is exorbitant. Prices were compiled from a number of sources, including auction houses, appraisers, dealers, jewelry store owners, and collectors. Pricing data was gathered from all over the country, but differences were often a result of the *type* of marketplace (e.g., an urban retail shop versus a rural flea market) rather than its locale.

If you see one of your possessions in this book (or a similar one) and wish to sell it—as a private party to a dealer, or as a dealer to a dealer—you should expect to receive approximately 35% to 40% of the value listed. If it cannot be resold quickly, expect even less; and it is possible that a dealer may not wish to purchase it at all. Collectors are very specialized; dealers work for years to assemble a list of collectors who will pay top dollar for an item. Try to be as objective about your item as possible. If it is an heirloom, its sentimental value may be greater than any dollar amount you could get for it.

BOARD OF ADVISORS

One person cannot be an expert in every type of jewelry. Many "specialists"—dealers, collectors, gemologists, appraisers, auction house directors, museum curators, researchers and historians—were consulted for the sections relating to their specialty. Some provided expertise in more than one field, or general gemological and/or historical information, as well as photos or items for photos and listings. Their names appear in the captions and at the end of their respective categories. Mailing addresses and/or phone numbers are listed in the front of this book. If you wish to buy or sell an item in their field or fields of expertise, send a note with a photograph or photocopy, description, and self-addressed stamped envelope (or call if no address given). If time and interest permit, they will respond.

OTHER CONTRIBUTORS

Other dealers and collectors who provided jewelry for the photos and listings are listed below. Note that the word "collection" in the photo captions can refer to a dealer who sells under his or her own name, or a collector (some people are both). Correspondence to any of them may be addressed in care of the author (see below).

Dealers: Allie Dickason, Mary Lou Diebold, Kathryn Ferguson, Lisa Hohlfeld, Neil Lane, Leigh Leshner, Dena McCarthy, Rochelle Mendle, Richard Noël, Connie Parente, Harriet Stein of HMS, Ltd., Ellen Stuart, Victoria Taylor, Vicki Telford, Kathy Toledo, Pamela Tonge and Dawn Usher.

Collectors: Joyce Albers, Ofelia Bucy, Jill Crawford, Corinne Durst, Margaret Levine, Delia Magaña, Cheri Mulligan, Sherry Shatz, Lucile Thompson.

COMMENTS INVITED

This is the first edition of *Warman's Jewelry*. Our readers are encouraged to send their comments and suggestions to Christie Romero, Christie's Treasures, P.O. Box 424, Anaheim, CA 92815-0424.

STATE OF THE MARKET REPORT

The economic realities of the recessionary early nineties hit the antique, period, and vintage jewelry market particularly hard. As a collectible, jewelry is relatively pricey, and the collector population is not as large, nor is the collecting tradition as long as, for example, glass or dolls. Costume jewelry collecting in particular is a relatively recent phenomenon. Prices began to soar as disposable income began to drop, resulting in a noticeable decrease in buying and selling activity on both wholesale and retail levels, especially in the middle market. Dealers were shocked to discover that they could not continue to count on increasing prices. What went up can, and did, go down.

While the middle market has languished, the high and low ends have continued to hold their own. Advanced collectors and foreign buyers who want the rarest and best fuel the upper end, while the very inexpensive pieces sell to bargain-hunters and beginners fearful of paying too much.

Proliferating repros, "marriages," and alterations have made collectors cautious. Prices have escalated to the point where mistakes are risky and costly. Beginning collectors, especially, are afraid of making mistakes. Collectors *and* dealers need to arm themselves with information and hands-on experience. It is much more acceptable for dealers to say "I don't know" than to make up a story that they hope gullible buyers will believe. When the buyer finds out the story is wrong, credibility is lost forever. Better yet for dealers to learn as much as they can about what they are buying and selling, and better, too, for their customers to be informed. Lack of information breeds lack of trust.

Midway through the decade and heading toward the next millennium, the overall picture appears to be brightening. There is a trend toward fine old pieces made of karat gold and gemstones. A certain segment of the market can be counted on to always buy gold and diamonds, sometimes for their intrinsic value alone, because these buyers believe precious materials are always "safe"; but there has been a growing appreciation for the workmanship, history, and beauty of fine antique jewelry as well. Victorian jewelry in particular has surged in popularity. Sentimental Victoriana (love tokens, memorial jewelry, etc.) as well as gold and gemstone-set pieces appear to be doing well in most parts of the country.

Another group of buyers makes purchases based on design, personal taste, and wearability. One of the most appealing aspects of old jewelry for many collectors is that they can *wear* items from their collection. In addition to the standard criteria (condition, craftsmanship, etc.), these fashion-conscious collectors want pieces that also look good on them and complement their wardrobes (some dedicated jewelry collectors buy clothes to go with their jewelry, rather than vice versa). The type of jewelry they buy is as much tied to their lifestyle as any other consideration. Career women, for example, tend toward classic, tailored brooches, bracelets, and earrings that go well with suits and other business attire. The Retro Modern style of the forties is especially popular with this group.

Yet another area of growing interest is in handmade, one-of-a-kind, or limited production pieces with unique, identifiable designs from Arts & Crafts to Postwar Modern. Although outside the scope of this book, it should be noted that ethnic jewelry from Africa, Asia, and the Middle East is also gaining favor.

A large segment of the collectible jewelry market is trend-oriented, and pricing is often dependent on the basic economic law of supply and demand—the currently "hot" and scarce pieces command the highest prices. Costume jewelry (see price notes in Costume Jewelry, Part III) is particularly subject to the ins and outs of fads and trends. Some fads are short-lived, while others make a comeback. Crosses came and went, but there has been renewed interest in Bakelite and other plastics after a leveling-off period that followed the initial collecting boom. As of this writing, colorless rhinestones were once again "in" for the holiday season, and silver was the metal (or at least the metal *color*) of choice. It remains to be seen if these trends will sustain themselves.

What probably will continue is a soft market for the average, ordinary, and common pieces that some dealers continue to price as rarities. Unless they are cheap enough for a beginner to take a chance on, chances are they will not sell. However, famous makers and designers, for better or worse, continue to carry clout. Whether it is a Tiffany diamond or a Trifari rhinestone, the name makes a difference in price and salability. The public's perception of value is an important factor in today's market. The average person believes that older is better than newer, and signed is better than unsigned, and more importance is often given to these aspects of a piece than others.

Regional variations in price were at one time considerable, but today, with a few exceptions, the market has leveled to the point that there is no part of the country where prices of comparable pieces sold in comparable marketplaces are significantly lower or higher than any other. Nationally distributed price guides, well-publicized auction results, and itinerant dealers have seen to that. Regional differences do exist in the *kinds* of jewelry that most readily *sell*, e.g., traditional versus avant-garde, conservative versus flamboyant. Advisors have also reported that middle market merchandise moves better in the middle part of the U.S., whereas high-end goods do well in urban coastal markets and upper-income tourist areas. Fad-oriented goods often peak in different parts of the country at different times, too. There is generally a time lag between East and West, Midwest and Southern regions.

Regardless of the vagaries of the marketplace, one maxim still holds true: buy what you like, buy the best that you can afford, but if you are thinking of buying for investment, buy stocks instead.

BOARD OF ADVISORS

Rosalie & Aram Berberian
ARK Antiques
P.O. Box 3133
New Haven, CT 06515
(203) 498-8572
American Arts & Crafts

Steve Cabella
The Modern i Gallery
500 Red Hill Ave.
San Anselmo, CA 94904
(415) 456-3960
Post-war Modernist

Melinda Churchfield, Collector
28227 Paseo El Siena
Laguna Niguel, CA 92677
(714) 498-1792
Hatpins

Dexter Cirillo
Dealer and Author
P.O. Box 8764
Aspen, CO 81612
Native American (Indian)

Milly Combs, Collector
c/o author
P.O. Box 424
Anaheim, CA 92815
Art Nouveau, Hatpins

Elizabeth M.C. Cook, G.G.
Director, Jewelry Department
Butterfield & Butterfield
7601 Sunset Blvd.
Los Angeles, CA 90046
(213) 850-7500 ext. 202

Samuel C. Gassman, G.G.
E. Foxe Harrell Jewelers
Clinton, IA 52732
(319) 242-3580 (by appointment)
Victorian

Gail Gerretsen, Dealer
Los Angeles, CA
(213) 622-9200 (by appointment)
American & European Arts & Crafts

Elayne Glotzer, Dealer
45 East 89th St.
New York, NY 10128
(212) 348-5221
Designer/Mfr Signed Costume

Toni Greenbaum
Jewelry Historian
248 West 88th St. # 3D
New York, NY 10024
(212) 721-6343
Post-war Modernist

Lael Hagan, G.G.
New York, NY
(718) 522-1843 (by appointment)
19th & 20th Century Fine

Ellen Hoffs
Before
P.O. Box 3637
Santa Monica, CA 90408
Post-war Modernist

Carmelita Garceau Johnson, Collector
(818) 885-6520
Hair and Hairwork

AUCTION HOUSES

Butterfield & Butterfield
Elizabeth Cook, Jewelry
7601 Sunset Blvd.
Los Angeles, CA 90046
213/850-7500 ext. 202
213/850-5843 FAX

Butterfield & Butterfield
Taryn Miller, Jewelry
220 San Bruno
San Francisco, CA 94103
415-861-7500 ext. 247
415-861-8951 FAX

Christie's
Simon Teakle, Jewelry
502 Park Ave. (at 59th St.)
New York, NY 10022
212-546-1133
212-980-8163 FAX

Christie's East
Susan Abeles, Jewelry
219 East 67th St.
New York, NY 10021
212-606-0400
212-737-6076 FAX

Christie's West
342 North Rodeo Dr.
Beverly Hills, CA 90210
310-275-5534
310-275-9748 FAX

William Doyle Galleries
Berj Zavian, Jewelry
175 East 87th St.
New York, NY 10128
212-427-2730

Dunning's Auction Service
William Milne, Jewelry
755 Church Rd.
Elgin, IL 60123
708-741-3483
708-741-3589 FAX

Freeman/Fine Arts of Philadelphia
1808 Chestnut St.
Philadelphia, PA 19103
215-563-9275

Grogan & Co.
Peter Shemonsky, Jewelry
890 Commonwealth Ave.
Boston, MA 02215
617-566-4100
617-566-7715 FAX

Leslie Hindman Auctioneers
215 West Ohio St.
Chicago, IL 60610
312-670-0010
312-670-4248 FAX

Phillips
Claudia Florian, Jewelry
406 East 79th St.
New York, NY 10021
(212) 570-4830
(212) 570-2207 FAX

Skinner, Inc.
Gloria Lieberman, Jewelry
2 Newbury St.
Boston, MA 02116
617-236-1700
617-247-2903 FAX

Sotheby's
John D. Block, Jewelry
1334 York Ave. (at 72nd St.)
New York, NY 10021
212-606-7000
212-606-7107 FAX

Sotheby's West
Carol Elkins, Jewelry
308 North Rodeo Dr.
Beverly Hills, CA 90210
310-274-0340
310-274-0899 FAX

John Toomey/Treadway Gallery
818 North Blvd.
Oak Park, IL 60301
(708) 383-5234
(708) 383-4828 FAX

Weschler's
909 E St. NW
Washington, DC 20004
202-628-1281
202-628-2366 FAX

ABBREVIATIONS

LISTINGS

Am	American	lt	light
appl	applied	mfr	manufacturer
approx	approximately	mkd	marked
bc	brilliant cut	mono	monogram
bg	background	MOP	mother of pearl
cab	cabochon	No	number
ct	carat or carats (stones)	#	numbered
ct or c	karat gold (Eng)	oe	old European cut
C	century	om	old mine cut
c.	circa	orig	original
circ	circular	pr	pair
constr	construction	pat	patent
curv	curvilinear	pc, pcs	piece, pieces
dam	damaged	pl	plated
dk	dark	plat	platinum
diag	diagonal	pts	points
dia	diameter	rect	rectangular
dwt	pennyweight	rev	reverse
emb	embossed	r.s.	rhinestone
Eng	English	rh pl	rhodium-plated
engr	engraved	rc	rose cut
Fr	French	sgd	signed
f.w.	freshwater (pearls)	sp	silver plated
geo	geometric	st yg	silver-topped yellow gold
Ger	German	sm	small
gf	gold-filled	sc	single cut
gp	gold plated	sq	square
grad	graduated	ster	sterling silver
hmk	hallmark	syn	synthetic
hp	hand painted	tl	total length
h	height	tw	total weight
imp	impressed	turq	turquoise
irid	iridescent	wg	white gold
Ital	Italian	wm	white metal
k	karat (gold)	w	width
lg	large	yg	yellow gold
l	length	ym	yellow metal

PHOTO POSITIONS

L	Left	TR	Top Right
C	Center	CL	Center Left
R	Right	CR	Center Right
T	Top	BL	Bottom Left
B	Bottom	BC	Bottom Center
TL	Top Left	BR	Bottom Right
TC	Top Center		

More than one piece in a position is assigned a number, reading left to right, e.g., *BL, 1* is the first piece on the left at the bottom, *BL, 2* is the second piece on the left at the bottom (to the right of the first piece).

Note: Some large pieces in the photographs are smaller than actual size due to space constraints. Some small pieces are larger than actual size in order to show details. Adjacent photos on the same page are not necessarily sized proportionately or to scale.

TIMELINE

LATE GEORGIAN PERIOD

Date	General History, Discoveries & Inventions	Date	Jewelry & Gemstone History, Discoveries & Inventions
		1819	Oxyhydrogen (gas) blowpipe invented (c.)
1820	George III of Great Britain dies, George IV becomes king		
		1824	Pinmaking machine patented in England by Lemuel Wellman Wright
1829–1837	Andrew Jackson is president of U.S.		
1830	India rubber elastic first appears in women's clothing *Godey's Lady's Book* first published French occupation of Algeria begins George IV of Great Britain dies, William IV becomes king		
1836	Edmund Davey discovers and identifies acetylene		

EARLY VICTORIAN (ROMANTIC) PERIOD

Date	General History, Discoveries & Inventions	Date	Jewelry & Gemstone History, Discoveries & Inventions
1837	Victoria becomes Queen of Great Britain The telegraph is patented	1837	Charles Lewis Tiffany founds company in New York City; becomes Tiffany & Co. in 1853
1839	Louis J. M. Daguerre perfects daguerreotype photographic process Charles Goodyear invents and patents (1844) vulcanized rubber; displays products at Crystal Palace (1851)		
		c. 1840	Scottish motifs in pebble (agate) jewelry popularized, continuing through the rest of the century Repoussé and machine stamping replace cannetille (gold filigree) Algerian knot motif introduced in Paris
1840	Victoria weds Prince Albert	1840	Electroplating commercialized; large-scale jewelry manufacturing begins in U.S.
1842	Gutta-percha introduced in Paris Excavations of ancient Assyrian capital of Nineveh begin		
		1846	Riker, Tay & Searing founded in Newark NJ, becomes Riker Bros. 1892
		1847	Cartier founded in Paris
1848	Balmoral Castle in Scotland purchased by Queen Victoria	1848	Caldwell & Bennett becomes J.E. Caldwell & Co. in Philadelphia

Date	General History, Discoveries & Inventions	Date	Jewelry & Gemstone History, Discoveries & Inventions
1849	California Gold Rush	1849	Gold electroplating patented
	The safety pin invented and patented by Walter Hunt of New York (patent #6,281)		Opals first discovered in Australia
1850	High tariff placed on foreign goods imported into U.S.	1850	Tube-shaped (trombone) safety catch patented by Charles Rowley of Birmingham, England
1851	First international exhibition, the Great Exhibition of the Works of Industry of All Nations, held at The Crystal Palace in London	1851	Artificial aventurine (goldstone) exhibited at The Crystal Palace
	Vulcanite/ebonite (hard rubber) developed by Nelson Goodyear in U.S. and Charles MacIntosh in U.K.		
	Gold first discovered in Australia		
1852	Louis Napoleon becomes Napoleon III; beginning of French Second Empire	1852	Tiffany & Co. introduces the English sterling standard to the U.S.
1853	Commodore Matthew Perry sails American fleet into Japan, opens East-West trade relations		
	Crystal Palace Exhibition held in New York, modeled after London exhibition		
1854	Results of first commercially successful aluminum reduction process published by Henri Ste. Claire Deville	1854	Use of 15, 12, and 9-karat gold made legal in England
1855	Paris Exposition Universelle is held	1855	Theodor Fahrner founds jewelry factory in Pforzheim, Germany
	Aluminum articles first exhibited		First aluminum jewelry made in France (c.)
	R.W. Bunsen develops gas-air burner		Kerr & Thiery, later Wm. B. Kerr & Co., founded in Newark, NJ
1857	Furnace to melt platinum and its alloys developed in Paris by Henri Ste. Claire Deville	1857	Snake-chain making machine patented in U.S.
	Financial "Panic of 1857" affects all U.S. industries		
		1858	Boucheron founded in Paris
1859	Construction of the Suez Canal begins	1859	Jewels of Queen Ah-Hotpe of Egypt discovered
	Comstock Lode (silver) discovered in Nevada		
		c. 1860–1900	Vulcanite used for jewelry

MID-VICTORIAN (GRAND) PERIOD

Date	General History, Discoveries & Inventions	Date	Jewelry & Gemstone History, Discoveries & Inventions
1861	U.S. Civil War begins [1861–1865]; Lincoln inaugurated		
	Prince Consort Albert dies; Victoria enters prolonged period of mourning	1861– c.1880	The wearing of mourning (black) jewelry required at British court
1862	International Exhibition held in London	1862	Archeological Revival gold jewelry exhibited by Castellani of Rome at International Exhibition
1863	Edward, Prince of Wales, marries Alexandra of Denmark		
1865	Lincoln assassinated	1865	Sapphires found in Missouri River in Montana

Date	General History, Discoveries & Inventions	Date	Jewelry & Gemstone History, Discoveries & Inventions
1866	First transatlantic cable laid		
1867	Paris Exposition Universelle is held	1867	Egyptian revival jewelry exhibited at Paris Exposition
			Diamonds discovered in South Africa
		1868	Demantoid (green) garnets discovered in Ural Mountains
			Gorham Mfg. Co., Providence, RI, adopts sterling standard of 925 parts per thousand
1869	First transcontinental railroad completed from Omaha to San Francisco	1869	*American Horological Journal* first published, merges with *The Jewelers' Circular* to become *The Jewelers' Circular and Horological Review,* 1873
	Suez Canal opened		
	Celluloid, the first successful semi synthetic thermoplastic, invented in U.S. by John Wesley Hyatt; commercial production begins in 1872; tradename registered, 1873		
1870	Fall of the French Empire	1870	*The Jewelers' Circular* founded, first issue published February 15
1870s	Recession in Europe	1870s	Influx of European craftsmen and designers into U.S. Japanese craftsmen introduce metal-working techniques and designs to the West
1872	International Exhibition held in London	1872	Black opals first discovered in Queensland, Australia
1873	Universal Exhibition held in Vienna		
	U.S. establishes gold standard		
1875	Arthur Lazenby Liberty founds Liberty & Co. of London	1875	The Celluloid Novelty Co. begins jewelry production
1876	Centennial Exposition held in Philadelphia		
	Wearing of swords banned in Japan		
	Queen Victoria becomes Empress of India		
	Alexander Graham Bell patents the telephone		
1877	Advent of bottled oxygen (liquified and compressed)	1877	Successful experiments with chemical manufacture of very small rubies and sapphires published by Frémy in Paris
1878	Paris Exposition Universelle is held	1878	Tiffany & Co. awarded gold medal for encrusted metals technique in the Japanesque style at Paris Exposition
			Tiffany Diamond discovered in South Africa
			Unger Bros. of Newark, NJ, begins the manufacture of silver jewelry
1879	T. A. Edison patents incandescent light bulb	1879	Gem expert George F. Kunz joins Tiffany & Co.

LATE VICTORIAN (AESTHETIC) PERIOD

Date	General History, Discoveries & Inventions	Date	Jewelry & Gemstone History, Discoveries & Inventions
1880	First electrically lit town, Wabash, Indiana (business district)	1880	Cecil Rhodes establishes the De Beers Mining Company in South Africa (renamed De Beers Consolidated Mines in 1888)
	Rational Dress Society founded in Britain		Mass production of wrist watches begins in Switzerland; introduced in U.S. in 1895; U.S. manufacture begins in 1907 (c.)

Date	General History, Discoveries & Inventions	Date	Jewelry & Gemstone History, Discoveries & Inventions
		1884	Krementz & Co. of Newark, NJ patents the one-piece collar button
		1885	First appearance of the Geneva synthetic ruby
1886	Gold discovered in South Africa (Transvaal) Statue of Liberty dedicated	1886	Tiffany setting for diamond solitaires introduced Richard W. Sears starts a mail-order company to sell watches (second company to sell jewelry and watches founded in 1889)
1887	Queen Victoria's Golden Jubilee is celebrated	1887	Gold extraction by cyanide process invented by John Stewart Macarthur and the Forrest brothers Birmingham (England) Jewellers' and Silversmiths' Association formed by manufacturers *The Keystone* magazine founded Tiffany & Co. purchases French crown jewels The Belais brothers of New York begin experimenting with alloys for white gold (c.); David Belais introduces his formula to the trade in 1917 (referred to as "18k Belais")
		1888	C.R. Ashbee's Guild of Handicraft founded in London, the first crafts guild to specialize in jewelry making and metalwork
1889	Paris Exposition Universelle is held, Eiffel Tower constructed (first structure to serve as landmark for an exposition)	1889	Tiffany & Co. exhibits enameled orchid jewels by Paulding Farnham at the Exposition Universelle Black opals discovered in New South Wales, Australia
1890	Sarah Bernhardt plays Cleopatra on stage Charles Dana Gibson's "Gibson Girl" first appears in the humor magazine *Life*	1890	Screwback earring finding for unpierced ears commercially marketed (c.)
1891	The marking of foreign imports with the name of the country of origin in English required by the enactment of the McKinley Tariff Act	1891	Power-driven bruting (girdling) machine patented for cutting diamonds; improved production of old European cut (round brilliant) diamonds Blue sapphires mined commercially in Montana
1892	*Vogue* magazine founded in U.S.	1892	Marcus & Co., formerly Jaques & Marcus, established in New York
1893	World's Columbian Exposition is held in Chicago	1893	Cultured pearls first developed by K. Mikimoto in Japan; first spherical pearls grown in 1905
1894	Thomas Edison's Kinetoscope Parlor (peepshow) opens in New York City		
1895	Samuel Bing opens his new Paris gallery of decorative art called *L'Art Nouveau* American Consuelo Vanderbilt marries the British Duke of Marlborough The wireless telegraph invented by Guglielmo Marconi (first transatlantic wireless signal in 1901)	1895	René Lalique exhibits jewelry at the Bing gallery and the Salon of the Societé des Artistes Français; begins work on a series of 145 pieces for Calouste Gulbenkian Daniel Swarovski opens glass stone-cutting factory in Tyrol, Austria
1897	Queen Victoria's Diamond Jubilee is celebrated Casein plastics marketed in Germany Boston and Chicago Arts and Crafts Societies founded	1897	Lacloche Frères established in Paris
1898	Alaska Gold Rush Spanish-American War		

Date	General History, Discoveries & Inventions	Date	Jewelry & Gemstone History, Discoveries & Inventions
		1899	Fred Harvey Company provides Native American silversmiths with sheet silver and precut turquoise to produce first Indian-made tourist jewelry for Harvey House curio shops
1899–		1899–	
1902	Boer War (South Africa)	1902	Diamond supplies curtailed by Boer War; prices for De Beers' reserve stock rise
1900	Paris Exposition Universelle is held Oxyacetylene torch invented by Edmund Fouché	1900	Synthetic rubies exhibited at Paris Exposition; Tiffany & Co. exhbits a life-size iris corsage ornament set with Montana blue sapphires The Kalo Shop, founded by Clara Barck Welles in Chicago, begins jewelry-making in 1905 and closes in 1970 Lever safety catch for brooches (c.)

EDWARDIAN PERIOD (BELLE ÉPOQUE)

Date	General History, Discoveries & Inventions	Date	Jewelry & Gemstone History, Discoveries & Inventions
1901	Queen Victoria dies; Edward VII becomes king (coronation in 1902) McKinley assassinated; Teddy Roosevelt becomes president Pan-American Exposition held in Buffalo, NY Gustav Stickley begins publishing his periodical *The Craftsman* (until 1916)		
1902	Vienna Secession Exhibition is held	1902	Flame-fusion process for synthesizing rubies presented in Paris by Verneuil, published and patented in 1904
1903	Wiener Werkstätte founded in Vienna, Austria by Koloman Moser and Josef Hoffmann		
1904	Louisiana Purchase Exposition held in St. Louis New York City subway opens	1904	Louis Comfort Tiffany exhibits his jewelry for the first time at the St. Louis Exposition Marshall Field & Co., Chicago, establishes a craft shop for jewelry and metalware (closed c. 1950) Georg Jensen opens his silversmithy in Copenhagen, Denmark
		1905	Forest Craft Guild founded by Forest Mann in Grand Rapids, MI
		1906	National Stamping Act passed in U.S. requiring marking of gold and silver content Van Cleef & Arpels founded in Paris
		1907	Tiffany & Co. establishes Art Jewelry Dept. with Louis Comfort Tiffany as director
1908	Henry Ford introduces the first mass-produced automobile, the Model T Couturier Paul Poiret opens "Boutique Chichi" and introduces corsetless dresses and the vertical line in fashion (c.)	1908	First spherical cultured pearls patented in Japan by Mikimoto (American patent granted in 1916)

Date	General History, Discoveries & Inventions	Date	Jewelry & Gemstone History, Discoveries & Inventions
1909	Leo H. Baekeland patents Bakelite, the first entirely synthesized plastic	1909	Cartier in New York is opened
	The Wright brothers begin large-scale manufacture of the airplane (patented 1906)		
1910	The Ballets Russes production of *Schéhérazade* presented in Paris	1910	B.A. Ballou & Co. patents the bullet safety catch for brooches
	Edward VII dies	c. 1910–	
		1920	Suffragette jewelry in green, white, and violet (first initials for "give women votes") is popular
		1911	Synthetic blue sapphires patented in U.S by Verneuil
1912	The *Titanic* sinks	1912	Oscar Heyman & Bros. founded in New York
1913	Suffragettes demonstrate for the right to vote in London		
1914	World War I begins	1914	Platinum banned for use in jewelry during wartime
	Panama Canal opens		
	The first U.S. fashion show is staged by Edna Woolman Chase, editor of *Vogue*		
1915	Panama-Pacific International Exposition held in San Francisco	1915	U.S. patent #1,165,448 granted to Dr. Richter & Co. for a white gold alloy of gold, nickel and palladium
1917	Theda Bara plays Cleopatra in first (silent) film version		
	The U.S. enters the war		
	Russian Revolution begins		
1918	First regular airmail service between Washington D.C. and New York City begins		
	World War I ends		
	Bohemia, Moravia and Slovakia become the Republic of Czechoslovakia		

THE MODERN ERA

Date	General History, Discoveries & Inventions	Date	Jewelry & Gemstone History, Discoveries & Inventions
1919	Bauhaus founded in Germany by Walter Gropius	1919	Marcel Tolkowsky publishes *Diamond Design*, detailing the cut of the modern brilliant (American or ideal cut)
	The Eighteenth Amendment to the U.S. Constitution is ratified (Prohibition)		
1920	The Nineteenth Amendment, giving women the right to vote, is ratified		
	First regular radio programs begin broadcasting in Pittsburgh		
1922	Howard Carter discovers King Tutankhamun's tomb in Egypt	1922	Raymond C. Yard, Inc. is founded in New York City
		1924	Frederik Lunning opens a shop for Georg Jensen in New York City
1925	Exposition Internationale des Arts Decoratifs et Industriels Modernes held in Paris	1925	Synthetic spinel, inadvertently produced by flame fusion process 1908, in wide commerical use (c.)
	Josephine Baker appears in the *Revue Nègre* in Paris		
1926	Motion pictures with sound first publicly shown		
	The first commercial injection molding machine patented by Eckert and Ziegler in Germany		

Date	General History, Discoveries & Inventions	Date	Jewelry & Gemstone History, Discoveries & Inventions
1927	Charles Lindbergh flies solo nonstop New York to Paris	1927	Cartier patents model with spring system for double clip brooch
1929	First Technicolor film, *On With The Show*, opens in New York (color process developed in 1922)	1929	*L'Exposition de Joaillerie et Orfèvrerie* (Precious Stone Jewelry and Goldwork) is held in Paris
	The Great Depression begins with stock market crash		Trabert & Hoeffer, Inc.-Mauboussin merger agreement
1930	Formation of the *Union des Artistes Modernes* in Paris	1930	Clipback earring finding for unpierced ears introduced (c.)
			The Duette pinback mechanism for double clip brooches patented by U.S. costume jewelry manufacturer Coro
1931	Empire State Building constructed	1931	William Spratling opens the first silver workshop in Taxco, Mexico
1932	Franklin D. Roosevelt elected president	1932	14k gold replaces 12k and 15k in Britain by decision of the Worshipful Company of Goldsmiths in London
	Radio City Music Hall opens		Harry Winston opens a retail jewelry business in New York City
1933	Construction begins on Golden Gate Bridge in San Francisco (completed 1937)	1933	The invisible setting (*serti invisible*) patented by Van Cleef & Arpels (introduced in U.S. 1936)
	Prohibition repealed		
	Gold taken out of circulation		
1934	Cecil B. De Mille's *Cleopatra* starring Claudette Colbert in title role	1934	Ernest Oppenheimer creates the De Beers Consolidated Mines Ltd. diamond cartel
			Synthetic emeralds (Igmerald) devloped by IG-Farben, Germany, first seen by gemologists
			Van Cleef & Arpels introduces the Ludo flexible strap bracelet
		1935	D. Lisner & Co. introduces Bois Glacé jewelry, their trade name for colorless phenolic plastic (Bakelite) laminated to wood
			The Jewelers' Circular merges with *The Keystone* to become *Jewelers' Circular-Keystone*
1936	Edward VIII of Britain abdicates the throne to marry American-born divorcée Wallis Simpson, becomes Duke of Windsor, succeeded by George VI		
	Margaret Mitchell's novel, *Gone With The Wind*, is published		
	Life magazine founded by Henry Robinson Luce		
	BBC inaugurates television service; general broadcasting begins in U.S. 1941		
1937	Du Pont de Nemours & Co. introduces acrylic plastic, trade name Lucite	1937	Paul Flato opens his Los Angeles establishment
	The International Exhibition of Arts and Techniques in Modern Life held in Paris		
	First feature-length animated film, Walt Disney's *Snow White and the Seven Dwarfs*		

Date	General History, Discoveries & Inventions	Date	Jewelry & Gemstone History, Discoveries & Inventions
1938	Du Pont develops nylon, the first all-synthetic fiber		
1939	*Gone With The Wind* premiers	1939	First commercially successful synthetic emerald process marketed by Carroll Chatham of San Francisco, CA (Chatham Created Emerald term first used 1963)
	The New York World's Fair, entitled "The World of Tomorrow," opens		
	World War II begins in Europe		The House of Jewels at the New York World's Fair is sponsored by Tiffany & Co., Black, Starr & Frost-Gorham, Udall & Ballou, Marcus & Co., and Cartier New York
	First nylon stockings marketed		
			Van Cleef & Arpels opens an office in New York City after exhibiting in the French Pavilion at the World's Fair
			Verdura opens his own shop in New York
1940	France falls under German occupation	1940	The Bank of France bans all gold trading
1941	The U.S. enters the war with the Japanese bombing of Pearl Harbor	1941	10% luxury tax on jewelry in U.S., raised to 20% in 1944
	Craft Horizons, the first national magazine for crafts, is published by the Handcraft Cooperative League (merged with the American Handcraft Council to become the American Craftsmen's Cooperative Council, 1942, American Craftsmen's Council, 1955, American Crafts Council, 1970)		Jean Schlumberger opens shop in New York, joins Tiffany & Co. in 1955
1942	Rationing of consumer products (sugar, coffee, gasoline) begins in U.S.	1942	Use of platinum for jewelry prohibited in U.S.
			White metal restricted by U.S. government, sterling silver used as substitute in costume jewelry
1943	Postal zones added to addresses of large cities in U.S.		
1945	World War II ends	1945	Suzanne Belperron forms partnership Herz-Belperron with Jean Herz in Paris
	United Nations is formed, holds first session in 1946		Mexican government requires marking of sterling silver with spread eagle assay mark (c.)
		1946	First national exhibit of American studio artists' jewelry held at Museum of Modern Art in New York City
			David Webb opens office in New York (salon in 1963)
1947	Couturier Christian Dior introduces The New Look	1947	Synthetic star rubies and sapphires (Linde) first marketed
			Metalsmithing workshop series for war veterans begins, continues through 1951
1948	Jewish State of Israel declared, admitted to U.N. in 1949	1948	De Beers Diamond Corp. launches the slogan "a diamond is forever"
			The Metal Arts Guild is organized in San Francisco
1949	German Federal Republic (West Germany) proclaimed	1949	Harry Winston's Court of Jewels exhibit opens in New York, tours U.S. for the next four years
1951	Color television is introduced in U.S.		
1952	George VI of Britain dies; succeeded by Elizabeth II		
1953	Marilyn Monroe sings "Diamonds Are a Girl's Best Friend" in *Gentlemen Prefer Blondes*		

Date	General History, Discoveries & Inventions	Date	Jewelry & Gemstone History, Discoveries & Inventions
		1954	De Beers institutes the annual Diamonds International Awards for original designs in diamond-set jewelry
			First successful production of synthetic diamonds at General Electric; process patented in 1960; large gem-quality crystals produced 1970
1955	Atomically generated power first used in the U.S.	1955	Swarovski Corp. introduces the aurora borealis color effect for rhinestones and crystal in collaboration with Christian Dior
1957	The U.S.S.R. launches the first "Sputnik" satellite on Oct. 4		
	Jack Kerouac's *On the Road* published, coins the term "Beat Generation"		
1961	Audrey Hepburn stars in *Breakfast at Tiffany's*	1961	International Exhibition of Modern Jewelry (1890–1961) held in London
			U.S. National Stamping Act amended, requiring a maker's trademark
1963	U.S. Post Office introduces the ZIP code		
	Elizabeth Taylor stars in *Cleopatra*		

References: David Bennett & Daniela Mascetti, *Understanding Jewellery,* Antique Collectors' Club, 1989; Shirley Bury, *Jewellery 1789–1910, The International Era,* Vols. I & II, Antique Collectors' Club, 1991; Bernard Grun, *The Timetables of History,* revised 3rd ed., Simon & Schuster/Touchstone, 1991; Hans Nadelhoffer, *Cartier, Jewelers Extraordinary,* Harry N. Abrams, 1984; Kurt Nassau, *Gems Made By Man,* Chilton Book Co., 1980; Penny Proddow, Debra Healy, Marion Fasel, *Hollywood Jewels, Movies, Jewelry, Stars,* Harry N. Abrams, 1992; Dorothy Rainwater, *American Jewelry Manufacturers,* Schiffer Publishing, 1988; Alfred M. Weisberg, *Why Providence?* Providence Jewelry Museum, 1992; *Information Please Almanac,* Houghton Mifflin Co., 1991; *Encyclopedia Americana; Microsoft Bookshelf CD-ROM Reference Library,* 1993, *Microsoft Encarta Multimedia Encyclopedia,* 1993 and *The Software Toolworks Multimedia Encyclopedia,* 1992 (CD-ROM).

Advisors: Leslie Kinder-Anderson, Lael Hagan, Karen Lorene, Elise Misiorowski, Tom Paradise, Myron Toback, Myra Waller, Janet Zapata.

PART I

Victorian Jewelry

INTRODUCTION

More jewelry was produced during the nineteenth century than in all previous centuries combined. There were several contributing factors: the Industrial Revolution and mass production, a growing middle class, and a changing social climate. For the first time, more women than men wore jewelry as symbols of wealth, although it was usually the men's wealth they were displaying. In contrast to the dandies of the eighteenth century, nineteenth century men were relatively conservative. While eighteenth-century gentlemen might have worn diamond-studded buckles, buttons, cravat pins, and other adornment, the primary decorative element for the nineteenth century gentleman was the pocket watch and all its accoutrements. Chains, fobs, seals, and charms dangled from his vest.

Jewelry has always been worn for other purposes in addition to social status. It can serve as a memento of loved ones living or dead. It also has a role as decorative and/or functional parts of clothing. A jewel can be worn as an expression of religious faith and as a talisman or amulet to ward off evil and disease. Souvenir jewelry and traditional jewelry symbolic of national or cultural origin or group membership are also common. In fact, more nonstatus antique jewelry, often made from nonprecious materials, survives today in its original form than does gemstone and gold jewelry. Jewelry with components of value was more likely to be broken up for its gemstones and precious metal and reworked into pieces in keeping with current fashion.

Fine and expensive high-karat gold and gemstone pieces from the late eighteenth and early nineteenth centuries certainly do turn up at auctions and high-end antique shows. However, most of the earliest accessible and affordable jewelry that exists today is early Victorian memorial and sentimental jewelry. This book begins with the period marked by Queen Victoria's ascension

to the throne of Great Britain. Although it may seem arbitrary, the year 1837 is generally recognized by jewelry historians as the beginning of a new era. There was, of course, a carryover of styles and types of jewelry from previous periods, called Late Georgian and Regency in Great Britain, circa 1800-1837. (In the United States, these periods correspond roughly to the Colonial and Federal periods.) Some pieces listed as early Victorian could actually date a bit earlier.

The timespan of the period is lengthy, so it is usually divided into three subperiods. While there is a difference of opinion as to the exact year that one subperiod ends and the next begins, there is consensus on their names: They are called the Early or Romantic, the Middle or Grand, and the Late Victorian or Aesthetic periods.

To more easily understand the great diversity and quantity of Victorian jewelry, the listings in this section have been grouped by types and/or materials. Each category is listed under the subperiod most closely associated with it, but individual listings may have earlier or later circa dates. Jewelry doesn't always fit neatly into a time slot or category. Styles tend to overlap, and newer versions of old designs continued to be made in later periods. Many materials, like coral, cut steel, and diamonds; motifs, such as snakes, flowers, and hands; and types of jewelry, like watch chains, bracelets and cameos, were worn throughout the nineteenth century. Precise dating can be difficult, unless there are clues like maker's marks, hallmarks with date letters, or engraved dated inscriptions. More often than not, nineteenth-century jewelry is unmarked. Identifying construction techniques and original findings can help to narrow the date range. Some findings, however, like the C-catch (a simple hook) and the tube hinge of brooch pin assemblies, were in use for the entire period, and often continued to be used in the twentieth century. Furthermore, pieces with intrinsic value (precious metals and stones) do not always survive intact. Alterations are common.

Several thematic threads were woven into the fabric of nineteenth-century society. Nature, history, symbolism, and above all, sentiment, were sometimes inextricably intertwined. In Victorian times, naturalism was expressed in jewelry with exact depictions of flora and fauna in gold and gemstones or other materials. Distasteful as it may seem today, real insects and birds' heads were sometimes made into jewelry. Flowers were symbols of sentiment and nature. Every flower had a specific meaning, and their definitions were cataloged in several flower dictionaries. One book, published in 1866, was appropriately called *The Language and Sentiment of Flowers*.

The second half of the nineteenth century was the age of the international exhibition—what later came to be known as world's fairs and expositions. Their historical importance should not be underestimated. In a period lacking mass communications media like television, exhibitions were the mass-marketing tool of the era. They made it possible for manufacturers and merchants to display their wares over a period of six months or more to hundreds of thousands of potential customers. The latest discoveries and developments, styles, and tastes were introduced to the general public at exhibitions. Instead of "as seen on TV," an item would be touted, for example, "as seen at the Paris Exposition." To have a booth at an exhibition conferred the highest status on the goods and their maker. Jewelry was exhibited by such prestigious firms as Froment-Meurice of Paris and Phillips of London at London's Crystal Palace Exhibition in 1851. Castellani of Rome exhibited at the International Exhibition in London in 1862 and at the Philadelphia Centennial Exposition in 1876; Tiffany & Co. of New York was also at the Philadelphia Centennial and at the Paris Exposition in 1867, 1878, 1889, and 1900. The designs of these and other exhibitors became fashionable by word of mouth and through reports in periodicals. They also inspired many imitators.

The period 1837-1901 is called the Victorian era in the United States as well as Great Britain. In spite of our country's independence from hers, Victoria's tastes influenced Americans as well as her own subjects. While the Western world looked to Paris for the latest styles and trends, English interpretations of French styles were acceptable to the more conservative American temperament. At times, these styles were modified even further by American artisans and manufacturers.

When Queen Victoria ascended the throne of Great Britain in 1837, the United States was a young country. Production of machine-made jewelry had begun in New England and New Jersey, but a distinct American style had yet to emerge. Most of it imitated the English or French styles. Some jewelers, in fact, tried to pass off their items as European. There were goldsmiths and silversmiths working in this country in the early eighteenth century, but, until the midnineteenth century, they produced mostly utilitarian wares. Personal adornment was largely limited to buckles, buttons, and clasps. Other types of jewelry that were worn were usually imported from Great Britain and Europe. In the early years of this country's history, distrust of the aristocracy and all that symbolized it—jewelry, for example—and the Puritan work ethic discouraged ostentatious displays of wealth. In fact, most Americans wore little except sentimental jewelry until after the Civil War. Washington's elite were sometimes the exception to this rule, however. Dolly Madison was known for her jewelled turbans sent from Paris (the War of 1812 notwithstanding). In the 1840s, President John Tyler's new wife, Julia, was the closest thing to royalty this country ever saw: She wore crowns and diamond tiaras.

References: Lillian Baker, *100 Years of Collectible Jewelry (1850-1950)*, Collector Books, 1978; Vivienne Becker, *Antique and Twentieth Century Jewellery*, 2nd ed., N.A.G. Press, 1987.

Necklace, enamel, 14k yg, c. 1830-40, oval and round scalloped edge links with multicolored champlevé enamel on both sides of links on engr scrollwork surfaces, 24" tl × ½", $2,090 (A). *Photo courtesy of Grogan & Co., Boston (3/30/93).*

EARLY VICTORIAN, ROMANTIC PERIOD C. 1837-1861

Queen Victoria set the tone for the era as the first woman to rule Great Britain since Queen Anne, who died in 1714. Like most women of her time, she was an incurable romantic—and she loved jewelry! The early years of her reign are aptly called The Romantic Period (also known as the Victoria and Albert period). Albert married Victoria in 1840, became Prince Consort in 1857, and died suddenly in 1861. The twenty-one years of their marriage were filled with love and devotion, and they were blessed with nine children. Symbols of romance were predominant in the jewelry that Albert designed and had made for Victoria. For example, her betrothal ring was in the form of a snake with its tail in its mouth, a symbol of everlasting love, a motif that recurs throughout the nineteenth century. The snake also symbolized eternity, guardian spirit, and wisdom. Snake (or serpent) jewelry was especially popular in the 1840s. The hand, another recurring romantic symbol in Victorian jewelry, had a variety of meanings depending on how it was depicted. Hands holding flowers conveyed the flower's message. Yew wreaths symbolized mourning. Clasped hands symbolized friendship. Good luck and evil eye hand-gesture amulets were carved in coral, ivory, jet, and mother-of-pearl. Hands were also used as clasps for bracelets and neckchains, especially in earlier period pieces.

Sentiment prevailed in the gifts of jewelry Victoria exchanged with others. She fostered the widespread practice of giving and wearing jewelry made with the hair of the giver. And no one thought it at all strange that she had a bracelet made from her children's baby teeth.

The Great Exhibition of the Industry of All Nations, held in London in 1851, was perhaps the single most important event of the early Victorian period. It was dubbed "The Crystal Palace" after the gigantic all-glass structure that housed it. Never before had there been a multinational exhibit of any kind. This monumental spectacle has been called "the focal point for the Victorian culture of the Western world." Its success spawned Crystal Palace offspring in Cork in 1852, in New York and Dublin in 1853, in Munich in 1854, and in Paris in 1855. In 1854, the Crystal Palace itself was recreated at Syndenham, outside London. The jewelers who took part in these exhibitions were the most highly esteemed trend setters of jewelry fashion. If it had been seen at the Crystal Palace, it was in style. In 1851, naturalistic diamond flower brooches and hair ornaments, Celtic annular (ring) brooches and Scottish granite bracelets, Berlin iron jewelry, and gemstone and enameled bracelets were among the pieces shown.

Early Victorian fashions determined the ways in which jewelry was worn. The dresses of the period were full-skirted, worn with petticoats, and often had long sleeves. Lace collars with brooches pinned at the throat were common. Necklines on dresses worn by younger women were cut low and wide across the shoulders. Velvet or silk ribbons were sometimes worn around the neck, crossed in front and pinned with a small brooch. Large jewelled brooches with pendent drops, called bodice brooches, were worn on low-cut gowns in the evening. Unless otherwise altered, early Victorian brooches have an extended pinstem (meant to be pushed back through the clothing to keep the brooch in place), C-catch and tube hinge. Gold and enamel or gem-set snake necklaces with flexible scalelike links were in vogue. In the late 1840s and early 1850s, bonnets were worn during the day, and for evening wear, center-parted hair covered the ears in loops or ringlets trimmed with ribbons or flowers. Consequently, earrings were seldom worn. Bracelets, worn in multiples on both wrists, were the most popular form of jewelry, especially snake-shaped coils or bangles. Stretchy expandable bracelets were introduced in the early 1840s, thanks to the invention of elastic, c. 1830. In spite of their prevalence, relatively few early Victorian bracelets survive today, having been subjected to considerably more wear and damage than brooches or necklaces might have been.

Romanticism inspired the revival of medieval and Renaissance motifs and decorative elements that continued throughout the century. Gothic architecture was translated into jewels. Gold was still in relatively short supply at the onset of the Early Victorian period. Most gold was hand-wrought filigree (called *cannetille*) or hollow-stamped or repoussé thin-gauge metal used as settings for gemstones or as frames for portrait miniatures and enamels. The Renaissance revival renewed the use of enamels in jewelry. The Swiss and the Italians excelled in enameling: The Swiss were known for painted enamels (sometimes called Geneva, Swiss, or *Limoges* enamel), and the Italians were noted for polychromatic *champlevé*.

References: *The Crystal Palace Exhibition Illustrated Catalogue,* reprint of the original Art-Journal publication, Dover, 1970; Carolyn Goldthorpe, *From Queen to Empress, Victorian Dress 1837-1877,* Metropolitan Museum of Art, New York (exhibition catalog), 1988.

Bracelet
  Snake
      18k yg, diamond, rubies, c. 1840-50, hinged
      bangle, hollow yg tube engr with scales
      (some dents), lg rc diamond on top of
      head, cab ruby eyes, illegible hmks on

Bracelet, hinged bangle, 18k yg, enamel, diamonds, rubies, c. 1840-50, snake, blue enameled head and body set with 58 om and rc diamonds, cab ruby eyes (minor loss to enamel), 2-¹/₂″ outside dia, head 1-¹/₄″ × ⁵/₈″ w, $4,313 (A). *Photo courtesy of Butterfield & Butterfield, San Francisco and Los Angeles (6/17/93).*

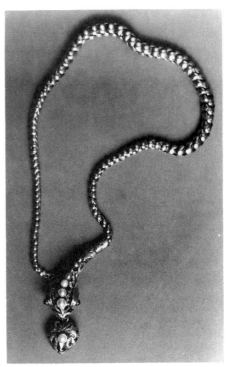

Necklace, 15k yg, pearls, enamel, garnets, wm, c. 1855-60, snake, grad scalelike links, blue enamel ground, appl yg and wm scroll and foliate design on head, garnet eyes, row of grad collet-set pearls on top of head, suspending blue enamel heart-shaped locket, pearl center, wm and yg scroll dec, rev glazed compartment containing woven cloth, box clasp on side of head, Eng, 17″ tl, head ³/₄″ w, heart ⁵/₈″ × ⁵/₈″, $1,800. *Author's collection.*

thumbpiece and spring catch of clasp, 2-¹/₄″ dia **1,100**

18k yg, rubies, c. 1860-70, woven yg mesh over a steel coil, ruby eyes, 3″ inside, 2″ w **2,800**

14k yg, rubies, c. 1860, engine turned, braided yg, three coils, ruby eyes, 2-¹/₂″ × 2″ dia . . . . **2,200 (A)**

14k yg, enamel, ruby, diamonds, c. 1860, green and yellow enameled hinged bangle, head set with an oval ruby surrounded by rc diamonds, diamond eyes, 2-¹/₄″ dia (some enamel dam) **2,500**

Brooch/Pin

14k yg, amethyst, c. 1830-40, lozenge-shaped scrolled openwork repoussé yg frame set with a lg oval cab amethyst, suspending a shield-shaped pendent drop of similar design, set with pear-shaped cab amethyst, 2-⁷/₈″ tl × 1-⁷/₈″ **1,100**

Yg, enamel, c. 1830-40, oval painted enamel miniature portrait depicting two young girls, one holding a bird, set in yg bezel and scrolled floral openwork frame, in fitted presentation box, C-catch, tube hinge, extended pinstem (repaired mounting), 1-⁷/₈″ × 1-⁵/₈″ . . . . **1,320 (A)**

Earrings, pendent

18k yg, enamel, c. 1830-40, openwork foliate surmount on earwire suspending lg drop of navette-shaped enamel plaque of female in native dress set in openwork scrolled and foliate frame, 3-¹/₂″ × 1″, pr . . . . . . **1,320 (A)**

Necklace

Snake

15k yg, garnet, green stones, c. 1860, cab garnet set in a chased and textured yg head, lt green stones in eyes, scalelike linking, Eng, 17″ × ¹/₂″ . . . . **1,980 (A)**

Yg, diamonds, cab red stones, c. 1840, flexible tapered body set with 240 om diamonds, head encrusted with om and rc diamonds (some simulated), red stone eyes, sm oval-shaped glazed locket compartment on underside of head, in fitted leather box, 15-¹/₂″ tl . . . . **21,850 (A)**

Suite: Necklace and Pendent Earrings

Enamel, 18k yg, c. 1830-40, necklace of nine grad oval Swiss painted enamel plaques of peasant scenes set in openwork floral and beaded yg frames alternating with beaded yg trefoils, floret centers, 16″ tl × 1-¹/₄″, earrings with openwork floret tops suspending oval painted-enamel plaques in yg frames, ⁵/₈″w × 1-¹/₂″ tl, suite . . . . **4,070 (A)**

CORAL

History: Coral was popular throughout the nineteenth century. Children wore coral necklaces to fend off disease and evil spirits because the Victorians held onto the ancient belief that coral had curative and protective powers. It also appealed to their interest in nature. Beads, carved

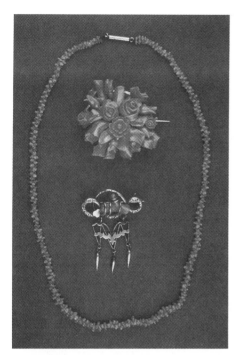

Coral, early, mid, late Victorian: Necklace, c. 1840, sm shaped cylindrical beads, yg tube clasp, 16" tl × ³/₁₆", $150; TC, Brooch/Pin, 14k yg, c. 1850-60, carved flower heads and leaves mounted on yg wire armature, C-catch, tube hinge, extended pinstem, 1-¹/₂" w × 1-³/₄", $400; BC, Brooch/Pin, c. 1880-90, gf, three open loops, wire-wrapped branch coral mounted in center, suspending pierced shaped plaque with three pendent drops; 1-³/₄" w × 1-¹/₄", $125. *Courtesy of E. Foxe Harrell Jewelers.*

cameos, floral motifs, good-luck charms, and natural branches were made into jewelry of all types. Italy, particularly Naples, was the primary source for coral, and most carvers were Italian. Desirable but rarer colors were deep red and pale pink.

The most prevalent surviving forms are those in which the coral is protected by a metal mounting or frame or beads. Intact examples of delicately carved all-coral pieces are more difficult to find.

References: Vivienne Becker, *Antique and Twentieth Century Jewellery,* 2nd ed., N.A.G. Press, 1987; Shirley Bury, *Jewellery, 1789-1910, The International Era,* Vol I, Antique Collectors' Club, 1991.

Bracelet
  Bangle, hinged
    18k yg, c. 1860-70, central medallion and tapered shoulders prong-set with grad round coral cabs, prongs tipped with yg beads, 2-³/₄" dia × 1-³/₄" . . . . . . **1,610 (A)**

14k yg, late Victorian, central oval cameo of a woman's profile, flanked by two curved coral segments of carved lions' heads, small cameo set in clasp, mounted in yg . . . . **1,430 (A)**
Link
  Yg, c. 1850-60, six carved coral masks depicting satyrs, joined by paired carved coral bars, terminating in a larger coral bacchant head carved in high relief in a rect coral plaque clasp, mounted in yg, safety chain, some chips to coral, 7-¹/₂" tl × ³/₄", clasp 1-³/₈" × 1-¹/₄" . . . . . **4,675 (A)**
Brooch/Pendant
  Cameo
    10k yg, c. 1900, woman's profile, engr oval frame, four seed pearls set at compass points, lever catch, swivel bail, 1" w × 1-³/₄" **350**
Brooch/Pin
  Gf, c. 1880-90, die-stamped and engr gf oval pretzel shape, twisting around central branch coral, terminating in sm heart shape, added safety catch, tube hinge, ⁷/₈" × ⁵/₈" **65**
  14k yg, mid-Victorian, carved head of a winged cherub, high relief, yg pin back, 2-¹/₈" × 1" . . . . **1,045 (A)**
  14k yg, c. 1850-60, carved cherub within carved floral, foliate and scroll motifs in high relief, mounted on yg armature, pin back, 2-³/₈" × 2-¹/₈" . . . . **1,210 (A)**
  Yg, c. 1880, round coral cabs mounted on yg armature in concentric ovals, ³/₄" × 1" **125**

Brooch/Pendant, cameo of woman s profile, coral, 14k yg, c. 1900, high relief cameo set in engr oval frame, lever clasp, swivel bail; 1-³/₈" w × 1-⁵/₈", $500. *Lucile Thompson collection.*

Earrings, pendent

    Yg, c. 1850-60, carved coral leaves and fruits mounted on jointed yg armatures, shepherd's hook earwires, 1-$\frac{1}{4}$" × $\frac{5}{8}$", pr . . . **350**

    Yg, c. 1850-60, cascading carved coral roses and leaves suspended from newer yg screwback findings with carved flowerhead surmounts, 1-$\frac{3}{4}$" tl × $\frac{5}{8}$", pr **275**

Hair ornament

    Gf, c. 1875, cornucopia shape mounted on two-pronged gf comb, with cascading carved coral fruits on gf wires, 5" × 1-$\frac{3}{4}$" l **275**

Necklace

    c. 1880, lathe-turned interlocking beads alternating with grad pearls, 18" tl **425**

    14k yg, late Victorian, fringe of 10 sm bezel-set cameos of women's profiles suspended from yg chain in grad pattern, 17-$\frac{3}{4}$" tl, 1-$\frac{1}{4}$" w at center . . . . **345 (A)**

Scarf pin

    Seed pearls, c. 1880, lg branch with string of seed pearls wrapped around branches, yg pinstem, 2" × 1-$\frac{7}{8}$" **300**

Suite: Brooch/Pin and Earrings

    Gf and yg, coral, c. 1850, die-stamped and engr, yg vine and leaf motifs suspending one round and three tapered beads, appl to oval open looped hollow gf brooch, C-catch, tube hinge, extended pinstem, ring for safety chain on brooch; 1-$\frac{1}{2}$" w × 1-$\frac{7}{8}$", matching drop e.r., soldered earwires, three tapered beads on each, 1-$\frac{1}{2}$" tl × $\frac{3}{4}$", suite **500**

    Yg, c. 1860, tapered shield-shaped yg plaque surmounted by textured yg floral and foliate motifs with a round coral cab in a flowerhead mount in the center, matching pendent earrings with flowerhead surmounts, brooch 1-$\frac{7}{8}$" × 1-$\frac{3}{8}$", earrings, 2" tl × $\frac{3}{4}$", suite . . . . **358 (A)**

STEEL, IRON, AND ALUMINUM

History: Jewelry made from riveted faceted beads or studs of polished steel dates at least as far back as the sixteenth century. Cut steel jewelry had its heyday in the late eighteenth century, when some of the most delicate and intricate ornaments were made to imitate the sparkle of diamonds. But it persisted as a craft and a fashion into the twentieth century. Much of what survives today was made in France, especially in the form of buckles for shoes and waists.

Some sources say that circa dating can be determined by construction methods and the number of facets on the studs. Earlier pieces have numerous (up to 15) facets, while later ones have as few as five. Machine-stamped strips instead of individually riveted studs are an indication of later, lower-quality, manufacture. But, according to other sources, multifaceted, individually studded examples of higher quality can also date as late as the 1900s. Factories in France were still turning out cut steel trinkets as recently as the 1940s.

Although buckles are the form most often seen today (for which there is less demand), bracelets, brooches, earrings, chains, and necklaces can also be found. Considering the intricacies of their design and craftsmanship and their relative scarcity, prices on these pieces remain quite reasonable.

Most of the black-lacquered lacy cast-iron jewelry known as Berlin iron is pre-Victorian. Its manufacture began around 1804, but a quantity of it was made in Germany during the Napoleonic Wars (1813-15). Some pieces continued to be made in the 1850s and were exhibited by German manufacturers at the Crystal Palace. Today it is extremely scarce and expensive.

Another type of iron jewelry that is more readily found dates to the later part of the century. It is inaccurately called gunmetal, perhaps because its smooth burnished bluish-grey surface resembles the barrel of a gun. Chains and lockets are the predominant forms.

Aluminum was scarce and classified as a precious metal in the midnineteenth century. Unlike silver, it was lightweight and did not tarnish. It was cast and riveted to gold or gilt metal in the 1850s and 1860s. The aluminum surface was often chased or engraved. As improved mining and processing methods increased available supply, the price of aluminum dropped and the novelty wore off. By the end of the century, aluminum had become déclassé. Today, the jewelry is difficult to find and pricey. An entirely different kind of handwrought aluminum jewelry made its appearance in the 1940s.

References: Vivienne Becker, *Antique and Twentieth Century Jewellery,* 2nd ed., N.A.G. Press, 1987; Shirley Bury, *Jewellery, 1789-1910, The International Era,* Antique Collectors' Club, 1991; Anne Clifford, *Cut Steel and Berlin Iron Jewellery,* Adams and Dart, 1971 (out of print); Ginny Redington Dawes & Corinne Davidov, *Victorian Jewelry, Unexplored Treasures,* Abbeville Press, 1991.

Bracelet, link

    Cut steel, late Georgian-early Victorian, layered and assembled central rosette flanked by six smaller single rosettes, set with sm round multifaceted studs, linked together and to box clasp with v-spring catch, center 1-$\frac{1}{2}$" dia, sides $\frac{1}{2}$" dia, 7" tl **525**

    Cut steel, composition, early Victorian, ivory-colored composition molded in a rose motif in centers of six linked medallions, frames set with cut steel studs, box clasp with v-spring catch, each link 1" × $\frac{3}{4}$", 7" tl **450**

Brooch/Pin
Cast iron, cut steel, early Victorian, polished iron cameo of classical bust set in frame with faceted studs riveted to metal backing in radial strips, C-catch, tube hinge, extended pinstem, 1" w × 1-¼" **350**
Cut steel, late Victorian, butterfly shape, pavé-set lg and sm studs with lg facets, C-catch, tube hinge, extended pinstem, 1-¾" w × 1" **325**
Buckle
Cut steel, c. 1880-90, two-piece, curved oval, round, and marquise faceted studs riveted to open, pierced backing, center hook-and-eye closure, metal bars for belt attachment on rev ends, 3-¼" w × 1-¾" **75**
Buckles, shoe
Cut steel, c. 1890, convex ovals, border of double row of sm round studs, central butterfly motif in pavé round and marquise faceted studs, riveted to pierced metal backing,

Buckle, cut steel, gunmetal, fabric, c. 1890, tapered shield shape bordered by double row of faceted and riveted cut steel beads, central motif of meandering rows of smaller faceted and riveted cut steel beads terminating in four star-shaped florets, mounted on black silk ground attached to gunmetal backing, long bar and double hook closure for belt on rev, 2-½" w × 5", $125. *Author's collection.*

metal bars for shoe attachment on rev, 1-⅞" w × 2-¾", pr **85**
Cut steel, fabric, c. 1890-1900, scalloped-edge rectangles, slightly convex, scrolled floral motif of small round faceted studs riveted to metal backing, mounted on black fabric background, metal bars for attachment to shoes on rev, mkd "Made in France," 2-⅞" w × 2", pr **100**
Earrings, pendent
Cut steel, mid to late Victorian, surmount of rosette with lg central stud surrounded by smaller studs mounted on shepherd's hook earwire, suspending large stud-set rosette, terminating in a fringe of three stud-set strips, 2-½" tl × ¾", pr **325**
Cut steel, mid to late Victorian, layered and assembled three-dimensional daisy motif surmount and drop, pavé-set with sm faceted studs, shepherd's hook earwires, 2" tl × ⅞", pr **325**
Hair comb
Cut steel, tortoiseshell, late Victorian, stud-set crown motif riveted to metal backing mounted on two-prong tortoiseshell comb, top 2" w × ⅞", 3" tl **185**
Neckchain
Steel, late Georgian-early Victorian, polished pierced links with star motifs, linked by a double row of tubular jump rings, ⅜" links, 28" tl **275**
Steel, early to mid Victorian, composed of bright-cut ovals with pierced scalloped-edge centers, linked by triple split rings, ½" × ¼" links, 28" tl **250**
Longchain and locket
Gunmetal, late Victorian, curb-link chain interspersed with sm round spectacle-set faceted glass stones, suspending circ locket from swivel hook, engr with mono front and back, 1-¾" dia, 60" tl **175**
Gunmetal, late Victorian, cable-link chain suspending heart-shaped locket from swivel hook, locket 1" × ⅞", chain 36" tl **150**
Pendant
Aluminum, 10k yg, c. 1860-70, Masonic pendant designed as a hinged orb that opens to form a cross, each aluminum section of pyramidal design enhanced with Masonic engr, joined with yg links and yg bail, 2-¼" tl × 1-⅝" . . . . **440 (A)**
Watch Pin
Gunmetal, c. 1890-1900, ribbon bow shape, swivel hook suspended from center knot, 1-⅜" w × 1" **95**

HAIR IN JEWELRY

History: One of the most popular expressions of Victorian sentimentality, on both sides of the Atlantic, was the making and wearing of jewelry with human hair, a practice that originated in the seventeenth century. These pieces were worn as memento mori (mourning) and also as love tokens.

The earliest type of hair jewelry was made with glass or rock-crystal-covered compartments to hold the hair of a loved one, living or deceased. Eighteenth and early nineteenth century mourning brooches might depict a funereal scene, complete with weeping willow, urn, and a despondent maiden standing forlornly by.

Portrait miniatures in painted enamel often have a lock of the portrayed loved one's hair enclosed in a compartment on the reverse. In other pieces, the hair is formed into curls, called "Prince of Wales plumes," or made into wheat sheaves, mounted on a white background. Another technique was to lay strands of hair flat on "goldbeater's skin," a type of adhesive backing, and cut out individual floral motifs that were then assembled as a three-dimensional picture under glass.

More commonly, locks of hair were simply braided or coiled, sometimes using more than one color (from different family members), and placed in compartments set into a frame and covered with glass.

On mourning pieces, the outer or inner frame could include a snake motif, symbolizing eternity. Seed pearls, symbolic of tears, were sometimes added, along with gold thread or wire tied around the lock of hair. In late Georgian and early Victorian pieces, the backs were gold or gold-filled and slightly convex. They were often engraved with names or initials, and dates of birth and/or death. This personalization of a piece is desirable to collectors, and of course it takes the guesswork out of placing the piece in its time frame.

Early mourning brooches or pins, c. 1820-40, were small, and worn pinned to black ribbon as a necklace or bracelet. They were bordered with pearls, garnets, coral, or black enamel around the glass-covered compartment. Later brooches were larger, worn at the throat or in the center of the bodice. Black onyx plaques or black enameled borders inscribed "In Memory Of" around a central hair compartment became standardized forms for mourning pieces.

References: Vivienne Becker, *Antique and Twentieth Century Jewellery*, 2nd ed., N.A.G. Press, 1987; Jeanenne Bell, *Answers to Questions About Old Jewelry*, Books Americana, 1992; Shirley Bury, *An Introduction to Sentimental Jewellery*, Victoria & Albert Museum, 1985.

Advisor: Carmelita Johnson.

Brooches/Pins, memorial, yg, hair: TL, c. 1820-40, rect, glazed compartment containing blond and brown braided hair (glass cracked), set in yg, closed back, seed pearl border, C-catch, tube hinge, extended pinstem, $^3/_4$" w × $^1/_2$", $150; TR, c. 1830, 10 round cab corals set in rect border, central glazed compartment containing braided brown hair, C-catch, tube hinge, extended pinstem, $^7/_8$" w × $^5/_8$", $220; BL, c. 1840, rectangle set with 14 round faceted garnets around border, central glazed compartment with hinged yg back for hair, bordered with seed pearls, C-catch, tube hinge, extended pinstem; 1-$^1/_8$" w × 1", $350; BR, c. 1835, eight table-cut garnets in oval setting, border of radiating points set with seed pearls, brown braided hair in central glazed compartment, yg mount, C-catch, tube hinge, extended pinstem, 1-$^1/_8$" w × $^7/_8$", $350. *Courtesy of E. Foxe Harrell Jewelers.*

Brooch/Pin

12k yg, hair, cloth, glass, enamel, c. 1855-65, two colors (blond and brown) flat-woven hair in a checkerboard pattern in front glazed compartment with beaded yg border, woven dk brown cloth in rev glazed compartment, mounted in oval yg frame with black enameled Greek key design, Eng, C-catch, tube hinge, extended pinstem, 1-3/4" w × 1-3/8"
. . . . **500**

14k yg, hair, MOP, seed pearls, glass, c. 1840-50, three-dimensional floral bouquet motif constructed from cut shapes of adhesive-backed blond and brown hair with added hp details, seed pearls in flower centers, mounted on MOP plaque set in an oval engr and *taille d'épargne* enameled yg frame, beveled glass cover, convex yg rev engr with mono, C-catch (repaired), tube hinge, 1-3/4" w × 1-5/8" **450**

14k yg, hair, glass, c. 1860, flat woven dk brown hair in front and back, covered with beveled glass, die-stamped and engr scalloped edge frame, C-catch, tube hinge, 1-1/4" w × 1-1/2" **225**

14k yg, enamel, diamond, half-pearls, hair, c. 1860-70, circ shape, center of blue enamel star surmounted by om diamond surrounded by half pearls, twisted wirework and enamel, rev glazed compartment containing lock of hair, 2" dia . . . . **495 (A)**

Black onyx, 14k yg, hair, oval onyx plaque with appl yg mono (cipher), rev glazed compartment containing dk brown braided hair, hook for watch, engr "Obt Dec 6th 1871," C-catch, tube hinge, 1-1/4" w × 1-5/8" . . . **400**

Black onyx, 9k yg, seed pearls, hair, c. 1860, oval framed bordered with seed pearls and oval cut stones set in sawtooth bezels, enclosing glazed compartment containing braided blond and gray hair, inscribed on rev, C-catch, tube hinge, Eng, 1" w × 1-1/2"
. . . . **350**

Garnets, hair, glass, gf, c. 1830-40, rounded rect, woven hair in glazed compartment bordered by flat-cut garnets set in gilt cut down collets, gf backing, C-catch, tube hinge, soldered ring with attached safety chain and pin on rev, 1" w × 7/8" **275**

Gf, hair, c. 1850-60, oval glazed compartments, front containing twisted lock of brown hair, rev containing woven cloth, set in beaded-edge gf frame, C-catch, tube hinge, extended pinstem, 1-1/4" w × 1-1/2"
. . . . **165**

Gf, hair, c. 1860-70, concentric rings of braided lt brown hair, dk brown hair in center, gf dividers, set in circ glazed compart-

Brooches/Pins, memorial: TL, c. 1860, Prince of Wales plumes of two colors hair and seed pearls on ivory ground, border of twist pattern ym within glazed compartment set in tubular ym frame enclosed by carved jet in branchlike pattern, one-piece hinge and catch pin assembly attached to rev, 1-3/8" w × 1-1/8", $275; **TC,** c. 1830-40, weeping willow and urn motif, black enamel on yg, urn with glazed compartment containing braided hair, white enamel accents, extended pinstem, C-catch, tube hinge, 7/8" w × 1", $350; **TR,** c. 1840, rounded-corner rect with inner and outer engr gf frame, foliate motif on black enamel bg, glazed compartment containing braided hair, C-catch, tube hinge, extended pinstem; 7/8" w × 1/2", $90; **BL,** "In Memory Of" in Gothic lettering on black enamel ground within lobed and scrolled yg frame, central glazed compartment containing braided hair within engr inner yg frame, rev inscribed "May Allen died May 18 1837. Aged 39," C-catch, tube hinge, 1" w × 5/8", $145; **BR,** c. 1840-50, rect, black enamel within inner and outer yg frame engr with foliate design, glazed central compartment containing braided hair, C-catch, tube hinge; 1" w × 5/8", $100. *Photo courtesy of Carmelita Johnson collection.*

Brooch/Pin, ym, hair, c. 1840-50, flower basket motif constructed from cutout shapes of adhesive-backed hair in three-dimensional design on flat off-white ground set in rect engr frame, glass cover, C-catch, tube hinge, 2" w × 1-³⁄₄", $450. *Photo courtesy of Carmelita Johnson collection.*

ment, plain gf frame, C-catch, tube hinge, extended pinstem, 1-⁵⁄₈" dia **175**

Gf, c. 1860-80, oval, swiveling central plaque containing "Prince of Wales plumes" of brown hair in glazed compartment on one side, photograph on the other, mounted in gf wire frame with appl foliate motifs and hollow batons on top, bottom and sides, C-catch, tube hinge, extended pinstem, 1-³⁄₄" w × 2-¹⁄₄" **200**

Hair, yg, oval yg framed glazed compartment containing three colors of coiled hair, rev inscribed: "My dear Mother, precious will be her memory while being lasts, died 12 April 1852 aged 85 years 6 mo," C-catch, tube hinge, 1-¹⁄₄" w × 1-⁵⁄₈" **185**

Hair, yg, elongated oval yg framed glazed compartment containing braided gray-brown hair, rev inscribed: "My beloved grandmother, Mrs. M. Dummer, died 12 April 1852, aged 85 years 6 mo," C-catch, tube hinge, added rings for safety chain, 1-⁵⁄₈" w × 1" **145**

Yg, hair, glass, c. 1840-50, octagonal yg framed oval glazed compartment containing braided brown hair, C-catch, tube hinge, ³⁄₄" w × 1-¹⁄₈" **145**

Yg, enamel, cloth, c. 1830, *Limoges* enameled plaque depicting portrait of dog's head on blue bg, set in repoussé and *cannetille* circ frame, rev glazed compartment for hair containing woven brown cloth backing, C-catch, tube hinge, extended pinstem, ⁷⁄₈" dia **450**

Yg, hair, seed pearls, c. 1840-50, oval glazed compartment containing twisted lock of reddish-brown hair, mounted in yg frame set with scalloped-edge double row of seed pearls in cut-down collets, 1-¹⁄₂" w × 1-³⁄₈" **275**

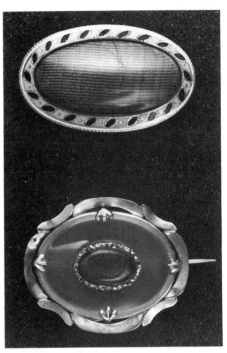

Brooches/Pins, memorial, c. 1840: T, yg, enamel, elongated oval yg frame, lt and dk blue enamel border, center compartment containing woven lt brown hair, convex glass cover, C-catch, tube hinge, attached ring for safety chain on rev; 1-⁵⁄₈" w × 1", $250; B, gf, beveled oval translucent chalcedony prong-set in shaped gf frame, surmounted by central oval glazed compartment containing woven brown hair set in engr bezel, C-catch, tube hinge, extended pinstem, 1-¹⁄₂" w × 1-¹⁄₄", $300. *Courtesy of E. Foxe Harrell Jewelers.*

Yg, black enamel, 15k, pearls, scrolled border, central forget-me-not motif, glazed compartment for hair on rev, inscribed "In Memory of G. Watson, Obt 27th April 1851 at 76," Eng, C-catch, tube hinge, extended pinstem, 1-¹⁄₂" w × 1-³⁄₄" **300**

Yg, black enamel, 10k, c. 1850, lobed, scrolled and serrate raised border, "In Memory Of," in Gothic letters around central glazed compartment containing two colors braided hair, convex yg backing engr with two sets of initials, C-catch, tube hinge, safety chain loop, 1-⁷⁄₈" × 1-¹⁄₂" **350**

Pendant

Agate, 15k yg, hair, c. 1860-70, oval tablet-cut dendritic agate set within twisted-wire frame outlined with appl yg beads, rev hair compartment (glass replaced with plastic), Eng, 1-⁵⁄₈" w × 2-¹⁄₈" tl . . . . **1,100 (A)**

Agate, gf, hair, c. 1850-60, Maltese cross of banded grey agate segments set into sq gf center glazed compartment containing

Pendant, black onyx, MOP, hair, yg, c. 1860-80, central floral motif constructed from cutout shapes of adhesive-backed hair mounted on MOP plaque set into oval onyx pendant, glass crystal, yg bezel and bail, 1-¼" w × 1-⅞", $325. *Mary Lou Diebold collection.*

braided brown hair, pendant bail riveted to one agate segment, 1-¼" sq **300**

Painted miniature, yg, hair, c. 1830, depicting frontal portrait of a young woman, rev glazed compartment containing plaited hair, set in plain yg bezel and frame, pendant bail, in original leather case, 2" w × 2-¾" . . . . **715 (A)**

Painted miniature, 9k rose gold, ivory, hair, portrait of a youth with long flowing blond hair painted on ivory, sgd "C.T.," dated 1890, rev enclosing a lock of blond hair, mounted in plain rose gold frame, 3-⅛" w × 4-¾" tl . . . . **1,035 (A)**

Pendant and Chain

Yg, *pietra dura,* hair, seed pearls, c. 1860-70, oval central glazed compartment containing brown hair arranged in "Prince of Wales plumes" on white bg, tied with gold thread, seed pearls, rev plaque of *pietra dura* floral bouquet motif (one flower missing), set in 14k yg frame with rope-twist border, pendant bail, married to 9k yg chain with raised rect fancy links, pendant 1-¼" w × 2" tl, chain 15-¾" × ¼" . . . . **460 (A)**

Ring

9k yg, hair, c. 1860-70, flat-woven brown hair channel-set in flat band with raised borders, covered with three rect engr yg plaques mounted at intervals, central scrolled plaque for mono, inside mkd "M.G., 9ct," Eng, ¼" w **150**

Yg, c. 1860, woven hair mounted in center of flat band with raised edge, covered with X-shaped engr yg plaques spaced at intervals, some wear, ¼" w **175**

Man's, yg, hair, enamel, late Georgian to early Victorian, black cloisonné enameled tapered shank set with rect black glass head with central glazed compartment containing woven hair, inside engr inscription, ½" w × ⅝" **375**

Scarf pin/Stickpin

Yg, black enamel, hair, garter motif, "In Memory Of" inscribed in enamel border, central glazed compartment containing braided white hair, rev engr with name, date of death (1842) and age of deceased, 2-¾" tl × ½" dia **125**

Suite: Brooch/Pin and Earrings, yg, hair, enamel, seed pearl, c. 1850-60, three-dimensional sheaves of wheat motifs constructed from hair appl to flat off-white ground enclosed in glazed compartments set in yg frames with Greek key design in black enamel; brooch 1-⅝" w × 1-⅜", matching drop earrings (findings converted to screwbacks), ⅝" × ⅞", $650. *Photo courtesy of Carmelita Johnson collection.*

HAIRWORK

History: Hairwork is a second type of hair jewelry in which the entire piece is made of woven hair with the addition of gold or gold-filled fittings and decorative elements. These pieces were not necessarily meant for mourning. They were made by and for women and men out of their own or a loved one's hair and given as mementos or love tokens.

The technique involved the use of a type of worktable on which individual strands of hair were weighted and woven together to form hollow tubes around a solid core of cording and/or wire. This core was sometimes removed, and the tubes were then tied or enclosed with gold rings at intervals to form spherical or elliptical hollow beads. After processing and weaving, the hairwork could then be made into necklaces, bracelets, earrings, or brooches. A commonly found form is a watch chain in which the tube or rope of hair is woven in a spiral pattern, with an added gold or gold-filled swivel hook and bar and fob charms (sometimes also made of hair).

Hairwork jewelry was made for more than 50 years commercially, as well as by "loving hands at home" from instructions found in women's magazines of the day, such as *Godey's Lady's Book* or *Peterson's Magazine*. Fittings for hair watch chains were advertised in Sears catalogs as late as 1911, but the practice of making and wearing hair jewelry reached its peak of popularity in the 1850s and 1860s, and had waned considerably by the 1880s.

While the thought of human hair jewelry may be distasteful to some, collectors find both the idea and its execution fascinating. In recent years, there has been a growing appreciation for this lost art, as well as interest in reviving it.

The value of hair jewelry is in the workmanship; solid gold fittings enhance the value only slightly over gold-filled. Watch chains are the form most usually found, and necklaces and earrings are scarce. Brown is the most common hair color. Blond and white are scarce, and red is rare, not only because redheads are in the minority, but also because red hair was attributed to women of ill repute.

Damaged pieces are difficult to repair. To date, only one qualified restorer has been found, so be sure to check condition carefully.

References: Lilian Baker Carlisle, "Hair Jewelry," in *The Antique Trader Weekly*, May 2, 1990; Anita and Phil Gordon, "Hair Jewelry: Much More Than Mourning," in *Jewelers' Circular-Keystone/Heritage*, February 1990 (Chilton); Jules and Kaethe Kliot, eds., *The Art of Hairwork, Hair Braiding and Jewelry of Sentiment* (reprint of book by Mark Campbell, 1875), Lacis Publications, Berkeley, Calif., 1989.

Bracelet, hair, gf, yg, c. 1840-60, 3 cords of braided hair braided together, ends held in place by three-part cylindrical hinged engr gf clasp, suspending yg heart charm containing Prince of Wales plumes of hair in glazed compartment, 3-1/2″ dia, heart 5/8″ w × 3/4″, $400. *Photo courtesy of Carmelita Johnson collection.*

Collectors' Club: Hair Art International Restorers (H.A.I.R.) Society, Ruth Gordon, restoration craftsperson and president, 24629 Cherry Street, Dearborn, Mich. 48124 (313) 277-2479.

Museums: Bennington Museum, Bennington, Vt.; Fleming Museum, Burlington, Vt.; Pine Forest Historical Museum, Edmore Mich.; Henry Ford Museum and Greenfield Village, Dearborn, Mich.

Advisor: Carmelita Johnson.

Bracelet
   Gf, c. 1860-70, flat woven band of brown hair terminating in engr gf oval front clasp, 7" tl × 7/8" **275**
   Gf, c. 1860-70, flat band of woven brown hair terminating in rect front clasp with glazed compartment containing braided grey hair, 7-1/2" tl × 5/8" **300**
   Gf, c. 1860-70, band of woven brown hair in two (outer and inner) patterns, lobed flower-petal-shaped end caps, front clasp of oval glazed compartment containing braided hair set in lobed petal frame, safety chain, 7-1/4" tl × 1", clasp 1-1/8" × 7/8" **425**
   Yg, enamel, c. 1850-70, braided band of dk brown hair joined by front clasp of engr and black enameled yg, central glazed compartment containing braided hair, 2-1/2" dia, clasp 1-1/2" w **450**
   Yg and gf, micromosaic, c. 1850-60, flat band of woven brown hair terminating in gf rect

end caps, oval front clasp with micromosaic of King Charles spaniel in off-white bg set in plain yg frame, safety chain, 7-1/2" tl × 3/4", clasp 1-1/8" × 3/4" **575**
Link
   Yg, enamel, c. 1850-60, segmented sections of braided dk brown hair with rect end caps of engr and black and white enameled floral and foliate motifs, linked together and terminating in engr and enameled clasp suspending sm engr and enameled puffed heart, 7-1/2" tl × 5/8" **475**
Brooch/Pin
   Yg, c. 1850-60, bow shape, multiple thin braided segments of dk brown hair held together at ends and center by engr rect yg plaques mounted on pin assembly, C-catch, tube hinge, 1-3/4" w × 1" **150**
Bar
   Gf, c. 1870-80, three cords of tight-woven brown hair braided together, mounted on gf bar, held in place by engr gf bands at center and ends, C-catch, tube hinge, 2-1/8" w × 3/8" **125**
Earrings, drop
   Yg, c. 1860-70, single hollow lt brown hairwork lantern-shaped beads, yg caps at each end, orig yg earwires, 1-3/4" tl × 3/4", pr **175**
   Yg, c. 1860-70, lantern-shaped drops of hollow woven brown hair enclosed in yg wire cages,

Bracelet, snake, hair, yg, green stones, c. 1840-60, tightly woven hair encasing central core of cord-covered wire, heavily engr yg head and tail, green stone eyes; 16" l uncoiled, 3/8" w, 3" dia, $575. *Photo courtesy of Carmelita Johnson collection.*

Brooches/Pins, hair, c. 1850-60, woven hollow work: L, coiled pretzel design with appl engr gf foliate and floral motifs, C-catch, tube hinge; 2″ w × ⁷/₈″, $125; C, cross motif, beads formed by yg rings, yg beads on ends; 1-¹/₄″ w × 1-⁵/₈″, $150; R, bow motif, two loops clasped by engr gf central plaque, pendent drops with segments tied at intervals, yg tube tips; 2-³/₈″ w × 1-³/₈″, $125. *Photo courtesy of Carmelita Johnson collection.*

suspended from circ domed surmounts of similar design, mounted on earwires, 1-⁷/₈″ tl × ⁵/₈″, pr **200**

Yg, seed pearls, c. 1860-70, scalloped-edge hollow hair disks enclosed in yg wire cages, central engr yg flowerheads with seed pearl centers, suspended from surmounts of similar design, mounted on earwires, 1-⁵/₈″ tl × 1″, pr **285**

Necklace

Gf, c. 1860-70, narrow cord of tightly woven dk brown hair terminating in a tube clasp, suspending an anchor pendant of woven hair wrapped with gf foxtail chain, domed and arrow-shaped end caps, 16-¹/₂″ tl × ¹/₄″, pendant 1-¹/₈″ w × 2-¹/₄″ **285**

Gf, c. 1860-70, hollow tube of woven dk brown hair tied at intervals to form beads, gf clasp, central engr gf rect plaque suspending cross pendant of similar hollow bead constr, gf end caps, 17-¹/₂″ tl, cross 1-³/₈″ w × 2-¹/₂″ **425**

Ring

Gf, c. 1860-70, flat woven band of brown hair, top of stamped scrolled gf plaque with central compartment containing blond hair, band ¹/₄″ w, top ³/₄″ × ¹/₂″ **150**

Scarf pin/Stickpin

Gf, c. 1870-80, horseshoe charm of woven brown hair, gf end bands, suspended from top of pinstem with gf bead finial, 2-¹/₄″ tl, charm ⁵/₈″ w × ³/₄″ **100**

Yg, c. 1840-50, snake in coiled S-shape of tightly woven dk brown hair, yg head, seed pearl eye, mounted on yg pinstem, 3″ tl, snake 1-³/₈″ × ⁷/₈″ **225**

Suite: Brooch/Pin and Earrings

14k yg, c. 1860-70, lozenge-shaped brooch of

Necklace, hair, 14k yg, c. 1860, hollow woven tube tied at intervals forming beads, suspending rect engr yg front clasp and three acorn-shaped pendent drops of woven hair, 20″ tl, clasp 1-¹/₂″ l, $500. *Lucile Thompson collection.*

Rings: L, yg, hair, c. 1850-60, domed center, engr and cutout sections enclosing woven hair, inner engr inscription "H to E," ¼" × ⅝" dia, $160; C, memorial, woven hair channel-recessed in yg ring with rolled edges, engr cover plate with initials "G.W.," inside engr reads "GELE 18 Marz 1818 - GERST 6 July 1854," ³/₁₆" × ⅞" dia, $190; R, c. 1860, woven hair in belt/buckle motif with ym buckle, tip and keeper, adjustable; ³/₁₆" w, $100. *Photo courtesy of Carmelita Johnson collection.*

woven hair enclosed with twisted yg wire, yg floral and foliate motifs on sm plaques at center and ends, suspending three woven hair pendent drops, 1-¾" w × 1-½", matching lantern-shaped drop earrings suspended from earwires, 1-⅝" tl × ⅜", suite **400**

14k yg, c. 1860-70, hollow woven hair tubes formed into bow-shaped brooch enclosed with engr yg center knot, 2" w × ⅞", drop earrings of hollow woven beads suspended by yg cones from circ woven hair surmount with appl spiral yg decor, 10k yg screwback findings added later, 1-¾" tl × ½", suite
. . . . **400**

Watch Chain

Gf, c. 1860-70, fancy pattern woven hair, engr gf findings, bar and swivel, 13-½" tl **75**

Gf, mid to late Victorian, longchain of dk brown woven hair, spiral pattern, gf slide and swivel hook for watch, 34" tl × ⅛" **100**

14k yg, enamel, ym, c. 1840-50, dk brown woven hair, spiral pattern, engr and black *taille d'épargne* enamel end and center fittings, bar for vest buttonhole, eyescrew swivel suspending circ engr daguerreotype locket, tight-woven acorn drop fob charm suspended from center fitting, 14-⅞" tl × 1"
. . . . **200**

T-B:. Brooch/Pin, hair, gf, c. 1850-60, oval with twisted gf wire forming pinwheel cage around oval center button, enclosing woven brown hair, gf backing, suspending two acorn-shaped drops of hollow hairwork from chains, C-catch, tube hinge, extended pinstem, 1" w × 1-½" tl, $150, *Author's collection;* Watch Chains, hair: gf, c. 1860, dk brown woven hair with hair horseshoe charm suspended from center, gf bar and swivel, 9" tl, horseshoe ½" × ¾", $100, *Vicki Telford collection* ; gp brass, MOP, c. 1860-80, spiral pattern woven hairwork, engr fittings, red stone in center, MOP on horseshoe-shaped fob charm, missing bar and swivel from ends, 10" tl, fob ½" × ⅝", $75, *Author's collection* ; yg, c. 1840-60, lt brown chain suspending dk brown cross and heart charms, engr fittings, early hook and clasp, 13" l, cross 1-¼" l, heart ¾" w, $275, *Cheri Mulligan collection;* Pendent Earrings, hair, yg, c. 1860-70, three hollow beads with yg caps suspended from a scrolled, pierced yg plaque, hairwork bead surmount on orig yg earwire, two colors brown hair, 2" tl × ⅞", pr, $250, *Kathryn Ferguson collection.*

SCOTTISH JEWELRY

History: Gothic and Celtic revivals were already well under way when Victoria ascended the throne. Her own romantic attachment to ancient and medieval history was certainly influential in furthering the public's preoccupation with the past. Britain's, particularly Scotland's, past was romanticized by historical novels, like those of Sir Walter Scott. And after Victoria purchased Balmoral, a castle in Scotland, in 1848, everyone became enamored of Scottish motifs. Circular Scottish plaid pins, heraldic crests, dirks and claymores (knives and swords), thistles and St. Andrew's crosses (Scottish national emblems), and the Order of the Garter strap and buckle (symbol of the chivalric order headed by Victoria)—all were made into jewelry with pebbles (agates), cairngorms (dark yellow-amber faceted quartz), and amethysts set in engraved silver or gold.

Unless a piece is hallmarked with a British date letter (and many pieces are not), precise dating of Scottish jewelry is difficult. Earlier pieces tend to be more faithful to traditional Scottish motifs. Mid-Victorian pieces incorporated anchors, hearts, serpents, arrows, and other non-Scottish forms. Subtle differences can be seen in later nineteenth-century pieces, such as the cut of the stones and the absence of ornate engraving. Some traditional forms continued to be made, and C-catches and tube hinges continued to be used as brooch findings well into the twentieth century.

But rhodium plating and cast mountings are sure signs of more recent vintage and lesser quality. Brooches are the most common form; bracelets are scarcer, but they do turn up; earrings and buckles are rare, necklaces extremely rare. Scottish jewelry is very wearable with today's fashions, consequently, demand is high, especially for larger pieces.

References: Vivienne Becker, *Antique and Twentieth Century Jewellery*, 2nd ed., N.A.G. Press, 1987; Shirley Bury, *Jewellery, 1789-1910, The International Era*, Antique Collectors' Club, 1991; Ginny Redington Dawes and Corinne Davidov, *Victorian Jewelry, Unexplored Treasures*, Abbeville Press, 1991. Contains many excellent (albeit mostly rare) examples, beautifully photographed.

Bracelet, link
  Agate, sterling, c. 1860, curved sq links set with brown and white stones in engr mounts, lg working buckle clasp, links ³/₄" sq, 8" tl **800**
  Agate, citrine, silver, c. 1870-90, scalloped oval silver links set with lg citrines, alternating with carved trefoil links of pink/white agate, padlock clasp set with pink agate, links ⁵/₈" × ⁷/₈", 7" tl **975**
  Agate, c. 1880, interlocking carved, curved brown and white agate links hinged with steel pins, ⁵/₈" × ³/₄", 6-¹/₂" tl **300**
  Agate, white metal, c. 1890, converted from watch fob, grad brown and white agate

Brooches/Pins, Scottish agate, silver, c. 1850: L, target plaid type, scalloped edge, variegated stones cut to fit around center domed crystal compartment possibly containing heather, C-catch, tube hinge, extended pinstem, 1-³/₄" dia, $300; **R,** Scottish claymore and shield shape, stones set flush in engr mount, C-catch, tube hinge, 2-³/₈" l, $250. *Corinne Durst collection.*

squares set in wm frames, swivel hook clasp,
5-½" tl **375**

Brooch/Pin

Agate, citrine, 14k yg, c. 1850, in the form of a
dirk (dagger), three round citrine briolettes,
jasper and bloodstone set in engr yg handle
and blade, 2" tl × ⅜" **500**

Agate, cairngorms, silver, c. 1850, St. Andrew's
cross X-shape set with lozenge-shaped grey/
white agates, mounted on sq engr silver
backing set with cab cairngorms in bezels on
four corners between the arms of the cross,
1-¾" sq **350**

Agate, silver, c. 1850-60, annular (doughnut-
shaped) target plaid brooch, flat wedge-
shaped segments of beige, rust, and brown
veined agate mounted flush in engr inner and
outer silver frame and backing, C-catch, tube
hinge, extended pinstem, 2" dia **275**

Agate, jasper, silver, c. 1850-60, claymore
(Scottish broadsword) shape, with engr ster
cage over red jasper hilt, engr ster fleur-de-lis
band enclosing bloodstone blade, C-catch,
tube hinge, 3-½" tl × ¾" **250**

Agate, citrines, silver, c. 1850, Celtic annular
(ring) brooch, curved sections of gray/white
agate set in engr mounting, engr trefoils set
with cab citrines at joined ends and center
point of ring, 2-¼" dia **300**

Agate, silver, c. 1860, annular shape, flat, polished piece of grey and white banded agate
in an eight-pronged silver mounting, with
engr silver Order of the Garter strap and
buckle motif in center mounted around sm
opening, C-catch, tube hinge, extended
pinstem, 2-¼" dia **300**

Agate, yg, c. 1860-70, circ design, Order of the
Garter strap and buckle motif of inlaid seg-

Brooch/Pin, Scottish Agate, silver, c. 1850-60, quatrefoil ring brooch with disk and cone-shaped segments of
multicolored stones bezel-set, flat backing, 1-¼" dia,
$150. *Lucile Thompson collection.*

ments of bloodstone and jasper, striped and
banded agate, in engr yg setting, 1-¾" ×
1-½" **700**

Agate, silver, c. 1860-70, anchor shape,
bloodstone and rust and grey agates set flush
in engr mounting, 2-¾" × 2" **400**

Agate, silver, c. 1860, annular oval, Maltese
cross set with multicolored agates mounted
in center, flanked on two sides by pyramid-
shaped agates, oval cabs above and below,
curved sections set in ring, engr mounting,
1-½" w × 2-¼" **550**

Sterling, citrine, date letter for 1948, annular
shape, Celtic knot motifs in die-stamped
frame, lg round faceted citrine mounted on

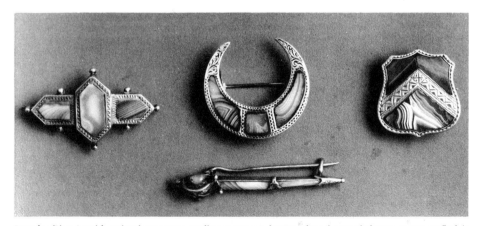

Brooches/Pins, Scottish, striated grey agate, sterling, c. 1860: L, lozenge-shaped crossed plaques, stones set flush in
engr mounting, beaded edge, 1-⅝" w × ⅞", $150; TC, segmented stones set flush in engr crescent shape, C-catch;
1-¼" × 1-⅛", $175; BC, dirk (dagger) shape, tapered stone in engr mounting, C-catch, tube hinge, 2" × ½", $150,
Cheri Mulligan collection; R, shield shape, stones set flush in engr mounting, C-catch, 1" × 1", $125, *Mary Lou
Diebold collection.*

crossbars in the center, Glasgow (Scotland) hmks, C-catch, tube hinge, extended pinstem, 1-¹/₂″ dia **150**

Earrings, pendent

Agate, silver, mid-Victorian, grey agates set in flat urn-shaped drops and St. Andrew's cross X-shaped surmounts, shepherd's hook earwires, 1-³/₄″ × ⁵/₈″, pr **575**

Scarf pin/Stickpin

Agate, citrine, yg, c. 1850, alternating bloodstone and jasper in garter motif, center citrine, ⁵/₈″ w × ¹/₂″, 3″ tl **425**

Agate, 14k yg, mid-Victorian, bloodstone disk set in yg frame with pierced and beaded border, surmounted by quadrate cross set with agates in engr yg, ⁷/₈″ dia, 2-³/₄″ tl **450**

Brooches/Pins, sterling, date letter for 1950: Traditional Celtic brooches continued to be made in Scotland in the twentieth century. T, Dove of Peace motif in center of annular garter shape bearing Latin motto "VIRTUTE TUTUS," Edinburgh (Scotland) hmks, C-catch, tube hinge, 1″ × 1-¹/₄″, $75; B, annular Order of Garter strap and buckle motif bearing Latin motto: "PER MARE PER TERRAS," cross and gauntlet in center, hmkd for Edinburgh (Scotland), C-catch, tube hinge, 1-⁵/₈″ × 1-⁷/₈″, $100. Joyce Albers collection.

MID-VICTORIAN (GRAND PERIOD) C. 1861-1880

The Romantic Period ended abruptly with the death of Prince Albert in 1861 and the beginning of the Civil War in the United States—causes for deep mourning on both sides of the Atlantic. The wearing of black was more than correct form for mourning; it became fashionable. Fashion, as always, played an important role in the changing look of jewelry. The voluminous skirt, supported by crinolines, or hoops, was introduced in the mid-1850s and became the look of the 1860s. This wider silhouette required larger jewelry. Brooches were massive and bracelets widened and were often worn in pairs, one on each wrist. Lower necklines prompted the wearing of necklaces and large lockets. Lockets and brooches often contained photographs, which gradually overtook portrait miniatures as a form of memorial jewelry. Hairstyles changed to once again reveal the ear, and earrings returned, growing to greater lengths toward the end of the period. Trains, bustles, ruffles, pleats, flounces, and fringe adorned the skirts of the 1870s. Tassels and fringe appeared in jewelry to complement the look.

By the 1860s, revivalism was in full swing. Women were piling on Etruscan-style amulets and other classical ornaments to the point of being satirized by the press. Revivalist Castellani's goldwork was displayed at the International Exhibition in London in 1862. Egyptian-style jewels were seen at the Exposition Universelle in Paris in 1867.

International exhibitions whetted appetites for exotic jewels from exotic places, like India. Mogul jewelry, Jaipur enamel, and gold-mounted tiger's claws from Calcutta became the rage in the 1870s, especially after Queen Victoria was proclaimed Empress of India in 1876. These pieces also inspired the work of English, European, and American jewelers.

After the Civil War, it became acceptable for American women to wear jewelry in greater quantities. Prosperity was growing, and with it the desire to display signs of wealth. What better way for a man to proclaim his status than to bedeck his wife in jewels? For the upper classes, at least, The Grand Period was indeed grand.

Working-class women were also decking themselves in baubles, bangles, and beads, although they were of the mass-produced imitation variety. Obviously fake costume jewelry was still an unheard-of idea. Even if it wasn't real, women wanted it to look like it was. Manufacturers were now capable of turning out machine-made goods in quantity to satisfy their demand. Electroplated trinkets set with glass stones were made to look like gold and diamond jewels.

Men continued to drape their vests with the requisite watch chains and fobs. Cuff links, also known as sleeve buttons, tie pins (also called scarfpins, stickpins, stockpins, cravat pins), signet rings, collar buttons, and shirt studs were additional forms of male adornment. Most of these were gold or gold-filled. Gemstones were added on occasion, particularly to stickpins.

By the 1860s, Tiffany & Co. had established itself as America's most prestigious and reputable firm, first by importing the best of European goods, then by manufacturing their own wares of the highest quality. From 1867 until the end of the century, it exhibited and won medals at international expositions in Paris and the United States. Tiffany promoted an appreciation of American artisanship and resources by exhibiting pieces with American themes and newly discovered American gemstones like Montana blue sapphires and Maine tourmalines. It also displayed newly discovered diamonds from South Africa and opals from Australia.

The Centennial Exposition in Philadelphia was a landmark event in American jewelry history, giving Tiffany and other American jewelers the opportunity to display their artistry in a grand manner and capture the world's attention. It furthered the recognition of the United States as an industrial nation with a talent for invention and production.

Pendent Earrings, 18k yg, tiger's claws, c. 1880-1985, granulated yg circ plaque surmounts on earwires suspending tiger's claws mounted in openwork design of granulated yg; sgd "Tiffany & Co.," 1-¼" tl × ⅝", pr, **$4,830 (A).** *Photo courtesy of Christie's New York (4/22/93).*

References: Joan Younger Dickinson, *The Book of Diamonds,* Avenel (Crown), 1965 (out of print); Penny Proddow and Debra Healy, *American Jewelry, Glamour and Tradition,* Rizzoli, 1987; Kenneth Snowman, ed., *The Master Jewelers,* Abrams, 1990 (Contains a chapter on Tiffany & Co. by Janet Zapata.).

Pendant
 Vinaigrette
  Yg, tiger claw, c. 1870-80, top surmounted by figure of a tiger holding a round faceted garnet, pendant bail, tiger claw set in chased foliate yg frame, 2-¼" × 1-⅞"
  . . . . **3,850 (A)**

BLACK (MOURNING) JEWELRY

History: Sentiment was the glue that held Victorian lives together. It was also the preservative that has saved many pieces of jewelry from being discarded or sold for scrap. Surely one prevailing sentiment was that of bereavement. Victoria had an unswerving sense of propriety and issued rules and regulations governing strict codes of behavior for herself, her family, her court, and her subjects. These rules of etiquette included dress codes for all occasions, particularly for mourning, including the proper jewelry to be worn.

After Prince Albert died, Victoria went into a period of mourning that lasted for the rest of her life, a full 40 years. For much of this time, all members of the royal court were required to wear black. This funereal atmosphere spread throughout the populace, creating a demand for black jewelry, the only color permitted during periods of full mourning. An entire industry grew up around the mining and carving of jet—the material of choice—a fossilized coal found near the town of Whitby, England. The area became famous for its artisans, and tourists went to Whitby to watch them work. They brought home jet souvenirs, sometimes personalized with the names of loved ones—not necessarily departed.

Brooches, bead necklaces, and bracelets were the most commonly worn types of jet jewelry. Bracelets were often of the stretchy type, strung on elastic and usually worn in pairs (as were many types of bracelets). Pendent earrings were worn, but are not found as often today as are brooches and bracelets.

Jet jewelry became so popular that it spawned a number of imitations. Two of the most common were black glass, misleadingly called "French jet," and vulcanite, a hardened (vulcanized) rubber that is sometimes erroneously called gutta-percha. (Gutta-percha is a natural substance from the Malayan palaquium tree, occasionally used for jewelry, but little survives.) Bog oak, from the peat bogs of Ireland, is sometimes included in this group of imitations, but although it is black to dark brown and carved (usually with Irish motifs) or heat press molded, it was never meant to be a substitute for jet.

True jet jewelery tends to command higher prices than do comparable pieces made from its imitations. Many dealers do not know how to tell the difference. The word "jet" has become synonymous with "black," so any black shiny jewelry material may be misidentified as jet.

Black onyx is another material used in mourning jewelry, and it causes some confusion among collectors. Gemologically, the correct name is black-dyed chalcedony. Onyx by definition is a banded, or layered stone, most often seen carved into cameos. The black color is almost always a result of soaking in a sugar solution and heating in sulphuric acid, a process that was known to the Romans.

At times, it can be difficult to determine the distinction between mourning and fashion in black jewelry. Massive necklaces, diamond-enhanced brooches, and elaborately carved bracelets might lead one to question the depth of the wearer's mourning. But considering that some women wore black for most of their adult lives, it is not surprising that they would want to enliven their attire with a bit of fashionable elegance. Because it *was* fashionable, black jewelry was also worn by women who were not in mourning.

References: Helen Muller, *Jet Jewellery and Ornaments,* Shire Publications, Ltd., 1986. This little 36-page booklet is chock-full of information on the history and identification of jet and its imitations, including a list of British museums exhibiting jet. See also chapters on mourning and Celtic jewelry in Shirley Bury, *Jewellery, 1789-1910, The International Era,* Vol. II, and Vivienne Becker, *Antique and Twentieth Century Jewellery,* 2nd ed.; Ginny Redington Dawes and Corinne Davidov, *Victorian Jewelry, Unexplored Treasures,* Abbeville Press, 1991. For gemological information on jet and onyx, see Walter Schumann, *Gemstones of the World,* N.A.G. Press, 1990.

Bracelet, elastic
Jet, MOP, c. 1850-60, carved center `oval plaque, with appl carved jet star shape on MOP disk, triangular carved side plaques tapering to faceted lozenge-shaped beads, drilled and strung with black elastic, 1-½" w at center, beads ¼" w **300**
Jet, c. 1850-60, carved center domed rect plaque, triangular carved side plaques tapering to faceted lozenge-shaped beads, drilled and strung with black elastic, 1-⅜" w at center, beads ⅜" w **275**
Bangle, hinged
Black onyx, 14k pink gold, c. 1890-1900, table-cut rect onyx plaques in millegrained pink gold mount, safety chain, 2-⅞" × ½" . . . . **935 (A)**
Brooch/Pin
Black enamel, diamonds, 18k yg, c. 1880-90, navette-shaped, black enamel ground, central scrolled quatrefoil motif set with oe diamonds, border of engr scroll design and smaller oe diamonds, tw approx 1.15 ct., rev hinged locket, C-catch, tube hinge, 1-¾" × 1-⅛" . . . . **2,070 (A)**
Black glass (French jet), seed pearls, ym, c. 1880-90, fancy shape molded bar, center

Bracelets, elastic, jet, c. 1860-70: L, carved center and two side plaques, scrolled and foliate design, strung on black elastic, center plaque 1-½" sq, pr, $575, *Allie Dickason collection;* R, sq plaques of faceted jet, drilled and strung with black elastic, 2-¾" dia × ⅝", pr, $200, *Author's collection.*

Bracelet, elastic, bog oak, c. 1860-80, seven pierced disks carved with Gothic arches and castle motifs, drilled and strung with elastic, Irish, 6 disks 1-⅛" dia, one larger disk 1-½" dia, $300. *Allie Dickason collection.*

set with row of seed pearls in ym, flanked by ym bead on each end, 2-½" × ½" **65**

Black onyx, 14k yg, seed pearls, c. 1870-80, central rect onyx bar set in a yg frame bordered by trefoil clusters of bezel-set cut onyx, surmounted by yg plaque set with seed pearls, and a yg quatrefoil mounted on a central onyx disk, three teardrop-shaped onyx drops and yg swag chains suspended from bottom edge of outer frame, C-catch, Am, 1-¾" w × 1-⅝" **450**

Bog oak, c. 1860-70, circ shape, fuchsia flower and leaves motif carved in high relief, textured bg, C-catch, tube hinge, 2-¼" dia **145**

Bog oak, gilt ym, c. 1860-70, oval annular plaque, carved notched border set in ym frame, Irish harp motif, carved and framed in ym, mounted in center, 1-½" w × 2" . . . **200**

Jet, ym, c. 1860-70, oval plaque, cameo of a woman's profile carved in relief, carved beaded edge, C-catch, tube hinge pin back on ym plate mounted on rev, 1-⅞" w × 2-⅜" **300**

Jet, c. 1860-70, circ disk, central acorn and oak leaf motif carved in high relief, 1-½" dia **125**

Gf, photograph, c. 1850, central swiveling compartment containing photo on each side, die-stamped oval frame, wheat sheaf motifs, C-catch, tube hinge, extended pinstem, 1" w × 1-⅛" **145**

Vulcanite, c. 1870-80, molded in the shape of a cuffed hand holding a funereal wreath (yew), C-catch, tube hinge, 3-¼" w × 1-⅛" **125**

Vulcanite, c. 1870-80, molded fuchsia motif mounted in center of plain flat oval plaque, C-catch, tube hinge on ym plate glued to rev, 1-⅜" w × 1-¾" **85**

Vulcanite and horn, c. 1870, molded vulcanite floral design joined to carved horn ring-shaped plaque, C-catch, replaced hinge mounted on plaque rev, 1-⅞" w × 2-⅛" **125**

Brooches/Pins, jet, c. 1860-70: T, memorial, cross shape, with shaped and engr gf end caps, C-catch, tube hinge, ¾" w × 1-¼", $65; C, memorial, oval, with pierced and lobed border, domed center carved with name "Smith," one-piece pin assembly of metal bar with C-catch and tube hinge appl to rev, Eng, 1-⅞" w × 1-¼", $125, *Author's collection;* B, grapes, leaves, and vines carved in high relief, ribbed and ropetwist carved oval border, appl metal pinback, C-catch, tube hinge, extended pinstem; 1-¾" w × 2", $175, *Terrance O'Halloran collection.*

Yg, enamel, glass, cloth, c. 1840-60, rect yg closed-back frame, black enamel border, central glazed compartment containing brocaded cloth, C-catch, repaired hinge, 1" w × 1-¼" **125**

Bar

Black onyx, diamonds (45 pts ea), 14k yg, pearl, c. 1890-1900, fancy yg scrollwork and engr center set with pearl, flanked by two oval onyx plaques each set with an

Brooches/Pins, Bar, black glass (French jet), c. 1880-90: T-B, bar set in millegrained low-karat yg frame with beaded border, triangular segments mounted on four sides, safety catch added later, tube hinge; 2-³⁄₈″ × ⁵⁄₈″, $125; satin finish rounded bar, diagonal ends, three parallel incised grooves at each end, safety-pin C-catch (enclosed), tube hinge mounted on gf plate on rev; 2-¹⁄₄″ × ¹⁄₄″, $50; faux seed pearls set in fancy shaped bar with oval shell ends, C-catch, tube hinge mounted on gf plates riveted to rev; 2-¹⁄₂″ × ³⁄₈″, $85; arrow shape, individual faceted glass beads riveted to black lacquered metal backing, wire C-catch; 3-³⁄₄″ × ⁷⁄₈″, $95. *Author's collection.*

Chatelaine, vulcanite, lacquered metal, c. 1890, molded frontal bust of a woman mounted on shield-shaped plaque, suspending swivel hook, lg lacquered metal hook for belt riveted to rev; 1-³⁄₄″ w × 3″ tl, $150. *Author's collection.*

om diamond, lever catch mkd 14k, Am, 2-¹⁄₄″ w × ¹⁄₂″ **1,100**

Brooch/Pin and Buckle
   Vulcanite, c. 1870-80, molded in the shape of wheat sheaves tied with ribbon, brooch, C-catch, tube hinge, same size matching buckle divided in two, black lacquered metal hook, eye, and loop assembly for belt mounted to rev with screws, 2-¹⁄₄″ w × 2″, each **125**

Earrings, pendent
   Jet, yg, c. 1860-70, teardrop shape, carved cameo of woman's profile suspended from ring-shaped jet surmounts, orig yg hook earwires, 2″ tl × ³⁄₄″, pr **225**

Locket and Chain
   18k yg, black onyx, c. 1870, shield shape, stone cut to shape and set flush in engr frame, engr and *taille d'épargne* enameled slide, fine cable-link yg chain, 18″ tl, locket (closed) ⁷⁄₈″ w × 1 ¹⁄₄″ **475**
   Vulcanite, yg, c. 1860-70, cable-link chain of gold overlay links alternating with plain vulcanite links, 20″ tl, suspending an oval locket with appl yg mono ''V,'' 1″ w × 1-¹⁄₂″ . . . . **303 (A)**

Lockets
   Vulcanite, lacquer, c. 1870, matching sm and lg convex oval hinged pendants with appl floral motifs, black lacquered outer surfaces,

Earrings, black onyx, 14k yg, seed pearls, c. 1870, onyx disk surmounts, pearl centers on earwires, suspending teardrop shape onyx drops, central yg floral motifs, seed pearls set in flowerheads; 1-³⁄₄″ tl x ¹⁄₂″, pr, $450. *Mary Lou Diebold collection.*

sm 1" w × 1-$\frac{1}{4}$", lg 1-$\frac{1}{8}$" w × 1-$\frac{7}{8}$" .... **100 and 125**

Necklace

Bead

Jet, micromosaic, 9k yg, double strand of carved 7mm jet beads suspending an oval plaque of floral bouquet in multicolored micromosaic set in yg frame, sgd "Crouch," 14-$\frac{1}{2}$" tl, plaque 1-$\frac{3}{8}$" w × 1-$\frac{3}{4}$" .... **546 (A)**

Bib

Black glass (French jet), black lacquered metal, c. 1880, openwork fringed bib of round and navette-shaped faceted flat glass beads suspended from three openwork lobed glass plaques and double row of round faceted flat glass beads mounted on black lacquered metal backing, front part of bib 5-$\frac{3}{4}$" w × 6", 18" tl **500**

Dog collar choker

Black glass (French jet), ribbon, c. 1890-1900, sm black faceted glass beads strung on wire in open lacy scalloped-edge pattern, 7-$\frac{1}{2}$" l × 1-$\frac{1}{2}$" w, threaded on black grosgrain ribbon, 31" tl × $\frac{3}{4}$" **95**

Pendant

Jet, mid-Victorian, oval plaque, central eight-pointed star motif carved in high relief, ym wire bail, 1-$\frac{1}{2}$" w × 1-$\frac{7}{8}$" **150**

Pendant, cross

Vulcanite, c. 1870-80, molded lilies motif appl to plain cruciform shape, 2" w × 3-$\frac{1}{2}$" **150**

Pendant and Chain

Black onyx, low karat gold, seed pearls, c. 1880, millegrained bezel-set cut onyx, teardrop shapes in grape motif pattern, suspended from a fine cable-link chain, 16" tl, pendant $\frac{7}{8}$" w × 1-$\frac{3}{8}$" **125**

Ring

Black onyx, diamonds, 14k yg, c. 1880-90, rounded corner rect plaque set with three om diamonds (approx 60 pts tw) in pronged flowerheads, reeded flat band shank with rope-twist center, Am, $\frac{3}{8}$" w × $\frac{5}{8}$", shank $\frac{1}{8}$" **850**

Suite: Brooch/Pin and Earrings

Black onyx, pearls, yg, mid- to late-Victorian brooch with curved onyx tablet top surmounted by scrolled knife-edge yg wirework in fan shape set with half-pearls, suspending sm shield-shaped and lg rev teardrop black onyx plaque from scrolled knife-edge wirework set with half-pearls, matching

Locket and Bookchain, 14k yg, gf, enamel, diamonds, c. 1860-70, oval hinged pendant locket with rc diamond flowerhead cluster center, plain black enameled ground and bail, yg, married to gf fancy geo link bookchain necklace (not orig), 20" tl, locket 1-$\frac{1}{4}$" w × 2-$\frac{1}{8}$", $650. *Joyce Albers collection.*

Pendant and Chain, vulcanite, c. 1875, cross pendant with scrolled foliate and lobed ends (faded to dk brown), suspended from black circ link chain by ym bail and jumpring (probable marriage), 27-$\frac{1}{4}$" tl, cross 2" × 3-$\frac{3}{8}$", $250. *Joyce Albers collection.*

drop earrings of shield and rev teardrop plaques with yg and pearls, added screwback findings, brooch 2-¹/₂" w × 2", earrings 1-¹/₂" tl × ¹/₂", suite ...... **825 (A)**

Black onyx and seed pearls, yg frame and mounting, c. 1870-80, center oval stone, engr quatrefoil and seed pearl in center, flared and navette-cut stones set in surrounding bezels, accented with yg beads, earrings with scrolled yg wire suspending teardrop stones, brooch 1" w × 1-¹/₄", earrings 1-¹/₂" tl × ³/₄", suite **850**

TORTOISESHELL AND PIQUÉ

History: Tortoiseshell was another popular nineteenth-century jewelry material. It was also considered suitable for half-mourning. Lockets, haircombs, and bracelets were made from this natural material taken from the shell of the hawksbill turtle (now an endangered species).

A technique known as piqué, originally used in ornamental objects in the seventeenth century, was applied to jewelry and popularized in the mid to late nineteenth century. After softening it with heat, the tortoiseshell was inlaid with gold and/or silver in floral or geometric patterns. The technique using inlaid strips of metal cut into ornate designs is called *piqué posé*. *Piqué point*

refers to dots or other small geometric shapes inlaid in an overall pattern.

Animal rights was not a big issue in Victorian times. Animals or parts of animals were used with impunity. It is now illegal to buy or sell tortoiseshell in the United States, but antique pieces are exempt. Not all mottled brown lightweight material is tortoiseshell, however. Toward the end of the nineteenth century, many haircombs and other jewelry and objects were made of celluloid in imitation of tortoiseshell.

References: Vivienne Becker, *Antique and Twentieth Century Jewellery,* 2nd ed., N.A.G. Press, 1987; Ginny Redington Dawes and Corinne Davidov, *Victorian Jewelry, Unexplored Treasures,* Abbeville Press, 1991.

Bracelet, link
    Piqué, yg, silver, c. 1860-70, seven ring-shaped links, each suspending a 6mm bead, with yg and silver *piqué point* inlay of Xs and dots, 14k findings, safety chain, links 1" dia, 7-¹/₄" tl **550**
Bracelets
  Bangles, hinged
    Piqué, yg, c. 1880, strips of yg inlaid around edges of ³/₈" w ovals, ³/₁₆" thick, 2-¹/₂" inside dia, pr **475**
Brooch/Pin
    Piqué, yg, silver, c. 1860, domed circle, flat back (hollow), inlaid with two intersecting quatrefoils of foliate and floral design (*piqué*

Brooches/Pins, tortoiseshell piqué, yg, c. 1860, (top left) butterfly with inlaid yg foliate and filigree design, (top right) stylized six-pointed star with *piqué point* inlay, (bottom center) domed faceted round pin with inlaid *piqué posé* floral design, central hexagonal honeycomb pattern. Butterfly 3-¹/₄" × 2", star 3-¹/₄", round, 1-³/₄" dia, three, $1,320 (A). *Photo courtesy of Skinner, Inc., Boston (12/14/92).*

Bangle Bracelets, hinged, 14k yg, c. 1880, Etruscan revival, each decorated with bead and wirework scrolled motifs; slight damage, 1876 patent date on inner metal strip of hinge mechanism, Am, 2-⅞" dia × ¾", pr, $1,150(A). *Photo courtesy of Butterfield & Butterfield (4/1/93).*

posé) in yg and silver, C-catch, tube hinge, extended pinstem, 1-⅝" dia **325**
Earrings, pendent
  Piqué, yg, c. 1860-70, concentric tapered oval hoops, inlaid with scalloped floral design *(piqué posé)* in yg, suspended from earwires with oval piqué surmounts, 1-½" tl × ⅞", pr
  . . . . **600**
  Piqué, yg, silver, c. 1860-70, elongated pyramid shape, inlaid floral and foliate motifs *(piqué posé)*, suspended from piqué bead surmounts on earwires, 2" tl × ⅜", pr
  . . . . **300**
  Piqué, yg, c. 1870-80, teardrop shape with inlaid honeycomb pattern *(piqué point)*, suspended from piqué bead surmounts on earwires, 1-¾" × ½", pr **275**
Haircomb
  Late Victorian, carved dragon motif surmounting four-tooth comb, Chinese import, 4-½" tl, top 3-½" w × 2-¼" **275**
  Piqué, yg, c. 1870-80, curved narrow rect top inlaid with geo pattern *(piqué point)*, surmounting five-tooth comb, top 3-⅝" w × ½", 2-½" tl **225**
Locket and Chain
  Mid-Victorian, cable links suspending oval locket with pierced scrolled and foliate design in center, gf spring-ring clasp, chain 24" tl × ⅝", locket 1-⅛" w × 1-¾" **250**
  c. 1860-70, oval locket, chain 21" tl
  . . . . **193 (A)**
Scarf pin/Stickpin
  Piqué, yg, c. 1880, domed disk inlaid with yg circles, set in plain yg bezel mounted on yg pin with central spiral ridge, 2-½" tl, head ⅜" dia **200**

REVIVALIST JEWELRY

Victorians were fascinated with ancient history. Archeological discoveries and published accounts of ancient historical events and epics prompted revivals of jewelry styles from ancient and medieval cultures: Assyrian, Celtic, Egyptian, Etruscan, Gothic, Greco-Roman, Mogul (India), Moorish, and Renaissance. Exact copies were favored over interpretations. With few exceptions, originality and creativity were not notable characteristics of Victorian style, although exquisite workmanship and attention to details often were.

A number of noted jewelers of the mid to late nineteenth century worked in the revivalist mode, copying ancient forms. Among these, the most famous were the Castellani family of Rome and Carlo Giuliano and sons Carlo and Arthur of London.

Castellani

ETRUSCAN

Revivalism reached its height during the 1860s and 1870s. A mania for all things Italian promoted the popularity in particular of Etruscan revival jewels, most closely associated with what is generically called the "archaeological style." The discovery of gold treasures from antiquity in Tuscany, in west-central Italy, near Rome, instigated the attempt to copy the ancient technique of granulation. Minute beads of gold were applied side by side to a gold surface to create a design. The difficulty lay in soldering the beads to the surface without melting them. The Castellani, while unable to duplicate the technique exactly, came closest to perfecting it. Twisted, or corded, wirework was also applied to gold jewels in the Etruscan style. Others made the attempt at granulation and wirework but were usually less successful.

The ancient jewels themselves were copied by the Castellani as well as the techniques. The bulla, a two-sided round pendant worn by the Etruscans as an amulet, and the fibula, a safety-pin-type brooch used to fasten garments, were among the favorite forms.

The popularity of the Castellanis' work was of course a motive for their imitators—copyists of copyists, as it were. Skill in craftsmanship, or the lack of it, is what separates the wheat from the chaff. Some craftsmen were very skilled indeed, but the range of quality in Etruscan-style jewels is wide. Although quality workmanship is of primary consideration, a signature can add a great deal of value. The Castellani marks, back-to-back overlapping Cs, are important ones to know. It is also important to note that their marks as well as their techniques were copied.

Large numbers of pieces in the archaeological style were produced by anonymous manufacturers throughout the last half of the nineteenth century. Many unsigned examples of varying quality can be found today of Etruscan decoration on gold and gold-filled pieces.

John Brogden

RENAISSANCE

The Giulianos were revivalists of another sort. They specialized in jewels in the Renaissance style and were famous for their enameling. One trademark was an enameled white background with black dots, or black with white dots. Carlo Giuliano's work reached its peak in the·1870s. Although he too used granulation as well as other ancient techniques, unlike most revivalists, he was an interpreter of the style. He improved upon techniques and forms with original ideas rather than produce exact copies. He signed his pieces C.G. in an applied or impressed oval plaque.

Sons Carlo and Arthur (mark: C.& A.G.) carried on after their father's death in 1896, but changing styles affected their business. Early twentieth-century pieces were not as successful, and the business closed in 1914. Both Giuliano marks have been copied.

Other noted archaeological and Renaissance revivalist jewelers were John Brogden of London, Ernesto Pierret of Rome, and Jules Wièse and son Louis of Paris.

Austrian and Hungarian Renaissance Revival jewelry was produced in quantity in the late nineteenth and early twentieth centuries. It is cruder in execution and materials—usually silver gilt, enamel, low-quality gemstones (sometimes glass), and freshwater pearls. Nevertheless, these pieces have a certain appeal and are of growing interest, particularly among collectors of costume jewelry. Accordingly, prices have risen. Most pieces are unmarked, but sometimes a piece will have an Austro-Hungarian silver quality hall-

Bracelets, Link, silver gilt, Hungarian Renaissance Revival, c. 1890-1900: L, openwork flowerhead links set with round rubies, teardrop tourmalines, pearl centers, linked to lozenge-shaped spacers set with teardrop tourmalines, v-spring clasp, 7-1/2" tl × 7/8", $600, *Mary Lou Diebold collection;* R, ornate scrolled, foliate and floral motifs, center section set with lg and numerous small cab garnets and seed pearls, flanked on each side by three sections set with smaller cab garnets, hmk for 800 silver (dog's head), 6" tl, center 1-1/2" × 1", $450, *Joyce Albers collection.*

mark, a dog's head in a coffin-shaped lozenge, or the head of the goddess Diana in a cartouche. (See Tardy, *International Hallmarks on Silver*, English translation, Paris, 1985.)

EGYPTIAN

The discovery of the tomb and treasures of Queen Ah-Hotpe and the start of construction of the Suez Canal in 1859 (completed 10 years later), inspired the return of the Egyptian style, which had been revived once before in the late eighteenth and early nineteenth centuries. Familiar Egyptian symbols—scarabs, pharoahs, lotus blossoms, falcons, and vultures—found their way into jewels by Castellani, Giuliano, Brogden, Robert Phillips, and several famous French jewel houses, including Froment-Meurice and Boucheron. These pieces were worked in gold, enamel, gemstones, and mosaics in much the same manner as other revivalist jewelry.

Revivalism caught on in the United States too, although somewhat later. When Alessandro Castellani exhibited his family's work at the 1862 International Exposition in London, America was in the the throes of the Civil War. But in 1876, at the Centennial Exposition in Philadelphia, Castellani presented his ideas and his jewelry to the receptive American public. Soon after, classical motifs and Etruscan worked gold began making their appearance in American-made jewelry, most of it mass-produced.

Today, it is not unusual to find American pieces, both signed and unsigned, that reflect the widespread appeal of the past during the mid to late Victorian era.

References: Bennett and Mascetti, *Understanding Jewellery*, Antique Collectors Club, 1989; Shirley Bury, *Jewellery 1789-1910, The International Era*, Vol. II, Antique Collectors Club, 1991; Geoffrey Munn, *Castellani and Giuliano, Revivalist Jewellers of the Nineteenth Century*, Trefoil, 1984 (out of print); Kenneth Snowman, ed., *The Master Jewelers*, Abrams, 1990 (chapter by Geoffrey Munn). See also Tom R. Paradise, "Jewelry's Archaeological Style," in *Jeweler's Circular-Keystone/Heritage*, November 1990 (Chilton).

Museums: The Villa Giulia in Rome houses a collection of 600 pieces of Castellani jewelry (limited public access). Some of the ancient jewels that inspired the Castellani can be seen at the British Museum in London. A selection of Giuliano's work is at the South Kensington Museum. The Victoria and Albert Museum in London has an extensive collection of revivalist jewels.

Reproduction Alert: Faked signatures and reproductions are common. Signed pieces should be authenticated by an expert.

Bracelet
　Bangle, hinged
　　15k yg, c. 1870-80, with a wire-twist edge

and beaded top, wire-twist and beaded starburst motifs in center sections, 14.4 dwt, Eng, 2-⅛" dia × ⅝" .... **880 (A)**
　15k yg, c. 1860-70, Etruscan revival, hollow tube surmounted by a concave disk with a flowerhead shape outlined in appl yg wirework and beads, appl yg beads on each shoulder, sgd "JB" for John Brogden, Eng, 2-⅜" dia × ¼", disk ¾" dia .... **4,070 (A)**
　Yg, gemstones, c. 1895, archeological revival, foliate motifs, distressed yg surface and borders, set with oval cab ruby, four circ cab sapphires, two oval and two circ cab emeralds, two circ cab garnets in irregular distressed bezels, Fr lozenge hmk, sgd "Wièse" (Louis), 3" dia × ¾" .... **7,475 (A)**
Bangle, coiled
　18k yg, mid-Victorian, Etruscan revival, braided mesh, single coil, two spherical terminals with appl bead and wirework, sm turq and seed pearls, 11.3 dwt, ¼" dia, terminals ½" dia .... **825 (A)**
Strap
　18k yg and silver, faience, diamonds, c. 1890, Egyptian revival, faience scarab with blue, red, green enamel on yg wings, three om diamonds set in silver on each wing, cen-

Brooches/Pins, yg, Etruscan Revival, c.1860-70: T, 18k, concentric ovals, convex center, wirework and die-stamped border, rev glazed compartment for hair, C-catch, tube hinge, extended pinstem, 1-½" × 1-¼", $300; B, 15k, garnets (carbuncles), domed disks with appl twisted wirework, bezel-set center cabs, C-catches, tube hinges, extended pin stems, attached rings for safety chains, foxtail chain tassel, ⅝" l, suspended from smaller brooch, ⅞" dia; larger brooch 1-⅛" dia, Eng, pr, $500. *Courtesy of E. Foxe Harrell Jewelers.*

tered on woven yg mesh strap, 7-1/2" × 7/8"
.... **1,980 (A)**

Brooch/Pin

18k yg, c. 1860-70, Etruscan revival, circle pin terminating in a ram's head, suspending a hollow urn within the circle, (hole in urn), sgd "Castellani," 1-1/4" dia ..... **1,540 (A)**

18k yg, mosaic glass, c. 1860-70, circ shape, quatrefoil design outlined in gold wire cloisons inlaid with turq micromosaic within yg twisted wire frame, sgd "Castellani," 1-1/8" dia .... **2,310 (A)**

18k yg, c. 1860-70, in shape of a horseshoe, 4.7 dwt, signed "Brogden," Eng, 1-1/8" × 1"
.... **1,100 (A)**

Yg, c. 1860, Etruscan revival, a three-dimensional bull's head within a concave disk attached to hollow bar that suspends overlapping grad disks terminating in the head of Bacchus, with appl beads and wirework over all, foxtail chain suspended from bar, sgd "Pierret, Ernesto," 2-1/4" w × 4-3/8" tl
.... **30,800 (A)**

Bar

14k yg, faience, c. 1890, Egyptian revival,

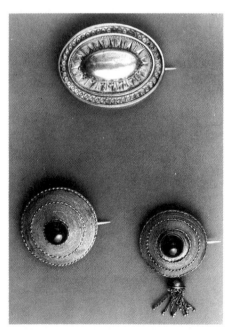

Brooches/Pins, yg, Etruscan Revival, c.1860-70: T, 18k, concentric ovals, convex center, wirework and die-stamped border, rev glazed compartment for hair, C-catch, tube hinge, extended pinstem, 1-1/2" × 1-1/4", $300; B, 15k, garnets (carbuncles), domed disks with appl twisted wirework, bezel-set center cabs, C-catches, tube hinges, extended pin stems, attached rings for safety chains, foxtail chain tassel, 5/8" l, suspended from smaller brooch, 7/8" dia; larger brooch 1-1/8" dia, Eng, pr, $500. Courtesy of E. Foxe Harrell Jewelers.

center of faience scarab framed by two serpents and pharoah's head, flanked by raised and engr lotus motifs on each end, Am, sgd "JEC & Co" for J.E. Caldwell (Philadelphia), 2-1/2" w × 1-1/8" **2,500**

18k yg, c. 1860-70, Greco-Roman revival, ancient coin, 3/4" dia, flanked by two smaller coins, 3/8" dia, with male profiles, within bezel-set mounts with bead terminals, mounted on round bar, sgd "Pierret," 2-1/4" w × 1-1/8" .... **3,520 (A)**

18k yg, c. 1890-1900, Gothic revival, quatrefoil of four interlaced rings, each containing a floral sprig, sgd "Wièse" (Louis) on rev and in a lozenge on the catch, 1-1/4" w × 1" .... **1,980 (A)**

Fibula

18k yg, enamel, c. 1870-80, Etruscan revival, granulated yg crescent set with blue, green, and white enamel flowers, joined to a tapering cylinder of similar design with a white enamel cupid astride, terminating in a lion's head, pinstem enclosed in cylinder, 2-1/2" w × 7/8" .... **3,680 (A)**

Cuff Links

18k yg, enamel, c. 1900, Egyptian revival, concave oval disks containing blue, green, pink, and red *basse-taille* enamel scarabs, joined by hollow oval tubing, 7/8" × 5/8", pr
.... **1,540 (A)**

Earrings, pendent

14k yg, c. 1870, Etruscan revival, in the shape of two-handled urns with stopper-shaped surmounts, wire-twist and bead decoration, 4.4 dwt, 1-3/8" tl × 3/4", pr .... **990 (A)**

Pendent Earrings, 15k yg, c. 1870: L, Etruscan Revival, ram's heads suspending amphorae with wirework detail, earwires, 5.1 dwt., Eng, 2-1/2" × 3/4", pr, $1,980 (A); R, teardrop shape with appl wire-twist, foliate motif suspended from a 6 mm. dome, 2.8 dwt., 2-1/4" × 3/8", pr, $468 (A). Photo courtesy of Skinner, Inc. (3/14/93).

Pendent Earrings, 18k yg, c. 1860-70, Etruscan Revival, a spade-shaped surmount on earwire, suspending a vertical ring of reeded yg to which are attached a scrolled opposed wing-shape above and a heart-shape within a lg tapered hoop, the whole accented with wirework and beading, 2-³/₈" tl × 1-¹/₄", pr, $4,600 (A). Photo courtesy of Butterfield & Butterfield (4/1/93).

18k yg, c. 1860, Etruscan revival, spherical drops suspended from earwires with bead surmounts, appl bead and wirework, 1-⁵/₈" tl × ³/₄", pr . . . . **880 (A)**

Yg, c. 1870-80, Etruscan revival, hollow disks with scrolled plume design, suspended from single leaf-shaped surmounts on earwires, bead and wirework decoration, 1-¹/₂" tl × 1", pr . . . . **1,320 (A)**

Yg, mid-Victorian, Etruscan revival, scrolled hoops terminating in sculpted women's heads in the round (hollow), appl bead and wirework, suspended from flowerhead surmounts on shepherd's hook earwires, 1-³/₈" tl × ³/₈", pr . . . . **2,640 (A)**

Yg, seed pearls, c. 1870, Etruscan revival, full-figured urns with wire-twist detail and beadwork suspended from shepherd's hook earwires, chains terminating in seed pearls suspended from tops of urns, 8.4 dwt, 2" × ³/₄", pr . . . . **4,400 (A)**

Hair Ornaments

Yg, ivory, c. 1860, Etruscan Revival, each surmounted by a hollow yg ram's head with cab ruby eyes, collars of three hollow yg disks with appl yg bead and wirework of grad lg to sm size in succession behind heads, mounted on tapering ivory stems, sgd "Castellani," 6" × 1", pr . . . . **9,900 (A)**

Locket

Yg, enamel, natural pearl, c. 1870, Renaissance revival, heart-shaped, with center of a white-faced cherub with golden hair, white wings on black bg, within a black dot on white frame, white-on-black festoon pattern enameled outline, radiating pin-set pearls, black dot on white bail, sgd "Giuliano," 1-³/₈" w × 1-⁷/₈" . . . . **20,735 (A)**

15k yg, c. 1870-80, horseshoe shape, with textured hoof, compartment containing a five-leaf clover and engraved, 11.7 dwt, sgd "Pierret," 1-¹/₄" w × 1-³/₄" . . . . . . **1,320 (A)**

Necklace

18k yg, c. 1860-70, woven strap style with appl yg bead work, 17-¹/₄" tl × ³/₈" **800**

18k yg, c. 1870, Etruscan revival, fringe of grad amphora suspended from a gold chain with spiral link spacers completed by an S-clasp, attributed to Ernesto Pierret . . . . . . **8,800 (A)**

18k yg, c. 1870, Etruscan revival, foxtail link chain suspending a fringe of hollow urn shapes from round domed plaques and from lg central and two sm side domed and shield-shaped pendants with appl bead and wirework suspended by foxtail chain joined at sides of necklace, 16-¹/₂" tl × 2-¹/₄" . . . . **3,410 (A)**

18k yg, lapis, c. 1860-70, Etruscan revival, fringe of lapis beads, 10 to 12mm, with yg bead and wirework finials suspended from

Necklace, 14k yg, c. 1870, Etruscan Revival fringe necklace, beaded and woven chain suspending bead-tipped baton links, 10.3 dwt, 17-¹/₂" tl with extension × 1", $715 (A). Photo courtesy of Skinner, Inc. (3/14/93).

Necklace, 18k yg, c. 1870, Etruscan Revival, woven yg mesh terminating in bead and wire-twist ends with tiny frog centers, suspending a fringe of yg urns, (missing one urn), hmkd "JB" for John Brogden, in fitted box, Eng, $7,150 (A). *Photo courtesy of Skinner, Inc. (3/14/93).*

yg foxtail chain, clasp mkd "Roma," 15-$\frac{1}{2}$" tl × 1-$\frac{1}{4}$", with pr of earrings made to match in 14k yg, 1-$\frac{1}{2}$" tl × $\frac{1}{2}$" . . . . **2,750 (A)**

Yg, c. 1860, Etruscan revival, woven foxtail neckchain suspending 22 hollow yg urns from flowerhead bails with appl bead and wirework, sgd "Castellani," 13-$\frac{1}{2}$" tl × 1-$\frac{1}{8}$" . . . . **16,500 (A)**

Pendant

Yg, c. 1860-70, Etruscan revival, circ domed, floral plaque outlined with appl yg wirework and polished rim, converted from brooch/ pin, sgd "Castellani," $\frac{3}{4}$" dia . . . . . **1,870 (A)**

Yg, enamel, c. 1900, in the shape of a five-petal flowerhead, pink and green enamel, jump- ring bail sgd "C & AG" for Carlo & Arthur Giuliano, in fitted leather box, Eng, 1-$\frac{1}{8}$" tl × $\frac{3}{4}$" . . . . **1,210 (A)**

Bulla

18k yg, c. 1860-70, Etruscan revival, circ bottom and tapering top joined by a hinge to similar rev, opening to covered com- partment, appl granulation and wirework, Roman numerals and mono, 1" w × 1-$\frac{5}{8}$" **1,500**

Yg, c. 1860-70, Etruscan revival, two-sided, hinged at top, tapering top section with appl yg bead and wirework, terminating in convex disks, the word "AMOR" in raised letters on one side, "ROMA" on the other, sgd "Castellani," $\frac{7}{8}$" w × 1-$\frac{3}{8}$" . . . . **3,850 (A)**

Yg, Roman coins, c. 1860, Etruscan revival, one side set with gold coin depicting Hadrian Aureus, Rome, A.D. 134–138, IOVI VICTORI, Jupiter seated holding scepter on rev, back side set with silver coin depicting Rome Republic, L. Ivli, Denarius, Rome (101 B.C.), head of Roma, chariot driven by Victory on rev, mounting

Pendant, sapphire, pearls, rubies, diamonds, citrines, yg, enamel, c. 1860-70, Renaissance Revival, with cen- ter oval sapphire bordered with seed pearls within a scrolled lozenge-shaped blue, black and white enam- eled openwork frame set with rubies and pearls, sus- pending an inverted triangular enamel drop set with a rc diamond, citrine and cab ruby, enameled bail set with a rc diamond, citrine ruby (repair evident), 1-$\frac{7}{8}$" w × 3-$\frac{3}{4}$", $4,140 (A). *Photo courtesy of Christie's New York (4/22/93).*

decorated with yg granulation and wirework, maker's mk for Castellani (entwined Cs), in red velvet box, 1-¹/₂" w × 2"
.... **9,900 (A)**

Cross

15k yg, c. 1870, lobed ends, beaded and wire-twist detail, reeded bail, Eng, 1-³/₈" w × 2-³/₈" **300**

Pendant and Chain

Cross

15k yg, seed pearls, c. 1870, chain of reeded and polished circ links, ornate clasp, approx 15" tl, suspending a cross with wirework and seed pearls, Eng, 1-³/₈" w × 2-¹/₄" .... **1,045 (A)**

Scarf pin/Stickpin

Jasper, 18k yg, c. 1900, Egyptian revival, carved jasper bust of pharoah mounted on a yg pinstem, Fr hmks, 3-¹/₂" tl × ¹/₂" .... **1,100 (A)**

Suite: Brooch/Pin and Earrings

Garnet, yg, seed pearls, c. 1860-70, domed-disk with appl wirework, center cab garnet (carbuncle) bordered with seed pearls, sus-

Pendants, silver gilt, Hungarian Renaissance Revival, c. 1890-1900: T, scrolled openwork enameled plaque set with pearls, rubies and emeralds, suspended from bail by two chains, pendent drops on bail and base of plaque, 1" w × 2-¹/₂" tl, $450, *Mary Lou Diebold collection;* B, Pendant/brooch, Hungarian *násfa* (traditional bodice pendant/brooch), collet-set garnets, green beryls, baroque pearls within triangular scroll and foliate design, sq-cut green beryl and enamel center, suspending a baroque pearl flanked by two pear-shaped garnet drops, 1-¹/₂" w × 2-³/₄" tl, $750, *Ellen Stuart collection.*

Suite: Bangle Bracelet, Brooch, Pendent Earrings, Buttons, 15k yg, garnets (carbuncles), c. 1860. Bangle with central disk set with carbuncle, wire-twist and bead decoration, matching brooch suspending foxtail chain tassel, earrings with wire-twist bows on crossbars suspending carbuncles, and two buttons in fitted case. Bangle 2-³/₈" dia × 1-¹/₈", brooch 2-¹/₂" × 1-¹/₄", earrings 1-¹/₂" × ⁵/₈", $3,850 (A). *Photo courtesy of Skinner, Inc. (3/14/93).*

Suite: Brooch/Pendant and Pendent Earrings, yg, c. 1860-70, Etruscan Revival. Brooch/pendant with center of lion's head in high relief in a beaded and wire-twist starburst medallion, matching earrings, brooch/pendant bears Castellani mark after 1861, 3″ tl with bail (removable) × 2″, earrings 2-¹/₂″ tl × ⁷/₈″, $7,975 (A). *Photo courtesy of Skinner, Inc. (12/14/92).*

pending a bell-cap coiled wirework tassel from two lengths of chain, 1-³/₈″ dia × 2-¹/₄″ tl with tassel, matching drop earrings, ⁵/₈″ dia × 1-³/₈″ tl with tassels, suite . . . . . . **990 (A)**
15k yg, mid-Victorian, Etruscan revival, oval-shaped yg brooch, decorated with granulation and filigree accents accompanied by a pr of matching earrings, completed by 14k yg backs of later addition, Eng, suite . . . . **1,150 (A)**

CAMEOS AND INTAGLIOS

History: The cameo has come to be known as a classic form of jewelry, the epitome of the old-fashioned look. But its widespread popularity began in the nineteenth century as a tourist souvenir. Hardstone cameos date to ancient Greece and Rome. Eighteenth century Neoclassicists revived the art, but it was the Victorians who popularized the cameo made from a variety of materials—shell, lava, coral, ivory, jet, as well as gemstones—as a part of a Greco-Roman revival that remained in vogue from midcentury onward.

Travelers taking the Grand Tour of Europe helped promote cameo-carving to the point of mass production. Italy was a favorite destination, especially, because of the Victorian fascination with ancient history, the ruins of Pompeii at

Mount Vesuvius. Lava cameos were purchased as souvenirs. The material, actually a form of limestone, was found in the region and associated with the volcano that was Pompeii's downfall. Nearby, in the seaside town of Torre del Greco, Italian cameo carvers made shell and coral cameos for the tourists, as they continue to do today.

A true cameo is a miniature sculpture in relief, carved from a single piece of material. When the material is layered, as are agate, onyx, and shell, the carver uses the light and dark layers as contrasting background and foreground. The subject matter can range from classic mythological and Biblical scenes, to floral bouquets and landscapes, or to the more commonly seen heads or busts of women or men.

A woman's profile is the motif most closely associated with cameos by their wearers today. These can date anywhere from 1840 to the present. Their look is usually in keeping with the style of the times. One favorite technique for dating a cameo is to look at the nose of the woman in profile. Aquiline, or romanesque, noses are found on the classic beauties of the midnineteenth century. Pert, turned-up noses are found on twentieth-century interpretations of female attractiveness.

The most common material for cameos is shell, which is soft and easy to carve. Portrait cameos were sometimes made with the depicted woman wearing a necklace or other jewelry set with a small diamond. These are called cameos *habillés* (French for "dressed up") and are still being made.

Nineteenth century lava and coral cameos are also found today, although not as abundantly. While most shell cameos are carved in bas-relief, because of the relative shallowness of the material's layers, lava and coral, being monochromatic, can be and often are carved in high relief. The protruding noses on these cameos are most susceptible to damage.

Some of the best and most highly prized cameos are made from hardstone, which is more difficult to carve. Hardstone cameos are occasionally carved within a concave depression in the stone, where the edge of the stone is level with the highest part of the cameo itself. *Chevet*, or *chevée*, and cuvette, or curvette, are the terms used interchangeably for this type of cameo.

The quality of a cameo's carving can range from breathtaking to abysmal. Values also range widely, depending on the skill of the carver, depicted subject, size, and the materials used for the cameo and the mounting or frame. Ultrasonic machine-made stone cameos have been produced for the past 20 years. Their quality and value are low. Pseudocameos are molded from natural or synthetic materials and laminated to a backing or set in a metal frame.

Brooches are the usual form, but cameos can also be found set into necklaces, bracelets, earrings, rings, and stickpins.

Intaglios, which actually preceded cameos in ancient times, are the opposite of cameos, in that the design is recessed or carved into the stone below the surface. The most common association is with seals, or signet rings, in which the intaglio is used to create an impression in relief when pressed into sealing wax. These seals and rings are also worn for ornamental purposes, but the carved design is less perceptible than that of a cameo. Intaglios are carved from hardstone or glass, never shell or other soft material. Molded

glass imitation intaglios are found in inexpensive jewelry.

Reverse-painted crystal intaglios were popular in the mid to late nineteenth century, especially in sporting jewelry featuring animal motifs. Dogs, horses, or other animals were carved into the backs of rock crystal quartz cabochons. The intaglios were then painted in realistic colors and backed with mother-of-pearl before setting. From the front, the animals appear three-dimensional. These were later imitated with molded and painted glass.

References: Vivienne Becker, *Antique and Twentieth Century Jewellery*, 2nd ed., N.A.G. Press, 1987; Anna Miller, *Cameos Old & New*, Van Nostrand Reinhold, 1991; Michael J. Weinstein and Ed Aswad, *Shell Cameos*, Books Americana, 1991.

Museums: Boston Museum of Fine Arts, Boston, Mass.; J. Paul Getty Museum, Malibu, Calif.; Indiana University Museum, Bloomington, Ind.; Lizzadro Museum of Lapidary Arts, Elmhurst, Ill.; Metropolitan Museum of Art, New York, N.Y.; University Museum, University of Pennsylvania, Philadelphia, Pa.; Walters Art Gallery, Baltimore, Md. (See Anna Miller's book, listed above, for further information on these and other cameo collections.)

Bracelet, link

Lava, silver gilt, c. 1870, nine oval plaques, alternate tan, beige, charcoal shades, low-relief carved women's profiles set in plain linked bezels, safety chain, 7-1/2" tl × 7/8" **300**

Lava, ym, c. 1860-70, five oval plaques, shades of brown, detailed high relief carved women's profiles (some chips), set in plain linked bezels, 7" tl × 1-3/8" **500**

Charm

Gemstones, yg, gf, 9k yg curb links and heart charm clasp, suspending a collection of ten seals: 9k, 14k, 18k yg, and gf, variously set with carnelian, citrine, agate,

Bracelet, link, lava cameos, silver, c. 1860-70, seven carved plaques of women's profiles in shades of grey, beige, and tan set in linked bezels, safety chain, 6-1/2" × 3/4", $300. *Ofelia Bucy collection.*

bloodstone, sardonyx, and onyx intaglios, c. 1820-1850 . . . . **1,955 (A)**

Gemstones, two silver gilt lockets and five hardstone intaglio seals suspended from silver gilt curb link bracelet **375**

Brooch/Pendant

Coral, 10k yg, c. 1900, profile bust of a female warrior in high relief, bezel set in an engr yg frame, swivel bail, 1-½" w × 1-⅞" **350**

Hardstone, 14k yg, c. 1860-70, oval onyx cameo of a woman's profile set in shield-shaped yg frame with appl bead and wirework, hinged pendant bail, 1-¾" w × 2-⅜" tl . . . . **880 (A)**

Hardstone, 14k rose gold, c. 1870-80, cameo of a woman's profile in rose gold frame with appl scrolls and beadwork, 10k yg pinstem, 1-⅝" w × 2" . . . . **935 (A)**

Lava, 14k yg, c. 1860-70, cameo of a full-figured winged god holding a garland standing on platform with pedestal and urn in high relief set in pierced Greek key pattern yg frame, 2" w × 2-⅜" . . . . **715 (A)**

Brooch/Pin

Citrine, 9k yg, c. 1900, elongated hexagonal-shaped faceted citrine *chevet* (curvette) cameo, mounted on a yg frame, 1-½" w × 1-¼" . . . . **920 (A)**

Hardstone, 12k yg, c. 1890-1900, black onyx oval cameo set in engr shield-shaped frame flanked by tapering, pierced and scrolled yg plaques with appl engr textured foliate motifs, three appl beads at top of frame, Eng, 1-½" w × ⅞" **300**

Hardstone, 18k yg, c. 1850-60, oval banded agate depicting profile bust of a woman with grape leaves in her hair, high relief, set in fancy bezel with openwork scrolled and beaded frame, 1-⅜" w × 1-¾" **1,500**

Brooch/Pin, hardstone cameo, 15k yg, c. 1860-70, profile of a warrior in a polished yg oval frame with appl wire-twist and bead design of circ and lozenge shapes, 1-½" × 1-¾", $1,045 (A). *Photo courtesy of Skinner, Inc. (12/14/92).*

Hardstone, diamonds, pearls, st yg, enamel, c. 1840, circular pink chalcedony cameo depicting the front bust of a female bacchante framed by rc diamonds set in silver, black enamel rim, border of natural pearls, yg back, 1" dia **2,000**

Hardstone, 18k yg, c. 1860-70, circ outline, set with sardonyx cameo depicting a female profile within a granulation and wirework yg frame, 1-¾" dia . . . . **1,955 (A)**

Reverse intaglio, rock crystal quartz, 14k yg, seed pearls, c. 1890, circ rev painted intaglio depicting a jockey riding a race horse, set in

Brooch/Pin, composition, gf frame, wm back, c. 1850-60, landscape and columned building motif, molded in imitation of carved lava, C-catch, tube hinge, extended pinstem (some damage to frame), 2" × 1-¾", $175. *Ellen Stuart collection.*

Brooch/Pin, shell cameo, yg, c. 1860-70, classic profile of a woman with flowers in her hair, set in beaded and coiled wirework yg frame, added safety catch, 2-¼" × 2-⅝", $1,100. *Ellen Stuart collection.*

Cameos, shell, 14k, c. 1910-1915: Note the difference in the appearance of these women compared to shell cameo on page 34. **L** Brooch/Pin, profile of a bacchante with grape leaves in her hair, set in rounded lozenge-shaped engr yg frame with four pearls set at compass points, lever catch, 1-½″ × 1-⅞″, $450; **TC**, Brooch/Pendant, profile of a woman, yg filigree frame, swivel pendant bail, lever catch, 1″ × 1-⅜″, $375, *Cheri Mulligan collection*; **BC**, Brooch/ Pendant, profile of a woman with flowers in her hair, wearing dog collar necklace set with sm oe diamond (cameo *habillé*), set in octagonal wg filigree frame, swivel pendant bail, lever catch mkd 14k, 1-½″ × 1-¾″, $550, *Margaret A. Levine collection*; **R**, Brooch/Pin, profile of a woman with flowers in her hair and on shoulder, set in engr yg frame, lever catch, 1-¼″ × 1-¾″, $400, *Cheri Mulligan collection*.

yg bezel encircled by frame with riding crop and ribbon bow motifs, bordered with seed pearls, 1-¼″ dia . . . . **1,540 (A)**
Shell, yg, c. 1870-80, front bust of a woman, bezel set within an independent tubular frame with bead and leaf motifs appl to top and bottom, new 18k yg clasp, 1-⅜″ w × 1-¾″ **400**
Shell, 18k yg, c. 1860-70, full-figure cameo of woman with drapery set in oval yg frame of notched squares with granulation and wirework, 1-⅝″ w × 2″ . . . . **1,870 (A)**
Shell, 15k yg, c. 1860-70, cameo depicting the figure of a woman holding a dove, within a yg frame of two undulating snakes set with turquoise and red eyes, (some crazing to shell). 2-⅛″ w × 2-¼″ **800**

Cuff Links
Reverse intaglio, rock crystal quartz, MOP, 14k yg, c. 1890-1900, pr of round buttons with MOP bg, brown horse and multicolored polo players on green grass in rev intaglio joined by rings to yg bar, ½″ × ½″, pr . . . . . **495 (A)**
Reverse intaglio, rock crystal quartz, 14k yg,

late Victorian, four-leaf clovers within a yg bg, Hungarian hmks, pr . . . . **385 (A)**
Earrings, pendent
Coral, yg, mid-Victorian, pear-shaped drops with carved frontal portrait cameos of women set in wire-twist yg frames with saw-tooth bezels, suspended from replaced earwires, 2″ tl × ¾″, pr **400**
Locket
Hardstone, 18k yg, c. 1860-70, sardonyx cameo of a man's profile set in oval yg locket with rope-twist and beadwork border and bezel, 1-⅛″ w × 1-¾″ tl **700**
Neckchain and Intaglio
18k yg, hardstone, mid-Victorian, circular-link chain, T-bar toggle and ring closure, with sardonyx intaglio of warrior's head, rev of black onyx, suspended between uneven lengths of the chain, 17-¾″ tl, intaglio ¾″ w × 1″ . . . . **2,090 (A)**
Pendant and Chain
18k yg, ym, hardstone, mid-Victorian, Etruscan revival, circ sardonyx cameo of classic woman's profile set in circ frame decorated

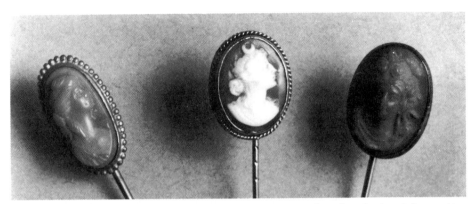

Scarf pin/Stickpins, shell and coral cameos, gold over brass, c. 1900. L, coral, $^1\!/_2''$ × $^3\!/_4''$, 1-$^1\!/_2''$ tl; C, shell, yg, goddess Diana, $^1\!/_2''$ × $^5\!/_8''$, 2-$^1\!/_2''$ tl; R, $^3\!/_8''$ × $^3\!/_4''$, 2-$^3\!/_4''$ tl. $50-100 ea. *Ellen Stuart collection.*

with appl bead, strap, and scrollwork, rev locket compartment for photograph, suspended from fancy figure-eight ym chain (not orig), pendant 1-$^5\!/_8''$ w × 2-$^1\!/_4''$ tl
.... **1,980 (A)**

Ring

Hardstone, 18k yg, half pearls, c. 1850-60, top of oval black onyx cameo outlined by nine half-pearls, continuing to sculpted foliate shoulders, hair compartment on rev (cracked), illegible hmk, $^3\!/_8''$ × $^3\!/_8''$ **300**

Hardstone, yg, mid to late Victorian, man's, rect three-layer cameo depicting dual profiles of male warriors, brown bg, white and black cameos in high relief, set in plain yg ring, size 9-$^1\!/_2$, 1" × $^7\!/_8''$ **450**

Hardstone intaglio, 18k yg, mid Victorian, oval sardonyx intaglio of profile of Hercules and Omphale, open back collet set, continuing to a ribbed shank, sgd, attrib to J. Graves, Boston, $^3\!/_4''$ × $^5\!/_8''$ .... **1,100 (A)**

Shell, yg, c. 1870-80, oval cameo of flower bouquet carved in detail, bezel set within a yg twisted-rope border, mounted on yg shank, ring size 5, 1-$^1\!/_8''$ w × 1-$^1\!/_4''$ **300**

Scarf pin/Stickpin

Coral, gf, c. 1900, carved cameo depicting a woman's profile, $^1\!/_2''$ w × $^3\!/_4''$, 2-$^1\!/_2''$ tl **50**

Hardstone, yg, late Victorian, oval white on black cameo of a dog in high relief set in plain yg bezel, $^5\!/_8''$ w × $^3\!/_4''$ **250**

Reverse intaglio, rock crystal quartz, 18k yg, depicting jockey silks in blue and white

Suite: Brooch/Pin and Pendent Earrings, lava cameos, silver, low kt yg, c. 1860-70. Brooch 3/4 profile of a bacchante in high relief set in plain yg frame, 1-$^1\!/_2''$ × 1-$^7\!/_8''$, earrings with carved flowerhead in surmount, full-face head of woman in drop, ropetwist gp frame, earwires, $^5\!/_8''$ × 2-$^1\!/_4''$ tl, $550. *Ofelia Bucy collection.*

Suite: Brooch/Pin and Pendent Earrings, sardonyx cameos, pearl, 18k yg, c. 1860-70. Brooch, cameo of a woman's profile suspended from within two eccentric oval tubular rings, each set with a pearl, surmounted by a yg trefoil, C-catch, tube hinge, extended pinstem, matching earrings on earwires, French hmks. Brooch 1″ × 1-⁵⁄₈″, earrings ⁷⁄₈″ × 1-⁵⁄₈″, $2,185 (A). *Photo courtesy of Butterfield & Butterfield (4/1/93).*

Watch Fobs/Seals, 9k yg, hardstone intaglios (1 all gold), c. 1860-80. Assortment of 10 fobs, chased and engr, set with intaglios of bloodstone, carnelian, citrine, amethyst, chalcedony, sardonyx, engr with various monograms, coats-of-arms, mottos; Eng, size range ³⁄₄″ to 1″ h, ³⁄₈″ × ¹⁄₂″ to ¹⁄₂″ × ³⁄₄″ at base, $150–300 ea. *Mary Lou Diebold collection.*

Watch Fob/Key, 9k yg, c. 1855, carnelian intaglio seal, monogram and chess knight one side, rev engr with motto: "time passes, but friendship remains" in French, swivel mechanism to allow use of seal, Eng, ⁷/₈" w × 2-¹/₄" tl closed, 2-⁵/₈" open, $375. *Mary Lou Diebold collection.*

polka dots with yellow helmet, rev dated April 6, 1899, Fr hmks . . . . **825 (A)**

Reverse intaglio, rock crystal quartz, 14k yg, c. 1900, depicting the head of a hound . . . . **138 (A)**

Reverse intaglio, rock crystal quartz, yg, c. 1890-1900, depicting dog's head, bezel-set within yg frame of twisted wire and beaded edges, orig box, 3" × ⁷/₈" . . . **770 (A)**

Suite: Bracelet and Pendent Earrings
  Lava, silver, c. 1860-70, bracelet of seven three-quarter profile cameos of women set in linked bezels with matching pendent earrings in silver mounts, lava cameo drops and surmounts on earwires, bracelet 6" × ⁷/₈", earrings ³/₈" × 2" tl, suite **750**

Brooch/Pin and Pendent Earrings
  Lava, yg, c. 1860-70, oval cameo depicting a full-figure putti holding a rabbit, carved in high relief, together with matching oval pendent earrings, cameo heads in surmounts on earwires in plain yg frames, (silver pinstem), brooch 1-¹/₈" w × 1-³/₈", e.r. 1-³/₈" tl × ¹/₂", suite . . . . **550 (A)**

MOSAICS IN JEWELRY

The rise and fall of mosaics paralleled that of cameos. Also based on ancient Roman techniques and revived by neoclassicists, mosaics of the late eighteenth and early nineteenth centuries were miniature works of art in glass or stone, resembling paintings. Like cameos, mosaics reached their height of popularity in the midnineteenth century, during the revivalist rage for all things Italian. And like cameos, too, the tourist trade brought them to that height and was their downfall in terms of quality.

There are two types of Italian mosaics: Roman, in which tiny bits of colored glass called tesserae are pieced together to form a picture, held in place with cement in a glass or stone background;

and Florentine, or *pietra dura* (literally, "hard stone," plural: *pietre dure*), in which thin slices of colored stones are cut in shapes and fitted together like a jigsaw puzzle to produce a picture, usually using a bed of black marble as the foundation.

The subject matter for mosaics is also of two distinct types. Roman mosaics, catering to the tourist trade, often depict Roman ruins and landscapes or are copies of ancient mosaics, like the Capitoline doves, often called "Pliny's doves." Mythological and religious figures are also seen in Roman mosaics. Florentine mosaics usually have floral motifs.

Value depends on quality of workmanship and condition. Mosaics are easily cracked or otherwise damaged. In Roman mosaics, the size of the tesserae helps determine age and quality. Micromosaics that look less like pieces of glass and more like a painting to the naked eye are usually earlier and better.

Entire parures, or suites, of jewelry were made from both types of mosaics. Demi-parures of pendant or brooch and earrings are also found. The brooch is the most common single type of mosaic jewelry. Mosaics continue to be made in Italy today, still for tourists, but with much larger tesserae and much lower quality.

Reference: Vivienne Becker, *Antique and Twentieth Century Jewellery*, 2nd ed., N.A.G. Press, 1987; Lael Hagan, "Mosaic Jewelry: Heir to a Long Artistic Tradition," in *Jewelers' Circular-Keystone/Heritage*, November, 1991.

Museum: The Los Angeles County Museum of Art, Los Angeles, Calif., houses one of the world's finest collections of Roman and Florentine mosaics—objects, paintings, furniture, and jewelry— The Gilbert Collection. The museum has published an accompanying catalog, *The Art of Mosaics, Selections from the Gilbert Collection.*

Bracelet
  Bangle
    Micromosaic, 18k yg, c. 1860-70, central floral bouquet motif in multicolored tesserae on white lozenge-shaped ground, flanked by two oval mosaics each depicting a pr of doves, yg bead and wirework on remaining surface, baluster finials at hinge and clasp, 2-¹/₄" dia × ⁷/₈", finials 1-¹/₈" . . . . **3,025 (A)**
  Link
    Micromosaic, malachite, 14k rose and yg, c. 1870-80, six circ multicolored mosaic plaques depicting Roman ruins and landmarks in malachite borders within plain rose gold frames, linked with a double row of yg floral motifs, 6-³/₄" tl, plaques ⁷/₈" dia . . . . **3,075 (A)**
Brooch/Pin
  Micromosaic, 14k yg, c. 1860-70, oval mosaic of "Pliny's doves" on blue ground, set in yg

frame with rope-twist wire decoration, C-catch, tube hinge, extended pinstem, 1-¹/₂" w × 1-⁷/₈" **750**

Micromosaic, 18k yg, c. 1870-80, oval mosaic of white, red, yellow, and pink flowers on black ground, bezel set within a yg tubular frame with appl bloomed yg ivy leaves on top, bottom and sides, C-catch, tube hinge, 2-¹/₄" w × 2" **1,000**

Micromosaic, yg, c. 1870-80, Egyptian revival, sq on sq, central scarab motif in greens and reds on circ white ground, blue border with scrolled wire in each corner, set in yg frame with beaded corners, superimposed on a sq with red and white mosaic corners, blue and white floral trefoils at ends of side corners, 2-¹/₄" w × 2-³/₄" . . . . **1,870 (A)**

Micromosaic, silver, c. 1890, oval black glass plaque set in plain bezel, center design of bird and flowers in multicolored tesserae, 1-³/₄" w × 1-³/₈" **250**

Pietra dura, gp ym, c. 1900, oval plaque, black stone ground with green, white, turq and mottled stone inlay in flower motif, ribbon-twist frame, appl pear and leaf motifs, 2" w × 1-⁵/₈" **200**

Pietra dura, 14k yg, c. 1870-80, oval plaque, white flower on black bg, glazed compartment for hair on rev, set in spiral wire frame, 1-³/₄" w × 1-¹/₄" **400**

Pietra dura, 18k yg, c. 1860-70, multicolored floral bouquet motif in black ground, set in oval yg frame with cabled wire decoration, 1-³/₄" w × 1-¹/₄" . . . . **715 (A)**

Earrings, pendent

18k yg, c. 1870, multicolored micromosaic dragon motifs within lozenge-shaped plaques, lobed sides, terminating in three

teardrop-shaped drops, suspended from disk-shaped surmounts with micromosaic faces in yg frames, 2-³/₄" tl × ⁷/₈", pr . . . . **3,575 (A)**

Pendant/Brooch

Micromosaic, 20k yg, c. 1860-70, oval shape, depicting a madonna, terminating in three micromosaic star and floral motif teardrop-shaped pendent drops, hinged pendant bail, 1-¹/₄" w × 3-¹/₈" tl . . . . **1,840 (A)**

Micromosaic, 14k yg, c. 1860-70, circ multicolored mosaic plaque of two doves on a perch, floral and foliate sprays on blue ground set in a twisted wirework frame suspending a central trefoil flanked by two lozenge-shaped floral mosaic pendent drops, 1-¹/₂" w × 2-⁵/₈" **2,500**

Pendant

Pietra dura, silver, c. 1870-80, oval plaque with rounded edge, white, blue, and brown floral and foliate motif on black ground, silver pendant bail, 1-¹/₄" w × 1-⁷/₈" tl **350**

Suite: Brooch/Pin and Pendent Earrings

Micromosaic, 15k yg, c. 1860-70, circ brooch of a medusa in mosaic suspending a lozenge-shaped mosaic pendent drop, in a yg wire-twist frame, with matching lozenge-shaped pendent earrings, 14k yg findings (replacement earwires), brooch 1-¹/₄" dia × 2-⁷/₈" tl, earrings ³/₄" × 2-¹/₄" tl, suite . . . . **2,090 (A)**

Brooch/Pin, micromosaic, glass, 18k yg, c. 1865, dove of peace in white, grey, and green, the word "PAX" in gold tesserae inlaid in blue glass ground, granulation and wirework yg frame, C-catch, tube hinge, extended pinstem, 1-³/₄" dia, $1,000. Ellen Stuart collection.

Pendent Earrings, micromosaic, 18k yg, ym, c. 1870, double-tier drops of multicolored micromosaic depictions of doves and cherubs, suspended from double chains, each terminating in three teardrop-shaped pendants, new post tops (possible marriage, some repair evident), ³/₄" × 2-⁵/₈" tl, pr, $1,840 (A). Photo courtesy of Butterfield & Butterfield (4/1/93).

L, Suite: Brooch/Pin and Earrings, micromosaic, gf, c. 1860, multicolor flower motif on goldstone ground, brooch 1-¹/₂″ × 1″, earrings 1-¹/₄″ tl, $400; TR, Pendent Earrings, micromosaic, 14k yg, seed pearls c. 1870, circ micromosaic plaques depicting Roman ruin, black glass ground, grad seed pearl fringe, suspended from double chains, sq faceted black glass surmounts on earwires (added later), plaques ⁵/₈″ dia, 2-¹/₂″ tl, $950, *Cheri Mulligan collection;* BR, Brooch/ Pin, micromosaic, gf, c. 1860, Roman scene in mosaic on black glass ground set in plain frame (dam), 1-¹/₈″ × ⁷/₈″, $125, *Ellen Stuart collection.*

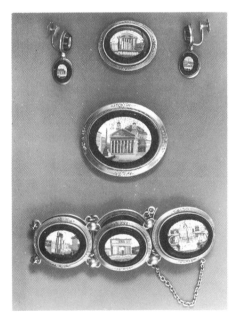

Suite: Bracelet, Earrings, Brooch, Pin, micromosaic, silver gilt, c. 1890, oval plaques, black glass ground, various Roman ruins, tourist scenes, set in engr silver gilt frames, earrings with screwbacks mkd 800; linked plaques bracelet, 7-³/₄″ tl, plaques 1-¹/₄″ × 1-³/₈″, clasp 1-¹/₄″ × 1-⁵/₈″, brooch 2″ × 1-⁵/₈″, pin 1-³/₈″ × 1-¹/₈″, earrings 1-¹/₄″ × ¹/₂″, $1,000. *Cheri Mulligan collection.*

Necklace, Brooch/Pin and Pendent Earrings
Micromosaic, 18k yg, c. 1850-60, necklace of oval plaques depicting Roman ruins and scenes in multicolored tesserae set in reddish-brown glass in plain yg bezels, joined with double lengths of elongated cable-link chain, 15″ tl, center plaque 1-¹/₂″ w × 1-¹/₄″, side plaques 1-¹/₈″ w × 1″, matching brooch, 1-¹/₈″ w × 1″, and pendent earrings, pear-shaped drops suspended from circ surmounts on earwires, 1-⁵/₈″ tl × ⁵/₈″, suite . . . . **4,125 (A)**
Pendant/Brooch and Pendent Earrings
Micromosaic, yg, c. 1875, brooch depicting the Lamb of God in a central oval mosaic plaque of multicolored tesserae, within an oval gold bead and wirework frame with quatrefoil border of shell and arrow motifs interspersed with scrolled wirework, suspending an urn-shaped drop with mosaic of floral sprays, rev glazed locket compartment, hinged pendant bail, 1-⁷/₈″ w × 3-³/₄″ tl, matching pendent earrings with central mosaic plaques depicting doves, floral mosaic disk surmounts on earwires, ⁷/₈″ w × 2-⁵/₈″ tl, within a fitted case stamped "A. Tanfani, Roma, 166 Corso-Via Della Vite 9, Via Condotti 2," suite . . . . **4,400 (A)**

Suite: Bracelet, Pendant, Bar Pin, Earrings, *pietra dura,* 18k yg, gp metal, c. 1860. Pendant and earring drops suspended from floral surmounts, hinged plaque bracelet and bar pin all in yg bead and scrolled wire frames, back plates gp metal, in orig fitted box, die-stamped "Cesare Guglifini, Firenze" (Ital), bracelet 5-³/₄" × 1-¹/₄", pendant 2-¹/₂" × 1-³/₈", pin 2" × ⁷/₈", $5,280 (A). *Photo courtesy of Skinner, Inc. (12/14/92).*

MANUFACTURED GOLD, GOLD-FILLED, AND GOLD-PLATED JEWELRY

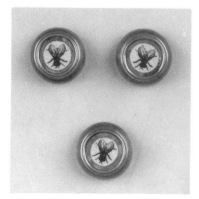

Shirt Studs, micromosaic, malachite, 18k yg, mid-Victorian, three yg disks, fly motifs in mosaic centers, malachite border, ¹/₂" dia, $935 (A). *Photo courtesy of Skinner, Inc. (12/14/92).*

History: The revivalists inspired an interest in goldwork. All-gold jewelry was a novelty in the midnineteenth century. Before discoveries in California and Australia in 1849 and 1851 made larger quantities of gold more accessible, gemstones were the focal point of most jewelry. Gold was used sparingly in very thin filigree (*cannetille*) or repoussé work in the early part of the century. Later, heating, rolling, pressing, and then electroplating, made a little gold go a long way and gave machine-made articles the look of gold without the expense.

By the 1830s, the Industrial Revolution had come to jewelry manufacture. Birmingham became a major center for machine-made goods in England. The invention of electroplating in 1840 helped launch what was to become a huge costume jewelry industry in England and the United States (although the term "costume jewelry" wasn't coined until the early twentieth century).

In the United States, manufacturing centers grew along the Eastern seaboard: in Philadelphia, New York, Boston, and especially in Providence, Rhode Island, the neighboring towns of Attleboro and North Attleboro, Massachusetts, and in Newark, New Jersey. Some of these manufacturers are still in business today.

It is worth noting that during the height of mid-Victorian revivalism, several Newark firms produced quality pieces in revivalist styles, comparable to those made in Europe. These jewels met with acceptance, however, only when they were sold as French or English-made. America's wealthy believed their own country's product was inferior to that of Europe. Perhaps this was because A...ricans excelled in the mass production of inexpensive gold and gold-filled or plated items. Many of the factories that made these items were in Newark and Providence. Although the pieces were mass-produced, there was still some artisanship involved. The forms may have been die-stamped by machine (the preferred method at the time), but engraving, enameling, and finishing were done by hand.

Stamped jewelry backed with a flat plate is sometimes called "hollow work," and resembles hand-raised repoussé metalwork, in which the metal is worked from the back to create a design in relief. Engraving or chasing may be added to the front of the piece. This is the type of work that many today consider typically Victorian, probably because it was produced in such quantities that a great deal of it has survived. Often, particularly in American pieces, the engraved depressions were partly filled with black enamel to enhance the design, called *taille d'épargne,* or black enamel tracery.

The addition of gold fringe or bead-tipped foxtail chain tassels was common in pieces of the 1870s, a time when women's dresses were trimmed with abundant quantities of fringe. Long pendent earrings were in vogue and were especially well-suited to tassels and fringing.

Garter bracelets, or *jarretières,* of gold or gold-plated brass mesh with fringed and tasseled ends, were worn in pairs. The bracelets were secured with an ornamental slide, often engraved and enameled, or set with a small cameo. They are sometimes referred to as slide bracelets, which can be confusing because another type of bracelet, made up of a collection of slides from longchains (see below), is also called a slide bracelet. This practice began earlier in this century after longchains went out of fashion. These slide bracelets became (and still are) popular enough to have been reproduced. The reproductions are fairly easy to detect: They don't have the hodgepodge look of a piece made up of old parts, as the originals are. Sometimes each slide is hallmarked in exactly the same way—a dead giveaway.

Hinged hollow bangles, both gold and gold-filled, are another kind of bracelet that remained

Bracelets, garter (*jarretière*), 10k yg, enamel, seed pearls, c. 1870, chain mesh, foxtail chain tassels suspended from engr and *taille d'épargne* enameled caps, bow-shaped engr and enameled slides set with seed pearls in center plaques, Am, 7-1/2" tl × 5/8", slides 1" × 1-1/8", pr, $2,300. *Mary Lou Diebold collection.*

popular throughout the Victorian period. They have become a classic form and are still made today. Widths and decorative elements vary from wide and ornately engraved or decorated to narrow and plain. The bypass or crossover design, in which decorated ends of a narrow tubular bangle cross parallel to one another at the top, gained favor in the later part of the century.

One variety of necklace of typically Victorian manufacture is called a book-chain necklace. Stamped, flat, folded-over rectangles, resembling the shape of a book, form the links of a double-sided chain, usually engraved or decorated on both sides. The chain is held together in front by an ornate clasp or slide, often with a small cameo set in it, the ends extending like tassels. The design may have evolved from the practice of wearing a ribbon around the neck, pinned with the ends crossed in front.

Gold and gold-filled longchains and slides were practical as well as popular. A watch, lorgnette, or other useful (or decorative) item could be attached by means of a swivel hook and suspended from the chain. The ornamental slide was drawn up and the pendent piece pinned or tucked into a pocket or belt, causing the chain to drape attractively.

Lockets, another classic jewelry form, were popular throughout the nineteenth century, varying in size and shape. Large oval gold and gold-filled lockets on wide or thick chains were in

Bangle Bracelets, hinged, yg: L 15k, c. 1860-70, with appl wirework decoration and safety chain, approx. 33.2 dwt, probably Eng, 2-¼″ dia × ¾″, pr, $1,430 (A); R, 14k, c. 1870-80, an etched geo and floral design with black *taille d'épargne*, enamel tracery, Am, 2-½″ dia × ¾″, pr, $1,760 (A). *Photo courtesy of Skinner, Inc. (12/14/92).*

keeping with style proportions of the Grand Period, 1860-80. Round and somewhat smaller lockets appeared toward the end of the century.

Gold-filled and electroplated jewelry was affordable to nearly everyone. It was manufactured in the same forms and styles as solid gold jewelry. Unless there is enough wear on a piece to reveal base metal (usually brass), jewelry should be tested to determine if it is gold or gold-filled. Gold-filled pieces sell for a little more than half the price of their all-gold counterparts.

Occasionally, one hears the term "pinchbeck" used to refer to gold-filled or gold-plated brass jewelry (more commonly heard in Britain). This is a misnomer. In reality, pinchbeck is an alloy of metals formulated in the early eighteenth century by Christopher Pinchbeck as an inexpensive imitation gold. It fell out of favor as a substitute for gold when electroplating was invented (c. 1840), and truly met its demise when 9 karat gold was made legal in Britain in 1854. It was not much used in the United States. Pre-Victorian pieces made from real pinchbeck are rarely seen today, despite some dealers' claims. If genuine, they are highly collectible and expensive.

Nineteenth century gold jewelry is often unmarked. If hallmarks are present, however, they can help determine age and country of origin. The United States had no legal standards until 1906, but 14 and 10 karats were the most common alloys for mass-manufactured gold of the Victorian period. A few prestigious firms, such as Tiffany & Co., used 18k exclusively; others used it occasionally. The British used 9, 12, and 15 karat gold after 1854, when standards were lowered from 18 karat. According to some experts, unassayed (unmarked) gold before 1854 can be lower than 18k. Britons spell karat with a c; the abbreviation is "c" or "ct." If a British piece is hallmarked, the date of assay is indicated by a letter.

Assayed French gold is never lower than 18k; the hallmark is an eagle's head. Maker's marks are in a lozenge. Other European countries use three-digit numbers that are karat equivalents in thousandths, for example, 750 equals 18k, 585 is 14k, etc.

References: Jeanenne Bell, *Answers to Questions About Old Jewelry,* Books Americana, 1992; Duncan James, *Old Jewellery,* Shire Publications, 1989. Marks: Any book on English hallmarks can decipher them, but the venerable *Jackson's Hallmarks,* Ian Pickford, ed., Antique Collectors' Club, 1992, is now published in a portable pocket-sized edition. French and many other countries' hallmarks on gold and platinum are in Tardy's *Poinçons D'Or et de Platine,* Paris, 1988 (in French, no translation). Dorothy Rainwater, *American Jewelry Manufacturers,* Schiffer, 1988, is an indispensable source of information on American-made jewelry and marks.

Museum: Providence Jewelers' Museum, Providence, R.I.

Bracelet
Bangle
14k yg, diamond, sapphires, late Victorian, raised foliate motif on satin-finish ground, set with one sm diamond, 2 sm sapphires,

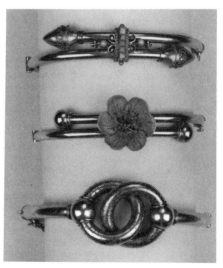

Bangle Bracelets, hinged, gold, c. 1890: T, 15k yg, turquoise, pearls, bypass design, tapered bulbous ends accented by twisted wirework, center set with turquoise and pearls, 8.2 dwt, Eng, 2-⅞″ dia × ¾″, $358 (A); C, 15k yg, ruby, bypass design, hollow tube with spherical ends, central textured flower motif with a ruby center, 6.5 dwt., Eng, 2-⅞″ dia, flower 1″ × ⅞″, $358 (A); B, 14k pink gold, hollow tube with center knot of etched interlocking hollow rings, minor dents, 11.7 dwt, 3″ dia, center 1-¾″ × 1″, $330 (A). *Photo courtesy of Skinner, Inc (3/14/93).*

sgd "Krementz," Newark, N.J., 2-1/2" dia
× 1/4" w . . . . **1,045 (A)**
Bangle, hinged
  9k yg, c. 1880, rounded hollow oval,
    Etruscan-style beadwork decoration on
    front half, 2-3/4" × 2-3/8" × 3/8" w **450**
  14k yg, ym, enamel, c. 1870-80, strap and
    buckle motif, engr and *taille d'épargne*
    enameled, safety chain, Am, 2-1/2" dia ×
    5/8" . . . . **259 (A)**
  15k yg, enamel, c. 1870-80, engr and *taille
    d'épargne* enameled floral and foliate de-
    sign with Greek key border, safety chain,
    Eng, 2-1/4" inside dia × 1/2" **575**
  Gf, c. 1900, oval, engr scrollwork on front
    half, button opening mechanism, 2-5/8" ×
    2-1/4", 7/8" w **125**
  Gf, c. 1890, round, engr and chased ornate
    floral and feather pattern, center mono
    "A," Am, mkd "J F S S Patent" on inner
    metal band hinge mechanism, 2-1/2" dia ×
    3/4" **300**
  Gf, oval, appl scrolled pierced quatrefoil
    center, surmounted by sq plaque engr with
    scrollwork and mono, flanked by four appl
    grad teardrop shapes on bangle shoulders,
    Am, inside mkd " J.M.F. & Co." for J. M.
    Fisher & Co., Attleboro, Mass., "Pat Jan 2
    06," button opening mechanism, 2-1/2" ×
    2" × 1/4" w, top 3/4"w **200**
  Gf, c. 1890, tapered oval, bezel-set purple
    faceted glass in the center, engr floral and
    foliate design around bezel and on bangle
    shoulders, Am, mkd " F. M. Co." for
    Finberg Mfg. Co., Attleboro, Mass., button
    opening mechanism, 2-3/4" × 2-1/4", top 1"
    w, tapering to 1/4" **200**
  Gf., c. 1890, oval, concentric lozenge
    shapes, foliate ends, engr on front, button
    opening mechanism, 2-5/8" × 2", 7/8" w
    . . . . **95**
  Gf, c. 1890, oval, engr with scrolls and name
    "Ella," Am, mkd "F.M. Co." for Finberg
    Mfg. Co., 2-1/2" × 2", 5/8" w **85**
  Gf, c. 1880, rose color, oval, chased and
    engr textured geo and floral motifs across
    front, button opening mechanism, Am,
    2-3/4" × 2-3/8", 1" w **300**
Flexible
  14k yg, c. 1840, mesh band terminating in
    two textured gold hands with blue enam-
    eled cuffs holding interlocking oval hoops,
    European hmk, 17.6 dwt, band 3/8" w,
    hands and hoops 2-1/4" × 1" . . . **1,980 (A)**
  Yg, diamonds, turq, c. 1860-80, strap and
    buckle design, oval tubular links terminat-
    ing in foxtail chain tassel, buckle set with
    rc diamonds and oval turq cabs, 7" × 1"
    . . . . **3,410 (A)**
Garter (*jarretière*)
  14k yg, enamel, seed pearl, c. 1870, woven
    yg mesh, 5/8" w, rect slide with scalloped

and lobed edge, engr and black *taille
  d'épargne* enamel, surmounted by appl
  six-pointed star set with a seed pearl, suspending a foxtail chain tassel with engr
  and enameled cap, terminating in matching chain tassel, slide 1" × 3/4" **1,250**
  15k yg, black enamel, c. 1860-80, flexible
    mesh bracelet with slide and foxtail tas-
    sels, highlighted by *taille d'epargne*
    enamel tracery, 19 dwt, Eng **900**
  Gold over brass, hardstone cameo, c. 1870,
    matching pr, chain mesh with die-stamped
    and engr slides set with sm carnelian
    cameos in centers, 3/8" w, slides 1/2" × 3/4",
    pr **450**
  Yg, seed pearls, c. 1870-80, matching pr,
    woven yg mesh, 5/8" w, lobed lozenge-
    shaped engr slides, raised central plaques
    set with seed pearls, engr capped ends and
    slides terminating in bead-tipped foxtail
    chain tassels, slides 1-1/8" × 7/8", pr
    . . . . **2,310 (A)**
Slide
  Yg, assorted gemstones, slide bracelet made
    from 16 watch or longchain slides of oval,
    triangular, navette, circular, and cushion
    shape, three are set with diamonds, nine
    with seed pearls, four with red cabochons,
    two with opals, one with coral cameo,
    strung on two lengths of double loop
    chain, 7" × 1/4" **1,400**
  Yg and gf, assorted gem and glass stones,
    made from nine slides of rect, lozenge,
    heart, and teardrop shape set with seed
    pearls, enamel, garnets, opal, red, blue,
    and green glass, one with an onyx cameo,
    separated by yg bead spacers, strung on
    two lengths of chain, 7" tl, center slide
    (largest) 3/4" × 1/2" **600**
Brooch/Pin
  10k yg, carnelian, c. 1890, die-stamped and
    engr, scalloped border, tapered ends, sm cab
    center stone, C-catch, Am, 1-1/4" w × 7/8"
    . . . . **95**
  14k yg, amethysts, c. 1890, in shape of a horse-
    shoe with engr floral decoration set with five
    amethysts in yg, 6 dwt., 1-1/4" w × 1-3/8"
    . . . . **350**
  14k yg, diamonds, c. 1900, bouquet of four yg
    five-petaled flowers, each set with one cen-
    tral diamond within raised yg pistils, at-
    tached to a yg stem, 7/8" w × 1-1/2"
    . . . . **468 (A)**
  18k yg, oe diamonds, enamel, silver, late Victo-
    rian, flower bouquet, black enamel petals,
    diamond centers, stems tied with silver rope-
    twist wire, sgd "Tiffany & Co.," 1-1/8" w ×
    2-1/2" . . . . **2,200 (A)**
  18k yg, diamonds, silver, c. 1890, in the shape
    of three full figure swallows pavé-set with di-
    amonds perched on a yg branch, 2" × 1-1/8"
    . . . . **990 (A)**

Brooches/Pins and Collar Button, engr and *taille d'épargne* enamel, Am., c. 1870-80: L, gf, oval, quatrefoil design (some enamel loss), C-catch, tube hinge, soldered ring for safety chain, 1-¼" × 1", $50; TC, Watch Pin, gf, serrate oval, prong-set center pearl, suspending foxtail chain tassel with engr and enameled cap, Moorish influence, rev hook for watch, C-catch, tube hinge, 1-⅛" × 1-½" tl, $125; R, yg, circ with enameled honeycomb pattern, central bow motif set with seed pearls, loop for safety chain on rev, C-catch, tube hinge, extended pinstem, 1" dia, $225; BC, Collar Button, yg, quatrefoil motif, ⅝" dia, $75. *Author's collection.*

Gf, c. 1900, hollow constr, die-stamped floral and foliate motifs in relief, open oval swirl frame, C-catch, tube hinge, 1-¼" w × 1-¾"
. . . . **65**

Gp base metal, garnets, seed pearls, c. 1890-1900, crescent shape, engr ends, center buff-top garnet, star-cut set, four grad seed pearls alternating with two sm garnets on each side, C-catch, tube hinge, 1-⅝" w × ¼" **125**

Low-karat yg, late Victorian, die-stamped hollow vine and leaf motif in open scrolled pretzel shape, C-catch, tube hinge (repaired), 1-⅞" w × 1-¼" **75**

Brooch/Pin, 14k yg, pearls, rubies, diamonds, c. 1870-80, oblong yg plaque with center band of scrolled openwork, beaded edge, surmounted by central sq plaque set with pearls and gemstones in quatrefoil pattern, C-catch, enclosed end for pinpoint, Am, 1-¾" × ⅝", $350. *Mary Lou Diebold collection.*

Bar

9k, yg, garnet, date letter for 1896, die-stamped and engr floral design, scallop edge, tapered ends, hollow contr, center stone star-cut set, C-catch, Eng, 1-⅝" × ½"
. . . . **100**

15k, yg, c. 1880-90, wirework and flowerhead motifs, beaded edge, tube clasp with enclosed end for pinpoint, mkd "15ct," Eng, 1-½" × ⅝6" **155**

Gf, enamel, c. 1870-80, stamped and engr, flared ends, black *taille d'épargne* enamel border, scroll and quatrefoil design, wide C-catch, tube hinge, hook for watch or pendant on rev, 2-⅛" w × ⅝" **95**

Gf, garnet, c. 1880-90, stamped and engr, scrolled, and foliated motifs, double lozenge-shaped ends, raised center set with sm rc garnet, 2-¼" w × ½" **85**

Gf, tiger's eye, c. 1900, bezel-set oval tiger's eye cameo center flanked by two engr disks, wirework scrolled ends, C-catch, flanged hinge, worn to base metal, 2" w × ⅝" **65**

Gp base metal, blue glass, c. 1890, stamped, center hemisphere with appl wirework set with row of sm glass cabs on diagonal, lotus flower shaped ends with appl Etruscan-style decoration, wide C-catch,

Earrings, yg: TL, c. 1870-80, hinged ring, scalloped wire border, with seed pearl in center of engr and *taille d'épargne* enameled strap-shape threaded through center of ring, engr and enameled surmount on earwire, 1-¹/₂" tl × ¹/₂" dia, $400; TR, c. 1880-90, disks, appl bow-shaped center, engr with black *taille d'épargne* enamel tracery, earwires, possible conversion from collar buttons, ⁵/₈" dia, $275; Brooches/Watch Pins, yg, c. 1870-80: BL, articulated scroll, engr and *taille d'épargne* enameled (some enamel damage), appl center plaque with seed pearls and scrolled wirework, Moorish influence, C-catch, tube hinge, extended pinstem, hook for watch, 1-¹/₄" × 1-⁵/₈", $400; BR, 10k, engr oval with appl diagonal cross motif, center seed pearl, 1-¹/₈" w × ³/₄", $185, *Cheri Mulligan collection*

tube hinge, hook for watch or pendant on rev, 2-³/₈" w × ⁵/₈" **95**

Yg, enamel, diamond, c. 1900, stylized flowerhead outlined in black enamel, om diamond center, mounted in center of yg bar, 2" w × ¹/₂" **350**

Brooch/Watch Pin

14k yg, c. 1890-1900, pretzel-twist knot of hollow tubing, hook for watch on rev, C-catch, tube hinge, some dents, 2" w × 1" **225**

Cuff/"Handy" Pins

Gf, c. 1900, hollow die-stamped, one scallop edge, raised foliate design in center, enclosed C-catch, tube hinge, 1" × ¹/₄", pr **45**

Earrings

14k yg, c. 1880, engr spheres with *taille d'épargne* enamel, suspended from (replaced) earwires, ⁵/₈" dia, pr **275**

15k yg, diamonds, c. 1890, hollow pendent ovals, die-stamped scrolled design, star-cut set sm rc diamond centers, shepherd's hook earwires, probably cuff link conversions, Eng, ¹/₂" w × ³/₄", pr **295**

18k yg, c. 1860, each designed as an arch with applied wire twist detail and textured gold leaf center, suspending three sm oval bead drops, 7.8 dwt, ³/₈" w × 1-¹/₂" tl, pr .... **523 (A)**

Gp, c. 1890-1900, Creole hoops (tapered ring),

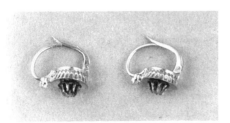

Earrings, yg, c. 1890: L, 14k, sm round-cut diamonds, disks with hinged Fr-back earwire, high-pronged setting, ³/₈" dia, $350; R, disks with appl fan-shaped motif set with seed pearls, hinged Fr-back earwire, mkd "14k," ¹/₂" dia, $250, *Cheri Mulligan collection.*

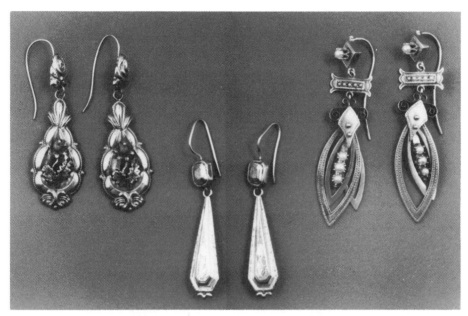

Pendent Earrings, yg: L, sm coral beads, c. 1860-70, pear-shaped drops, scalloped edge, stamped hollow constr with appl leaves and flower, coral bead center, earwires soldered to floral surmount, 2" tl × ⁵/₈", $375; **C,** 12k, c. 1860-70, die-stamped and engr hollow teardrop suspended from octagonal surmount on earwire, probably Eng, 1-¹/₂" tl × ³/₈", $250; **R,** 14k, seed pearls, c. 1870-80, concentric navette shapes with three seed pearls in center, suspended from rect plaque with seed pearls and diamond surmount with pearl center, mkd 14k, Am, 2" tl × ¹/₂", $900, *Cheri Mulligan collection.*

allover engr design on flattened sides, earwires attached to ends of hoops, Am, ⁷/₈" dia, pr **45**

Yg, c. 1890-1900, Creole hoops, faceted hollow tapered rings, Am, ³/₄" dia, pr **150**

Locket

Gf, c. 1870-80, oval, prong-set black/white onyx full-figure cameo set in concave center, flanked by S-scroll wirework, plain raised central frame bordered with raised Etruscan-style design, similar rev with plain concave center, 1" w × 1-⁵/₈" **125**

Gf, c. 1870-80, elongated oval, allover engr floral and foliate design, *taille d'épargne* enamel in royal blue, turq, red, white on front, rev engr with name "Bessie," ³/₄" w × 1-¹/₈" **125**

Gf, late Victorian, oval, allover engr, raised quatrefoil and scroll design in center, rev raised scroll for mono, ⁵/₈" w × ⁷/₈" **75**

Locket and Chain

Gf, seed pearl, c. 1870-80, oval, surface covered in Etruscan-style scrolled wirework and beading with seed pearl prong-set in center, 1" w × 1-³/₈", with gf double loop-in-loop chain (not orig), 16" tl **175**

Gf, seed pearls, c. 1870-80, rounded oval, twisted wirework in scrolled design, raised vertical panel set with three seed pearls in

Locket, daguerreotype, gilt metal, c. 1840-50, round, engr with engine-turned design, hinged cover, compartment for photo (daguerreotype), ring for attachment to watch chain, 1-¹/₄" dia, $125. *Author's collection.*

Locket and Chain, 9k yg, enamel, 1880, oval hinged locket, engr front and back, blue champlevé enameled front, two inside photo compartments, suspended from cable-link chain, tube clasp, inscribed "C.L. Sep 30 80," Eng, chain 19" tl, locket $^7/_8$" × 1-$^1/_8$", $350. *Mary Lou Diebold collection.*

Neckchain and Pendant, 10k yg, enamel, seed pearl, c. 1870, shield-shaped pendant/front clasp, engr, with black *taille d'épargne* enamel tracery, suspending foxtail chain tassel, engr and enameled cap, Moorish influence, split-ring double-link cable chain, 22" tl, clasp $^7/_8$" × 1-$^1/_2$", $450. *Mary Lou Diebold collection.*

center, sm raised trefoils set in a fan shape across bottom front, 1-$^1/_8$" w × 1-$^1/_2$", married to gf longchain with swivel hook and heart-shaped slide set with a pearl, opal, and garnet cluster, slide $^3/_4$" × $^3/_4$" **475**
Gf, red stones and seed pearls, c. 1870-80, oval, pink and yellow gold color, stamped and engr, appl foliate and scroll design between raised curved sections, raised vertical panel in center set with sm red stones and seed pearls, red stone prong-set at base of front, 1" w × 1-$^1/_4$", married to gf book chain with engr foliate motifs appl to textured rings, 18" tl × $^1/_4$" **375**
Gf, c. 1880-90, oval with appl knife-edge wire

scrollwork on concave surface, raised plaque set with four seed pearls in center, $^7/_8$" w × 1", reeded cable-link chain, 15-$^1/_2$" tl **150**

Neckchain

14k yg, early Victorian longchain, foxtail links, engr indented rect slide, terminating in a gloved hand holding gp swivel, 15.2 dwt, 54-$^1/_2$" tl **375**

14k yg, c. 1870, longchain and slide, fancy cable links terminating in two bead-tipped foxtail chain tassels with engr domed caps surmounted by fluted disks, engr tricolor gold shield-shaped slide with appl knife-edge scrollwork in center, 32" tl × $^1/_8$", slide 1" × $^7/_8$" . . . . **1,610 (A)**

15k yg, mid Victorian, circ star-engr links, Eng, 17" × $^1/_4$" . . . . **660 (A)**

15k yg, mid to late Victorian, longchain and slide, fancy links with bead terminals, scalloped-edge slide with appl three-dimensional floral and foliate motif, 46.7 dwt, 60" tl × $^3/_{16}$", slide 1-$^1/_8$" × $^7/_8$" . . . . **1,320 (A)**

Necklace

Bookchain

14k yg, black onyx, c. 1860-80, stamped and engr links clasped by lozenge-shaped slide set with white on black hardstone cameo, terminating in two tasseled ends, 18" tl , slide $^7/_8$" × $^5/_8$" **450**

Gf, c. 1870-80, stamped and engr rect links with reeded, engr and *taille d'épargne* enameled oval front clasp, terminating in two ends stamped to look like tassels, 21" tl × $^3/_8$", clasp $^3/_4$" × $^1/_2$" **250**

Gf, c. 1870-80, stamped and engr rounded

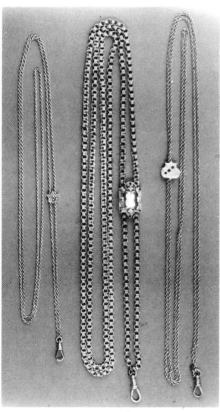

Longchains and Slides: L, gf, seed pearls, c. 1890, foliate motif, rope-twist chain, slide with seed pearls, 48" tl, $125; C, gf chain, 18k yg slide, hardstone cameo, c. 1890, flower motif surrounding rect bezel, *taille d'épargne* enamel, chain 62" tl, slide $^5/_8$" w × 1", $450, *Cheri Mulligan collection* ; R, 14k yg, seed pearls, c. 1880, rope-twist chain, shield-shaped slide set with three seed pearls (1 missing) on diag, 64" tl, $300, *Vicki Telford collection.*

Necklaces, Bookchains, gf, c. 1870: L, coral, seed pearl, die-stamped and engr links suspending stamped and engr shield-shaped pendant clasp with carved coral cameo, seed pearl center, scrolled wirework border, 18" tl, pendant 1" × 1", $250, *Cheri Mulligan collection;* C, hardstone, enamel, die-stamped and engr, chain 5/16" w, *taille d'épargne* enameled pendent drop with hardstone cameo, 1" × $^5/_8$", 21" tl, $275, *Ellen Stuart collection* ; R, red stones, narrow book chain, stamped and engr links, round front clasp with three sm faceted red stones in center, single tassel, 17" tl, $125, *Cheri Mulligan collection.*

Pendant and Chain, 14k yg, pearl, enamel, c. 1870, die-stamped and engr domed disk with appl tapering crossbars and scrolled top suspended from cable-link chain, pearl set in six-pointed star mounted in center, terminating in a foxtail chain tassel with engr and *taille d'épargne* enameled cap, tube clasp, Am, pendant 1" w × 2-1/2", 16-1/2" tl, $750. *Cheri Mulligan collection.*

11 seed pearls and one red stone eye, mounted on yg shield-shaped brooch/pendant, matching drop earrings with gf clips (added), brooch/pendant 1-1/8" w × 2-1/4", earrings 1-5/8" tl × 3/4", suite .... **633 (A)**

Suite: Brooch/Pin and Earrings
Gf, coral, c. 1890, oval pin engr with scroll design, coral baton through center ring, 7/8" w × 5/8", matching disk earrings (screwback findings added later) 3/8" dia, suite **185**

Suite: Brooch/Pin and Pendent Earrings
14k yg, c. 1870, die-stamped and engr lobed plaques suspending fringe of pear-shaped drops from scrolled wire and beadwork frame, C-catch, Am, brooch 2" w × 1-1/4", earrings 1-3/4" tl × 3/4", suite **750**

Watch Chain
9k yg, c. 1890, cable link with tubular center segment, 1/4" w, swivel hook, no bar, can be worn as bracelet, Eng, 7-3/8" tl **250**
9k yg, c. 1890, round box link and fancy segments, swivel and bar, Eng, 8-1/4" × 3/16" **275**
14k yg, c. 1890-1900, paper-clip style, 14" tl × 1/8" **400**
14k yg, c. 1890, fancy oval and elongated open links with matching fob and swivel clasp, 22 dwt, 15" l × 1/4" **500**

Scarf or Handkerchief Holder, 14k yg, late Victorian, engr scalloped-edge tongs with slide for opening and closing, end loop for attachment of chain and finger ring, 1-5/8" tl × 5/8", $150. *Mary Lou Diebold collection.*

rect links, oval front clasp with stamped scrollwork and beaded edge, carnelian cameo prong-set in center, terminating in two ends stamped to look like tassels, 20" tl × 1/4", clasp 7/8" × 3/4" **300**

Pendant
15k yg, enamel, seed pearl, c. 1900, domed oval center, turq enamel, star-cut set center seed pearl, twisted yg wire, scrolls and beads around border, Eng, 5/8" × 3/4" **145**

Suite: Brooch/Pendant and Earrings
14k yg, seed pearls, mid-Victorian, three-dimensional bird and floral motif with approx

Suite: Brooch/Pin and Earrings, 14k yg, blue enamel on chased yg, c. 1850-60, Algerian knot motif, brooch 1-½" × 1", earrings 1-¼" tl × ⅝", $850. *Cheri Mulligan collection.*

Suite: Brooch/Watch Pin and Pendent Earrings, 14k yg, enamel, seed pearls, c. 1870, brooch of die-stamped, engr and *taille d'épargne* enameled plaque set with seed pearls accented with beadwork, suspending tassel of foxtail chains, engr and enameled cap, hook for watch on rev, C-catch, Am, 1-¼" × 2" tl, matching earrings with beaded disk surmounts on orig earwires, 2-¼" tl x ¾", $1,200, *Mary Lou Diebold collection.*

15k yg, mid Victorian, alternating plain circ and flattened oval shaped links with appl bead and wirework, 19.4 dwt, 14" tl × ½" .... **660 (A)**

18k yg, c. 1880-90, fancy rect openwork segments interspaced with tubular links, chain and spring ring added for wear as necklace, illegible hmks, Eng, 16-¾" tl × ⅜" **850**

Watch Chains

9k yg, c. 1890, fancy rect segments joined to faceted links, bars and swivels, altered for

Watch Fob and Chain, gp brass, carnelian, c. 1890-1900, scrolled clasp suspending metal mesh and rope-twist chain, monogrammed scrolled plaque, and scroll-top fob with oval carnelian intaglio seal; attached cable chain with swivel mkd "S.O.B. Co," sq engr and mono locket, 4-½" × 1", chain 6-⅛" tl, locket ¾" sq, $125. *Joyce Albers collection.*

wear as bracelets, Eng, 7-$\frac{3}{4}$" tl × $\frac{1}{4}$", pr
. . . . **700**
Watch Pin
Gf, c. 1900, fleur-de-lis motif, die-stamped,
mkd "A&Z 1/20 12k G.F." on rev hook for
watch, $\frac{7}{8}$" w × 1" **45**

Gp base metal, green enamel, c. 1900, fleur-de-lis, die-stamped, $\frac{7}{8}$" w × 1-$\frac{1}{8}$", suspending black grosgrain ribbon, 4" × 1", and fob of a working compass set in ym (marriage), 1-$\frac{1}{8}$" dia **65**

LATE VICTORIAN (AESTHETIC PERIOD) C. 1880-1901

By the 1880s, Victorian society was beginning to change. In celebration of 50 years on the throne in 1887, Queen Victoria was willing to relax her strict rules of mourning a little, much to the relief of her subjects. Fashions had changed, too. Victoria was no longer as influential as her beautiful daughter-in-law, Princess Alexandra, who was already a trend-setting, fashionable woman—in much the same way that today's Princess of Wales, Diana, outshines dowdy, matronly Queen Elizabeth II.

In keeping with a new aestheticism, lines were simpler and fabrics lighter. Flounces and trains were abandoned in favor of smooth curves. Delicate lace replaced heavy fringe. After a short period of protruding emphasis, the bustle became a vestige of its former self as fullness transferred to leg-o'-mutton and balloon sleeves. Collars grew higher and tighter. The tailored look was in vogue: Women were becoming more active, in the work force and at leisure, and required proper attire. Their only remaining extravagance was their headgear. Hats were large and decorated profusely with bows, ribbons, lace, flowers, plumes, and feathers—sometimes entire birds. Ornamental hatpins grew to great lengths to keep them in place.

Attitudes about jewelry were also affected. Elaborate ostentation gave way to refined simplicity. Heavy, dark, somber, massive, and ornate jewelry was losing favor. Lighthearted, light-colored, and delicate pieces took its place. Silver replaced gold for daytime wear. Many female aesthetes—early feminists rebelling against constricting fashions and protesting the notion of woman as decorative object—no longer wore any jewelry at all during the day. Diamonds continued to be the evening jewels of choice among most women of wealth and status, however.

Jewelry in general was reduced in dimension even when worn in quantity. Brooches were smaller and often worn in multiples. Some had utilitarian purposes as veil, lace, hat, bodice, skirt, or cuff pins. These were also called handy pins or beauty pins. Earrings shrank to diminutive proportions. Sometimes they were nothing more than a single small stone, pearl, or stud. Until the 1890s, earrings were made for pierced ears. By the end of the century, however, women were beginning to look upon ear-piercing as a barbaric practice. The screwback finding was invented as a solution. Its use gradually superseded the earwire and stud post; by the 1920s, screwbacks were predominant.

Necklaces were fringes or festoons of linked gemstone drops and chains. Princess Alexandra was the instigator of the dog-collar necklace, a high, wide choker, usually of diamonds and/or pearls, which became an Edwardian trademark when she became Queen. In the United States, the American "royal," Consuelo Vanderbilt (who became the Duchess of Marlborough in 1895), popularized the look with her dog collar of 19 rows of pearls and diamond clasps. Both women had the requisite long slender necks for wearing such a jewel. Bracelets continued to be worn in multiples, growing narrower toward the end of the period. Bangles were tubular or open knife-edge wires joined by an ornamental device in front. Curb-link bracelets in gold or silver were also fashionable, often joined with a heart-shaped padlock clasp. Small waists were a fashion focal point; wide belts and ornamental buckles were commonly worn.

Sporting jewelry grew in popularity as women became more involved in outdoor activities. Horseshoes and animal motifs—fox and hounds, horses, game birds, etc.—were worn with tailored clothing. Both women and men wore reverse-painted crystal intaglios, an often-used dec-

Brooch/Pin, lead crystal (paste), silver, c. 1890-1900, grad om-cut stones bead set within crescent-shaped base and frame, tube hinge, added safety catch, 1-$\frac{3}{8}$" × 1-$\frac{1}{4}$", $125. *Joyce Albers collection.*

oration for stickpins, cuff links, and small brooches.

Japanese motifs and designs gained approval after new trade relations were opened with Japan in the 1850s, and Japanese decorative arts and crafts were introduced to the West at international exhibitions in the 1860s and 1870s. Interest in things Japanese coincided with the growth of the Aesthetic movement in Britain, France, and the United States. The tenets of the movement embraced the Oriental approach to design: simplicity of form and inspiration from nature. Japanese fans, bamboo, scenes, and other ornamental devices, collectively referred to as *japonaiserie* (also called Japanesque and japonisme), began to crop up in jewelry, particularly in silver and mixed-metals, imitating the Japanese sword-making techniques of shibuichi and shakudo. Tiffany & Co. won the Grand Prix for their Japanesque mixed-metals designs in silverware at the Paris Exposition of 1878. They applied the same techniques to jewelry.

International expositions continued to play an important role in the dissemination and marketing of new ideas and trends in fashion and jewelry. Two more Expositions Universelles were held in Paris in 1889 and 1900. The World's Columbian Exposition in Chicago in 1893 was another exhibition that brought international prestige and recognition to the United States. Tiffany and Gorham each had their own pavilion, and numerous other American and European manufacturers were well-represented with displays of jewelry.

SILVER AND MIXED METALS

History: Silver as a metal for jewelry has fluctuated in popularity and application. In the eighteenth and nineteenth centuries it was customarily used for setting diamonds and colorless paste, or, disguised with gilding, for making imitation jewels look real. It wasn't until the latter part of the nineteenth century that silver began to be used as a material for its aesthetic and sculptural qualities alone. Changing fashions, historical events and discoveries, and the Aesthetic movement itself contributed to the metal's appreciation.

The discovery of the Comstock Lode in Nevada in 1859 made silver readily available to manufacturers in the United States and Britain. Its relatively low cost meant that silver jewelry was now affordable to almost everyone. The *japonaiserie* craze of the 1870s and early 1880s led British and American manufacturers to produce stamped silver trinkets engraved with Japanese motifs. In the United States, it was permissible to include copper in a fashion similar to *shibuichi* (copper and silver) and *shakudo* (copper and gold), but assay

laws prohibited British manufacturers from doing so. Touches of gold were added to British silver for a mixed-metals effect.

The locket and the hinged bangle were favorite forms in silver. They were stamped, engraved, and embellished with beaded edges and applied motifs such as buckles, flowers and leaves, crosses and anchors.

After a decline in the wearing of daytime jewelry in the mid 1880s, silver jewelry regained favor in the waning years of the century. Message and love brooches were all the rage among the working class. These were stamped and engraved with the names of loved ones or other endearing terms. A Biblical reference, "Mizpah," sent the message: "The Lord watch between me and thee when we are absent one from another." The language of flowers was also used to send sentimental signals to loved ones—forget-me-nots (remembrance), ivy (friendship), and roses (a different meaning for every variety). Other popu-

Watch Fobs and Chains, silver, niello, c.1890: C & L, heart shape with floral scroll design, working compass in center, suspended from double-hinged links with dotted design, 5-1/2" tl × 9/16" w, fancy-link chain, helix pattern design, swivels on ends, 20-1/4" tl × 1/8" w, $400; R, round fob with working compass, niello enamel in checkerboard pattern, 7/8" dia, suspended by a spring ring from chain of long silver/niello and cabled copper links, oversize silver/niello spring ring and swivel clasp attached to chain, 18-1/2" tl, $350. *Joyce Albers collection.*

lar symbols were the anchor of hope, the cross of faith, the heart of charity, the good-luck horseshoe, and lovebirds.

Silver belts, buckles, clasps, and chatelaines were frequently worn during the aesthetic period. Chatelaines were derivatives of a chain worn by medieval keepers of keys. They are waist ornaments that serve a utilitarian purpose—a sort of housewife's tool kit. Various implements are suspended by chains from a decorative clasp that hooks over a belt or waist sash: Scissors, needle cases and other sewing tools, notepads and pencils, match safes, coin purses, and other assorted useful items could be hung from swivel hooks on a chatelaine. Most of these were decorated with repoussé or engraving. Chatelaines, made from an assortment of materials, came in and out of fashion throughout the century. Those made of silver appealed to aesthetic tastes, especially after the trend-setting Princess Alexandra was seen wearing one.

A technique known as "niello" was applied to silver ornaments in the late nineteenth century. Based on a medieval Russian technique, niello is a greyish-black mixture of silver, lead, copper, and sulphur that is applied to engraved designs on the silver's surface, then fired and polished smooth. Allover geometric or floral patterns yielded the best effect. An alloy of 800 silver (parts per thousand) was usually used because it withstands firing temperatures better than higher grades of silver.

Like gold, nineteenth-century silver jewelry is not always hallmarked. When marks are found, however, they can be helpful clues. The American standard for silver was 900 parts per thousand until 1906. Pieces marked "standard" or "coin" are of 900 silver. Some manufacturers, notably Tiffany and Gorham, used the British sterling standard of 925 considerably earlier and marked pieces "sterling." The British mark for sterling is a lion passant, or walking lion. The place of assay and date letter hallmarks correspond to those used on gold. European countries used alloys ranging from 750 to 950, with various devices used as indications of silver content hallmarks.

References: Vivienne Becker, *Antique and Twentieth Century Jewellery*, 2nd ed., N.A.G. Press, 1987; Ginny Redington Dawes and Corinne Davidov, *Victorian Jewelry, Unexplored Treasures*, Abbeville Press, 1991; Marks: *Bradbury's Book of Hallmarks* (on British and Irish silver, gold, and platinum), J.W. Northend Ltd., 1987; Tardy, *International Hallmarks on Silver*, English translation, Paris, 1985. Includes the silver hallmarks of many European countries and Great Britain.

Bracelet
　Bangle
　　Sterling, c. 1900, circ hollow tube, chased and engr scroll and foliate design covering

outside surface, Am, 2-³/₄" dia × ¹/₄"
　. . . . . **145**
Bangle, hinged
　Sterling, rose and yg, c. 1870-80, *japonaiserie*-style appl and engr floral and insect motifs accented with gold, beaded edge on scalloped border, 2-¹/₄" inside dia, 1-³/₈" w **500**
　Sterling, c. 1880, oval, stamped and engr with bird and floral motifs within engr circles and borders, 2-¹/₂" × 2" × 1-¹/₄" w **350**
　Sterling, c. 1880, stamped and engr "Mizpah" in center of floral and foliate motifs, scalloped inside borders and beaded edges, 2-³/₈" inside dia, 1-⁷/₈" w **475**
Link
　Sterling, c. 1890-1900, curb links suspending three heart-shaped padlocks with keyhole centers bordered with stamped scrollwork, padlocks ⁷/₈" w × 1-¹/₈", 7" tl × ⁵/₈" **250**
　Sterling, c. 1900, chased curb links with clasp of stamped scrollwork heart-shaped padlock with keyhole center and key, Am, padlock ⁵/₈" w × ⁷/₈", 7" tl × ¹/₂" **225**
Brooch/Pin
　Sterling, c. 1880-90, circ stamped and engr, raised floral and foliate motifs in center, raised Gothic arches around border, beaded edge, 1-³/₈" dia **125**
　Sterling, pink gold, c. 1880, stamped and engr in the shape of a hand holding an open fan, asymmetrical flower and bird motifs overlaid with pink gold (*japonaiserie*), 2-¹/₄" w × 1-¹/₂" **250**
　Sterling, c. 1890-1900, horseshoe motif, stamped and engr "Good Luck," scalloped edge, appl riding crop motif, C-catch, tube hinge, 1-¹/₄" × 1-¹/₄" **150**

Bracelet, hinged bangle, 900 silver, c. 1870-80, oval bangle, front half decorated with appl roses and leaves, engr checkerboard pattern, zigzag border, back half smooth, mkd "standard" (for 900 silver) on inside of box clasp, Am, 2-¹/₂" dia × 1-¹/₄", $200. *Author's collection.*

Bracelets, Link: T, sterling, c. 1900, links engr with family names and initials, mkd "pat appl for," 6-³/₄" tl, ¹/₄" w, $50; B, silver, c. 1895, U.S. and Canadian coins, love token charms, engr one side with family monograms and ciphers, "Mother," "Father," some with dates 1871-93, nine coins of grad size linked to form bracelet, suspending five coins as charms, 7-³/₄" tl, lgest coin 1" dia, $175. *Joyce Albers collection.*

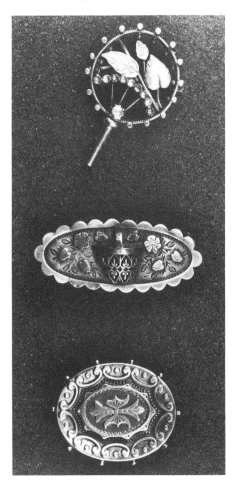

Sterling, c. 1900, lozenge-shape, stamped and engr with floral border, name "Rose" in center cartouche, 1-³/₄" w × ⁷/₈" **100**

Sterling, c. 1900, handy pin, rect with scrolled corners, center stamped name "Pet," Eng, 1-¹/₄" w × ¹/₄" **50**

Bar

MOP, silver gilt, c. 1890, carved in the shape of two clasped hands (*fede* motif: friendship, trust), mounted on pin back assembly with silver gilt bands around wrists, Am, 2-¹/₂" w × ¹/₂" **100**

Silver and silver gilt, c. 1890, in the shape of a cuffed hand with pointing finger wearing a ring, stamped, engr and appl details, 2-¹/₄" w × ³/₈" **145**

Sterling, c. 1870-80, stamped engr arrow shape with cutout fancy engr scrollwork feather, C-catch, tube hinge, 2-³/₄" w × 1" **200**

Sterling, c. 1880-90, plain round hollow center bar with spherical midsection, ter-

Brooches/Pins: T, mixed metals, rc glass pastes, c. 1880-90, in shape of circ Japanese fan with border of ym rods, open center of mixed metal foliate motifs mounted on wires, collet-set stones in arch beneath leaves, three knife-edge wires radiating from larger prong-set stone at base, C-catch, tube hinge, 1-³/₈" × ⁷/₈", $75, *Author's collection;* C, Watch Pin, sterling, yg, date letter for 1890, die-stamped and engr scalloped-edge ellipse, three-dimensional openwork basket motif mounted in center, flanked by engr flower sprays, yg accents, hook for watch, C-catch and tube hinge, Birmingham (Eng) hmks, 1-³/₄" × ³/₄", $150, *Joyce Albers collection;* B, sterling, date letter for 1891, die-stamped and engr oval, raised center, C-scroll border design, beaded edge, Birmingham (Eng) hmks, 1-¹/₄" × 1", $100, *Cheri Mulligan collection.*

Brooch/Pin, sterling, enamel, c. 1870-80, engr oval and St. Andrew's cross bisecting four lobed segments mounted on outer edge, lt and dk blue enamel, C-catch and tube hinge, 1-⁵⁄₈″ × 1-¼″, $175. *Joyce Albers collection.*

Brooch/Pin, 900 silver, h.p. porcelain, c. 1886, center plaque of scene depicting a gentleman assisting a lady in debarking a ship, set in ornate openwork scrolled silver frame with brass beading, Austrian hmk for 900 silver (in use 1886-1922), 1-⁵⁄₈″ × 1-⁷⁄₈″, $200. *Joyce Albers collection.*

Brooches/Pins, sterling, name, Eng, late Victorian: TL, date letter for 1890, flower spray, cutout letters, "Mizpah" (Biblical reference) over cutout heart shape, mounted on branch-shaped bar, 1-³⁄₄″ × ⁵⁄₈″, Birmingham hmks, C-catch, tube hinge, $125; TR, round, pierced center with cutout foliate and bird motifs, "Clara," within engr and beaded-edge border, mkd "sterling," C-catch, tube hinge, 1-¹⁄₂″ dia, $150, *Leigh Leshner collection;* BL, round, pierced center with cutout shamrocks and leaves, "Dora," within notched and beaded-edge border, 2″ dia, $175, *Richard Noël collection;* BR, bar, date letter for 1909, die-stamped lozenge shape with cutout border, engr heart and flowers, "Lily," Birmingham (Eng) hmks; 1-⁵⁄₈″ × ¹⁄₂″, $125, *Author's collection.*

Brooch/Pin, copper, wm, ym, c. 1886-90, Statue of Liberty motif in the center of a recessed disk, notched and engr border in tricolor metals laminated to ym backing, C-catch, soldered ring with chain joining stickpin with engr cube-shaped head, Am, 1-1/4" dia, chain 3-1/2" l, stickpin 1-1/4" l, $175. *Joyce Albers collection.*

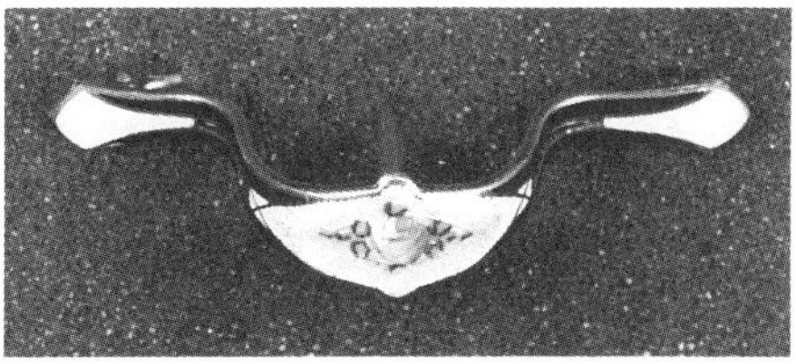

Brooch/Pin, bouquet pin, sterling, enamel, c. 1900, bowed-out shape with spike protruding from rev center to hold bouquet of flowers, black/white enamel with center pink/green enamel rose motif, mkd "sterling," C-catch, 1-7/8" × 3/8", center front to back 3/4", $100. *Author's collection.*

minals of repoussé, chased and engr lions' heads, each suspending a bead from mouth, C-catch, flanged hinge, 2-7/8" w × 5/8" **150**

Buckle

Silver, 14k rose gold, faceted gemstones, c. 1890-1900, rect with foliate scroll motifs, gold swiveling hasps, blue and pink faceted collet-set stones in opposing corners, sgd "Bolin," Russian hmks, 3-1/4" w × 1-1/4" **300**

Buckles

Sterling, c. 1890-1900, rect with scrolled edges and cut-in scroll motif decor, double hasps, sgd "Tiffany & Co.," 1-3/4" w × 1-1/8", pr **325**

Chatelaine

Silver, c. 1890-1900, tubular scrolled top clasp suspending five chains, each terminating in a swivel hook with: a rect locket surmounted by a stamped raised rooster motif, 1-1/8" w × 1-1/4", a clamshell-shaped pincushion, 1-1/4" w × 2", a retractable pencil, 2-7/8" l × 1/4", a notepad with a cover of stamped raised male and female profiles and engr foliate corners, 1-3/8" w × 3-3/8", and a hat charm (possibly of later addition), 1-1/8" w × 1-1/2", 7-3/4" tl × 2-3/4" . . . . **715 (A)**

Silver, c. 1890-1900, top clasp of three figural openwork plaques suspending seven implements: hand mirror, coin purse, pencil, comb case, glove button hook, stamp box, and perfume flask case, Eng and Fr hmks, 9-1/2" tl × 4" w . . . . **825 (A)**

Locket and Chain

Sterling, c. 1880-90, die-stamped oval locket with raised center engr with belt/buckle and scrollwork motifs, suspended from snake chain of lg star-punched links, 17-3/4" tl × 1/4", locket 1-3/4" w × 2-5/8" **375**

Lockets and Chains, sterling: L, c. 1880-90, die-stamped and engr locket with beaded edge, rev mkd "sterling," "W RR H," joined by spring ring to chain of engr and beaded links, 17-1/2" tl × 1/2", locket 1-3/8" × 2", $400; C, c. 1880-90, die-stamped and engr locket, raised center, floral design border, beaded edge, engr cable link chain, Eng, chain 18" tl, $300, *Mary Lou Diebold collection;* R, Locket and Necklace, sterling, date letter for 1889, die-stamped and engr oval locket and matching necklace joined by spring rings, central oval plaque of locket engr with *japonaiserie* motifs, border and necklace decorated with punched stars, beaded edges, Birmingham (Eng) hmks on rev of locket, necklace 17" tl × 5/8", locket with extension 1-1/2" w × 3-7/8" tl, $425, *Author's collection.*

Sterling, c. 1880, die-stamped and engr oval locket, scroll and foliate motifs, rev mkd "H W," suspended from fancy cable-link chain, 28" tl, locket 1-½" w × 2-¼" ..... **431 (A)**

Sterling, date letter for 1930, Victorian revival, oval locket, die-stamped and engr vertical ridges accented with ym corded wire, Birmingham (Eng) hmks on rev, suspended from engr fancy link chain, 17" tl, locket 1-¼" w × 1-½" .... **173 (A)**

Sterling, date letter for 1890, oval locket with beaded edge, allover engr scrollwork, Birmingham (Eng) hmks on rev, 1-½" w × 2", married to plain flat link book chain, 18" tl × ³/₈" **375**

Neckchain

Shakudo, c. 1880, longchain of continuous floral and open rect links, 50" × ⅛" .... **1,760 (A)**

Necklace

Shakudo, c. 1880, grad linked discs of naturalistic scenes in the Japanese mixed-metals style, silver gilt mounts, terminating in a pendent drop shaped like a Japanese fan, 17-½" tl, largest disk 1-¼" dia .... **2,970 (A)**

Sterling, c. 1880, collar of stamped and engr tubular links with inner and outer beaded edges, inside borders of appl sm cross motifs, box clasp and v-spring catch, Eng, 16-½" tl × ⅞" **400**

Suite: Bangle, Brooch, Earrings, Locket, and Necklace

Sterling, c. 1880-90, hinged bangle with beaded edge, appl scrolled wirework, center rect plaque engr with foliate motif, 2-½" × 2-¼", matching rounded rect brooch with glazed compartment containing hair on rev, 2" w × 1", matching drop earrings, cushion shape, suspended from bead surmounts on earwires, 1-½" tl × ½", matching oval locket, 1-½" w × 1-⅞", chain necklace of reeded links each suspending a hollow urn shape, beaded inside border, large spring ring clasp, extension terminating in a second spring ring for attaching locket, in orig fitted box, Eng hmks (illegible), suite ..... **990 (A)**

Suite: Brooch and Earrings

Sterling, c. 1880-90, brooch a die-stamped disk with raised center engr with floral and foliate wreath and thistle motifs, ridged bor-

T, Watch Chain and Fob Charm (can be worn as necklace), sterling, date letter for 1901, fancy links and rect openwork segments, suspending a domed tassel and fob charm with shield-shaped center for mono, Eng hmks on fob, "JS" and star on swivel; 17" tl × ¼", fob 1-⅛" w, $200, _Mary Lou Diebold collection._ Date letters tell the story: many traditional forms (like fob charms) continued to be made well into the twentieth century. B, Fob Charms (five), silver, L-R: monogrammed urn, mkd "800"; shamrock within wreath, Dublin import hmk, 1927 date letter; shield shape within floral border, Birmingham (Eng) hmks, 1894 date letter; shield shape within circle-in-square border, Birmingham hmks, 1923 date letter; diver and ocean, ribbon border, Birmingham hmks, 1931 date letter, $30-50 ea, _Joyce Albers collection._

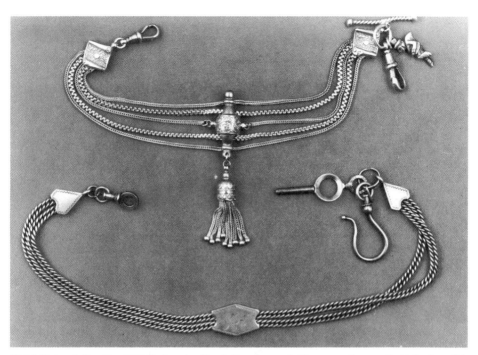

Watch Chains, sterling: T, c. 1870-80, domed and beaded tassel suspended from central urn motif with five fancy-link chains threaded through and attached to scrolled sq ends, bar and swivel hooks with Eng hmks (no place of assay), added wm figural charm, 8-3/4" tl × 2-1/2", $250; B, c. 1875-90, double curb chain with lozenge-shaped slide, mono one side, attached to triangular ends, engr borders, lg hook and watch key (sp brass, mkd "ptd 1874") on one end, lg threaded split ring on other, 13-1/2" tl × 1/2", $125. *Joyce Albers collection.*

Sword Jabot, silver, diamonds, rose gold, silver sword with engr rose gold hilt, appl rope-twist wire on handle set with rc diamonds, suspending a foxtail chain tassel terminating in an acorn drop, bearing the inscription: "J.B.W. from P.H.P., 1879," 4" × 1", $690 (A). *Photo courtesy of Christie's New York (4/22/93).*

der, C-catch, tube hinge, 1-3/8" dia, matching earrings suspended from kidney wires, 3/4" dia, suite 200

Sterling, yg, c. 1880, circ brooch with beaded scalloped edge, stamped and engr with floral and foliate motifs accented with yg (*japonaiserie*), matching oval earrings suspended from bead surmounts on earwires, brooch 1-5/8" dia, earrings 5/8" × 1-1/4" tl, suite 450

Watch Chain
Sterling, c. 1890-1900, curb links suspending bar and swivel hook, cross pendant, 5/8" w × 1-1/8", chain 12" tl × 1/4" 125

DIAMOND AND COLORED GEMSTONE JEWELRY

History: The diamond has been the stone of choice among nobility and the wealthy for centuries. Although the eighteenth century has been called The Age of Diamonds, improved cutting and setting techniques to enhance the diamond's brilliance were developed in the nineteenth and twentieth centuries. Until the use of platinum found favor as a metal for setting diamonds at the end of the nineteenth century, silver was used to complement the stone's whiteness, and it was almost always laminated to a yellow gold backing (sometimes called silver-topped yellow gold).

Closed-back and foiled settings were still in use at the beginning of the century. Openbacked (à jour) mounts gradually replaced them. It was discovered that brilliance was increased when light was reflected from the back as well as the front of the stone. The shape and cut of the diamond also evolved. Flat-backed rose cuts and cushion-shaped old mine cuts were eventually outnumbered (but not entirely replaced) by the circular old European brilliant cut toward the end of the century. The introduction of the power-driven bruting (girdling) machine in 1891 made production of circular stones faster and easier.

The discovery of diamonds in South Africa in 1867 increased the stone's availability. Subsequent discoveries led to greater supplies and lower prices in the early 1880s. In spite of a worldwide depressed economy, diamond-encrusted jewels were well represented at the 1889 Paris Exposition and found favor among the wealthy. By the 1890s, the De Beers Company had begun to control prices and dominate the South African diamond market, as it does today.

Diamonds have always been considered formal jewels for important occasions, usually reserved for nighttime wear. The Victorians had strict rules of etiquette concerning when diamonds should be worn and who should wear them. They were considered inappropriate for unmarried young women; most married matrons reserved them for fancy dress balls and court appearances.

When electric lighting was introduced in the 1880s, sparkling diamond-set jewelry became even more desirable. At the turn of the century, the fashion for pale fabrics and colorless platinum-set jewels further heightened the demand for diamonds.

Diamonds found their way into every conceivable form of jewelry, from tiaras to rings. The diamond brooch lent itself to a variety of motifs that reflected the Victorian preoccupation with nature. Flower bouquets and sprays were worn throughout the nineteenth century, sometimes with parts mounted en tremblant, on springs or wires that trembled when the wearer moved. Animal and insect motifs were popular in the 1880s and 90s, as were crescents and stars. These were often worn scattered about the neckline, or as veil or lace pins. Figural motifs remained in vogue through the turn of the century.

In 1886, Tiffany & Co. introduced the Tiffany setting for diamond solitaires. The high-pronged mount elevated the stone to show off its brilliance to the best advantage. It became the standard setting for engagement rings.

Other gemstones were in and out of style according to the vagaries of fashion. In the 1830s, the romantic notion of the "language of stones," like that of flowers, gave rise to pieces with messages spelled out by the initial letter of the stone's name. "Regard," the most commonly expressed sentiment, was represented by ruby, emerald, garnet, amethyst, ruby, and diamond. This idea was revived at the end of the century.

Pavé-set small turquoise cabochons were used extensively in jewelry of the 1840s, particularly in snake motifs. Turquoise made a return appearance in the 1890s.

Besides their familiar use in Scottish pebble jewelry, agates, variegated varieties of quartz, are found in other types of Victorian jewelry. Idar-Oberstein in Germany (the actual source of many a so-called Scottish pebble) has been a primary center for the cutting and polishing of agates for three centuries. The soaking and heating processes for staining the stones has been done there as well. During the mid to late nineteenth century, color-enhanced banded agates, often used for cameos, were also formed into beads and figural or geometric shapes. Although agate's value as a gemstone is low, Victorian agate jewelry is valued for its design, craftsmanship, and collectiblity.

Both faceted and cabochon garnets were popular at various times. Among the several varieties and colors of garnets, the types most closely associated with the Victorian period are the reddish-brown pyrope and the reddish-purple almandine. In the early nineteenth century, memorial brooches were often set with flat-cut pyrope or almandine garnets around a compartment containing hair. Large almandine cabochons, called carbuncles, are most often seen in mid-Victorian revivalist pieces. In the later part of the century, small faceted rose-cut and single-cut pyropes (also called Bohemian garnets) were set in low-karat gold and gilt base metal or silver. This type of jewelry was mass-produced in Bohemia, and is being reproduced today. Green demantoids were discovered in the Ural Mountains in 1868 and are found in late nineteenth century pieces. The green color was especially favored for the salamander and lizard brooches that were in vogue at the time. Garnets are of modest value, except for demantoids, which are rarer, more desirable, and costly.

Opals were also popular in the late Victorian era, their wearers having overcome the superstition that the stone brought misfortune. In keeping with the pale look of the period's fashions, moonstones were worn, sometimes carved as cameos. The man in the moon was a favorite motif. Pearls, another pale gem, were worn as necklaces alone or in combination with diamonds, setting the tone for what would become the classic Edwardian style of the early twentieth century.

References: Vivienne Becker, *Antique and Twentieth Century Jewellery*, 2nd ed., N.A.G. Press, 1987; David Bennett and Daniela Mascetti, *Understanding Jewellery*, Antique Collectors

Club, 1989; Eric Bruton, *Diamonds,* 2nd. ed., FGA, 1978; Joan Younger Dickinson, *The Book of Diamonds,* Avenel (Crown), 1965 (out of print); Margaret Flower, *Victorian Jewellery,* A.S. Barnes & Co., 1951 (out of print); Gilbert Levine and Laura L. Vookles, *The Jeweler's Eye, Nineteenth-Century Jewelry in the Collection of Nancy and Gilbert Levine,* catalog of an exhibition at The Hudson River Museum, Yonkers, N.Y., 1986; Basil Watermeyer, *Diamond Cutting,* 4th ed., Johannesburg, 1991 (self-published; includes history of cuts).

Museums: The most extensive collections are British, housed at the Victoria and Albert Museum and the British Museum, London; in the United States, the Cooper-Hewitt Museum and Metropolitan Museum of Art, New York, and the Smithsonian Institution, Washington, D.C., have noteworthy collections.

Reproduction Alert: Late Victorian garnet jewelry is mass-reproduced. Wholesalers advertise in antique trade papers such as *The Antique Trader Weekly.* Other gemstone-set reproductions are imported from Portugal, South America, Germany, and Thailand. Some pieces are good enough to fool the experts.

Bracelet
  Bangle, hinged
    Sapphires/diamonds, 14k yg, c. 1890-1900, knife-edge wire oval, prong set on top half with four round sapphires, 1.8 ct tw, alternating with three oe diamonds, 1 ct tw, 2-½" × 2-¼" .... **2,200 (A)**
    Garnets, silver, c. 1900, oval, three rows of rc stones, 2-³⁄₈" × 2-⅛", ³⁄₈" w **175**
  Flexible
    Tourmaline, 14k yg, c. 1900, central pink tourmaline quatrefoil flanked by prs of pink tourmaline trefoils, each terminating with one oval pink tourmaline joined to yg foliate links, safety chain, 6" × ⁵⁄₈" .... **825 (A)**
  Link
    Garnets (almandine), silver, c. 1900, grad oval clusters of rc and sc stones, connected by double row of links, safety chain, 6-½ × ⅞" **200**
Brooch/Pendant
    Diamonds, st yg, c. 1880, tapering openwork scrolled foliate design set with oe, om, and sc diamonds throughout, larger collet-set oe diamond drop and top, pendant loop, 1-¼" w × 1-⁵⁄₈" .... **1,100 (A)**
    Turq, diamond, st yg, c. 1880, crescent shape set with grad oval turq cabs alternating with rows of two or three oe or om diamonds, pendant bail, 4" × ³⁄₈" **2,500**
Brooch/Pin
    Agate, banded, mid Victorian, rect plaque, elongated notched bottom side, suspending a tapered pendent drop from center, a sm

Brooch/Pendant, diamonds, 18k yg, enamel, c. 1890, oe diamond floret within an oe diamond, black enamel and yg round frame with scalloped edge in yg (with pendant hoop), 1-⅛" dia, with low-karat yg rope link chain, 9-¼", $2,990 (A). *Photo courtesy of Christie's New York (4/22/93).*

Brooch/Pendant, diamonds, st yg, c. 1890-1900, pavé-set diamond five-pointed star, circ-cut diamond center, circ-cut diamond rays (with pendant hoop), 2" × 2-⅛", $5,750 (A). *Photo courtesy of Christie's New York (4/22/93).*

round bead suspended from each end, C-catch, tube hinge, 1-¼" w × 1-½" tl **250**
    Demantoid garnets, 18k yg, platinum, diamond, ruby, c. 1890-1900, lizard shape, pavé set with demantoids, stripe of diamond-set plat down back, cab ruby eyes, Fr hmks, C-catch, 1-½" × ⅝" **3,000**
    Demantoid garnets, diamonds, rubies, st yg, c. 1890-1900, salamander shape, body set with a row of demantoids bordered by a row of diamonds, diamond-set legs and tail, with ruby eyes, 2-⅝" × ¾" .... **6,050 (A)**
    Demantoid garnets, diamonds, st yg, c. 1900, salamander shape, center row of demantoids flanked by rows of om and rc diamonds, two demantoids on each leg, cab ruby eyes, locking C-catch, barrel hinge, in fitted velvet box, 2-¼" × ¼" .... **6,490 (A)**

Brooch/Watch Pin, turq and seed pearls, 800 silver, gilt, c. 1880, fleur-de-lis shape, pavé stones, hook at base on rev for watch or pendant, C-catch, tube hinge, 1-½″ × 2″, $250. Courtesy of E. Foxe Harrell Jewelers.

Diamonds, 15k yg, enamel, c. 1880-90, round with scalloped fluted edge, set with nine om diamonds, approx 2.25 ct tw, black enamel in starburst pattern around center stone, with attached safety chain and stickpin, Eng, ⁷⁄₈″ dia **1,600**

Diamonds, 15k yg, pearl, c. 1890-1900, yg four-loop ribbon knot set with om diamonds, pearl center, locking C-catch, tube hinge, Eng, 1″ w × ⁵⁄₈″ . . . . **1,210 (A)**

Diamonds, cab ruby, platinum, c. 1900, in the shape of a swallow in flight, open oval frame extending from wing tips on one side, pavé set oe and sc diamonds, sgd "Gattle" for E. M. Gattle, New York, N.Y., 2″ w × 1-³⁄₈″ . . . . **7,370 (A)**

Diamonds, rubies, 18k yg, late Victorian, in the shape of a rose with yg petals, diamond and ruby-set pistils and stamen, stem and leaves (one stem removable), pavé rc diamond-set bird *en tremblant* atop petals, removable, 1-⅛″ w × 2-⅛″ . . . . **3,025 (A)**

Diamonds, rubies, sapphires, pearls, green glass, st yg, c. 1880-90, butterfly shape, diamond and pearl body, rc diamond, ruby, sapphire-set wings, green glass eyes, 1-³⁄₄″ w × 1-¼″ . . . . **1,650 (A)**

Brooch/Pin, diamonds, st yg, early Victorian, flower spray, with oe diamond center weighing approx 0.50 ct, and set throughout with rc and om diamonds; 2″ × 2-½″, $2,640 (A). Photo courtesy of Skinner, Inc. (3/14/92).

Diamond, 14k yg, c. 1870-80, hand shape, holding an om diamond of approx. 1.10 cts, *taille d'épargne* enamel on cuff, 1″ × ³⁄₈″ . . . . **1,430 (A)**

Diamonds, 14k yg, enamel, c. 1870-80, modified lozenge shape, center star set with om diamonds, blue enameled scrolls at tapered ends, flanked on either side with star set diamonds, 23 dwt., 1-¼″ w × 1″ . . . . **1,650 (A)**

Brooch/Pin, rc and table-cut diamonds, 14k yg, c. 1855, flower spray, closed back settings, Dutch hmk for 14k on pinstem (oakleaf, in use 1853-1906), two missing diamonds replaced with marcasites, 1-⁷⁄₈″ × ⁷⁄₈″, $700, Ellen Stuart collection.

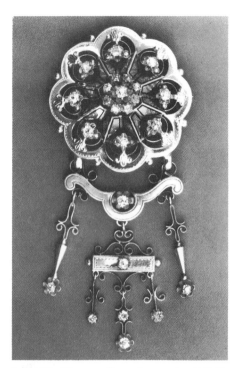

Brooch/Pin, 14k yg, om diamonds, enamel, c. 1860-70, central starburst motif with black enamel accents within scalloped border, suspending a detachable pendent section of three scrollwork drops, set throughout with om diamonds in flowerhead mounts, 1-$\frac{1}{2}$" × 3-$\frac{1}{2}$" tl, $2,200. *Mary Lou Diebold collection.*

Brooch/Pin, diamonds, st rose and yg, c. 1880, flowerhead brooch with oe diamond pistil, surrounded by rc and oe diamond petals, 1-$\frac{5}{8}$" dia, $3,220 (A). *Photo courtesy of Christie's New York (4/22/93).*

Brooch/pin, 18k yg, diamonds, silver, c. 1890, in the shape of three full-figure swallows pavé-set with diamonds perched on a yg branch, 2" × 1-$\frac{1}{8}$", $990 (A). *Photo courtesy of Skinner, Inc (3/14/93).*

Diamonds, rubies, seed pearls, button pearl, st yg, c. 1890-1900, turtle shape, with center row of round rubies flanked by rows of oe and rc diamond-set legs and head, attached to newer 2" yg chain set with five seed pearls and one button pearl, $\frac{3}{4}$" × $\frac{5}{8}$" . . . **1,600 (A)**

Diamonds, sapphire, rubies, silver, 14k pink gold, c. 1880-90, bee shape, body and wings of pavé-set om diamonds, circ-cut sapphire in center, ruby eyes, mounted in silver with pink gold legs, 1-$\frac{7}{8}$" × 1-$\frac{1}{4}$" . . . . . **3,850 (A)**

Diamonds, sapphires, ruby, syn ruby, glass, 10k yg and wg, c. 1890-1900, in the shape of a realistic floral bouquet of chased yg leaves, stems and flowerheads set with dk and lt brown diamonds centering and outlining flowerheads and leaves, ruby and syn ruby, sapphires and blue glass at base, 1-$\frac{1}{4}$" w × 2-$\frac{7}{8}$" . . . . **2,310 (A)**

Diamonds, st yg, c. 1880, crescent shape outlined with a row of larger om diamonds, filled with rows of smaller om diamonds, 3" × $\frac{3}{8}$" **2,500**

Diamonds, st yg, c. 1890-1900, in the shape of a horse and carriage, set throughout with rc diamonds, in fitted case stamped "I.J. Mazure & Co. Ltd., Antique Dealers, The Silver Vaults, 53 Chancery Lane, London, WC2A1QS," C-catch, 2-$\frac{1}{8}$" × $\frac{3}{4}$" . . . . **2,000 (A)**

Emeralds, pearls, 15k yg, mid-Victorian, scrolled three-dimensional quatrefoil threaded with snake chain terminating in two beaded tassels, emerald-cut emerald, 1.75 ct, flanked by four pearls set in concave oval center, four smaller emeralds and pearls at outer edges, 15.8 dwt, 1-$\frac{7}{8}$" w × 3" tl . . . . **3,850 (A)**

Emeralds, rubies, diamonds, opal, yg, c. 1900, gem-set butterfly with diamond-set wings, each centered with one cushion-shaped emerald, the top two outlined with round rubies, the body of one round ruby outlined with diamonds, one cab opal (crazed) below, ruby eyes, diamond antennae, encl C-catch, tube hinge, 2-$\frac{3}{8}$" w × 2-$\frac{1}{4}$" . . . . **11,000 (A)**

Garnets, silver gilt, mid to late Victorian, oval convex plaque pavé-set with lg and sm rc garnets surrounding center carbuncle (cab garnet), suspending an open swagged, tapered pendent drop set with sm rc and round bezel-set garnets, terminating in an inverted teardrop-shaped cab garnet, 1-⅞" w × 4" tl .... **1,210 (A)**

Opal, diamonds, yg and platinum, c. 1900, central bezel-set oval white opal outlined with circ brilliant and oe diamonds, sgd "Tiffany & Co.," 1" w × 1-¼" ...... **2,970 (A)**

Rubies, emeralds, diamonds, st yg and yg, c. 1850, three-dimensional design of two birds on a leafy branch, one mounted *en tremblant*, set with cushion-shaped rubies and emeralds and rc diamonds (several stones missing), 2" × 1-¼" ...... **7,475 (A)**

Bar

Diamonds, sapphires, rose gold, c. 1890-1900, knife-edge rose gold bar, each end terminating in an oe diamond, surmounted by a crescent outlined with grad sapphires, center of grad sc diamonds, C-catch, 1-⅞" w × ⅝" .... **715 (A)**

Diamonds, platinum and yg, c. 1900, yg bar surmounted by a plat bull terrier head set throughout with rc diamonds, sgd provenance: estate of Marian Anderson, 1-¼" .... **850 (A)**

Opal, garnets, 14k yg, c. 1900, central pear-shaped boulder opal flanked by grad round garnets, handmade mount, 1-⅝" w × ⅝" .... **523 (A)**

Opal, 14k yg, c. 1900, oval cab-cut grey opal (crazed) as center of tapering yg bar .... **357 (A)**

Opals, demantoid garnets, rc diamonds, 15k yg, c. 1890, pr of oval white opals, each outlined with round demantoids alternating with rc diamonds, mounted on a bar flanking a central larger oval demantoid topped and bottomed with a demantoid and two rc diamonds, 1-⅝" w × ¾" .... **1,210 (A)**

Buckle

Amethyst, plat, yg, c. 1900, oval shape, channel-set with step-cut amethysts, four larger trapezoidal stones at top, bottom, and sides, pierced gallery, double yg hasps, sgd "F.W.L.," 1-½" w × 2-⅜" ...... **1,650 (A)**

Cuff Links

Yg, green and pink tourmaline, c. 1900, pair of two-sided links alternately set with two cushion-shaped green and two cushion-shaped pink tourmalines within yg frames of conforming shape, each link ½" × ⅜", pr .... **3,450 (A)**

Earrings

Diamonds, sterling, late Victorian, central prong-set oe diamonds, approx .95 ct each, within flower head mounts on earwires, ¾" tl × ⅜", pr .... **3,410 (A)**

Diamonds, st yg, 14k, c. 1880-90, cluster of om diamonds mounted within silver tops with yg backing and hinged Fr-back earwires, ¾" tl × ½", pr .... **2,750 (A)**

Pearls, diamonds, st yg, late Victorian, pearl buttons encircled by om diamonds (2.4 ct tw), 14k yg earwires, ⅝" dia, ⅞" tl, pr .... **1,760 (A)**

Earrings, pendent

Agate, 14k yg, c. 1860, tiered shaped multi-colored agate plaques surrounded by beaded

L, Pendant, garnets, silver gilt, beveled glass, mid-Victorian, oval with clusters of lg and sm rc stones, glazed hinged compartment for hair on rev, 1-⅞" × 1", $150, Lucile Thompson collection; Brooches/Pins, garnets, gilt metal: C, c. 1880-90, curvilinear, with scrolled arabesque design, flat and rc stones, appl findings, 2-¼" × 1", $125; R, c. 1890-1900, round starburst with center domed plaque of prong-set table-cut and rc stones, 1-¼" dia, $75, Joyce Albers collection.

Early Victorian, c. 1840–1860: TL, Brooch/Pin, a shell cameo depicting the bust of a bearded man, set in a serrate engr bezel within a hollow stamped relief yg frame with a pierced foliated scroll design, suspending two inverted drop-shaped f.w. pearls, flat backing, C-catch, tube hinge, 2" w x 1³/4" tl, **$750; TR, Mourning Brooch/Pin,** a beveled glazed compartment containing woven brown silk, in a deeply engr rect yg inner frame set within a yg outer frame with Greek key and foliate design on black enamel ground, engr initials on convex back, C-catch, tube hinge, 1¹/2" w x 1¹/4", **$400; CL, Brooch/Pin,** circ micromosaic of a scarab beetle within a six-lobed rosette, mounted in black glass in a yg frame, ⁷/8" dia, **$450; C, Brooch/Pin,** molded blue *pâte-de-verre* (glass) cameo or "tassie" depicting the bust of a young woman, set in a ym frame with ropetwist wire and beaded decoration, C-catch, tube hinge, extended pinstem, 1¹/2" w x 2", **$450; CR, Brooch/Pin,** Limoges enamel portrait of a dog's head set within a *cannetille* yg frame, glazed compartment on rev, C-catch, tube hinge, extended pinstem, ⁷/8" dia, **$425; B, Necklace,** a carbuncle (cab garnet) encircled by seed pearls set within a yg *cannetille* mount with ropetwist loops forming a quatrefoil, suspending a carbuncle and flanked by two smaller carbuncles in lobed oval *cannetille* mounts, joined to a hollow flexible tubular chain, terminating in a tube clasp, 18" tl, center 2¹/4" w x 1¹/4" tl, **$1200.** *Courtesy of E. Foxe Harrell Jewelers.*

Mid-Victorian, c. 1860–1880: TL, Brooch/Pin, stamped yg quatrefoil with appl wirework and beaded decoration, the center set with eight circ-cut rhodolite garnets, hollow back, tube hinge, added safety catch, 1½" dia, **$800; TC, Brooch/Pin,** light brown hairwork tubes in a double pretzel-twist knot caught by yg rings at sides, central engr yg leaf above an engr yg bow motif, C-catch, tube hinge, extended pinstem, 1¾" w x ¾", **$200; TR, Brooch/Pin,** engr snake motif in a triple-looped yg flat-backed hollow tube, the head bezel-set with a lg faceted oval pyrope garnet, suspending an engr heart-shaped locket with a sm garnet center, C-catch, tube hinge, extended pinstem, 2" w x 1⅞" tl, **$800; CL, Pendent Earrings,** hollow stamped and backed yg, opposed S-scrolls with blue and white *champlevé* enameled foliate centers, each suspending a yg bead, fishhook earwires, ½" w x 1¼" tl, **$225; C, Brooch/Pin,** enameled porcelain portrait of the bust of a young woman set in a yg ropetwist frame with cabled wire around the bezel, C-catch, tube hinge, extended pinstem, 1⅞" w x 2¼", **$350; CR, Pendent Earrings,** carved coral flowers, fruit, and leaves mounted on articulated yg armatures, fishhook earwires, ¾" w x 1⅝" tl, **$400; B, Bracelet,** Scottish, banded agate and jasper, linked fluted sq cylinders and one spherical bead, terminating in a heart-shaped lock clasp of banded agate set in silver, engr on rev, 7" tl, lock ⅞" w x 1½", **$300.** *Courtesy of E. Foxe Harrell Jewelers.*

Late Victorian, c. 1880–1900: TL, Ring, circ-cut syn spinel bezel-set in center encircled by seed pearls and circ-cut sapphires in yg scallop-edge mount, foliate engr gallery and shoulders, narrow shank, Hungarian hmks (partially obliterated), approx size 6½, ⅞" dia, **$400; TC, Brooch/Pin,** Egyptian Revival, silver gilt stamped relief pharoah's head, *champlevé* enamel, flat backing, mkd "900," ⅞" w x 1", **$300; TR, Brooch/Pin,** bead-set flat-cut and rc pyrope garnets in silver gilt, motifs symbolizing Faith (cross), Hope (anchor), and Charity (heart), 1¼" x 1¼", **$450; CL, Cravat Pin,** enamel on porcelain depicting the head of a fox, set in 9k yg frame with ropetwist wire and beaded edge, mkd "9 ct," sgd "W.B. Ford," dated 1884, handmade safety catch, ⅞" dia, 2" tl, **$300; C, Brooch/Pin,** six-rayed star, st 18k yg set with a green tourmaline in the center of appl central star shape set with natural blue spinels, rays set with golden topaz and white sapphires, six pink spinels set in cut-down collets at the ends of knife-edge wires radiating from the center, 1⅞" dia, **$2900; CR, Ring,** yg friendship or wedding band with geo faceted and engr surface, mkd "W" (turned sideways) "xxx" for J.R. Wood & Sons, New York, NY, approx size 8, ⅜" w, **$225; B, Necklace,** almandine garnets set in a grad fringe of linked clusters forming flowerheads, C-scrolls, trefoils and quatrefoils, terminating in teardrop-shaped drops, joined to a chain of linked lg and sm collet-set garnets, in brass, 17" tl, center 2" top to bottom, **$500.** *Courtesy of E. Foxe Harrell Jewelers.*

Arts & Crafts, c. 1890–1920: L, 1 Pendant & Chain, pansy motif in iridescent blues, greens, and yellow enamel on a silver plaque within a twisted wire frame decorated with C-scrolls and beading, rev mkd "Newlyn enamel" for the Newlyn Industrial Class, Cornwall (Eng), suspended from a silver paper clip chain, 24" tl, spring ring clasp, pendant 1 1/2" w x 1 3/4", **$950; L, 2 Brooch/Pin,** convex tapered rect ster plaque with a central cipher (T flanked by A and H, encircled by C) surrounded by pooled blue enamel within a silver frame embossed with the motto "NEGLECT NOT THE GIFT THAT IS IN THEE," rev mkd "W.H.H." for W. H. Haseler, Birmingham (Eng) hmks, date letter for 1918, 1 1/2" w x 7/8", **$750; L, 3 Brooch/Pin,** heart shape flanked by pierced Celtic knot motifs, a central inverted heart shape in yellow and orange enamel, surrounded by blue/green enamel with silver stud accents, rev mkd "silver," with logo for Murrle, Bennett & Co (Eng), added safety catch, 1 1/2" w x 1", **$800; TC, Brooch/Pin,** oval silver plaque with full-figure polychrome enameled portrait of an angel on iridescent blue ground, flanked by two lg cast silver wings and suspending a garnet cab drop, unmkd, 4" w x 2 3/4" tl, **$2500,** *Terrance O'Halloran collection;* **BL, Sash Ornament,** sp brass, shield shape, cusped at the top, with hammered and acid-etched border, bright green molded glass scarab bezel-set in center, flanked by raised scallop and scroll motifs, appl metal plate on rev imp "Made In Our Craft Shop Marshall Field & Co." (Chicago), wide C-catch, tube hinge, thick pinstem, 2 7/8" x 2 1/8", **$475; C, Festoon Necklace,** eight tapered shield-shaped plaques with chamfered corners, of grad size, enameled in dk blue shading to purple, linked to triple, double, and single silver chains, the four larger central plaques suspending collet-set blister pearls, 14 1/2" tl x 3 1/4" center top to bottom, **$650; BR, Brooch/Pin,** an openwork gilt metal plaque with a lg green glass cab center encircled by smaller blue glass cabs and suspending six pendent drops, each set with a sm green glass cab, in the Viennese style, unmkd, trombone catch, 2 1/4" w x 2 1/2" tl, **$750; R, 1 Pendant & Chain,** hammered and pierced pear-shaped ster plaque, a central oval faceted amethyst set in a yg bezel, encircled by MacGregor rose motifs, surmounted by a trefoil and suspended from three linked volutes and a trace and paper clip chain, T-bar clasp, pendant rev mkd "950," logo for Murrle, Bennett & Co (Eng), 7/8" w x 1 3/8", 2 3/4" tl, chain 16 1/2" tl, **$900,** *Gail Gerretsen collection;* **R, 2 Pendant & Chain,** blue-green and lt green enamel on a textured silver plaque with a raised branch and berry design surrounding a central oval amethyst cab and suspending a smaller oval amethyst cab drop from a short chain, two fine silver chains attached to top of pendant, 1 1/2" w x 2" tl, 16" tl, **$500,** *Terrance O'Halloran collection.*

Art Nouveau, c. 1895–1910: TL, Brooch/Pin, circ scene of sun rising (or setting) in water in *plique-à-jour* enameled shades of aqua, green, yellow & lavender, silver fish in foreground with green glass cab in its mouth, mkd "900," C-catch, tube hinge, extended pinstem, 1" dia, **$900; TC, Belt Buckle,** a peacock feather in shades of blue, green and brown matte enamel with a bezel-set kidney-shaped blue glass cab as the "eye," on a cut-to-shape and pierced convex gilt brass groundplate, Fr, rev mkd with a sword motif flanked by "P. Fs" for Piel Frères, *"Déposé"* (registered), 4 1/2" x 2 1/2", **$1000; TR, Brooch/Pin,** in the shape of a dragonfly, translucent iridescent pink & green *plique-à-jour* enamel wings, body set with a grad row of opals, garnet eyes, mkd "900," C-catch, tube hinge, 2" x 2", **$1700; CL, Sash Ornament,** water lilies, leaves and curv border in shades of white, green, and yellow *basse-taille* enamel on a convex cut-to-shape and pierced groundplate, rev mkd "sterling," with hmks of a crown, Gothic W and a lion for Watson, Newell Co., Attleboro, MA, wide C-catch, 2 7/8" x 1 1/2", **$275; C, Brooch/Pin,** carved ivory bust of a "Gibson Girl" with a rhinestone collar, mounted in the center of a gp metal openwork frame in a stylized spider motif, C-catch, 1 7/8" w x 2", **$850; CR, Sash Ornament,** lg irises, leaves and border in shades of purple and green *basse-taille* enamel, shades of yellow ground on a convex cut-to-shape groundplate, rev mkd "sterling, G.S. pin," safety catch (added later), 3" x 1 7/8", **$275; B, Pendant & Chain,** enamel portrait, after Alphonse Mucha, on a circ silver plaque, unmkd, suspended from a fancy wiretwist silver chain, 20" tl, pendant 1 1/4" dia, **$800.** *Terrance O'Halloran collection.*

Edwardian, c. 1890–1920: L, Lavalier, c. 1910, two chains of oe diamonds, millegrained bezel-set in platinum, joined at the top to a millegrain-set diamond bail, linked to an open navette-shaped center set with a row of oe diamonds across the top, a row of calibré rubies across the bottom (illusion of a three-dimensional ring shape), continuing to two oe diamond chains suspended *négligée*, each terminating in a diamond and ruby-set bow suspending a pear-shaped natural pearl, one white, one grey, suspended from a fancy link fine plat chain, sm plaque at top of chain mkd "plat," 18" tl, pendant 2⅞" tl x ¾" w, **$4000; TC, Flexible Bracelet,** c. 1910, articulated pierced sections forming an undulating tapered band pavé-set with oe and sc diamonds, engr gallery, a natural black pearl set in the center, flanked by smaller pink, grey, and cream pearls, continuing to a narrow flexible band, v-spring and box clasp, safety chain, 7½" tl, ⅜" w at center, **$4000; C, 1 Bar Pin,** c. 1910, a slightly tapered open plat bar with three horizontal rows of seed pearls flanking a vertical row of three carré-set oe diamonds, two sq-cut sapphires in millegrained bezels at each terminal, pierced plat gallery, yg pinstem, lever safety catch mkd with opposed "A&A" for Allsopp & Allsopp, Newark, NJ, 2½" w x ¼", **$1400; C, 2 Bar Pin,** c. 1905, a tapered rounded plat-topped yg bar with a center row of grad cream-colored natural pearls set within a row of calibré rubies forming waisted sections between each pearl, surrounded by pavé diamonds, pierced gallery, trombone catch, 2⅜" w x ¼", **$1800; BC, Necklace,** c. 1890–1900, a chain of knife-edge links joining grad prong-set turquoise cabs alternating with grad oe diamonds set in cut-down st yg collets, suspending a grad fringe of turquoise and diamonds on knife-edge wires, v-spring and box clasp, 15" tl, 1" top to bottom at center, **$5000; R, Pendant/Brooch & Chain,** c. 1910, an oval garland-style wreath of oe diamonds set in plat, a bell-shaped cab emerald, approx 9.00 cts, in a diamond-set plat frame suspended from a diamond-set bail in the center of wreath, diamond-set pendant loop, lever catch on rev, added seed pearl and plat chain, 18" tl, pendant 1¼" w x 1¾" tl, **$15,000.** *Courtesy of Neil Lane Jewelry.*

Fine Jewelry, c. 1920–1935: L, 1 Bar Pin, c. 1925, tapered plat bar with a center rect black onyx cab flanked by a grad horizontal row of sq onyx cabs turned 45° in millegrained bezels, trapeze cab onyx terminals, pavé-set throughout with bc diamonds, pierced plat gallery, trombone catch, 3⅛" w x ½", **$3000; L, 2 Jabot Pin,** c. 1925, a cut-corner triangle of carved jade surmounted by a diamond-set plat bolute, scallop and scroll motifs, outlined at the top with calibré-cut black onyx, plat pinstem terminating in a plumed spear-shaped cap of pavé diamonds and jade, 2½" tl x ⅝", **$2600; C, Flexible Link Bracelet,** c. 1920, a center bow motif set with oe and bc diamonds and calibré sapphires, continuing to a line of Fr-cut sapphires on one side and carré-set oe diamonds on the other, engr settings, v-spring and box clasp, safety chain, 7¼" tl x ⅜" w, **$8000; TR, 1 Pendent Earrings,** transitional, c. 1915–1920, a single carré-set oe diamond surmount suspending a flexible geo diamond-set shaft, terminating in a navette shape outlined in calibré sapphires, pierced geo center in a brickwork pattern, carré-set with oe diamonds, in plat-topped yg, orig post and clutch findings, clutch mkd "*Promis Nice France-Étranger*," Fr hmks and export mks, 1⅝" tl x ⅜" w, pr, **$5500; TR, 2 Ring,** c. 1935, a center raised band set with diagonally opposed horizontal rows of bc diamonds and calibré rubies, a row of bc diamonds pavé-set above and below, continuing to a tapered shank, mkd "900 Plat 100 Irid," by Oscar Heyman & Bros., approx size 5½, ½" w, **$4000; BR, Brooch/Pin,** c. 1925, a flower basket motif, pierced and cutout plat set throughout with oe and bc diamonds, a row of baguette diamonds at the base, interspersed with carved ruby, sapphire, and emerald leaves, lever catch, 1⅜" w x 1½", **$7000.** *Courtesy of Neil Lane Jewelry.*

Costume Jewelry, c. 1920–1935: L, 1 Pendant/Necklace, c. 1925, a prong-set rect blue glass plaque with beveled edges, suspending three baguettes, suspended from a chain of alternating metal baton links and glass baguettes, Czech, 17¹/₂" tl, pendant 1" w x 2¹/₄" tl, **$125; L, 2 Link Bracelet,** c. 1930, balustered half-cylinders of orange Bakelite set in chrome links, mkd "Germany," v-spring and box clasp, 7¹/₄" x ⁵/₈", **$125; TC, Bar Pin,** dk green painted enamel on chrome, overlapping disks bisected by a chrome stripe, 2¹/₂" w x ³/₄", **$75; C, Dress Clip,** c. 1930, slightly concave dk green Bakelite disk with a hemispherical chrome bead center, surmounting a heavy wire wm frame, tapering to an appl stepped curved triangular segment, a domed crossbar in the center, flat-backed hinged clip on rev, 1" w x 3¹/₈", **$125; BC, Pendant/Necklace,** c. 1925, a cushion-shaped chrome plaque, lobed at the base, surmounted by a D-shaped Bakelite "cab," a swag and scallop pattern enameled design below, suspended from spiral-fluted ellipsoid glass beads linked to hollow capsule-shaped chrome beads, continuing to a long V-link chrome chain, mkd "Made in France" on rev of plaque, 1⁵/₈" w x 2", 32" tl, **$225; R, 1 Link Bracelet,** c. 1935, "tank track" links of red Bakelite with chrome centers, slot and bar clasp, 7³/₄" tl x 1", **$95; R, 2 Necklace,** c. 1930, paired circ links joining chrome annular disks with arc-shaped cutouts, bezel-set green glass cabs in centers, continuing to a chain of navette-shaped links and sm green glass beads, v-spring clasp mkd "Checho Slovakia," 18¹/₂" tl, disks ³/₄" dia, **$245.** *Charles Pinkham collection.*

Plastic and Novelty, c. 1930–1950: TL, Bangle Bracelet, c. 1930, rare six-color laminated Bakelite, marbled butterscotch, brown, dk red, yellow, green, marbled amber, 2⁵/₈" inside dia, 1³/₈" w, **$450; TC, 1 Brooch/Pin,** c. 1940, "nuts and bolts man," jointed, articulated arms and legs, wm screws, bolts, and springs, painted plastic head, beads for hands and feet, 1¹/₄" w x 4¹/₂" tl, **$325; TC, 2 Brooches/Pins,** c. 1940, pearlized and painted pastel multicolored thermoplastic Dutch boy and girl with articulated arms and legs connected with ym jump rings, girl 2¹/₂" w x 3¹/₄", boy 2¹/₂" w x 3⁷/₈", pr, **$500,** *Kirsten Olson collection;* **TR, Charm Bracelet,** c. 1935, circ ym links suspending various Bakelite fruit and leaves, 7" tl, banana charm 1³/₈" l, **$175; TC, 3 Pendent Earrings,** c. 1950, glass and cardboard in the shape of thermometers, suspended from wm surmounts, clipbacks, mounted on orig card that reads "Mini Thermometer Earrings, They Actually Work!," 2" tl x ³/₈", pr, **$45; BL, Brooch/Pin,** c. 1940, carved and painted wood head of a *"bandido"* smoking a cigar, red cord chin strap, 2¹/₂" w x 2¹/₄", **$95,** *Author's collection;* **BC, 1 Brooch/Pin,** c. 1940, carved and painted Bakelite in the shape of an eagle surmounting crossed spears and suspending a drum from red, white and blue cord with tassel, 2¹/₄" w x 3¹/₂" tl, **$375; BC, 2 Dress Clip,** c. 1935, two carved blue plastic dogs with glass eyes, flat-backed hinged clip mkd "Pat Apld For," 1¹/₂" w x 1¹/₈", **$85; BC, 3 Brooch/Pin,** c. 1935, carved green Bakelite elephant with wm saddle, mounted on cut-to-shape chromed wm plaque, 2" w x 1¹/₄", **$125; BR, Dress Clip,** c. 1935, rev carved and painted domed Bakelite disk with yellow and green flower design, flat-backed hinged clip on rev, 1³/₈" dia, **$75,** *Kirsten Olson collection;* **B, Necklace,** c. 1940, painted red and dk brown cylindrical and disk-shaped wooden beads with stamped gp brass rosette caps forming lantern-shaped drops, suspended from circ celluloid and brass link chain, 16¹/₂" tl x 1¹/₂", **$75,** *Author's collection.*

Fine Jewelry, c. 1935–1945: TL, Brooch/Pin, 14k rose and yg bow with diamond-set plat "knot," mkd "14k" on catch, 2³/₄" w x 1", **$1200; TC, Brooch/Pin,** 10k rose and yg scrolled ribbon, mkd "Forstner 10 kt" for Forstner Chain Corp., Irvington, NJ, 2³/₈" w x 2¹/₄", **$300; TR, Brooch/Pin,** 14k rose and yg ribbon bow with emerald-cut amethyst center, mkd "14k" on rev, 2" x 1¹/₄", **$450; CL, Earclips,** 14k yg ribbon bows, center of each set with three diamonds, a spray of three sapphires on wires radiating from center, mkd "14k EK" (conjoined), ³/₄" w x 1¹/₈, pr, **$750; C and CR, Suite: Clips and Earclips,** in the shape of maple leaves, 18k yg enameled in cobalt blue, a single bc diamond set on each leaf, double-pronged hinged clips mkd "18 kt," 1³/₄" w x 1⁷/₈", earclips mkd "pat pend 18kt," ³/₈" w x 1", suite, **$3000; B, Necklace,** alternating 14k rose and yg slightly convex chevron-shaped links, mkd with conjoined "WAB" for Allsopp-Steller, Inc., Newark, NJ, 15¹/₂" tl x ³/₄", **$2800.** *Elizabeth Cook collection.*

Fine Jewelry, c. 1950–1965: TL, Brooch/Pin, textured 18k yg feather with five bc diamonds set in plat prongs at the base, rev mkd "Sterlé Paris," # 5.218, Fr hmks, trombone catch, 3³/₈" x ³/₄", **$3200; TC, Link Bracelet,** 18k yg, six tightly woven flexible mesh oval plaques with raised moiré pattern of concentric curves on a textured ground, mkd "V.C.A. France" for Van Cleef & Arpels, # 2V638-3 on rev of box clasp, 7¹/₂" tl x 1³/₄" w, **$18,000; TR, Pendent Earrings,** a lg oval hematite cab enclosed in a 18k yg wire "cage," surmounted by a bc diamond linked to a pearl center, suspended from a "caged" hematite bead and bc diamond surmount, post and clip findings, rev sgd "Verdura," mkd "18k," 2" tl x ³/₄", pr, **$7400; CL, Brooch/Pin,** 18k textured yg cat with cat's-eye chrysoberyl eyes, coral nose, diamond-set plat collar, yg wire whiskers, mkd "Tiffany & Co., 18k," 1¹/₈" w x 1³/₄", **$3700; C, 1 Cuff Links,** "dumbbell" type, solid textured 18k yg nugget shapes, each front set throughout with fifteen various size bc diamonds in plat prongs, similar smaller back set with three bc diamonds, approx 2.30 cts tw in pr, connected with a split shank, sgd "Ruser" in script for William Ruser, Los Angeles, mkd "18k, 10% irid plat," front ⁷/₈" x ⁵/₈", pr, **$3000; C, 2 Brooch/Pin,** a spray of five 18k yg tulips with textured and beaded surface, each set with two circ-cut rubies, a ribbon of four bc diamonds set in plat enclosing stems at the base, appl plaques on rev mkd "Tiffany" and "18k," 1¹/₂" w x 3", **$4000; C, 3 Earclips,** openwork textured 18k yg trefoils, each with a center rosette of seven circ-cut rubies, appl plaque on one mkd "Tiffany," "18k" on the other, open wire clipbacks, 1" x 1", pr, **$3500; CR, Brooch/Pin,** stylized moderne cat, Florentine finish 14k yg, circ-cut ruby nose, rev mkd "14k," "EB" in a lozenge for Engel Bros, Inc., New York, NY, 1" w x 2¹/₂", **$450; BL, Ring,** 18k yg tiger with dk amber enamel stripes, emerald cab eyes, a larger emerald cab encircled by diamonds on top of head, mkd "18k," approx size 5¹/₂, ⁷/₈" w x 1¹/₈", **$2800; BC, Suite: Necklace and Flexible Bracelet,** necklace of linked grad convex textured 18k yg leaf shapes, alternating center leaves each set with two bc diamonds in plat, matching bracelet of same size links, Fr hmks (eagle, rhino, dog heads), maker's mk in a lozenge on tongues of v-springs, box clasps, necklace 16¹/₂" tl x 1" at center, bracelet 7³/₄" tl x 1¹/₈" w, suite, **$18,000; BR, Brooch/Pin,** 18k yg bird with textured feathers, body set throughout with cab rubies, bc diamond eye, polished yg beak, mkd "18k TLI," 1" w x 1³/₄", **$2500,** *Courtesy of HMS, Ltd.*

Post-War Modernist, c. 1945–1955: TL, Money Clip or Tie Bar, c. 1952, a folded tapered ster bar with triangular section bezel-set with a circ faceted amethyst, appl angled round wire, stamped "ed wiener sterling," 2³/4" x 1¹/2", **$200; TC, Brooch/Pin,** c. 1947, a rect black walnut plaque with a row of five vertical lengths of sq wire mounted free-swinging on front surface, stamped "Cooke" for Betty Cooke, 2³/8" w x 2", **$250; TR, Link Bracelet,** c. 1947, hinged brass, copper and ster rect boxes, biomorphic shapes cut out from top surface, revealing patinated lower layer, heavy safety chain, sgd "Macchiarini" for Peter Macchiarini, 7⁷/8" tl x 1¹/4" w, **$900; CL, Brooch/Pin,** c. 1950, cast ster elliptical double volute, stamped "Art Smith," 3" w x 1¹/2", **$300; CR, Brooch/Pin,** c. 1945, cutout ster plaque surmounting two overlapping textured and oxidized ster triangles, a bezel-set jade cab mounted at one end, stamped "de patta" for Margaret De Patta, 3¹/4" w x 1³/4", **$950; BL, Brooch/Pin,** c. 1954, cast ster curv freeform with oxidized concave surfaces, a cultured pearl set in lower left curve, by Bob Winston, unsgd, 2" w x 1³/8", **$250; BR, Brooch/Pin,** c. 1952, forged ster wires, some bead-tipped, some with flattened ends, forming a three-dimensional starburst, stamped "renk" for Merry Renk, 2³/8" dia, **$550; B, Necklace,** c. 1955, three rounded-corner rect ster plaques with crossed flat wires framing framed sections with oxidized surfaces, some sections cut out or set with gemstones: turquoise, jade, opal, moonstone, pearl, citrine, continuing to a forged flat wire chain of open rounded rect links, stamped "Lobel" for Paul Lobel, 15¹/2" tl x ⁷/8" w, **$950.** *Photo courtesy of The Modern i Gallery.*

Designer/Manufacturer Signed Costume, c. 1935–1955: TL, Pendent Earrings, c. 1950, a grad cluster of beige faux pearls and colorless r.s. linked to ym chain, forming articulated bunch of grapes motif, with r.s.-set gp ym filigree leaves, screwbacks mkd "Miriam Haskell," 2¹/4" tl x 1", pr, **$150,** *Author's collection;* **TC, Suite: Brooch/Pin and Earclips,** c. 1950, brooch a foliate spray, each leaf bezel-set with green glass molded in a grid pattern imitating "invisible setting," pavé colorless r.s. stems on gp wm, 1¹/2" w x 2³/8", earclips, each a looped ribbon similarly set with molded green glass and colorless r.s., 1" w x 1¹/8", all pieces mkd "Trifari ©," suite, **$425; TR, Pendent Earrings,** c. 1950, a cluster of iridescent faceted black glass beads suspended from two rows of beads strung on wire, linked to a circ disk surmount with pavé beaded surface, unmkd, clipbacks, 1¹/2" w x 2¹/2" tl, pr, **$95; CL, Clip,** c. 1940, volute with reeded ster vermeil center, pavé faux turq glass cabs and colorless r.s., grad tapered rods alternating with marquise-cut red r.s.-tipped wires radiating from outer half of spiral, double-pronged hinged clip on rev, mkd "Pat Pend sterling," #2364, logo for Marcel Boucher (bird's head surmounting "MB"), 2¹/8" w x 2¹/2", **$225; C, Brooch/Pin,** c. 1940, painted enamel, gp wm, and pavé colorless r.s. tulip spray, center stamens and pistils *en tremblant,* rev mkd "Coro, Pat No. D.115043" (1939), 2¹/2" w x 4", **$195; CR, Brooch/Pin,** c. 1955, in the shape of a ballerina, gp wm, skirt set with baroque pink and white faux pearls, coloress r.s., rev mkd "Chanel" (script mark), 2" w x 2¹/4", **$500; BL, Bead Bracelet,** c. 1950, textured cylindrical green glass beads capped with gp rondelles, brass bead spacers alternating with faux pearls, v-spring and box clasp with faux pearl cluster, mkd "Miriam Haskell," safety chain, 7¹/2" tl x ⁵/8", $135; **BR, Link Bracelet,** c. 1955, molded pink glass in the shape of acorns set in gp wm frames interspersed with sm colorless r.s., foldover clasp mkd "Trifari," 7¹/4" tl x ¹/2", **$175,** *Charles Pinkham collection;* **BC, Necklace,** c. 1945, two gp wm ribbon and foliate loops, each set with four cobalt blue glass circ cabs and sm colorless r.s. flanking a larger central blue glass cab, suspending a ribbon loop and ropetwist pendant set with a central row of colorless baguette r.s., continuing to a sq cobra chain, appl plaque on rev mkd "Schiaparelli" (script mark), 16" tl, center 1¹/2" top to bottom, **$275,** *Author's collection.*

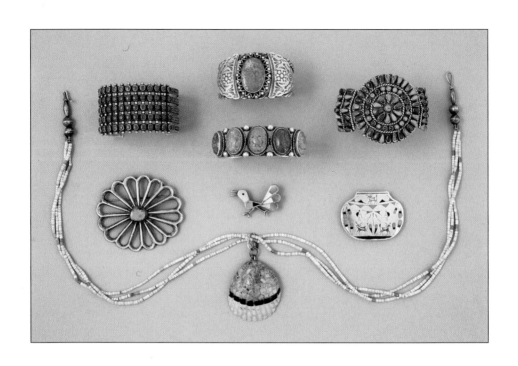

Native American (Indian): TL, Cuff Bracelet, Zuni, c. 1950, five rows of sm circ turq cabs mounted on ster bands with sm circ and lenticular-shaped stampwork, beaded edges and connecting crossbars, 2³/8" inside dia, 1¹/2" w, **$300; TC, Cuff Bracelet,** Fred Harvey, pre-W.W. II, lg flat oval turq cab with bead and serrate pattern flat silver wire frame encircling bezel, flanked by scallop-edge triangular sections decorated with stampwork in cross, arrow, and plume patterns, mounted on three tapered flat ropetwist wires with stampwork decorated solid tips, 2¹/4" inside dia, 1¹/2" w, **$250; TR, Cuff Bracelet, Zuni,** c. 1940, cluster work, varicolored petit point and sm circ turq, ropetwist silver wire separating rows, 2" dia circ medallion flanked by V-shaped rows of petit point turq mounted on three round wires soldered together to form tapered cuff, 2⁵/8" inside dia, **$450,** Terrance O'Halloran collection; **C, Cuff Bracelet, Navajo,** c. 1950, five varicolored oval turq cabs bezel-set in ropetwist wire frames, beading between each cab, mounted on a half-round wire tapered band with flattened ropetwist wire center, 2³/8" inside dia, 1" w, **$500,** Margaret Levine collection; **BL, Brooch/Pin, Navajo,** tufa-cast oval scallop-edge sunburst with irreg flat oval turq cab center, 2³/4" w x 2³/8", **$125; BC, Brooch/Pin, Zuni,** bird motif, inlaid MOP, turq, jet, and spiny oyster, 1¹/2" w x ⁷/8", **$85,** Terrance O'Halloran collection; **BR, Brooch/Pendant, Hopi,** bulbous vase-shaped plaque with inlaid turq, jet, MOP, coral and overlay flute-player and deer motifs, 2" w x 1¹/2", **$75,** Margaret Levine collection; **B, Necklace and Pendant,** Santo Domingo, scallop shell pendant with mosaic overlay of turq, coral, and jet (some missing pieces), suspended from three-strand heishi necklace interspersed with turq beads, terminating in round and lenticular silver beads and hook clasp, shell 1⁵/8" w x 2", necklace 25" tl, **$250,** Terrance O'Halloran collection.

Mexican, Taxco School, c. 1935–1960: TL. Brooch/Pin, c. 1950, pre-Hispanic warrior and serpent motif, cut-to-shape *metales casados* (married metals), rev stamped "Los Castillo, Made by Chato," # 36, 2³/4" x 1¹/2", **$275; TC, Link Bracelet,** c. 1940, alternating ster and bronze links, oblongs with one rounded end, raised ridged centers, forming a fish-scale pattern, rev imp with pre-1945 maker's mark for William Spratling, "sterling," 6³/4" x 1", **$1100; TR, Bola Tie,** c. 1950, grooved ster disk slide surmounted by a polychromatic enameled snake head, rev mkd "Margot de Taxco," government assay mark eagle with "16" in the center, encircled by "sterling Made in Mexico," # 5554, enameled bola tips in the shape of snake's tails, on braided black leather cord, approx 40" tl, slide 1" dia, tips 2¹/2" l, **$450; CL, Brooch/Pin,** c. 1940, conjoined bird and fish motif, repoussé ster feathers and scales, fish with amethyst cab eye, rev imp "Hand Made sterling Hubert Harmon Made in Mexico," maker's mark (winged feet), 2³/4" x 3¹/2", **$650; C, 1 Brooch/Pin,** c. 1935, folded silver ribbon bow, center set with a lg beveled sq amethyst flanked by vertical rows of sm turq cabs, rev imp "silver Mexico," conjoined "FD" for Frederick Davis, 3¹/2" w x 1³/4", **$1000,** Jill Crawford collection; **C, 2 Earclips,** c. 1955, slightly curved teardrop shape with inlaid obsidian triangles flanking ridged center, rev imp "Ledesma" for Enrique Ledesma, "925, Taxco Mexico," government assay mark, # 268, ³/4" w x 1¹/8", pr, **$45; CR, Pendent Earrings,** c. 1955, a three-dimensional articulated caricature of a chicken, with cutout wings, feet and tail linked to a cutout head mounted on a concave disk surmount, rev imp "sterling Mexico, Salvador" for Salvador Terán, # 175, screwbacks, 1" w x 2" tl, pr, **$145; BL, 1 Brooch/Pin,** c. 1940, hand hammered and incised 940 ster flower with beaded center, rev imp with conjoined "HA" for Héctor Aguilar, "Taxco 940," 2³/4" w x 2¹/2", **$250,** Author's collection; **BL, 2 Ring,** c. 1940, lg emerald-cut amethyst bezel-set within a silver ropetwist wire frame flanked by baton-shaped vertical bars, stepped shoulders, tapered narrow shank, rev imp with conjoined "FD" for Frederick Davis, ⁷/8" x ⁷/8", **$500; BC, Pendant & Chain,** c. 1955, pendant of intertwined serpents, ster inlaid with azur-malachite, suspended from elongated ster tubes strung on foxtail chain, pendant imp with post-1947 maker's mark for William Spratling "925," 3" w x 2¹/2", chain 17" tl, **$2800,** Jill Crawford collection; **BR, 1 Brooch/Pin,** c. 1955, S-shaped with cutout center, set with a cultured pearl, rev imp "Sigi Tasco, Hecho En Mexico, sterling" # 81, government assay mark, ³/4" w x 2⁷/8", **$150,** Author's collection; **BR, 2 Brooch/Pin,** c. 1940, repoussé bird, floral and foliate motifs, three coral cabs bezel-set at the base, rev imp "Matl" in script for Matilde Poulat, "925," 1⁷/8" w x 2", **$250; B, Chain Necklace,** c. 1945, lg oval links, twelve with beveled rect turq centers, joined with flanged circ links, terminating in a v-spring and box clasp imp "Hecho en Mexico, sterling Mexico, silver 980," maker's mark for Antonio Pineda ("Antonio Taxco" in crown shape), 25" tl x ⁵/8" w, **$1800,** Jill Crawford collection.

Scandinavian: L, Suite: Pendant & Chain and Ring, Finnish, each bezel-set with a flat red jasper disk, the pendant with a radiating abstract design, the ring with a beaded frame, each imp with Finnish hmks, maker's mark for Kultateollisuus Ky (winged hammer), Turku, date letter for 1971, pendant mkd "Made in Finland," 1⁵/₈" dia, suspended from orig cable link chain, 24" tl, ring ⁵/₈" dia, suite, **$150; TL, Brooch/Pendant, Norwegian,** c. 1960, cast ster vermeil stylized flowerhead enameled in cobalt blue, rev mkd with mfr's logo (scales), "D-A" for David-Andersen, designer name (illegible), "925S sterling," 1⁷/₈" w x 1³/₄", **$125; TC, Brooch/Pin, Norwegian,** c. 1950, stamped ster vermeil hummingbird and flower motif, multicolored *basse-taille* enamel, rev mkd "David-Andersen Norway sterling 925S," 2¹/₄" w x 1¹/₄", $145; **TR, Cuff Links, Danish,** c. 1950, rounded triangular bas-relief pyramid shapes, shafts mkd "925S sterling Danmark, Bluitgen," 1" x 1", **$65; CL, Brooch/Pin, Danish,** c. 1960, slightly convex-sided rect plaque with a stylized snake motif forming a figure 8, matte blue and red enamel, rev imp "Poul Warmind, Denmark, sterling, Z," # 24, 2" w x ⁷/₈", **$175; C, Brooch/Pin, Danish** *skønwirke,* c. 1910, a repoussé silver foliate wreath forming an open-centered rounded lozenge shape around a central oval amber cab, two smaller circ chrysoprase cabs below, set within the foliage in the style of Evald Nielsen, terminating in two long oval jump rings suspending an elongated floral bud set with an amber cab at the base, flat backing imp "ARN 830 S," C-catch, tube hinge, extended pinstem, 3" w x 3³/₄" tl, **$750,** *Author's collection;* **CR, Brooch/Pin, Danish,** c. 1950, a cast and shaped ster stylized fish design, with two rows of grad turq *champlevé* enameled ellipses radiating from the slightly concave center, rev mkd with post-1945 mark for Georg Jensen, "925S," "HK" for Henning Koppel, designer, # 343, 2³/₈" w x 1³/₄", **$450,** *Courtesy of Imagination Unlimited;* **BL, Brooch/Pin, Danish,** open C-scrolls enclosing two flowerheads flanking a lg oval amethyst cab set in a scallop-edge bezel, two smaller circ amethyst cabs above and below, rev imp with post-1945 mark for Georg Jensen, # 236A, 1⁵/₈" w x ⁷/₈", **$475,** *Kirsten Olson collection;* **BC, Link Bracelet, Danish,** c. 1940, die-stamped and backed links, dove motif alternating with rect foliate design set with three sm coral cabs, oval box clasp bezel-set with a coral cab, rev imp "GJ" for Georg Jensen, "925 sterling Denmark" (1933–1944 mark), #24, 7¹/₄" x ⁵/₈", **$1500,** *Courtesy of Imagination Unlimited;* **BR, Earrings, Danish,** stamped relief scrolled flower bud with a cluster of four moonstones at the base, screwbacks, mkd "Georg Jensen, sterling Denmark" (post-1945 mark), # 32B, ³/₄" w x 1¹/₈", pr, **$325; R, Pendant, Norwegian,** c. 1960, hatchet-shaped with rounded base, shades of dk to lt violet *basse-taille* enamel in central imbricated (fish-scale) depressions, tapering to a narrow shaped shank with pendant loop (added chain), rev mkd "David-Andersen Norway sterling 925S," 1¹/₂" w x 2", **$95,** *Author's collection.*

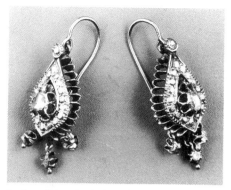

Earrings, diamonds, 9k yg, c. 1860-70, teardrop shape, one lg center rc stone, 16 smaller rc and table-cut stones around border, openwork scalloped edge frame suspending three rc stones, Eng, 1" × ³/₄", pr, $750, *Cheri Mulligan collection.*

14k yellow gold mounts, 2-¼" tl × ½", pr
. . . . **1,540 (A)**
Garnets, 14k yg, c. 1870, kite-shaped yg pendent drops with pierced under-bezels, pear-shaped cab garnets set in center collets with added beading, suspending snake-chain fringe tapering up from center, replaced earwires, 2-½" tl × ⁵/₈", pr . . . . . . **1,650 (A)**
Garnets, silver gilt, c. 1870-80, tiered pendent drops (girandole) of oval, round, and teardrop cab and rc garnets suspended from oval

Hatpins, moonstone and 14k yg, diamonds and rubies, c. 1890, round cone cab moonstones in prong bezels, accented with alternating diamonds and rubies in a yg wire-twist and beadwork mount, Austrian hallmarks, heads measure 1" × ⁵/₈" and ⁷/₈" × ½", pr, $1,650 (A). *Photo courtesy of Skinner, Inc. (3/14/93).*

surmounts of lg cabs surrounded by sm rc (possible marriage), 2-⁷/₈" tl × ³/₄", pr
. . . . **605 (A)**
Lavalier
Blister pearl, round oe diamonds, st yg, late Victorian, drop-shaped blister pearl in center of pear-shaped pendant drop bordered with oe diamonds of grad size set in independent frame, held in place by scrolled prongs set with oe diamonds, suspended from a plume-shaped bail set with oe diamonds, 17" silver cable-link chain, provenance: estate of Marian Anderson, 1" w × 2-½" tl . . . . **2,700 (A)**
Necklace
Citrine, 14k yg, c. 1890-1900, fine-link chain suspending a fringe of round bezel-set citrines from yg florets, 14-½" tl × 1-³/₈"
. . . . **800**
Garnets, 15k yg, mid Victorian, festoon style, draped yg chains suspending three convex oval engr yg plaques, each set with a rhodolite garnet cab and suspending a yg urn drop, an additional garnet suspended from bottom of center plaque, 18" tl, center plaque 1-³/₄" tl × ³/₄", side plaques 1" × ½"
. . . . **990 (A)**
Opals, rubies, yg, c. 1900, fringe of seven oval opals set at the base of grad open scrollwork drops topped with sm round collet-set rubies, alternating with eight smaller oval opals set at ends of grad baton-shaped drops, all linked and suspended from fine cable-link chain, 15" tl × 1-⅛" . . . . **2,300 (A)**
Bead
Banded agate, yg, c. 1860-70, 37 beads with bead clasp, 24" tl . . . . **660 (A)**
Pendant
Opal, diamond, yg, c. 1900, centered with round opal of approx 4.5 ct surrounded by

Locket, diamonds, 18k yg, c. 1890-1900, heart-shaped locket pavé-set with oe diamonds suspended from scrolling ribbon diamond-set bail, mounted in yg (one diamond missing), 2" × 1-⅛", $8,050 (A). *Photo courtesy of Christie's New York (4/22/93).*

Necklace, garnets, ym (brass), c. 1900, linked star and flower motifs with three pendent drops of four stones each, 19-½″ tl, center with drop, ⅝″ × 1-⅛″, $350. *Joyce Albers collection.*

12 oe diamonds, set in yg, suspended from a diamond-set bail, approx 6.8 ct tw (opal chipped and slightly crazed), sgd "Tiffany & Co.," incl mounting to convert to ring (added later) . . . . **8,800 (A)**

Pendant and Chain

Diamonds, rubies, platinum, and yg, c. 1900, heart shape concentrically set with lg and sm oe, rc, and sc diamonds with calibré-cut rubies in heart-shaped outline, border of sm round diamonds, rev compartment for photograph, suspended from diamond-set platinum link chain, 16″, pendant ⅝″ w × 1″ . . . . **3,300 (A)**

Rubies, diamonds, st yg, c. 1840, heart-shaped pendant set with rubies and sm sc diamonds with diamond-set bow suspended from neckchain of collet-set oval rubies alternating with scrolling navette-shaped diamond-set links, neckchain 15″, pendant 1″ w × 2″ . . . . **7,250 (A)**

Ring

14k yg, hardstone cameo, c. 1870-80, white cameo on black onyx, triple-beaded edge setting, die-stamped and engr, ½″ w × ⅝″ **275**

15k yg, ruby, seed pearl, c. 1890, carré-set stones (bead-set in recessed squares), engr design on shoulders, Chester (Eng) hmks, date letter worn, probably 1888, ⅜″ **250**

18k yg, bloodstone, c. 1890-1900, rect stone set in pierced and engr bezel and shank, ⅜″ w × ½″ **200**

18k yg, diamonds, ruby, c. 1880, plain flat band, appl rounded rect plaque set with four rc diamonds, star-cut set center ruby, Eng, ⅜″ w **250**

18k yg, syn sapphires, diamond, c. 1900, band with star-cut set sc diamond and two sm syn sapphires, tapering to chased foliate shoulders, Eng hmks (illegible), ¼″ × ¾″ **125**

22k yg, sc and om diamonds, c. 1880, star-cut bead settings, engr scrolls on shank, Birmingham (Eng) hmks (illegible), ¼″ **350**

Rings, yg, c. 1890: L, 15k yg, seed pearls and sapphires, date letter for 1890, engr tapered band, Birmingham (Eng) hmks, ½″ w, ring size 5, $225; C, quatrefoil design of opals interspaced with seed pearls, tapering to die-stamped shank, ring size 5, $275; R, 15k, seed pearls and rubies, date letter for 1890, engr tapered band, Birmingham (Eng) hmks, ⅜″ w, ring size 5-1/2, $225, *Cheri Mulligan collection.*

Amethyst, diamonds, 14k yg, c. 1900, central oval faceted amethyst within an octagonal frame outlined by bc diamonds, quartered by finely detailed engr yg foliate motifs, 1-⅛″ w × 1-½″ . . . . **1,540 (A)**

Cat's eye chrysoberyl, 9k yg, c. 1880-90, bezel-set oval cat's eye, thin shank, Eng **325**

Chalcedony and turq, yg, c. 1890-90, stone engr and overlaid with gold, set with sm turq, moon and star motif, engr shank, ½″ w × ¾″ **250**

Demantoid garnet, diamonds, 18k yg, late Victorian, navette shape, center of oval demantoid surrounded by pavé-set oe diamonds, mounted on yg shank with sculpted shoulders, head ¾″ w × ⅞″, ring size 7 . . . . **2,200 (A)**

Diamonds, 14k yg, c. 1880, om diamond, 1.1 ct, flanked by two sm sc diamonds set within a lotus flower motif, ⅜″ w × ⅝″, ring size 8-½″, with added 18k ring guard . . . . **1,210 (A)**

Diamonds, 14k yg, enamel, c. 1900, lozenge-shaped panel of prong-set oe diamonds, .9 ct tw, within scalloped openwork border, dk blue enamel on border and shoulders, ⅝″ w × ⅞″ **1,100**

Diamonds, st yg, late Victorian, snake ring, om, circ, and sc diamond-set hoop with snake head at the top set with a larger oe diamond, 1.75 ct tw, ring size 7 . . . . **2,500 (A)**

Diamonds, st 18k yg, late Victorian, one oe diamond, .6 ct tw, flanked by eight sc diamonds on shoulders, ring size 6 . . . . **1,200 (A)**

Diamonds, st yg, late Victorian, cluster ring, center oe diamond, .9 ct, surrounded by smaller oe diamonds, ⅝″ dia, ring size 6 . . . . **1,650 (A)**

Gemstones and pearl, st yg, c. 1830-40, cluster top of ruby, emerald, garnet, amethyst, ruby, diamond (initial letters spell "regard") encircling one grey pearl, mounted on replaced yg shank, ¼″ × ½″ **200**

Rubies, seed pearls, 15k yg, c. 1890, three lozenge-shaped bezel-set sq-cut rubies with seed pearls set between each bezel, Eng **275**

Sapphire, diamonds, plat, late Victorian, cluster ring, center round pink sapphire, encircled by 20 rc diamonds, ⅜″ dia, mounted on plat shank, ring size 5-¼ . . . . **660 (A)**

Sapphire, diamonds, yg, late Victorian, narrow navette shape set with a marquise-cut blue sapphire framed by om diamonds, mounted in yg on narrow shank . . . . **4,313 (A)**

Scarf pin/Stickpin

Diamond, 14k yg, seed pearl, c. 1900, lozenge-shaped frame set with one sm oe diamond, seed pearl in frame at base, mounted on yg pinstem, 1-⅜″ tl × ⅜″ w **75**

Diamond, plat, yg, c. 1900, one oe diamond, 1.15 ct, set in plat prongs mounted on yg pinstem, 2-¾″ tl . . . . **1,980 (A)**

Pearl, enamel, yg, late Victorian, head in the shape of a lighthouse, enameled black and orange, on f.w. pearl base, within a fitted velvet box, ⅝″ w × 1″ . . . . **715 (A)**

Suite: Bracelet, Bar Pin, Pendent Earrings, Studs, Hairpins, and Cuff Links

Malachite, silver, 15k yg, c. 1860, flexible bracelet of hinged oval plaques with yg screw heads in center of each, yg buckle motif on clasp, silver gilt back, bar pin with yg buckle in center, suspending a pear-shaped drop, matching pendent earrings, cuff links, shirt studs, hairpins, buttons, with yg accents, Eng hmks, in fitted box, suite . . . . **2,200 (A)**

Suite: Bracelet and Pendent Earrings

18k yg, garnets, c. 1900, flexible yg chain mesh bracelet suspending one lg rc garnet, 7″ tl × ½″, matching pendent earrings married to Art Nouveau mount and earwire, 1-⅝″ tl × ½″, suite **600**

Suite: Brooch and Earrings

Garnets, silver gilt, c. 1890-1900, brooch of three concentric circles bead set with rc garnets enclosed with ribbon-loop motif at top, C-catch, tube hinge, extended pinstem, 1-⅝″ w × 1-⅞″, matching earrings suspended from circ garnet-set surmounts on screwbacks of later addition, 1-⅛″ w × 1-¾″, in fitted velvet case . . . . **880 (A)**

Suite: Pendant and Pendent Earrings

Amethyst, 15k yg, c. 1850-60, repoussé yg shield-shaped pendant, foliate motif, centered with prong-set oval buff-top amethyst, suspending a repoussé lozenge-shaped drop set with a keystone-shaped buff-top stone, 1-½″ w × 3″, matching pendent earrings with oval stones in lozenge-shaped surmounts and pear-shaped stones in drops, 3″ tl × 1″ . . . . **2,090 (A)**

PART II

Turn-of-the-Century Jewelry

INTRODUCTION

The year 1900 did not signal the beginning of a new era so much as the continuation of the old and the continuing evolution of the new. The Victorian age did not end with the Queen's death in 1901; it held sway until World War I. But while a large proportion of the populace continued to cling to late Victorian fashions, three more stylistic trends emerged to establish themselves among various segments of society by the turn of the century. This did not happen overnight. Edwardian style had already begun to make its mark on fashionable society long before Edward became king. Aesthetic influences that led to the Arts and Crafts movement and the beginning of modernism had made their presence felt as early as the midnineteenth century. And the "new art" had made its debut in Paris in the 1890s. So, in fact, at the turn of the century, there were four concurrent jewelry styles: Victorian, Edwardian, Arts and Crafts, and Art Nouveau.

This section is divided into the three latter styles. As with nineteenth-century jewelry, it can be difficult to clearly identify turn-of-the-century pieces as one particular style or another. At times, two or more styles are commingled in a single piece of jewelry. Most of us have a need to pigeonhole and label, but this is not always possible. While an attempt has been made to categorize the pieces in the listings, individual interpretations vary. Up until recently, historians usually grouped all turn-of-the-century art jewelry under Art Nouveau. Now, most make a distinction between Art Nouveau and Arts and Crafts. But one person's Arts and Crafts is another's Art Nouveau, and Edwardian pieces sometimes include Art Nouveau elements. Some stylistic details clearly belong in one or the other category. These will be described in the sections that follow. It is more important to understand the part that each style played in jewelry history, to recognize its characteristic components, and to

see how the styles influenced one another and evolved over time.

As always, events and fashion trends played an important part in the evolution of *fin de siècle* jewelry design. The pace of change was quickened by new developments: The advent of the automobile and the airplane revolutionized transportation and increased mobility. Motoring became a fashionable pastime. The wireless telegraph and the telephone improved communications. The motion picture industry made its humble debut as the peepshow at Thomas Edison's Kinetoscope Parlor in New York City. By 1910, thousands of movie theatres were showing films whose stars were already influencing fashion. Jewelers advertised their wares in the new trend-setting fashion magazine, *Vogue*.

The 1900 Paris Exposition Universelle heralded the pinnacle of Art Nouveau. Sarah Bernhardt's stage jewels by René Lalique and Georges Fouquet inspired many designers. The 1904 St. Louis Exposition showcased the remarkable jewels of Louis Comfort Tiffany for the first time.

In 1890, artist Charles Dana Gibson introduced the public to what was to become the epitome of turn-of-the-century American womanhood, the Gibson Girl. Her hair, figure and attire were considered the height of fashion in a trend that continued through the early 1900s.

The head and neck were emphasized with large hats, upswept bouffant hairdos, and high collars for day, décolletage for evening. Hatpins, haircombs, tiaras, dog collar chokers, and delicate lace pins and watchpins complemented the look. Festoon necklaces and pendants and their diminutive form, the lavalier, also focused attention on the neck. The lorgnette, usually worn suspended from a chain, became a symbol of period sophistication. Corsage, or bodice, ornaments decorated "pouter pigeon" bosoms. The waist was a focal point of the hourglass silhouette, and anything that adorned it was fashionable. One- and two-piece buckles, sewn onto fabric or leather belts, were often-worn accessories. Large brooches known as sash ornaments were also worn at the waist. Many have open centers; some include a simulated hasp. The pinstem is invisible when the brooch is pinned to a ribbon or belt, and the brooch imitates the look of a buckle. Cuff links and scarf pins continued to be worn by both sexes. Mainstream and avant-garde designs alike were rendered in these forms and were made from both precious and nonprecious materials.

References: Lillian Baker, *Hatpins and Hatpin Holders, An Illustrated Value Guide,* Collector Books, 1983, 1992 value update; Vivienne Becker, *Antique and Twentieth Century Jewellery,* 2nd ed., N.A.G. Press, 1987; Shirley Bury, *Jewellery 1789-1910, The International Era,* Vol. II, Antique Collectors' Club, 1991; Deanna Farneti Cera, ed., *Jewels of Fantasy, Costume Jewelry of the 20th Century,* Harry N. Abrams, 1992; Charlotte Gere, *American & European Jewelry, 1830-1914,* Crown Publishers, 1975 (out of print); Alison Gernsheim, *Victorian and Edwardian Fashion, A Photographic Survey,* Dover Publications, 1981; Penny Proddow and Debra Healy, *American Jewelry, Glamour and Tradition,* Rizzoli International, 1987; A. Kenneth Snowman, ed., *The Master Jewelers,* Harry N. Abrams, 1990; Janet Zapata, "Authenticating Tiffany Jewelry," article in *Jewelers' Circular-Keystone/Heritage,* August, 1988.

ARTS & CRAFTS C. 1890-1920

History: Arts and Crafts was more than a style—it was called a movement, which encompassed a philosophy, an attitude, and a way of living. The practitioners of the movement were revivalists of a sort, but unlike the Etruscan and Greco-Roman revivalists, they were not copyists, but interpreters of the past. They revived the ideas of handicraft, medieval guilds, and individual craftsmanship. Their philosophical point of view influenced their creative impulses, which found expression in a number of different forms and incorporated a variety of stylistic elements. So Arts and Crafts is not one style, but many.

Historians usually classify the various interpretations of Arts and Crafts by country of origin. While it may be that an identifiable characteristic approach to design is shared by artisans of the same nationality, it is dangerous to generalize. Without documentation or identifying marks—and many Arts and Crafts pieces are unmarked—attribution to country or maker is a guessing game at best. In terms of history, however, it can be useful to trace the movement as it developed from its origins in Great Britain and spread to Europe and the United States.

objects. They also rebelled against the excesses of Victorian ornament, setting the stage for the advent of modernism at the beginning of this century. The rebellion had its roots in Great Britain, then the greatest of the industrialized nations. The Crystal Palace Exhibition of 1851 had shown the world the achievements of the British in the use of the machine. For some, it was the beginning of the end of artisanship. John Ruskin and William Morris, generally recognized as the founders of the movement, went on to formulate a rather utopian philosophy that would eventually become the Arts and Crafts movement. The earliest application of the philosophy was in architecture, interior design, and furnishings. Jewelry making wasn't included until C.R. Ashbee founded his Guild of Handicraft in London in 1888.

The Aesthetic movement of the 1870s may have given impetus to Arts and Crafts and Art Nouveau. The influence of Japanese art began with the aesthetes and also found expression in the later styles. The adherents of the Aesthetic movement were a splinter group of intellectuals that included the Pre-Raphaelites of the art world and the advocates of dress reform, such as members of The Rational Dress Society in Britain and The Free Dress League in the United States. While mainstream fashion kept women tightly corseted, boned, and laced into hourglass figures, clothing reformers attempted to liberate fashion from the confines of the corset. Reform dress for Arts and Crafts proponents was loose and highwaisted in the medieval or Renaissance style. This was part of their preoccupation with the past—recalling simpler, idealistic times in the hopes of liberating themselves from the dehumanizing mechanized world. Types of jewelry made to complement the clothing were primarily necklaces and pendants, buckles, sash ornaments, and brooches. Hatpins, hair ornaments, and tiaras, an important part of period fashion, were also interpreted by Arts and

Liberty and Co.

Murrle, Bennett & Co.

GREAT BRITAIN

As early as the 1870s when Victorian classical revivalists were in the majority, there were those who rebelled against the Industrial Revolution, with its increased mechanization and mass production, and the consequent loss of the human touch in the making of decorative and utilitarian

Crafts designers. Rings and bracelets were less commonly made and earrings rarely.

The central idea of the Arts and Crafts movement purists was for one artisan to make everything entirely by hand from start to finish. No matter how varied the style, the one thing they all had in common was the desire for their handcraftsmanship to be apparent. Hammer marks and irregularities were left intact as evidence of human handiwork. Simplification of line and form, and the use of stylized organic motifs were also common.

Staunch social idealists, the leaders of the movement hoped to bring art to the people "in an acceptable form at realistic prices." In jewelry, the intrinsic value of the materials was of secondary importance to design and workmanship. Most Arts and Crafts artisans preferred silver to gold and inexpensive cabochon gemstones like turquoise and moonstone to faceted diamonds and rubies. Enameling was a favorite technique of many. Some worked in brass, copper, and glass.

Although the materials were inexpensive, the time and workmanship involved in producing entirely handmade pieces made them too labor intensive to be affordable for any but the well-to-do. The rejection of the use of all machinery made production in multiples difficult and expensive. The guild artisans were unable to produce sufficient quantities of jewelry to supply the masses. The irony was that the very manufacturers whose techniques they rejected were successful where the purists failed. British firms such as Liberty & Co., W. H. Haseler, Murrle, Bennett & Co., and Charles Horner commercialized the style, but in so doing made it affordable.

Foremost among the success stories was Liberty & Co., founded by Arthur Lazenby Liberty in 1875 as an importer of Near and Far Eastern goods. The company's own popular Cymric (pronounced "kim'-rik," from the word for the Celts of Wales) line of metalware and jewelry was first exhibited in 1899. Liberty employed a number of designers to create what were then called modern designs. The Liberty Style, which really *was* the people's style, was mass-produced interpretations of one-of-a-kind handmade pieces and was much more accessible and affordable to the middle and working classes. The prototypes for these pieces were designed by talented artists whose names were kept from the public at the time, but who are well-known today. Liberty's principal designer, whose work is most sought after, was Archibald Knox (1864-1933). Knox's work is characterized by Celtic knot motifs (also called *entrelac*) and whiplash curves in silver and enamel. In his pieces, he popularized the use of intermingled floating blue and green enamels pooled in central depressions. He occasionally worked in gold. Some other known designers who worked for Liberty were Jessie M. King, Oliver Baker, and Arthur and Georgie Gaskin.

Brooches/Pins, Eng, W. H. Haseler, sterling, enamel, c. 1900: TL, shaped cutout plaque with hammered surface, three blue-green *cloisonné* enameled leaf motifs, rev mkd "WHH silver," C-catch, 1-¼" × 1-¹/₁₆", $500; TR, pierced trefoil design, green enamel, rev mkd "WHH silver," 1" × ⅝", $350; BL, c. 1900, mushroom-shaped plaque flanked by Celtic knot motifs, with enameled center of blue and green shading to orange-yellow over a central knot motif, unmkd, C-catch, tube hinge, 1-⅛" × 1-¹/₁₆", $350; BC, c. 1900, navette-shaped bar terminating in Celtic knots at each end, enameled oval center in shades of blue and green, rev mkd "silver WHH," C-catch, tube hinge, 1-⅝" × ½", $650; BR, date letter for 1905, lozenge-shaped Celtic knot design with enameled raised oval center of red-orange and green, rev mkd "WHH," Birmingham hmks, C-catch, 1-¼" × ¾", $600. *Terrance O'Halloran collection.*

These same designers also worked independently, creating entirely handmade pieces. When Liberty appropriated their designs, the pieces were made by machine, but with hand-finished details. They retained the look of the hand-wrought designs, and except by purists' standards, are still considered Arts and Crafts. Unfortunately, the pieces were marked only with one of several Liberty hallmarks ("L & Co.," "Ly & Co.," and "LC&C Ld"). Attribution is based on characteristic motifs and techniques, and at times, archival documentation in the form of drawings and company records.

W. H. Haseler and Murrle, Bennett & Co. also produced designs for Liberty's retail establishment. In 1901, W. H. Haseler, a Birmingham manufacturer, formed a partnership with Liberty to produce their Cymric line. Pieces can be marked for . Liberty or "W.H.H." for Haseler. Murrle, Bennett & Co. was founded in 1884 as a wholesale distributorship. It was based in England but also had manufacturing connections in Pforzheim, Germany, where it imported pieces for Liberty and also worked with Theodor Fahrner. Its mark is a conjoined "MB" inside a large C, followed by a small o, which is often used together with British hallmarks or Fahrner's marks. Some pieces are marked "M.B. & Co." Charles Horner produced silver and enamel jewelry that was entirely made by machine. They were known for small brooches, pendants and chains, and hatpins. The winged scarab, Celtic knot, and thistle were favorite motifs. Horner pieces had the look of Liberty, if not the quality of execution. They are marked "C.H.," often with Chester assay marks and date letters. For more on these four firms, see "Liberty and His Rivals" in Becker's *Antique and 20th Century Jewellery*.

Theodor Fahrner
(Germany)

Wiener Werkstätte
(Austria)

GERMANY AND AUSTRIA

By the late 1890s, the Arts and Crafts movement had found its way across the English Channel to Europe, where it was interpreted and renamed by German, Austrian, and Scandinavian artisans. In Germany and Austria, it was called *Jugendstil* ("young style"). Scandinavians called it *skønvirke*, which will be described in the section on Scandinavian silver. Most Italian artisans still produced classic revival jewelry but the few practitioners of the new style called it *Stile Liberty*.

German *Jugendstil* jewelry has been classified both as Arts and Crafts and as Art Nouveau. It seems best, however, to analyze each piece individually rather than to judge the entire body of work. Certain pieces exhibit English Arts and Crafts influence while others take inspiration from French Art Nouveau. If it is possible to generalize at all, the *Jugendstil* look, whether abstract or figural, is characterized by strong lines and bold designs. A number of individual artists worked independently or anonymously. Several manufacturers also produced *Jugendstil* jewelry. The most well-known of these was Theodor Fahrner of Pforzheim, who brought the work of many individual designers to the attention of the general public.

Theodor Fahrner could be called the Liberty of Germany, although Fahrner manufactured jewelry exclusively, while Liberty traded in a variety of goods. What the two had in common was employing skilled freelance designers to produce modern designs for a commercial market. The designs themselves were sometimes the same, thanks to the connection with Murrle, Bennett & Co. Unlike Liberty, however, many of Fahrner's pieces produced between 1900-1919 were also signed by the designers. Most of these designers came from the Darmstadt Colony, an artists' community founded on the same philosophical ideals as the British guilds. It is during this period that Fahrner's *Jugendstil* jewelry was produced. Today, it is highly sought after, especially if it is signed by the artist. Some important designers were Patriz Huber, Max Gradl, Franz Boeres, and Georg Kleemann.

Founded in 1855 in Pforzheim, the company's distinctive mark, a conjoined "TF" in a circle, was not introduced until 1901. The death of Theodor Fahrner (Jr.), son of the company's founder, in 1919 brought changes to the factory. Keeping up with new styles under new ownership, the company went on to become known as a producer of Art Deco fashion jewelry in marcasite, enamel and gemstones set in silver. The firm closed in 1979. A great deal of information, painstakingly compiled by its authors, can be found in the book on Fahrner cited in the references below.

In Austria, Vienna was the center of *Jugendstil* activity. Among its practitioners, the best-known is a guild of multimedia craftspeople who were part of the Vienna Secession, The Wiener Werkstätte (Viennese Workshop). Founded in 1903 by Josef Hoffmann (1870-1956) and Koloman Moser (1868-1918), it was patterned after C.R. Ashbee's Guild of Handicraft. The style that evolved there is geometric and simplified—a harbinger of modernism. Jewelry by any of the Wiener Werkstätte designers, especially the work of Hoffman and Moser, is now highly collectible. The most often-seen of the shop's marks is a superimposed "WW." An extensive history and

Brooch/Pin: c. 1910, disk of black glass with painted enamel design depicting a woman's head with ribbons in her hair, ground of blue and green leaves and orange spirals and dots, mounted in plain brass frame, rev mkd with superimposed "WW" for Wiener Werkstätte (Austria), a leaf design and artist's initials "M.W." in enamel, C-catch, 1-³/₄" dia, $450. _Terrance O'Halloran collection._

examples of both German and Austrian _Jugendstil_ can be found in Becker's _Art Nouveau Jewelry,_ listed in the references below.

The Art Silver Shop

UNITED STATES

British and European Arts and Crafts jewelry has been well-documented in several books. American Arts and Crafts jewelry, however, has been given relatively little attention. Aside from brief chapters in two books, the only other sources of information are articles in periodicals, exhibition catalogs, and the semiannual sales catalogs published by Rosalie and Aram Berberian of ARK Antiques. There are a great many more extant, accessible examples of American Arts and Crafts jewelry than some historians would lead one to believe. Consequently, the listings in this book are weighted heavily toward them. Some examples are by makers about whom very little published information exists, but whose work is available on the market today.

The handicraft aesthetic caught on a bit later in the United States and lasted longer. Some say it never stopped, but that is a matter of personal interpretation. It began with guilds of craftspeople

inspired by and patterned after British models. The most well-known are the Roycrofters and Gustav Stickley's Craftsman group. Perhaps because these guilds were not known for jewelry making explains why some collectors are unaware that American Arts and Crafts jewelry was made by many others. The movement's jewelry makers were concentrated in the Northeast (Boston, New York), the Midwest (especially Chicago), and California. Arts and Crafts societies were founded in several major cities and promoted the work of their members.

In Boston, the Society of Arts and Crafts was the guiding light of the movement. Founded in 1897, the Society began conferring the award and title of Medalist to their most highly skilled members in 1913. Four of these Medalists were jewelers whose oeuvre is recognized today as the best of American Arts and Crafts. This Boston group seems to have been directly inspired by the British in terms of design and execution, if not use of materials. Their pieces incorporate organic motifs, wire, and beadwork in open, delicate, and refined designs. Unlike their British counterparts, however, they worked primarily in gold, and used faceted stones of high intrinsic value, as well as cabochon gemstones and pearls. They relied on stones and metal for color, rather than enamel. But like the British, their pieces are not always signed. Documentation in the form of drawings or photographs in the Society's archives have aided attribution.

Among the earliest recipients of the Medalist award was Josephine Hartwell Shaw (1865-1941), to whom it was given in 1914. Examples of her work are rare and sought after today. Margaret Rogers (?—c. 1945) became a Medalist in 1915. She exhibited in Boston and at the annual exhibitions sponsored by the Art Institute of Chicago. Frank Gardner Hale (1876-1945) studied at C.R. Ashbee's Guild of Handicraft in England and in Europe, and his work reflects the influence of his studies. He won the Medalist award in 1915. Edward Everett Oakes (1891-1960) studied under both Shaw and Hale. The youngest and most prolific of the four, he was awarded the Society's medal in 1923. Even though he was a latecomer, his pieces retained the motifs and the aesthetic of Arts and Crafts. He developed distinctive repoussé leaf and flower forms that were combined with wire tendrils and beadwork in layers around gemstones. He used his own alloys of colored gold, particularly green gold, and also worked in combinations of gold and silver. His mark is his last name within an oak leaf, but, like the others, he did not always sign his work.

In New York, the eccentric artistic genius Louis Comfort Tiffany (1848-1933), son of the founder of Tiffany & Co., turned his attention from interior design to jewelry after his father's death in 1902. His pieces were first exhibited at the St. Louis Louisiana Purchase Exposition in 1904. Until

Bracelet, link, 14k green gold, c. 1925, alternating convex-sided rect and sq links in an openwork quatrefoil, scroll and foliate design, by Edward Everett Oakes, Medalist of the Boston Society of Arts & Crafts, clasp sgd "Oakes" in an oak leaf, 7-½" × ⅝", $6,500. *Photo courtesy of ARK Antiques, New Haven, Conn.*

many, including Oriental, Islamic, Egyptian, and Byzantine motifs and, especially, the colors and forms found in nature. Tiffany was such an individual artist that the diverse body of his work defies classification. However, Zapata considers his jewelry to be very much in keeping with Arts and Crafts philosophy: "Louis's conception of jewelry was at odds with the pieces being made at Tiffany & Co. To him, color was paramount; gemstones were to be selected for their polychromatic effects, not for their monetary value." (Zapata, p. 40). She goes on to state that "each piece was hand-crafted . . . nothing was stamped out or cast. This craftsmanship ideal was followed at the time by Arts and Crafts designers in England and Boston." (Zapata, p. 100).

Marcus & Co. was a New York firm whose output included both British-influenced Arts and Crafts and French-influenced Art Nouveau. They are noted for their enameled gold, gemstone, and pearl jewelry, but they occasionally made sterling pieces.

In upstate New York, Heintz Art Metal Shop of Buffalo, in business from 1906 to 1929, made jewelry and decorative objects of patinated bronze with sterling overlay in cutout patterns. Their style is so distinctive that, although their mark was not used on jewelry, it is readily identifiable.

The Chicago Arts and Crafts Society was founded in 1897, the same year as Boston's, and fostered a number of Arts and Crafts silversmiths and jewelers (many of them were both). Collectors were made aware of their work as a result of an exhibition and catalog entitled *The Chicago Metalsmiths*, sponsored by the Chicago Historical Society in 1977. The catalog is still the best source of information on this group of artisans and shops. The largest and best-known of these is The Kalo Shop, in operation from 1900 to 1970. Their early jewelry designs are the essence of simplicity in line and form. Most are sterling, often set with blister or baroque pearls, mother of pearl or abalone shell, coral, moonstones, or other inexpensive gemstones. Pendants are suspended from handmade paper-clip chains, so called because of the elongated oval shape of the links. This is a typical type of chain used by turn-of-the-century Arts and Crafts designers. In the 1920s and 1930s, the look changed to cutout and pierced repoussé floral and foliate motifs with engraved details. The word "Kalo" in block letters is found as part of the mark on all of their pieces. Some are numbered with order or design numbers.

Some other noted Chicago shops and silversmiths who also made jewelry were the Art Silver Shop (later Art Metal Studios, still in business), the T.C. Shop, James H. Winn, Madeline Yale Wynne, Frances Glessner, and Matthias W. Hanck. Lebolt & Co., a retail jewelry establish-

1907, his jewelry was made by his own firm, Tiffany Furnaces. After 1907 and until 1933, all L.C.T. pieces were made by and marked Tiffany & Co. There is ongoing controversy over the identification of L.C. Tiffany jewelry made after 1907, particularly when a Tiffany & Co. piece of the period comes up for sale at auction. An authentic, identifiable piece of Louis Tiffany jewelry sold at auction today might bring tens of thousands of dollars.

Perhaps because of his association with the most prestigious jewelry firm in the country, some may find it difficult to reconcile Tiffany's jewelry with the Arts and Crafts movement's tenets. Many classify it as Art Nouveau, along with his glass, lamps, and other decorative art objects. Jewelry historian and L.C. Tiffany biographer Janet Zapata points out that his sources and influences were

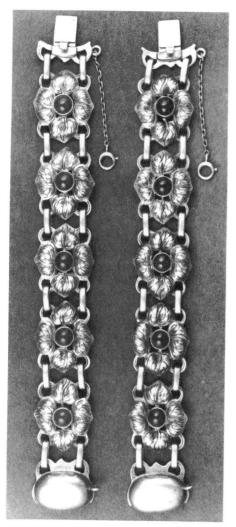

Bracelets, link, sterling, green chalcedony/carnelian: c. 1930, five engr and repoussé quatrefoil plaques, bezel-set stones (chalcedony in one, carnelian in the other) in centers, joined with flat oval jump rings, oval box clasps, safety chains, mkd "Kalo Hand Wrought Sterling" on clasp rev, 7-½" tl × 1", each, $1,000. *Terrance O'Halloran collection.*

ment founded in 1899, installed a workshop around 1912 to produce its own line of hand-wrought silver and jewelry.

Marshall Field & Co., a Chicago-based department store, catered to the demand for handcrafted metalware and jewelry by opening its own Craft Shop around 1904. It made jewelry in silver and brass using acid-etching and patination, techniques that were apparently unique to American Arts and Crafts jewelry. These two processes were usually combined to create a design on a shaped plaque of hammered raised metal. The effect was an antique, aged look, more crude and rough in appearance than the polished, refined pieces of the Boston jewelers.

Other midwestern shops made brass, copper, and nickel silver (German silver) jewelry of the same genre: Carence Crafters of Chicago (who also made sterling and gemstone pieces), George W. Frost of Dayton, Ohio, and the Forest Craft Guild in Grand Rapids, Michigan, founded by Forest Mann around 1905. Most, but not all, pieces are marked.

Pasadena, California silversmith Clemens Friedell (1872-1963) worked for Gorham Co. in Providence, Rhode Island before coming to California in 1910. His style has the Art Nouveau overtones of that company's Martelé line. His earlier work was mostly commissioned silverware, but he opened a retail shop in 1929 that carried jewelry as well as a large array of decorative silver objects and hollowware.

As with any other type of jewelry, one should always evaluate an Arts and Crafts piece on its own merits, regardless of where, when, or by whom it was made. Because so much Arts and Crafts jewelry is unmarked, and often unattributable, this may not be just the first, but the only method of evaluation. Many an amateur hobbyist made handcrafted jewelry in the Arts and Crafts mode. Some of it is well done, some is not.

References: Edith Alpers, "Edward Everett Oakes (1891-1960), a master craftsman from Boston, Massachusetts," in *Jewellery Studies* Vol. 3, The Society of Jewellery Historians, Great Britain, 1989, and "F.G. Hale: Master Craftsman/Jeweler," article in *Jewelers' Circular-Keystone*/Heritage, August, 1989; Vivienne Becker, *Art Nouveau Jewelry,* E.P. Dutton, 1985 (out of print); Malcolm Haslam, *Collector's Style Guide: Arts and Crafts,* Ballantine Books, 1988; Sharon S. Darling, *Chicago Metalsmiths,* Chicago Historical Society, 1977; Charlotte Gere and Geoffrey C. Munn, *Artists' Jewellery—Pre-Raphaelite to Arts and Crafts,* Antique Collectors' Club, 1989; Wendy Kaplan, "The Art that is Life," in *The Arts & Crafts Movement in America, 1875-1920,* Museum of Fine Arts, Boston, 1987; Elyse Zorn Karlin, *Jewelry & Metalwork in the Arts & Crafts Tradition,* Schiffer Publishing, 1993; Catherine Kuland and Lori Zabar, *Reflections: Arts & Crafts Metalwork in England and the United States,* exhibition catalog, Kurland-Zabar, New York, 1990; Mervyn Levy, *Liberty Style, The Classic Years: 1898-1910,* Rizzoli International, 1986; Gloria Lieberman, "Artistic Adornment, Arts and Crafts Jewelry," in *Antiques & Fine Art,* May/June 1990; Don Marek, "Light and Line: The Art of Forest Emerson Mann," in *Arts & Crafts Quarterly,* Vol. VI, No. 3; Kevin McConnell, *Heintz Art*

Metal, Schiffer Publishing, 1990; Joseph Sataloff, *Art Nouveau Jewelry*, Dorrance & Co., 1984; Ulrike von Hase-Schmundt et al., *Theodor Fahrner Jewelry, between Avant-Garde and Tradition*, Schiffer Publishing, 1991; Janet Zapata, *The Jewelry and Enamels of Louis Comfort Tiffany*, Harry N. Abrams, 1993.

Periodicals: *Arts & Crafts Quarterly*, 9 South Main Street, Lambertville, N.J. 08530; *Fine Early 20th Century American Craftsman Silver, Jewelry & Metal* (semiannual catalog with prices), ARK Antiques, Box 3133, New Haven, Conn. 06515.

Museums: British Arts and Crafts jewelry: Birmingham Museums and Art Gallery, Birmingham, The Fitzwilliam Museum, Cambridge, and The Victoria and Albert Museum, London, England. The Schmuckmuseum (Jewelry Museum) in Pforzheim, Germany has an extensive collection, including examples of both German and Austrian *Jugendstil*. Museum of Fine Arts, Boston, Mass. American Arts and Crafts jewelry.

Advisors: Rosalie and Aram Berberian (American), Gail Gerretsen, Terrance O'Halloran (British), Janet Zapata (American).

Bracelet
  Bangle
    Silver, carnelian, c. 1910-15, hammered surface with six appl semicirc looped bands of silver alternating with round cab carnelians set in ropetwist framed bezels, unmkd, 2-5/8" dia, 1" w **250**
  Bangle, hinged
    Sterling, turq, c. 1915-20, smooth silver with oval turq in matrix cab flanked by cutout and pierced stylized lotus motifs, slot and tab clasp, rev mkd "sterling," 2-1/2" dia, 1" w **450**
  Cuff
    Silver, agate, c. 1915-20, cutout foliate design, hammered surface with incised veining on leaves with shaped and curved tips, pierced center band, tapering to the back, lg round brown and turq agate cab bezel-set in the center within a beaded frame, 2-1/4" dia, 1-1/4" w **250**
  Cuff, wraparound
    800 silver, c. 1910-20, hand hammered with a thin repoussé line outlining the shape, tapering outward from the back to wide opposed curv cusped ends with domed centers in front, mkd "800," "Handarb" (abbrev for *handarbeit*, Ger for handwrought), maker's mark, #24, 2-3/8" dia, 3" top to bottom in front, tapering to 1-1/8" in back **275**
  Link
    Gp sterling, dyed agate, c. 1910-20, bezel-set blue cab agate links alternating with rounded rect links of gp ster with raised appl oak leaf and acorn motifs, spring ring clasp, 6-3/4" tl × 5/8" **350**
    Opals, pearls, 18k yg, c. 1925, oval plaques

collet-set with opal doublets alternating with round blister pearls set within yg foliate mounts, box clasp with v-spring sgd "Oakes" within an oak leaf for Edward Everett Oakes, 6-1/2" tl × 1/2" . . . **4,070 (A)**
    Star sapphires, citrines, peridots, white sapphires, 14k yg, c. 1910-1920, gemstone-set flowerhead links, lg central link flanked by smaller links, centers of bezel-set round star sapphires surrounded by smaller oval faceted gemstones as petals, mkd· "14k," 7" tl × 7/8" **3,650**
    Sterling, baroque pearl, black onyx, c. 1910-20, central oval plaque with collet-set oval black onyx surmounted by a collet-set baroque pearl flanked by silver floral and scrolled vine motifs, continuing to oval hammered links joined with flat oval jump rings, spring ring clasp, Am, mkd "W.N. Brooks," 7-1/4" tl × 5/8" **325**
    Sterling, c. 1930, five engr and repoussé quatrefoils joined with flat oval jump rings, oval box clasp, safety chain, mkd "Kalo Hand Wrought Sterling" on clasp rev, 7" tl × 1" . . . . **495 (A)**
    Sterling, c. 1930, three flowerheads alternating with three vine and berry motifs, engr and repoussé, joined with flat oval jump rings, oval box clasp, safety chain, mkd "Kalo Hand Wrought Sterling" on clasp rev, 7" tl × 1-1/2" . . . . **550 (A)**
    Yg, c. 1915-20, 11 hollow domed cushion shapes, linked with pairs of jump rings, the top surfaces covered with appl heart-shaped leaves, scrolls and sm flowerheads, v-spring and box clasp, sgd "F.G. Hale" for Frank Gardner Hale, medalist of the Boston Society of Arts and Crafts, 7-1/4" tl × 1/2" **4,900**
Brooch/Pendant
    Silver, green stone (quartz), c. 1900, pierced and engr kidney-shaped plaque with three lg round green cabs bezel-set in a triangular pattern, suspending another round green cab from a cable-link chain, C-catch, flanged hinge, swiveling pendant bail, 1-3/4" w × 1-7/8" tl **325**
Brooch/Pin
    14k yg, citrine, pearls, c. 1910, lozenge-shaped frame with an oval faceted citrine in the center, flanked by an openwork yg leaf and vine design set with sm golden-toned pearls, 2" w × 1/2" . . . . **330 (A)**
    800 silver, amethyst, enamel, rose gold, c. 1900, highly stylized winged insect design, cutout scrolled antennae, pierced tapering body, central oval faceted amethyst set in millegrained bezel, flanked by lavender enameled wings, two rose gold spots below, mkd "800 MM," Ger or Austrian, C-catch, flanged hinge, extended pinstem, 1-3/8" w × 5/8" **400**
    900 silver, amber, c. 1910, oval repoussé de-

Brooches/Pins, Eng, Charles Horner, sterling, enamel:
T, date letter for 1909, blue/green enameled segments at the base of a foliate design within a pierced oval, mkd "CH," Chester hmks, C-catch, 1-$\frac{1}{8}$" × $\frac{7}{8}$", $285; B, c. 1910, winged scarab motif, blue/green enamel on body and wings, mkd "CH," Chester hmks, date letter illegible, C-catch, tube hinge, 1-$\frac{3}{4}$" × $\frac{3}{4}$", $295. *Charles Pinkham collection.*

Patinated brass, c. 1910-15, repoussé rect plaque with hammered edge, acid-etched abstract free-form design in the center, unmkd, pinned to a piece of leather, in orig box mkd "Forest Craft Guild," wide C-catch, flanged hinge, 2-$\frac{3}{4}$" w × 1-$\frac{1}{2}$" **225**

Patinated brass, c. 1910, hammered convex rect plaque, acid-etched grapes and grapevine motif, green patinated bg, rev mkd "Frost" in a triangle for George W. Frost, Dayton, Oh., wide C-catch, flanged hinge, 2-$\frac{3}{8}$" w × 1-$\frac{3}{4}$" **295**

Pearls, diamonds, 14k yg, c. 1920, grapevine motif with lg and sm pearls and diamonds set among yg leaves and tendrils within a rect frame, attributed to Edward Everett Oakes, medalist of the Boston Society of Arts and Crafts, 1-$\frac{3}{4}$" w × 1-$\frac{1}{8}$" . . . . **7,150 (A)**

Silver, opals, enamel, c. 1901, rounded triangular plaque with pierced and cutout center flanked by two oval opals, blue and green enamel in recessed surfaces around a central raised flame-shaped design, suspending an

Brooches/Pins, Eng, c. 1900, Ruskin Pottery (founded by Wm. Howson Taylor in 1898, inspired by, but not related to, John Ruskin): three oval convex mottled turq green plaques of glazed ceramic set in plain brass bezels, C-catches, tube hinges, one rev mkd "Ruskin Pottery," 1-$\frac{7}{8}$" × $\frac{7}{8}$", another mkd "Ruskin," 1-$\frac{1}{2}$" × 1-$\frac{1}{8}$", third unmkd, 1-$\frac{3}{4}$" × $\frac{7}{8}$", each, $175. *Photo courtesy of Butterfield & Butterfield, Los Angeles.*

sign of a lg flowerhead with its center a bezel-set oval orange amber cab in a ropetwist wire frame, flanked by a lg foliate motif on one side, a row of beading on the other, pierced side, rev mkd "Handgetriebeit [hand-raised], AM 900" around octagonal mk for Adolf Meyer, Frankfurt, Germany, C-catch, 2-$\frac{1}{8}$" w × 1-$\frac{3}{4}$" **225**

900 silver, c. 1900, hammered convex rect, repoussé sailing ship motif, beaded border, rev mkd "handarbeit [handwrought] 900," Ger hmks, trombone catch, flanged hinge, 2-$\frac{1}{8}$" w × 1-$\frac{3}{8}$" **275**

Boulder opals, yg, c. 1910, elongated oval yg frame strung with opal beads suspending a larger opal bead from chain, 1-$\frac{3}{4}$" w × 1-$\frac{1}{2}$" . . . . **330 (A)**

Brass, glass, c. 1910, hand hammered, convex six-sided shield shape, oval coral-colored glass cab bezel-set in the center surrounded by an acid-etched freeform design, rev mkd "Forest Craft Guild" (Grand Rapids, Mich.), wide C-catch, flanged hinge, 2-$\frac{5}{8}$" w × 1-$\frac{1}{2}$" **250**

Brass, glass, c. 1910, hand-hammered six-sided convex shield shape with round coral-colored glass cab bezel-set in center, acid-etched geo design, unsgd, attributed to Forest Craft Guild, wide C-catch, flanged hinge, 2-$\frac{3}{8}$" w × 1-$\frac{3}{4}$" **195**

Brooches/Pins, Ger, Theodor Fahrner, c. 1910-14: T, heart-shaped leaves and vine design with three millegrained collet-set citrines between and above each leaf, rev mkd "TF" in a circle, "935," C-catch, 1-³/₄" × 1", $800, *Gail Gerretsen collection;* B, domed oval with cutout and appl foliate, floral motifs and scrolled wire, oval green chalcedony and MOP bezel-set at top center and right, rev mkd "TF" in a circle, "800," 2" × 1-¹/₄", $1,000, *Terrance O'Halloran collection.*

oval opal drop, designed by Georg Kleemann, rev mkd "TF" for Theodor Fahrner (Ger), 1" × 1" tl . . . . **633 (A)**

Silver, enamel, c. 1900-10, disk with mottled blue, green, and purple enameled center encircled by sm raised quatrefoils within a beaded edge, C-catch, tube hinge, 1-¹/₂" dia **150**

Silver, European, c. 1910, horizontal whiplash curv design forming three irregularly shaped openings, sm round cab garnet collet-set in center opening, suspending teardrop cab garnet, rev mkd "800," C-catch, 1-¹/₂" × 1" **345**

Silver, European, c. 1920, open tapered rect with horizontal center bar, rect cab agate bezel-set in center, flanked by vertical cross bars, unmkd, C-catch, 1-³/₄" × ⁷/₈" **135**

Sterling, jade (nephrite), c. 1915-20, modified lozenge shape, oval green nephrite cab flanked by die-stamped raised stemmed foliate motifs, hammered surface, flat backing, mkd "sterling," and "S" bisected by an arrow for Spies Bros., Chicago, IL, safety catch, 1-³/₈" w × ⁵/₈" **95**

Sterling, c. 1930, cutout, pierced, repoussé, and engr oval with stylized foliate design of two lg leaves and two buds with scrolled vines, rev mkd "Handwrought Sterling Kalo," safety catch, 2-¹/₄" w × 1-³/₄" **400**

Sterling, moonstone, c. 1940, pierced and cut out, slightly convex irregular oval, a round moonstone in the center of a sm stylized flowerhead on one side, trailing curv polished ribbons with looped ends forming the rest of the brooch, rev mkd "Handwrought Sterling Kalo," safety catch, 3" w × 1-³/₄" **450**

Brooches/Pins, 900 silver, enamel, c. 1905: oval plaques with raised stylized mouse motif on recessed textured surface, one (L) filled with dk blue *champlevé* enamel, rev imp with superimposed "WW" for Wiener Werkstätte (Austria), design by Koloman Moser, enclosed C-catch, tube hinge, 1-¹/₈" × ⁷/₈", enameled, $1,800, plain, $1,500. *Terrance O'Halloran collection.*

Brooch/Pin, c. 1900, bezel-set scarab beetle in the center of a winged motif of sawn, pierced, engr and stippled patinated copper, maker's mark "JC," C-catch; 1-⁷/₈" × 1", $150. *Joyce Albers collection.*

Brooches/Pins, Am, c. 1910: T, hammered and raised copper disk with round translucent green glass cab bezel-set in recessed center, acid-etched design, rev stamped "Forest Craft Guild" (Grand Rapids, Mich.), wide C-catch, flanged hinge, 2-¹/₂" dia, $235; C, hammered and raised brass triangle with round green glass cab bezel-set in center, surrounded by an acid-etched design resembling Oriental calligraphy, rev stamped "Forest Craft Guild," wide C-catch, flanged hinge, 3" × 1-⁷/₈", $235; B, hammered and raised brass shield or scarab shape with acid-etched geo design, appl metal plate on rev imp "Made In Our Craft Shop Marshall Field & Co." (Chicago), wide C-catch, flanged hinge, 2" × 2-¹/₄", $250. *Gail Gerretsen collection.*

Sterling, enamel, date letter for 1907, sm Tudor rose shape with red and green enamel center, mkd "RC," Birmingham (Eng) hmks, C-catch, ³/₄" dia **45**

Thomsonite, oxidized wm, c. 1900, oval cab thomsonite bezel-set in irregularly shaped recessed center, cutout foliate motifs at each end, Am, rev mkd "W," C-catch, 2-¹/₄" w × ¹/₂" **200**

Thomsonite, patinated copper, c. 1900, one lg, one sm, oval cab thomsonite, bezel-set in a tapering shield-shaped plaque with pierced center, appl foliate design flanking lg cab, Am, rev mkd "W," C-catch, 2-⁵/₈" w × 1-¹/₂" **250**

Tourmaline, pearls, green gold, c. 1930, lg bezel-set rect-cut green tourmaline flanked by gold foliate and scroll motifs interspersed with collet-set pearls and seed pearls, attributed to Edward Everett Oakes, 1-¹/₂" w × ⁵/₈" **3,800**

Wm, ceramic, c. 1917-20, hammered disk surmounted by smooth sq with riveted corners, circ dk pink ceramic disk mounted in center (probably Ruskin pottery), rev mkd

"Rd 662862 [1917 British registry no.] S & Co. Platondor," Eng, 1-¹/₂" dia **250**

Bar

15k yg, moonstones, c. 1900, a central lg oval moonstone flanked by yg grape clusters and leaves, a smaller oval moonstone at each end, within a yg beaded wirework frame, 2-¹/₂" w × ⁵/₈" . . . . **605 (A)**

800 silver, glass, c. 1910, slightly curv rounded-end bar with cutout center sections, round blue glass cab at one end set behind circ cutout cage, rev mkd "800 silver," C-catch, 2-¹/₂" w × ¹/₂" **100**

Brass, c. 1910, convex tapered and cusped bar with acid-etched floral motifs and oxidized incised outlines on hammered ground, appl metal plate on .rev imp "Made In Our Craft Shop Marshall Field & Co." (Chicago), safety catch, 2-⁵/₈" w × ⁷/₈" **185**

Copper, c. 1900, acid-etched landscape design with two trees and mountains, unmkd, C-catch, 2-¹/₄" w × ¹/₂" **85**

Hammered brass, c. 1910, geo design of brackets and squares within a recessed

Brooches/Pins, Am, attributed to Edward Everett Oakes, Medalist of the Boston Society of Arts & Crafts, c. 1925: L, bezel-set oval faceted citrine flanked by clusters of sm yg flowerheads and beading, 1-1/4" × 1/2", $1,500; C, oval 14k green-gold frame with a half pearl center flanked by domed and chased three-lobed leaves, 1-1/4" × 1/2", $1,200; R, bezel-set rect faceted smoky quartz flanked by a tapering yg flower and scroll design, 1-1/4" × 1/2", $1,350, *Photo courtesy of ARK Antiques, New Haven, Conn.*

Brooch/Pin, bar, lapis lazuli, 18k yg, c. 1920, three oval lapis cabs set within a yg mount of grapes and grape leaves motifs, sgd "Tiffany & Co." on appl plaque, mkd "18k," attributed to Louis Comfort Tiffany, 3-1/4" w × 1", $4,400 (A). *Photo courtesy of Skinner, Inc. (9/21/93).*

Brooches/Pins, Am, c. 1910, attributed to Heintz Art Metal Shop, Buffalo, NY: T, sm freeform copper leaf shape, ster overlay border and scroll design, unsgd, C-catch, 1" × 1/2", $65, *Gail Gerretsen collection;* T-B, 2, convex shaped copper bar tapering to cusped ends, ster overlay border, geo and scroll design, unsgd, C-catch, 2-1/4" × 3/8", $85, *Author's collection;* T-B, 3, rect bronze plaque, ster overlay in scroll and trefoil design, unsgd, wide C-catch, 3-1/8" × 1-3/8", $175; T-B, 4, Watch fob, convex bronze rect plaque, ster border and overlaid narrow rect with cutout design of two candles, suspended from tapered bronze and sterling plaque with levered clasp on rev for attachment to clothing, mkd "sterling" on front, 3-3/4" tl × 1-1/4", $250, *Gail Gerretsen collection.*

acid-etched and patinated center, mkd with perpendicular overlapping C's for Carence Crafters, Chicago, C-catch, 3" × 1/2", ... **175**

Patinated brass, glass, c. 1910-15, hammered and repoussé rect with a bezel-set round coral-colored glass cab in the center, unmkd, pinned to a piece of leather, in orig box mkd "Forest Craft Guild" (Grand Rapids, Mich.), C-catch, flanged hinge, 1-1/8" w × 1/2" **125**

Sterling, glass, c. 1910, hammered convex rect bar with sq blue glass cab bezel-set in center, rev mkd "M" in a lozenge, "sterling," 2-1/4" w × 3/8" **95**

Bouquet pin

Bronze, sterling, c. 1910, bowed-out bronze bar with sterling overlay in a zigzag design with vertical crossbars, spike protruding from center rev for securing flower bouquet, unsgd, attributed to Heintz Art Metal Shop, Buffalo, N.Y., C-catch, 3-$\frac{1}{2}$" w × $\frac{1}{4}$", 1" center front to pinstem **110**

Sash ornament

Gp, patinated copper, glass, c. 1910, lobed rect plaque with four triangular Greek meander motifs at hammered corners, an oval mottled green and rust-colored glass cab bezel-set in the center, flanked by cutout leaf shapes and surrounded by six sm raised spade-shaped Greek meander motifs, rev mkd "Grecian copper," maker's mark, Am, wide C-catch, flanged hinge, 3" w × 2-$\frac{1}{8}$" **125**

Patinated brass, c. 1910, rect plaque with central acid-etched foliate design on hammered ground, unmkd, pinned to a sq piece of leather in orig box mkd "Forest Craft Guild" (Grand Rapids, Mich.), wide C-catch, flanged hinge, 2-$\frac{3}{4}$" w × 2-$\frac{1}{4}$" **275**

Patinated copper, glass, c. 1910, rounded lozenge-shaped plaque with raised and indented corners, appl pierced navette-shaped Celtic motif in the open cutout center, flanked by a bezel-set lg round green glass cab on one side, a raised Billiken motif on the other, on an acid-etched abstract pattern ground, appl disk on rev mkd "Trade Mark Billiken" around imp Billiken mk (elfin character originally designed and patented by Florence Pretz, trademarked by The Craftsman's Guild of Chicago, 1908), wide C-catch, flanged hinge, 3" w × 2-$\frac{1}{8}$" **150**

Brooches/Pins

Sterling, c. 1930, masks of comedy and tragedy, cutout, repoussé and chased, mkd "sterling Kalo," each 1" w × 1-$\frac{1}{2}$", pr **350**

Handy pins

Bronze, sterling, c. 1910, sm bar pins with sq terminals, sterling overlay border, attached to orig card mkd "Sterling on Bronze, Handmade," logo for Heintz Art Metal Shop (mono HAMS within a lozenge), in orig box, C-catches, 1" w × $\frac{1}{4}$", pr **95**

Buckle

Copper, c. 1900-10, one-pc, lg rect plaque with hand-hammered and raised asymmetrical vine and floral design, appl hook and loop for belt attachment on rev, 3-$\frac{7}{8}$" w × 2-$\frac{1}{4}$" **225**

Copper, enamel, c. 1900-10, two-piece, convex rounded triangles, with *basse-taille* enameled yellow-orange centers and alternating red and green sqs above, hook and

Buckle, sterling, enamel, date letter for 1906, two-piece curv stylized lotus design, hammered surface with recessed areas filled with blue-green *champlevé* enamel, rev mkd "L & Co." in lozenges for Liberty & Co., "22," Birmingham (Eng) hmks, 3-$\frac{3}{8}$" × 2-$\frac{1}{8}$", $750. Terrance O'Halloran collection.

eye, bars for belt attachment on rev, 2-$\frac{1}{2}$" w × 1-$\frac{3}{4}$" **275**

Patinated brass, c. 1910, one-pc, hammered convex rect with acid-etched design of trefoils within triangles, green patinated ground, appl hook and bar for belt attachment on rev, mkd "Forest Craft Guild," 2-$\frac{7}{8}$" w × 2" **275**

Sterling, c. 1900, one-pc, open oval composed of two lg and 10 sm circ knots of partly chased heavy-gauge wire joined at the sides, triple hasp in open center, mk for Gorham & Co. (lion, anchor, Gothic G), 2-$\frac{1}{2}$" w × 3-$\frac{1}{2}$" **375**

Yg, c. 1900, one-pc, slightly convex rect with curved sides, rect cutout center with hasp, hammered surface with appl riveted strapwork design, bar for belt attachment on rev, 2-$\frac{1}{4}$" w × 1-$\frac{1}{2}$" **650**

Chain

Silver, enamel, c. 1900-10, longchain, handmade cable links interspersed with six two-sided tapered rect plaques with lavender enameled centers surrounded by bead and spiral design, terminating in a swivel hook, 62" tl, plaques 1-$\frac{1}{4}$" × $\frac{3}{8}$" **1,200**

Silver, onyx, c. 1900-10, paper clip longchain linked to two pierced navette-shaped plaques set with dyed green cab onyx, 50" tl . . . . **605 (A)**

Sterling, c. 1910, paper clip longchain, six slightly tapered rect plaques with overlaid cutout double arrow shapes, evenly spaced three to a side, one plaque mkd "Kalo Sterling," terminating in a spring ring, 55" tl, plaques 1-$\frac{1}{4}$" × $\frac{1}{2}$" **750**

Sterling, c. 1920, alternating wide flat oval and round wire links, simple hook clasp, adjoining link mkd "Kalo Sterling 12," 24-$\frac{1}{2}$" tl **700**

Cuff links

Enamel, silver, c. 1900, handmade from but-

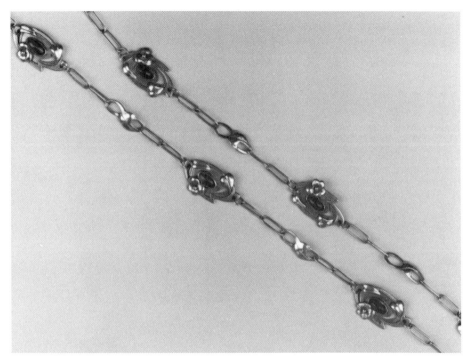

Chain, yg, c. 1900-10, paperclip longchain interspersed with oval cab citrines set in stylized floral and foliate yg plaques, 30 dwt, 44" tl, $3,300 (A). *Photo courtesy of Skinner, Inc. (3/14/93).*

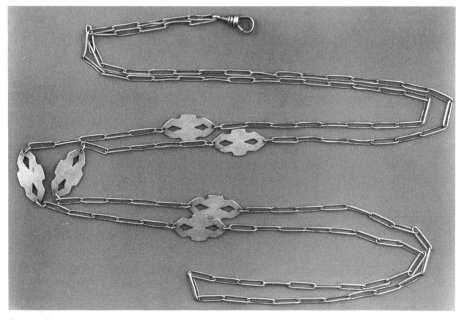

Chain, sterling, Am, c. 1910, paperclip longchain with six cutout and pierced lozenge-shaped plaques evenly spaced three to a side, one plaque mkd "Kalo Sterling," terminating in a swivel hook, 56" tl, plaques 1" × ½", $750. *Gail Gerretsen collection.*

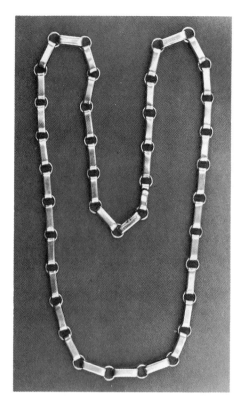

Chain, sterling, Am, c. 1920, alternating wide flat oval and round wire links, simple hook clasp, adjoining link mkd "Kalo Sterling 12," 24-½" tl, $700. _Gail Gerretsen collection._

Cuff links, sterling, c. 1901, dumbbell-type link, sterling disks with raised hammered centers encircled by a floral and foliate design in lilac and green _champlevé_ enamel, shank mkd "TF" in a circle for Theodor Fahrner (Ger), "935," ¾" dia, pr, $650. _Photo courtesy of Butterfield & Butterfield, Los Angeles._

tons, circ, turq, green, and white _cloisonné_ swirled design, Eng, 1-⅛" dia, pr **250**

Thomsonite, oxidized wm, c. 1900, dumbbell-type link, oval with cutout foliate motif, oval cab thomsonite (stone cracked) bezel-set in centers, curved stem terminating in plain oval button, Am, mkd "W" on rev, 1-¼" × ½", pr **125**

Earrings

Sterling, moonstones, c. 1930-40, button style, with three round moonstones bezel-set in a triangular pattern flanked by domed ster disks and beads, combination screwback/clip findings (altered), ⅞" dia, pr **200**

Earrings, pendent

14k yg, turquoise, seed pearls, c. 1910-20, elongated teardrop-shaped yg plaque with feather motif design, bezel-set with an oval turq below a vertical row of three seed pearls, suspended from a sq surmount bezel-set with a sq turq, screwback findings, rev mkd "14 A" within a stemmed trefoil (clover leaf) for Alling & Co., Newark NJ, ½" w × 1-½" tl, pr **975**

Hatpin

German silver (wm), c. 1910, irregular convex oval disk with an acid-etched stylized five-petal flower in the center, mk for Carence Crafters, Chicago (perpendicular overlapping Cs) on rev, head 1-¼" × 1", 10" tl **195**

Patinated copper, c. 1900-10, lg rust-colored convex sq, cutout bg designs with appl flowerhead and cattail motifs in red and green, 2-⅛" sq, 8" tl **185**

Silver, enamel, 1907 registry no, vinaigrette/perfume holder, hollow silver ball surmounted by appl Tudor rose motif with blue and green enamel, pierced holes to allow scent to escape, Eng, mkd "WJH Silver, Rd 507468," head ⅞" × 1", 7-½" tl . . . **1,100**

Sterling, enamel, blister pearl, date letter for 1912, circ with raised beaded edge (stamped), blue and green _basse-taille_ enamel with collet-set blister pearl center, rope twist ster border, mkd "C.H." for Charles Horner, Chester (Eng) hmks, swiveling head 1" dia, 9-¼" tl **250**

Sterling, enamel, date letter for 1909, Tudor rose motif, turq enameled petals, hinged head, mkd "JF" for James Fenton, Birmingham (Eng) hmks, 1-⅛" dia, 10-¼" tl **200**

Sterling, copper, c. 1906, head in the shape of a mortarboard with tassel, appl copper numbers "06" on flat top, mkd "Sterling pat apld for," accompanied by documented provenance in a typed note: "Graduation gift given me when I graduated in piano at Lexington College at Lexington Mo in 1906, Lavinia St. Clair," head ⅞" × ⅝", 8" tl **100**

Sterling, c. 1915, head in the shape of a golf club iron, (mashie), mkd "Alvin" for Alvin Silver Co. (now a division of Gorham), 1" × ¾" × 1-¾", 9-¼" tl **80**

Sterling, c. 1910, head in the shape of a golf

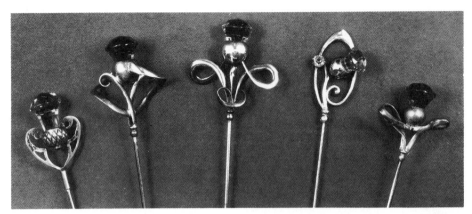

Hatpins, sterling, glass, Eng, c. 1907-11: L-R, 1, date letter for 1908, thistle motif with amber-colored faceted glass center, within pierced and scrolled ster heart shape, mkd "P&T" for Pearce & Thompson, Birmingham hmks, head $^{7}/_{8}$" × 1-$^{1}/_{8}$", 7-$^{1}/_{4}$" tl, $165; L-R, 2, date letter for 1911, scrolled and twisted flattened sterling wire encircling thistle motif with purple faceted glass center, mkd "C.H." for Charles Horner, Chester hmks, head 1" × 1-$^{1}/_{4}$", $185; L-R, 3, date letter for 1910, thistle motif with amber-colored faceted glass center, flanked by double twisted loops, mkd "C.H." for Charles Horner, Chester hmks, head 1-$^{1}/_{4}$" × 1-$^{3}/_{8}$", 10" tl, $185; L-R, 4, date letter for 1907, thistle motif with amber-colored faceted glass center mounted on branched stem, prong-set round amber-colored faceted glass on the other branch, within a scrolled and cusped oval sterling loop, mkd "C.H." for Charles Horner, Chester hmks, head 1-$^{3}/_{8}$" × $^{3}/_{4}$", $175; L-R, 5, c. 1910, thistle motif with purple faceted glass center, surmounting four twisted loops of flattened ster wire, mkd "C.H." for Charles Horner, Chester hmks, date letter illegible, $165. *Milly Combs collection.*

Hatpins, Am, c. 1900-10: L, patinated brass rect with acid-etched design of a tree, hammered edge, rev mkd "Frost" in a triangle for George Winfield Frost, Dayton OH, 1-$^{3}/_{8}$" × 1-$^{5}/_{8}$", 10" tl, $150; R, irregular six-sided polygon of hammered brass with an acid-etched design, mottled lt blue and brown glass cab bezel-set in the center, rev mkd "Frost" in a triangle, 1-$^{1}/_{2}$" × 1-$^{1}/_{4}$", 9" tl, $150; BC, circ freeform brass head with freeform cutout swirls and raised hobnail design, round peacock-eye glass cab bezel-set off-center, rev mkd "Forest Craft Guild" (Grand Rapids, Mich.), 1-$^{3}/_{8}$" dia, 10" tl , $175, *Milly Combs collection;* TC, sq head with acid-etched abstract Oriental design on a hammered surface, crimped border, green patinated bg, 1" sq, 10" tl, $135, *Terrance O'Halloran collection.*

Locket and Chain, sterling, c. 1930-40, oval locket with engr acorn and leaf design, beaded edge, mkd "Sterling Kalo 8" on bottom outside edge, suspended from a chain of stylized flower links alternating with elongated flat links, mkd "Kalo Sterling 25," terminating in a spring ring front clasp, 24" tl, locket 1-⁵/₈" w × 2-³/₄", $1,600. Gail Gerretsen collection.

club driver (woody) with golf scene stamped in relief on top surface, ⁷/₈" × ¹/₂" × 1-⁷/₈", 8-³/₄" tl **115**

Sterling, c. 1910, hollow bead (one side dented) surmounted by stamped flame or plume motif, mkd "C.H. 925" for Charles Horner, ³/₈" × ³/₄", 7" tl **65**

Sterling, date letter for 1908, sword hilt motif, handle mkd "C.H." for Charles Horner, Chester (Eng) hmks, head ³/₄" × 1-¹/₄", 9" tl **95**

Sterling, c. 1910, open inverted heart shape, slightly twisted, with center loop mkd "Sterling" and "C.H." for Charles Horner, head ¹/₂" × ⁵/₈", 6-¹/₂" tl **75**

Necklace

14k green gold, tourmalines, c. 1900-10, three geo plaques with sq cut green tourmalines in millegrained mounts flanked by appl scroll and foliate motifs, alternating with four smaller plaques with appl scroll and foliate

motifs, joined to a fancy link chain, European, mkd "585" and maker's mark, spring ring clasp, 16-¹/₂" tl × ³/₈" **800**

950 silver, enamel, c. 1910, central six-sided plaque with two lg flowerheads within looped vines, on a blue-green enameled ground, suspending a tapered swirl enameled pendent drop, suspended at the top from two double cable-link chains each joined to a triangular Celtic knot with blue-green enamel center, continuing to a single cable-link chain, rev mkd "MB" for Murrle, Bennett & Co., Eng, 17" tl, center plaque 1-¹/₈" w × 1-¹/₂" tl with drop **850**

Turquoise, 14k yg, c. 1915, a lg oval turq cab, flanked by two smaller oval cabs set in millegrained bezels within plain yg frames joined with baton links and continuing to a cable link chain, the center cab with a cutout yg Greek meander motif at the base suspending a similarly set oval cab linked to a pear-shaped turq drop and flanked by two pear-shaped turq drops, 26" tl, center 4" top to bottom × 1-³/₈" w . . . . **1,210 (A)**

Yg, amethysts, c. 1910-15, nine grad shield-shaped pendent drops of pierced scroll and foliate design, each set with a teardrop-shaped faceted amethyst, suspended from an oval and circ link yg chain, lgest drop sgd "F.G. Hale" for Frank Gardner Hale, medalist of the Boston Society of Arts and Crafts, 15" tl . . . . **3,850 (A)**

Necklace, sterling, freshwater pearls, blister pearls, c. 1910, paperclip chain suspending five pierced and raised lobed plaques with collet-set blister pearls in the centers, alternating with six f.w. pearls, spring ring clasp, 17" tl, plaques ⁵/₈" × ⁷/₈", $750. Terrance O'Halloran collection.

Necklace, sterling, carnelian, c. 1920, slightly convex hammered oval linked plaques suspending an asymmetrical oval pendant with a cutout and appl abstract design, bezel-set with an oval cab carnelian, mkd "Sterling Handmade," mk for Art Silver Shop (superimposed A over T, flanked by two Ss), Chicago, 14-1/2" tl, pendant 1-5/8" × 1", $500. *Gail Gerretsen collection.*

Necklace, silver, MOP, pearls, enamel, sapphires, c. 1900, cable-link chain set at intervals with rect and oval enameled collets in shades of blue and yellow, suspended from waisted enameled plaque with baroque pearl drop and two chains suspending a double dragon motif surrounding an oval MOP drop, terminating in three collet-set oval faceted sapphires and linked baroque pearls, 13" tl, 1-1/4" × 2-3/4", $2,875 (A). *Photo courtesy of Christie's New York (4/22/93).*

Festoon
Silver, amethyst, c. 1900, central oval plaque with stylized foliate, vine and bead motifs, oval cab amethyst bezel-set in center, foliate and bead motif pendent drop and two side plaques joined by double swagged chains and beaded links continuing to a single chain, 16-1/2" tl × 2" . . . **475**
Pendant
14k yg, rhodolite garnets, seed pearls, diamonds, c. 1915, three lg cushion-shaped faceted garnets collet-set in an inverted triangle formation in the center of an openwork shield-shaped yg pendant with pierced scrolls and cutout foliate motifs, set with seed pearls and sm diamonds, attributed to Frank Gardner Hale, 1-1/4" w × 1-3/4" . . . **7,700 (A)**
Silver, gp silver, turq, f.w. pearl, c. 1900-15, oval turq with matrix framed by cast grapevine design, gp leaves, suspending f.w. pearl drop, 1-5/8" w × 1-3/4" tl **450**
Silver, enamel, seed pearls, baroque pearls, c. 1900-15, stylized insect motif with scrolled silver wire antennae, baroque pearl center and pendent drop, mottled red enameled body, suspended from double chain of seed pearls joined to bail, 3" tl × 1-1/2" **475**

Sterling, enamel, date letter for 1903, die-stamped circ Tudor rose motif, recessed areas filled with translucent green enamel, rev mkd "P&S" for Pearce & Sons, Birmingham (Eng) hmks, 1" dia **75**
Sterling, MOP, c. 1910, vasiform plaque, with elongated oval iridescent blue-green MOP bezel-set within appl curv foliate and vine design, surmounted by two sm three-petaled flowerheads, rev mkd "Sterling Hand Made," 2-3/8" tl × 1" **1,200**
Wm, enamel, date letter for 1909, pink, blue, and green enameled shield shape surmounted by three flowerheads, rev mkd "DM&Co.," Birmingham (Eng) hmks, 1" × 1-1/2" **65**
Pendant and Chain
14k yg, opals, enamel, pearls, c. 1910, shield-shaped pendant enameled in shades of green

Pendant, 14k yg, blister pearl, tourmalines, emeralds, c. 1905, heart-shaped pierced scroll and foliate design around a lg central bezel-set pink and green-toned blister pearl with a beaded frame around the bezel, flanked by rect-cut pink tourmalines, sq-cut light green emeralds above and below, beaded pendent drop and accents throughout, sgd "F.G. HALE" for Frank Gardner Hale, Medalist of the Boston Society of Arts & Crafts, 2-½" tl × 1-½", $5,500. *Photo courtesy of ARK Antiques, New Haven, Conn.*

and yellow, surmounted by a tablet shape with a collet-set oval opal in the center, three pearls at the top, one at the bottom, flanked by three horizontal bars of grad lengths, tapering in to scrolled terminals, suspending a collet-set round opal in a tapered-out drop, a flared bail suspended from a chain interspersed with enameled navette-shaped links, chain 26" tl, pendant 2" tl × 1"
. . . . **990 (A)**
Brass, green stone, c. 1900-10, lozenge-shaped metal plaque with curled top and side edges, pierced and textured surface, oval green cab stone set in the center, suspended by two short chains from a smaller-waisted plaque set with a smaller round green cab stone, suspended from chain continuing to a spring ring clasp, 16-½" tl, pendant 2-½" tl × 1-½"
. . . . **245**
Silver, moonstones, c. 1900, pierced quatrefoil silver plaque, open circ center with cross-hatched silver wire surmounted by a cush-

ion-shaped moonstone, terminating in a round moonstone pendent drop, suspended at top corner from double cable-link chains joined to an oval moonstone, continuing to a single cable chain interspersed with six spectacle-set oval moonstones, 18" tl, pendant 3-⅝" tl (including double chain) × 1-¼"
. . . . **1,200**
Silver, enamel, chrysocolla, c. 1900-15, open oval green enameled frame surmounted by appl enameled quatrefoil in turq shading to white, center bezel-set with oval cab chrysocolla, counter enameled, suspended from a paper clip chain linking turq enameled batons, 22" tl × ⅛", pendant 2-½" tl (incl enameled bail), × 1-½" **350**
Sterling, coral, c. 1910, center oval coral cab flanked by arrow-shaped leaf clusters

Pendants and Chains, sterling, *champlevé* **enamel, Eng:** L, date letter for 1908, trefoil shape with interlocking design, dk and lt blue-green enamel, Birmingham hmks, added chain, 1" × ⅞", $195; C, date letter for 1908, handled vase form with scroll design, blue and green enamel in center, cable-link chain joined to an enameled disk, continuing to a double S-hook clasp, rev mkd "CH" for Charles Horner, Chester (Eng) hmks, chain 15-¾" tl, pendant 1-½" × ⅞", $295; R, date letter for 1909, pierced elongated trefoil design, blue and green enamel within a navette-shaped frame, cable-link chain joined to an enameled disk and silver bail continuing to a larger link chain, box clasp, rev mkd "CH" for Charles Horner, Chester hmks, chain 20" tl, pendant ⅞" × 2-½" tl, $295. *Charles Pinkham collection.*

Pendants and Chains, silver, enamel, c. 1910-20: L, sq plaque with repoussé floral design around central cross motif filled with blue-green enamel, suspending a moonstone drop from two chains at bottom corner, suspended from top corner and sides by a double fancy-link chain joined to two moonstones, continuing to a single chain, T-bar clasp, chain 20-1/2" tl, pendant 7/8" sq, 2-1/2" tl, $475; C, flat disk with off-center collet filled with a raised enamel cab in iridescent shades of blue, green, white, suspending three enameled circ pendent drops from chains, suspended from double cable-link chains joined to a single chain, spring ring clasp, 18-1/2" tl, pendant 1-3/8" dia × 2-1/4" tl, $275; R, triangular pendant with chamfered corners, suspended from sm sq plaque by three lg jumprings, raised hammered surfaces enameled in translucent shades of blue, green, yellow, and pink, rev mkd "S&E," illegible Eng hmks, joined to a fine cable-link chain, tube clasp, 16" tl, pendant 1-1/8" × 1-1/2", $475. *Gail Gerretsen collection.*

Pendants and Chains, sterling, c. 1910-15: L, bell-shaped plaque with appl scroll and whiplash curv design surrounding turq colored glass of conforming shape, suspended from bail of stylized lily design, re-placed chain, rev mkd "925," 7/8" × 2", $450; C, vasi-form pierced plaque with appl foliate motifs surrounding a central bezel-set oval cab turq, suspended from a paperclip chain, 28" tl, pendant 1" × 1-5/8", $375; R, coffin-shaped pendant, an oval cab azur-malachite bezel-set in the recessed center, with rect cutout top extending above a raised edge forming atttachment for a paperclip chain, continuing to a T-bar clasp, 15-3/4" tl, pendant 5/8" × 1-3/8", $375. *Gail Gerretsen collection.*

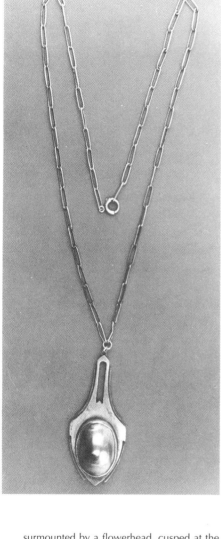

Pendant and Chain, green gold, pearl, diamond, c. 1910, circ grapevine design around a collet-set golden pearl with a collet-set diamond in a pendent drop, suspended from bail and paperclip chain with interspersed grape leaf motifs, and a clasp of two grape leaves, attributed to Josephine Hartwell Shaw, medalist of the Boston Society of Arts & Crafts. Chain 17" tl, pendant 1-½" tl, $3,300. *Photo courtesy of ARK Antiques, New Haven, Conn.*

Pendant and Chain, sterling, blister pearl, c. 1910, cut-out and pierced shield shape tapering to a narrow top, an irregular oval blister pearl collet-set in the center, suspended from a paperclip chain, spring-ring clasp, rev mkd "sterling Kalo," ⅞" × 2", chain 17-½" tl, $950, *Gail Gerretsen collection.*

surmounted by a flowerhead, cusped at the base, suspended from a paperclip chain, sgd "Kalo," 20" tl, pendant 1-⅛" w × 1-⅛" . . . . **1,540 (A)**
Sterling, shell, c. 1910, oval abalone shell surmounted by an appl floral and foliate design, suspended from a paper clip chain, 15" tl, sgd "Kalo," ⅝" × 1-⅛" **$715**
Yg, opals, enamel, diamonds, c. 1910, triangular shape surmounted by a trefoil motif, a lg oval opal in the center within a frame of green and blue enamel, three rc diamonds set at the base, suspending a smaller drop of similar design set with a pear-shaped opal, suspended from a paper-clip chain, 20" tl, pendant ¾" × 2-¾" tl . . . . **2,860 (A)**

Ring
  18k yg, garnets, c. 1915, three oval cab garnets bezel-set within a trefoil-shaped hand-wrought yg wire frame, ¾" × ¾" . . . **330 (A)**
  Sapphires, 14k yg, c. 1925, a round yellow sapphire, 9 mm, collet-set off-center within a yg foliate mount set with sm lt blue sapphires, attributed to Edward Everett Oakes, ¾" × ½" . . . . **2,750 (A)**
  Silver, opal, c. 1900, oval white opal prong-set in pierced shield-shaped mount, pierced shank, ⅝" × ½" **175**
Scarf pin/stickpin
  German silver (wm), c. 1910, triangular-shaped head with acid-etched design of three arrows radiating from the center, ¾" w × 1", 2-⅞" tl **75**

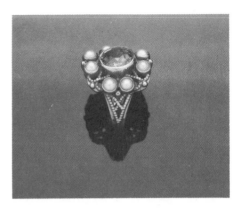

Rings, silver, gemstones, Eng: L, c. 1910, lg open rect with appl scroll, leaf and berry design, six sm cab garnets set among leaves, round moonstone center, shank studded with sm yg disks, in the style of the Gaskins, top ³/₄″ × 1-¹/₄″, $800; R, c. 1915-20, oval carbuncle set in a shaped bezel surrounded by scrolls, gilt leaves, and bezel-set teardrop-shaped rc colorless stones appl to curved rect supporting base, mkd "G.H." for George Hunt, ³/₄″ × ⁵/₈″, $850. *Terrance O'Halloran collection.*

Ring, opal, 14k yg, c. 1910-15, oval boulder opal within an elongated oval floral and foliate yg mount, sgd "Kalo," ³/₄″ × 1-⁵/₈″, $2,640 (A). *Photo courtesy of Skinner, Inc. (3/14/93).*

German silver (wm), c. 1910, arrowhead-shaped head bezel-set with an oval turq cab, engr swastika motif below, ¹/₂″ w × ³/₄″, 2-¹/₂″ tl **85**

14k yg, almandine garnet, c. 1910, oval cab garnet set within horizontal lozenge-shaped yg plaque with scrolled and beaded design, with vertical pierced navette shape below, mkd "14k" with superimposed "TC" for The T.C. Shop, Chicago, ¹/₂″ w × 1″, 3″ tl ... **250**

14k yg, scarab, c. 1915-20, scarab set within stepped and notched yg mount, Am, sgd "Winn" for James H. Winn, Chicago, ¹/₂″ w × ⁷/₈″, 2-³/₄″ tl .... **440 (A)**

Brass, c. 1910, trapezoid-shaped head with acid-etched abstract geo design, green patinated ground, ⁵/₈″ w × ¹/₂″, 2-³/₄″ tl **95**

Sapphire, enamel, 14k gold, c. 1915-20, mushroom-shaped head with center collet-set sap-

Rings, yg, Margaret Rogers, Medalist of the Boston Society of Arts & Crafts: T, sapphire, pearls, 18k, c. 1915, center bezel-set round faceted blue sapphire surrounded by eight collet-set pearls in a quatrefoil pattern, in a yg crisscrossing openwork design with simulated granulation, sgd "MR" (conjoined), approx ⁵/₈″, $4,500; C, lapis lazuli, moonstones, 14k, c. 1910, a lg oval bezel-set lapis cab flanked by yg leaf, scroll, and bead motifs around round moonstones, attributed to Margaret Rogers, approx ³/₄″, $3,250; B, black opal, 18k, c. 1910, lg oval bezel-set black opal flanked by beaded trefoils, sgd "MR" (conjoined), approx ³/₄″, $3,000. *Photos courtesy of ARK Antiques, New Haven, Conn.*

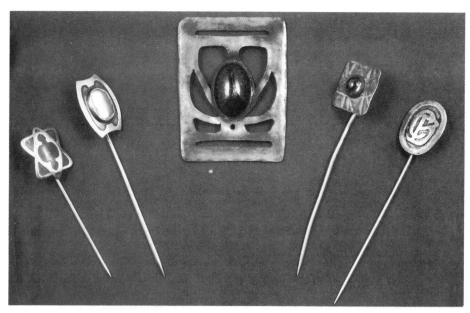

Scarf pins/Stickpins, Am, c. 1900-10: L, six-pointed star shape in copper bordered with silver overlay, cutout silver lozenge in center, unmkd, attributed to Heintz Art Metal Shop, Buffalo, N.Y., ½" w × ¾", 2" tl, $95; L-R, 2, shield-shaped head with a collet-set blister pearl in recessed oxidized center, mkd "sterling," ½" w × ¾", 2-½" tl, $75, *Terrance O'Halloran collection;* C, Watch fob ornament, rect hammered brass plaque with an oval peacock-eye glass cab bezel-set in the center of a cutout stylized flowerhead design, slots for attachment to a leather strap, mkd "Forest Craft Guild," 1-¾" × 1-¼", $300, L-R, 4, acid-etched patinated copper, sq plaque bezel-set with a round peacock eye glass cab, mounted on a brass pin, head ½" sq, 2-⅝" tl, $65, *Milly Combs collection*; R, oval patinated brass acid-etched head with mono "CB" in the center, ½" w × ¾", 2-⅝" tl, $65; *Terrance O'Halloran collection.*

Suite, brooch and earrings, sterling, c. 1930-40, fuchsia motif, brooch mkd "sterling," 1-⅞" × 3", screwback earrings sgd "Clemens Friedell," Pasadena, Calif., ¾" × ⅞", $750. *Charles Pinkham collection.*

phire, blue enamel, in a yg mount, $\frac{1}{2}$" × $\frac{1}{2}$",
2-$\frac{1}{2}$" tl . . . . **220 (A)**
Suite: Pendant, Chain, and Bracelet
  900 silver, enamel, c. 1910-15, rect enameled
  plaque with orange grapes and leaves design
  on red *basse-taille* enameled ground, suspended from a paper clip chain, rev mkd
  "900 Germany," maker's mk a script M
  bisected by a horizontal line, matching link
  bracelet of five enameled plaques joined
  with lg circ wire links. Pendant 1-$\frac{1}{4}$" w ×
  1-$\frac{3}{4}$", chain 21" tl, bracelet 7-$\frac{3}{4}$" tl × $\frac{3}{4}$"
  . . . . **450**

Watch Fob, sterling, black leather, abalone, c. 1910,
shield-shaped, pierced, and repoussé plaque, foliate design surrounding irregular oval abalone collet-set in the
center, mounted on a leather strap with a top bracket
for chain and swivel hook, 3-$\frac{7}{8}$" tl, plaque 1-$\frac{1}{8}$" × 1-$\frac{3}{4}$",
$450. *Gail Gerretsen collection.*

ART NOUVEAU C. 1895-1910

Wm. B. Kerr (America)

Unger Bros. (America)

History: In 1895, Samuel Bing (1838-1905)
converted his Oriental art gallery in Paris into a
gallery for a new style, which gave the style its
name, *L'Art Nouveau.* The Art Nouveau style
caught fire and burned with a passion for a short
while at the turn of the century. Its rise and fall
spanned less than 20 years, but Art Nouveau had
quite an impact on jewelry history. The essence of

Art Nouveau was distilled by the French, but the
ingredients for its heady mix of line and form
came from the British Arts and Crafts movement.
It was the British insistence upon artistic integrity
and individual expression that inspired the
French to break away from constricting, traditional, imitative realism. This may explain the difficulty in determining which elements constitute

which style. The two have much in common: the use of inexpensive gemstones and other materials, enameling, the whiplash curve, motifs taken from nature, and Japanese influence. But something changes in the translation from English to French. French pieces are figural and more three-dimensional and asymmetrical. The female face and body (naked and clothed) are predominant subjects for Art Nouveau interpretation, nearly absent in Arts and Crafts. Other favorite Art Nouveau motifs include dragonflies and butterflies—some with female bodies, writhing snakes, and mythical creatures (chimera). The peacock and peacock feathers have been interpreted by both the British and the French in different ways. Irises, poppies, winged sycamore seeds, waterlilies, and trailing vines are part of the botanical repertoire of Art Nouveau. Arts and Crafts floral and foliate motifs are stylized, and the designs are more abstract and controlled. Art Nouveau motifs have an element of fantasy, with exaggerated lines and sensual overtones. It might be an oversimplification to say that if it's British, it's Arts and Crafts, if it's French, it's Art Nouveau. It would be fair to say, however, that the British retained too much of their Victorian sensibility to embrace Art Nouveau wholeheartedly. The French, on the other hand, were more than willing to take off in Art Nouveau's exuberant and, some say, decadent direction. Other countries followed: Belgium, Spain, and to a lesser extent, Russia. In Germany, Austria, and the United States, both British and French influences were felt.

Although there were many practitioners of the style in France, the work of one man has come to represent everything that Art Nouveau jewelry is about: René Lalique (1860-1945). His life has been well-documented and his work well-preserved (see references below). The few Lalique pieces that have come up for sale in the United States recently are his later, much less elaborate molded and engraved glass plaques. These were made after 1910, when he turned his attention primarily to glassmaking. A student of jewelry history should be familiar with his earlier work, however, because to understand Lalique is to understand Art Nouveau at its finest. Some earlier, circa 1900 Lalique pieces were auctioned in Geneva, Switzerland in 1993.

Other important French Art Nouveau designers and houses include Maison Louis Aucoc, under whom Lalique apprenticed, Georges Fouquet, Lucien Gaillard, Lucien Gautrait, and Vever.

Enameling is one of the most important decorative elements in Art Nouveau jewelry. One of the techniques that Lalique was noted for, and which became closely associated with Art Nouveau, is plique à jour enameling. The usual explanation is that it looks like a stained glass window; a piece has no metal backing and the enamel colors are translucent. Plique à jour is particularly effective when used to depict insect wings (butterflies,

dragonflies) and landscapes with sky and water. It is a difficult technique, and the results are fragile. Intact pieces are scarce.

When an enameled piece does have a backing, or groundplate, there are several other possible techniques, all of which were used in Art Nouveau as well as other styles of jewelry: basse-taille, champlevé, cloisonné, and Limoges or painted enamel are the ones most commonly seen. An explanation of these techniques can be found in the glossary. Basse-taille and champlevé enameled flowers on sterling or brass plaques, resembling miniature paintings, are often found in American Art Nouveau brooches and sash ornaments.

In the United States, Americans were torn between English pragmatism and French chic. While Arts and Crafts jewelry was gaining popularity in Boston, Chicago, and other cities, Newark, New Jersey jewelry makers were turning out pieces influenced by Art Nouveau. In the spirit of American entrepreneurship, the style was commercialized with great if short-lived success, particularly by two Newark silver manufacturers, Wm. B. Kerr and Unger Bros. Both firms were noted for their die-stamped relief designs that imitated repoussé handwork. They are easily recognized and circa-dated. The pieces are backed with flat soldered-on sterling plates that bear the companies' marks. Kerr used a fasces, a bundle of rods bound around a battle-ax; Unger Bros.' mark is its interlaced initials, UB. Typical motifs were women's faces with flowing hair and flowers, particularly poppies, waterlilies, and irises. Kerr was bought out by Gorham in 1906. Unger Bros. stopped making Art Nouveau designs in 1910. Pieces by either firm sell in the $500 to $900 range today. Other manufacturers, some based in Providence, Rhode Island and Attleboro, Massachusetts, produced similar die-stamped jewelry in sterling and silver-plated brass. The quality varies. Inexpensive pieces are usually made from a single thin sheet of unbacked metal.

Several notable Newark manufacturers specialized in gold jewelry in the Art Nouveau style, often enameled and/or set with gemstones: Alling & Co., Carter, Gough & Co., Krementz & Co., Larter & Sons, William Link Co. (also sterling), Riker Bros, and Whiteside & Blank, to name a few. All of their marks, along with notes on the companies' histories, can be found in Dorothy Rainwater's American Jewelry Manufacturers.

In New York City, both Tiffany & Co. and Marcus & Co. produced beautiful enameled and gemstone-set Art Nouveau jewels.

The style itself was a departure from what had gone before, but jewelry forms followed fashion's dictates. Hatpins, haircombs, necklaces and pendants, ornamental plaques de cou for dog collars, brooches, sash ornaments and buckles, and to a lesser extent, bracelets, cuff links, rings, and stickpins, were all interpreted by Art Nouveau designers. Another commonly seen form is sometimes referred to as "medal" jewelry. This was a French idea that was also popular in the United States. It replaced the classic cameo with a medallion in gold or silver of the profile, full face, or torso of a woman or man in repoussé, stamped, or cast relief. Borders and backgrounds were appropriately decorated with undulating vines, leaves, and flowers in the Art Nouveau style. The medallion could be a pendant, locket, brooch, or scarf pin. Less expensive versions were made in gilt base metals.

The commercialization of Art Nouveau also brought about its demise. Perhaps its stylistic excesses, like a rich dessert, became difficult to digest in large quantities. After 1910, relatively little Nouveau jewelry was produced. By 1915, it was completely out of fashion.

References: Lillian Baker, *Art Nouveau & Art Deco Jewelry*, Collector Books, 1981, 1990 value update; Vivienne Becker, *Art Nouveau Jewelry*, E.P. Dutton, 1985 (out of print); Vivienne Becker, *The Jewellery of René Lalique*, exhibition catalog, Goldsmiths' Company, London, 1987; Elyse Zorn Karlin, *Jewelry & Metalwork in the Arts & Crafts Tradition*, Schiffer Publishing, 1993; M. Koch et al., *The Belle Époque of French Jewellery 1850-1910*, Thomas Heneage & Co. Ltd., 1990; Elise Misiorowski and Dona Dirlam, "Art Nouveau: Jewels and Jewelers," in *Gems & Gemology*, Winter 1986; Gabriel Mourey et al., *Art Nouveau Jewellery & Fans*, Dover Publications, 1973 (reprint of *Modern Design in Jewellery and Fans, 1902*); Joseph Sataloff, *Art Nouveau Jewelry*, Dorrance & Co., 1984; Janet Zapata, "The Legacy of Value from Newark Jewelers," in *Jewelers' Circular-Keystone/Heritage*, November 1993.

Museums: The Walters Art Gallery, Baltimore, Md.; Metropolitan Museum, New York, N.Y.; Musée des Arts Décoratifs, Paris, France. The Calouste Gulbenkian Museum in Lisbon, Portugal, houses the René Lalique collection created for its namesake between 1895-1912.

Reproduction Alert: Since the 1960s revival of Art Nouveau, many cast knockoffs of die-stamped period pieces have been made, especially in sterling. The reproduced pieces are solid instead of hollow, and the details are not as sharp. Reproductions of gold and gemstone Nouveau jewels can be cast or stamped, but also lack detail and signs of wear. Enameling is not as skillfully done.

Advisors: Elise Misiorowski, Janet Zapata.

Belt
  Sterling, ribbon, c. 1900, six grad ster plaques of busts of women with flowing hair, joined together at top and bottom by double chains, all attached to a satin ribbon, mk for Wm. B. Kerr Co., Newark N.J. (fasces), 24" tl .... **715 (A)**
Bracelet
  Bangle, hinged
    14k yg, diamonds, c. 1900, central lily motif

set with diamonds, approx .45 ct. tw, flanked by smaller diamonds within foliate motifs, tapering to a narrow stem, flanked by knife-edge flattened wire forming the bangle, 20.7 dwt, 3-1/4" dia × 1" .... **1,320 (A)**
  14k yg, f.w. pearls, c. 1900, central three-dimensional sculptured iris and foliate motif set with three f.w. pearls, tapering to engr scrolled sides, 2-3/8" dia × 1-1/8" at top, 1/4" at sides .... **715 (A)**
  Yg, opal, diamonds, demantoid garnets, glass, c. 1900, openwork tapering bangle with appl yg foliate design around bangle and forming prongs for an oval blue opal (possible replacement) and set with three om diamonds, seven demantoid garnets, and three faceted blue glass stones, tapers from 1" to 3/8" .... **3,000 (A)**
Link
  18k yg, enamel, pearls, diamonds, c. 1900, alternating circ and rect links with blue *guilloché* enameled frames and appl foliate motifs with pearl and rc diamond centers, joined with three rows of pearls linked with eyepins, sm white enamel flowerheads with diamond centers in center rows, sgd and mkd "Gautrait, France" for Lucien Gautrait, box and v-spring clasp, 7-1/2" tl × 5/8" .... **14,300 (A)**
  Platinum, 18k yg, diamonds, c. 1900, straight line of openwork rect yg links with stylized foliate motifs diagonally bisected by rc diamond-set plat bands, Fr hmks, # 7214, 8" tl × 1/2" .... **3,410 (A)**

Bangle bracelets, yg, c. 1900: T, 14k, chased and engr floral and foliate motifs set with three lozenge-shaped faceted sapphires, 2-1/2" dia × 1/4", $1,210 (A); B, chased waterlilies and lilypad motifs, incorporating rounded square plaques spaced at intervals around bangle, polished finish, mk for Riker Bros (R above a scimitar), Newark, N.J., 2-7/8" dia × 3/8", $1,100 (A). *Photo courtesy of Skinner, Inc. (12/14/92).*

Bracelets
Bangles,
14k yg, oe diamonds, rubies, c. 1900, raised iris motifs with curv foliage encircling wavy-edged bangles interspersed with cushion-shaped plaques set with alternating diamonds and rubies in one bangle, the other without stones, mk for Riker Bros (R above a scimitar), Newark N.J., each ³/₈" w × 3" dia, pr . . . . **4,400 (A)**

Brooch/Pendant
Diamonds, st yg, c. 1890, openwork whiplash and foliate motif, set throughout with prong-, bead-, and tube-set oe diamonds, hidden pendant attachments, girdle of largest diamond chipped, 7 dwt, 1-¹/₄" w × 1-³/₄"
. . . . **2,200 (A)**

Brooch/Pin
10k yg, enamel, f.w. pearl, diamond, c. 1900, five-petaled flowerhead in shades of orange, yellow, and green enamel with f.w. pearl center, sm diamond at the base of an open foliate frame 1-¹/₄" w × ³/₄" **250**
14k yg, enamel, f.w. pearl, c. 1900, daisy flowerhead enameled in shades of green and white with f.w. pearl center, within an open oval yg frame with scroll and foliate accents, mkd "Larter" (Newark, N.J.), 1-¹/₄" w × ⁷/₈"
. . . . **300**
14k yg, oe diamonds, pearl, c. 1900, open-winged dragon with sword through its body, sword handle set with 6 oe diamonds and one round pearl, one oe diamond on ea wing, ruby eye, locking C-catch; 1-³/₈" w × 1-¹/₈" . . . . **770 (A)**

Brooch/Pin, enamel, ym, c. 1900, circ plaque, Limoges enamel on metal, depicting the profile of the Princesse Lointaine (a role played by Sarah Bernhardt) with red, pink, and green flowers in her blonde hair, rust-brown bg with gold accents, scalloped and sawtooth gilt-wire frame around a plain bezel, C-catch, tube hinge, 1-³/₄" dia, $400. *Terrance O'Halloran collection.*

14k yg, red cab, c. 1900, in the shape of a flying griffin with a sword through its body, red cab eye, with overall engr detail, obliterated maker's mk, 4.8 dwt C-catch, tube hinge, 1-³/₈" w × 1-¹/₄" . . . . **440 (A)**
18k yg, st yg, diamonds, garnets, c. 1900, dragonfly shape with st yg wings set with 46 rc diamonds, garnet eyes, trombone catch, 2" w × 1-¹/₄" . . . . **1,495 (A)**
18k yg, topaz, emeralds, c. 1910, navette-shaped mount with a scrolling vine frame, with appl orange and yellow enameled leaves and sm yg flowerheads surrounding a cushion-shaped faceted topaz flanked by sq step cut emeralds in the center, sgd "Tiffany & Co.," 1-³/₄" w × ¹/₂" . . . . **4,125 (A)**
18k yg, enamel, diamonds, plat, colored stones, c. 1910, heart shape outlined with 20 rc diamonds set in plat, a raised yg female profile in the center within a field of three yg flowers, each set with one sm faceted colored stone, yellow-green *plique à jour* enamel bg, Fr hmks, 1" w × ⁷/₈" . . . **3,300 (A)**
800 silver, c. 1890, an oval cutout scrolled foliate frame, hinged at the top, attached to an oval compartment for a photograph or miniature, pinback mounted on the rev, mkd "G.A.S." for Georg Anton Scheidt (Viennese mfr), Austrian hmk for 800 silver (dog's head in a coffin-shaped lozenge), C-catch, tube hinge, extended pinstem, 1-⁵/₈" w × 1-⁷/₈"
. . . . **250**
Brass, c. 1910, sash ornament, shield shape with green glass center surrounded by die-stamped scroll and wirework, wide C-catch, flanged hinge, 2-¹/₂" × 2-⁵/₁₆" **60**
Brass, c. 1910, sash ornament, bombé oval with an openwork center of vine and grapes motifs within a four-lobed frame, scrolled and beaded border, wide C-catch, flanged hinge, 2-³/₄" × 2" **80**
Brass, enamel, c. 1900, cast brass circ plaque with scallop and scroll border, profile of a woman wearing an Egyptian-style headress in the center, red, blue, green, and pink painted enamel, C-catch, 1" dia **95**
Citrine, 14k yg, oval faceted citrine, measuring approx. 21.5mm × 15.1mm, held by two yg cherubs on each side, a collet-set diamond at top center and within yg ribbon mount below, 1-⁵/₈" w × 1-¹/₈" . . . . **1,980 (A)**
Enamel on sterling, c. 1900-10, sash ornament, sm irises and leaves in shades of green and yellow *basse-taille* enamel, white bg, on a cut-to-shape engr flat ground-plate, rev mkd "sterling," wide C-catch, 1-⁷/₈" × 1-¹/₈"
. . . . **125**
Enamel, 14k yg, diamond, c. 1900, in the shape of a rose blossom enameled with transparent iridescent pink to pale yellow enamel, oe diamond collet-set on one petal, 1" w × 1-³/₈" . . . . **1,320 (A)**
Glass, brass, c. 1900, lg oval clear cab glass

Brooches/Pins, sterling, c. 1900: L, full-face head of a woman with flowing hair in die-stamped high relief, flat backing with appl oval disk mkd "sterling #1716," mk for Wm. B. Kerr & Co. (fasces), Newark, N.J., new pin back assembly (converted from a belt ornament), 1-³/₄" × 1-¹/₄", $200, *Author's collection;* C, c. 1900, profile of a woman with a Gibson Girl hairstyle surrounded by sycamore seed motifs, appl oval disk mkd "sterling #1703," mk for Wm. B. Kerr & Co. on rev, wide C-catch, lg tube hinge, thick pinstem, 2-¹/₂" × 2-⁵/₈"; $400, *Kirsten Olson collection;* R, circ die-stamped raised design of the profile of a woman with a waterlily in her flowing hair, a lilypad, vine, bud, and water in the bg, flat backing mkd "F & B Sterling" for Theodore W. Foster & Bro. Co., Providence, R.I., wide C-catch, tube hinge, 1-¹/₂" dia, $135, *Author's collection.*

Brooches/Pins, sterling, Unger Bros, c. 1900: L, caricature of an octopus, die-stamped in relief, green glass eyes, flat backing plate mkd with interlaced "UB" for Unger Bros, Newark, N.J., "sterling 925 fine," C-catch, 1-⁵/₈" × 1-¹/₂", $500; R, bouquet of flowers, die-stamped in relief, flat backing plate mkd with interlaced "UB" for Unger Bros, "sterling 925 fine," wide C-catch, flanged hinge, 2-¹/₄" × 1-⁵/₈", $300. *Terrance O'Halloran collection.*

with rev-painted castle design (moisture damage), bezel-set within an asymmetrical brass frame depicting the head of a woman on one side, long flowing hair in whiplash curves around frame, wide C-catch, 2-¹/₂" w × 1-⁵/₈" **200**

Gp brass, rhinestone, c. 1900, irregularly shaped cast plaque depicting the head of a woman with an exotic headress, flowing hair and flowers, a r.s. in her hair, sgd "F.Stiasny" on the front, wide C-catch, flanged hinge, 2-¹/₈" × 2-¹/₈" **250**

Silver, enamel, f.w. pearls, c. 1900, open curv

design with a central motif of a laurel wreath filled with blue-green *plique à jour* enamel, two crossed silver wires topped with f.w. pearls in the open center, terminating in a f.w. pearl drop flanked by two sm foliate motifs in *plique à jour* enamel, rev mkd "Germany," illegible maker's mk, C-catch, 1-³/₈" w × 1-¹/₈" **400**

Silver, c. 1900, die-stamped raised design of bust of a woman surrounded by vines and flowers, unbacked, C-catch, 1-¹/₄" w × 1-¹/₂" **115**

Sp base metal, c. 1900, stamped oval plaque

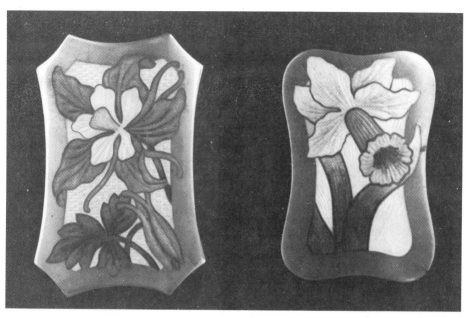

Brooches/Pins, enamel on sterling, Am, c. 1900: L, flower, leaf, and stem in shades of lavender, green, and white *basse-taille* enamel on white bg, plain silver border, shaped rect with convex sides and chamfered corners, rev mkd "sterling," safety catch (added later), tube hinge, 1-5/8" × 2-3/8", $200; R, shaped rounded rect with convex sides, daffodil design in white, green, and yellow *basse-taille* enamel, white bg, plain silver border, rev mkd "sterling," "S" in a circle for Shepard Mfg. Co., Melrose, Mass, wide C-catch, 1-1/2" × 2-1/8", $250. *Terrance O'Halloran collection.*

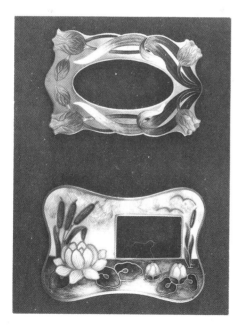

Brooches/Pins, sash ornaments, enamel on sterling, Am, c. 1900: T, tulips and leaves in shades of coral and green *basse-taille* enamel on plain silver bg around cutout oval center, cut-to-shape groundplate, rev mkd "sterling," wide C-catch, tube hinge, 3" × 2", $175; B, waterlilies and cattails, water, sky and clouds in shades of white, blue, green, pink, and brown *basse-taille* enamel on shaped convex rect groundplate with off-center rect cutout, rev mkd "sterling top," "CMR" in lozenge, for Charles M. Robbins Co., Attleboro, Mass., wide C-catch, tube hinge, 3-1/4" × 2-1/8", $350. *Terrance O'Halloran collection.*

bordered with whiplash swirls, center depicting a woman and child with flowers and clouds, 2" w × 2-3/8" **100**

Sp brass, glass, c. 1900, stamped raised design of a woman's face with flowing hair and whiplash curves around and within an open and pierced shield shape, three round green glass cabs bezel-set below face, C-catch, tube hinge, 1-3/4" w × 2-1/8" **125**

Sp brass, c. 1900, die-stamped relief profile of a woman wearing a bonnet (worn to base metal), unbacked, C-catch, 2-1/8" w × 2-1/2" **50**

Sp brass, c.1900, die-stamped design of two full-figured females with drapery forming an oval annular shape, C-catch, extended pinstem, 2-1/8" w × 2-1/2" **100**

Sterling, wm, c. 1900, die-stamped circ raised design of woman's head in center of a flower, backed with flat wm plate mkd "sterling front," C-catch, 1-1/2" dia **150**

Sterling, c. 1900, die-stamped flowerhead in high relief, flat backing with appl oval plate hmkd for Wm. B. Kerr and Co. (fasces), Newark NJ, "sterling," wide C-catch, tube hinge, 1-3/4" × 1-1/2" **300**

Sterling, die-stamped flowerhead in relief, flat backing mkd "sterling," C-catch, tube hinge, 1-1/2" × 1-1/4" **95**

Sterling, enamel, c. 1910, navette-shaped plaque with red *basse-taille* enamel ground, central design of three Easter lilies in white, green, and yellow, rev mkd "Genuine Cloisonné," mk for Watson, Newell Co. (crown, Gothic W, lion), Attleboro, Mass., C-catch, tube hinge, 2-1/2" w × 7/8" **125**

Sterling, enamel, c. 1910, elongated oval plaque with white *basse-taille* enamel ground, central design of three bluebells in blue, yellow, and green, rev mkd "Genuine Cloisonné," mk for Watson, Newell Co., safetypin C-catch, tube hinge, 2" w × 7/8" **100**

Brooch/Pin, sterling, c.1902, circ openwork design, center depicting the profile of a woman wearing an exotic headdress framed by two curv snake and vine motifs, sgd "William Link © 1902" (Newark, N.J.), 1-3/8" dia, $413 (A). *Photo courtesy of Skinner, Inc. (3/14/93).*

Sterling, enamel, c. 1910, disk with concentric rings of enamel, white *basse-taille* moiré-patterned ground with pink scroll and foliate design, green border and inner circle, rev mkd "Champlevé Sterling," mk for Charles M. Robbins Co. (R in a lozenge, shield with arm holding sword, bird in a square), Attleboro, Mass., safetypin C-catch, 1-1/2" dia **125**

Sterling, enamel, c. 1900-10, elliptical plaque with aqua *basse-taille* enamel over sun ray patterned groundplate, with cutout oval center surmounted by a shield-shaped plaque with an Easter lily in shades of white, green, and yellow enamel on ground of aqua shading to white, ster beaded border around inner and outer edges, rev mkd "Sterling Chicago" around "N" in a circle, for F.H. Noble & Co., replacement lever catch, flanged hinge, 2-1/4" w × 1" **150**

Yg, f.w. pearls, c. 1900, in the shape of a serpent with a f.w. pearl in its mouth and a long articulated seaweed tail set with f.w. pearls, 1" w × 3-5/8" . . . . **1,980 (A)**

Yg, enamel, c. 1899, curved rect plaque of four repoussé cherubs within a pierced diamond-set frame with pink and green enamel flowers and vines, repoussé by E. Becker (minor enamel loss), Fr, sgd "Maison Louis Aucoc," 2-3/8" w × 1-1/2" . . . . **6,325 (A)**

Yg, amethyst, enamel, seed pearls, diamond, c. 1900, oval faceted amethyst mounted in the center of an open circ frame with enameled foliate accents at compass points, three seed pearl cluster above, one sm diamond below millegrained bezel, 1" dia . . . **770 (A)**

Enamel, brass, c. 1910, rect plaque depicting a peacock in a field in *basse-taille* enamel, blue sky, green landscape, dk and lt blue, green, rust, and yellow peacock, C-catch, 1-1/4" w × 3/4" **190**

Bar

Enamel, brass, c.1910, white *basse-taille* enamel on diaper pattern groundplate, peacock motif in shades of blue, green, and yellow, safety pin C-catch, 2-5/8" w × 5/16" **200**

Enamel, brass, c. 1915, tapered bar, "San Francisco 1915" flanked by green and orange poppies on lavender ground in *basse-taille* enamel (dam), souvenir of Panama-Pacific International Exposition, safetypin C-catch, 2-1/2" w × 1/4" **125**

Gp brass, c. 1900, row of three women's profiles with flowing hair in cast gp metal, C-catch, 1-3/4" w × 5/8" **85**

Gp metal, rhinestones, c. 1900, in the shape of a dragonfly, engr scroll design on wings set with purple r.s., green r.s. eyes, 2-3/8" w × 1/2" **95**

Opal, diamonds, emeralds, 18k yg, plat, c. 1915-20, an openwork serpentine

Brooches/Pins, sash ornaments, gp brass, glass, c. 1900-10: T, double overlapping lozenge shape with squared ends, cutout center, simulated hasp, mottled red/green glass cabs (one chipped) bezel-set at top and bottom center, flanked by various shaped motifs with stamped Oriental design appl to hammered-textured ground (machine made), wide C-catch, flanged hinge, 3-³/₄" × 2-¹/₄", $75, *Kirsten Olson collection;* CL, folded butterfly wing shape with cutout center, three sm purple faceted glass stones bezel-set diagonally across the center, cast gp design of flowerheads, batwings, scroll and foliate motifs, wide C-catch, flanged hinge, 3" × 1-³/₄", $85, *Author's collection;* C, open modified lozenge-shaped plaque, with pierced flowerhead within circ center set with round coral-colored glass cab and four seed pearls, flanked by iris motifs set with smaller glass cabs, 3-¹/₈" × 1-³/₄", $150, *Milly Combs collection ;* CR, rect plaque with cutout oval center surmounted by bezel-set oval topaz-colored faceted glass, four gp salamanders at corners, with heads extending over glass, and waterlilies appl to engr ground, wide C-catch, 3" × 1-¹/₄", $125, *Kirsten Olson collection;* BL, rounded rect with appl foliate and floral motifs on bg of lilypads, abalone leaves at compass points around center bezel-set oval topaz-colored faceted glass, wide C-catch, flanged hinge, 2-⁵/₈" × 2", $150; BR, brass ginkgo leaves and bezel-set blue faceted glass within an open oval frame, C-catch, flanged hinge, 2-⁷/₈" × 2", $125, *Milly Combs collection.*

frame of overlapping textured yg foliate motifs and plat wire, centrally prong-set with an oval opal, approx 19.7 × 16 × 6.8mm, approx 12 ct, flanked by four white and ten fancy colored yellow marquise-cut diamonds, and sq-cut emeralds, rev appl plaque imp "Tiffany & Co.," 2-³/₈" w × 1-¹/₈" . . . . **13,225 (A)**

Bouquet pin

Enamel, sterling, c. 1910, waterlily motif in shades of white, pink, and green enamel on bowed groundplate, tapering to turned-up ends, pierced sides, mk for Watson Newell Co. (crown, Gothic W, lion), spike for holding a flower bouquet missing, C-catch, 2-¹/₄" w × ⁵/₈", 1" at bowed-out center **85**

Sash ornament

Brass, glass, c. 1900-10, elongated open rect with cast floral and foliate design, bezel-set rounded rect faceted lt blue glass at one end of open center, simulated hasp at the other, wide C-catch, 4" w × 1-¹/₂" **95**

Gp brass, celluloid, c. 1900-10, open oval with stamped raised floral and foliate design, oval coral-colored celluloid cab (hollow) bezel-set in center, C-catch, 3" w × 2-¹/₄" **75**

Gp copper, c. 1900-10, rect with scalloped-edge chamfered corners, oval cutout center, four raised scrolled fret motifs at sides, top and bottom on patinated ridged ground, wide C-catch, lg flanged hinge, thick pinstem, 2-⁵/₈" w × 1-⁷/₈" **65**

Silver, white metal, c. 1900-10, fancy-shaped open rect, peaked top and bottom, lobed sides, die-stamped with incised scroll, spiral and Greek key motifs on raised silver front, cutout center follows shape, simulated hasp appl to one side,

flat wm backing, wide C-catch, flanged
hinge, 2-⅝" w × 1-⅞" **50**

Sterling, enamel, c. 1900-10, open rect with
bombé sides, white *basse-taille* enamel
over diaper pattern groundplate, pink and
green floral/foliate motifs in each corner,
plain ster simulated hasp, rev mkd "Sterling R," wide C-catch, heavy tube hinge,
2-¾" w × 2" **95**

Sterling, white metal, c. 1900, annular oval
with die-stamped relief design of lilies of
the valley and scrolled, undulating leaves,
simulated hasp appl at one end, rev mkd
"sterling front," wide C-catch, flanged
hinge, 2-¼" w × 1-¾" **85**

Watchpin

14k yg, enamel, diamond, c. 1900, a pair of
yg herons flanking a spray of three cattails
enameled in shades of green, peach, and
brown with an oe diamond in the center,
hook for pendent watch on rev, mk for
Krementz & Co., Newark, N.J., 1" w ×
1-⅛" .... **2,300 (A)**

14k yg, enamel, seed pearl, c. 1900, in the
shape of an iris framed by curv leaves,
enameled in shades of purple and green,
with a seed pearl center, hook for watch at
the base, mk for Bippart, Griscom &
Osborn, Newark, N.J., (torch), 1" w ×
1-⅛" .... **1,840 (A)**

Brooch/Watch pin, 14k yg, c. 1910-15, crescent shape
set with grad seed pearls, a three-quarter profile head of
a woman with flowers in her flowing hair, twisted hook
for pendent watch on rev, C-catch mkd "14k," "C" in
an arrowhead for Carter, Gough & Co, Newark, N.J., 1-
⅜" × ¾", $850. *Elizabeth Cook collection.*

Gf, c. 1900, open triangular shape with a
tapered-out scrolled and reeded center
flanked by looped wire at the top,
surmounting scrolled feather motifs, hook
for pendent watch on rev, C-catch, tube
hinge, 1-⅛" w × 1" **75**

Sterling, c. 1900, slightly convex circ disk,
die-stamped relief design depicting the
frontal torso of a woman with flowing hair

L, Brooch/Watch pin, sterling, c. 1900, iris motif in die-stamped relief, flat backing with appl oval plate mkd "sterling
#1690," mk for Wm. B. Kerr & Co. (fasces), Newark, N.J., C-catch, hook for pendent watch on rev, 1" × 1-¼", $145,
Kirsten Olson collection; C, Buckle, sterling, c. 1900, two irises and two buds in die-stamped relief mounted on
swirled wire, flat backing with appl oval plate mkd "sterling # 1844," mk for William B. Kerr & Co., two bars and sm
sharp hook for belt attachment on rev, 4-½" × 2-¾", $450, *Milly Combs collection.*

and gown, reading a book, flanked by lilies and undulating leaves, rev mkd "sterling" within a fish holding the letter L in its mouth, for Fishel, Nessler & Co., New York, hook for pendent watch, C-catch, flanged hinge, 1" dia **175**

Buckle

Brass, c.1900, two-pc, cast, raised fuchsia motif, sp ground, hook and eye closure, bars for belt attachment, 2-$\frac{1}{2}$" w × 2" **100**

Brass, glass, c. 1900, one-pc, rect with concave sides and chamfered corners, four oval green glass cabs bezel-set in corners, appl scrolled twisted wire and bead design on the surfaces between each cab, double hasp mounted in cutout center, mkd "F & B" for Theodore W. Foster & Bro. Co., Providence, R.I., 3-$\frac{1}{4}$" w × 2-$\frac{3}{4}$" **95**

Gp base metal, glass, c. 1900, one-pc, curv freeform outline with beaded edge, five lg round faceted purple glass stones bezel-set à jour on a diagonal metal strip, rev mkd "Vanlines," appl hook and bar for belt attachment, 2-$\frac{3}{4}$" w × 2" **115**

Gp base metal, glass, c. 1900, two-pc butterfly shape, framed by open-mouthed snakes, three oval green faceted glass stones bezelset within mouths, sm red cab glass in eyes of snakes and butterfly, rev mkd "66," appl hook and eye and bars for belt attachment, 4-$\frac{1}{4}$" w × 2-$\frac{3}{8}$" **275**

Gp brass, glass. r.s., c. 1900, one-pc annular oval in the shape of a snake holding a lt blue bezel-set glass cab in its mouth, pink r.s. eye, double hasp, hook for belt on rev mkd with mono "E A & Co" in a circle, 2-$\frac{1}{2}$" w × 2" **125**

Sp brass, c. 1900, one-pc, convex rect diestamped relief design of flowers and buds on reeded stalks and leaves appl on openwork bg of undulating reeded vines, rev mkd "F.N. & Co." in crowned coat of arms, for Fishel, Nessler & Co., New York, appl flat bars for belt or sash, 4-$\frac{3}{4}$" w × 1-$\frac{3}{4}$" **125**

Silver, c. 1900, open asymmetrical curv rect, die-stamped high relief depicting the torso of a woman in profile in medieval dress and head ornament, surrounded by undulating vines, leaves, and flowers, flanking an offcenter oval cutout with double hasp, flat backing, unmkd, probably Fr, 2-$\frac{1}{4}$" w × 3-$\frac{1}{2}$" **350**

Sterling, c. 1900, slightly convex annular oval with allover engr scroll and floral design, double hasp, mkd "Sterling," script L with crossbar (Eng pound sign), for La Pierre Mfg Co, Newark, N.J. and New York, (later International Silver), 4" w × 3" **350**

Sterling, c. 1900, one-pc, cut in the shape of two draped winged nymphs, facing each other with arms outstretched, hands touching above cutout center, mk for Gorham & Co. (lion, anchor, Gothic G) on rev, 1-$\frac{3}{4}$" w × 2-$\frac{1}{2}$" **375**

Cuff links

14k yg, turq, c. 1900, dumbbell-type link, cab turq in millegrain setting with yg snake motif frame, $\frac{3}{4}$" × $\frac{1}{2}$", pr **275**

14k yg, c. 1900, dumbbell-type link, cast relief of ladies' heads with flowing hair, $\frac{3}{4}$" × $\frac{1}{2}$", pr **250**

18k yg, c. 1900, lions' heads, each with a bezel-set diamond in its mouth, within curv hexagonal frames, linked to elliptical backs

Buckles, enamel, gp brass, c. 1900: T, two-pc design of swallows and flowers in aqua, blue, green, and rust *basse-taille* enamel on a cut-to-shape and pierced gilt groundplate, rev mkd "metal gilt," 3-$\frac{3}{4}$" × 1-$\frac{7}{8}$", $275, *Terrance O'Halloran collection;* B, two-pc floral and foliate design in champlevé and *basse-taille* enameled shades of green, white, lt and dk blue, dk red, and lt orange on a cut-to-shape and pierced groundplate (some enamel dam), hook and eye, wire bars for belt attachment on rev, 4-$\frac{1}{4}$" × 2", $150, *Author's collection.*

Buckles, sp base metal, c. 1900: TL, two-pc, raised die-stamped design of the head of a woman with flowing hair in the center of four flowers with undulating leaves, hook and eye, bars for belt attachment appl to rev, 2-½" × 1-½", $100, *Kirsten Olson collection;* TR, sp brass, one-piece, die-stamped mermaid with flowing hair and water, irregular shape, appl hook and bars for belt attachment, 2-³⁄₈" × 1-⁵⁄₈", $90, *Milly Combs collection;* B, sp brass, two-pc, five die-stamped overlapping grad disks, curving upward, with raised floral and undulating vine borders, heads of women with Gibson Girl hairstyle in centers, worn to base metal, hook-and-eye closure, bars for belt attachment on rev, 4" × 1-½", $65, *Author's collection.*

Hair comb, horn, diamonds, silver, c. 1900, dragonfly motif, cut-to-shape, pierced and molded in relief, body tinted green, rc diamond set in silver on each top wing, surmounting a toothed comb, 4-½" × 3-¼", $285. *Terrance O'Halloran collection.*

with open curv design, ½" × ½", 1" tl, pr
.... **550 (A)**
Earrings
14k yg, enamel, pearls, c. 1900, waterlily motifs enameled in shades of lt and dk green, a 4mm pearl in the center of each flowerhead, screwbacks, mkd "Krementz" (Newark, N.J.), 1" w × ½", pr .... **440 (A)**
Hatpin
Brass, glass, c. 1900, two-sided design of a woman's head with an Egyptian headress surmounted by flowers and leaves, bezel-set oval topaz-colored faceted glass within lotus motif below, 1" × 2-½", 8" tl **275**
Brass, glass, c. 1900, lg open three-dimensional quatrefoil with a pierced design of butterflies and scrolls surmounted by a lg bezel-set oval smoky topaz-colored faceted glass stone, head 3" × 1-½" × 1-¼", 11-½" tl
.... **250**
Brass, glass, c. 1900, two-sided iris and reeded leaves motifs in pierced scrolling shape, ⅞" × 1", 8-⅞" tl **100**
Brass, glass, c. 1900, two-sided design of a pierced Celtic knot surmounted by an acanthus motif within a scrolled arch, flanked by

Hatpin, sterling, glass, c. 1900, fibula or safetypin type, three appl flowerheads with green glass centers, and curv ribbon and bow design, 7-¹/₂″ × 1″, $225. *Charles Pinkham collection.*

Hatpins, sterling, wm, c. 1900-10: TL, head of a woman wearing an exotic headress, full face in stamped relief, rev mkd "sterling front," 1″ × 1-¹/₈″, 8-¹/₄″ tl, $175; TR, circ shape, die-stamped relief profile of a woman with a waterlily in her flowing hair, a lilypad, bud, and water in the bg, rev mkd "sterling top Ger. silver back," 1-¹/₈″ dia × 7-¹/₈″ tl, $175; C, profile of a woman in the center of a full-blown flower with leaf and stem, rev mkd "sterling front," 1″ × 1-¹/₈″, 6-¹/₂″ tl, $175; BL, high relief die-stamped head of a grinning girl wearing a hat (Flora Dora), rev mark partially obscured by pin stem mount, mkd "sterling," probably Unger Brothers, 1-³/₈″ × 1-¹/₄″, 7″ tl, $225; BR, girl's head, full face in stamped relief, flowing hair surrounded by cattails and a waterlily, pierced bg, rev mkd "sterling" and interlaced "UB" for Unger Brothers, Newark, N.J., 1″ dia, 7″ tl, $200. *Milly Combs collection.*

bezel-set oval purple faceted glass, ⁷/₈″ × 1-³/₄″, 11-¹/₂″ tl **135**

Gp brass, glass, c. 1900, star-shaped head with turq glass center, ⁷/₈″ dia, 5-¹/₂″ shank **45**

Enamel, yg, seed pearls, c. 1900, shades of green and orange enamel in the form of a flower set with five pearls, gold filigreed stem **550**

Sterling, c. 1900, "The Eternal Question," design by Charles Dana Gibson, based on "The Girl in the Red Velvet Swing," Evelyn Nesbit, two-sided head, in profile with flowing hair forming the shape of a question mark, in hollow die-stamped relief, ³/₄″ w × 2″, 9-⁵/₈″ tl **275**

Sterling, c. 1900, die-stamped relief design, head of a woman wearing a hat within a curved and tapered shaped top, ⁷/₈″ w × 1-¹/₂″, 9-¹/₄″ tl **145**

Sterling, c. 1900, die-stamped flowerhead in relief, flat backing mkd "sterling," 6″ shank, head 1-³/₄″ × 1-³/₈″ **110**

Locket

14k yg, c. 1900, a circ medallion with a raised design of the torso of a Native American Indian tending a fire with a kettle suspended from a branch, curling smoke in the bg, pendant bail, 1-⅛″ dia . . . . **440 (A)**

Sterling, c. 1910, oval locket with die-stamped relief design of the profile of a woman with flowers in her flowing hair, inside mkd "sterling," 1-⅛″ w × 1-⅝″ **125**

Locket and Chain

14k yg, sapphires, diamonds, c. 1910, circ locket with a central stylized foliate design flanked by six collet-set sapphires within recessed ovals (three on each side) and two sm diamonds below, suspended from fancy chain with a collet-set sapphire within each of three navette-shaped links, mkd "S14C" for Strobell & Crane, Newark, N.J., chain 20″ tl, locket 1-¼″ dia . . . . **1,650 (A)**

Lorgnette

10k yg, c. 1900, raised whiplash motif, mono in block letters on one side, 22.3 dwt, 5″ × 1-¼″, case . . . . **275 (A)**

Necklace

Dog collar

14k yg, enamel, citrines, pearls, c. 1900, vertical bars with pink and green enameled scrolled foliate motifs, a baroque pearl in the center of each, alternating with sm sq yg plaques turned 45 degrees and set with sq-cut citrines, joined by fancy yg links, mkd with a torch flanked by "14" and "K"

Lorgnette, sterling, c. 1900, two-sided, heads of women and gargoyles in high relief within a scrolled shaped handle, button mechanism for releasing folded spectacles, mk for Unger Bros on inside of compartment, pendant bail for chain, handle 5-¼″ × 1-¼″, 4-½″ open, $650. *Charles Pinkham collection.*

Locket, sterling, c. 1900, heart-shaped, with die-stamped front depicting the Drowning Ophelia, waterlilies and irises, inside imp with Unger Bros. mk, "sterling 925 fine," 1-½″ × 1-¾″, $400. *Terrance O'Halloran collection.*

Necklace, 18k yg, enamel, pearl, diamonds, rubies, c. 1900, yg foliate link chain set with round diamonds joined with green enameled lilypads (with detachable shortener), suspending a detachable pendant with appl cutout yg oak leaf motifs on a green *plique à jour* enamel ground set with pavé round and oe diamonds and collet-set circ cab rubies, the cusped base suspending a pearl and rc diamond drop, mounted in yg, Fr hmks; 21″ tl, $9,200 (A). *Photo courtesy of Christie's New York (4/22/93).*

Necklace, 800 silver, c. 1900, lg center, flanked by two smaller filigreed plaques, matching clasp, with flowerhead centers surrounded by domed, beaded disk and foliate motifs, connected by swagged round cable-link chains (five from center, four from side plaques), 18" tl, center 1-⅝" × 1-⅜", $250. *Joyce Albers collection.*

for Bippart, Griscom & Osborn, Newark, N.J., 13-¾" tl × 1-¼" . . . . **5,175 (A)**

800 silver, rhinestones (paste), c. 1910, six rows of curb-link chain joined with front center ornamental clasp, a rounded sq with central scrolled filigree set with colorless, pink, and green stones, rev mkd "800," "Germany," approx 14-½" tl, clasp 1-⅝" sq **175**

Gp silver, MOP, c. 1905, pierced shield-shaped central and curv side plaques with carved MOP wheat-ear motifs bezel-set in the centers, joined by five rows of fine cable-link chain, the center plaque suspending a carved MOP inverted pear-shaped drop, Prague hmks, approx 2-¾" top to bottom at center, 14" tl **575**

Pendant

14k yg, enamel, garnet, pearls, c. 1900, navette-shaped frame of tapering pierced segments filled with blue-green *plique à jour* enamel, a sq-cut garnet bezel-set in the open center, enameled fleur-de-lis above and two lilies with seed pearl centers below shading off-white to pale green, suspending a f.w. pearl, Am, rev mkd "14k," a stylized rose mk, probably for Untermyer-Robbins Co., N.Y., ⅝" w × 1-⅝" tl **600**

18k yg, opals, c. 1900, lobed oval, foliated C-scroll design framing three collet-set oval opals and suspending a collet-set pear-shaped opal drop, fleur-de-lis bail, 1-¾" w × 2-¾" tl . . . . **1,100 (A)**

18k yg, enamel, diamonds, pearl, c. 1900, in the shape of a three-lobed lily-of-the-valley leaf in green enamel encasing the head and torso of a woman with flowing hair, the center lobe encircled by a sprig of lilies-of-the-valley set with om diamonds, suspending a pearl drop, Fr, 1-½" w × 1-½" tl . . . . **2,070 (A)**

Glass, foil, ym, c. 1910-15, crystal oval plaque molded with lilies and three grasshoppers (*sauterelles*), backed with green foil in ym mount with pendant bail, imp "Lalique," 2" w × 3" . . . . **1,320 (A)**

Cross

Brass, faux seed pearls, c. 1910, beaded scroll design set with 10 faux seed pearls, central motif of a woman's profile with flowing hair; 1-⅝" w × 2-¾" **150**

14k yg, sapphires, c. 1900, 16 collet-set sapphires forming a cross within a double-helix yg frame, 1-½" w × 2-½" . . . . . . **1,540 (A)**

Pendant & Chain

14k yg, enamel, c. 1900, circ plaque depicting

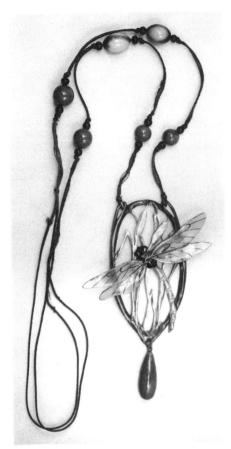

Pendant/necklace, horn, glass beads, cord, c. 1900, pierced oval horn plaque surmounted by a dragonfly with hp wings, cattails in bg, suspended from a thin braided cord interspersed with round mottled blue glass and hollow oval horn beads, sm blue wooden bead spacers, a teardrop-shaped blue glass bead suspended from base of pendant, probably Fr, attributed to Elizabeth Bonté, pendant 4-³/₄" tl × 3-¹/₂", necklace 31-¹/₂" tl, $1,100. *Kirsten Olson collection.*

Pendant and Chain, c. 1900, scrolled shield-shaped beaded silver filigree plaque suspended from a pendant bail by two chains and filigree top, center prong-set with an oval faceted amethyst, terminating in a heart-shaped, beaded pendent drop, added chain, 20" tl, pendant 3"x 1", $250. *Terrance O'Halloran collection.*

the profile of an eagle framed by foliate motifs, bg of green and red *plique à jour* enamel, one sc diamond in eagle's eye, suspended from a twisted link chain, 13" tl, plaque ⁷/₈" w × 1-¹/₄" tl .... **225 (A)**

18k yg, enamel, diamond, emerald, ruby, c. 1900, in the shape of a winged female-headed serpent wearing a cobra headdress enameled in shades of blue, green, and white with grey *plique à jour* enameled wings, suspending an unfaceted emerald drop and surmounted by an oval-cut ruby suspended from a diamond-set sunburst motif flanked by coiling serpents, continuing to a yg oval link chain and later-added 14k yg

clasp, pendant rev sgd "L. Gautrait" for Lucien Gautrait, approx 15" tl, pendant 2-³/₄" w × 4-¹/₄" tl .... **26,450 (A)**

Gp brass, glass, pearls, c. 1910, triangular die-stamped openwork pendant set with a round faceted purple glass flanked by two genuine pearls (possibly added) suspending three purple glass drops, two lengths of gp chain with four spectacle-set faceted purple glass stones suspended from top corners of pendant, 19-¹/₂" tl **125**

Silver gilt, enamel, faux pearl, paste, c. 1900, flowerhead shape with simulated pearl center, blue *plique à jour* enamel bg set upon a silver gilt scrolling knife-edge frame set with

Pendants, crosses, c. 1900: L, sp brass, two sided die-stamped floral and foliate motifs, 3" × 1-⁷/₈", $100; C, chrysanthemum motif, cast brass, faceted round yellow glass bezel-set in center, 2-¹/₂" × 1-³/₄", $150; R, sp brass, two sided die-stamped floral motif, 2-⁷/₈" × ⁷/₈", $125. *Milly Combs collection.*

Pendant and Chain, sterling, seed pearls, garnets, c. 1900, pendant of curv trefoil design in a textured finish, four seed pearls set in center, bezel-set cab garnets in pendent drop and at top center, suspended from double chains joined to garnet beads and continuing to a single chain, pendant 1-¹/₄" tl × 1-¹/₈", $715 (A). *Photo courtesy of Skinner, Inc. (3/14/93).*

Pendant and Chain, enamel, pink sapphires, 18k yg, wg, diamonds, c. 1910, openwork pendant with an oval faceted pink sapphire in center flanked by lg foliate motifs enameled in shades of yellow, pink, and green, with pavé-set diamonds along edges and in pierced sections above and below, suspending an oval faceted pink sapphire pendent drop, mounted in yg, attached to a wg cable link chain, 15-¹/₂" tl, pendant 1-³/₈" × ³/₄", $2,070 (A). *Photo courtesy of Christie's New York (4/22/93).*

Pendant and Chain, 18k yg, enamel, peridot, pearls, c. 1910, tapering curv plaque depicting a female figure with outstretched arms and flowing robes in yg, sunset, and waterlilies in shades of green, yellow and white *plique à jour* enamel, suspending a pear-shaped peridot drop, attached to a yg paper clip link chain with flowered *plique à jour* enamel plaques, and cultured pearls, 15-³/₄", pendant 3" tl × 1-¹/₂", $10,925 (A). *Photo courtesy of Christie's New York (4/22/93).*

paper-clip chain, 10.0 dwt, pendant 1-¹/₄" w × 2-¹/₂", 24" tl . . . . **935 (A)**

Cross

18k yg, diamonds, pearl, c. 1910, acanthus and flowerhead motifs set with rc diamonds, central flowerhead within a circ frame set with a button pearl, suspended from a fancy oval link chain, 22" tl, cross 1-¹/₄" w × 2" . . . . **880 (A)**

Pendant and Cord

Glass, silk cord, c. 1910-15, crystal disc molded with a curv scroll motif on sienna tint ground, inscribed "R. Lalique" in script, mold pierced with two holes at top for cord, one hole at bottom for tassel, disc approx 2" dia, approx 6" tl with tassel . . . . **413 (A)**

Pendant/Necklace

Horn, glass beads, cord, c. 1900, carved horn pendant in the shape of a poppy set with a purple glass cab, an irregular navette-shaped horn pendent plaque at the base, suspended from a cord interspersed with purple glass beads and horn discs, incised signature on rev of pendant (illegible), approx 32" tl, pendant 3-¹/₂" w × 4-¹/₂" tl **900**

Ring

Diamond, 18k yg, c. 1900, yg with one cushion-shaped om diamond within a sculpted shoulder mount depicting a pair of dolphins, 1.5 ct, 6.1 dwt, ³/₈" × ³/₄", ring size 5 . . . . **2,860 (A)**

Lapis, 18k yg, c. 1900, an oval lapis cab bezel-set in a tapering sculptured foliate yg mount, ³/₄" × ⁵/₈" . . . . **413 (A)**

Opal, 18k yg, enamel, diamonds, c. 1900, a lg oval opal prong-set within an elongated organic freeform yg mount in green *basse-taille* enamel, set with sm diamonds, sgd "Marcus & Co," New York, ³/₄" w × 1-¹/₄" . . . . **3,850 (A)**

Scarf holder

Silver, gp silver, c. 1900, open tapered gp tube with central silver poppy spray motif, sm

Ring, 14k yg, c. 1910, set with a pear-shaped opal doublet with oe diamonds mounted in sculpted yg (bearing an inscription), 1-¹/₈" × ¹/₂", $5,750 (A). *Photo courtesy of Christie's New York (4/22/93).*

paste stones, suspended from a link chain, 18" tl . . . . **770 (A)**

Silver, enamel, tourmaline, glass, c. 1900, *plique à jour* enameled foliate design in shades of green and pink, with one central bezel-set tourmaline, surrounded by sm round pink stones, suspending an additional lg oval pink stone, attached at each end to a

spike protruding from rev hinged bar mounted on back of tube, mkd "*Deposé*," probably Fr, 1″ w × 1-³/₄″ **100**
Scarf pin/Stickpin
14k yg, diamond, c. 1900, head in the shape of an iris with oe diamond dewdrop, ¹/₂″ w × ³/₄″, 2-³/₈″ tl . . . . **127 (A)**
14k yg, sapphire, c, 1905-15, a collet-set sapphire in the center of an oval yg frame surmounted by a trefoil between two Greek key motifs curving into a foliate motif at the base, mk for Whiteside & Blank, Newark,

N.J. (arrow bisecting a crescent), head ¹/₂″ × ³/₄″, 2-¹/₂″ tl . . . . **358 (A)**
Gp metal, rhinestone, c. 1900, head of a woman with a Gibson Girl hairstyle, r.s. in her hair, ³/₈″ dia, × 2-¹/₄″ tl **45**
Gp metal, c. 1900, profile of a woman with flowing hair and exotic headdress, ³/₈″ dia × 2-³/₈″ tl **30**
Gp metal, c. 1900, medallion of the profile of a Roman warrior mounted in the center of an open curv scrolled frame, ³/₄″ dia × 2-¹/₄″ tl **25**

EDWARDIAN C. 1890-1920

History: Historically, the Edwardian period lasted for only the nine years that King Edward VII was on the throne, 1901-1910. The style known as Edwardian, however, began to evolve more than 10 years earlier and continued to be seen for about 10 years after Edward's death. By the time Edward and Alexandra became king and queen, they were past middle age, and the style they influenced was firmly entrenched.

The period was a time of social reform, but it also saw the rise of an incredibly wealthy upper class, in Great Britain as well as the United States. Unlike Victoria, who was the people's queen, Edward and Alexandra set the tone for an international high society separated from the lower classes by a social whirl of balls, sporting events, yachting, and all the other pursuits of the well-to-do. Elegance and delicacy were the watchwords of the day. Jewels, of course, were an important part of the trappings.

Edwardian jewelry contrasts markedly with other concurrent styles. While Arts and Crafts and Art Nouveau were part of the aesthetic avant-garde, Edwardian jewelry clung to tradition. The former attracted the intellectual elite, the latter, the social elite. Arts and Crafts and Art Nouveau emphasized design and workmanship over intrinsically valuable materials. Edwardian emphasized diamonds, pearls, and platinum, in skillfully worked designs. Arts and Crafts and Art Nouveau jewelers used enamels and gemstones in a palette of colors. Edwardian jewels were monochromatic, mostly white or colorless. Arts and Crafts jewelry was inspired by the medieval and Renaissance periods; Edwardian looked back to the neoclassical and rococo of the eighteenth century and the French courts of Louis XV and Louis XVI.

One of the most distinctive aspects of Edwardian jewels is their lacy, delicate appearance, made possible by the use of platinum, an extremely strong and ductile metal. Although platinum had been used earlier, demand for it—and consequently its value—was not as high, nor was it worked in the same way as it was at the turn of

the century. (For awhile, jewelers continued to treat platinum as they had silver, laminating it to gold. This was unnecessary, because platinum does not tarnish and is strong enough to be used alone. Experts speculate that jewelers were striving to maintain the tradition of nineteenth-century diamond jewels set in silver-topped gold.) The Edwardian look is characterized by knife-edge platinum wires joining millegrained collet-set diamonds in openwork designs and saw-pierced platinum plaques set throughout with diamonds. The colorless all-diamond and pearl-and-diamond jewels complemented the all-white and pale pastel feminine fashions of the period, which were made of lightweight fabrics and lace.

The style's emphasis on diamonds coincided with improvements in diamond-cutting technology, which gave rise to new cuts, such as the marquise or navette, the emerald cut, and the baguette. The term "calibré cut" was used to refer to any stone cut to a special shape to fit a setting. The briolette cut, a three-dimensional teardrop shape, was often used for stones meant to be suspended, for example, in earrings or lavaliers. All of these cuts were also used for other transparent gemstones. Colored stones were often combined with diamonds and pearls in Edwardian jewelry, particularly amethysts, peridot (Alexandra's and Edward's favorites, respectively), blue sapphires, demantoid (green) garnets, rubies, opals and turquoise.

It should be noted that while the French were the source of the Edwardian style, they would never give it the name of a British king. In France, the style is called *belle époque* (beautiful era), *fin de siècle* (end of the century), or *style guirlande*, (the garland style). The latter name is taken from the floral and foliate motifs found on eighteenth-century French furniture, architecture, and decorative objects. The motifs were usually in the shape of wreaths or swags, that is, garlands. These were combined with bows, tassels and lace motifs to produce the jewelry forms of the day: dog collars, fringe and festoon necklaces, brooches, corsage ornaments and larger bodice ornaments (also called stomachers), tiaras, lavaliers, pendants, and earrings.

The *négligée* pendant and the *sautoir* were uniquely Edwardian jewels of the period. A variation on the lavalier, the defining feature of the *négligée* is a pair of pendent drops suspended from unequal lengths of fine chain, usually joined to a small gem-set plaque. The drops are often pear-shaped pearls or gemstones. The *sautoir* is a long necklace terminating in a tassel or pendant. The necklace can be a rope or woven band of seed pearls or a platinum chain interspersed with diamonds; the tassels are usually made of pearls with diamond-set caps, and the pendants are pierced diamond-set plaques.

The most famous practitioner, if not the originator of the garland style, was Louis Cartier (1875-1942), who designed for an international clientele of the rich, royal, and famous. American bankers and industrialists, as well as French aristocrats and English nobility, commissioned jewels from Cartier's atelier in Paris. The firm was so successful with their new line of garland-style diamond and platinum jewelry (introduced in 1899), that they soon expanded, opening branches in London in 1902 and New York in 1909.

Other famous French houses working in the garland style were Lacloche Frères, Boucheron, Chaumet and Mellerio. Georges Fouquet, best known for his Art Nouveau designs, also made Edwardian-style jewels.

Peter Carl Fabergé (1846-1920), the celebrated jeweler of the Russian Imperial court, was noted for his objects of virtu. Most of his jewels could be classified as Edwardian, but others have definite Art Nouveau lines and motifs. A master of enameling and a technical perfectionist, Fabergé was capable of great versatility. His clientele, however, tended toward the traditional in jewelry, and his jewels reflect a certain restraint. Because the Fabergé name on a piece brings high prices, there are many fakes and forgeries to be wary of.

In the United States, by the first decade of this century, Tiffany & Co., Marcus & Co., Black, Starr & Frost, Udall & Ballou, and Dreicer & Co. all had retail establishments on Fifth Avenue in New York City, where their Edwardian-style jewels found favor with the wealthy denizens of that prestigious neighborhood.

For those unable to afford the opulence of Cartier et al., more modest adornments were available. Even if she owned no other piece of fine jewelry, a woman might have a diamond and platinum or white gold ring in the elongated oblong or navette shape and pierced scrollwork of the Edwardian style. Bar brooches were very much in vogue; stars and crescents, sporting, and novelty jewelry continued to be popular, as were slim bangles and narrow flexible and link bracelets with pierced or filigree plaques; inexpensive gold lavaliers were also prevalent. Most of these pieces were also set with small diamonds and

seed pearls. Moonstones, opals, peridots, demantoid garnets, and amethysts were also used. Synthetic sapphires made their appearance around 1910. White gold came into common usage during World War I, when platinum was appropriated for the war effort and banned for use in jewelry.

Less expensive still was imitation jewelry (the term "costume jewerly" had yet to be coined) jewelry in colorless rhinestones (paste), glass, and silver made to look exactly the same as real jewelry. It has been overlooked by many of today's costume jewelry collectors because of its small size and delicacy, but the current trend toward the Edwardian look may increase demand and raise prices. Nonprecious jewelry in the Edwardian style has not survived in quantity. Whether little was made to begin with, or it was discarded, is unclear. Edwardian pieces made of nonprecious materials are grouped separately in the listings, because they forecast the development of costume jewelry as an accepted form of ornament and a major collectible classification.

The latter part of the period, c. 1910-1920, interrupted by war, saw both gradual and abrupt stylistic changes. It has been called a transitional period, from Edwardian to Art Deco, in both fine and costume jewelry. The transitional style continued through the 1920s, becoming more geometric, but retaining the open, lacy filigree and white or pale palette of high Edwardian, moving toward Art Deco's stronger contrasts in black and white and red and white. Aiding this change was what is considered a landmark event: the presentation in Paris of the Ballets Russes *Schéhérazade* in 1910. The ballet's Oriental-inspired costumes, stage design, and vibrant colors influenced trend setters such as Paul Poiret, the progressive couturier, whose designs changed the fashion silhouette from curvilinear to vertical. Tassels and turbans were favorite Poiret accessories, and tasseled pendants and long pendent earrings were complementary jewelry forms. The *sautoir* evolved into long diamond-set geometric chain links and pendants, eventually reaching the masses as tasseled flapper beads in faceted glass.

References: David Bennett and Daniela Mascetti, *Understanding Jewellery*, Antique Collectors' Club, 1989; Joyce Jonas, "The Elegant Edwardians," in *Jewelers' Circular-Keystone/Heritage*, August 1988; Michael Koch et al., *The Belle Époque of French Jewellery 1850-1910*, Thomas Heneage & Co. Ltd, 1990; Elise Misiorowski and Nancy Hays, "Jewels of the Edwardians," in *Gems and Gemology*, Fall 1993; Hans Nadelhoffer, *Cartier, Jewelers Extraordinary*, Harry N. Abrams, 1984; Diana Scarisbrick, *Ancestral Jewels*, Vendome Press, 1989; A. Kenneth Snowman, *Fabergé Lost and Found*, Harry N. Abrams, 1993; Alexander von Solodkoff, *The Art of Carl Fabergé*, Crown Publishers, 1988.

Advisors: Joyce Jonas, Elise Misiorowski.

FINE JEWELRY

Bracelet
  Bangle
    Pearl, diamonds, platinum, yg, c. 1910, center button pearl flanked by two om diamonds and a row of smaller diamonds, 2.5 ct tw, in a plat-topped yg mount, Austrian hmks, 2-½" dia × ¼" . . . . **2,530 (A)**
    Sapphire, diamonds, 18k yg, c. 1910, an oval blue sapphire, approx 1.3 ct, encircled by om diamonds, flanked by four collet-set om diamonds, in the center of a double row of rc and om diamonds, 1.75 ct tw, set in a divided bangle top, Austrian hmks, 2-⅝" dia × ½" . . . . **2,860 (A)**
    Sapphire, diamonds, 18k yg, c. 1900, center oval sapphire, 2.2 ct, surrounded by 29 om diamonds in a fluted, foliate engr basket mount, with tapering diamond-set shoulders on a knife-edge bangle, Fr hmks, in orig fitted box; 3-¼" dia × ¾" . . . . **4,235 (A)**
  Bangle, hinged
    14k yg, sapphires, pearls, plat, c. 1910, the top half set with five round sapphires, pearls and pierced plat leaves, mk for Hagerstrom & Chapman Company (H over C), Newark, N.J., 2-¼" dia × ¼" . . . . **770 (A)**
  Flexible
    Diamonds, platinum, c. 1915, a line of grad oe and om diamonds, collet-set within an openwork, tapered, flexible center, at-

Bracelet, hinged bangle, sapphire, diamonds, platinum-topped yg, c. 1905, a tapered pavé oe and rc diamond-set band, cutout oval sections with knife-edge openwork and diamond-set quatrefoils on the sides, a cushion-cut blue sapphire, approx 14.3 cts, prong-set in the center, flanked by cutout circ sections with knife-edge openwork and diamond-set trefoils, 2-⅝" dia × ⅞", $6,900 (A). Photo courtesy of Christie's New York (4/21/93).

tached to a strap of openwork rect links, each set with one diamond within a navette-shaped mount, terminating in a push clasp with safety chain, 7" tl . . . . **3,800 (A)**
  Moonstones, yg, c. 1900, a grad row of nine collet-set oval moonstones, continuing to narrow rect links, v-spring and box clasp, 7-½" tl × ½" **200**
  Seed pearls, diamonds, platinum, c. 1900, central rect plaque of pierced openwork in

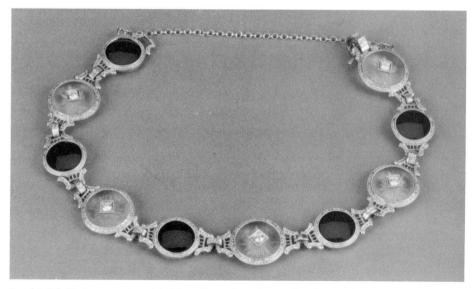

Bracelet, link, black onyx, rock crystal, 14k yg, diamonds, c. 1915-20, five circ carved rock crystal quartz plaques each set with one circ-cut diamond alternating with five round black onyx plaques set in textured and openwork yg bezels and lyre-shaped links plated with white metal; 6-½" × ½", $1,093 (A). Photo courtesy of Butterfield & Butterfield (4/1/93).

navette and quatrefoil design, set with circ-cut diamonds flanked by nine rows of seed pearls joined by plat wire, matching clasp, 7″ tl . . . . **2,640 (A)**

Seed pearls, diamonds, platinum, c. 1900, a band of seed pearls strung with plat chain joined with plat eyepins, terminating in a diamond-set bar clasp, .28 ct tw, 7-⅛″ × 1″ . . . . **3,025 (A)**

Link

Diamonds, platinum, c. 1910, delicate openwork rect links with pierced foliate motifs, each set with five circ-cut diamonds, sgd "T. Kirkpatrick & Co.," 7-¼″ × ¼″ . . . . **4,620 (A)**

Brooch/Pendant

Yg, platinum, diamonds, seed pearls, c. 1900, annular shape set with an inner and outer ring of oe and om diamonds, 10 seed pearls evenly spaced between rings, pendant bail, ⅞″ dia . . . . **1,980 (A)**

Pearls, demantoid garnets, diamonds, 14k yg, c. 1900, an openwork quatrefoil outlined in diamonds with four demantoid-set foliate motifs radiating from the center set with a 6 mm pearl, four smaller pearls between each lobe, 1-⅜″ × 1-⅜″ . . . . **2,200 (A)**

Pearls, diamonds, platinum, c. 1910, lozenge-shaped outline with central quatrefoil and openwork rc diamond design, set with pearls, suspending three baroque pearl and diamond drops, pendant bail, 1-⅝″ w × 2-¼″ . . . . **2,185 (A)**

Platinum and 14k wg, diamonds, c. 1915, heart shape, pierced scroll and foliate openwork,

Brooch/Pendant, diamonds, rubies, pearl, platinum-topped yg, c. 1910, a navette-shaped frame, the lower half set with rc diamonds, the upper with calibré-cut rubies, interlaced with a floral scroll of rc and oe diamonds in knife-edge and pavé settings, terminating in a pearl drop, Fr, 2″ × 1-⅝″, $4,888 (A). Photo: © 1993 Sotheby's, Inc. New York (4/19/93).

set throughout with oe and sc diamonds, approx 3.75 ct tw, pendant bail, 1-⅝″ w × 1-¾″ . . . . **1,800 (A)**

Brooch/Pin

Diamonds, platinum topped 18k yg, c. 1900, garland style, open quatrefoil shape of a foliate motif outlined by diamond collets and bead set within foliate elements with smaller diamonds, five larger oe diamonds, terminating in a pendent drop set with one lg oe diamond, 4.4 ct tw, 1-⅛″ w × 1-⅞″ . . . . **5,500 (A)**

Diamonds, c. 1900, horseshoe shape set with a

Brooch/Pendant, yg, diamonds, pearl, c. 1900, garland style wreath set throughout with rc diamonds, suspending a baroque pearl in the center, trombone catch, 1-¼″ × 1-½″, $850. Cheri Mulligan collection.

Brooch/Pendant, 18k yg, diamonds, sapphires, c. 1910, open knife-edge wirework flowerhead design, four sapphires, six oe and om diamonds set around a center sapphire in pronged flowerhead mounts, swivel bail, lever catch; 1-¾″ dia, $3,500. Mary Lou Diebold collection.

Brooch/Pin, c. 1900, central oval opal (46.5 × 24.7 × 13.8 mm), framed by calibré-cut rubies, rc and French-cut (sq-cut) diamonds, mounted in platinum and yg, sgd "Lacloche Fres., Paris," # 33705, 2-¼" × 1-⅜", $12,650 (A). Photo: © 1993 Sotheby's, Inc. New York (4/19/93).

row of seventeen oe diamonds, 3.30 cts tw, and six cushion-cut sapphires of grad size interspaced within the row, three on each side, platinum mount, lever catch, 1-⅜" × 1-⅜" . . . . 1,725 (A)

Diamonds, platinum topped yg, c. 1900, crown design, points topped with four lg oe diamonds, (2 ct tw), interspaced with three diamond-set trefoils, pavé-set with smaller oe diamonds at the base, 1-¼" w × ⅝" 3,500

Diamonds, syn sapphires, platinum, c. 1910-15, lozenge shape with rounded ends, outlined in oe diamonds around knife-edge openwork, central oe diamond flanked by tapered elongated pentagonal sections pavé-set with oe diamonds, enclosed by eighteen calibré-cut syn sapphires in a lozenge-shaped outline, with five oe diamonds set in a curved row above and below, approx 2.35 ct tw, 1-¾" w × ⅞" . . . . 1,700 (A)

Diamonds, platinum, c. 1910, buckle shape set with 140 diamonds, approx 6.85 ct tw in a

Brooch/Pin, c. 1906, platinum crescent shape set with 41 oe diamonds, approx 3 cts tw, inscribed on the inside rim with name and "11-28-1906," 1-⅝" dia, $3,163 (A). Photo: © 1993 Sotheby's, Inc. New York (4/19/93).

flexible plat mount, 2-⅝" w × 1-⅛" . . . . 4,290 (A)

Diamonds, platinum, 14k wg, c. 1915, curv ribbon bow shape, pierced and set throughout with oe diamonds, 7.5 ct tw, 1-¾" w × 3" . . . . 5,400 (A)

Diamonds, platinum, c. 1910, elongated quatrefoil, pierced, with knife-edge filigree, center tapering row of oe diamonds in octagonal mounts set throughout with smaller oe diamonds, 2-⅜" w × 1" . . . . 2,100 (A)

Diamonds, platinum, c. 1910, pierced and engr plat bow set throughout with thirty-three oe and om diamonds, approx 4 ct tw, pierced gallery, lever catch, 2-⅛" w × 1" . . . . 4,313 (A)

Diamonds, platinum, c. 1910, pierced eye-shaped plat plaque with center pupil of one

Brooch/Pin, c. 1910, lozenge shape, one circ-cut collet-set diamond in the center, and approx 26 round diamonds in a pierced, openwork, and knife-edge platinum filigree setting, yg pin stem, 2-¾" × ¾", $1,265 (A). Photo courtesy of Butterfield & Butterfield (4/1/93).

Brooch/Pin, c. 1900, tapered bar, pierced scrolled openwork design with a central pansy motif, pavé-set with rc and om diamonds, suspending a diamond-set flowerhead drop, mounted in platinum and 18k yg (two stones missing), 2-³/₄″ × 1-¹/₂″, $2,530 (A). *Photo courtesy of Christie's New York (4/22/93).*

Brooch/Pin, c. 1910, navette-shaped outline with openwork floral design on knife-edge wire ground, set throughout with oe and rc diamonds mounted in platinum, 2-¹/₈″ × 1-³/₈″, $2,990 (A). *Photo courtesy of Christie's New York (4/22/93).*

oe diamond, 1.95 ct, within radiating rows of sm oe diamonds, outlined in diamonds with two fan-shaped elements at top and bottom, approx 100 diamonds, 3.95 ct tw, lever catch, 2-³/₄″ w × 1″ . . . . **6,900 (A)**

Diamonds, plat, c. 1910, crescent-shaped, with a line of oe, om, and sc prong-set grad diamonds, sgd "T.B. Starr," for Theodore B. Starr, New York, N.Y., 4.4 dwt, 1″ w × ⁷/₈″ . . . . **1,210 (A)**

Diamonds, platinum, c. 1915, in the outline of a bow with an open center, pavé-set with diamonds, 2.8 cts tw, sgd "Cartier #2915564," 1-¹/₂″ w × ³/₄″ . . . . . **2,970 (A)**

Moonstone, diamonds, platinum, c. 1910, lg central circ moonstone cameo of a woman sculpting a bust within a navette-shaped pierced platinum setting with 42 circ-cut and oe diamonds, sgd "Walton Co.," 1-¹/₂″ w × ⁷/₈″ . . . . **3,163 (A)**

Opal, plat, diamonds, rubies, demantoid

garnets, c. 1910, navette-shaped, handmade pierced mount, floral motif, one central lg oval bezel-set opal, outlined with floral elements collet set with circ-cut sc and brilliant-cut rubies, diamonds, and demantoid garnets, millegrain detail, 6.7 dwt, 2″ w × 1″ . . . . **3,850 (A)**

Sapphire, diamonds, plat-topped 18k yg, c. 1906, in the the garland style, a central oval blue sapphire, approx 7.35 ct, bordered with diamonds and encircled by diamond-set floral and foliate motifs within an oval diamond-set frame, lobed top and bottom, approx 2 ct tw, sgd "J.E. Caldwell," Philadelphia Pa., accompanied by original receipt dated January 25, 1906. 1-³/₄″ w × 1-¹/₄″ . . . . **14,300 (A)**

Bar

9k yg, diamond, c. 1915-20, plain tapered bar, sm sc diamond set in center, safety catch, Eng, 2″ w × ¹/₄″ **60**

Brooch/Pin, c. 1910, circ knife-edge and pierced openwork design, concentric quatrefoils set with circ-cut and oe diamonds and pearls (not tested), platinum mount, 1-³/₄″ dia, $4,600 (A). *Photo courtesy of Christie's New York (4/22/93).*

Brooch/Pin, c. 1915, scroll and foliate design set throughout with 33 diamonds, approx 1.5 cts tw, set in an inverted triangular openwork 14k wg and platinum mount, safety catch, 2″ w × 1-¹/₂″, $1,035 (A). *Photo courtesy of Butterfield & Butterfield (6/17/93).*

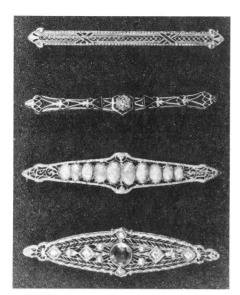

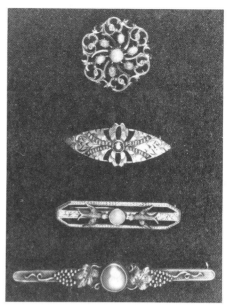

Brooches/Pins, bar, c. 1910-20: T, platinum-topped 14k yg, geo openwork in a helix pattern with two pierced X-shapes, trefoiled ends, lever catch, 2-³/₈″ × ³/₁₆″, $175; T-B, 2, 14k openwork, geo scroll with hexagonal center set with a diamond, flanked by two triangular syn blue sapphires, mkd "14k," "S" in a heart for E.L. Spencer Co., Providence, R.I., lever catch, 2-³/₈″ × ¹/₄″, $175; T-B, 3, platinum and wg, filigree scroll design with ten grad oval opals prong-set on a shaped and tapered bar, mkd "14k & plat" on lever catch, 2-¹/₂″ × ¹/₂″, $1,200; B, filigreed 14k wg, lozenge shape with center faceted amethyst, oe diamonds and seed pearls, mkd "14k" on lever catch, 2-¹/₂″ × ⁵/₈″, $750, *Cheri Mulligan collection.*

Brooches/Pins, yg, c. 1900-10: T, scrolled foliate open-work wreath design, six oval opals prong-set around a round center opal, wide C-catch, ⁷/₈″ dia, $175; T-B, 2, 14k, lace or handy pin, pierced and engr lozenge shape, scroll and foliate design with center syn sapphire, and four curved rows of seed pearls, mkd C over T (superimposed), for Crane and Theurer, Newark, N.J., lever catch, 1-³/₈″ × ⁹/₁₆″, $250; T-B, 3, 14k, rect open triple bar, chamfered corners, engr, pr of bird motifs with sm opals set in wings flanking a bezel-set opal mounted on center bar, lever catch, 1-¹/₂″ × ³/₈″, $250; B, tapered 10k bar, central grapevine motif surrounding a collet-set baroque pearl, feather-pattern ground, lever catch, 2-¹/₂″ × ³/₈″, $225. *Cheri Mulligan collection.*

9k yg, seed pearls, date letter for 1908, bird and foliate motifs set with seed pearls, appl to narrow bar, Chester (Eng) hmks, C-catch, 1-¹/₂″ w × ¹/₂″ **125**

10k yg, amethyst, c. 1910-15, rounded lozenge shape, cut-out crescent and bar design, lozenge-shape faceted amethyst bezel-set in center, mkd "CRR" for C. Ray Randall & Co., North Attleboro, Mass., "10k" on C-catch, 1-¹/₈″ w × ³/₈″ **65**

10k and 18k yg, diamond, c. 1900, four-leaf clover, om diamond-set center, mkd "18k" on underside, mounted on center of bar, lever clasp mkd "CXK" for Champenois & Co, Newark, N.J., "10k," 2″ w × ¹/₂″ **275**

14k wg, diamonds, mabé pearl, c. 1915, oval openwork mount, center mabé pearl flanked by larger diamonds, outlined and set throughout with smaller diamonds, .75 ct tw, 1-³/₈″ w × ¹/₂″ . . . . **1,100 (A)**

18k yg, oe diamonds, emeralds, c.1910-15, oval yg bar, cutout center with appl diamond-set leaves, one oe diamond within a

box mount in the center, flanked top and bottom by sq cut emeralds, 2-¹/₈″ w × ³/₈″ **450**

Diamonds, platinum, c. 1910, openwork, tapering bar set with a line of grad circ-cut and rc diamonds, diamond-set scrolled terminals, damaged gallery, 2-³/₄″ w × ³/₈″ . . . . **413 (A)**

Diamonds, platinum, yg, c. 1900, pierced bar with trefoiled ends, central cartouche set with one larger oe diamond, and set throughout with slightly grad oe and om diamonds, 2″ w × ¹/₄″ . . . . **2,200 (A)**

Diamonds, platinum, 18k yg, c. 1900, scal-loped-edge ends tapering to a point, pierced central lozenge-shape flanked by a pierced stylized bird design, each with larger collet-set oe diamond as the head, set throughout with oe, om, and sc diamonds, 7.5 ct tw, 2-¹/₄″ w × ⁷/₈″ . . . . **6,875 (A)**

Diamonds, platinum, yg, c. 1910, tapered

bar with scrolled spade-shaped terminals, a .9 ct oe diamond set in the center, flanked by smaller diamonds, 1.4 ct tw, within a pierced plat mount, yg pinstem .... **2,420 (A)**

Diamonds, sapphires, platinum, c. 1910, oe diamond, approx. 1.55 ct, flanked by 12 oe diamonds, approx 2.8 ct tw, and four collet-set sapphires in plat frame, central portion conforming to shape and size of center stone, 3″ w × ³/₈″ ...... **4,050 (A)**

Plat-topped 14k yg, diamonds, sapphire, pearls, c. 1900, open scrollwork bar set with oe and om diamonds, suspending an oval faceted sapphire, approx 1.15 ct, encircled by circ-cut diamonds and flanked by two pearls, 1-³/₈″ w × 1-⁵/₈″ tl ...;...................... **1,600 (A)**

Platinum, c. 1910-20, pierced tapered bar with trefoil terminals, center set with oe diamond, 1.45 cts, and set throughout with eighteen smaller oe diamonds, lever catch, 2-¹/₄″ × ¹/₄″ .... **3,163 (A)**

Platinum, 14k wg, diamonds, c. 1915, grad row of 17 oe diamonds, 2 ct tw, set in plat and yg frame (bent, dam on rev), 3-¹/₄″ w × ¹/₄″ .... **900 (A)**

Yg, amethyst, seed pearls, c. 1910, openwork scroll and foliate design, bezel-set oval faceted amethyst in center, flanked by seed pearls, added safety catch, 1-³/₄″ w × ³/₈″ **75**

Lace

Yg, seed pearls, blue stone, c. 1910, circ frame with bg of yg honeycomb openwork, quartered by radiating bars tapering outward, each set with three grad seed pearls, a collet-set faceted blue stone in the center, replaced safety catch, ⁷/₈″ dia.......................~.... **65**

Cuff links

18k yg, enamel, date letter for 1912, double-sided yg oval links with painted enamel hunting scenes, Birmingham (Eng) hmks, ³/₄″ × ¹/₂″ w .... **1,495 (A)**

Plat-topped 18k yg, oe diamond, c. 1900, pr of two linked plat-topped yg disks, ea with oe diamond in center, .5 ct tw, millegrain frames, Fr hmks, ³/₄″ dia .... **700 (A)**

Earrings, drop

Diamonds, platinum, 14k wg, c. 1915, garland style laurel wreaths suspended from a stepped surmount, set with 74 round diamonds, wg screw back findings, ⁵/₈″ w × 1-¹/₄″ tl, pr .... **978 (A)**

Earrings, pendent

Emeralds, yg, c. 1915, inverted open heart-shaped drop pavé-set with circ-cut emeralds,

Cuff links, Am, c. 1900-20: TL, MOP disks set in wm frames, blue r.s. in centers, ¹/₂″ dia, pr, $20, *Richard Noël collection;* TR, abalone disks set in engr wm, millegrain-set faux seed pearls in centers, rev ym mkd "Krementz" (Newark, N.J.), ¹/₂″ dia, pr, $50; C, centers of white *basse-taille* enamel, foliate and geo pattern, set into linked MOP disks, ¹/₂″ dia, pr, $50, *Terrance O'Halloran collection;* BL, engr MOP disks set in engr 14k wg frames, yg backs, mkd "14" within a "C" for Carrington & Company, Newark, N.J., ¹/₂″ dia, pr, $150; BR, engr platinum frame, MOP center, blk enamel border, yg backs, mkd "C" in an arrowhead for Carter, Howe & Co., Newark, N.J., ¹/₂″ dia, pr, $125, *Richard Noël collection.*

terminating in a cluster of three emeralds, suspended by yg chain from surmount set with one circ-cut emerald, screwback findings, ³/₄″ w × 1-¹/₂″ tl, pr **350**

Diamonds, syn sapphires, platinum, yg, c. 1910, teardrop faceted blue syn sapphire outlined in sc diamonds suspended from articulated diamond-set chain and Fr earwires, mounted in plat-topped yg, ³/₈″ w × 1-¹/₄″ tl, pr **1,150**

Lavalier

14k yg, diamond, pearls, c. 1900, scrolled frame tapering out from a trefoil surmount set with a pearl, center strip of tapered foliate motifs terminating in an oe diamond, suspended from an oval link yg chain in-

Lavaliers, yg, c. 1900, without chains: TL, 10k, open concave lozenge shape, tapering to bail, f.w. pearls at top and bottom, a flowerhead with a seed pearl center, within a central lozenge-shaped frame, 1-¹/₂″ tl × ⁵/₈″, $100; BL, pierced V-shape set with seed pearls, suspending a f.w. pearl, flowerhead center with prong-set faceted blue glass, tapering to a double-loop pendant bail, mkd "10k," 1-³/₄″ tl × ⁵/₈″, $100; with chains: L, tapering scrolled yg wirework and floral motifs set with seed pearls, suspending hexagonal drop set with faceted lt blue glass, rev mkd "14k," suspended from fine yg chain, 18″ tl, pendant 1-³/₈″ × ¹/₂″, $150; C, narrow 10k latticework plaque with green enameled accents suspending a briolette-cut amethyst from a foliate cap, set throughout with seed pearls, suspended from a fancy-link yg chain, 16″ tl, pendant 2″ × ¹/₄″, $250; R, open scrollwork teardrop shape with red faceted glass, pendent f.w. pearl, mkd "O 10k B" on bail for Richard Oliver & Bloomfield, N.Y., 1-⁵/₈″ × ⁵/₈″, chain mkd 14k, 19-¹/₂″ tl, $150, *Cheri Mulligan collection.*

Lavaliers, c. 1900-10: L, frosted rev carved hexagonal rock crystal plaque, bezel-set, four sides bordered with 14k yg filigree, suspended by two chains from filigreed trefoil surmount, four syn blue sapphires set in surmount, top, center, and bottom of plaque, chain 20″ tl, pendant 1″ × 1-¹/₈″, $150; C, two pendent drops with knife-edge segments terminating in collet-set oe diamonds suspended *negligée* from a lozenge-shaped plaque set with oe and rc diamonds, two lengths of fine chain joined to loops at top of plaque, in platinum-topped yg, European hmks, pendant 1-¹/₂″ × ¹/₂″, chain 16-¹/₂″ tl, $1,500; R, 10k yg bow set with seed pearls, oe diamond center, suspending two pearl drops from chains, orig neckchain joined to loops at top of bow, 16″ tl, pendant 1-¹/₂″ tl × ⁵/₈″, $200. *Cheri Mulligan collection.*

terspersed with five oval seed pearls, mkd "14k," pendant ¹/₂″ w × 1-⁵/₈″, chain 14-¹/₂″ tl . . . . **500 (A)**

Diamonds, platinum, c. 1910, an elongated triangle pavé-set with oe diamonds, with two linked oe diamonds suspended from cutout center and from cusped base, 1.25 ct tw, suspended from wg cable-link chain, 17″ tl (chain probably not orig) . . . . **1,540 (A)**

Emerald, diamonds, pearl, plat-topped yg, c. 1900, an emerald-cut emerald, approx 4 ct, set in the center of an open quatrefoil frame with clusters of three collet-set diamonds on all four sides, terminating in a drop of two diamonds and a pearl, suspended from a plat chain, approx 15" tl, pendant ⅞" w × 1-½" tl . . . . **2,640 (A)**

Platinum, diamonds, c. 1910, openwork vasiform, tapering out to a flared base set with a curv row of five sm oe diamonds, and a vertical row of five sm diamonds in the center, ¾" w × 1-⅜" tl . . . . **385 (A)**

Platinum, diamonds, c. 1910, two collet-set oe diamonds, approx .77 ct tw, suspended *négligée* from two flexible rows of collet-set oe diamonds, joined near the top by a diamond-set foliated scroll, completed by a plat chain, longest row of diamonds 2-⅜", scroll ⅝" w, 16" approx tl . . . . **1,650 (A)**

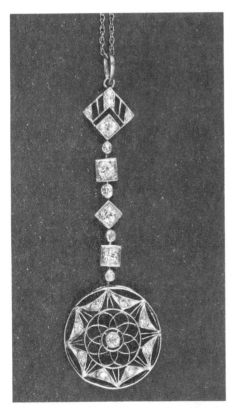

Lavalier, platinum, diamonds, c. 1910, pierced sq knife-edge top set with one lg and four sm oe diamonds, suspended from one corner by a pendant bail, suspending a row of collet-set alternating with bead-set oe diamonds in box settings, terminating in a circ openwork and pierced plaque set with nine oe diamonds around one collet-set diamond in the center of eight swagged segments within a plat frame with a pierced gallery, 2-⅝" tl × ¾", $850. *Elizabeth Cook collection.*

Lorgnette

14k yg, c. 1900, case and handle with allover chased and engr scrolled feather and floral des, folded, 1-¼" w × 5-¼" . . . . . . **880 (A)**

Platinum, diamonds, enamel, c. 1910, set with pavé rc diamonds and diamond and black enamel barrel slides completed by black cord, rc diamond handle, signed "Cartier" on bail, lorgnette, folded with handle, 2" × 1" . . . . **3,850 (A)**

Platinum, diamonds, c. 1915-20, folding spectacles within platinum frames, attached to a tapered engr plat handle with scrolled terminals top and bottom, pavé-set with 106 oe diamonds, loop for chain at the base, spectacles 3-¼" w open, handle 2-½" × ¾" . . . . **3,163 (A)**

Necklace

Diamonds, c. 1910, two pear-shaped diamond drops, approx 4.25 cts tw, suspended *négligée* from circ-cut collect-set diamond and knife-edge platinum link chains, continuing to a similarly set chain necklace, 50 diamonds, approx 1.00 cts tw, approx 15" tl, longest drop approx 2¼" . . . . . **$27,500 (A)**

Peridots, yg, seed pearls, c. 1900, grad circ yg filigree plaques, a collet-set peridot in the center of each, a seed pearl suspended from each connecting link, the lg center plaque suspending five smaller plaques set with peridots from grad chains linked with seed pearls, 16-¼" tl . . . . **2,090 (A)**

Diamonds, platinum topped yg, c. 1900, fine yg chain suspending six oe diamonds, two linked together in the center, flanked by two single drops on each side, 8 cts tw, in double circ knife-edge frames suspended from sm foliate motifs set with sc diamonds, 15" tl × 1-½" . . . . **11,000 (A)**

Dog collar

Seed pearls, st yg, c. 1900, composed of 18 strands of seed pearls attached at intervals to five rect openwork st yg plaques, a vertical row of four four-petaled flowerheads within each frame set throughout with sm rubies and rc diamonds, approx 14" tl × 2-¾" w . . . . **3,850 (A)**

Seed pearls, platinum diamonds, c. 1900, a network of plat links strung with seed pearls attached to six openwork scrolled foliate plat bars, each set with four pearls and two sm collet-set diamonds, converts to two bracelets, approx 14" tl × 1-½" . . . . **3,740 (A)**

Festoon

Freshwater pearls, diamonds, platinum, c. 1910, lg center f.w. pearl and lg pendent pearl drop suspended from multiple swagged plat chains interspersed with smaller f.w. pearls and sm spectacle-set diamonds, 14" tl × 2" . . . . **1,650 (A)**

Necklace, c. 1905, in the garland style, a chain of X-shaped and tapered diamond-set platinum links suspending swagged floral and foliate motifs and a knife-edge-linked fringe of similar motifs set throughout with sc and oe diamonds, terminating in nine grad pear-shaped diamond drops, each within a diamond-set frame, 16-½" tl × 2", $68,500 (A). *Photo courtesy of Christie's New York (4/21/93).*

Necklace, dog collar, c. 1910, a central slightly convex rect platinum plaque of pierced scroll, fan and geo design, with a horizontal row of five full-cut diamonds, 1.65 cts tw, four circ-cut diamonds in corners, and set throughout with numerous sm rc diamonds, flanked by nine strands of cultured pearls with 14k wg diamond-set spacers and wg clasp (pearls, spacers, and clasp probably not orig), plaque 2" × 1", approx 13" tl, $6,325 (A). *Photo courtesy of Butterfield & Butterfield (6/17/93).*

Moonstones, yg, c. 1900, a collet-set oval cab moonstone suspended from vertically linked lg and sm round cab moonstones in the center of a grad row of eight collet-set oval moonstones each suspended from a round moonstone linked together and continuing to a fine yg chain, 15" tl × 1-⅛" **300**

Topaz, pearls, diamonds, platinum, c. 1900, a central yellowish-brown rect-cut topaz prong-set within an open scrolled foliate mount set with diamonds and pearls, suspending a pear-shaped yellow topaz drop, flanked by swagged plat chains interspersed with seed pearls joined to two yellow topaz and continuing to a single chain, 17" tl × 2" . . . . **1,540 (A)**

Sautoir

Platinum, seed pearls, onyx, rock crystal, c. 1915, a plat chain interspersed with seed pearls suspending an onyx and pearl chain with a rock crystal and seed pearl drop, 30" tl . . . . **715 (A)**

Seed pearls, diamonds, st yg, c. 1900, multiple strands of seed pearls twisted together in a double rope, attached to two rc diamond-set st yg terminals suspending seed pearl tassels with rc diamond-set st yg caps, 41" tl . . . . **4,025 (A)**

Seed pearls, diamonds, platinum, c. 1900, multiple strands of seed pearls braided together and attached to two diamond-set plat terminals suspending seed pearl tassels with diamond-set plat caps, 57" tl . . . . **5,225 (A)**

Pendant

Pearl, diamonds, sapphires, plat-topped yg, c. 1910, a center teardrop-shaped pearl suspended within a frame of channel-set sapphires, surrounded by a garland style diamond-set wreath in a plat-topped yg mounting, sgd "B.S.& F." for Black, Starr & Frost, 1" w × 1-½" . . . . **3,190 (A)**

Pendant and Chain

Diamonds, platinum, c. 1910, plat bars set with rc diamonds suspending a small open baton-shaped diamond-set pendant with an appl X-shaped center, three diamonds missing, 25" tl . . . . **2,750 (A)**

Necklace, sautoir, c. 1915, a platinum pear-shaped plaque pendant, with pierced rows of scallops outlined in pavé rc diamonds, suspending a pear-shaped diamond from each scallop, suspended from three diamond-set triangular openwork elements attached to an openwork ribbon of seed pearls and platinum chain, 25-½" tl, pendant 2-⅛" w × 2-⅞", $17,250 (A). *Photo courtesy of Christie's New York (4/21/93).*

Diamonds, pearls, platinum, c. 1910, an openwork plat quatrefoil with a diamond in the center encircled by smaller diamonds, .75 ct tw, outlined with a seed pearl border, suspended from a cable link chain, 21" tl, in a fitted leather box sgd "Watherston & Son," pendant 1-⅜" × 1-⅜" . . . . **2,640 (A)**

Cross, Diamonds, platinum, c. 1910, Celtic cross pendant with flared ends, each end collet-set with three oe diamonds, center oe diamond quartered by four smaller diamonds, one larger diamond below and bead-set sc diamonds throughout, 10 ct tw, sc diamond-set bail, 1-½" w × 2-¼", suspended from a curb link chain, 17" tl . . . . **7,700 (A)**

Ring

Amethyst, 9k yg, rc diamonds, date letter for 1912, one oval center, two round side stones in gypsy setting, pierced gallery, Chester (Eng) hmks, ½" w **200**

18k yg, sapphire, diamonds, date letter for

Necklace, sautoir, c. 1900, twisted multistrands of seed pearls terminating in two rc diamond and seed pearl tassels, 31" tl, $2,530 (A). *Photo courtesy of Christie's New York (4/22/93).*

Pendant/Necklace, c. 1915, a pendant of two concentric rings of collet-set circ-cut diamonds with a lg collet-set diamond in the center, suspended from a double row of collet-set diamonds forming a Y with a lg collet-set diamond encircled by smaller collet-set diamonds at the center, continuing to a delicate sc and circ-cut diamond and calibré-cut emerald link chain, plat mount, suede fitted case mkd Van Cleef & Arpels, 14" tl, pendant ³/₄" dia, 2-¹/₄" tl, $14,950 (A). *Photo courtesy of Christie's New York (4/21/93)*

1911, a sapphire flanked by two diamonds in a scalloped prong setting, Chester (Eng) hmks, ¹/₂" w **250**
Black opal, diamonds, 14k wg, c. 1915, prong-set oval opal cab outlined by oe diamonds in a millegrain setting, continuing to a polished wg shank, Am, sgd "Marcus," ⁷/₈" × ³/₄" . . . . **3,080 (A)**

Demantoid garnet, diamonds, 18k yg, c. 1900, navette-shaped top with oval faceted demantoid garnet center, pavé-set with oe diamonds, polished yg shank with sculpted shoulders, ⁷/₈" × ³/₄" . . . . **2,200 (A)**
Diamonds, platinum, c. 1910, tapering top of openwork plat, center row of two larger oe and one bc (replacement) diamonds, 1 ct tw, surrounded by smaller sc diamonds, .35 ct tw, ³/₈" × ³/₄" . . . . **1,100 (A)**
Diamonds, platinum, c. 1900-10, top of openwork platinum with center row of three oe diamonds, 1.9 ct tw, in ocatagonal mounts outlined with sc diamonds, center stone flanked by diamond baguettes set vertically, continuing to a polished platinum shank (bent), ¹/₂" × ⁷/₈" . . . . **1,300 (A)**
Diamonds, 18k wg, c. 1915, tapering wg band with center row of three prong-set oe diamonds, 2.15 ct tw, ³/₈" × ³/₄" . . . . . **2,000 (A)**
Diamonds, platinum, c. 1915, navette-shaped top set throughout with bc and sc diamonds, continuing to a diamond-set shank, 1.15 ct tw, ⁵/₈" × ³/₄" . . . . **550 (A)**
Diamonds, platinum, c. 1910, pierced convex navette-shaped top with a vertical row of three oe diamonds, set throughout with smaller diamonds, pierced gallery, tapering to a platinum shank, ³/₄" × ⁵/₈" . . . . . **500 (A)**
Diamonds, platinum, c. 1900, pierced bombé shape with a center row of three oe diamonds, 1 ct tw, sc diamonds set throughout in foliate motifs, ³/₈" × ⁷/₈" . . . . **2,420 (A)**
Diamonds, platinum, c. 1900, an oe diamond, approx 1.5 ct, in the center of a pavé-set diamond quatrefoil, ³/₄" × ³/₄" . . . . **3,575 (A)**
Diamonds, platinum, c. 1910, openwork sq top, rounded corners and center set with larger oe diamonds, smaller diamonds pavé-set in formée (equilateral) cross motif, approx 1.5 ct tw, ⁵/₈" sq . . . . **4,400 (A)**
Diamonds, platinum, 18k yg, c. 1900, 39 oe diamonds, 1.3 ct tw, set within a pierced, scalloped-edge navette-shaped plat-topped

Ring, c. 1910, rounded oblong platinum plaque set with a grad vertical row of five oe diamonds, with concentric borders of calibré-cut rubies and sm diamonds, mounted on a balustered yg shank, 1" × ¹/₂", $4,600 (A). *Photo: © 1993 Sotheby's, Inc. New York (4/19/93).*

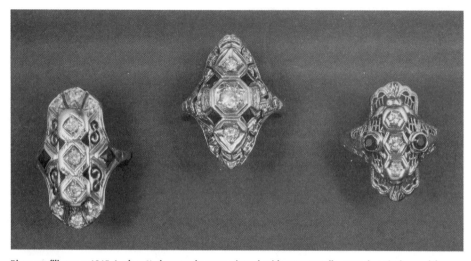

Rings, wg filigree, c. 1915: L, elongated convex lozenge, pierced, with cutout scrolls, central vertical row of three oe diamonds flanked by two bezel-set sq blue syn sapphires, three sc diamonds at top and bottom, tapering to a thin wg shank, mkd "18k," $600; C, convex navette shape, pierced and engr, an oe diamond in a central octagonal mount, smaller oe diamonds above and below, quartered by four sq-cut syn sapphires, tapering to an engr wg shank, Am, mkd "UR-18k" for Untermeyer-Robbins Co., N.Y., 1" × ³⁄₄", $600; R, elongated convex lozenge, pierced, stamped and engr with center vertical row of three sc diamonds flanked by two circ-cut blue sapphires, tapering to a thin wg shank, mkd "14k," ⁷⁄₈" × ¹⁄₂", $475. *Dena McCarthy collection.*

yg mount with central six-petaled flo-werhead design, ³⁄₄" w × 1" ..... **2,300 (A)**

Jadeite, diamonds, platinum, c. 1910, an oval jadeite cab, 13.9 × 9.8 × 5.85mm, bezel-set within a pierced plat foliate motif mount set with 66 oe and sc diamonds, ⁷⁄₈" × ³⁄₄" .... **11,500 (A)**

Moonstone, diamonds, platinum, c. 1910, a navette-shaped moonstone within a dia-mond-set foliate frame, tapering to a narrow shank, ⁵⁄₈" w × 1" .... **770 (A)**

Shell, 14k wg, diamond, onyx, c. 1915, oval cameo *habillé*, profile bust of a woman wearing necklace set with om diamond, bezel set, swivels to rev of oval black onyx plaque set with sc diamond, ⁷⁄₈" × ⁵⁄₈" **350**

Scarf pin/Stickpin

14k yg, demantoid garnets, c. 1900, in the shape of a lizard, set with garnets on the head and back, chased detailing, ³⁄₄" × ⁵⁄₈", 2-¹⁄₂" tl .... **660 (A)**

Diamond, platinum, yg, c. 1900, head of one oe diamond, 1.15 ct, plat prong-set on yg pinstem, 2-³⁄₄" tl .... **1,980 (A)**

Diamonds, rubies, platinum, rose and yg, c. 1910, rose gold stem topped with a crowned openwork oe, rc, and sc diamond-set shield within a border of calibré-cut rubies mounted in yg, in a fitted box stamped "Cartier," ¹⁄₂" w × 2-³⁄₄" tl .... **770 (A)**

"IMITATION" (COSTUME) JEWELRY

Bracelet

Flexible

Sterling, glass, c. 1915-25, stamped filigree, wider center section set with oval faceted blue glass flanked by triangular blue glass in millegrained settings, tapering to sm sq hinged plaques, box clasp mkd "sterling," 7-³⁄₄" tl × ³⁄₄" **110**

Sterling, rhinestones, c. 1920, strap and buckle motif, rows of three r.s. each set in hinged box mounts, pavé buckle (hinged), mkd "sterling pat 3-20-17," safety bar, 7-¹⁄₄" tl × ³⁄₈" **125**

Sterling, rhinestones, enamel, c. 1920, pierced rect plaques in quatrefoil design, rounded edges, two plaques with appl r.s.-set lozenges bordered in black enamel, v-spring box clasp, mkd "S.W. Sterling," 7-¹⁄₂" × ¹⁄₂" **115**

Brooch/Pin

Silver, rhinestones (paste), c. 1910, in the shape of a butterfly, pierced openwork wings set throughout with colorless r.s., pavé r.s. body, 1-⁵⁄₈" w × 1-¹⁄₈" **125**

Rhinestones (paste), sterling, c. 1910-15, 12-petaled daisy flowerhead, bead-set pavé r.s., mkd "925," 1-⁵⁄₈" dia **135**

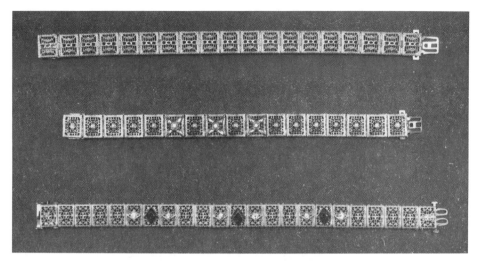

Bracelets, flexible, sterling, stamped filigree, c. 1915-25: T, sm rect hinged plaques, each with curved floral and foliate motifs accented with pink and green painted enamel, similar motifs engr on gallery, hinged box clasp mkd "sterling," 7" tl × ³/₈", $75, *Richard Noël collection;* C, sm rect hinged plaques, scrolled gallery, three center plaques bezel-set with four triangular green faceted glass stones around center r.s., hinged box clasp mkd "sterling," 6-⁵/₈" tl × ³/₈", $145; B, sm rect hinged plaques, engr gallery, three plaques set with lozenge-shaped green faceted glass in millegrained bezels, each flanked by plaques with round colorless faceted glass bead-set within lozenge-shaped frames, hinged box clasp mkd "sterling" and "G" in a lozenge, probably for J.A. & S.W. Granbery, Newark, N.J., 7-¹/₄" tl × ³/₈", $165, *Charles Pinkham collection.*

Bracelets, hinged bangles, transitional, c. 1920-30: L/T, gp base metal, pierced stamped openwork, appl lozenge with prong-set pink faceted glass in center, safety chain, 2-¹/₂" dia, ¹/₂" w, $55; C, wm, pierced filigree, central octagonal colorless faceted glass set in a millegrained bezel, bordered with seed pearls, enameled trefoils top and bottom, flanked by blue, yellow, and red *cloisonné* enameled plaques with bird and floral motifs, 2-¹/₂" dia × ³/₄" w, $150; R/B, gp wm, pierced and stamped scrollwork, front hinged clasp set with oval citrine-colored faceted glass (chip), plating worn, Am, inside mkd "Samsan pat pend," 2-¹/₂" × ¹/₂", $85; *Terrance O'Halloran collection.*

Brooches/Pins, figural, c. 1900-10: TL, salamander, a row of green r.s. down center of its back, green r.s. eyes, set throughout with colorless r.s., mkd "sterling," 2-³/₈" × ⁵/₈", $95; TR, silver swallow, colorless circ-cut r.s. set throughout, mk worn, 1-¹/₈" × 2-¹/₈", $95; C, flower spray with pearl centers, sm turq glass cabs set throughout, C-catch, 1-⁷/₈" × ¹/₂", $75; *Dena McCarthy collection;* BL, 10k wg filigree bow, lever catch mkd "10k," Am, 1-⁷/₈" × ⁵/₈", $90, *Terrance O'Halloran collection;* BR, bow, black enameled surface set with 12 seed pearls, mkd "sterling," C-catch, 1-⁷/₈" × ¹/₄", $65, *Dena McCarthy collection.*

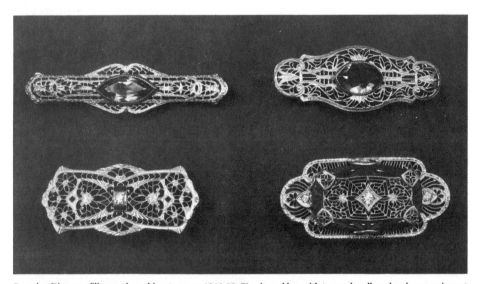

Brooches/Pins, wm filigree, glass, rhinestones, c. 1910-20: TL, pierced bar with tapered scalloped ends, marquise-cut amber-colored faceted glass in central millegrained bezel, lever catch, 2-¹/₈" × ¹/₂", $45; TR, lobed and scrolled pierced lozenge shape, wide marquise-cut green faceted glass in central millegrained bezel, pierced gallery, lever catch, 1-³/₄" × ⁵/₈", $65; BL, fancy shaped rect, pierced wm, center set with circ-cut colorless r.s. and two dk blue baguettes, lever catch, 1-⁵/₈" × ³/₄", $65; BR, rounded rect with bombé ends, pierced and filigreed plaque surmounted by an oval ring of molded carnelian glass, a r.s. in a lozenge center and on each side of glass, held in place with pierced strapwork, pierced gallery, lever catch, 1-³/₄" × ³/₄", $95. *Terrance O'Halloran collection.*

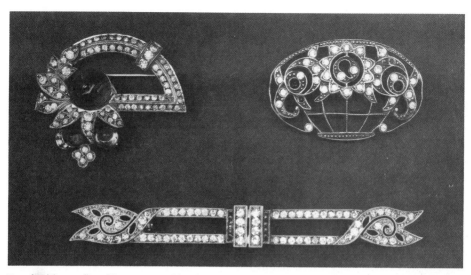

Brooches/Pins, sterling, rhinestones, transitional, c. 1920: T/TL, open center semicircle with an off-center cross bar, pavé-set with colorless r.s., floral motif on one side with lg blue, med red, sm green glass cabs, rev mkd "sterling" (rhodium plated), 1-³/₈" × 1-¹/₈" , $125; C/TR, stylized flower basket motif, pierced and set throughout with colorless r.s., 1-¹/₂" × ⁷/₈", $65; B, pavé-set colorless r.s. double bar, with center verticals set with colorless r.s. flanked by a row of calibré-cut red glass stones set *à jour*, terminating in a scrolled foliate design at each end, rev vertical mkd "sterling Germany," rhodium plated, lever catch, tube hinge, 3-¹/₈" × ³/₈", $250. *Terrance O'Halloran collection.*

Bar
    Gp base metal, glass rev intaglio, c. 1910, bar in the shape of a riding crop, rev intaglio of a fox mounted in the center, 2-¹/₈" w × ³/₈" **135**
    Yg-topped base metal, c. 1910, in the shape of a tennis racquet, engr handle, rev mkd "Gold Top," 1-¹/₄" w × ³/₈" **75**
Sash ornament
    Sterling, enamel, c. 1910, flared rect, rect cutout center, red *basse-taille* enamel (sm chip) on inside and outside border around white *basse-taille* sunburst pattern, three ym fleurs-de-lis spaced along each end, mkd "sterling," mk for Watson, Newell Co. (crown, Gothic W, lion) Attleboro, Mass., 1-⁷/₈" w × ³/₈" **75**
Earrings, pendent
    Silver, rhinestones (paste), c. 1910, articulated row of paste-set links of sm double leaves alternating with single collet-set stones, suspending a daisy flowerhead with lg center stone and petals set with smaller stones, original earwires, flowerhead ³/₄" dia, approx 2-¹/₂" tl, pr **175**
    Sterling, chrysoprase, marcasites, c. 1920, lg cushion-shaped faceted chrysoprase at the base of an elongated drop set with marcasites within a garland style ster mount, suspended from a marcasite-set surmount with screwback findings, 1" w × 2-³/₄" tl, pr **225**

Pendent Earrings, rhinestones, pot metal, c. 1910-20, chandelier style, five strands of articulated links suspended from a scrolled center plaque, two sm foliate motifs linked to a flowerhead cluster surmount, set throughout with colorless r.s., new posts, 4" × 1-¹/₄", pr, $125. *Joyce Albers collection.*

Pendent Earrings, rhinestones, pot metal, transitional, c. 1920, articulated garland style row of r.s.-set foliate motifs suspending a pierced geo kite-shaped drop from a flowerhead surmount, pavé-set throughout with colorless r.s., original screwback findings, 3-⅝" tl × 1-⅛", pr, $150. *Author's collection.*

Lavalier

  Sterling, rhinestones (paste), glass, c. 1910, a tapered r.s.-set bail suspending a flowerhead and two r.s.-set garlands curving out to an open pavé r.s. Greek key motif on each side of a lozenge-shaped faceted blue glass stone, continuing to a V-shaped base suspending two sm r.s.-set drops, rev mkd "sterling," 1-⅛" w × 2" tl **125**

Necklace

  Sterling, rhinestones (paste), c. 1910-15, three articulated pendent drops of foliate design, pavé-set stones, suspended from attached floral link ster chain (possible marriage), 16-½" tl, pendant 2" **125**

Dog collar

  Silver, rhinestones (paste), glass, c. 1900, hinged openwork plaques of lacy scrolled design set throughout with colorless pastes, with a lg cushion-shaped turq-colored glass cab bezel-set in the center of each, forming a collar terminating in a v-spring and box clasp, approx 13" tl × 2-½" w **575**

Pendant and Chain

  Silver, rhinestones (paste), faux pearls, c. 1910, a paste-set bow and a row of three collet-set colorless pastes suspending a tassel of articulated rows of colorless paste and faux pearls with a cone-shaped cap of pavé-set colorless and red pastes, two lengths of fine cable-link silver chain attached to loops at the top of the bow, approx 22" tl, pendant ¾" w × 2-½" tl **150**

  Silver, rhinestones (paste), c. 1910, a circ openwork design incorporating a central pavé-set navette shape surmounted by a pavé-set fan shape, a lg collet-set red stone in the open center with a smaller red stone above and below, encircled by a row of colorless stones, flanked by open paste-set scrollwork

Lavaliers, silver, glass, rhinestones, c. 1900-10: L, faceted navette-shaped pink glass set in a silver frame with a pierced gallery, faux seed pearl border, pendant bail set with r.s, 1-⅞" × ¾", $85, *Terrance O'Halloran collection;* C, open modified tapered shield, outlined in sm pavé r.s., center of bezel-set round green faceted glass and sm r.s. in a knife-edge setting, terminating in a bezel-set r.s. drop, suspended from a fine twist-link chain, spring ring mkd "sterling," 18", pendant 2" tl × ¾", $145, *Leigh Leshner collection;* R, circ, millegrained and knife-edged with inner quatrefoil outline, garland style floral and foliate motifs and center drop set with r.s. in millegrained mounts, r.s.-set pendant bail, 1-⅛" dia, 1-½" tl, $115, *Terrance O'Halloran collection.*

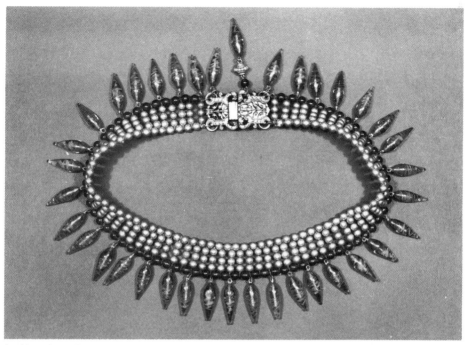

Necklace, dog collar, c. 1910-20, four rows of faux pearls and a row of red glass beads suspending a fringe of green glass drops, terminating in an ornate scrolled ym clasp ,13-3/8" tl × 1-1/2", $150. *Terrance O'Halloran collection.*

Festoon Necklace, glass, seed pearls, gp base metal, c. 1900, double-tiered center and two side elements bezel-set with rect, oval, and teardrop-shaped faceted purple glass in scrolled ym filigree mounts set with seed pearls, suspended from double swagged chains, continuing to a single chain, spring ring clasp, 18" tl × 3", $200. *Terrance O'Halloran collection.*

and an outer row of colorless stones, suspended from a paste-set plume-shaped bail and two lengths of fine cable-link silver chain, Fr hmks, approx 20" tl, pendant 1-½" dia **225**

Silver (800), rhinestones (paste), c. 1910, in the shape of an openwork flower basket set with colorless, green, pink, and topaz-colored stones, terminating in a teardrop-shaped collet-set pink stone drop, suspended from two lengths of fine cable-link silver chain, mkd "800," approx 21" tl, pendant 1-¼" w × 1-⅞" tl **125**

Necklace, sautoir, c. 1910, faux pearl tassel with cap of green glass, silver collar, and bail set with marcasites, faux pearls, and green glass beads interspersed on silver chain; 30-½" tl, tassel 3" tl, $150. *Joyce Albers collection.*

PART III

Twentieth-Century Jewelry

INTRODUCTION

The twentieth century truly began with World War I, a cataclysmic event that transformed society. Women would never be the same after "the war to end all wars." When the smoke cleared, the Gibson Girl had become Thoroughly Modern Millie. Her fashions, her attitude, her way of life, were marked departures from all that had gone before. The war, and—at last—the right to vote gave American women a stronger voice in the affairs of the country and a greater awareness of the affairs of the world. This worldly sophistication was aided by the advent of radio, the growth of fashion magazines and popular culture periodicals, and perhaps most importantly, the motion picture industry. Changes in fashion occurred at an ever-accelerating pace.

Although Paris continued to be regarded as a fashion mecca through the midcentury, British and European royalty were no longer as influential as America's Hollywood elite. Movie stars were the new royals. What they wore was closely monitored, reported, and emulated. Purveyors to these new royals achieved instant fame and success by association. Names of designers attained new importance, and name-dropping became a pastime of a new social class.

Indeed, "new" and "novelty" were watchwords of the day. The latest was considered the best. In jewelry, new designs and materials were incorporated into manufacturers' repertoires. Except for a hiatus during World War II, diamonds and platinum still ruled, but the avant-garde opted for chrome, rock crystal, glass, and that most novel of materials, plastic. Costume jewelry was given the stamp of approval by Coco Chanel and other haute couturiers. It was no longer looked down upon as a mere imitation of the real thing, although there were surely many rhinestone and rhodium knockoffs masquerading as diamonds and platinum. Obviously fake jewels, however, were now being worn to complement one's outfit, or costume.

Stylistic trends also evolved more rapidly in the twentieth century. Whereas a nineteenth century style could span several decades, after World War I each decade was characterized by a different look. And while the general term "modernism" can be applied to the entire era, we tend to group the changing styles within it by 10-year periods; i.e., the 1920s, 1930s, 1940s, 1950s, etc. This is not necessarily an accurate classification, nor are the appellations Art Deco, Streamline Moderne, or Retro Modern correctly applied to each decade. These are styles, not periods, which, as always, tend to overlap and coexist along with revivals and traditions. It can be said, for example, that Art Deco was a popular style in the 1920s, but certainly not the only style. Consequently, rather than label each of the following subdivisions of twentieth-century jewelry with a style name, they are divided by period and prefaced with an explanation of the predominant styles in each.

In this section, it is also necessary to introduce a separate classification based on certain materials from which some jewelry was made. Costume jewelry is too all-encompassing and unwieldy a term for the several types of nonprecious jewelry that proliferated from the 1920s onward. Therefore, there is a special category for plastic and novelty jewelry, the whimsical and fun costume jewelry that does not fall clearly into any other stylistic category. Costume jewelry that imitates fine jewelry is grouped separately in its respective period. The classification of "designer signed" costume jewelry, however, spans several decades.

References: Vivienne Becker, *Antique and Twentieth Century Jewellery*, 2nd ed., N.A.G. Press, 1987, and *Fabulous Costume Jewelry*,

Schiffer Publshing, 1993; David Bennett and Daniela Mascetti, *Understanding Jewellery*, Antique Collectors' Club, 1989; Barbara Cartlidge, *Twentieth-Century Jewelry*, Harry N. Abrams, 1985; Deanna Farneti Cera, ed., *Jewels of Fantasy, Costume Jewelry of the 20th Century*, Harry N. Abrams, 1992; Roseann Ettinger, *Popular Jewelry, 1840-1940*, Schiffer Publishing, 1990; Peter Hinks, *Twentieth Century Jewellery, 1900-1980*, Faber & Faber, London, 1983; Graham Hughes,

Modern Jewelry, an International Survey, 1890-1967, Crown Publishers, 1968 (out of print); Jane Mulvagh, *Costume Jewelry in Vogue*, Thames and Hudson, 1988; Penny Proddow and Debra Healy, *American Jewelry, Glamour and Tradition*, Rizzoli International, 1987; Penny Proddow, Debra Healy, and Marion Fasel, *Hollywood Jewels*, Harry N. Abrams, 1992; Jody Shields, *All That Glitters, The Glory of Costume Jewelry*, Rizzoli International, 1987.

FINE JEWELRY C. 1920-1935

History: After a period of wartime austerity, the woman of the 1920s burst forth with a frenetic exuberance. She cut off her hair, her sleeves, and her hems; bound her chest and dropped her waistline to become *la garçonne*, the female boy. She celebrated her new postwar prosperity and freedom by piling on the jewels. Bare arms and waistless dresses changed fashion's focus from the wide waist-cinching belts and sash and corsage ornaments of the *belle époque* to multiple bracelets and small plaque brooches or jeweled ornaments worn at the hips and shoulders. There were endless variations of the diamond and platinum bracelet variously referred to as the plaque, flexible link or box, strap, band, or straight line. Some were accented with natural or synthetic sapphires or rubies, emeralds, or a combination of these. Short hairstyles gave rise to long pendent drop earrings. The screwback finding (called the "French back" by some in the trade) was now the norm, as most women no longer pierced their ears. Large hats, hatpins, tiaras, and haircombs disappeared, to be replaced by bandeaux and cloche hats embellished with small hat ornaments. The *sautoir* remained, but in modified modernized form, becoming more geometric. It was often made entirely of diamonds and platinum, terminating in a diamond-set drop instead of a tassel, and it was convertible, forming bracelets, choker, and a pendant. Lorgnettes continued to be fashionably suspended from long chains or cords; in the 1930s, they adapted for wear as clips. Tasseled ropes of gemstone beads were also worn. Pearls remained popular, worn as *sautoirs* or long ropes, or twisted about the wrist. The recenty marketed cultured pearl was affordable to the middle classes, although it caused a furor among natural (Oriental) pearl merchants. Dog collars narrowed to become short delicate necklaces, often worn in addition to a *sautoir*. The bar pin and plaque brooch continued to be worn as transitional jewels in addition to the new circle brooch and jabot pin. Pierced platinum or white gold and diamond rings retained the elongated outline of the past two decades, but became increasingly geometric in design. New ring shapes were hexagonal or octagonal, with colored gemstones and diamonds set in domed or stepped mounts.

The excesses of the 1920s were sharply curtailed by the 1929 stock market crash and the onset of the Great Depression. But even though it was out of reach for most people and its production diminished, precious jewelry continued to be made. The elite of Hollywood and New York could still afford it; women of wealth everywhere continued to wear their status symbols. Indeed, jewelry grew larger and more three-dimensional as fashions became less severe. During the early 1930s, the waistline returned, sleeves grew longer and/or fuller, and a woman's curves were emphasized by bias-cut gowns in soft and satiny fabrics.

The dress clip became the most important jewelled accessory of the 1930s. Usually worn in pairs at the neckline, they were held in place by means of a flat-backed hinged mechanism that snapped shut over the fabric's edge. The story goes that Louis Cartier came up with the idea for the clip while watching a woman use clothespins to hang laundry out to dry. These versatile ornaments could also be worn on jacket lapels, hats, purses, belts, and, with the attachment of an additional pinback mechanism, a pair could be joined for wear as a brooch.

The all-white look of diamonds and platinum that began with the Edwardians at the turn of the century persisted well into the 1930s, with the additional use of colorless rock crystal. Over the years, geometric forms competed with, and then replaced, the garland style. By the early 1920s, diamond cutting had advanced to such a degree that unusual shapes, such as the half-moon, the obus, or bullet (a narrow pentagon), the epaulet (a wide pentagon), the trapeze, and the triangle, could be produced for added geometric interest in all-white jewels. At the same time, color was injected into some jewelry designs in the form of rubies, emeralds, sapphires, jade, coral, lapis, onyx, and enamels, as the style that later came to be known as Art Deco exerted its influence.

Art Deco itself was influenced by a number of design sources: Oriental, Persian/Islamic, East Indian, ancient Egyptian, pre-Hispanic Mexican,

African, American Indian, and, most directly, by turn-of-the-century Austrian and German secessionist and *Jugendstil* designs.

While the commonly held view is that the Art Deco style arose as a result of the 1925 Paris exposition from which it derives its name, *L'Exposition Internationale des Arts Décoratifs et Industriels Modernes*, in fact, its ascendance is really a culmination of developments that occurred throughout the previous two decades. It should be noted that the outbreak of war forced the exposition's postponement. It was originally planned for 1916, the idea having been discussed since 1907, according to Sylvie Raulet in her book *Art Deco Jewelry*, cited below. So we see the seeds of modernism being planted at the turn of the century and reaching full flower after World War I. Still, the popularization of the style was not widely felt in the United States until after the exposition—an event in which it did not participate. (Herbert Hoover, Secretary of Commerce at the time, was noted as saying this country did not have any modern decorative arts, and therefore could not meet the entry requirements of newness and originality.)

The name Art Deco was not applied to what was then called "modernistic" or "moderne" until 1968, when it appeared in the title of a book by Bevis Hillier, *Art Deco of the Twenties and Thirties*. This probably explains why there are several different interpretations of what the style really is, and why there is debate over the period in which it flourished. For some, it is an all-encompassing label that includes what others separate into Art Deco, Zig-Zag Moderne, Streamline Moderne, and the International Style. Some say the style ended in 1925; others claim it spanned the entire period between the world wars. Hillier takes the inclusive, evolutionary point of view that although "There was a difference in character between the 'twenties and the 'thirties . . . Art Deco was a developing style . . . There was a strong continuity." (from the introduction to *The World of Art Deco*, catalog of an exhibition at the Minneapolis Institute of Arts, 1971).

The credo of the modernists was "form follows function," and all excess ornamentation was to be avoided, on a parallel with the tenets of the Arts and Crafts movement. Unlike the purists of that movement, however, the modernists espoused and embraced the use of the machine. The style is characterized by the simplification and stylization of motifs from nature and the introduction of abstract, nonrepresentational, structural, and geometric forms. Futuristic and speed-associated motifs were also part of the repertoire. Suffice it to say that whatever the label, there is general agreement that the design developments of the period between the wars were as much a departure from Victorianism as the chemise was from the hoop skirt.

In jewelry, too, one often hears the term Art Deco applied to everything from slight variations on Edwardian pierced platinum-and-diamond plaque brooches to starkly simple abstract metal and enamel pendants or bangles. The tendency is to call any piece from the 1920s or 1930s Art Deco—a matter of subjective interpretation. In fact, the evolution of the style in jewelry can be traced through several different lineages, from the traditional French *haute joailliers* to the avant-garde artist-designers, continuing to popular adaptations and modifications by American jewelers inspired by the French designs.

Cartier is the most famous of the former for its version of Art Deco, which tended toward the figurative and exotic Eastern-influenced designs. Notable were Cartier's use of carved gemstones in multicolored fruit salad arrangements of leaves and berries in flexible band bracelets, flower vase brooches, and double clip brooches (patented by Cartier in 1927).

Van Cleef and Arpels also contributed a great deal to the genre. It was particularly known for its Egyptian Revival motifs executed in calibré-cut colored gemstones and pavé diamonds on strap bracelets, which were inspired by the discovery of Tutankhamen's tomb in 1922 (an event that launched a general mania for Egyptian motifs). The firm also excelled at creating convertible diamond and platinum jewels in the prevailing geometric forms, for example, a *sautoir* necklace that separated into bracelets and a pendant.

Other famous French houses whose pieces come up for sale at important jewelry auctions include Boucheron, Mauboussin, Chaumet, and Lacloche. More rarely seen is the work of the French avant-garde designers: Jean Després (1889-1980), Jean Dunand (1877-1942), Georges Fouquet (1862-1957) and son Jean Fouquet (b. 1899), Gérard Sandoz (b. 1902), Raymond Templier (1891-1968), and Paul Brandt. When a significant piece by any of these houses or designers is offered, it can command prices in five or six figures.

Several American firms made and sold noteworthy Art Deco jewels inspired by the French, especially after the 1925 exposition: the manufacturing jewelers William Scheer, Inc., Oscar Heyman & Bros., and Raymond C. Yard; retailers J.E. Caldwell & Co., Black, Starr & Frost, Tiffany & Co., Marcus & Co., C.D. Peacock; and the New York branches of Cartier and Van Cleef & Arpels.

Many anonymous French and unsigned American-made pieces of the period are sold at auction. Price is often determined by the number, size, quantity, and quality of the gemstones used, as much as, if not more than the design, which can be repetitious and unoriginal. Less important commercial pieces signed by the famous houses are also auctioned regularly. Their names often cause an escalation in price, but astute buyers always evaluate a piece on its own merits before taking its marks into consideration.

References: J. Mark Ebert, "Art Deco: The Period, The Jewelry," in *Gems and Gemology,* Spring, 1983; Melissa Gabardi, *Art Deco Jewellery, 1920-1949,* Antique Collectors' Club, 1989; Neil Letson, "Art Deco Jewelry, Its Past, Present and Future," in *Jewelers Circular-Keystone/Heritage,* August, 1988; Daniela Mascetti and Amanda Triossi, *Earrings from Antiquity to the Present,* Rizzoli International, 1990; Hans Nadelhoffer, *Cartier, Jewelers Extraordinary,* Harry N. Abrams, 1984; Sylvie Raulet, *Art Deco Jewelry,* Rizzoli International, 1985; Janet Zapata, "Jewelry and Accessories," in *The Encyclopedia of Art Deco,* Alistair Duncan, ed., E.P. Dutton, 1988.

Museum: Musée des Arts Décoratifs, Paris.

Reproduction Alert: The Art Deco revival that began in the early 1980s has generated a plethora of knockoffs and Deco-style pieces that never existed during the 1920s and 1930s. Many of these come from Thailand and Hong Kong, where the workmanship is rarely as good as the originals, but European and American manufacturers are producing quality reproductions, some of which defy detection. Among them: Branca de Brito of Portugal, Hermes of Munich, Germany, and Authentic Jewelry in New York City. A quantity of this jewelry is now coming onto the secondary market. Ask questions, read auction catalog warranties, conditions, and descriptions carefully—if a piece is described as "Art Deco style," it is not of the period—and examine pieces thoroughly. Be aware that descriptions are the opinions of the auction houses.

Bracelet
Flexible
14k wg, syn sapphires, c. 1920, rect filigree hinged plaques bezel-set at intervals with five marquise-cut syn blue sapphires, hinged box clasp, tongue mkd "14k," 7-1/8" × 1/4" **225**
Diamonds, syn sapphires, platinum, c. 1920, a strap of circ bead-set diamonds with a zigzag pattern of channel-set syn sapphires, two sapphires missing, 16 dwt, 7-3/8" × 3/8" . . . . **2,640 (A)**
Diamonds, platinum, c. 1920, a straightline of hinged plaques with central pierced

lozenge-shapes, pavé-set with one hundred thirty-five circ diamonds, approx 10 cts tw, 7" × 3/8" . . . . **6,875 (A)**
Diamonds, platinum, blue stones, c. 1920, engraved plat straight-line set with 21 oe diamonds, approx 1.05 ct tw, and 21 rect-shaped blue stones, 7" × 3/16" . . **1,035 (A)**
Diamonds, sapphires, platinum, c. 1920, straightline with a center row of 56 calibré-cut sapphires flanked by two rows of circ diamonds, bisected by a central and two side diamond-set foliate motifs, 136 circ diamonds, approx 7.2 ct tw, 7-1/4" × 3/8" . . . . **11,500 (A)**
Diamonds, emeralds, platinum, c. 1920, articulated sq plaques set with alternating rows of diamonds and emeralds in geo pattern, 108 rect-cut emeralds and 132 circ diamonds, 5.3 ct tw, Fr hmks, 7-1/2" × 3/8" . . . . **11,500 (A)**
Diamonds, 18k wg, c. 1920, a strap of uniform width, pierced with two rows of double helix pattern, set throughout with sm oe and sc diamonds, 7-1/4" × 1/2" . . . . **4,950 (A)**
Diamonds, 14k wg, syn sapphires, c. 1925, a uniform line of box-style links, set with bc diamonds, 4.3 ct tw, framed by calibré-set step-cut syn sapphires, one sapphire missing, 19.8 dwt, 7" × 3/8" . . . . **4,240 (A)**
Diamonds, emeralds, platinum, c. 1925, a wide tapering openwork strap with a central marquise-cut diamond, continuing to a series of links, each with a central marquise-cut diamond with rows of circ diamonds alternating with links of circ diamonds in a geo pattern including calibré-cut channel-set emeralds, engr on hidden push-tongue clasp "May 1904-1924," two emeralds missing, 23.2 dwt, 7-1/4" × 5/8" . . . . **9,240 (A)**
Diamonds, syn sapphires, platinum, c. 1925, 23 tapering rect hinged plaques, each with pierced curved lines at top and bottom, pavé-set with 13 oe and 284 rc diamonds, two triangle-cut syn sapphires flanking center diamond in each of 16 central plaques, engr gallery, safety chain, 7-1/2" × 3/8" . . . . **3,450 (A)**

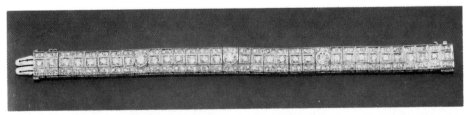

Bracelet, flexible, diamonds, platinum, c. 1920, articulated platinum plaques carré-set with 165 circ diamonds in three rows, three larger collet-set diamonds evenly spaced in center row, 5.8 cts tw, 7" × 1/2", $3,450 (A), *Photo courtesy of Butterfield & Butterfield, San Francisco and Los Angeles (6/17/93).*

Bracelet, flexible, diamonds, platinum, c. 1925, slightly tapering articulated plaques, central floral motif flanked by cutout curv rows with scalloped edges, center oe diamond approx 0.95 ct, and pavé-set with approx 252 circ diamonds, approx 12.6 cts tw, v-spring and box clasp, 6-½" × ¾", with fitted box, $18,400 (A). *Photo courtesy of Butterfield & Butterfield, San Francisco and Los Angeles (6/17/93).*

Diamonds, sapphires, platinum, c. 1925, two articulated panels of pavé-set oe diamonds, each with Fr-cut (sq) sapphire T-shapes at each end, two triangular sapphires at center edges, four Fr-cut sapphires in the corners, alternating with two open rect links set with Fr-cut sapphires, joined with diamonds-set bar links, sgd "Boucheron," 7" × ½" ...... **14,950 (A)**

Diamonds, sapphires, platinum, c. 1925, an oe diamond twin line band sectioned by five oe diamond and calibré-cut sapphire scallop motifs, each flanking a larger diamond center, 7-¼" × ⅜" ..... **17,250 (A)**

Diamonds, platinum, c. 1930, a row of pierced S-shapes bisected top and bottom by two horizontal pierced rows on hinged plaques of uniform width set throughout with circ diamonds, Fr hmks, v-spring and box clasp with safety clasps, approx 7 ct tw, 7-½" × ⅞" .... **9,350 (A)**

Diamonds, sapphires, platinum, c. 1930, a wide band, with three pierced foliate-patterned navette shapes, a lg collet-set diamond in each center flanked by triang-cut sapphires, alternating with geo pierced openwork, set throughout with sc and oe diamonds, pavé diamond borders, 7-½" × ⅞" .... **14,950 (A)**

Diamonds, platinum, c. 1930, a band of uniform width with a pierced X-pattern set throughout with sc and circ-cut diamonds, a slightly grad center line of larger diamond collets, mounted in plat, leather case, 7" × ⅝" .... **14,950 (A)**

Rubies, diamonds, syn rubies, platinum, c. 1925, central boss with a millegrain-set oval ruby cab, approx 15.2 × 14.2 × 8.5 mm outlined in diamonds, flanked by pierced triangular sections, a central row of approx 58 calibré-cut syn rubies, and a row of diamonds on each side of a tapering articulated band, approx 154 full-cut diamonds, approx 7.5 ct tw, 6-¾" × ⅞" .... **18,400 (A)**

Flexible link

Emerald, diamonds, platinum, 14k yg, c. 1920, an emerald-cut emerald, approx 2.8 ct, bezel-set in the center of a rect plaque framed by circ diamonds, flanked

by two oval-cut diamonds, approx 0.75 ct and 0.7 ct, collet-set within hinged shield-shaped diamond-set plaques continuing to articulated grad diamond-set chevrons tapering to narrow open baton-shaped plat links, 54 circ diamonds, approx 1.35 ct tw, 7" × ¾" .... **2,875 (A)**

Link

Diamonds, platinum, c. 1920, sq links set with double rows of diamonds, alternating with four collet-set diamonds and diamond-set foliate and X-shaped links (some solder), approx 4 ct tw, 7" × ¼" .... **4,400 (A)**

Diamonds, platinum, c. 1920, 38 full-cut diamonds set in a row of articulated box links approx 2.65 ct tw, engr gallery, safety chain, 7" × 3/16" .... **5,463 (A)**

Diamonds, platinum, c. 1920, three articulated pierced elongated rect segments, each set with one oe diamond in the center, approx 2.8 ct tw, and pavé-set with approx 196 oe and marquise-cut diamonds, approx 6.5 ct tw, 7-¼" × ½" .... **11,500 (A)**

Diamonds, enamel, platinum, c. 1925, alternating arched pavé-set diamond and circ sc diamond links, black enamel borders, (enamel slightly chipped), sgd "Cartier, Paris," # 01560, 6-¾" × ½" .... **27,600 (A)**

Diamonds, sapphires, rubies, platinum, c. 1925, three sc, baguette and circ-cut diamond panels, each with a larger sq diamond center flanked by two triang buff-top sapphires and one ruby set in a triang pattern on each side, alternating with buff-top sapphire twin rect links joined with diamond-set bar links, sgd "A.Marchak," for Alexandre Marchak, Paris France, # 1483, 7" × ⅜" .... **19,550 (A)**

Diamonds, platinum, c. 1930, three openwork plaques, each with a central marquise-cut diamond, set throughout with circ diamonds joined by open rect links set with circ diamonds and a pr of baguette diamonds, sgd "Peacock" for C.D. Peacock, Chicago IL, 16.3 dwt, 7" × ⅜" .... **7,150 (A)**

Diamonds, emeralds, platinum, c. 1930,

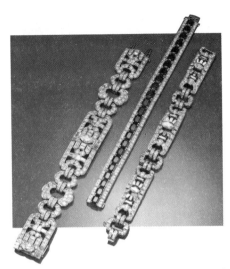

Bracelets, link, platinum, c. 1930: L, two elongated openwork rect segments (one divided in two for the clasp), centers set with two marquise-cut diamonds, approx 2.5 cts tw, alternating with a flared annular oval link flanked by two smaller annular ovals, joined by double bar links, set throughout with 36 baguette and 244 circ diamonds, approx 17.5 cts tw, 7-1/4" × 1", $26,450 (A); C, a flexible straight line of 24 emerald-cut sapphires, approx 36 cts tw, flanked by borders of oe diamonds, 7" × 5/8", $35,650 (A); R, three elongated, articulated openwork rect segments, joined by sm rect and double bar links, each center set with a marquise-cut diamond, approx 1.5 cts tw, flanked by baguette diamonds (30 total), set throughout with 192 circ and sc diamonds, 12.5 cts tw, 7" × 3/4", $12,650 (A). *Photo: © 1993 Sotheby's, Inc., New York (4/19/93).*

Bracelet, link, diamonds, platinum, c. 1930, three articulated, openwork, tapered oblong plaques joined by smaller paired links, set throughout with 306 oe, sc, sq-cut, and baguette diamonds, approx 16 cts tw, Fr, 7" × 3/4", $11,500 (A). *Photo: © 1993 Sotheby's, Inc., New York (4/19/93).*

three pierced panels pavé-set with circ diamonds, each with a central marquise-cut diamond within an equilateral cross formed by baguette diamonds, alternating with open fancy-shaped rect links, joined by wide bar links pavé-set with diamonds and calibré-cut emeralds, approx 11.5 ct tw, 7-3/4" × 5/8" . . . . **12,650 (A)**

Diamonds, platinum, c. 1930, three openwork rect panels with collet-set and carré-set circ and baguette diamonds throughout, alternating with pavé diamond-set opposed D-shapes joined with double bar links, flanking open curved links with marquise-cut diamond centers, 7" × 5/8" . . . . **9,200 (A)**

Diamonds, 14k wg, c. 1930, three rect openwork panels set throughout with baguette and circ-cut diamonds, each with a horizontal row of three lg circ diamonds in the center, joined with prs of diamond-set bar links to open shaped diamond-set rect links, 7-1/2" × 3/4" . . . . **15,525 (A)**

Diamonds, emeralds, onyx, platinum,

c. 1930, two pierced and cutout elongated rect panels with rounded corners, each with five marquise-cut diamonds set in a V-shaped pattern in the center, flanked by grad rows of buff-top emeralds and onyx and pavé-set with circ diamonds, joined to diamond-set open rect links by pierced rect pavé-set diamond links, approx 248 diamonds, plat mount, 7-7/8" × 5/8" . . . . **17,600 (A)**

Platinum, diamonds, black onyx, c. 1925, five open oval plat links, a circ disk set with alternating rows of black onyx and rc diamonds mounted in the center of each link, sgd "Yard" for Raymond C. Yard, New York, N.Y., foldover clasp, approx 7" tl × 1/2" . . . . **4,675 (A)**

Brooch/Pendant

Diamonds, simulated emeralds, platinum, c. 1920, a pierced geo and foliate design plaque, rect with chamfered corners, set throughout with oe diamonds, three circ-cut diamonds in the navette-shaped center framed by calibré-cut simulated emeralds, a short row of sim emeralds on each side, continuing to a tapering hinged element of similar design surmounted by a pendant loop, 3/4" w × 3" . . . . **2,530 (A)**

Bar

Diamonds, sapphires, platinum, c. 1920, a tablet-shaped bar with lobed ends, a tapering row of seven oe diamonds in the center of a pierced plat plaque pavé-set with sc

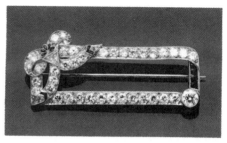

Brooch/Pin, diamonds, platinum, blue stones, c. 1920, an open rect shape, rounded upper right corner, a cut-out bow in the upper left corner, a larger collet-set oe diamond in the lower right corner, pavé-set with 41 oe, triangular, and kite-shaped diamonds, approx 3.75 cts tw, bow and one short side accented with 13 pear-shaped and calibré-cut blue stones, lever catch, 2" w × ³/₄", $1,725 (A). *Photo courtesy of Butterfield & Butterfield, San Francisco and Los Angeles (6/17/93).*

Brooch/Pendant, diamonds, syn sapphires, platinum, c. 1920, a rect bar with engr foliate design set throughout with circ collet-set diamonds, suspending two open lozenge-shaped wire links with collet-set diamond centers joined at the top of an elongated octagonal pierced geo and scroll pendant set throughout with circ diamonds, 45 diamonds, approx 2.6 cts tw, and vertical rows of sm calibré-cut syn sapphires (one diamond missing), 1-³/₄" w × 2-⁷/₈" tl, $1870 (A). *Photo courtesy of Dunning's, Elgin, Ill. (5/16/93).*

diamonds, top and bottom trimmed with Fr-cut (sq) sapphires, concealed pendant hoop, 2-¹/₂" w × ¹/₂" . . . . **8,050 (A)**

Brooch/Pin

Amethyst, diamonds, rock crystal, platinum, c. 1930, an octagonal, beveled-edge rock crystal frame quartered with four bead- and channel-set sc and baguette diamond and plat elements, top and bottom vertical bars and fan-shaped sides, with a central rect prong and bezel-set step-cut rect amethyst, 24 × 19 × 12.8mm, some broken diamonds, sgd "Lambert," 19.3 dwt, 1-⁵/₈" w × ³/₈" . . . . **5,500 (A)**

Diamonds, platinum, c. 1920, a hand-constructed three-masted sailing ship, set throughout with sc and baguette diamonds, 1.5 ct tw, millegrain details, trombone catch, Fr hmks, 4.4 dwt, 1-¹/₄" × 1-¹/₄" . . . **3,960 (A)**

Diamonds, platinum, c. 1920, a cusped navette-shaped plaque with a central lg prong-set oe diamond within a sq diamond-set frame, flanked by pierced spade-shaped designs, each with larger and smaller oe diamonds, and framed with smaller bead-set oe diamonds, quartered by larger oe diamonds, 5.3 ct tw, 7.3 dwt, 1-⁷/₈" w × 1" . . . **4,400 (A)**

Diamonds, emeralds, platinum, c. 1920, an open rect frame set with diamonds, a cutout diamond- and emerald-set flower and ribbon motif on the left side projecting into the open center, triangular-cut emeralds in the four corners, diamonds approx 1.15 ct tw, 1-⁷/₈" w × 1-¹/₈" . . . . **1,650 (A)**

Diamonds, platinum, c. 1920, an openwork oval within a rect plaque, one marquise-cut diamond in the center, approx 0.7 ct, flanked by pierced foliate motifs, set throughout with approx 70 oe, baguette, and sc diamonds, approx 2.15 ct tw, (slight damage), 1-⁷/₈" w × ³/₄" . . . . **2,070 (A)**

Diamonds, platinum, c. 1920, a gondola shape with scrolled ends, geo pierced design pavé-set with circ diamonds, a curved row of five

Brooch/Pin, diamonds, onyx, platinum, c. 1920, in the shape of an urn, two carved black onyx plaques in a diamond-set frame and base, surmounted by a diamond-set quatrefoil flanked by diamond-set vines and cascading articulated grad floral motifs, approx 80 circ diamonds, 3.55 cts tw, lever catch, 1-¹/₂" w × 1-³/₄", $5,750 (A). *Photo courtesy of Butterfield & Butterfield, San Francisco and Los Angeles (6/17/93).*

Brooch/Pin, diamonds, platinum, c. 1920, an open rectangle with notched corners and a central bow and trailing ribbon motif, pavé-set with 55 circ diamonds, approx 4.9 cts tw, 2-¹/₈" w × ³/₄", $3,850 (A). Photo courtesy of Dunning's, Elgin Ill. (11/7/93).

larger collet-set circ-cut diamonds in the center, 2-⁷/₈" w × ¹/₂" . . . . **5,290 (A)**

Diamonds, platinum, c. 1925, an openwork and pierced plaque, rect with lobed ends, concave top and bottom, with two central oe diamonds, approx 0.90 ct tw, and set throughout with fifty-one oe, baguette and circ diamonds, approx 2.00 cts tw, lever catch, 1-¹/₂" w × ¹/₂" . . . . **2,300 (A)**

Diamonds, 18k wg, c. 1930, a rect geo openwork and pierced plaque with notched corners, a central collet-set diamond flanked by lg cutout plume and scroll motifs and smaller cutout palmette motifs at top and bottom, bead- and carré-set throughout with circ-cut diamonds, 1-¹/₂" w × 1" . . . . **5,750 (A)**

Jadeite, diamonds, platinum, c. 1920, an oval pierced and carved floral and foliate motif jadeite plaque, 39 × 17 × 2mm, prong-set, framed at each end with curv plat elements set with two triangular-cut and eight circ diamonds, lever catch, 1-⁷/₈" × 1-¹/₈" . . . . **8,050 (A)**

Jadeite, seed pearls, enamel, 14k yg, c. 1920, an oval jadeite plaque with carved and pierced floral and foliate motifs, prong-set in a black enameled lozenge-shaped frame set with three seed pearls at top and bottom, one

Brooch/Pin, diamonds, platinum c. 1920, a navette-shaped geo pierced and openwork plaque with scalloped edges, set throughout with om and oe diamonds, 2-¹/₂" w × 1-³/₈", $14,950 (A). Photo courtesy of Christie's New York (4/21/93).

seed pearl at each end, mkd "14k," 2" w × 1-¹/₈" . . . . **1,725 (A)**

Jadeite, diamonds, platinum, wg, c. 1925, a carved and pierced annular jadeite disk flanked by D-shaped plat elements, each set with a half-moon diamond, with an inner ring of 14 sc diamonds set in plat, wg findings, lever catch, sgd "Walton & Co.," 1-¹/₂" w, disk 1-¹/₈" dia . . . . **2,300 (A)**

Jadeite, diamonds, platinum, c. 1930, a rounded oblong jadeite plaque with a pierced and carved floral and foliate motif, approx 49 × 18.5mm, within a foliate and geo frame of conforming shape, set throughout with sm circ and baguette diamonds, approx 4 ct tw, 2-⁵/₈" w × 1-³/₈" . . . . **13,200 (A)**

Rock crystal, onyx, enamel, diamonds, platinum, 14k yg, c. 1920, a lozenge-shaped fluted rock crystal plaque, a sm circ collet-set diamond in the center, prong-set within an onyx and blue enamel frame, flanked by rows of three diamonds each, bordered with green and black enamel (minor enamel loss), 1-⁵/₈" w × ³/₄" . . . . **1,045 (A)**

Sapphires, diamonds, 18k wg, c. 1920, an open navette, with a line of circ bead-set diamonds at top and bottom, clusters of circ prong-set sapphire cabs at tapered ends, sgd "Cartier # 1149," 1.1 dwt, 1-³/₈" w × ⁵/₈" . . . . **1,980 (A)**

Bar

Diamond, platinum, c. 1920, a straight bar with cusped ends, a row of six oe diamonds, 1.5 ct tw, each set within a box mount and separated by a line of three smaller bc diamonds, .6 ct tw, 6 dwt, 3-¹/₈" × ¹/₄" . . . . **2,090 (A)**

Diamonds, platinum, 18k wg, rubies, c. 1920, a row of tapering diamonds in three sections, separated by channels of calibré-cut rect rubies, safety-pin style catch, Fr hmks, # 3665, 6.5 dwt, 4" w × 4.8mm to 3mm . . . . **3,850 (A)**

Diamonds, sapphires, syn sapphires, platinum, c. 1920, tapered plat bar, rounded ends, pierced with a concentric oval and scroll design, a grad row of seven oe diamonds in the center framed and flanked by calibré-cut sapphires and Fr-cut (sq) syn sapphires, pavé-set with sc diamonds, sgd "Shreve & Co.," San Francisco, Calif., # A 2357, 3-¹/₄" w × ¹/₂" . . . . . . **5,175 (A)**

Rubies, diamonds, platinum, c. 1920, a line of seven collet-set oval-cut rubies alternating with eight oe diamonds, approx 1.5 ct tw, within a pierced frame set with 66 rc diamonds, in a tapering plat bar with open circ center and cusped ends, 2-³/₄" w × ⁵/₈" . . . . **3,163 (A)**

Sapphires, 14k yg, platinum, diamonds, c. 1920, open rect channel-set with sq

Brooch/Pin, bar, 18k yg, carnelian, enamel, c. 1925, Egyptian revival, a bezel-set oval carnelian cab flanked by opposed crested bird motifs with green, red, and blue *champlevé* enameled chests, and engr falcon wings, rev mkd "Tiffany & Co.," lever catch, 1-³/₄" w × ³/₄", $1850. *Victoria Taylor collection.*

step-cut sapphires, with two bead-set oe diamond bars at each end, .4 ct tw, 3.3 dwt, 1-¹/₄" w × ¹/₂" . . . . **1,760 (A)**

Circle

Diamonds, platinum, onyx, c. 1925, outer circ edge set with diamonds, inner edge with Fr-cut (sq) onyx, surmounted by a diamond-set bow with trailing ribbon in open center of circle, 73 diamonds, approx 2.25 ct tw, 1-¹/₂" dia . . . . **2,860 (A)**

Diamonds, platinum, sapphires, c. 1925, outer edge set with circ diamonds, approx 1.75 ct tw, inner edge with calibré-cut sapphires, a pierced diamond-set fan-shaped motif on each side, mkd "J.E.C. & Co." for J.E. Caldwell, Philadelphia, Pa., # K5609, 1-¹/₂" dia . . . . **6,050 (A)**

Cuff Links

Platinum, sapphires, yg, c. 1920, a pr of double links, plat disks with engr stripes and dot-and-dash patterned blue enamel borders, each center set with a sapphire cab, linked with yg findings, ¹/₂" dia, pr . . . . **523 (A)**

Platinum, diamonds, onyx, yg, c. 1920, a pr of double links, each an octagonal plat plaque with black onyx border and a central row of sc diamonds, yg findings, ¹/₂" × ¹/₂", pr . . . . **1,093 (A)**

Double Clip Brooch

Diamonds, platinum, c. 1930, each clip an openwork fan-shaped quadrant set throughout with baguette and oe diamonds, forming a semicirc brooch, a total of 78 oe and 44 baguettes, approx 15 ct tw, and a single oe diamond at the top, approx 1.1 ct, flat-backed hinged clips with a detachable pinback mechanism, (one stone missing), 3-¹/₄" w × 1-¹/₂" joined . . . . **12,650 (A)**

Diamonds, platinum, c. 1935, each clip an opposed scroll, pavé-set with circ and baguette-cut diamonds, connected with a detachable pinback mechanism, 2-³/₈" w × 1-¹/₄" joined . . . . **9,200 (A)**

Diamonds, platinum, 18k wg, c. 1935, a pr of asymmetrical geo pierced shield-shaped clips, each with one zigzag edge, set throughout with baguette and circ diamonds (one missing), approx 9.75 ct tw, double-pronged hinged wg clips can be joined with a wg pinback mechanism for wear as a brooch, 2-¹/₂" w × 1-¹/₈" when joined . . . . **8,250 (A)**

Dress Clip

Diamonds, platinum, c. 1930, scalloped fan shape, pierced geo design set throughout with 47 circ and baguette diamonds, approx 1.95 ct tw, flat-backed hinged clip on rev, mkd 950, sgd "Garrard, London," 1-¹/₄" w × ⁵/₈" . . . . **1,840 (A)**

Diamonds, platinum, c. 1930, triangular with three pierced vertical bars across the top, tapering scalloped pattern below, bead-set throughout with oe and om diamonds, 4 ct tw, 10 dwt, 1" w × 1-¹/₂" . . . . **1,870 (A)**

Diamonds, platinum, c. 1930, a pierced, inverted stepped triangle surmounted by a horizontal bar, set throughout with circ and baguette diamonds, approx 2.5 ct tw, sgd "Cartier, France," # 03371, in a leather box, 1-¹/₄" w × 1-¹/₈" . . . . **8,250 (A)**

Lapis lazuli, turquoise, diamonds, platinum, c. 1930, annular shape with serrated and lobed edge, a cluster of four round turquoise beads with sm diamond centers mounted in the open center, with five lapis lazuli beads in a semicircle below, surmounted by two sm angular baguette diamond-set tabs, sm circ-cut diamonds pavé-set throughout, 1" dia . . . . **3,220 (A)**

Sapphires, platinum, wg, diamonds, c. 1930, a shield-shaped plaque with cusped base, the top edge enclosed by an open rect frame, the plaque set with a center vertical row of three grad collet-set oval and circ sapphires, 2 ct tw, alternating with two circ diamonds, the lower portion framed by pierced rays, and bead-set throughout with circ, oe, om, and sc diamonds, 2.1 ct tw, 9.1 dwt, ³/₄" w × 1-³/₄" . . . . **4,675 (A)**

Dress Set: Cuff Links, Shirt Studs, and Buttons

Rock crystal quartz, diamonds, platinum, gold, c. 1920, each double link a frosted rock crystal disk, a horizontal row of three rc diamonds at each center edge, mounted in plat and gold, two matching studs and four buttons, (one disk slightly chipped), leather fitted case, sgd "Cartier, Paris," # 9980, 0407, links and buttons, ¹/₂" dia, set . . . . . **3,680 (A)**

Earrings

Clip

Coral, silver, gold, enamel, diamonds, c. 1930, coral and black enamel ladybugs with diamond spots on their backs, earclip backs convert to dress clips, fitted leather, silk, and velvet box, stamped "Cartier," slight enamel loss at ends of legs. Provenance: collection of Marian Anderson, 8.5 dwt, ³/₄" w × ⁵/₈", pr . . . . **8,500 (A)**

Diamonds, platinum, c. 1930, geo stylized butterfly shape set with a total of 40 oe and sc diamonds, approx 2.6 ct tw, Fr (open wire) clipbacks, ³/₄" w × ³/₄", pr . . . . **2,588 (A)**

Pendent

Coral, diamonds, enamel, platinum, c. 1925, elongated red coral drops capped by three rows of sc diamonds surmounted by black enamel C-scrolls and lozenge-shaped surmounts of red and black enamel, joined by collet-set diamonds, mounted in plat, 1-⁵/₈" tl × ³/₈", pr . . . . **4,600 (A)**

Onyx, diamonds, platinum, c. 1920, an elongated trapezoidal onyx plaque, slightly curved at the base, surmounted by a pavé diamond-set plat T-shape, continuing to a shank of a vertical row of diamonds suspended from a diamond-set fanshaped onyx surmount, Fr hmks, 2" tl × ⁵/₈", pr . . . . **4,290 (A)**

Pearls, diamonds, platinum, c. 1925, a pr of natural pearl drops, each approx 10.5 × 9.2mm, suspended from a flexible chain of sq-cut and bullet-shaped diamonds, open triangular surmount set with sm circ diamonds, mounted in plat, 2-³/₈" tl, pr . . . . **7,475 (A)**

Pearls, diamonds, platinum, c. 1920, two baroque natural pearls, each approx 15 ×

Pendent Earrings, emeralds, diamonds, platinum, c. 1920, each earring set with a drop-shaped emerald cab, with diamond-set bail, within a circ-cut diamond and calibré-cut emerald independent frame, suspended from a row of fancy and baguette-cut diamonds, plat mounting, ¹/₂" w × 2", pr, $16,100 (A). *Photo courtesy of Christie's New York (4/21/93).*

Pendent Earrings, sapphires, diamonds, platinum, c. 1930, each with a cushion-shaped sapphire drop within an octagonal frame set with baguette and sc diamonds, suspended from articulated segments of oe, sc, and baguette diamonds, a single oe diamond surmount, 2" tl × ³/₄", pr, $6,325 (A). *Photo © 1993 Sotheby's, Inc., New York (4/19/93).*

12.2mm, surmounted by a cone-shaped cap set with sm diamonds, suspended from a cluster of four collet-set oe diamonds and a row of three slightly grad pierced trefoil links set with sm oe and sc diamonds, a single collet-set oe diamond surmount, mounted in plat, 2" tl, pr . . . . **16,100 (A)**

Jabot Pin

Amazonite, wg, diamonds, c. 1920, carved stone depicting the bust of an Oriental man wearing a pierced diamond headdress and rc diamond necklace, sitting upon a diamond-set base, continuing to a pinstem terminating in a diamond-set cap, one broken diamond, 4 dwt, $^5/_8$" × 2-$^3/_8$" tl . . . . **660 (A)**

Diamonds, rubies, spinels, platinum, wg, c. 1920, curved top set with a curved center row of calibré-cut rubies and red spinels, and pavé-set with circ diamonds and baguettes, a short wg pinstem terminating in a spade-shaped ruby and diamond cap, diamonds approx 2 ct tw, 1-$^1/_4$" w × 1-$^3/_8$" tl . . . . **2,750 (A)**

Diamonds, 18k wg, sapphires, c. 1920, three tassels of grad lengths of diamond-set chains, each terminating in a sq-cut sapphire, one tassel at each end of a wg pinstem, the center tassel suspended from a diamond link chain swag, 45 circ diamonds, approx 1.2 ct tw, and ten sq-cut sapphires, 1-$^3/_4$" w × 2" tl . . . . **2,588 (A)**

Diamonds, sapphires, platinum, c.1920, flying geese motif, one lg and two sm pavé-set with rc diamonds with buff-top sapphire collars, mounted at each end of a plat pinstem, fitted leather case, sgd "Cartier, Paris," # 02048, 2-$^1/_4$" w × $^1/_2$" . . . . **4,025 (A)**

Jadeite, diamonds, platinum, 14k yg, c. 1920, an annular jadeite disk mounted at one end of a yg pinstem, encased through the center and part way down the stem with a pierced plat double helix and balustered tube, set with 108 sc diamonds, approx 1 ct tw, teminating in a removable plat arrowhead, disk 1" dia, 4" tl . . . . **2,185 (A)**

Lorgnette

Diamonds, platinum, c. 1920, a pr of folding spectacles in a pierced scroll and X-pattern elongated hexagonal plat case set throughout with diamonds, tapering up to a diamond-set handle and bail, $^5/_8$" w × 2-$^1/_2$" closed . . . . **2,860 (A)**

Diamonds, black onyx, platinum, c. 1925, a baton-shaped rc diamond and black onyx 1" handle terminating in a spring-ring clasp for chain attachment, extending a pr of rect lenses with chamfered corners, within a rc diamond and black onyx frame, mounted in plat, (black onyx slightly damaged), sgd "Cartier," 3-$^1/_2$" w × $^3/_4$" open . . . . **4,025 (A)**

Platinum, pearl, onyx diamond, c. 1920, a pr of

circ folding spectacles with an onyx and diamond handle suspended from a chain of seed pearls interspersed with onyx beads, navette-shaped links, 41" tl . . . . . **1,760 (A)**

Platinum, diamonds, enamel, onyx, c.1920, a pr of circ folding spectacles in plat frames, hinged nosepiece set with 36 rc diamonds and black enamel accents, rect thumb piece set with 34 rc diamonds around a black onyx center, serves as an unlocking trigger, suspending a carved black onyx rect link, attached by a rc diamond-set plat oval link to a black nylon cord, terminating in a carved black onyx, rc diamond-set plat slide, attributed to Cartier, (loss to enamel), spectacles and handle 5-$^1/_4$" w × 1-$^1/_2$" open . . . . **1,840 (A)**

Sapphires, diamonds, c. 1920, a pr of circ folding spectacles in pierced openwork frames, with a tapered scrolled handle bezel-set with heart, marquise, and triang-cut sapphires, and sm circ diamonds, 1-$^5/_8$" w × 3-$^1/_4$" closed . . . . **2,090 (A)**

Clip

Platinum, diamonds, onyx, c. 1930, a pr of folding spectacles in an onyx lozenge-shape cover with an oe diamond, approx 1.9 ct, in the center of a rect pavé-set diamond plaque outlined in black onyx, can be worn as a clip, (clasp needs repair), $^5/_8$" w × 2-$^1/_4$" closed . . . . **5,775 (A)**

Rock crystal quartz, diamonds, wm, c. 1930, a pr of folding spectacles in a tapered, three-lobed rock crystal cover etched with the profile of a dancing female, the openwork scrolled foliate handle set throughout with diamonds, can be worn as a clip, 19.7 dwt, 2-$^1/_2$" w × 1" closed . . . . **2,090 (A)**

Neckchain

Platinum, diamonds, c. 1920, two lengths of elongated bar links joined by a spring-ring clasp, interspersed with 10 openwork navette-shaped links, each with a circ diamond in a millegrained hexagonal setting, joined to an openwork triangular diamond-set link and continuing to a single bar and openwork link chain terminating in a spring ring for a pendant, 12 diamonds, approx .6 ct tw, 30" tl . . . . **935 (A)**

Platinum, diamonds, sapphires, c. 1920, bar links interspaced with two foliate clusters set with sm circ diamonds and pear-shaped sapphires, joined to a central scrolled trefoil set with a heart-shaped and a pear-shaped sapphire and sm circ diamonds, suspending a single chain with one foliate cluster, and terminating in a swivel hook, 30" tl . . . . **3,300 (A)**

Necklace

Lapis lazuli, diamonds, platinum, wg, c. 1925, a lg circ lapis cab joined on each side by

diamond-set geo links to two smaller lapis cabs, geo links suspending a lg pear-shaped lapis drop, continuing to a later-added wg chain, 18" tl, 2-¼" center top to bottom
. . . . **2,090 (A)**

Choker
    Seed pearls, sapphires, diamonds, platinum, c. 1925, a narrow band of woven seed pearls with a central geo bow composed of 56 seed pearls with a central horizontal and vertical row of 14 sq-cut sapphires, and three circ-cut diamonds set at evenly spaced intervals, terminating in a plat, sapphire, and diamond clasp, 13" tl × ½"
. . . . **4,888 (A)**

Pendant and Chain
    Diamonds, 18k wg, sapphires, platinum, c. 1925, three articulated concentric rings of 73 rc diamonds, 33 calibré-cut sapphires, and one oe diamond, suspended from a cable-link plat chain, pendant 1" dia
. . . . **2,588 (A)**

    Diamonds, sapphires, platinum, c. 1920, in the shape of a knotted, draped, and folded scarf, pavé-set with circ-cut diamonds with borders of calibré-cut sapphires, sm pierced foli-

Pendant, diamonds, syn sapphires, platinum, c. 1920, a flared, cusped diamond and syn sapphire-set bail suspending a stylized draped handkerchief-shaped pendant with a pierced geo, foliate, and scroll design, a center vertical row of grad carré-set diamonds flanked by two curved horizontal rows of sm calibré syn sapphires and a V-shaped row at the base, set throughout with circ diamonds, 38 diamonds, approx 2 cts tw, 1" w × 2-¾" tl, $1,540 (A). *Photo courtesy of Dunning's, Elgin Ill. (5/16/93).*

Pendant and Chain, yellow sapphire, diamonds, platinum, c. 1920, a prong-set cushion-shaped yellow sapphire, 89.89 cts, surmounted by pendant loops and arrow-shaped links set with sc and oe diamonds, suspended from a plat baton-link chain interspersed with singly set diamonds and joined at midpoint to a diamond-set open heart-shaped motif, pendant sgd "Cartier" # 251428, 2-⅝" tl × 1" w, chain unsgd, approx 24" tl, $26,450 (A). *Photo © 1993 Sotheby's, Inc., New York (4/19/93)*

ate designs scattered throughout, suspending a lg pear-shaped diamond within a pierced foliate pear-shaped frame pavé-set with circ-cut diamonds, attached to a fine baton-link plat chain, pendant ³/₄″ w × 3-¹/₈″ tl, 15″ tl . . . . **6,670 (A)**
Jadeite, diamonds, platinum, c. 1920, a three-dimensional oval jadeite plaque, approx 47 × 31mm, pierced and carved with an asymmetrical foliate motif, suspended from black enameled, open lozenge and kite-shaped diamond-set links, attached with a swivel clasp to a chain of diamond-set navette-shaped plat filigree links, 24″ tl . . . . **7,150 (A)**
Pendant/Brooch and Chain
    Diamonds, platinum, pearls, 14k yg, c. 1920, an oval-shaped pierced scroll and foliate design pendant/brooch with scalloped edge, set throughout with om and rc diamonds, approx 2.75 ct tw, suspended from a 30″ baton-link plat chain interspersed with cultured pearls, yg brooch attachment, pendant/brooch, 1″ w × 1-¹/₂″ . . . . **3,300 (A)**
Pendant and Cord
    Diamonds, platinum, c. 1920, a kite-shaped plaque with undulating edges, pierced scroll, ribbon, and trefoil design set throughout with oe diamonds, tapering up to a trefoiled bail, suspended from a black cord with a lozenge-shaped diamond-set plat slide, 3.84 cts tw, 15″ tl, pendant, 1″ w × 2-¹/₂″ . . . . . **4,125 (A)**
Ring
    Diamonds, 14k wg, c. 1920, a wide pierced band with two bezel-set oe diamonds surrounded by smaller diamonds, 2.2 dwt, ¹/₂″ w × ³/₄″, ring size 4 . . . . **425 (A)**
    Diamonds, platinum, 14k wg and yg, c. 1920, an open lozenge-shaped top with one lg oe collet-set diamond, 1.5 ct, in the center, framed by 12 smaller oe diamonds, 1.75 ct tw, continuing to a polished shank, 3.2 dwt, ⁵/₈″ × ⁵/₈″, ring size 6 . . . . **2,700 (A)**

Ring, diamonds, platinum, 14k wg, blue stones, c. 1920, an elongated octagonal plaque with a vertical center row of four oe diamonds, approx 1.7 cts tw, outlined with 19 calibré-cut blue stones and bordered by 29 full-cut diamonds, approx 0.95 ct tw, one diamond missing, pierced and scrolled wirework gallery, mounted on a wg shank, ¹/₂″ w × 1-¹/₈″ × ¹/₄″ depth, $2,588 (A). *Photo courtesy of Butterfield & Butterfield, San Francisco and Los Angeles (6/17/93).*

Diamonds, platinum, 14k wg, c. 1920, a sq top with a central lg oe diamond, 1.1 ct, framed by two concentric sqs of sm circ diamonds, 1.75 ct tw, continuing to a tapered shank, 3 dwt, ⁵/₈″ × ⁵/₈″, ring size 6 . . . . . . **2,200 (A)**
Diamonds, platinum, blue stones, c. 1920, an oe diamond, approx .5 ct, in the center of an octagonal frame, surrounded by 36 sm calibré blue stones and bordered by 22 circ diamonds, mounted on a narrow shank, ¹/₂″ w × ¹/₂″ . . . . **2,875 (A)**
Diamonds, sapphires, platinum, c. 1920, a central oval-cut sapphire, approx 3.95 ct, surrounded by 24 oe diamonds, approx 1.5 ct tw, pavé-set in a rounded rect plaque with pierced lines radiating from the center, and in tapered shoulders, pierced gallery, ³/₄″ w × ⁷/₈″ . . . . **6,325 (A)**
Diamonds, 18k wg, sapphires, platinum, c. 1920, two openwork concentric rings set with 21 oe diamonds and 16 calibré-cut sapphires, ⁵/₈″ dia . . . . **1,840 (A)**
Diamonds, platinum, sapphires, c. 1925, a tapering domed mount with a central collet-set oe diamond, .6 ct, framed by a diamond-set crescent at top and bottom within a quatrefoil of 20 calibré sapphires, shoulders set with additional diamonds, pierced and engraved gallery and shank, slight nick on central diamond, 2.8 dwt . . . . **5,775 (A)**
Diamonds, sapphire, platinum, c. 1925, a circ sapphire, approx .85 ct, encircled by two concentric rows of oe diamonds, approx 1.15 ct tw, in a scalloped-edge mount, ⁵/₈″ dia . . . . **2,420 (A)**
Diamonds, onyx, 18k wg, c. 1925, a central bc diamond, approx .8 ct, set in a barrel-shaped carved black onyx plaque with two rows of sm circ-cut diamonds in an X-shape across the top, diamond-set shoulders, 22 diamonds, approx .3 ct tw, mkd "750 D," ¹/₂″ w × ⁵/₈″ . . . . **2,070 (A)**
Diamonds, blue stones, platinum, c. 1925-30, a domed tapered mount with an oe diamond, approx 3.1 ct, surrounded by calibré-cut blue stones and 36 oe diamonds, a line of 34 oe diamonds set around the tapered shank, ³/₄″ × ¹/₂″ . . . . **34,500 (A)**
Diamonds, platinum, c. 1930, openwork bombé-shaped mount with pierced zigzag pattern encircling a rect bezel-set diamond, 1.45 ct, set throughout with circ diamonds, ¹/₂″ w × ³/₄″, ring size 6-³/₄ . . . . . . **2,090 (A)**
Diamonds, sapphires, platinum, c. 1930, a lozenge shape tapering to a narrow shank, an oe diamond, approx. .85 ct, collet-set in the center, encircled by V-shaped sections of calibré-cut sapphires radiating from it, and set throughout with circ diamonds, ³/₄″ × ³/₄″ . . . . **2,750 (A)**
Diamonds, platinum, 14k yg, black onyx, c. 1930, a plat topped yg collet-set oe dia-

Ring, diamonds, platinum, c. 1930, a rounded oblong plaque with a vertical row of three lg oe diamonds, 2 cts tw, surrounded by 51 smaller pavé-set oe diamonds, approx 3 cts tw, pierced gallery, mounted on a narrow shank, approx size 5-1/2, ⁵/₈" w × 1-¹/₈", $4,800.
Courtesy of E. Foxe Harrell Jewelers.

mond, .3 ct, in the center of a black onyx beveled oval plaque, bordered with 14 smaller oe diamonds, .7 ct tw, mounted on a tapered yg shank, 4.4 dwt, ⁷/₈" w × ⁵/₈" .... **990 (A)**

Emerald, diamonds, platinum, c. 1925, an emerald-cut emerald, approx 1 ct, flanked by two trapezoid-cut diamonds approx 1.25 ct tw, in a diamond-set pierced plat mount, ³/₄" w × ³/₈" .... **5,500 (A)**

Jadeite, platinum, sapphires, diamonds, c. 1920, a prong-set oval cab, 17.2 × 11.7mm, framed by calibré-cut sq sapphires, flanked by diamond-set shoulders, engr shank, ³/₄" w × 1" .... **4,400 (A)**

Jadeite, diamonds, wg, c. 1925, rect jadeite plaque with chamfered corners, 18.02 × 13.9mm, prong-set, flanked by baguette and triangular-cut diamonds, tapered shank, 4.1 dwt, ring size 6-¹/₄ .... **2,530 (A)**

Jadeite, platinum, c. 1930, a prong-set oval cab, approx 19.5 × 13.5mm, flanked by three baguette diamonds, approx .8 ct tw, continuing to a tapered shank, ⁷/₈" w × 1" .... **7,700 (A)**

Jadeite, diamonds, platinum, c. 1930, an oval cab, approx 28 × 19 × 10mm, prong-set in a tapering diamond-set plat mount, 1" w × 1-¹/₄" .... **23,100 (A)**

Sapphire, platinum, diamonds, c. 1930, an oval prong-set sapphire cab, 6.15 ct, flanked by a vertical row of sc diamonds, each shoulder set with three sc diamonds, 3 dwt, ⁵/₈" w × ³/₄", ring size 5 .... **1,980 (A)**

Sapphire, platinum, diamonds, c. 1930, a central rect step-cut sapphire, approx 10.8 × 6.3mm, flanked by two channel-set baguette-cut diamonds, continuing to a line of four sq channel-set Fr-cut diamonds on the shoulders, Tiffany & Co., shank repaired, 2.4 dwt, ring size 5-¹/₄ .... **9,625 (A)**

Sapphires, platinum, diamonds, c. 1925-30, central circ bezel-set sapphire, encircled by eight bead-set oe diamonds, .8 ct tw, and four sc diamonds, outlined with a scalloped edge of semicirc-cut sapphires continuing to an open foliate shoulder shank, 3.2 dwt, ¹/₂" w × ³/₈", ring size 9-¹/₄ .... **3,850 (A)**

Star sapphire, platinum, diamonds, c. 1930, a central circ prong-set star sapphire, 30 ct, set within a pierced mount, surrounded by bead-set sc and channel-set baguette diamonds, 7.4 dwt, ⁷/₈" w, ring size 7 .... **1,320 (A)**

COSTUME JEWELRY C. 1920-1935

History: When Coco Chanel (1883-1971) reputedly declared in 1924, "It does not matter if they are real, as long as they look like junk!," costume jewels had already begun to enjoy widespread acceptance by women at all social levels. Both Chanel and her arch rival, Elsa Schiaparelli, were foremost among Parisian couturiers in designing and promoting the wearing of faux jewelry as an accessory to clothing, and as a means of self-expression. Today we call it "making a statement."

Because they were made from nonprecious materials, costume jewels gave manufacturers and designers a greater freedom to experiment

with designs and the opportunity to cater to fashion's whims, trends, and fads. Consequently, we see a far greater diversity in costume jewelry of the period compared to fine jewelry.

To be sure, many directly imitative pieces were made, substituting paste or rhinestones, and molded or cut glass, for gemstones, and silver or white pot metal (tin alloyed with lead) for platinum. Some of these pieces were remarkably well made. The metal was often rhodium-plated for an even closer resemblance to platinum (rhodium is one of the six metals in the platinum group). Stones were prong- or bead-set; occasionally, millegrained settings were used. At a short distance, one would find it difficult to discern them from the real thing. Verbatim translations of the period style from fine to costume jewelry include flexible and linked plaque bracelets, bead *sautoirs* (sometimes called flapper beads), pendent earrings, geometric brooches and pendants, dress clips, and double clip brooches.

As with fine jewelry, Art Deco costume pieces originated in Europe, where the *Jugendstil,* Bauhaus, Wiener Werkstätte, and Liberty styles had already made a case for modernism, emphasizing design over intrinsically valuable materials. But even in France, where *haute joaillerie* and Cartier reigned, the more adventurous Art Deco artist-designers turned to silver, chrome, glass, lacquer and enamel, and plastics. Although a separate section on plastic and novelty jewelry is included elsewhere in this book, German and French Art Deco pieces in chrome and plastic are included here because the modernity of their design classifies them with similar period pieces made of other materials.

Some French Art Deco costume jewelry is of the faux diamond and platinum variety, usually referred to as "French paste," set in silver, extremely well made. The transitional path of Edwardian to Art Deco can be followed in these all-white pieces, along the same route as fine jewelry. Similarly styled bracelets, clips, buckles, and brooches in rhinestones and white metal were made in the United States, by costume jewelry manufacturers such as Trifari, Krussman and Fishel, later known simply as Trifari (see section on designer/manufacturer signed costume jewelry). Ciner Mfg. Co., in business since 1892, made both fine and costume jewelry. They produced rhinestone and sterling pieces in the French mode during the 1920s and 1930s. The White Metal Casters' Association made inexpensive rhinestone and pot metal buckles and clips as dress accessories in the 1930s.

The French and the Germans also excelled at designing modern-looking jewelry in sterling set with inexpensive gemstones and marcasites, small faceted bits of iron pyrite. Theodor Fahrner, already famous for its early twentieth-century *Jugendstil* designs (as mentioned in the Arts and Crafts section), kept up with fashion by producing fine quality Art Deco pieces in high-grade silver set with marcasites combined with amazonite, smoky quartz, rock crystal, onyx, carnelian, chrysoprase, lapis, or coral. Other less well-known German manufacturers also made jewelry in this style, most commonly using dyed blue or green chalcedony (imitating chrysoprase) with marcasites and sterling.

Most accounts of fashion history tend to focus on what was original about the 1920s and 1930s, but all was not geometry and streamline. The Victorians did not have a monopoly on revivals; in fact, Victorian fashion and historicism itself were revived beginning in the late 1920s, and

growing in popularity in the 1930s and early 1940s. Period films and their stars helped set the mood: Mae West in *She Done Him Wrong* (1933), Greta Garbo in *Camille* (1936) and *Conquest* (1937), Bette Davis in *Juarez* (1939), and of course, Vivien Leigh in the immortal *Gone With The Wind* (1939). The clothes and the jewelry (much of the latter created by Eugene Joseff, aka Joseff of Hollywood [see the section on designer/manufacturer signed costume jewelry] may not have always been authentically of the period portrayed, but they inspired a 1930s trend for softer, more romantic dresses with longer hems, peplums, puffy sleeves and such Victorian staples as cameos and jet (imitated in glass and plastic), ornate metal filigree, and flower jewelry.

The exotic influences of the period that permeated the work of Cartier, Van Cleef and Arpels, et al., found widespread expression in costume jewels as well. The Egyptomania instigated by the discovery of King Tut's treasures and sustained by Hollywood films (e.g., *Cleopatra* in 1934), was especially prevalent. Enameled silver or gold-plated metal winged scarabs, falcons, vultures, and other motifs were produced in several European countries and the United States. The slave bracelet, of enameled metal links set with glass cabochons or molded scarabs, was an extension of the craze. One of the primary sources for Egyptian-themed pieces was Czechoslovakia. Here, the medium was usually glass, but celluloid and metal pieces, or a combination of materials, were also produced.

After World War I, Bohemia, long renowned for its glasswork, beads, and garnet jewelry, became part of the new country called Czechoslovakia, created in 1918. In the period between the wars, quantities of glass beads, faceted and molded glass stones, and stamped metalwork were produced and exported, some in the form of finished jewelry and some for use in jewelry manufacturered in other countries. The center of this production was a town called Gablonz, now known as Jablonec. Because the country was taken over by the Germans during World War II (exports were curtailed in 1939), the glass and jewelry makers were dispersed to other areas, such as Neugablonz, Germany. Today, the boundaries have been redrawn once again, and Czechoslovakia is now divided into the Czech Republic and Slovakia. Jewelry marked "Czechoslovakia" is easily circa-dated, and has recently become quite sought after. Prices have risen accordingly.

Czechoslovakia was the source of several types of costume jewelry. Stamped gilt metal filigree necklaces, bracelets, brooches, buckles, clips, earrings and rings were set with glass cabochons and embellished with enameled foliate motifs, resulting in an ornate look that was more Victorian revival than Art Deco. The Art Deco style was not ignored, however. Geometric-cut pieces of glass resembling gemstones were prong-set in short necklaces and pendent earrings. Glass buckles, clasps, and clips were made in simple modern designs. Small faceted glass stones were often silver-plated to imitate marcasites. Oriental-inspired pieces were made with molded and pierced glass plaques imitating carved jade and carnelian. Glass bead *sautoirs* were another Czech product. Some Czech pieces are marked in difficult-to-read places, like the circumference of a jump ring. Other unmarked pieces are so characteristic of Czech glass and metalwork that they are unmistakable. Still others may have Czech components but were assembled elsewhere and may be hard to identify.

References: Lillian Baker, *Art Nouveau and Art Deco Jewelry,* Collector Books, 1981, 1992 value update; Stella Blum, *Everyday Fashions of the Twenties,* Dover Publications, 1981, and *Everyday Fashions of the Thirties,* Dover Publications, 1986; Deanna Farneti Cera, ed., *Jewels of Fantasy, Costume Jewelry of the 20th Century,* Harry N. Abrams, 1992; Ulrike von Hase-Schmundt et al., *Theodor Fahrner Jewelry, Between Avant-Garde and Tradition,* Schiffer Publishing, 1991; Sibylle Jargstorf, *Baubles, Buttons and Beads, The Heritage of Bohemia,* Schiffer Publishing, 1993, and *Glass in Jewelry,* Schiffer Publishing, 1991; Jane Mulvagh, *Costume Jew-*

elry in Vogue, Thames and Hudson, 1988; Penny Proddow, Debra Healy, and Marion Fasel, *Hollywood Jewels,* Harry N. Abrams, 1992; Jody Shields, *All That Glitters, The Glory of Costume Jewelry,* Rizzoli International, 1987.

Periodical and Collectors' Club: *Vintage Fashion & Costume Jewelry Newsletter* and Club, P.O. Box 265, Glen Oaks, N.Y. 11004, published quarterly.

Museums: Glass and Costume Jewelry Museum, Jablonec nad Nisou, Czech Republic; Jewelers' Museum, Providence, R.I.

Reproduction Alert: The same conditions and caveats apply for costume jewelry as for fine jewelry, particularly marcasite and silver, which has been reproduced in mass quantities. Again, quality varies widely. Some British and German exports are very well made. Wholesalers specializing in reproductions advertise in antiques trade papers.

Bracelet
Bangle
Brass, glass, enamel, rhinestones, c. 1920, stamped brass filigree, two appl plaques with faux lapis centers flanked by round green glass cabs, sm blue glass cabs and green r.s., white enamel scrolls, bezel-set oval green cabs flanked by sm faux lapis

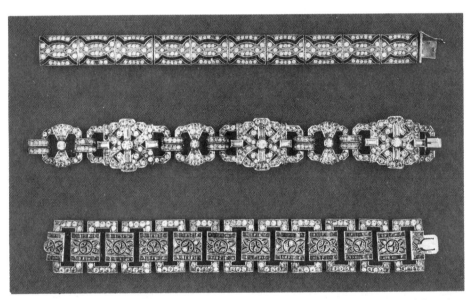

Bracelets, link, paste, sterling, French: T, c. 1920, hinged rect plaques bead-set with colorless pastes and channel-set with sq faux blue glass sapphires in geo swagged pattern, pierced gallery, mkd "935," Fr import marks (swan), makers mark "LEL" and stylized rose in oval reserve on v-spring, box clasp, safety clasp, 6-7/8" × 5/8", $150; C, c. 1930, three pierced and openwork stepped rect plaques alternating with three smaller open squares with bow-shaped centers linked with double bars, set throughout with colorless circ and baguette pastes, Fr hmks on v-spring, box clasp, 7-1/2" × 1", $350; B, c. 1925, open rect links of bead-set colorless pastes joined with center sq plaques of pierced paste-set foliate design flanked by horizontal rows of channel-set sq-cut green pastes, Fr hmks on v-spring, box clasp, 6-7/8" × 1", $350, *Connie Parente collection.*

cabs and brass shell motifs, Czech, 2-3/4"
dia × 7/8" **150**

Flexible

Wm, bronzed ym, c. 1935, four domed wm
disks with raised volute and triangle pattern in ym centers, appl to a flexible band
of faceted wm batons with rounded ends
strung together on monofilament, v-spring
and box clasp, metal tag mkd "Denaive
Paris," 6-7/8" × 1-1/4" **165**

Rhinestones, white pot metal, c. 1930, a
wide flexible band of articulated rect
plaques pierced and pavé-set with circ
and baguette colorless r.s. in stepped and
circ geo pattern, v-spring and box clasp
mkd "F.N.Co." for Fishel, Nessler & Company, N.Y., safety chain, 7-1/2" × 1-5/8"
. . . . **350**

Sterling, glass, c. 1920, hinged sq plaques of
stamped ster filigree alternating with colorless and black sq domed glass cabs with
molded scrolled and foliate designs, set in
millegrained bezels, box clasp mkd "O.B.
sterling" for Otsby & Barton Co., Providence, R.I., 7" × 1/2" **165**

Glass, sp brass, rhinestones, enamel,
c. 1920, wm hinged plaque bezel-set with
three rounded rect red glass cabs in ropetwist frames within black enamel scroll

and floral design, silvered r.s. (imitation
marcasite), set in bosses and bezels, terminating in snake chain at each end, springring clasp, rev mkd "Czechoslovakia,"
7-1/2" × 1" **85**

Flexible link

Sterling, paste (rhinestones), c. 1920, three
flexible hinged panels carré-set with colorless pastes, joined with circ paste-set links
terminating in a box clasp with a paste-set
articulated buckle ornament, rev mkd
"sterling Pat March 20, 1917 Diamonbar," Am, 7-1/4" × 1/2" **165**

Hinged

Sterling vermeil, chalcedony, enamel,
c. 1930, three lg open squares with convex top surfaces outlined in black enamel,
joined with six millegrained bezel-set
green-dyed chalcedony cabs in hinged
prs, box clasp, v-spring mkd "France sterling," safety chain, 7-1/2" tl × 1-7/8" . . . **750**

Hinged bangle

Sterling, rhinestones, c. 1920, sq-cut colorless r.s. channel-set in an oval ster bangle
with engr scroll, floral and foliate design
on sides, cutout chevron pattern on inside
surface, mkd "sterling," v-spring and box
clasp, safety clasp, 2-3/8" dia × 3/16" . . . **150**

Sterling, rhinestones, c. 1920, sq-cut blue

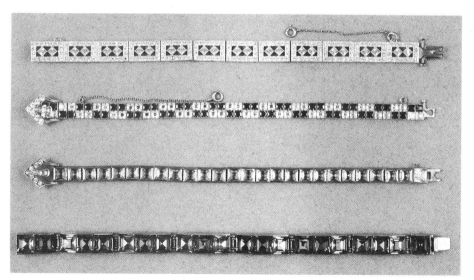

**Bracelets, flexible, rhinestones, American: T-B, 1, c. 1930, rh pl wm, straight line of hinged rect pierced plaques, each
with two millegrain-set sq colorless r.s. at 45° in open center, frames pavé-set with sm r.s., engr gallery, box clasp mkd
"EB" in lozenge for Engel Bros., Inc., New York, N.Y., safety chain, 7" × 3/8", $175; T-B, 2, c. 1920, two rows of sq-cut
dk blue and colorless r.s. millegrain-set in opposed prs forming checkerboard pattern, terminating in buckle-shaped
box clasp, rev mkd "sterling Pat. 3.20.17 Diamonbar," safety chain, 7" × 1/4", clasp 1/2" w, $250; T-B, 3, c. 1920,
straight line row of lg sq-cut colorless faceted r.s. set à jour in hinged mounts, engr scrolled foliate sides, terminating in
buckle-shaped box clasp, rev mkd "Diamonbar sterling," 7-1/4" × 1/4", $125; T-B, 4, c. 1930, sterling vermeil, slightly
convex hinged rect segments each set with a row of three lg sq-cut red r.s., v-spring and box clasp, mkd "sterling,"
7-3/8" × 3/8", $200, Victoria Taylor collection.**

and colorless (three alternating with three) r.s. channel-set in an oval ster bangle, with engr scroll, floral and foliate design on sides, cutout chevron pattern on inside surface, mkd "sterling," v-spring and box clasp, safety chain, 2-3/8" dia × 3/16" **225**

Sterling, rhinestones, c. 1920, sq-cut green r.s. channel-set in an oval ster bangle, with engr scroll, floral and foliate design on sides, cutout chevron pattern on inside surface, mkd "sterling, Diamonbar," v-spring and box clasp, 2-1/2" dia × 3/16" **175**

Link

835 silver, black onyx, c. 1920, five lobed rect plaques with raised beaded zig-zag and sun ray designs, each plaque prong-set with a flat chamfered-corner rect polished onyx slab, joined with open rect silver links, v-spring mkd "835," box clasp, 7-1/8" × 3/4" **175**

Chrome plated wm, plastic, c. 1930, three lg open oval chrome links alternating with three lg annular red plastic links joined with reeded elliptical chrome links, spring ring clasp, 7-1/2" tl × 1" **125**

Chrome plated wm, Bakelite, enamel, c. 1930, three domed rect segments of orange Bakelite alternating with four domed rect chrome segments, each with an orange enameled triangle at each end , 7-1/4" tl × 3/8" **125**

Glass, brass, c. 1930, nine rect faceted green

glass stones alternating with eight prs of vertically stacked rect faceted colorless glass stones, prong set, open backs, replaced spring ring clasp, 7" × 1" **65**

Glass, sp brass, enamel, c. 1930, rect blue faceted glass in millegrained bezels in the centers of four linked openwork plaques, flanked by sm blue and white enameled flower motifs terminating in chain loops with spring-ring clasp, unmkd, probably Czech, 7-1/4" × 2-5/8" **75**

Glass, sterling, c. 1920, five lt blue glass convex rect plaques prong-set in engr ster frames alternating with prong-set sq-cut open-backed colorless lead crystal stones, spring-ring clasp mkd "sterling," 7" × 1/2" **85**

Glass, sterling, c. 1925, three rect green glass plaques with molded floral design set in millegrained bezels, reeded links joining a colorless open rect with incised ridges, spring-ring clasp mkd "sterling," 7-1/4" × 5/8" **95**

Gp brass, glass, c. 1925, lg cushion-shaped red glass cabs and sm red truncated crescents bezel-set in convex rect plaques of stamped scrolled gp filigree, box clasp mkd "Made in Czechoslov," 6-7/8" tl × 3/4" **125**

Rhinestones, rh pl wm, c. 1930, open rect links with three horizontal bars pavé-set with colorless circ r.s., joined with prs of baguette-set links, double foldover clasp, 7-1/4" × 5/8" **75**

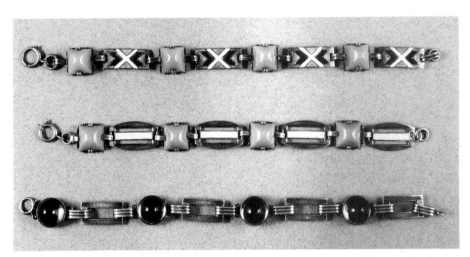

Slave Bracelets, link, silver, glass, *basse-taille* enamel, c. 1925: T, four pierced rect links with chevron-shaped cutouts flanking white enameled X-shapes on blue-green enameled ground, alternating with four high-domed cushion-shaped green glass cabs prong-set in flat-backed links, spring-ring clasp mkd "sterling," 7-7/8" × 1/2", $145; **C,** four convex rect red *basse-taille* enameled links, each with a cutout center bar of yellow enamel on a floral motif groundplate, alternating with four cushion-shaped red glass cabs in prong-set links, rev mkd "sterling," spring-ring clasp, 7-1/4" × 1/2", $145; **B,** four open rect green enameled silver links alternating with four bezel-set high-domed circ green glass cabs, joined with reeded oval silver links, 8" × 1/2", $125, *Charles Pinkham collection.*

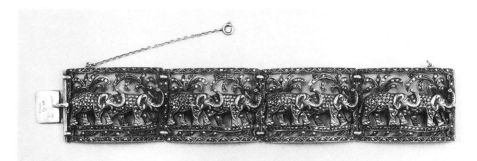

Bracelet, link, 900 silver, marcasites, red cabs, date letter for 1938, four rect panels linked together, each depicting two elephants on cutout bg of palm trees within scalloped pattern frames, pavé-set marcasites, red cab eyes, v-spring and box clasp, mkd "900," Egyptian silver hmks, date letter, maker's mark on tongue of v-spring, safety chain, 7-⅛" × ¼", $1,200. *Author's collection.*

Sterling, rhinestones, c. 1930, articulated bar links in tank-track pattern, each link bead-set with three sm circ colorless r.s., foldover clasp mkd "sterling," "EB" in a lozenge for Engel Bros., Inc., New York, 7" × ⅜" **125**

Brooch/Pin

Brass, c. 1930, streamlined design of a central domed disk surmounting a lacquered black flat disk and larger semicirc plaque, bisected by three rods soldered together at uneven lengths, 4-⅞" × 1-⅜" **100**

Brass, glass, rhinestones, c. 1920, rounded lozenge-shaped plaque, yellow star satin glass cab center with beaded frame around bezel, four amber-colored r.s. at compass points in stamped filigree and textured metal ground, safety catch, Czech, 1-¾" × 1-⅛" **65**

Glass, rhinestones, rh pl wm, c. 1930, circ openwork floral and foliate design with molded glass flowerheads and leaves in opalescent pastel shades of pink, blue, and green, within colorless pavé circ and baguette r.s. setting, 1-⅞" dia **65**

Gp brass, glass, enamel, c. 1920, stamped filigree lobed oval plaque with central bezel-set oval purple faceted glass framed by white seed beads encircled by five sm purple glass stones bezel-set in rope-twist frames, and sm yellow enamel flowerheads suspending a pear-shaped faceted purple glass drop from enameled cap, safety catch, rev mkd "Czech," 1-½" × 2-⅛"tl **95**

Marcasites, sterling, c. 1930, pierced rect with initials "C S R," geo design in two corners, pavé-set with marcasites, trombone catch, mkd "Made in France, sterling," 1-½" w × ¾" **85**

Marcasites, wm, enamel, c. 1930, rect openwork stepped and geo design, pavé-set with marcasites, blue enameled corners, lever catch, 1-⅛" w × 1-¾" **45**

Paste (rhinestones), sterling, c. 1930, open ta-

pered rect, geo pattern pavé-set with color-less pastes, trombone catch, pinstem mkd "Made in France," 1-¾" w × ⅞" **125**

Rhinestones, glass, wm, c. 1920, lg rect open-work design, three flowerheads with blue faceted glass centers, five lg oval blue faceted glass stones prong-set within scroll and foliate design set throughout with silvered r.s. (imitation marcasite) in wm frame, safety catch, Czech, 2-½" × 1-½" **85**

Rhinestones, glass, wm, c.1920, openwork butterfly motif, foliate and floral design within rope-twist rect wm frame with round, sq, rect and lozenge-shaped blue glass prong-set in upper left corner, set throughout with silvered r.s. (imitation marcasite), trombone catch, Czech, 1-⅞" × 1-¼" **65**

Rhinestones, rh pl wm, c. 1930, geo bowknot and sash, pavé-set with sq red r.s. and circ colorless r.s., 3" × 1" **60**

Rhinestones, rh pl wm, c. 1930, rect plaque with bombé sides, cutout and pierced arrow

Brooch/Pin, 800 silver, enamel, c. 1920, Egyptian revival, in the shape of a vulture grasping the Egyptian symbol of infinity in its talon, stamped and pierced sections filled with aqua, yellow, and green *plique à jour* enamel, rev mkd "800," added safety catch, tube hinge, 2-¼" w × 1-⅝", $500. *Terrance O'Halloran collection.*

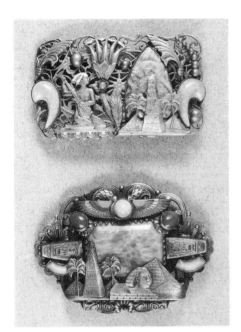

Brooches/Pins, brass, glass, enamel, Czech Egyptian revival, c. 1925: T, rect stamped filigree plaque with appl
Egyptian motifs: pyramids, palm trees, obelisk, lotus,
musician, and set with molded green glass and sm red
glass cabs, rev mkd "Czechoslovakia," safety catch,
2-1/2" w × 1-1/2", $245; B, oval stamped filigree plaque
with appl Egyptian motifs: sphinx, vulture, cartouches,
pyramids, obelisk, palm trees, and set with oval red,
round, crescent, and lg rect green glass with beveled
edges and chamfered corners, in millegrained and filigree bezels, green, blue, and red painted enamel details,
safety catch, rev mkd "Czecho," 2-3/4" tl × 1-7/8", $275,
Charles Pinkham collection.

Brooch/Pin, bar, glass, sp brass, rhinestones, enamel,
c. 1920, central elliptical molded and pierced floral and
foliate carnelian-colored glass plaque, prong-set in an
open-backed mount, flanked by black enameled arrow
motifs with colorless r.s. and sp centers, rev mkd
"Czechoslovakia," C-catch, 2-1/4" w × 3/4", $145.
Charles Pinkham collection.

Brooches/Pins, paste (rhinestones), sterling: T, c. 1920,
pierced oval plaque, central rosette within sm
flowerhead and swag motifs, slightly lobed frame, pavé-
set with colorless pastes, rev mkd "sterling Germany
4A," 1-7/8" w × 1-3/8", $200; C, c. 1925, Cartier-in-
spired, faceted colorless glass ring horizontally bisected
by a pierced scrolled bar tapering out from the center,
set with marquise-cut colorless r.s., and pavé-set with
sm circ r.s., rev mkd "Ciner sterling" (Ciner Mfg Co.,
New York, N.Y.), 1-3/4" w × 1-1/4", $125, *Victoria Taylor
collection;* B, Double Clip Brooch, c. 1930, a pr of
pierced stepped inverted triangles pavé-set with sm circ
colorless r.s. and bezel-set with marquise and baguette
r.s., flat-backed hinged clips mkd "Ciner sterling" on
rev, can be joined opposed with pinback mechanism for
wear as a brooch, forming notched lozenge shape, 2-1/4"
w × 1", $125, *Connie Parente collection.*

Brooches/Pins, sterling, marcasites, Theodor Fahrner, c. 1925-30: T, a scalloped-edge bar with pierced S-scrolls across center, a rect coral cab set in a millegrained bezel at each end, rev mkd "Germany sterling," conjoined "TF" in a circle for Theodor Fahrner, Pforzheim, replaced safety catch, 1-^{3}/$_4$" × ^{3}/$_8$", $450, *Terrance O' Halloran collection*; B, a center vertical row of sq amazonite cabs flanked on each side by a lg triangular-cut smoky quartz prong-set within a stepped marcasite-set frame, rev mkd with conjoined "TF" for Theodor Fahrner, "935," 2-^{1}/$_4$" w × 1", $900, *Victoria Taylor collection.*

and fan patterns pavé-set with colorless circ r.s. around a center millegrained bezel-set r.s., 2-^{3}/$_8$" w × 1-^{1}/$_4$" **55**

Rhinestones, white pot metal, c. 1930, T-shaped, tapering to a point at the bottom, pavé-set with sm and med circ r.s., C-catch, 1-^{1}/$_2$" w × 2-^{1}/$_2$" **35**

Bar

Gp brass, glass, enamel, c. 1925, a lg oval red glass cab bezel-set within a rope-twist frame, mounted on a scrolled and pierced stepped rect stamped gp brass plaque, flanked by sm oval and round red glass cabs and green enameled C-scrolls, rev mkd "Czechoslovakia," safety-pin catch, 2" w × ^{7}/$_8$" **45**

Gp ym, scarab, rhinestones, c. 1925, Egyptian revival, genuine scarab prong-set in the center of an opposed pair of gp falcon wings and birds' heads with green r.s. eyes, rev mkd "Made in France," safety-pin catch, 2-^{7}/$_8$" w × ^{3}/$_4$" **100**

Paste (rhinestones), glass, white pot metal, c. 1920, pierced fancy-shaped bar with cusped ends, pavé-set with colorless pastes, tapered center bezel-set with blue glass, safety catch, 2-^{3}/$_4$" w × ^{1}/$_2$" **65**

Buckle

Rhinestones, white pot metal, c. 1930, two-pc, pavé-set colorless r.s., one pc a wide triangle with two sm cut-out triangles, the other an opposed narrow triangle with a cut-out arrow in the center, hook-and-eye closure, bars for belt attachment on rev, mkd "WMCA" for White Metal Casters Association, Inc., New York, N.Y., 3-^{3}/$_4$" w × 2-^{1}/$_4$" **45**

Rhinestones, white pot metal, c. 1930, two pcs forming four double columns of pavé-set round colorless r.s., each column with a lg sq r.s. in the center, and baguette-set domed crossbars at the top and bottom, hook-and-eye closure, bars for belt attachment on rev, 2-^{1}/$_8$" w × 2-^{1}/$_8$" **75**

Rhinestones, white pot metal, c. 1930, two-pc, pierced and scrolled opposed shield shapes with cutout centers, pavé-set with colorless r.s., a pair of green baguette r.s. at centers and each end, rev mkd "WMCA" for White Metal Casters Assoc, New York, N.Y., # 19, hook-and-eye closure, bars for belt attachment, 3-^{3}/$_8$" × 1-^{3}/$_4$" **50**

Rhinestones, white pot metal, c. 1930, two-pc, in the shape of a lg bow, pavé-set with colorless r.s. (some missing), rev mkd "WMCA" for White Metal Casters' Assoc, New York, N.Y., hook-and-eye closure, bars for belt attachment, 3" w × 2-^{1}/$_4$" **45**

Rhinestones, glass, white pot metal, c. 1935, two-pc, stylized leaf shapes with openwork design set throughout with colorless r.s., appl molded dk blue, green, and white glass flowerheads with r.s. centers, hook-and-eye closure, bars for belt attachment, 3-^{1}/$_2$" w × 1-^{1}/$_4$" **95**

Cuff Links

Wm, MOP, enamel, c. 1920, snap-apart type, two-sided octagons with circ MOP centers surrounded by blue enamel scallops, further surrounded by white enamel, mkd "Kum-A-Part, Registered Baer & Wilde" (Attleboro, Mass. company founded in 1897, mfr of men's jewelry exclusively after 1918, became Swank, Inc. in 1940), ^{1}/$_2$" dia, pr . . . **25**

Double Clip Brooch

Rhinestones, glass, rh pl wm, c. 1936-40, a pr of scrolled shield-shaped dress clips pavé-set with sm circ and baguette colorless r.s. around center clusters of circ pearlescent blue glass cabs, with a detachable pinback mechanism for joining as a brooch, mkd "U.S. Pat No. 2034129 (1936) other pat. pend," 2-^{1}/$_4$" w × 1-^{1}/$_4$" joined **65**

Rhinestones, wm, c. 1937-40, a pr of shield-shaped dress clips with geo pierced design set throughout with r.s., flat-backed hinged clips can be joined with a sliding pinback mechanism for wear as a brooch, mkd "Pat 2066969" (1937), 2-^{7}/$_8$" w × 1-^{1}/$_2$" joined **80**

Rhinestones, white pot metal, c. 1937-40, a pr of dress clips, rounded triangles with openwork floral and foliate design set throughout with colorless r.s., flat-backed hinged clips can be joined with a sliding pinback mechanism for wear as a brooch, clips mkd "Made in USA, Pat 2085548" (1937), 3" w × 1-¼" joined **90**

Dress Clip

Glass, gp brass, c. 1930, Egyptian revival, molded in the shape of a sphinx, green glass with painted orange accented details, set in a

Chrysoprase, sterling, marcasites, Germany: T, Dress Clip, c. 1930, a carved and pierced floral and foliate oval chrysoprase plaque, prong-set within a geo and lobed openwork beaded ster frame set with marcasites, a flat-backed hinged clip with serrated rev edges mounted on rev, mkd "Drem Germany," 1-¼" w × 1-⅝", $135; Brooches/Pins, c. 1920-25: C, a lozenge shape formed by two prong-set triangular stones separated by a vertical marcasite-set ster bar in the center, pierced gallery, rev mkd "sterling," 1-½" w × ½", $80; B, four beveled rect cabs prong-set in a square around a circ cab prong-set in the open center, trefoiled ster triangles bead-set with marcasites within inside and outside angles formed by stones, rev mkd "Wachenheimer sterling," lever safety catch, 1-½" × 1-½", $235, Terrance O' Halloran collection.

flat-backed gp bezel, engr flat-backed hinged clip on rev, Czech, 1-¼" w × 1-¾" **65**

Glass, rhinestones, wm, enamel, c. 1930, set with multicolored round cabs and sm colorless r.s., scalloped edge outlined in black enamel, surmounted by a pavé r.s.-set bow, flat-backed hinged clip on rev, 1-⅜" w × 2" **30**

Rhinestones, white pot metal, c. 1930, half oval tablet, three sq r.s. set at 45° angles in the center of a pavé r.s. ground, flat-backed hinged clip, rev mkd "WMCA" for White Metal Casters Association, 2" w × 1-½" **60**

Rhinestones, white pot metal, c. 1935, fan-shaped with domed center disk, pavé r.s., flat-backed hinged spring clip, mkd "pat 1852188" (1932), 2-⅞" w × 1-¾" **50**

Sterling, wm, c. 1930, domed disk, cutout off-center, raised beads, appl wire and teardrop shapes in swirled pattern around textured edge, rev mkd "sterling," engr flat-backed hinged clip mounted on rev, 1-⅞" dia **125**

Wm, enamel, c. 1930, tapered shield shape with cutout navette-shaped center in white champlevé enamel framed by red basse-taille enameled sections, a cutout flat-backed hinged clip on rev, 1-½" w × 2-¼" **50**

Dress Clips

Rhinestones, rh pl wm, c. 1930, each a lg pierced, lobed, and cusped convex shield shape, two sq-cut colorless r.s. at top center, set throughout with various sizes of circ colorless r.s., flat-backed hinged clip mounted on rev, 2" w × 2-⅜", pr **150**

Rhinestones, rh pl wm, c. 1930, each a narrow vertical plaque, cusped at the base, pavé-set with sm circ colorless r.s. with a center vertical row of four baguettes set end-to-end, surmounted by a domed stepped rect with a vertical center row of horizontally set baguette r.s. flanked by two rows of pavé circ r.s., flat-backed hinged clip mounted on rev, ⅝" w × 1-⅞", pr **60**

Rh pl 800 silver, marcasites, c. 1930, pierced shield shapes with scroll motifs pavé-set with marcasites, rev mkd "800," flat-backed hinged clips, 1" w × 1-⅛", pr **50**

Earrings

Clip

800 silver, marcasites, c. 1935, slightly domed disks pavé-set with marcasites, clipbacks, rev mkd "800," ½" dia, pr **60**

Sterling, marcasites, c. 1935, leaf shapes pavé-set with marcasites, clipbacks, rev mkd "sterling," ½" w × 1-⅛", pr **50**

Drop

Glass, ym, c. 1925, Egyptian revival, two-

Dress Clips, rhinestones, glass, white pot metal, c. 1930-35: T, convex semicirc bands with a vertical row of dk pink sq cabs flanked by two rows of pavé colorless r.s., flat-backed hinged clips mkd "Pat 1801128" (1931), ½" w × 1-¼", pr, $85, *Terrance O'Halloran collection;* BL, three lg green glass cabs prong-set in triangular pavé r.s.-set mount with open grid design, flat-backed hinged clip on rev, 2" × 2", $45; BC, center vertical row of three grad flowerheads set with pear-shaped colorless r.s. and sm center circ r.s., flanked by curv rows of oval r.s., engr flat-backed hinged clip on rev, 1-½" w × 3", $55; BR, pierced ruffled semicirc shield shape set throughout with circ colorless r.s., flat-backed hinged clip, 2-⅛" w × 1-½", $30, *Richard Noël collection.*

sided molded cobalt glass pear-shaped plaques with painted green-accented relief design of an Egyptian goddess, later added shepherd's hook earwires, Czech, 1" w × 1-¾", pr **50**

Hoop

Brass, rhinestones, enamel, c. 1920, stamped filigree with white enamel foliate motifs alternating with round purple r.s., findings converted to posts, Czech, ¾" dia × ⅜" w, pr **30**

Pendent

Glass, brass, c. 1920, a chain of faceted tubular red glass beads linked with jump rings and eyepins suspending a pierced cone-shaped brass filigree and red glass bead drop, later added shepherd's hook earwires, 2-⅞" tl × ⅜", pr **65**

Glass, brass, faux pearls, rhinestones, c. 1925, polygonal geo-cut faceted colorless glass drop suspended from a beaded bail linked to a faux pearl and a fine chain, r.s.-set surmount, screwback findings mkd "Czechoslovakia," 2-¼" tl × ⅝", pr . . . **55**

Glass, brass, r.s., c. 1925, articulated shank section formed from a brass baton linked

above and below an open brass rect, pavé-set with sm colorless r.s., suspending a rect-cut prong-set blue glass drop, suspended from a r.s.-set surmount with screwback findings, mkd "Czechoslovakia," 2-½" tl × ½", pr **125**

Lead crystal, rh pl wm, c. 1935, elongated triangular drop prong-set with six crystal baguettes and five circ crystals in open-backed mounts suspended from a crystal-set surmount, screwback findings mkd "Czechoslovakia," 1-¾" tl × ½", pr . . . **55**

Lead crystal, sterling, c. 1920, three grad, stepped, articulated vertical rows of cushion-cut prong-set open-backed crystals, suspended from a cushion-cut crystal surmount, screwback findings, setting mkd with a star and "H & H" for Hamilton & Hamilton, Jr., Providence, R.I., (in business through 1922), 2-½" tl × ¾", pr **175**

Silver, paste (rhinestones), c. 1920, chandelier style, three narrow tapered drops suspended from a triangular plaque with a pierced center, linked to an X-shaped shank suspended from a triangular

Pendent Earrings, glass, brass, enamel, Czech, c.1920: L, mottled green glass cabs and enamel leaves on tapered stamped brass drop suspended from stamped brass surmounts, screwback findings, 1-⁷/₈″ × ⁵/₈″, pr, $75, *Leigh Leshner collection;* C, circ red glass cab bezel-set at the base of a black enameled scrolled foliate drop set with sm r.s. in the center, suspended from surmount with sm red glass center, screwback findings mkd "Czechoslovakia," 2-¹/₈″ tl × ³/₄″, pr, $95, *Author's collection;* R, cone-shaped stamped filigree drop terminating in a pear-shaped opaque dk blue glass bead, suspended from a blue faceted glass bead and surmount, screwbacks, 2-¹/₈″ × ³/₈″, pr, $85, *Leigh Leshner collection.*

Pendent Earrings, glass, butterfly wing, sterling, 9k yg, c. 1920, a pear-shaped drop with white sulphide (bas-relief clay figure) of a draped nude goddess in colorless glass with irid blue butterfly wing ground, set in a rounded-back ster bezel with gadrooned border, suspended from a fancy link chain, flowerhead surmount, yg screwback findings mkd "9c," backs of drops mkd "sterling silver England," 2-³/₄″ tl × ⁵/₈″, pr, $175. *Terrance O'Halloran collection.*

surmount, set throughout with colorless pastes, shepherd's hook earwire, 2-⁵/₈″ tl × ¹/₂″, pr **125**

Sp brass, glass, c. 1920, slightly domed disk drop surmounted by a smaller appl hammered (stamped) disk set with an orange glass cab in a millegrained bezel, linked to a hammered baton flanked by orange glass half-round cabs, suspended from a glass bead and surmount set with an orange cab in a rope-twist frame, screwback findings mkd "Czechoslovak," 2-¹/₈″ tl × ³/₄″, pr **85**

Sterling, c. 1920, three lozenge-shaped beveled carnelians, prong-set with a C-scroll and stepped ster mount set with one lg and one sm marcasite, suspended from a r.s.-set surmount, fr earwires, 2″ tl × ¹/₂″, pr **150**

Sterling, c. 1920, long briolette-cut green glass suspended in the center of a scrolled open r.s.-set frame, r.s.-set trefoil surmount and shepherd's hook earwires, fram mkd "sterling," 3″ tl × ⁵/₈″, pr **150**

Sterling, c. 1920, beveled rect dyed blue chalcedony cabs prong-set in openwork suspended from stamped and pierced scrolls and heart shaped links, surmount set with marcasites, screwback findings, mkd "sterling Germany," 2-¹/₄″ tl × ³/₈″, pr **175**

Locket and Chain

Wm, glass, c. 1925, Egyptian revival, oval locket with allover raised floral and foliate design, central motifs of a pharoah's head, two snakes and a pyramid, four faux lapis

Pendent Earrings, rhinestones: L, c. 1935, rh pl wm, flared drop set with grad prs of marquise-cut colorless r.s. with circ r.s. centers, terminating in a lg inverted pear-shaped r.s. and five sm circ prong-set r.s., suspended from a flowerhead surmount of one lg collet-set r.s. encircled by sm collet-set r.s., triangular engr clipbacks mkd "Pat. 1967965" (1934), Am, 2" tl × ⅝", pr, $65; C, c. 1925, chandelier style, three articulated drops with baguette, circ and, marquise-cut pastes in millegrained bezels suspended from a horizontal bar set with three sq-cut pastes, surmounted by a paste-set arch with a pentagonal articulated drop suspended from a sq-cut paste in a millegrained bezel, circ paste-set surmount, rev mkd "sterling," mkd "10k" on yg screwback findings, 2-¾" tl × ⅝", pr, $195; R, c. 1925, two articulated chains of paired paste-set foliate motifs terminating in flowerhead drops, each with a lg open-backed colorless paste encircled by prong-set sm r.s., suspended négligée from similarly set flowerhead surmounts, screwback findings mkd "sterling," 2" tl × ⅞", pr, $195, *Kirsten Olson collection.*

glass cabs in millegrained bezels at center top and bottom, suspended from a textured oval link chain, 18" tl, locket 1-½" w × 2-½" tl **225**

Necklace

Brass, glass, c. 1925, linked triangular brass plaques prong-set with alternating red and black triangular glass cabs, unmkd, probably Czech, 15-⅛" tl × ½" **135**

Brass, glass, c. 1925, stamped brass filigree hexagonal plaques alternating with prong-set open-backed faceted green triangles, jump rings added for length, unmkd, probably Czech, 16-½" tl × ⅞" **95**

Chrome plated wm, glass, enamel, c. 1930, a hexagonal stepped and faceted green glass plaque prong-set in an open-backed frame in the center of a necklace of articulated flat rect chrome bicycle chain riveted links, alternate center links enameled lt green, suspending a tapered-out articulated jabot of chrome and enameled chrome links terminating in three bezel-set molded green glass ziggurats, 15-½" tl, pendent section 1" w × 3" **200**

Chrome plated wm, Bakelite, c. 1930, two lg faceted cone-shaped chrome drops terminating in a black and a green Bakelite bead suspended from a necklace of alternating black and green beads, long wm tubes and short sq wm tubes strung on fine chain, 19-½" tl, drops 2-½" tl × ⅝" **245**

Chrome plated wm, Bakelite, c. 1930, tapered chrome chain mesh joining a domed trapezoid flanked by two domed rect segments of dk red Bakelite, spring-ring clasp, oval jump ring mkd "Germany," 16-½" tl, ¾" w at center **200**

Chrome plated wm, Bakelite, c. 1930, alternating chrome and black Bakelite domed rect segments with chrome bead spacers, strung on fine chain joined to wm herringbone chain, barrel clasp, jump ring mkd "Germany," 16-½" tl × 1" **225**

Glass, sp brass, c. 1925, nine sq reeded translucent green glass plaques prong-set and linked to inverted stepped triangular sp brass plaques, each set with four silvered black faceted glass stones (imitation marcasites) terminating in a v-spring and box clasp mkd "Czechoslov," 15-½" tl × ½" **100**

Glass, sp brass, c. 1925, linked and prong-set grad domed rect plaques of molded translucent green glass, silvered sections imitating marcasites, suspending a stepped rect center plaque of similar design, continuing to a sp

Lorgnette, sterling, marcasites, enamel, c. 1920, a pr of folding spectacles in hexagonal frames, engr hinged nosepiece, collapses into a pentagonal engr ster case pierced in geo fan and triangle design, pavé-set with marcasites, black enameled shield-shaped center, red enameled sections above and below, continuing to an annular handle, jump rings for chain attachment, spring release mechanism on handle rev, Fr hmk on nosepiece, maker's mark "DD" in lozenge, # 1073801E, 2-¹/₂″ × 1-¹/₈″ closed, 6″ tl open, $650. *Kirsten Olson collection.*

round and oval link trace chain, spring-ring clasp, rev of center plaque mkd "M. I. Czechoslovakia," 20-³/₄″ tl × 1-¹/₄″ **175**

Glass, brass, c. 1925, 10 molded and faceted shield-shaped plaques of carnelian-colored glass, prong-set and linked together, six navette-shaped brass spacers with raised reeded X-design terminating in a spring-hook clasp, probably Czech, 15″ tl × ³/₄″ **125**

Glass, sp brass, c. 1925, one lg faceted cusped shield shape flanked by six medium pentagonal and 18 sm sq silvered black glass plaques, prong-set and linked together terminating in a spring-ring clasp and jump ring,

Necklaces, glass bead, c. 1920: L-R, 1, grad dk blue glass spheres alternating with tapered tubular faux pearls joined with eye pins and jump rings, suspending a lg dk blue faceted glass teardrop pendant from a filigree bail, necklace 19-¹/₄″ tl, pendant 2-¹/₈″ × 1″, $125; L-R, 2, lt blue glass beads, faceted ellipsoids with fancy wm caps, smooth tubes, shaped cylinders, and spheres joined with eyepins, suspending a wm pendant with lg emerald-cut blue glass prong-set in the center of a wm wreath and bow, set with blue and silvered r.s. in millegrained bezels, surmounted by a navette-shaped plaque with blue faceted glass and r.s., rev mkd "Czechoslovakia," 25″ tl, pendant 2-¹/₂″ × 1-¹/₄″, $150; L-R, 3, lg and sm faux pearls alternating with sm ellipsoid and spherical black glass beads joined with eyepins, suspending a pendant with a lg faceted black and colorless glass center flanked by stepped rows of faux pearls, black and colorless r.s., surmounted by a black and colorless r.s. stepped cap, black r.s.-set bail, wm backing, spring-ring clasp, necklace 19-¹/₂″ tl, pendant 3-¹/₄″ × 1-¹/₄″, $175; L-R, 4, medium blue beads, long faceted cylinders, smooth ellipsoid and sq cylinders joined with eyepins and jump rings to stamped sp domed disk, suspending a pendant with lg circ blue faceted glass in millegrained bezel, framed by sp foliate motifs, faux pearls, and blue r.s., 17-³/₄″ tl, pendant 2-⁷/₈″ × 1-³/₈″, $150, *Leigh Leshner collection.*

Necklaces, glass, Czech, c. 1925: T-B, 1, colorless faceted inverted triangles, open wm backs, unmkd, 16-⅛″ tl × ½″; T-B, 2, blue geo faceted rectangles, sp brass backs, prong-set, 16-¼″ tl × ⅜″; T-B, 3, purple foiled-back geo-cut inverted triangles prong-set, closed brass backs, jump ring mkd "Czechoslov," 15-¾″ tl × ⅝″; T-B, 4, green foiled-back geo stepped triangles, 14-¾″ tl × ½″, each, $95, *Charles Pinkham collection.*

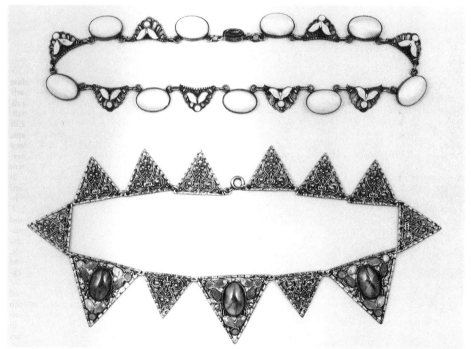

Necklaces, Czech glass, sp brass, enamel: T, c. 1925, bezel-set yellow satin glass oval cabs alternating with enameled foliate motifs in triangular stamped filigree plaques, terminating in an oval box clasp set with amber-colored faceted glass, rev mkd "Czechoslovakia," 15″ tl × ½″, $125, *Leigh Leshner collection;* B, c. 1930, three bezel-set medium blue satin glass oval cabs imitating star sapphires, each flanked by three sm blue enameled foliate motifs, appl to stamped sp brass filigree triangles linked to smaller filigree triangles, spring ring clasp, unmkd, 15-⅛″ × 1-¼″, $150, *Author's collection.*

mkd "Made in Czechoslovakia," 15" tl × 1"
.... **100**
Glass, wm, c. 1930, stepped rect molded black
glass plaque with silvered triangular side elements, flanked by wm bead spacers and two
tapered drape design black glass plaques
with incised silvered lines, continuing to a
wm curb link chain, spring-ring clasp,
Czech, 16" tl × 1-³/₈" **85**
Gp brass, glass, c. 1920, grad stepped stamped
gp links with geo and Greek key design,
lower six links prong-set with rect faux jade
glass cabs, suspending a center plaque
prong-set with molded and pierced rect faux
jade glass, rev mkd "Czechoslov," barrel
clasp, 17-¹/₂" tl, center 1-¹/₄" w × 1" **175**
Rh pl wm, glass, c. 1920, three prong-set oval
blue foil backed cabs alternating with four
inverted stepped wm triangles joined to baton-shaped links, 17" tl × ⁵/₈" **165**
Rh pl wm, glass, c. 1920, a central inverted
ziggurat formed of rect and sq bezel-set red

Necklace, gp brass, glass, enamel, rhinestones, c. 1930,
linked grad shield-shaped gp plaques with central pendant of three vertically linked plaques: two scrolled
quatrefoils with carnelian-colored glass cabs flanked by
green enameled foliate motifs and purple r.s. in millegrained bezels, and one shield-shaped, each shield
shape surmounted by a green enameled flowerhead
with purple r.s. center, oval and round carnelian-colored glass cabs in millegrained bezels within wire-twist
frames, probably Czech, 16-¹/₄" tl, pendant 3-¹/₄" tl × 1",
$375. *Kirsten Olson collection.*

Necklace, glass, brass, enamel, c. 1930, eight lg sq-cut
aqua glass stones set in serrated bezels mounted at 45°
on stamped openwork brass plaques surmounted by sm
white and blue enameled foliate motifs and sm aqua r.s.,
linked together and suspended from a double flat-
twisted link chain interspersed with white enameled
teardrops flanking aqua r.s., spring-ring clasp, Czech,
15-³/₄" tl × 1", $200. *Cheri Mulligan collection.*

glass cabs flanked by prong-set molded red
trapezoids linked together and continuing to
a chain of pierced rh pl inverted stepped
triangles, jump ring mkd "Germany," 16-³/₄"
× 1" **125**
Bead
Glass, gp brass, c. 1920, marbled blue glass
beads, lg balustered cylinders with green
enameled brass collars, sm spheres with
tubular brass filigree spacers joined with
brass eyepins, two strands suspended
négligée from a central plaque by a jump
ring mkd "Czechoslov," plaque bezel-set
with sm round and lg hemispherical marbled blue glass, continuing to necklace of
similar design with a barrel clasp, necklace 18" tl, longest strand 7" l **175**
Glass, c. 1920, amber-colored beads, lg
briolettes, bicones, lg and sm faceted sph-

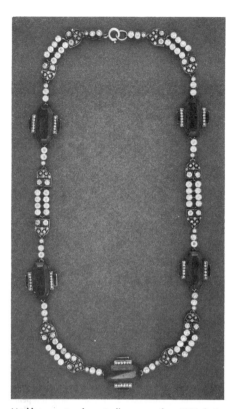

Necklace, paste, glass, sterling, enamel, c. 1920, lg tapered rect-cut green glass stones in open-backed bezels
flanked by parallel stepped rows of sm pastes and black
enamel, linked to articulated tablet-shaped plaques
with pierced paste-set rounded ends flanking a double
row of bezel-set colorless pastes, and a vertical row of
three bezel-set pastes, rev mkd "Made in France," Fr
hmks, 19-½″ × ¾″, $750. *Connie Parente collection.*

eres terminating in *négligée* briolette
drops, 31″ tl, longest drop 3-½″ l **100**
Glass, sp brass, c. 1920, sq green glass cylinders and sm spheres flanked by sp rondelles, joined with eyepins and jump rings to
baton-shaped sp links, terminating in two
green glass drops suspended *négligée*,
spring-ring clasp, 22″ tl, longest drop 4″ tl
. . . . **125**
Glass, c. 1920, sm red faceted spheres interspersed with lg and sm cones forming
symmetrical pairs, red and black faceted
disk spacers, hand knotted, 62″ tl **100**
Bead sautoir
Glass, c. 1920, four strands of black seed
beads strung with round black bead spacers, molded red glass disks, terminating in
a sq plaque and tassel of black seed beads
and red tapered oval beads, 32″ tl, plaque
and tassel 6-½″ tl × 1-¾″ w **50**

Glass, c. 1920, crocheted translucent yellow
seed beads forming a rope terminating in
two yellow, green, and red Venetian glass
beads and looped seed bead tassels, 65″ tl
× ½″ **75**
Glass, c. 1920, a strand of pale translucent
yellow seed beads terminating in a two-
strand tassel, interspersed with sm pink
faceted spheres, two lg disks and six
rounded bicone pink and yellow wedding
cake Venetian glass beads flanked by sm
pink spheres, ym clasp, 24″ tl, pendant
6-½″ **125**
Glass, c. 1920, translucent red beads, sm
and lg faceted spheres, lg briolettes, tassel
of sm round faceted beads and seed beads,
32″ tl, 5-½″ tassel **125**
Glass, c. 1920, lg black briolettes, faceted
spheres and ellipsoids, sm faceted lavender spheres, tassel of black seed beads and
lavender spheres, 30″ tl, 5″ tassel **150**
Glass, c. 1920, sm and lg translucent green
faceted spheres, faceted bicones, tassel of
sm round faceted beads and seed beads,
37″ tl, 4″ tassel **100**
Glass, c. 1925, Egyptian revival, two red
molded two-sided sarcophagi with
painted yellow accented details and sm
round red bead hand-knotted on yellow
thread teminating in a rect red plaque with
molded pharoah's head and painted yellow accented details, 34-¾″ tl, sarcophagi
⅝″ w × 1-½″, plaque 1-⅛″ w × ⅝″ . . . **75**
Glass, c. 1925, Egyptian revival, two-sided
molded yellow glass scarab beads with
cobalt blue rondelle spacers suspending a
rounded triangular cobalt plaque pendant
with molded relief design of an Egyptian
falcon god, painted green accented details, Czech, 26″ tl, pendant 1-⅛″ × 1-⅛″
. . . . **175**
Glass, c. 1925, Egyptian revival, two molded
two-sided sarcophagi, green with painted
gilt accented details (hieroglyphics and
other decoration) hand-knotted on a
strand of sm round green beads suspending a rounded triangular plaque pendant
with a two-sided molded design of an
Egyptian tomb painting accented with
painted gilt, Czech, 30″ tl, pendant 1-¼″ w
× 1-⅞″ **150**
Glass, c. 1925, Egyptian revival, two Assyr-
ian figures in two-sided molded relief, cobalt blue with painted green accented details, hand-knotted with green thread on a
strand of sm round cobalt beads joined to
an octagonal one-sided molded relief
plaque of a pharoah's head, rev mkd "Registered," continuing to a short strand of sm
beads terminating in a molded two-sided
relief pendant of an Assyrian head, Czech,
35-¾″ tl, pendant ⅞″ w × 1-⅝″ **225**

Necklace, brass, c. 1930, seven stamped brass plaques, inverted ziggurats, linked together and continuing to a lg cable-link chain, hook clasp, 21" tl × 1-¹/₂", $75. *Author's collection.*

Glass, c. 1925, Egyptian revival, sm round white beads interspersed with six larger oval jade-green beads strung with colorless seed bead spacers and joined to a molded white pharoah's head plaque with brown details, terminating in two white and green bead strands suspending *négligée* two lg white teardrops with brown accented spiral patterns, 31-¹/₂" tl, plaque including drops 3-³/₄" tl × 1-¹/₈" w **100**

Choker

Glass, c. 1930, Egyptian revival, 13 sm rect black glass plaques, each with a molded pharoah's head, white accented details and bg, strung with black faceted rondelle spacers and colorless seed beads and suspending black faceted briolettes, Czech, spring-ring clasp, 15" tl, 1" top to bottom **145**

Sautoir

Celluloid, sp brass, ribbon, c. 1925, Egyptian revival, a black velvet ribbon interspersed with four yellow celluloid tapered baton-shaped beads and two lacquered black celluloid round beads, and a round black bead sliding shortener, suspending a triangular pale yellow celluloid pendant with a central appl stamped relief sp brass pharoah's head, terminating in three tapered baton-shaped yellow and lacquered black drops, 38" tl, pendant 2-³/₄" tl × 1-⁵/₈" **200**

Gp copper, enamel, c. 1925, Egyptian revival, cut-to-shape cast pendant of crossed hands holding a crook and flail (symbols of pharoah's rule) with dk blue champlevé enamel accents, suspended from a gp chain of flat tapered and reeded cast links, 30" tl, pendant 2" w × 3" **125**

Pendant

Glass, ym, c. 1925, Egyptian revival, triangular molded two-sided plaque with a central relief figure of a pharoah flanked by hieroglyphics and brick-pattern design, red glass with painted green accented details, ym pendant bail, Czech, 1-¹/₂" w × 2-¹/₄" **50**

Pendant and Chain

Chrome plated wm, Bakelite, enamel, c. 1930, tuxedo bow of black Bakelite with articulated chrome and black enamel ribbon ends, suspended from a sq link wm chain, v-spring and box clasp, 16-³/₄" tl, pendant 1-¹/₄" w × 2-¹/₄" tl **245**

Gp brass, glass, enamel, c. 1920, oval stamped filigree pendant bezel-set with sm circ, triangular and L-shaped cabs of blue and green glass around a lg central oval green cab in an open lozenge-shaped frame with painted blue and green enamel and gp stars, suspended from a triangular trefoiled plaque and a stamped scrolled oval link chain, unmkd, probably Czech, 26" tl, pendant 1-¹/₈" w × 2-¹/₂" **145**

Pendant/Necklace

Bakelite, wm, c. 1930, center of three dk blue Bakelite segments riveted to wm forming an inverted ziggurat, joined with eyepins to grad conical dk blue beads and wm bead spacers, continuing to oval link trace chain, 15-¹/₄" tl, center 1-¹/₈" w × 1-¹/₂" **225**

Bakelite, chrome plated wm, c. 1930, half-rods of orange and black Bakelite held by grooved sq prongs in stepped and balustered chrome plaques, joined with eyepins and sm orange and black tubes, continuing to baton-shaped chrome links, jump ring and rev of plaque mkd "Germany," 14-¹/₂" tl × ³/₄" **250**

Bakelite, chrome plated wm, c. 1930, center of articulated green Bakelite segments and a chrome bead riveted together with wm plates forming an inverted ziggurat, joined with eyepins to grad conical green beads, continuing to a chain of chrome rods and

Pendants and Chains, sterling, c. 1920: L, an oval-cut citrine prong-set in the center of a rect filigree plaque with chamfered corners, engr foliate design set with marcasites, suspended from a sm open trefoil with rosette center, rev mkd "sterling," 1" w × 1-3/4" tl, added chain, $195; C, an oval green chrysoprase cab prong-set in an octagonal frame with geo design in green, red, and black champlevé and *basse-taille* enamel, suspended from a reeded bail and cable-link chain, 24" tl, pendant 1" w × 1-1/2" tl, $200; R, a navette-shaped faceted green glass plaque with an inset camphor glass (frosted white) plaque with sm r.s.-set navette-shaped ster center, prong-set within a stepped angular navette-shaped frame, rev mkd "sterling H" flanked by two triangles, suspended from three filigree plaques linked to bezel-set circ and baguette green r.s., continuing to an oval-link chain, filigree clasp mkd "Pat 1257158" (1918), "sterling H," Am, 16-1/4" tl, pendant 1" w × 2-1/2" tl, $95, *Victoria Taylor collection.*

Pendants/Necklaces, rh pl wm, c. 1920: L, camphor glass, rhinestones, rect links of stamped wm filigree and two chamfered-corner sq plaques bezel-set with frosted glass, rev cut with sun ray pattern centers, each set with a sm r.s., suspending an oval pendant bezel-set with a similar frosted glass plaque, 17-1/2" tl, pendant 7/8" × 1-7/8" tl, $175; R, circ links of stamped wm filigree terminating in a clasp mkd "Pat 1257158" (1918), suspending a lobed rect filigree pendant with center of lg oval cobalt blue faceted glass set in a millegrained bezel, flanked top and bottom by bezel-set triangular colorless faceted glass, within a scalloped, palmette, floral, and foliate motif frame, Am, 16-1/4" tl, pendant 1" w × 2-7/8" tl, $225, *Charles Pinkham collection.*

Pendant and Cord, amazonite, black onyx, sterling, marcasite, c. 1920, long articulated pendant constructed of sections of three sm onyx cabs, vertical amazonite and onyx bars, onyx ring, and round bead, joined with marcasite-set ster links to an elongated rect pendant with prong and bezel-set shaped onyx and amazonite rect cabs separated by a marcasite-set band, terminating in a bell-shaped onyx, marcasite, and amazonite bead drop, suspended from a marcasite-set bail mkd "sterling Germany," 26-½" black cord, pendant 6-⅝" tl × ½", $995. *Kirsten Olson collection.*

jump rings, 18" tl, center 1-⅛" w × 1-⅜"
.... **225**
Chrome plated wm, enamel, c. 1930, a lg domed disk surmounted by a sm domed disk with dk blue enamel on opposing halves, suspended vertically from sq cobra chain, 16" tl, pendant 1" w × 2" tl **265**
Bead
Glass, brass, c. 1920, necklace of lg and sm red glass spheres and bicones, two lg and two sm brass filigree beads, joined with eyepins and hand-knotted, suspending a stamped brass pendant, circ frame with central urn motif flanked by lg foliate motifs set with red r.s., 34" tl, pendant 1-⅝" × 2" **125**

Glass, sp brass, enamel, c. 1920, lt blue glass cones and sm spheres and brass filigree beads joined with eyepins, suspending a rect sp brass pendant with lg oval marbled blue glass cab, sm white and blue enameled flowers in corners, filigree prongs over glass at top and bottom, 26" tl, pendant 1-⅞" × 1-½" **135**
Rh pl wm, glass, enamel, c. 1920, flat chamfered corner rect wm links, centers stamped with a volute pattern and enameled lt blue, suspending a molded and pierced lt blue glass rect plaque in a pronged setting, terminating in a spring-ring clasp and jump ring mkd "Germany," 15-½" tl, pendant ⅞" w × 2" tl **195**

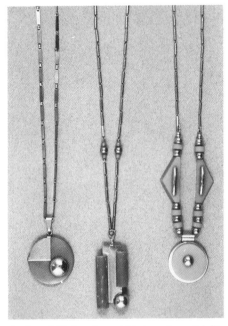

Pendants & Chains, chrome plated wm, brass, Bakelite, Germany, c. 1930: L, pendant of an orange Bakelite disk with appl chrome quarter sector and off-center domed disk, suspended from a chain of baton-shaped flat links, jump ring mkd "Germany," 24-½" tl, pendant 1-⅜" dia × 2" tl with bail, $195; C, pendant of a rect chrome plate vertically bisecting a short and a long green Bakelite cylindrical rod, one on each side, a chrome ball in lower corner, suspended from a chain of chrome tubes, brass and Bakelite beads joined with eyepins, jump ring mkd "Made in Germany," 24" tl, pendant 1" w × 2-¼" tl, $225; R, pendant of a green Bakelite disk with a sm center chrome hemispherical bead, riveted to a slightly larger chrome disk backing and tubular bail, suspended from a strand of sm Bakelite cylinders with chrome bead spacers, and two lg triangular Bakelite segments with appl chrome fins, strung on fine chain, and continuing to a tubular chrome link chain, 17-¼" tl, pendant 1-⅛" dia, 1-½" with bail, $225, *Charles Pinkham collection.*

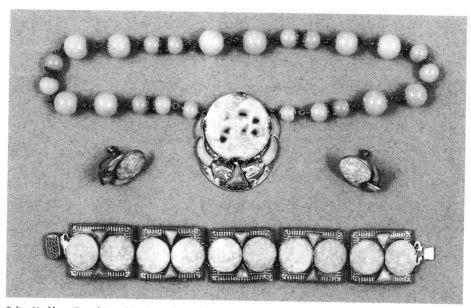

Suite: Necklace, Bracelet, and Earrings, glass, gp brass, c. 1935, bracelet of molded pink glass disks and triangles bezel-set in linked stamped brass rect plaques, one lg molded pierced glass disk prong-set in the center plaque of the necklace of alternating lg and medium spherical pink glass beads joined with eyepins and brass filigree rondelles, pr of matching earrings with screwbacks, bracelet mkd "Made in Czechoslov," 7-1/8" × 1-1/8", necklace mkd "Czechoslova-kia," 16" tl, pendant 1-5/8" w × 1-7/8", earrings mkd "Czechoslov," 3/4" × 1", suite, $350. *Charles Pinkham collection.*

Sterling, onyx, marcasites, c. 1920, a pendant in the shape of a draped handkerchief, borders pavé-set with grad marcasites, a prong-set cusped triangular black onyx plaque in the center, surmounted by rigid sq ster links in an open V-shape joined to pierced navette-shaped links with marcasite centers and sq plaques set with onyx and marcasite continuing to a geo and floral ster link chain, spring-ring clasp, rev of pendant mkd "sterling," 16-1/2" tl, pendant 2-1/4" tl × 7/8"
. . . . **300**

Ring

Marcasite, c. 1925-30, oval mottled blue "Swiss lapis" (dyed jasper) cab set in a millegrained bezel in the center of a stepped oval mount with four V-shaped accents, hollow and open on rev, bead-set throughout with marcasites (some missing), engr shoulders tapering to a narrow shank, inside mkd "sterling" (worn), 1-1/4" × 3/4", approx ring size 4 . . . . **100**

Marcasite, c. 1925-30, bow shape flanked by three-lobed scallops pavé-set with marcasites, narrow shank mkd "silver," 1/2" × 1", approx ring size 5-1/2 . . . . **38**

Marcasite, c. 1925-30, snake motif bead-set with marcasites tapering to a narrow shank, mkd "925," 5/8" × 1/2", approx ring size 5-1/2
. . . . **30**

Marcasite, c. 1925-30, navette-shaped plaque, pavé-set with marcasites, pierced gallery, tapered marcasite-set shoulders continuing to a narrow 9k yg shank, mkd "9ct and sil," Eng, 3/8" × 7/8", approx ring size 6-1/2 . . . . . **85**

Marcasite, c. 1925-30, rect silver plaque with chamfered corners pavé-set with marcasites, pierced gallery, narrow shank, 5/8" × 7/8", approx ring size 5-1/2 . . . . **75**

Marcasite, c. 1925-30, double entwined snake motif bead-set with marcasites tapering to a narrow shank, mkd "silver," 5/8" × 3/4", approx ring size 6 . . . . **100**

Wm, glass, rhinestones, c. 1920, stamped filigree bezel-set with lg oval dk blue glass cab flanked by sm blue r.s., 3/4" × 1/2" **65**

Shoe Buckles

Oxidized wm, paste (rhinestones), c. 1920, bowed rect frame with openwork floral and foliate design around central lozenge shape, pavé-set with colorless pastes, center vertical bar on rev for attachment to vamps of shoes, 2-1/8" w × 1-1/4", pr **48**

Suite: Dress Clips and Buckle

Rhinestones, white pot metal, c. 1930, a two-pc buckle and two dress clips, each pc a double-stepped triangle design, pavé-set r.s., openwork centers of vertical wm bars, flat-backed hinged clips, hook-and-eye closure on buckle, 3" w × 2", clips, 1-7/8" w × 1-1/2"
. . . . **75**

PLASTIC AND OTHER NOVELTY JEWELRY
C. 1920-1960

History: In her introduction to the chapter on jewelry in *Art Plastic,* Andrea DiNoto remarks, "If one word were needed to summon up the spirit of the twenties and thirties, 'novelty' would do nicely." For the first time, the idea of wearing jewelry for fun caught on. The ideal material for creating this new type of jewelry was plastic—lightweight, inexpensive, and colorful. Although jewelry had been made from celluloid, the earliest semisynthetic plastic, as far back as 1875, it was limited in style, made mostly in the form of imitation ivory, coral, amber, and tortoiseshell for naturalistic ornamental and utilitarian pieces. It was worn primarily by those who could not afford the real thing. It wasn't until the reckless, lighthearted attitude of the flapper came on the scene that we begin to see whimsical and flamboyant items appear, in decidedly unnatural colors.

In the first half of the twentieth century, many types of plastic were developed and given trade names by the manufacturers that produced them. Numerous different trade names were given to the same generic substance, as each manufacturer strove for proprietary identification of the material. Over the years, certain names came into generic usage in spite of the fact that they were registered trade names (like Kleenex and Xerox). The three names in most common usage today are celluloid (the word is now seldom capitalized) for pyroxylin-camphor thermoplastic, Bakelite (sometimes written lowercase) for thermosetting phenol formaldehyde resin, and Lucite (seldom lowercase) for thermoplastic polymethacrylates, or acrylics. Sometimes these labels are erroneously applied to other, related but not chemically identical, plastics. For example, cellulose acetate is often incorrectly called celluloid. Accurately identifying these materials requires a variety of tests, some of which are potentially destructive.

Some collectors believe that a piece of plastic jewelry is collectible and has value because of other factors, such as design and craftsmanship, and that the type of plastic used is of secondary importance. They believe that knowing exactly what a piece is made of is not worth the risks involved in testing. Others consider correct material identification an important part of classifying, circa-dating, and putting a piece in historical context, all of which serves to enhance the value of their collection. The middle ground—the one taken here—is making educated guesses based on nondestructive sensory tests, and grouping plastics by generic types (thermoplastics and thermosets) and their related trade names. For most collectible jewelry purposes, these are celluloid,

Bakelite, and Lucite. A brief explanation of each follows.

Thermoplastics are those that will soften or reliquefy with the application of heat. Once cooled they will again become solid. Thermosets are liquid (resinous) before they are molded or cast, but once they solidify, they remain solid. Thermoplastic scraps can be recycled. Thermosets cannot. All plastics can be classified in one or the other of these two categories.

CELLULOID

Celluloid, the first successful semisynthetic thermoplastic, is part natural fiber, or cellulose. Its generic names, pyroxylin-camphor thermoplastic, sometimes referred to as cellulose nitrate, are clues to its makeup: cellulose fiber mixed with nitric acid (nitrated) to which camphor is added and subjected to heat. Celluloid was first used as a substitute for natural materials, but its versatility, coupled with imaginative designs and new processes, later yielded a variety of forms. In 1902, a patent was granted for a process of setting rhinestones or metal into celluloid, thereby enhancing its decorative potential. In 1923, a synthetic pearl essence was invented, called "H-scale." It replaced the more expensive fish scale type of pearl essence (the coating on simulated pearls) for celluloid and was used on toilet articles, decorative accessories, and jewelry.

One of the major drawbacks of celluloid was its flammability due to the nitrocellulose it contained. In 1927, the Celluloid Corporation introduced Lumarith, their trade name for cellulose acetate, which substituted acetic acid (vinegar) for nitric acid and camphor. Except for its bright colors, in appearance and use cellulose acetate is the same as celluloid, but ·nonflammable. It is often labeled celluloid but technically and chemically this is incorrect. When warmed in hot water, the two materials can be differentiated: Celluloid smells like camphor; cellulose acetate, like vinegar. (This test should not be used on a piece set with rhinestones or other materials susceptible to water damage, nor should any piece be immersed in water for more than a few seconds.) The use of cellulose acetate coincided with the development of the injection-molding process, which made mass production of inexpensive plastic items possible.

Celluloid articles should be stored carefully in a dry and ventilated place. They are subject to disintegration if exposed to extremes of temperature, constant moisture, or corroding metal. Cracks, crystallization, and discoloration are signs of decomposition. Already damaged pieces are contagious and should be kept separate from others.

Much of the foregoing information on celluloid was recently brought to light by Julie P. Robinson, celluloid historian, who is currently researching and writing the history of celluloid and its inventor, John Wesley Hyatt. She has obtained copies of U.S. patents and perused the archives of the Celluloid Corporation and other pyroxylin plastics manufacturers and the Smithsonian Institution. Most material on collectible plastics published within the last 10 years has focused on Bakelite and later plastics, with sketchy—and sometimes conflicting—details about plastic's earliest developments. Therefore, the information on celluloid that Robinson has researched from original archival material has been the primary technical source for this section.

Haircombs and hatpins were among the earliest items of personal adornment made of celluloid, following fashion's currents at the turn of the century. (Leominster, Massachussetts was a center for haircomb production, first in natural materials, then plastics.) But when fashions changed, these lost popularity. Hatpins shrank to become hat ornaments, with a threaded pinpoint that was pushed through the hat and secured with a second ornamental head. Surprisingly, haircombs didn't completely disappear when the bob became the predominant hairstyle. Large and ornate Spanish-style backcombs, often embellished with rhinestones and painted enamel, were still occasionally worn, bound to the head, in the late 1920s, when the tango was all the rage, and Spanish lace, fringed shawls, and flounced skirts were part of a dancer's costume. A more typical 1920s head ornament was the headband, or bandeau. These too, were made of rhinestone-studded celluloid. Because the material is flexible, the headbands are adjustable, held by an ornamental celluloid clasp. Today, these are rare finds. Celluloid bangles, many ivory- or amber-colored, but in other colors as well, were worn from wrist to elbow, in the fashion made popular by heiress Nancy Cunard. The ones most sought after today have painted designs and/or geometric patterns of pavé rhinestones set into them. Whimsical figural pins, and short chain necklaces with dangling floral or figural motifs were also made of celluloid. Celluloid (pyroxylin plastics) continued to be used for jewelry well into the 1940s (post-World War II molded figural pieces marked "Occupied Japan" can still be found), but with the development of other less flammable and more easily mass-produced plastics, celluloid fell out of favor. After the Celluloid Corporation became part of Celanese in 1947, U.S. production was discontinued. Japan continued to make pyroxylin items during the 1950s.

BAKELITE

The first entirely synthesized plastic was invented by Leo H. Baekeland in 1908 (patented 1909). As with many inventions, it was accidental. He was searching for a formula for synthetic shellac, at which he failed miserably. Instead, he came up with "the material of a thousand uses," as the advertisers called it: thermosetting phenol formaldehyde resin. He christened it Bakelite. Other companies started manufacturing similar phenolics and came up with their own trade names, among them: Catalin, Marblette, Durez, and Prystal. Bakelite is the name that has stuck with collectors, although some purists insist on calling it by the generic name phenolic or the trade name Catalin (most jewelry made from this material was made by the Catalin Corporation).

Jewelry was not the first of its thousand uses. The Great Depression created a market for it, because it was cheap to manufacture, colorful, and lent itself to a wide range of styles and manufacturing techniques. It gave women a much-needed lift, to both their outfits and their spirits. Bakelite was well suited to the chunky, heavy jewelry styles of the 1930s. It could be laminated into geometric shapes (polka dots were a popular motif), set with rhinestones, clad or inlaid with metal, carved on a lathe, or made into the shapes of animals, fruits, or other realistic figurals. Colorless Bakelite (introduced in 1935 by the Catalin Corporation, whose trade name for it was Prystal) was carved on the back side with floral or figural designs. The carving was sometimes enhanced with paint. From the front, the designs look three-dimensional. "Reverse-carved" is today's name for this technique. Over time, the pieces have oxidized to a light amber color.

Bracelets of all types—solid and hinged bangles, link, elastic stretchies, cuffs, and charm—brooches, dress clips, shoe clips, buckles, earrings, rings, necklaces, beads, and pendants were all made from Bakelite. Bakelite jewelry and objects have been avidly collected for the past 10 years. Several books and magazine articles have covered the subject quite thoroughly (see the references following for some of them).

LUCITE

Although the German manufacturers Röhm and Haas are credited with being the first to formulate acrylic resin (1928), their trade name for it, Plexiglas, seems to be used mainly in reference to utilitarian and decorative objects. Lucite, introduced by DuPont in 1937, is the trade name most often heard in reference to jewelry. Lucite is water clear in its original form, but it is often tinted in a wide range of transparent to opaque colors. Jewelry made entirely of Lucite has only recently been recognized as collectible. Molded, tinted, and reverse-carved Lucite figurals are becoming nearly as sought after as their early 1940s Bakelite contemporaries. After the war, Bakelite was no longer cost-effective to produce, but Lucite, a thermoplastic, continued to be manufactured and is still in use today. Postwar jewelry forms, however, are quite different from earlier pieces.

Some circa 1940s novelty jewelry was made of Lucite combined with other materials such as Bakelite, wood, leather, and metal. One of the hottest items among costume jewelry collectors in recent years, jelly bellies, have Lucite as the center, or belly, of sterling animal pins. These were made in the 1940s by Trifari and other American manufacturers (see the section on designer/manufacturer signed costume jewelry). In the 1950s, pearlized Lucite bangles and button earclips, often rhinestone-studded, were popular accessories, as were laminated brooches, bracelets, and earrings encasing flowers or embedded with pastel-dyed shells and glitter. In the 1960s, Lucite was often used in colorless form for chunky rings, necklaces, and bracelets.

IDENTIFYING PLASTICS

Nondestructive sensory tests can reveal a plastic's identity. Smell: The aforementioned hot water test works for Bakelite as well as celluloid and cellulose acetate. The Bakelite smell is quite distinctively acrid (formaldehyde or carbolic acid); Lucite is odorless. Visual: Celluloid is generally thin-layered and delicate-looking. It can be transparent and colorless (with yellowish oxidation), but it is usually made opaque or translucent with fillers. Ivory, amber, and tortoise are common colors; pastels, red, blue, green, and black are also found. Cellulose acetate jewelry is often found in very bright shiny colors. Bakelite is opaque or translucent in a limited (oxidized) range of colors. Some Bakelite was also colorless and transparent originally, but it has turned light amber with age. Chalk-white plastic is not Bakelite, which becomes yellow over time. Lucite's colors are limitless. Touch: Celluloid is lightweight and brittle but slightly flexible and can be solid or hollow, molded or laminated. Bakelite is dense and heavy for its size and solid, never hollow as injection- or blow-molded plastics can be. Because most of it is cast, it will not have mold marks or lines. Lucite is solid and dense, but softer and lighter than Bakelite. Sound: Bakelite has a clunky sound when two pieces are knocked together. Other plastics have a higher-pitched sound.

As prices of collectible plastics, especially Bakelite, have skyrocketed over the past few years, it

is important to remember that plastics, unlike gold and gemstones, are not intrinsically valuable. The material itself is not collectible; what was made from it is. An unimaginative, plain, or downright ugly piece (even though it is genuine celluloid, Bakelite, or Lucite) will have little collector interest or value.

Other materials were used concurrently with plastics to produce whimsical novelty articles. In the 1940s, carved wood was a favorite material, alone or in combination with other materials. Western motifs were all the rage in wood as well as plastic, due once again to the movies' influence. Horses' heads are the most prevalent motif. During wartime shortages, with factories limited to military production and European sources cut off, many pieces were hand-carved and constructed. Ceramic or plaster composition, felt, yarn, leather, feathers, and sequins were combined to make fashion head brooches, some of them resembling popular movie stars. Others had exotic Oriental or African faces (some of these were also carved in wood). The Sears catalog of 1944 advertised "lapel 'pin-ups' in gay hand-painted ceramics"—cartoonish animals and people—with Lucite and yarn details. Once the war was over, this type of jewelry faded into oblivion. In the 1950s, cute replaced whimsical, and gold-plated metal and rhinestones were the usual materials of choice.

References: Lillian Baker, *Twentieth Century Fashionable Plastic Jewelry*, Collector Books, 1992; "Techniques and Materials," in Deanna Farneti Cera, ed., *Jewels of Fantasy, Costume Jewelry of the 20th Century*, Harry N. Abrams, 1992; Corinne Davidov and Ginny Redington Dawes, *The Bakelite Jewelry Book*, Abbeville Press, 1988; Andrea DiNoto, *Art Plastic, Designed for Living*, Abbeville Press, 1984; Sylvia Katz, *Early Plastics*, Shire Publications, Ltd., 1986, and *Plastics, Common Objects, Classic Designs*, Harry N. Abrams, 1984 (Katz' books contain little jewelry, but a great deal of information about plastics, including testing methods); JoAnne Olian, *Everyday Fashions of the Forties As Pictured in Sears Catalogs*, Dover Publications, 1992; Sheryl Shatz, *What's It Made Of? A Jewelry Materials Identification Guide*, self-published, 1991.

Museums: National Plastics Center and Museum, Leominster, Mass.; Smithsonian Institution, Washington, D.C.

Reproduction Alert: As with anything that becomes highly collectible and expensive, Bakelite jewelry is now being reproduced. The formula for the material is easily obtainable. The one saving grace for collectors is that producing a desirable piece is extremely labor intensive and requires a certain amount of artisanship. It is not likely, therefore, that mass quantities of reproductions will be entering the market. Marriages of old parts, and "fakelite" imitations (made of plastics other than Bakelite) are more common. Comparing a piece with a known old one and buying from reputable dealers who stand behind their merchandise are a collector's best protection.

Advisor: Julie Robinson (Celluloid).

Bracelet
Bangle
 Bakelite, painted enamel, c. 1930, yellow Bakelite with carved and painted black enamel harlequin motif, 2-⅝" dia × ¾" w
 . . . . **250**
 Bakelite, c. 1930, deep-carved rose and foliate motif in butterscotch-colored Bakelite, 2-½" inside dia, 1-¼" w **225**
 Bakelite, c. 1930, marbled butterscotch-colored triangular bangle with circ inside surface, ¾" w, 2-⅝" dia **125**
 Bakelite, wm, c. 1930, translucent butterscotch-colored, saucer-shaped, encircled with two rows of alternating inlaid black and wm rect strips in a checkerboard pattern, 2-⅜" inside dia, ⅝" w **200**
 Bakelite, c. 1930, pale yellow with inset faceted black domed disks, 2-⅝" inside dia, ⅞" w **225**
 Bakelite, c. 1930, cutout and notched dk yellow with center raised band of alternating laminated black and yellow sqs, 2-⅝" inside dia, ¾" w **275**

Celluloid, rhinestones, c. 1920, ivory colored with triangular pattern of red and colorless r.s., 2-⅝" dia × ½" w **150**
Celluloid, rhinestones, c. 1920, translucent dk green with rows of alternating blue and green r.s., 2-¾" dia × ¾" w **100**
Lucite, c. 1950, pearlized emerald green with convex surface, 2-½" dia × ⅞" w
. . . . **35**
Lucite, rhinestones, c. 1950, mottled opaque and translucent white, lg circ colorless r.s. spaced along each side of center ridge, 2-¾" dia × 1" w **65**
Lucite, c. 1960, thick, translucent fuchsia, molded with an undulating center ridge, 2-½" inside dia × 1-½" w **85**
Hinged bangle
 Bakelite, c. 1930, translucent blue-green Bakelite, cutout triple bars hinged with opening at the top, terminating in two lg carved circ flowerheads mounted with screws to each end, 2-¼" inside dia, 1-½" w . . . **200**
 Bakelite, rhinestones, c. 1935, oval green bangle, deep-carved floral and foliate design set with colorless r.s., plain back, 2-⅜" dia, 1" w **175**

Bangle Bracelets, celluloid, rhinestones, c. 1920-25: L-R, 1, tapered beige bangle with raised metal beads in lozenge flanked by triple-bar patterns, colorless and blue r.s., 3" dia × ⅝" w in front, **$200; L-R, 2,** ivory-colored with a row of black r.s. on black stripe flanked by rows of colorless r.s., 2-½" dia × ⅝" w, **$85,** *Connie Parente collection;* **L-R, 3,** ivory-colored with pavé red r.s. set in red ground, 2-⅝" inside dia, ¾" w, **$95; L-R, 4,** ivory-colored with a center row of colorless r.s. flanked by two rows of amber-colored r.s. separated by incised lines, 2-⅝" dia, ⅝" w, **$95,** *Kirsten Olson collection;* **L-R, 5,** dk red celluloid in the shape of a snake, set with cobalt blue r.s., carved head and tail, 2-½" dia × ⅝" w, **$150; L-R, 6,** amber-colored with a grid pattern of colorless r.s., 2-⅝" dia × ½" w, **$100; L-R, 7,** coated black pavé-set with colorless r.s., 2-⅝" dia × ¾" w, **$125; L-R, 8,** ivory-colored with diag carved lines and rows of amber-colored r.s. 2-⅝" dia × ⅝" w, **$175; L-R, 9,** ivory-colored pavé-set with colorless r.s. in silver-colored ground, 2-⅝" dia × ¾" w, **$100,** *Connie Parente collection.*

Hinged Bangle Bracelets, Bakelite, c. 1935: L, oval laminated lt amber-colored with green borders, folded ribbon design, reeded brass strip at top, 2-⅝" dia, 1-¼" w, $250; C, tapered oval green Bakelite bangle with appl two-layer carved wood and Bakelite flowerhead, 2-⅝" dia, 2" w at top, $200, *Connie Parente collection;* R, oval laminated red with black borders, folded ribbon design with reeded brass strip, 2-½" dia, 1-¼" w, $295, *Kirsten Olson collection.*

Chrome pl brass, Bakelite, c. 1935, a wedge-shaped chunk of red Bakelite in the center of fanned-out chrome blades continuing to a flat band with a spring-action hook closure, 2-⅜" dia × ⅞" w **250**

Thermoset plastic, rhinestones, c. 1955, ivory colored, front half inset with clusters of sm aurora borealis r.s., 2-⅛" inside dia × ¾"w **100**

Thermoset plastic, rhinestones, c. 1955, ivory colored, front half inset with lg multi-colored pastel r.s. and sm colorless r.s., ¾" w, 2-¼" inside dia **100**

Wood, bone, glass, c. 1940, three-dimensional carved dk brown wood head of an elephant with raised trunk, inset glass eyes and carved bone tusks, tapering to a back hinge joined to a carved tapered section completing the bangle, 2-⅜" inside dia, head 1-⅞" × 1" **150**

Wood, plastic, c. 1940, a carved dk brown wood disk surmounted by an appl lami-

Bracelets, Bakelite, c. 1935: L, elastic stretchy, alternating rounded rect plaques of polished black and rev-carved floral pattern amber-colored Bakelite, strung on two lengths of elastic, 1-¼" w, $175, *Kirsten Olson collection;* C, bangle, rev-carved and painted green, white, and yellow floral and foliate design in amber-colored Bakelite, 2-½" inside dia, ¾" w, $165; R, link, alternating black and rev-carved floral amber-colored disks joined with pairs of black celluloid links, spring-ring clasp, 7-½" × 1-⅜", $185, *Author's collection.*

nated black over red plastic disk molded in a swirled fluted pattern conforming to carved pattern in wood, mounted on a carved oval dk brown wood bangle, 2-3/8" inside dia × 1" w, disk 1-3/4" dia **125**

Bracelets

Bangles

Bakelite, c. 1930, one butterscotch-colored and one burnt-orange-colored Bakelite with matching deep-carved floral and foliate design, 2-5/8" inside dia, 7/8" w, each **175**

Brooch/Pendant

Bakelite, vinyl-coated cord, c. 1935, carved yellow Bakelite anchor, center post wrapped with lacquered dk blue vinyl cord, hole drilled through sides of post for wear as a pendant, safety catch, 1-5/8" w × 2-1/2" . . . **95**

Brooch/Pin

Bakelite, compass, c. 1935, deep yellow Bakelite anchor with a working compass set in the center, originally a button, 1-7/8" w × 2-3/8" **95**

Bakelite, c. 1935, carved black ship's wheel, 1-3/4" dia **45**

Bakelite, ym, paint, vinyl-coated cord, c. 1935, in the shape of a sea captain's hat of carved yellow and black Bakelite riveted together, with appl ym anchor, red vinyl cord, painted blue decoration on bill, 2-3/8" w × 1-7/8" **125**

Bakelite, gp ym, c. 1930, cutout and carved red Bakelite in the shape of a stylized horse's head with coiled ym wire mane, ym eye, new pinback, 2-3/8" w × 2-1/4" **250**

Bakelite, brass, wm, c. 1930, carved butterscotch-colored Bakelite racehorse's head with inlaid eye, goldtone painted bridle suspending a carved boot and two horseshoe charms with wm studs from brass eyepins, riveted pinback with C-catch, 2-1/4" w × 2-1/2" tl **175**

Bakelite, brass, c. 1935, carved translucent dk amber-colored Bakelite stylized horse's head with brass rivets at eye and mouth, C-catch, 2" w × 2-1/2" **85**

Bakelite, vinyl-coated cord, paint, c. 1935, pale yellow carved Bakelite horse's head with yellow and red painted eye, nose, and mouth, red vinyl cord bridle strung through holes drilled into the Bakelite, C-catch, 2-3/4" w × 3" **275**

Bakelite, chrome, c. 1930, black Bakelite annular disk with open center bisected by a chrome bar set with an off-center red Bakelite domed disk, bias-cut bar ends extending unevenly beyond the black disk edges, safety catch, 4" w × 2-1/4" **125**

Bakelite, rhinestones, paint, c. 1930, carved translucent amber-colored Bakelite in the shape of a sailfish, red r.s. eye, rev painted blue and white, safety catch, 2-3/4" w × 2-1/2" **125**

Bakelite, Lucite, paint, c. 1940, goldfish with red Bakelite body, painted eye, carved colorless Lucite fins, 2-3/4" w × 2-1/2" **160**

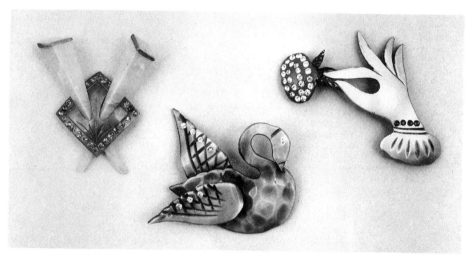

Brooches/Pins, celluloid, rhinestones, c. 1925-30: L, bluish-green sq with incised decoration and border of blue r.s., pierced with two ivory-colored spikes with gilt-edge sq tops, C-catch, 1-3/4" w × 3", $65, *Connie Parente collection;* **C,** in the shape of a swan, mottled green and pale yellow with a row of colorless r.s. on each wing, r.s. eye, 2-7/8" w × 2-1/2", $85, *Author's collection* ; **R,** in the shape of a stylized hand holding an apple, painted silver-grey coating, red and green apple with inset colorless r.s., hand with red r.s. at the wrist, C-catch, 3-1/2" × 1-1/2", $65, *Connie Parente collection.*

Brooches/Pins, figurals, c. 1935-40: TL, carved opaque brown and translucent dk amber-colored Bakelite winged insect, screw-mounted pinback, safety catch, 2-³/₄″ w × 1-¹/₂″, $125; TR, carved yellow Bakelite winged bug with lg green r.s. eyes, safety catch, 2-¹/₈″ × 1-¹/₄″, $150; BL, molded, carved and rev-carved colorless and translucent brown Lucite fly with yellow eyes, riveted pinback, C-catch, 2-⁷/₈″ w × 1-¹/₂″, $125; BR, molded, carved and rev-carved colorless and translucent red Lucite butterfly, C-catch, 3-¹/₄″ w × 2-³/₄″, $75, *Kirsten Olson collection.*

Bakelite, cotton string, c. 1935, carved green stylized foliate motif plaque, suspending seven tapered yellow cylinders (stylized bananas) on green cotton string threaded through a hole in plaque, appl wm pinback, C-catch, 2-¹/₈″ w × 4″ tl **450**

Bakelite, c. 1930, mottled green and yellow Bakelite plaque in the shape of a feather plume with incised details, 3-¹/₂″ × 1-³/₈″ **50**

Bakelite, glass, c. 1930, carved dk yellow Bakelite in the shape of a long narrow fish with pointed snout, two glass eyes, screw-mounted pinback, C-catch, 4-¹/₄″ × ⁷/₈″ **150**

Bakelite, glass, c. 1930, carved yellow Bakelite

Brooches/Pins, figurals with wood, c. 1935-40: L, carved marbled dk red Bakelite fox with glass eye emerging from a carved dk brown wood log, safety catch, 1-⁷/₈″ w × 1-⁷/₈″, $175, *Kirsten Olson collection;* C, carved dk brown wood head of a cocker spaniel, painted eye, C-catch, 2-³/₄″ w × 2-⁷/₈″, $65, *Author's collection* ; R, carved wood horse's head with glass eye, brass-studded leather collar, mounted with screws to a brass-studded translucent lt brown Lucite cutout oval frame, safety catch, 2-³/₄″ w × 1-³/₄″, $225, *Kirsten Olson collection.*

Western whimsy, c. 1940-45: L, Suite: Brooch/Pin and Earrings, wood, leather, paint, lacquer, twine, and celluloid brooch in the shape of a saddle with carved and hp details, appl leather strips and rope attached with metal studs and cutout celluloid stars, coated with clear lacquer, screwback earrings in the shape of cowboy boots, mounted on orig card mkd "hand carved," brooch 1-¹/₂" w × 2-¹/₄", earrings ¹/₂" × ¹/₂", suite, $50, *Author's collection;* C, Brooch/Pin, wood, metal, twine, carved saddle with appl rope, metal- and vinyl-coated trim, suspending a pr of carved boots from wm chains, saddle horn painted silver, 2" w × 4-¹/₄" tl, $100, *Connie Parente collection;* R, Brooch/Pin, injection molded and painted plastic in the shape of a cowboy clown, black, red, lt fleshtone with a silver-colored pistol suspended from a thin black cord, when pulled, eyes move and flashlight bulb nose lights up, compartment for battery on rev, 1-¹/₂" w × 4" tl, $165, *Kirsten Olson collection.*

in the shape of a swordfish with glass eye, riveted pinback, C-catch, 4" × 1-¹/₈" . . . **175**

Bakelite, paint, c. 1930, carved dk yellow Bakelite in the shape of a fawn, painted spots and features, 1-³/₈" w × 3-¹/₈" **65**

Bakelite, glass, paint, c. 1935, carved red Bakelite cartoonlike bulldog with enlarged head, bulging glass eyes, painted yellow collar, painted orange features, C-catch, 2-³/₄" w × 1-³/₄" **350**

Bakelite, paint, plastic, c. 1935, carved yellow Bakelite calliope on wheels, blue and red painted details with grad inset tabs of irid and colorless layers of thin plastic pipes, riveted pinback, C-catch, 1-⁷/₈" w × 1-³/₄" **350**

Bakelite, paint, c. 1935, irregular oval carved and pierced lt amber-colored Bakelite plaque with rev-carved and painted floral and foliate design in yellow, blue, red, green, pink, and white, 3-¹/₂" w × 2-¹/₄" **325**

Bakelite, leather, glass, c. 1940, turtle with green carved Bakelite shell appl to press-molded leather body, glass eyes, safety catch, 3-¹/₄" w × 2-⁵/₈" **350**

Celluloid, c. 1940, molded ivory-colored heads of three Scottie dogs, black, pink, and blue painted details, wm pinback, C-catch, 2" w × 1" **35**

Ceramic, paint, yarn, plastic, c. 1945, lapel pin-up in the shape of a cartoonlike white ceramic lamb's head with painted blue and red features and yarn and plastic bead pompon headdress, as advertised in 1944 Sears catalog, 2-¹/₂" × 2-¹/₂" **75**

Ceramic, paint, c. 1945, ceramic head of a woman wearing a head scarf and fruit, hp in dk fleshtone, red, cream, green, yellow, and gilt, paper labels on rev mkd "Carmen" and "California, Copa de Oro, Hand Decorated Ceramics," 1-¹/₄" w × 3" **85**

Lucite, paint, c. 1940, oval colorless Lucite plaque with rev-carved grid pattern and floral and foliate design painted red, blue, yellow, and black, riveted pinback, safety catch, 2-³/₈" × 1-³/₄" **50**

Lucite, paint, c. 1940, molded and carved mottled brown-green Lucite alligator with red, green, and white painted details, C-catch, 3-³/₄" w × 1-⁷/₈" **250**

Wm, c. 1925, cutout and engr plaque depicting a fashionable woman in a c. 1920s dress with a borzoi (Russian wolfhound) on a

Clips, Bakelite, c. 1930: TL, carved ridged lt amber-colored ovals with rev carved trellis and floral design, flowers tinted red, green, and yellow, flatbacked hinged dress clips on rev, 1-³/₈″ w × 2″, pr, $110, *Connie Parente collection;* TR, Shoe Clips, carved, rev carved and pierced lt amber-colored Bakelite in bow shapes with semi-circ centers of opaque yellow, folded-over wm clips for shoes on rev, pr, $40, *Author's collection;* BL, semi-circ plaque with cutout center, carved circ disk at top center flanked by sq-cut colorless r.s., two diagonal rows of r.s. below (one missing), flatbacked hinged wm dress clips mounted on rev with screws, 1-³/₄″ w × 1-¹/₈″, pr, $75, *Kirsten Olson collection;* BR, opposed J-scrolls, carved draped design in red Bakelite, flatbacked hinged wm dress clips on rev, 1-¹/₄″ w × 2″, pr, $35, *Richard Noël collection.*

leash, pinned to orig card mkd "Novelty Brooch, High Grade Finish," C-catch, 2-¹/₄″ w × 2-¹/₂″ **125**

Wood, Bakelite, c. 1940, a pr of stylized fish, marbled green Bakelite domed disks with carved and painted features, mounted on a single wood plaque with carved wood fins, 2-¹/₂″ w × 3″ **100**

Wood, Lucite, c. 1940, carved wood turtle with carved colorless Lucite shell, 3″ × 2″ **55**

Wood, fur, leather, ym, plastic, c. 1940, carved lt brown stylized horse's head with fur mane, red leather reins, red plastic eye, 2-¹/₂″ w × 3-¹/₄″ **40**

Wood, plastic, painted enamel, glass, c. 1940, carved dk brown horse's head with red vinyl-coated bridle, glass eye, red painted ears, nose, and mouth, 3-¹/₄″ w × 3-¹/₄″ **55**

Wood, leather, glass, ym, c. 1940, carved lt brown horse's head with brown leather reins and glass eye, 3″ × 3″ **35**

Wood, plastic, paint, c. 1940, fish with carved and painted wood body, pale transparent yellow fins with painted blue edges, C-catch, 2-¹/₂″ × 2-¹/₂″ **35**

Wood, Lucite, c. 1940, lobster with dk brown carved wood body and colorless Lucite claws, safety catch, 1-⁷/₈″ w × 3-¹/₄″ **45**

Wood, Lucite, painted enamel, c. 1940, fish of carved and painted wood with colorless Lucite fins, red, white, and blue painted details, 3-¹/₂″ w × 2-³/₄″ **35**

Bar

Bakelite, c. 1930, rev-carved grape motif on a lt translucent amber-colored bow-shaped plaque, safety catch, 2-⁷/₈″ w × ⁷/₈″ **95**

Bakelite, vinyl-coated cord, c. 1930, lt yellow bar carved in the shape of a riding crop suspending a pr of carved orange riding boots from cord, C-catch, 2″ w × 2-¹/₄″ tl **175**

Bakelite, c. 1930, lt yellow cylindrical bar with a row of four inset three-dimensional triangles in solid black, dk yellow, orange, and green, C-catch, 3-⁷/₈″ w × ¹/₂″ . . . **150**

Bakelite, brass, c. 1930, green Bakelite open rectangle with tapered domed top and bottom, two flat-backed domed saucer shapes with reeded brass centers mounted with screws to notched sides, safety catch, 3″ w × 1-¹/₄″ **195**

Bakelite, c. 1930, lt translucent amber-colored rounded rectangle with cusped ends, four inset green domed disks, safety catch, 3-¹/₂″ w × 1″ **95**

Chrome plated wm, Bakelite, c. 1930, open scalloped-edge wm rect with a scalloped

top strip of red Bakelite riveted in the center, C-catch, 1-⁷/₈" w × ⁵/₈" **85**

Brooches/Pins

Lucite, painted enamel, c. 1940, molded,
carved and rev-carved translucent lt amber-
colored Lucite crested birds on perches,
black painted eyes, C-catches, 1-³/₈" × 2-³/₄",
pr **95**

Buckle

Bakelite, c. 1930, one-pc, an open square with
carved and shaped corners, laminated dk
green framing deep yellow, center cutout
sections with bar for belt attachment, 2-¹/₄" ×
2-¹/₄" **50**

Bakelite, brass, c. 1930, two-pc deep-carved
butterscotch-colored Bakelite, floral and foliate design, brass hook-and-eye closure, bars
for belt attachment mounted with screws on
rev, 2-⁷/₈" w × 1-³/₄" **75**

Bakelite, brass, c. 1930, two-pc, each pc a red
Bakelite square divided diagonally, one-half
smooth, the other carved with rows of sm
squares that match when buckle is joined,
hook-and-eye closure, bars for belt attachment on rev, 4-³/₈" w × 2-¹/₈" **95**

Cuff Links

Sterling, MOP, c. 1945, in the shape of a western six-gun with revolving barrel, MOP handle, link back mkd "sterling," 1-⁵/₈" × ⁷/₈", pr
. . . . **100**

Dress Clip

Bakelite, wm, c. 1930, carved orange leaf with
laminated green stem, flatbacked hinged wm

clip mounted with screws to rev, 2-³/₈" ×
3-¹/₄" **100**

Bakelite, wm, c. 1930, carved translucent amber-colored Bakelite penguin, flatback wm
hinged clip, mkd "Bluette Deposée," Fr, ⁵/₈"
w × 1-³/₄" **70**

Dress Clips

Bakelite, wm, c. 1930, carved black Bakelite,
each in the shape of an acorn, flatback wm
hinged clips, 1-³/₈" w × 1-³/₄", pr **65**

Earrings

Clip

Lucite, rhinestones, c. 1955, domed Lucite
disks, painted black surface carved
through to colorless interior, set with lg
and sm colorless circ r.s., clipbacks, 1" dia,
pr **45**

Thermoset plastic, rhinestones, c. 1955, circ
domed disks of magenta plastic inset with
lg and sm colorless r.s., clipbacks, 1-¹/₈"
dia, pr **35**

Thermoset plastic, rhinestones, c. 1955, convex oval lt blue pl disks inset wth lg oval
aurora borealis r.s. and sm colorless circ
r.s., clipbacks mkd "Weiss," 1" w × 1-¹/₄",
pr **55**

Pendent

Bakelite, paint, glass, wm, c. 1930, a spherical translucent amber-colored Bakelite
drop painted with swirling red and black
lines, suspended from a wire strung with
amber-colored glass seed beads, and a
half-round hp amber-colored Bakelite

Pendent Earrings, assorted plastics, ym, c. 1920-25: L, red kite-shaped celluloid drops with pink, yellow, and blue molded plastic flowerheads in the center suspended from red bead and yellow flowerhead surmounts, screwback findings, 2-¹/₄" tl × ⁵/₈", pr, $45; C, amber-colored thermoset plastic hoops with molded and painted floral design in red, blue, and green suspended from wm chain and amber-colored bead and surmount, screwback findings, 2-¹/₂" tl, 1-¹/₄" dia, pr, $75; R, yellow Bakelite hemispheres sandwiching a molded plastic disk with multicolored flowerheads encircling outside edge, suspended from a ym chain and yellow plastic bead, plastic dome surmount, screwback findings, 2-³/₈" tl × ¹/₂", pr, $75, *Connie Parente collection.*

surmount similar to drop, screwbacks, 2″ tl, drop ⁵/₈″ dia, pr **75**

Bakelite, sp brass, c. 1950, each a lg ovoid plaque of black Bakelite with diagonally bevelled edges, suspended from a smaller surmount of similar shape, clipbacks, 3″ tl × 1-³/₈″ w, pr **40**

Haircomb

Celluloid, rhinestones, c. 1915, lt amber-colored, lg open cutout scrolled design outlined in green r.s., blue r.s. on painted blue ground, 5-¹/₂″ w × 6-⁷/₈″ tl **100**

Hat Ornament

Bakelite, wm, c. 1930, translucent lt amber-colored cone shape topped with a laminated yellow disk at one end of a threaded wm pinstem (unscrews to push through hat), tapered curved lt amber-colored rod at the other, 5″ × 1″ **25**

Celluloid, wm, c. 1930, pearlescent ivory color and black two-tone angled cone shape and smaller bullet shape at the ends of a threaded wm pinstem, 3″ × ¹/₂″ **20**

Celluloid, rhinestones, metal, c. 1930, opposed notched lt brown triangles set with colorless r.s., threaded pinstem, 4-³/₄″ × ⁷/₈″ **30**

Horn, wm, c. 1930, molded yellow and brown faceted crescent and triangle at the ends of a threaded pinstem, 3″ × 1-¹/₈″ **25**

Necklace

Bakelite, celluloid, brass, c. 1935, nine tapered ¹/₂″ cubes of black Bakelite suspended individually by brass jump rings from a black celluloid chain, spring-ring clasp, 15-¹/₂″ tl, 1″ top to bottom **125**

Celluloid, sp brass, c. 1930, five lt pink and lt yellow flowerheads and leaves with amber-colored hollow spheres in centers suspended from sp brass cable link chain, 15-¹/₄″ tl × 1-⁵/₈″ **100**

Celluloid, pl, c. 1930, colorless celluloid chain suspending four flowerheads with pink plastic bead centers and three pink bell-shaped flowers with colorless hollow spheres in centers, 15-¹/₄″ tl × 1-¹/₂″ **100**

Ring

Bakelite, c. 1940, marbled blue-green tapered dome with laminated black dot center, ⁵/₈″ w, approx size 6 . . . . **55**

Bakelite, c. 1935-40, orange dome with yellow laminated polka dots, ⁷/₈″ w, approx size 5 . . . . **125**

Bakelite, c. 1935, dk green dome with deep-

Haircombs, celluloid, rhinestones, c.1915-20: L, lt amber-colored encasing black celluloid in the center, fan-shaped open grillework top surmounted by cutout disks, set throughout with green r.s., 5-¹/₄″ w × 7″, $100; **C,** imitation tortoiseshell teeth surmounted by a row of grad cutout disks with alternating blue and green painted ground and r.s., 5-³/₄″ w × 2-³/₄″tl, $100; **R,** lt amber celluloid in cutout stylized lotus design outlined in blue, green, red, and yellow r.s. and gilt paint, 4-¹/₂″ w × 6-¹/₄″ tl, $175, *Connie Parente collection.*

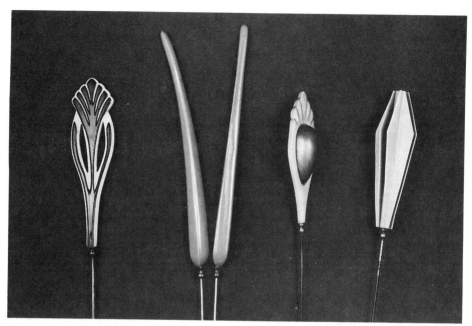

Hatpins, celluloid, c. 1918-20: L-R, 1, black and ivory-colored palmette motif, two-sided, head 3-⅛″x ⅞″, 8-½″ tl, $65; LR, 2, a pr of coral-colored tapering four-sided hollow rods, one slightly curved, 5″ × ⅜″, 9-¾″ tl, pr, $65; LR, 3, two-sided ivory-colored plume motif with center teardrop-shaped translucent amber-colored bubble (hollow), head 2-⅞″ × ⅞″, 8-½″ tl, $45; L-R, 4, three-dimensional paired coffin-shaped blades of beige celluloid, head 3″ × 1″, 8-½″ tl, $45. *Milly Combs collection.*

Headband, celluloid, rhinestones, c. 1920, blue r.s.-set cylindrical band of blue celluloid with overlapping ends held in place by an ivory-colored flowerhead-shaped clasp (adjustable) set with blue rhinestones, terminating in ovoid pearlescent white tips, clasp mkd "pat apld for," 1″ × 1″, band approx 26″ tl × ¼″, $175. *Connie Parente collection.*

Pendant/Necklace, Bakelite, cord, ym, c. 1925, cutout mushroom-shaped khaki-colored plaque with pierced and carved central floral bouquet flanked by a fringe of ym foxtail chains, suspended by eyepins and ym beaded caps from lt brown double cord with a carved Bakelite bead slide, 35" tl, pendant 2-1/4" w × 4-1/2"tl, $295. *Kirsten Olson collection.*

Suite: Pendant and Pendent Earrings, celluloid, rhinestones, paint, sterling, c.1920, an elliptical plaque of black celluloid with painted yellow vertical stripes and painted yellow, blue, red, and green foliate motifs, each section set with matching colored r.s., surmounted by a cutout circ pendant bail for a long cord or ribbon, pr of matching earrings, elongated drops suspended from ster chain and hemispherical celluloid surmounts, each set with a blue r.s., screwbacks mkd "sterling," pendant 1-1/4" w × 2-7/8", earrings 2-1/2" tl × 1/2", $75. *Author's collection.*

carved scalloped ridges, 7/8" w, approx size 4-1/2 . . . . **55**

Bakelite, c. 1930, oval yellow dome with carved swirled ridges, 1-1/8" w, approx size 4-1/2 . . . . **55**

Bakelite, c. 1930, carved yellow rectangle with diagonal opposed palmettes, top 3/4" × 1-1/8", approx size 5 . . . . **65**

Bakelite, c. 1935, smooth ridged green navette-shaped dome, 1-1/8" w, approx size 4 . . . . **40**

Suite: Bangle Bracelet, Bar Pin, and Pendent Earrings

Celluloid, rhinestones, c. 1930, ivory colored

with black colorant appl to half of each piece, colorless round r.s. set into ivory-colored halves, a pr of earrings, each a spherical drop suspended from a wm chain, domed disk surmount of black pl, screwbacks, bangle 3/4" w × 2-1/2" inside dia, bar pin 3-1/4" × 1/2", earrings 2" tl × 3/4" dia, suite **265**

Suite: Dress Clips and Buckle

Bakelite, wm, c. 1930, a pr of oblong olive green Bakelite clips, rounded at the base and deeply carved in a cross-hatched pattern of alternating smooth and textured sections, flat-backed wm hinged clips on rev, attached

to orig card, with orig price tag mkd "The May Co., 59¢," matching two-pc buckle with riveted wm hook and eye, bars for belt attachment on rev, each clip 1-⅛" w × 1-½", buckle 3" w × 1-½", suite **125**
Suite: Hinged Bangle and Clip Earrings
Thermoset plastic, rhinestones, c. 1955, ivory

colored, front half inset with lg and sm black r.s., hinge mkd "Weiss," matching pr of convex oval disk earrings, clipbacks mkd "Weiss," bangle ¾" w, 2-½" inside dia, earrings 1" w × 1-¼", suite **130**

FINE JEWELRY C. 1935-1945

History: The stylistic developments of the 1930s started taking a markedly different path about half-way through the decade. By the mid-1930s, the all-white look of diamonds and platinum that had been a mainstay of fine jewelry fashion since the turn of the century began to fade in popularity. Colored gold and gemstones gradually became more prominent, encouraged by changes in clothing styles and later, by wartime shortages and restrictions. The repeal of Prohibition and the abandonment of the gold standard in 1933 may have precipitated the change. Although the Great Depression had the nation as well as Europe in its grip for the duration of the 1930s, these two events may have sparked hope for better days ahead. Nightclubs were once again in business, and gold jewelry was once again in fashion, as publicized by Hollywood and its stars, the epitome of glamour. Jewelry was still desirable to own in hard times, not only as personal adornment, but also as portable wealth, a concept that remained true throughout the war years. In the make-do spirit of the period, however, fewer, less expensive, and imitation gemstones were used, including synthetic rubies and sapphires, and less expensive gold took the place of platinum, which became totally unavailable for jewelry during the war.

A resurgence of romanticism in the mid to late 1930s generated a desire for femininity in fashion and a return to old-fashioned Victorian sentimentality. There was even a reprise of British royal influence, which nearly upstaged all of Hollywood. The abdication of King Edward VIII in 1936, and his subsequent marriage to Wallis Simpson, was the "the most famous love story of modern times." Jewelry played a well-publicized, prominent, and sentimental role in that story. (Not to be outdone, Margaret Mitchell and Hollywood gave us *Gone With The Wind,* the most famous love story of Victorian times.) The Duke and Duchess of Windsor, as they became known, were the equal of Victoria in their influence on the jewelry-buying public. The most famous of the Duchess' jewels were made by Cartier and Van Cleef & Arpels, but designs by Suzanne Belperron, Harry Winston, Verdura, David Webb, and Seaman Schepps were also part of her collection. (All of these were sold by Sotheby's in

Geneva at its renowned record-breaking auction of April, 1987.)

Retro Modern is the somewhat controversial name recently coined for the fluid 1940s jewelry style that began around 1935. It is an appropriately oxymoronic term (its detractors might prefer to call it just moronic), carrying the suggestion of looking back and forward at the same time. The style's characteristics were truly an infusion of past and futuristic themes. The machine age, streamlined look of the late 1920s and early 1930s continued to evolve, becoming larger and more three-dimensional. However, geometric severity was tempered by curvilinear softness, asymmetry, and a return to naturalistic motifs, usually interpreted on a larger scale and in more stylized forms than their Victorian counterparts. In the gradual move away from abstraction, flowers, animals, and birds became increasingly popular. Buckles, bows, ribbons, and fabriclike folds were often executed in combined contrasting colors of gold alloys in overtones of pink (rose) and green as well as yellow (called bicolor and tricolor gold). Pieces were massive looking but hollow, and, especially during wartime, the gold was of a thin gauge. In German-occupied France, the customer supplied the gold and gemstones, and the government took a percentage of the gold's value. While the United States was under no such restriction on gold, patriotism dictated restraint. Patriotism itself was a prevalent theme in wartime jewelry, both in colors (rubies and sapphires, often synthetic, accented with small diamonds) and motifs (flags, eagles, and military insignia).

Elements of the machine age style that were reinterpreted in yellow and rose gold included large geometric link and wide strap bracelets in tank track and other repeating patterns. In 1934, Van Cleef & Arpels designed a flexible strap of honeycomb- or brickwork-patterned segments with a large ornamental buckle-shaped clasp. They christened it the Ludo bracelet, after Louis Ludovic Arpels, but it appears to have been inspired by Victorian gold mesh *jarretières,* or garter bracelets. The design was copied by many others and remained popular throughout the 1940s. Bangles were wide and three-dimensional, often with a single large rectangular-cut gemstone (aquamarine and citrine were favored) in the center of a scroll or bow of gold with small colored stone accents. Sentiment was expressed in charms of personal significance, some suspended from the traditional link bracelet, others mounted on wide hinged bangles or cuffs. Charms were also fine jewelry's form of whimsy. Disney cartoon characters became popular, especially after the appearance of the first feature length animated film, *Snow White and the Seven Dwarfs,* in 1937.

Dress clips, the ornamental mainstay of the early 1930s, became even more versatile as the central removable decoration of bangle bracelets, and as the *passe-partout* (another Van Cleef & Arpels invention introduced in 1938), an enhancer for a snake chain necklace. The ubiquitous double clip brooch also continued to be worn through the 1940s. Early 1930s pairs of clips were flat, geometric, symmetrical twins; later they became more three-dimensional and asymmetrical mirror images, or figurals. The double-pronged hinged clip finding took the place of the flat-backed clip by the end of the decade. This type of fastening continued to be used on fine jewelry, often with the addition of a safety catch for one or both prongs.

During the war years, clothing fashions grew more severe and masculine, but jewelry, especially brooches, became more feminine. Large floral sprays were prevalent, worn high on a square-shouldered jacket, like a corsage of real flowers. Bicolor gold ribbon bows were another favorite, as were gem-set birds and butterflies. Necklaces became a focal point, shortened to collarbone or choker length. The flexible, slinky, flattened gold tube, known variously as snake chain, gas pipe, or mouse tail, first exhibited in 1934, remained popular throughout the 1940s. Earrings became earclips with the introduction of the clipback finding in the early 1930s. The emphasis was on the lobe rather than below it. Multipetaled flowerheads, scrolls, and cornucopia were popular motifs. Pendent earrings continued to be worn at night, but were usually wider at the top and narrower at the bottom. Rings were massive, generally set with a large central colored gemstone flanked by scrolls of gold or small gemstones of contrasting color. Suites and demi-parures returned to favor after a hiatus of several decades, in matched brooches and earrings, clips and earrings, and necklaces, bracelets, and earrings.

French jewelers continued to be innovative and influential designers until 1940, when France fell under German occupation. Suzanne Belperron (1900-1983) was a celebrated French artist-jeweler whose distinctive style must be studied to be recognized, because she seldom signed her work. She favored inexpensive gemstones like citrine and rock crystal, often sculpturally carved or set in clusters. She worked briefly for Cartier and also ran her own shop; her

longest association was with Jean Herz, with whom she formed the partnership Herz-Belperron in 1945.

Van Cleef & Arpels was one famous firm whose designs came into prominence during the prewar period. In addition to the aforementioned creations, they are credited with the invention of the invisible setting of square-cut gemstones, used primarily for sapphires and rubies. Another of their well-known designs was the ballerina clip, or brooch. This design actually originated in the United States, executed in the early 1940s by John Rubel Co. for Van Cleef & Arpels, New York. It inspired a host of female figurals, which remained popular through the 1950s.

Cartier, long renowned for its impeccably crafted original designs, continued to produce distinctive, mostly figural pieces before the war, even managing to create some new designs during wartime. Its famous "Bird in a Cage" and "Liberated Bird" brooches, executed in 1942 and 1944, respectively, symbolized the occupation and the liberation of Paris.

After 1940, most European jewelry production was curtailed, although the large French houses managed to stay afloat with a limited output of mostly prewar designs. In contrast, American jewelers and their designs came to the fore. Some of these jewelers were transplanted Europeans, others were American born. One house, which became particularly well-known for their Retro Modern designs, was a merger of American and French firms: Trabert & Hoeffer-Mauboussin. Joining forces just after the stock market crash in 1929, the company became famous for their line of retro-styled jewels, named Reflection in 1938. The unique feature of this line was a standardized array of elements that the customer could arrange and combine to suit her fancy. While the firm of Trabert & Hoeffer, Inc. continues today, the association with Mauboussin was terminated in the 1950s.

Texas-born Paul Flato (b.1900) opened his first salon in New York in the late 1920s. His fame and fortune seemed assured when he opened a second establishment in Los Angeles in 1937, catering to Hollywood's elite. He was known for a wide variety of original, whimsical, naturalistic, and surrealistic designs. Fame and fortune were fleeting, however. His business closed in the early 1940s.

One of Flato's designers, a European émigré who had already made a name for himself working for Chanel in Paris, was Fulco Santostefano della Cerda, duc di Verdura (1898-1978), known simply as Verdura. After leaving Flato in 1939, he opened his own shop in New York and became known for his bold and imaginative designs and figural conceits. He emphasized design rather than large gemstones, the importance of which he dismissed, reputedly saying that "mineralogy is not jewelry." He occasionally incorporated shells and pebbles in his work. The firm founded by Verdura is still in business, under the ownership of Edward J. Landrigan, who continues to produce original Verdura designs.

Seaman Schepps (1881-1972), a native-born American, opened his first shops in California, but he moved to New York in 1921, where his establishment remained, except for a five-year hiatus from 1929 to 1934. His work reflects influences by Belperron, Flato, and Verdura in his sculptural and figural pieces. His most-often seen design is for clip earrings, a pair of gem-set turbo (snail-shaped) shells, inspired by Verdura.

Less well-publicized perhaps than their prestigious New York competitors, manufacturers in Newark, New Jersey, continued to produce well-made and affordable gold jewelry in the prevailing style of the period. Geared to conservative tastes, the pieces were more restrained examples of the tailored look that was popularly worn with suits at the time.

References: Annella Brown, "The Mysterious Madame Belperron," in *Heritage,* May 1992; John Culme and Nicholas Rayner, *The Jewels of the Duchess of Windsor,* Vendome Press/ Sotheby's London, 1987; Melissa Gabardi, *Art Deco Jewellery, 1920-1949,* Antique Collectors' Club, 1989; Lael Hagan, "The Retro Revival," in *Jewelers Circular-Keystone/Heritage,* May, 1994; Daniela Mascetti and Amanda Triossi, *Earrings from Antiquity to the Present,* Rizzoli International, 1990; Penny Proddow and Debra Healy, *American Jewelry,* Rizzoli International, 1987; Penny Proddow, Debra Healy, and Marion Fasel, *Hollywood Jewels,* Harry N. Abrams, 1992; Sylvie Raulet, *Jewelry of the 1940s and 1950s,* Rizzoli International, 1987; Kenneth Snowman, ed., *The Master Jewelers,* Harry N. Abrams, 1990; Sally A. Thomas, "Modern Jewelry: Retro to Abstract," in *Gems and Gemology,* Spring 1987; Janet Zapata, "The Legacy of Value from Newark Jewelers," article in *Jewelers Circular-Keystone/ Heritage,* November, 1993; auction catalog: "American Jewelry," Christie's New York, October 21, 1992 (biographies and background information on American jewelers and jewelry by Janet Zapata).

Advisor: Janet Zapata.

Bracelet
  Cuff
    18k yg, citrines, c. 1940, a row of five grad rect-cut citrines in pierced and cutout raised mounts, 2-¼" inside dia, ⅝" w
    . . . . **690 (A)**
  Flexible
    14k yg, diamonds, rubies, c. 1940, honeycomb pattern set throughout with diamonds, terminating in a polished yg buckle with a pavé-set diamond center and calibré ruby accents, mkd "T. & H. M." for Trabert & Hoeffer, Mauboussin,

Bracelet, flexible, 14k yg, diamonds, sapphires, c. 1940, a brickwork patterned strap with a buckle motif closure set with six oe-cut diamonds and nine calibré-cut sapphires, 8-½" tl × 1-⅛", $2,185 (A). *Photo courtesy of Butterfield & Butterfield, San Francisco and Los Angeles (6/17/93).*

    # 1813, diamonds approx 5.5 ct tw, 7" × 1" . . . . **11,000 (A)**
    14k yg, diamonds, rubies, c. 1940, a wide, lozenge-shaped pattern strap, with a central motif of two conical yg disks with off-center circ cutouts joined horizontally by a domed bar link set with a row of 12 sq-cut rubies flanked by two rows of 22 full-cut diamonds, approx 1.1 ct tw, foldover clasp mkd "14k," 7-¼" × 1-¼" . . . . **1,955 (A)**
    14k yg, diamonds, c. 1940, brickwork pattern yg strap with diamond-set buckle, sgd "Cartier," 25 dwt, 7" × 1" . . . . . **2,200 (A)**
    18k yg, diamonds, c. 1940, a wide honeycomb-pattern strap, terminating in a diamond-set buckle closure, 47.2 dwt, 7-⅛" × 1" . . . . **1,650 (A)**
  Flexible link
    18k rose gold, c. 1940, a wide strap of two lines of shell-shaped links, separated by rows of curved tubular elements and three rows of spheres, mkd "Regist," 59 dwt, 7-¼" × 1-½" . . . . **1,540 (A)**
    18k rose gold, c. 1940, strap of hollow, faceted, biconical-shaped links in a staggered two alternating with one pattern, Fr, sgd "J. Lacloche," 71.4 dwt, 7-¼" w × 1-¼" . . . . **3,850 (A)**
    18k yg, c. 1940, a wide strap of honeycomb links, buckle clasp, 100 dwt, 8" × 1-½" . . . . **3,080 (A)**
    18k yg, c. 1940, a wide strap with a spaced row of beveled bar links edged by rows of arching bar links, 89 dwt, 7-½" × ⅞" . . . . **2,860 (A)**
    18k yg, c. 1940, strap of domed, polished

links in a tank-track pattern, 57.2 dwt, 7-³/₄″ w × ⁷/₈″ . . . . **2,420 (A)**
Yg, c. 1940, a wide strap of honeycomb links, 54.8 dwt, 7-¹/₂″ × 1″ . . . . . . **900 (A)**

Hinged bangle
Yg, aquamarine, rubies, diamonds, c. 1940, a wide band surmounted by a lg bow motif with its center composed of an emerald-cut aquamarine, calibré-cut rubies and rc diamonds in four segments at compass points, flanked by a row of calibré-cut rubies along bow edges, each surmounting a curled yg ribbon, two ruby and diamond segments appl to the bangle shoulders, approx 70 dwt, 2-¹/₄″ inside dia, 1-¹/₄″ w . . . . **11,500 (A)**
Yg, diamonds, c. 1940, a stylized buckle motif with star-set oe diamonds on an open pear-shaped loop, the wide end surmounted by a domed rect clasp with a center row of diamonds, 2-³/₈″ inside dia, 1-³/₈″ w . . . . **4,140 (A)**
Yg, platinum, diamonds, enamel, onyx, colored stones, c. 1940, bypass design, a polished yg wide band with raised plat border, surrounded by seven appl plat charms of a heart, Minnie Mouse, two men in top hats, a Dutch girl, cowboy, and gondolier set with diamonds, onyx, and various colored stones, with enamel accents, (some stones missing), 2-¹/₄″ inside dia, 1-⁷/₈″ w . . . . **7,188 (A)**

Link
14k bicolor gold, c. 1940, stepped, tapered rect domed links alternating with sphere and annular links, Austrian hmks, 7-³/₄″ × ³/₄″ . . . . **1,430 (A)**
14k rose and yg, c. 1940, prs of domed horizontal bar links alternating with clusters of four circ domed links, approx 29.84 dwt, 7-¹/₂″ × 1″ . . . . **863(A)**
14k rose and yg garnets, c. 1940, yg floral and leaf motif links, each with a garnet-set center, alternating with flowerhead clusters of circ-cut garnets, 7-³/₄″ × ³/₄″ . . . . **403(A)**
14k rose gold, rubies, diamonds, c. 1940, a central scrolled buckle motif with a horizontal row of ruby cabs, approx 7 ct tw, encircled by an annular oval set with diamonds, continuing to a strap of articulated biconical meshed links, 41.5 dwt, 7″ × 1-¹/₄″ . . . . **4,125 (A)**
14k yg, crystal, c. 1940, Victorian revival, equestrian motif, three reverse crystal intaglios of foxes and hounds within horeshoe-shaped yg frames, joined by stirrup and snaffle bit links, mkd "Sloan and Co.," Newark N.J., 6-¹/₂″ × ³/₄″ . . . . **1,760 (A)**
14k yg, c. 1940, lg fluted domed links flanked by upright triangular links, safety

chain, 55.6 dwt, 7″ × 1-¹/₄″ . . . . **1,540 (A)**
14k yg, c. 1940, open chunky fancy-shaped rect links, gross weight, 2.65 oz, 7-³/₄″ × 1-¹/₄″ . . . . **1,495 (A)**
18k bicolor gold, c. 1940, a row of interlocking fluted cone-shaped links flanked by two similar rows in opposition, 55.9 dwt, 7″ × ⁷/₈″ . . . . **1,980 (A)**
18k rose and yg, c. 1940, seven rows of interlocking domed, faceted, ridged and smooth geo links, various shapes, 7″ × 1-¹/₂″ . . . . **2,645 (A)**
18k rose and yg, c. 1940, a line of stylized lotus flowers in stamped relief with raised bead centers, sgd "Birks" (Canada), 57 dwt, 7-³/₄″ × 1″ . . . . **2,420 (A)**
18k yg, c. 1940, hollow stylized bow-shaped links, Fr hmks, v-spring and box clasp, safety clasps, 7″ × ³/₄″ . . . . **2,300 (A)**
18k yg, c. 1940, hollow openwork ribbed rect links, flat polished back, foldover clasp, safety chain, several links dented, 22.2 dwt, 7-³/₄″ × ³/₄″ . . . . **550 (A)**
18k yg, c. 1940, tank-track hollow rect reeded links, foldover clasp, mkd "0750" in a lozenge, 7-³/₄″ × ⁷/₈″ . . . . . . **1,610 A)**

Bracelets
Cuffs
Citrines, silver, 18k yg, c. 1940, peaked pyramid-shaped silver cuffs, centered with channel-set rect step-cut citrines mounted in yg, Fr hmks, attributed to Suzanne Belperron, 34.8 dwt and 35.4 dwt, 2-¹/₂″ w and 3-¹/₂″ w, pr . . . . **23,100 (A)**
Brooch/Pin
14k bicolor gold, diamonds, rubies, syn ruby, c. 1940, a bow with trailing ribbon ends flanking a center ring, with a central knot of

Cuff Bracelet, 14k yg, diamonds, rubies, sapphires, platinum, c. 1940, a smooth wide band with raised edges, surmounted by six plat charms: a stork, a cowboy, a basket of flowers, a gondola with gondolier, a Dutch girl, and a pr of lovebirds, each set with a lg ruby cab, sm circ diamonds, calibré sapphires and rubies, ruby cab terminals, 2-³/₈″ inside dia, 2-¹/₄″ w, $4,730 (A).
Photo courtesy of Grogan & Co., Boston (12/6/93).

Double Clip Hinged Bangle Bracelet, diamonds, rubies, wg, c. 1935, a pair of detachable clips, each a pierced geo and scrolled heart-shaped plaque set throughout with circ and baguette diamonds, a calibré-cut ruby on each side, with a center vertical row of two collet-set ruby cabs and two calibré-cut rubies, mounted opposed on a tapered wg bangle with grad diagonal rows of circ diamonds radiating from one side of each clip, 210 diamonds, approx 5 cts tw, bangle 2-¹/₂″ inside dia, 1-¹/₄″ w, each clip 1-¹/₄″ w × 1-¹/₈″, **$6,050 (A).** *Photo courtesy of Dunning's, Elgin, Ill. (11/7/93).*

diamonds and rubies (one syn), mkd "Eckfeldt & Ackley," Newark, N.J., ³/₄″ w × 2-¹/₂″ .... **413 (A)**

14k bicolor gold, citrines, tourmaline, diamond, ruby, c. 1940, a butterfly with highly polished curved and scrolled wings, a center row of two citrines and a tourmaline, diamond eyes and ruby antennae, mfr's mk for Lester & Co. (an acorn), Newark, N.J., 2″ w × 1-¹/₂″ .... **825 (A)**

14k pink and green gold, ruby, c. 1940, a full-blown rose in polished pink gold with a circ-cut ruby in the center, green gold leaves and stem, sgd "Tiffany & Co.," 1-⁵/₈″ w × 2″ .... **880 (A)**

14k rose gold, rubies, c. 1940, two overlapping

Brooch/Pin, 14k rose and yg, amethyst, c. 1940, a polished gold ribbon bow with a lg prong-set cushion-cut amethyst center, 3-¹/₄″ w × 2″, **$460 (A).** *Photo courtesy of Butterfield & Butterfield, San Francisco and Los Angeles (6/17/93).*

annular disks with reeded surfaces joined by a polished yg dome with a central horizontal row of channel-set rubies, 15.9 dwt, 2-¹/₂″ w × 1-¹/₂″ .... **715 (A)**

14k yg, rubies, c. 1940, a floral and foliate spray, three flowerhead centers set with a total of 27 circ rubies, 1-⁵/₈″ w × 3-³/₄″ .... **1,725 (A)**

14k yg, sapphire, c. 1940, cutout, folded, twisted and scrolled yg in the shape of a stylized female figure with crossed hands holding a sapphire cab, sgd "Trabert & Hoeffer, Mauboussin," ¹/₂″ w × 2-³/₄″ .... **1,045 (A)**

14k yg, diamonds, sapphires, red stones, c. 1940, a diaper-pattern openwork three-dimensional bow surmounted by eight prong-set circ-cut sapphires and red stones, a row of five circ-cut diamonds across center knot, trombone catch, 1-⁷/₈″ w × ⁷/₈″ .... **431 (A)**

14k yg, c. 1940, highly polished double loop bow, sgd "Tiffany & Co.," 15.9 dwt, 3-³/₈″ w × 1-¹/₂″ .... **1,760 (A)**

14k yg, moonstones, sapphires, c. 1940, a yg flowerhead with foliated petals encircled by six prong-set oval moonstone cabs alternating with six prong-set sm circ sapphires mounted on yg wires, a cluster of circ sapphires in flower's center, 11.5 dwt, 2″ dia .... **150 (A)**

14k yg, diamonds, rubies, c. 1940, a slightly concave corrugated yg annular disk, a vertical polished yg band mounted from inner to outer bottom edge with a row of two circ prong-set diamonds and two circ prong-set rubies, sgd "Tiffany & Co.," 2.6 dwt, 1-¹/₄″ dia .... **495 (A)**

14k yg, citrine, c. 1940, a yg foliate spray flanked at the base by two trefoil clusters of prong-set circ citrines, stems encircled by an annular yg disk, mkd with conjoined "WAB" for Allsopp-Steller, Inc., successors to Wordley, Allsopp & Bliss Co., Newark, N.J., 9.9 dwt, 1-¹/₂″ w × 3-¹/₂″ .... **550 (A)**

18k rose gold, peridot, c. 1940, a scrolled ribbon motif with pierced center and coiled wire borders, a circ-cut peridot prong-set in the center, surmounting a bead-tipped wire sunburst motif, 1-⁷/₈″ w × 1-¹/₂″ .... **1,093 (A)**

Aquamarines, 14k yg, rubies, diamonds, c. 1940, a flower shape, petals formed from lozenge-shaped aquamarines with a cluster of circ-cut rubies and one round prong-set sc diamond in the center, curved polished yg stem, 15.2 dwt, 3″ w × 1-⁵/₈″ .... **3,520 (A)**

Citrine, 14k rose and yg, sapphires, c. 1940, a stylized bow with a central rect-cut citrine, flanked by folded ribbons and

Brooches/Pins, c. 1940: TL, 14k bicolor gold, diamonds, sapphires, rubies, a cutout curv, flared, cusped and scrolled design set with a semicirc, a star-cut, and V-shaped clusters of sm circ stones, approx 8.9 dwt, 2″ w × 1-⅛″, $523 (A); TR, rose gold, sapphires, diamonds, a gold multilooped ribbon bow with a center knot of pavé-set diamonds, a spray of circ-cut sapphires prong-set on wires radiating from the center, approx 16 dwt, 2-½″ w × 1-½″, $605 (A); B, 14k bicolor gold, citrines, sapphires, diamonds, a gold ribbon bow surmounted by six elongated trapeze-cut citrines, alternating with sm diamonds, radiating in a semicirc around center knot with a curv cluster of circ-cut sapphires below, approx 16.2 dwt, 2-¾″ w × 1-¼″, $550 (A); Earrings, clip, c. 1940: BL, 14k yg, amethysts, syn rubies, a scrolled yg ribbon with a central rect step-cut amethyst prong-set within a circ frame, a row of sm syn rubies surmounting grad rays on one side, clipbacks, 1″ × ¾″, pr, $495 (A); CL, 14k bicolor gold, sapphires, a ribbon bow with a center knot of calibré-cut sapphires, clipbacks, 1-⅛″ × ⅝″, $495 (A); CR, 14k yg, rubies, diamonds, a scrolled yg ribbon bow motif with a center knot of pavé-set diamonds, and a spray of sm circ rubies radiating from the center, clipbacks, 1-⅛″ × 1″, pr, $248 (A). *Photo courtesy of Dunning's, Elgin, Ill. (5/16/93).*

curved strips of yg, and clusters of circ and oval-cut blue, pink, and yellow sapphires, 3-¼″ w × 1″ .... **2,530 (A)**
Citrine, 18k yg, sapphires, rubelites, amethysts, aquamarines, peridots, c. 1935, an oval with a lg central bezel-set pear-shaped citrine, eight radiating rows of sq step-cut sapphires, spaces between rows filled with multicolored circ, oval, pear, and cushion-shaped bezel-set stones, sgd ''Chanel,'' attributed to Suzanne Belperron, 20.5 dwt, 2-½″ w × 2-¼″ .... **20,900 (A)**
Circle
14k bicolor gold, rubies, diamonds, c. 1940, a yg circ ring surmounted by an asymmetrical bicolor gold swirl and fan motif with a curved row of circ rubies along one edge, and four rows of diamonds spaced across the fan, 1-⅝″ dia .... **990 (A)**
Clip
14k yg, sapphires, diamonds, c.1940, a flowerpot design set with three pear-shaped

sapphires and 10 circ diamonds in the pot, one blue, and two yellow, lg oval sapphires and seven smaller circ diamonds prong-set on yg wires forming the flowers, undulating gold ribbon leaves, double-pronged hinged clip with lever catch on rev, 1-¼″ w × 2″ .... **1,265 (A)**
18k rose gold, diamonds, c. 1940, an asymmetrical yg scroll and leaf motif surmounting an open sq frame set with three oe diamonds, approx 1.9 ct tw, and pavé-set with 103 circ diamonds, approx 2.25 ct tw, double-pronged hinged clip on rev, 2-¼″ w × 1-¾″ .... **2,588 (A)**
18k yg, enamel, coral, diamonds, plat, c. 1940, a black enameled yg rose with an om diamond center and a yg stem held by a carved coral hand wearing a plat and rc diamond bracelet and a yg and black enamel bracelet, sgd ''Cartier Paris'' # 07053, Fr eagle's head hmk, double pronged hinged clip on rev, 1-⅛″ w × 1-⅞″ .... **5,463 (A)**
Citrines, 18k yg, c. 1940, pyramidal shape, set

with rect step-cut citrines, Fr hmks, attributed to Suzanne Belperron, some stones chipped, 22.8 dwt, 2-⅛″ × 1-½″ . . . . **10,450 (A)**

Clips

14k bicolor gold, diamonds, c. 1940, a pr of shield-shaped pierced geo and foliate motif clips set throughout with 138 oe, baguette, marquise, and sc diamonds, which fit into rose and yg and plat scrolled ribbon motif detachable frames set with 28 marquise and oe diamonds, 6.8 ct tw, double-pronged hinged clips, each clip and frame 1-¼″ w × 1-⅞″, pr . . . . **7,475 (A)**

14k rose gold, diamonds, c. 1940, plain polished yg circ disks, one with a diamond-set " + " (plus) sign in the center, the Fr word, *toujours* (always) engr above, the other with a diamond-set " − " (minus) sign and the Fr word, *jamais* (never), Am, sgd "Flato" for Paul Flato, 38 dwt, 1-⅜″ dia, pr . . . **4,510 (A)**

18k rose gold, c. 1940, in the shape of stylized cornucopia, double-pronged hinged clips, 1″ w × 2″, pr . . . . **863 (A)**

Diamonds, rubies, platinum, c. 1940, fan-shaped openwork ribbon motif set with circ bc and baguette diamonds, 6.6 ct tw, with curved rows of circ prong-set and rect calibré-cut channel-set rubies, 9.7 dwt, 1-¼″ w × 1-⅝″, pr . . . . **6,600 (A)**

Yg, sapphires, emeralds, diamonds, platinum, c. 1940, openwork shield-shaped yg fringe, with a center of carved rubies, sapphires, and emeralds in a fruit salad arrangement outlined in and interspersed with circ, triangular, and marquise-cut diamonds, sgd

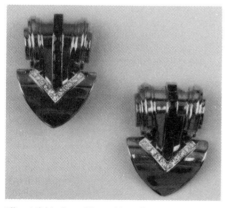

Clips, 14k bicolor gold, sapphires, diamonds, c. 1940, a pr of wide, short arrow motifs with shaped points and stepped, scrolled shafts, each with a vertical center row of baguette-cut channel-set sapphires terminating in a V-shaped row of circ diamonds, sgd "Tiffany & Co.," 17.1 dwt., double-pronged hinged clips on rev, 1″ w × 1-⅜″, pr, $2,875 (A). *Photo courtesy of Skinner, Inc., Boston (3/8/94).*

Double Clip Brooch, rubies, star rubies, diamonds, platinum, wg, c. 1935, a pair of triangular clips, geo pierced design set throughout with oe, baguette, and sc diamonds, a prong-set star ruby in the center of each, surmounting a cluster of carved oval rubies, with an armature for joining as a brooch, and a necklace armature set with a star ruby center surrounded by carved rubies and diamonds, to which the clips can be added (not pictured), diamonds approx 7 cts tw, each clip 1-¼″ w × 1-½″, $7,150 (A). *Photo courtesy of Grogan & Co., Boston (12/6/93).*

"Verdura," 28.1 dwt, 1-⅜″ w × 1-½″, pr . . . . **11,000 (A)**

Double Clip Brooch

18k yg, diamonds, c. 1940, a pr of clips of scrolled and folded ribbon design with pavé-set diamond borders, double-pronged hinged clips with a pinback mechanism for joining as a brooch, 2-¾″ w × 1-½″, joined . . . . **2,300 (A)**

Diamonds, sapphires, platinum, c. 1935, each clip set with four fan-shaped rows of three calf's head-cut (elongated trapezoid) varicolored sapphires interspersed with circ-cut diamonds, partially framed by a pavé-set diamond scroll, by Oscar Heyman & Brothers, connected with a detachable pinback mechanism, 2-¾″ w × 1-¼″ joined . . . . **8,050 (A)**

Earrings/Earclips

14k rose gold, aquamarines, rubies, diamonds, c. 1940, fan and scrolled ribbon motif, each with one emerald-cut aquamarine of approx 3 ct in the center, a row of five circ-cut rubies along one edge, and one circ-cut diamond in the scrolled base, converted to post and clutch backs, 1″ × ½″, pr . . . . **978 (A)**

14k yg, diamonds, rubies, c. 1940, polished yg annular hoop dotted with diamonds and rubies, snake chain fringe cascading from the open center, terminating in ruby beads, clipbacks, ½″ w × 1-¼″, pr . . . . . **1,650 (A)**

14k yg, ruby, c. 1940, five-petaled yg flowerheads, a lg ruby cab in each center, # 6456, screwbacks, ¾″, pr . . . . . . **920 (A)**

14k yg, ruby, turq, c. 1940, each a flowerhead with ruby center surrounded by sm circ turq cabs, surmounted by gold leaves, $\frac{1}{2}$" w × $\frac{3}{4}$", pr . . . . **770 (A)**

14k yg, sapphires, c. 1940, five-petaled yg flowerheads, centers set with 14 circ sapphire cabs, sgd "T. & H. M." for Trabert & Hoeffer, Mauboussin, # 6255, clipbacks, $\frac{5}{8}$"dia, pr . . . . **1,093 (A)**

18k rose gold, rubies, diamonds, c. 1940, stepped upswept scroll design, top edges set with buff-top rubies, each with a vertical row of pavé-set diamonds, mkd "T. & H. M." for Trabert & Hoeffer, Mauboussin, clipbacks, $\frac{1}{2}$" w × $\frac{3}{4}$" . . . . **1,650 (A)**

Pink gold, diamonds, rubies, c. 1940, abstract comet shape with a central triangular diamond surrounded by calibré-cut round rubies and smaller diamonds, clipbacks, $\frac{3}{4}$" w × 1-$\frac{1}{4}$", pr . . . . **1,650 (A)**

Rose and yg, c. 1940, fluted circ stylized flowerhead in rose gold with yg bead center, clipbacks, $\frac{3}{4}$"dia, pr . . . . **460 (A)**

Pendent

18k rose gold, pearls, diamonds, c. 1940, an open looped wire cloverleaf-shaped surmount with a diamond interspaced between each loop, a vertical center row of diamonds, suspending *négligée* a diamond-set double floral drop terminating in two cultured pearls, clipbacks, 1-$\frac{7}{8}$" tl × $\frac{3}{4}$", pr . . . . **1,100 (A)**

Necklace

14k · yg, c. 1940, snake chain, or gas pipe of uniform width, 16" tl × $\frac{1}{2}$" w . . . . . . **670 (A)**

14k yg, c. 1940, snake chain, or gas pipe of uniform width, 45 dwt, 16-$\frac{1}{2}$" × $\frac{3}{8}$" . . . . **880 (A)**

Necklace, choker, 14k yg, c. 1940, a tapered flexible gas pipe style collar, v-spring and box clasp, safety clasp, approx 65.6 dwt, 16" tl, 1-$\frac{1}{8}$" w at center, $1,540 (A). Photo courtesy of Dunning's, Elgin, Ill. (11/7/93).

14k yg, rubies, sapphires, diamonds, c. 1940, snake chain, or gas pipe of uniform width, with three appl flowerhead clusters of six circ rubies with circ diamond centers evenly spaced across center front, with a group of four prong-set circ sapphires flanking each cluster, sgd "Forstner," for Forstner Jewelry Mfg Corp., Irvington, N.J., approx 48 dwt, 15" tl × $\frac{3}{8}$" . . . . **3,450 (A)**

Tricolor gold, moonstones, sapphires, c. 1940, an X-shaped openwork center of crossed round wires radiating four to a side from two scrolled foliate motifs, terminating in eight pear-shaped moonstones, with two rows of three circ sapphires prong-set between the wires near the center, suspended from foliate links of green, yellow and rose gold, sgd "Tiffany & Co," 16" tl, center 2-$\frac{1}{4}$" w × 1-$\frac{3}{4}$" . . . . **2,588 (A)**

Ring

14k pink gold, rubies, diamonds, c. 1940, D-shaped buckle motif with a row of rubies set in the curve, a row of diamonds in the hasp, continuing to a narrow shank, top $\frac{3}{4}$" × $\frac{3}{4}$" . . . . **468 (A)**

14k rose gold, rubies, diamonds, c. 1940, 10 circ rubies and seven circ diamonds set within a scalloped-edge scrolled shell motif, tapered shank, 1" w × $\frac{3}{4}$" . . . . **633 (A)**

14k rose gold, star sapphire, syn rubies, diamonds, platinum, c. 1940, a wide, slightly concave yg S-shaped top, flanked by two rows of three prong-set circ-cut syn rubies, the surface bezel-set with a central oval star sapphire flanked by two rows of three sc diamonds pavé-set in plat, tapering to a shank mkd "14k 900 plat 100 irid," $\frac{3}{4}$" × $\frac{3}{4}$" . . . . **316 (A)**

14k rose gold, rubies, diamonds, platinum, c. 1940, a scrolled and stepped plat-topped yg head with a center row of sc diamonds flanked by two rows of six rect-cut rubies, two cab rubies set in scroll terminals, mkd "14k," $\frac{7}{8}$" w × $\frac{1}{2}$" . . . . **546 (A)**

18k rose gold, diamond, rubies, c. 1940, hollow, domed stylized bow tie design, with a collet-set oe diamond center flanked above and below by two collet-set circ rubies, $\frac{3}{4}$" w × $\frac{5}{8}$" . . . . **1,093 (A)**

Aquamarine, 14k rose gold, c. 1940, an emerald-cut aquamarine approx 20.25 ct, prong-set above a deep cutout gallery flanked by a plain tapered shank, 1" w × 1-$\frac{1}{4}$" . . . . **748 (A)**

Aquamarine, yg, rubies, c. 1940, a prong-set rect-cut aquamarine, approx 15.57 ct, flanked by vertical rows of cab rubies at the shoulders, continuing to a tapered shank, sgd "Seaman Schepps," $\frac{3}{4}$" w × $\frac{7}{8}$" . . . . **2,530 (A)**

Aquamarine, platinum, yg, rubies, diamonds, c. 1940, an emerald-cut, prong-set aquama-

Necklace/Bracelets, 14k rose and green gold, c. 1940, a row of bicolor gold ribbon bow motifs alternating with annular links, separates into two equal sections for wearing as bracelets, both sections imp with mfr's mk for Larter & Sons, Newark, N.J. (a spring-back shirt stud logo), 16-¼" tl × ¾", $4,750. *Photo courtesy of Janet Zapata.*

rine, 25 × 16 × 9.57mm, flanked by wide tapered scroll satin-finished yg shoulders, the lower portions set with four calibré-cut rubies and two baguette diamonds in plat bezels, 12.1 dwt, 1" w × ⅞", ring size 6-½
. . . . **1,980 (A)**
Citrine, 14k yg, rubies, c. 1940, lg prong-set rect-cut citrine, approx 30 × 21mm, flanked by rows of sm cab rubies in a scrolled yg mount, ⅞" w × 1-⅛" . . . . **330 (A)**
Citrine, 14k yg, syn rubies, c. 1940, a lg prong-

Ring, 18k rose gold, natural blue topaz, syn rubies, c. 1940, an emerald-cut blue topaz, 14 × 11.5 × 7.5 mm, prong-set, flanked by two flowerheads with syn ruby centers mounted on tubular shoulders, continuing to a split shank, 1" w × ½", $650. *Courtesy of E. Foxe Harrell Jewelers.*

set rect-cut citrine, tapering shoulders set with six grad rect-cut syn rubies, continuing to a split shank, ⅞" w × 1" . . . . **690 (A)**
Citrine, 14k yg, platinum, diamonds, c. 1940, a lg rect-cut citrine flanked by plat-topped yg cylindrical shoulders pavé-set with 10 oe diamonds, continuing to a tapered shank, 1-¼" w × ¾" . . . . **547 (A)**
Citrine, 14k rose gold, rubies, c. 1940, an emerald-cut citrine, approx 12.55 ct, prong-set in a rose gold ring set with four sq-cut rubies, mkd "14k," ¾" w × 1" . . . . **863 (A)**
Diamonds, rubies, 14k rose gold, c. 1940, double flower motif set with six circ diamonds and 10 circ rubies within a fluted yg S-scroll, tapered shank, 1" w × ⅜" . . . . **374 (A)**
Diamonds, rubies, platinum, c. 1940, a rounded flared top pavé-set with circ-cut diamonds and two diagonal rows of calibré-cut rubies, tapering and wrapping around to a polished plat shank and shoulder, ¾" × ¾"
. . . . **1,725 (A)**
Diamonds, yg, rubies, c. 1940, a domed yg top inset with an oe diamond center, approx 1 ct, and studded throughout with cab rubies and sm diamonds, continuing to a tapered band, ¾" w × ¾", approx ring size 5 . . . **4,025 (A)**
Diamonds, 14k wg, c. 1940, a pierced cushion-shaped top set with rows of sm diamonds, 1 ct tw, in a swirl pattern, a .6 ct

collet-set bc diamond mounted off-center, 4.6 dwt, ¹/₂″ w × ³/₄″, ring size 5-¹/₂ .... **1,300 (A)**

Topaz, rubies, diamonds, platinum, c. 1940, an emerald-cut yellow topaz flanked by two vertical rows of three oe diamonds and two curved horizontal rows of three baguette-cut rubies, 1″ × ¹/₂″ .... **805 (A)**

Suite: Clip and Earrings

14k yg, rubies, diamonds, c. 1940, starburst motif clip with polished yg spikes, diamond and ruby-set center, double-pronged hinged clip on rev, a pr of matching earrings with orig clipbacks, all pcs sgd "Tiffany & Co." (one ruby missing), a total of approx 33 circ diamonds and 80 circ rubies, brooch 1-⁷/₈″ w × 1-³/₄″, earrings 1-¹/₈″ w × 1-¹/₈″, suite .... **3,738 (A)**

Suite: Clips and Earrings

Pearls, diamonds, platinum, 14k wg, c. 1940, a pr of clips, each with a tapering cluster of pearls of various sizes and colors surmounted by a fan-shaped pierced plat scroll, set with a total of 36 circ diamonds, double-pronged hinged clips on rev, ³/₄″ w × 1-¹/₄″, pr of matching screwback earrings, ¹/₂″ w × ⁷/₈″ .... **3,450 (A)**

Suite: Clips, Earrings, Ring, and Bracelet attachment

14k yg, rubies, diamonds, c. 1940, convertible suite: a pr of textured yg ribbon and scroll shield-shaped clips, each with a spray of 23 oval-cut and circ-cut rubies and 14 sc diamonds, double-pronged hinged clips on rev, one clip fits into a wide yg bangle bracelet attachment, and a pr of matching clipback earrings, all pcs sgd "T.& H. M." for Trabert & Hoeffer, Mauboussin, and an unsgd ring with five rubies and 17 sc diamonds, one ruby missing, clips 1-³/₈″ w × 1-⁵/₈″, earrings ⁵/₈″ w × ³/₄″, suite .... **7,475 (A)**

Suite: Earrings and Brooch/Pin

18k yg, diamonds, c. 1940, fluted yg bow motifs with pavé-set rc diamond centers, a snake chain ribbon loosely knotted and looped around the center with bead and diamond-topped cone terminals, approx 50 dwt tw, Fr, in a fitted leather box, brooch 2 ¹/₄″ w × 4″ tl, earrings 1″ w × 2″ tl, suite .... **8,625 (A)**

Suite: Three Brooches/Pins, 18k yg, rubies, sapphires, emeralds, turquoise, c. 1940, scatter pins depicting three ladies holding baskets of ruby, emerald, and sapphire flowers, two with turquoise-dotted dresses and picture hats, ⁷/₈″ w × 2″; one with a diamond-set slip and porkpie hat, also holding a garland of sapphire flowers, 1-¹/₂″ w × 2″, Fr, each sgd "J. Lacloche," suite, $5,750 (A). Photo © 1993 Sotheby's, Inc., New York (4/19/93).

Suite: Earrings and Ring

Sapphires, rubies, emeralds, amethysts, citrines, yg, c. 1945, half-hoop clip earrings, ring with a bombé-shaped mount, each encrusted with faceted, cabochon, and carved sapphires, rubies, emeralds, amethysts, and citrines, earrings sgd "T & H. M." for Trabert & Hoeffer, Mauboussin, ³/₄″ w × 1″; ring 1″ × 1″ .... **5,750 (A)**

Suite: Necklace and Bracelet

14k yg, diamonds, rubies, emeralds, sapphires, c. 1940, a line of ¹/₂″ w yg flowerhead links, each center alternately prong-set with a circ ruby, sapphire, emerald, or diamond, a total of 44 stones, necklace 14-³/₈″ tl, bracelet 6-¹/₂″ tl .... **4,313 (A)**

FINE JEWELRY C. 1945-1965

History: History records wars as lines of demarcation. What happens after a war is usually a radical departure from what was happening before and during it. World War II was no exception. Postwar prosperity unleashed an indulgence in luxury long frustrated by deprivation. All aspects of popular culture changed, including a

marked change in fashion. Christian Dior introduced his New Look in 1947—long full skirts, nipped-in waist, unpadded, sloping shoulders, tight bodices and décolleté necklines. Femininity was back in style. To complement the look, jewelry had to change, too. In fact, jewelry design took off in two divergent directions, that of the traditionalists of fine jewelry, including the large houses and those who designed for them, and that of the new modernist designs of avant-garde studio artists (see the section on postwar modernists). Among the traditionalists, there was a return to an extravagant display of all kinds of gemstones, but especially, diamonds were a girl's best friend once again. In 1948, De Beers Corporation set the tone for the era with their now-famous slogan, "a diamond is forever." A nearly imperceptible flexible platinum wire setting (said to have been inspired by a holly wreath), pioneered by diamond magnate Harry Winston around 1946, allowed clusters of stones to dominate a jewel. Fancy cuts, such as marquise and pear, were particularly favored in diamond jewelry.

The motifs and forms of traditional jewelry in the 1950s and early 1960s were not a radical departure from those of the 1940s, but their execution was decidedly different. Where 1940s pieces had a heavy, solid, and smooth polished look (even though they may have been hollow and light in terms of actual weight), 1950s pieces were open and airy with textured surfaces such as Florentine (brushed metal), ropetwisted or braided wire, mesh, reeding, fluting, and piercing. Yellow gold was predominant except for all-diamond jewels, for which the preferred metal was once again platinum.

Following the trend for matching accessories, the suite returned in force as a full parure of necklace, bracelet, earrings, and brooch. Floral motifs were still in vogue, as well as a variety of leaf shapes, with increasing emphasis on gemstones and texture. Necklaces remained short as chokers, collars, or bibs. These could be draped, swirled, or fringed in gold or entirely gem-set. Bracelets were primarily of the flexible sort, often gemstone encrusted. Charm bracelets also maintained their popularity. Earrings were usually circular, floral, or foliate yellow gold clips for day and long fringes of gemstones, usually diamonds, for evening wear. Upswept styles that enveloped the ear were also common. Brooches in the forms of animals and people continued to amuse, more often as cartoonish caricatures than realistic portrayals. Stylized foliate sprays entirely set with numerous baguette, marquise and pear-shaped stones were another often-seen form. Modernism exerted its influence in the form of starburst and atomic shapes. Rings were domed clusters of gemstones, or one large stone surrounded by smaller stones, usually marquise or other fancy-cut diamonds.

The famous haute jewelry houses—Cartier, Van Cleef & Arpels, et al.—continued to produce opulent jewels in new designs as well as reprising prewar classics, which were finding a wider audience among the newly prosperous.

American jewelry firms achieved greater recognition during this period. Harry Winston (1896-1978), a retailer, broker, and manufacturer since the 1930s, made an even bigger name for himself with his touring "Court of Jewels" exhibit, which opened in 1949. He became known as the "King of Diamonds." Beginning in 1955 under Walter Hoving's directorship, Tiffany & Co. gained new distinction with designs by Jean Schlumberger (1907-1987), a former associate of Elsa Schiaparelli. Known for his use of colored gemstones, enamels, and motifs inspired by nature, Schlumberger became the first Tiffany designer whose jewels bore his signature. American-born Donald Claflin (d.1979), noted for his whimsical animal designs, joined Tiffany in 1965. Claflin had previously worked for David Webb. After opening an office in New York in 1946, and a salon in 1963, David Webb (1925-1975) came to prominence in the mid-1960s, when both clothing and jewelry styles were undergoing a significant change. He fostered, if not initiated, a trend for wearing quantities of large-scale, flamboyant jewels of Renaissance and fantasy-inspired design. Webb's animal motifs were influenced by Jeanne Toussaint of Cartier, creator of the famous panther jewels for the Duchess of Windsor and other wealthy clients.

Designers Verdura, Seaman Schepps and Suzanne Belperron remained active throughout the 1960s. Companies founded by Verdura, Schepps, Herz-Belperron, and Webb continue in business today.

In the late 1950s and 1960s, the fashion world turned to Italy, where clothing designers like Emilio Pucci were garnering attention. Italian jewelers were also creating a stir. The fashion for yellow gold created a new demand for Italian goldsmiths' talents. Foremost among Italian jewelers are the two family-run houses of Bulgari and Buccellati. The former is famous for its Renaissance-inspired colored gemstone pieces and classical designs incorporating ancient coins with heavy gold chains. Buccellati is known for its patterned texture engraving using a *bulino* graver, a technique also inspired by Renaissance goldwork, particularly that of Benvenuto Cellini. Both firms expanded to international branches, including the United States in 1952 (Buccellati) and 1970 (Bulgari).

Late 1950s and 1960s fine jewelry is the least well-defined of period genres. A few auction houses are beginning to recognize the 1950s as a period, including circa dates in their descriptions; others do not. Most 1960s jewelry is still described as contemporary or simply not dated. Auction house catalogs of important or magnificent (i.e., very expensive) jewelry usually include biographical information on designers and manufacturers, which can be quite helpful, but little other published data are currently available. A revised second edition of *Understanding Jewellery* (David Bennett and Daniela Mascetti, Antique Collectors' Club), with an additional chapter on 1960s and 1970s jewelry, was pub-

lished in December 1994. As the twenty-first century looms closer, historians will undoubtedly
acquire a clearer perspective on midtwentieth
century and later styles—perhaps someone will
even come up with names for them—and more
reference material will be published.

References: Graham Hughes, *Modern Jew-
elry, an International Survey, 1890-1967*, Crown
Publishers, 1968 (out of print); Penny Proddow
and Debra Healy, *American Jewelry*, Rizzoli In-
ternational, 1987; Penny Proddow, Debra Healy
and Marion Fasel, *Hollywood Jewels*, Harry N.
Abrams, 1992; Sylvie Raulet, *Jewelry of the 1940s
and 1950s*, Rizzoli International, 1987; Kenneth
Snowman, ed., *The Master Jewelers*, Harry N.
Abrams, 1990; Janet Zapata, "American Jewelry
Gains Ground at Auction," in *Jewelers Circular-
Keystone/Heritage*, March, 1993.

Advisor: Janet Zapata.

Bracelet
  Bangle
    Enamel, yg, c. 1962, hinged bangle of trans-
    parent yellow enamel accented with
    bands of ribbed yg and applied gold bead
    and lozenge shapes, sgd "Schlumberger,
    Paris," fitted leather case, ³/₄" w × 7"
    .... **18,700 (A)**
  Link
    18k yg, c. 1950, reeded intertwined oval
    links suspending a charm depicting Vec-
    chio Palazzio terminating in a push catch
    with safety, sgd "Tiffany & Co., Italy," 35
    dwt, ⁵/₈" w × 8" .... **2,640 (A)**
Brooch/Pendant
  18k yg, diamonds, c. 1960, elongated conical
  shape, satin finish yg topped with eight circ
  bc diamonds in a foliate design, pendant
  loop, sgd "Christian Dior," 8.3 dwt, ³/₈" w ×
  3-³/₈" .... **880 (A)**
  Jadeite, 18k yg, c. 1960, pierced and carved
  jadeite plaque, foliate motif within a yg hammered twisted rope motif frame, pendant
  loop, sgd "Webb," 35 dwt, 2-³/₄" w × 2"
  .... **2,420 (A)**
Brooch/Pin
  14k yg, rubies, c. 1950, a spray of flowers and
  leaves, ruby-set flowerhead centers and

**Brooch/Pin, yg, sapphires, diamonds, c. 1950, in the
shape of a pansy flowerhead with Florentine finish yg
petals, a center cluster of 24 prong-set circ blue sapphires, one curled petal edge pavé-set with six sm circ
diamonds, lever catch, unmkd, 1-³/₈" w × 1-⁵/₈", $1,100.
*Courtesy of E. Foxe Harrell Jewelers.***

round wire stems, 14.9 dwt, 1-³/₄" w × 2-¹/₂"
.... **605 (A)**
18k yg, enamel, diamonds, c. 1960, in the
shape of a tulip, petals *basse-taille* enameled
in yellow shading to orange with three dia-
mond-tipped stamens in the center, green
enameled leaf, and yg stem, rev mkd "18k
Italy," 1" w × 2-¹/₈" **650**
Coral, emeralds, diamonds, yg, plat, c. 1960, a
foliate spray of textured leaves and flower
buds, leaves terminating in diamonds set in
plat, with a flowerpod of an oval pink coral
cab, base of spray set with circ-cut and cab
emeralds, Am, sgd "Dunay" for Henry
Dunay, 17.2 dwt, 2-⁵/₈" w × 3" ... **3,300 (A)**
Diamonds, plat, 18k yg, c. 1950, foliate motif,
five diamond-set leaves, a marquise-cut diamond bud, collet-set diamond buds, and a sq
and baguette-cut diamond bud terminating
in a stem of baguette-cut diamonds, Fr,
attributed to Suzanne Belperron, 16.6 dwt,
102 diamonds, 1-⁷/₈" w × 2-¹/₄"
.... **13,200 (A)**
Diamonds, plat, 18k yg, c. 1960, pineapple

**Bracelet, flexible, rubies, sapphires, diamonds, 18k yg, c. 1945, of bombé form, encrusted with clusters of circ-cut
sapphire, ruby, and diamond flowers, sgd " Van Cleef & Arpels," # 49797, ³/₄" w × 6-¹/₂", $17,250 (A). *Photo © 1993
Sotheby's, Inc., New York (4/19/93).***

Brooch/Pin, platinum, diamonds, c. 1950, an irregularly shaped spray of plat wires with one curled edge, 22 baguettes, 2.3 cts tw, and 58 circ diamonds, 3.6 cts tw, scattered throughout, 1-¹/₂″ w × 2-³/₄″, $3,450 (A). Photo courtesy of Skinner, Inc., Boston (3/8/94).

shape in yg and plat set throughout with circ bc diamonds, 8.5 ct tw, sgd "David Webb," 27 dwt, 1-⁷/₈″ w × 3-¹/₄″ . . . . **9,350 (A)**

Diamonds, 18k yg, c. 1960, openwork leaf motif set throughout with circ bc diamonds, 3.5 ct tw, sgd "Tiffany & Co.," 18.6 dwt, 1-³/₄″ w × 2-⁵/₈″ . . . . **5,225 (A)**

Pearls, 14k yg, blue stones, c. 1950, a sculpted yg child holding a yg poodle, both with blue stone eyes, child standing on a cloud of freshwater pearls, back engraved "Friday's

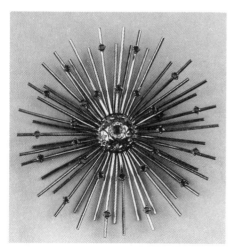

Brooch/Pin, 14k yg, rubies, diamonds, c. 1950, an atomic starburst of yg wires interspersed with prong-set rubies, radiating from a domed disk center set with sm diamonds around a ruby center, 3-³/₈″ dia, $978 (A). Photo courtesy of Skinner, Inc., Boston (3/8/94).

child is loving and giving," sgd "Ruser" for William Ruser, Beverly Hills, Calif., 20.4 dwt, 1-¹/₂″ w × 2-³/₈″ . . . . **2,420 (A)**

Sapphires, diamonds, platinum, c. 1950, a flower with invisibly set sapphire petals, diamond pistils in the center, and pavé-set diamond leaves with a baguette diamond stem, sgd by Van Cleef & Arpels, New York, # 31861, 1″ w × 1-¹/₂″ . . . . **18,700 (A)**

Earrings/Earclips

18k yg, sapphires, diamonds, c. 1950, star-shaped flowerhead with five reeded yg petals, sapphire and diamond center, clipbacks, 9.2 dwt, 1″ × 1″, pr . . . . **990 (A)**

18k yg, diamonds, c. 1950, each a five-petaled flowerhead of polished yg with diamond-set tips and center, 16.1 dwt, 1-¹/₈″ × 1-¹/₈″ . . . . **3,300 (A)**

Diamonds, 14k yg, c. 1960, each a flowerhead design with gold petals, one larger diamond in the center, interspersed with radiating smaller diamonds, 1.35 ct tw, screwbacks, ³/₄″ dia, pr . . . . **625 (A)**

Diamonds, 18k yg, c. 1950, overlapping leaf shapes with granulated yg tips, each pavé-set with 40 circ diamonds, approx 4.35 ct tw, within yg borders, sgd "Verdura, France," Fr hmk (Mercury's head), clipbacks, ⁷/₈″ w × 1-¹/₄″, pr . . . . **6,900 (A)**

Diamonds, emeralds, 18k yg, platinum, c. 1965, a pr of pear-shaped diamonds, approx 1.5 and 1.35 ct, each encircled by 18 channel-set calibré-cut emeralds framed by 28 circ diamonds within a four-row ropetwist yg wire mount of conforming pear shape, extending upward at the top, clipbacks, sgd "David Webb," ⁷/₈″ w × 1-¹/₄″, pr . . . . **9,775 (A)**

Diamonds, plat, 14k wg, c. 1950, each an upswept scroll motif with an oe diamond center, approx .9 ct tw, flanked by 25 grad circ diamonds accented by three baguette-cut and smalller circ diamonds, ⁵/₈″ w × 1-¹/₄″, pr . . . . **4,400 (A)**

Diamonds, sapphires, 18k yg and wg, c. 1960, flowerhead motif with a raised cluster of circ diamonds in the center, 5 ct tw, outlined with circ sapphires, within twisted gold wire frames, sgd "Van Cleef & Arpels" # 1881SO, 15 dwt, 1-¹/₄″ dia, pr . . . . **8,250 (A)**

Shell, rubies, sapphires, 14k yg, c. 1960, white turbo shell with spirals of yg tubing accented at each end with a cabochon sapphire or ruby, sgd "Seaman Schepps, P.S.V.," 1″ w × 1-¹/₄″, pr . . . . **3,080 (A)**

Turquoise, diamonds, yg, wg, c. 1955, stylized pinwheel motif, each with a raised center cluster of round turquoise cabs and circ diamonds, framed by radiating, spiraling reeded yg strips accented on the outside edges with tapered baguette-cut and circ diamonds, ap-

prox 3 ct tw, sgd "Cartier, Pat 2557200" (1951), clipbacks, 17.3 dwt, 1-¼" dia, pr
. . . . **7,150 (A)**

Necklace

18k yg, c. 1950, a line of interlocking oval links, each composed of fused, slightly twisted baton-shaped segments, sgd "M. Buccellati, Italy," 82 dwt, 17-¼" tl × ¾"
. . . . **3,520 (A)**

18k yg, c. 1960, fringe style, alternating textured and polished yg cylindrical elements accented with gold balls, Italian hmks, 36.6 dwt, 16-¾" tl × 1"w . . . . **880 (A)**

Pendant

Citrine, 14k yg, c. 1950, a very large circ-cut citrine, 46.75 × 30mm, surmounted by a yg stylized leaf spray at the top, continuing to a tapering yg bail, partial bezel at top and bottom, 56.4 dwt, pendant 1-⅞"dia
. . . . **440 (A)**

Ring

18k yg and wg, diamonds, c. 1950, a slightly rounded band encircled with a row of six circ diamonds set within starburst motifs, evenly spaced, with smaller engr starbursts in between, sgd "M. Buccellati, Italy," 3.3 dwt, ¼" w, ring size 4-¼ . . . . **1,760 (A)**

Cat's-eye chrysoberyl, diamonds, 18k wg, plat, c. 1950, crossover style terminating in two prong-set, round brown/black cabochon-cut cat's-eye chrysoberyls, a grad row of diamond baguettes on each shoulder, ¾" w × ⅝", ring size 4 . . . . **8,800 (A)**

Platinum, 18k yg, diamonds, c. 1965, a reeded yg dome with a domed plat center pavé-set with 83 sc diamonds, approx 1 ct tw, sgd "Webb" for David Webb, ⅝" dia
. . . . **2,070 (A)**

Suite: Brooch/Pin and Earrings

14k yg, amethyst, c. 1955, a pinwheel design brooch with an emerald-cut amethyst in the center, mkd "14k," and a pr of matching earrings with oval-cut amethyst centers, clipbacks mkd "Pat. No. 2583985" (1952), brooch 1-½" w × 1-¾", earrings ⅞", suite
. . . . **374(A)**

Suite: Pendant/Brooch, Necklace, Bracelet, Pendent Earrings, Ring

14k yg, pearls, diamonds, wg, c. 1960, Renaissance style, an openwork quatrefoil pendant/

Suite: Bracelet, Brooch/Pin and Earrings, 18k yg, diamonds, emeralds, c. 1960, a flexible bracelet of interlocking twisted wire flowerheads with emerald and diamond-set petals, 144 diamonds, approx 4.85 cts tw, sgd "Van Cleef & Arpels," # 5381, Fr hmks, v-spring and box clasp, approx 7-¼" × 1" (sold separately), $9,775 (A); matching brooch, a wire-twist yg foliate spray set with emeralds and 89 diamonds, approx 2.8 cts tw, and a pr of earrings set with emeralds and 42 diamonds, 1.75 cts tw, sgd "Van Cleef & Arpels," Fr hmks, brooch 2" w × 1-⅞", earrings ¾" × ⅞", suite, $9,200 (A). *Photo courtesy of Skinner, Inc., Boston (3/8/94).*

brooch with one lg oval baroque pearl in the center, quartered by similar baroque pearls, within a looped filigree yg frame accented with sm sc diamonds, 37.4 dwt, 3" × 3", a necklace of eight oval filigree plaques, each with a baroque pearl center, joined by heart-shaped links, sc diamond accents, loop for pendant, continuing to back links of similar design, detachable 7" extension can be worn as a bracelet, 20-½" l × 1", ring an open oval design with a baroque pearl center in a basket style mount attached to a fluted hoop shank, sc diamond accents, 18.3 dwt, size 6, pendent earrings, each suspending a plaque of similar design set with a baroque pearl, sc diamond accents, clipbacks, 11.7 dwt, 1-¾" w × 1-⅜", suite . . . . **4,500 (A)**

POSTWAR MODERNIST JEWELRY C. 1945-1965

Sam Kramer

Margaret De Patta

History: Just as the adherents of the Arts and Crafts movement rebelled against mainstream tradition at the turn of the century, so too did studio artists of the midcentury follow a path of their own. They reinterpreted the earlier movement's guiding principles in new forms with new approaches to design, creating a new definition of the word modern, with which the 1950s came to be identified. True to the Arts and Crafts philosophy, the emphasis was on design, hand-craftsmanship and accessibility to the public. Gold and precious stones were used on occasion, but sterling was the preferred metal, alone or in combination, most often with stones of the quartz family, cultured pearls, wood, brass, copper, and enamels. Although the jewelry was meant to be affordable for most people, the audience for these pieces was not wide. As was also the case at the turn of the century, this was not jewelry for the masses, but rather for an intellectual elite—the Beat Generation—that congregated primarily in urban centers on the East and West coasts. The beatniks were more ready and willing to accept the avant-garde designs that artist-jewelers produced than the average suburban housewife. Still, as the crafts movement gathered momentum, demand did grow, and some jewelers attempted to manufacture more commercialized production pieces. Many of their hand-crafted designs were not well-suited to mass production, however, and when demand increased, prices for one-of-kind pieces by well-known artists went up. Today these pieces—by important designers such as Sam Kramer and Margaret De Patta—command thousands of dollars.

The midcentury modernist movement had its roots in prewar Europe, under the influence of the Bauhaus and fine and applied arts "isms" such as Dadaism, Surrealism, Cubism, Biomorphism, and Constructivism. Several European painters and sculptors of these artistic schools also designed jewelry, among them: Salvador Dalí, Pablo Picasso, Jean Cocteau, and Georges Braque. In crossing the Atlantic, however, these influences were translated into a uniquely American idiom by artists who were jewelry makers as well as designers. This was true even when the European influences were more direct. Some American metalsmiths studied under leaders of the move-

ment who had come to the United States just before the war and set up schools of design or became directors of design programs at established schools and universities. Among them were Walter Gropius, Marcel Breuer, and László Moholy-Nagy of the Bauhaus. Other influences came from Scandinavia, where modernism flourished under the auspices of several important designers and their companies (see the Scandinavian jewelry section).

Still another source of education came, surprisingly, from the U.S. government. After World War II, many returning veterans entered into government-sponsored vocational programs. Workshops were led by metalsmith Margaret Craver Withers from 1947 to 1951. These helped to generate interest in pursuing the study of crafts further through the G.I. Bill. In response to this growing interest, a number of how-to books on jewelry-making were published from the late 1940s through the 1960s. Today, these books are invaluable resources for the historian, because they picture and give information about the work of modernist jewelers (see references following).

The overriding concepts characterizing the modernists' work were abstraction and nonobjective form, but each interpreted these concepts in different ways and with a variety of techniques. Artist-jeweler Philip Morton, author of a how-to book, *Contemporary Jewelry, a Studio Handbook,* in evaluating the work of midcentury metalsmiths, divides design into two groups, or expressive modes: rational and nonrational. Within each mode, he names several forms and techniques: plate-shape, linear, strip-plate, constructed, fused, forged, and cast. Each approach yielded a unique design, and yet for all their differences, there is an identifiable cohesiveness uniting the overall body of work by these artists. Space does not permit discussion of the finer points of all their work here. However, mention should be made of the seminal, influential, and important American studio jewelers whose work is collected today.

Sam Kramer (1913-1964), one of the first, and perhaps the most avant-garde studio artist of them all, began making jewelry in 1936, a full decade before the crafts movement was truly established. He opened a shop in New York City's Greenwich

Village in 1939. His work, and his personality, were a decided departure from the ordinary, a fact that he emphasized in advertising his wares as "fantastic jewelry for people who are slightly mad." He was called a "surrealistic jeweler" by *The New Yorker* magazine. Kramer was known for incorporating bizarre materials like taxidermists' glass eyes and found objects into even more bizarre biomorphic fused, cast, and constructed designs such as "Creature Brooch," "Skeletal Cuff," and "Pterodactyl Brooch." His mark, a mushroom inside a lobed circle, gave him the nickname, "Mushroom Sam"; like some of his pieces, the mushroom had erotic implications. Not all of Kramer's work were one-of-a-kind oddities. He did make some multiples of designs in a constructivist mode. Perhaps they were meant for his slightly less mad customers, but today these pieces bring slightly less money.

Several other studio artists set up shop in Greenwich Village in the 1940s and 1950s, taking advantage of the favorable intellectual climate there. Among them, Paul Lobel (1900-1983) successfully maintained a commercial production operation from about 1945 to 1964, making large cuff bracelets and brooches from cutout silver sheet and soldered forged wire. He was known for both nonobjective designs and abstract figurals such as musical instruments, animals, fruit, and leaf forms, all of which were given names in his catalogs. Art Smith (1917-1982), also worked in sheet and forged silver wire (as well as brass and other metals), and although he was influenced by Lobel, his work was more sculptural and biomorphic, using the human body as a point of departure or supportive framework for his designs. In 1948, Smith opened a shop in the Village, a few doors down from Lobel's. He signed his name in script on some, but not all, of his pieces. Ed Wiener (1918-1991), began working in his own shop in 1946, in Provincetown, Mass., but opened a store in New York City soon after, called "Arts and Ends." His long career, ending only with his death a few years ago, encompassed a succession of stylistic approaches, wrought or cast in silver and gold, often with the addition of gemstones. His signature is his name in lowercase print, but his jewelry is not always signed.

Ronald H. Pearson (b. 1924) was one of the founding fathers of Shop I in Rochester, N.Y. Opened in 1952, Shop I was the first independent gallery to exhibit and sell modern crafts exclusively. Pearson's work in forged or cast silver or gold is characterized by graceful simplicity of form, reminiscent of Scandinavian design. His successful commercial business still operates today. Pearson now resides and works in Deer Isle, Maine.

Other East Coast artist-jewelers of note (New York City unless otherwise specified): Harry Bertoia (1915-1978, Bally, Pa., formerly Detroit and Los Angeles), Jules Brenner, Alexander Calder (1898-1976), Betty Cooke (Baltimore), Ed Levin (b. 1921), Earl Pardon (1926-1991, Saratoga Springs, N.Y.), Olaf Skoogfors (1930-1973, Philadelphia), Henry Steig, (1906-1973), and Bill Tendler.

On the opposite coast, in Northern California, Margaret De Patta's rational approach was the opposite of Sam Kramer's nonrational one, but her influence on others was seminal, and possibly greater than his. A modernist pioneer, De Patta (1903-1964) began jewelry making in 1930 and had her own workshop by 1935. She established a studio in the San Francisco Bay Area in 1941, after studying with László Moholy-Nagy at his Bauhaus-oriented School of Design in Chicago. In 1946, disturbed by the fact that demand had driven up prices so that her jewelry was becoming inaccessible to the average person, De Patta and husband Eugene Bielawski responded by going into limited production of some of her designs using lost-wax casting methods. Each piece sold for less than $50. The energy and time-consuming tasks required to run the business caused them to abandon this endeavor in 1958.

De Patta's constructivist techniques yielded jewelry with optical effects achieved by combining specially cut or faceted transparent stones with metal rods, wire, sheet, or textured surfaces. Her pieces were three-dimensional spatial studies. She worked in both silver and gold, occasionally using diamonds, but more often rock crystal and rutilated quartz and other inexpensive gemstones. Her mark is a stylized M surmounted by a dot; she sometimes used her last name, with or without her mark. Today, most of De Patta's work sells for $1,000 and up.

In 1951, De Patta initiated the organization of the Metal Arts Guild in San Francisco, a resource, information, and support network for local metalsmiths. Joining this group were several artists who made names for themselves in the 1950s and 1960s. All of them give credit to De Patta as an inspirational and influential mentor. Some of them are still living and working today. Irena Brynner (b. 1917), who lived in San Francisco until 1956, started making jewelry in 1950. Her work there was constructivist and geometric. In 1956, she moved to New York, where she changed her techniques to lost-wax casting and welding, and her style became looser and more organic. She signs her pieces with her first initial and last name, alternately spelled with one or two n's.

One of Irena Brynner's early influences was Claire Falkenstein (b. 1908). While not a member of the Metal Arts Guild, Falkenstein was an inspiration to several members of that group (she lived in San Francisco before moving to Paris in 1950). She is a painter, and a metal sculptor who utilizes the same linear forging techniques applied to her larger works for her jewelry. Her work was exhibited at the Louvre in Paris, as well as in several galleries and museums in the United States. She made her first piece of jewelry in the mid-1940s. During the 1950s, she made a series of large neckpieces of forged silver or gold wire, incuding unusual inverted U-shaped and C-shaped pieces with undulating organic lines. Her mark is a superimposed CF. Falkenstein has not made jewelry for about 10 years, but she maintains a studio in Venice, Calif., where she lives and works as a painter.

Peter Macchiarini (b. 1909) made his first piece of jewelry in 1937, but it wasn't until after the war that he was able to set up a studio and workshop. He was one of the founding members of the Metal Arts Guild, and worked in the constructivist mode with a variety of materials, including ivory, ebony, brass, and copper. He signed his pieces with his first initial and last name, or last name alone. Macchiarini still lives and works in San Francisco's North Beach.

Merry Renk, another Metal Arts Guild founding member, has explored a number of techniques and forms, including *plique à jour* enamel, forged wire, lost-wax cast folded fabric, and solderless interlocking shapes. In 1947, she studied at the Institute of Design in Chicago, where she first exhibited in a gallery opened with two other students. Renk moved to San Francisco in 1948, where she still lives and works as a watercolorist, but she is no longer making jewelry. She signed her work with her last name in lowercase script.

When Florence Resnikoff moved to the San Francisco area from Chicago in 1951, she had already acquired the metalsmithing skills that would enable her to join the Metal Arts Guild and continue her development as a professional. Under the guild's influence, she studied structure, form, and color using a combination of materials and techniques such as forging and casting, acid-etching, repoussé, and fabrication. Her early work is primarily constructivist, but later pieces are a varied mixture of organic as well as geometric forms. Today, Resnikoff resides and works in Oakland, Calif.

Richard Gompf (b. 1928), who still lives in San Francisco, also credits De Patta with influencing his work, although, as the youngest of the group, he began a bit later than the others. His forms are Bauhaus-inspired, and his preferred technique is sand-casting, which gives weight and texture to his abstract shapes. He does not sign his pieces, but they have been exhibited and are pictured in a book on metal techniques by Marcia Chamberlain (see the references following).

Other notable West Coast artist-jewelers include Franz Bergman (San Francisco), Esther Lewittes (Los Angeles), Harry Osaki (Pasadena, Calif.), Coralynn Pence (Seattle, Wash.), Caroline Rosene (San Francisco), and Bob Winston (Oakland, Calif.).

In addition to these and other recognized met-

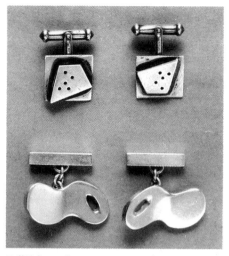

Cuff Links, sterling, c. 1950: T, a sq plaque surmounted by a pierced quadrilateral plaque, oxidized around edges, rev mkd "sterling," sgd "Rosene" for Caroline Gleick Rosene, San Francisco, Calif., hinged backs mkd "sterling, Pat. 2544893" (1951), ⅝" sq, pr, $75; B, a slightly concave irregular figure-eight-shaped plaque with a cutout oval at one end joined with cable links to a bar of heavy-gauge sq wire, rev mkd "Lewittes sterling" for Esther Lewittes, Los Angeles, Calif., 1-⅛" × ½", pr, $125, *Courtesy of Before Antiques.*

alsmiths, there were many lesser-known and unknown studio artists whose work has found its way into the collectibles marketplace. Because many studio artists supplemented their income by teaching classes in jewelry making, their students' work, much of it unsigned, has also filtered into the secondary market. Some unsigned pieces are very well made and designed, others are amateurish and imitative. A practiced eye will distinguish between the two.

Modernist midcentury jewelry is a specialized genre that does not appeal to everyone. But a dedicated and burgeoning corps of astute collectors, who, like the makers themselves, tend to be outside the mainstream, have caused interest to grow and prices to rise. Because the jewelry was mostly handmade and one or few of a kind, a limited quantity is available for sale today. Pieces by the most sought after artists are occasionally seen at twentieth-century decorative arts, rather than fine jewelry, auctions (Skinner's in Boston is the exception). Dealers who sell this type of jewelry are most often found at twentieth-century design shows and galleries in large cities.

Reproduction Alert: According to Steve Cabella, owner of The Modern i Gallery in San Anselmo, Calif., plagiarism does exist in modernist jewelry; there are some outright fraudulent copies being made. There are also authentic limited reproductions, which are openly advertised as such, as well as newly made pieces by the original artist being sold as old ones. These are not fakes, but most collectors prefer pieces to have the "historical patina" (Cabella's words) of the artist's earlier work. The usual caveats apply: When paying a substantial price for a piece, make sure there is substantial documentation for it as well, or that the dealer from whom the piece is purchased is reputable and knowledgeable enough to guarantee the authenticity and circa date of his or her merchandise.

References: Marcia Chamberlain, *Metal Jewelry Techniques,* Watson-Guptill Publications, 1976 (out of print); Graham Hughes, *Modern Jewelry, an International Survey, 1890-1967,* Crown Publishers, 1968 (out of print); Charles J. Martin, *How to Make Modern Jewelry,* Musuem of Modern Art, 1949 (out of print); Philip Morton, *Contemporary Jewelry, A Studio Handbook,* Holt, Rinehart and Winston, 1970 (out of print); Robert von Neumann, *The Design and Creation of Jewelry,* revised ed., Chilton Book Co, 1972; Sylvie Raulet, *Jewelry of the 1940s and 1950s,* Rizzoli International, 1987; Ralph Turner, *Contemporary Jewelry, a Critical Assessment, 1945-1975,* Van Nostrand Reinhold, 1976 (out of print); Oppi Untracht, *Jewelry Concepts and Technology,* Doubleday, 1985; exhibition catalogs: Martin Eidelberg, ed., *Design 1935-1965, What Modern Was,* Harry N. Abrams, 1991; *The Jewelry of Margaret De Patta,* The Oakland Museum, 1976; *Jewelry By Ed Wiener, Retrospective Exhibition,* Fifty-50 Gallery, New York, 1988; *Structure and Ornament, American Modernist Jewelry, 1940-1960,* Fifty-50 Gallery, New York, 1984.

Periodical: *Metalsmith,* quarterly journal of the Society of North American Goldsmiths, 5009 Londonderry Drive, Tampa, Fla. 33647. Over the last dozen years, past issues have published monographs on many noted midcentury and later metalsmiths, as well as more general articles on the history of metalsmithing in the United States and abroad. A great deal of the information for this section was obtained from these articles. From 1987 to 1992, monographs on Betty Cooke, Claire Falkenstein, Ed Levin, Paul Lobel, Peter Macchiarini, Art Smith, Ed Wiener, and Byron Wilson were authored by Toni Lesser Wolf (now known as Toni Greenbaum). Back issues are available at the above address.

Museums: The American Craft Museum, New York City; The Renwick Gallery at the Smithsonian Institution, Washington D.C.; The Oakland Museum, Oakland, Calif., houses an extensive collection of jewelry by Margaret De Patta; Schmuckmuseum, Pforzheim, Germany; Le Musée des Arts Décoratifs de Montréal, Québec, Canada, maintains a collection of modern decorative arts, including jewelry, that was part of the touring exhibit, "Design 1935-1965, What Modern Was," 1991-1993. A comprehensive exhibition of American studio jewelry, c. 1940-1960,

with catalog by guest curator Toni Greenbaum, will open at the Montreal museum in May, 1995, and travel worldwide through March, 1998.

Advisors: Steve Cabella, Toni Greenbaum, and Ellen Hoffs.

Bracelet
  Bangle
    Sterling, c. 1965, solid cast undulating form with an oxidized incised center groove of corresponding form, mkd "Reed & Barton © sterling," sgd "Pearson" for Ronald H. Pearson, Rochester, N.Y., 2-⅝" inside dia, ½" w at widest point **145**
  Cuff
    Sterling, c. 1960, a tapered flat band with appl round wire looped and bent around one edge of band, terminating in a lg ster bead soldered to front surface off-center, mkd "Orb sterling" on front of one end for Orb Silversmiths (Otto R. Bade, New Hope, Pa.), 2-¼" inside dia, 1-⅛" tapering to ⅝" end-to-end **100**
    Sterling, c. 1950, sandcast, tapered and ridged asymmetrical sculptured cuff, by Richard Gompf, San Francisco, Calif., 2" inside dia × ⅜" **250**
    Sterling, c. 1950, cuff formed from a tapered ster strip bisected horizontally by a length of heavy-gauge sq wire wrapped with

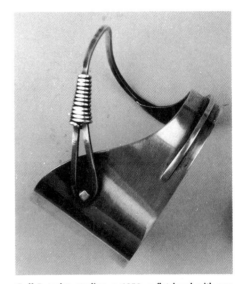

Cuff Bracelet, sterling, c. 1950, a flat band with one curved edge tapering from 2" w at one end to ½" w at the other, a length of sq wire appl to half of front surface and continuing outward in an extended curve, terminating in a wire-wrapped loop attached to a sq peg mounted on wide portion of cuff surface, sgd "Lobel" for Paul Lobel, New York, N.Y., 2-½" dia, $2,415 (A).
Photo courtesy of Skinner, Inc., Boston (3/8/94).

three coils of round wire with bead-tipped ends, evenly spaced across center front, mkd "sterling," sgd "Jules Brenner," New York, N.Y., 2-¼" inside dia, 1" w tapering to ⅝"(end to end) **350**

Flexible

Silver, brass, copper, c. 1950 design, hinged sq boxes, brass sides, silver top and bottom, copper center in layers with a central cutout freeform design cut through each layer, appl green patina on surfaces of inner layers, rev sgd "Macchiarini" for Peter Macchiarini, San Francisco, Calif., v-spring and box clasp, safety chain, 7-¼" × ¾" **1,000**

Brooch/Pendant

Sterling, c. 1950, circ cast bas-relief design of a sun face, rev sgd "Olaf Skoogfors," Philadelphia, Pa., 1-½" dia **200**

Brooch/Pin

Brass, enamel, c. 1950, convex-sided rect plaque, cloisonné enameled design of overlapping vasiform shapes in shades of periwinkle blue, purple, and pink on red ground, rev counter-enameled, unsgd, 2-⅛" w × 1-½" **150**

Brass, enamel, c. 1950, rounded sq convex plaque, cloisonné enameled wheel design with radiating spokes forming sections in alternating shades of dk and lt green, unsgd, 1-⅝" × 1-⅝" **150**

Copper, silver, brass, fire opal, c. 1950, stylized fish shape, a cutout copper plaque surmounted by a silver disk with appl brass beads, coiled copper wire, and an oval bezel-set fire opal eye, sm notch in disk for mouth, rev sgd "Loyola Fourtane Sausalito California" in engr script, 1-⅞" w × 1-¾" **175**

Sterling, c. 1950, an oxidized triangular plaque with one rounded corner, raised edge on two sides, surmounted by an ovoid concave plaque with a central bezel-set circ moonstone mounted off-center and projecting over the flat edge of the triangle, rev sgd "ed wiener," New York, N.Y., 2" × 2" **450**

Sterling, c. 1950, a single piece of forged wire formed into concentric squares, sgd "ed

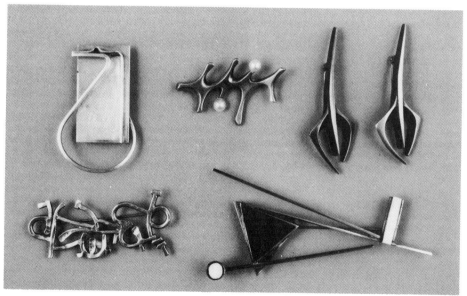

TL, Brooch/Pendant, c. 1950, a flat rect plaque with a perpendicular angled and folded strip mounted edgewise, joined at one side to an angled and curved length of sq wire projecting out and around to back of rectangle, rev mkd "sterling," sgd "Lobel" for Paul Lobel, New York, N.Y., 2-⅛" × 1-¼", $175; Brooches/Pins, sterling: TC, c. 1950, a cast abstract branch-like form, a cultured pearl mounted on the ends of two branches, rev sgd "Osaki" for Harry Osaki, Pasadena, Calif., 1-¾" × 1-⅛", $300; TR, c. 1960, a matched pr, each a slightly curved tapered vertical bar flanked at the base by opposed shaped tapered and cusped crescents, cast with polished and oxidized textured surfaces, rev mkd "sterling" and "S" for Christian F. Schmidt, Minneapolis, Minn., ⅞" w × 2-½", pr, $150; BL, c. 1950, an openwork abstract hammered wire design of conjoined loops and bars of varying lengths, rev mkd "sterling Levin" for Ed Levin, New York, N.Y., 2-½" × 1", $125; BR, c. 1950, constructed of angled, slightly tapered bars of ster and copper, a lg ebony triangle bezel-set and mounted on a brass triangle, a baton, and sm disk of ivory bezel-set in brass mounted at ends of bars, rev sgd "P Macchiarini" for Peter Macchiarini, San Francisco, Calif., 4" w × 1-⅝", $500, *Courtesy of Before Antiques.*

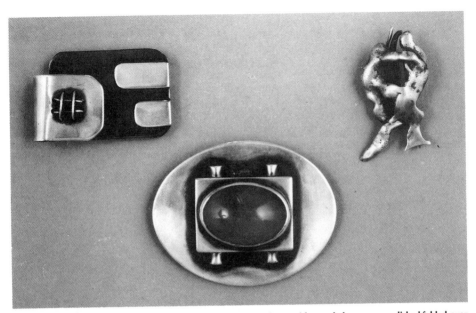

Brooches/Pins, sterling, Sam Kramer, c. 1950: L, an oxidized rect plaque with rounded corners, a polished folded-over extension on one side set with a sq-cut carnelian within a ster wire cage in the center, two rounded rect polished flat segments of unequal length soldered on opposite side, rev mkd "sterling," maker's mark for Sam Kramer, New York, N.Y. (a mushroom within a lobed circle), 1-⅞" w × 1-¼", $650, *Author's collection;* C, a flat oval plaque, oxidized center, surmounted by a rect plaque mounted on two vertical rods and bezel-set with a translucent beige and caramel-colored oval agate cab, rev mkd "sterling," maker's mark, 2-⅝" w × 2", $850; R, a cast abstract design of an embracing male and female couple with an oxidized bg of pierced undulating reed shapes, maker's mark, 1" w × 2", $750, *Courtesy of Before Antiques.*

weiner," originally designed in 1946, 2" w × 2-¼" **375**

Sterling, c. 1950, a heart shape with cutout center and scalloped edges, numerous criss-crossing incised lines on polished surface, rev mkd "sterling," maker's mark for Sam Kramer, New York, N.Y. (mushroom in a lobed circle), 2" w × 2-½" **475**

Sterling, glass eye, c. 1950, an irregularly shaped ster plaque with a center bezel-set yellow glass eye surmounted by an appl grooved ster crescent shape resembling an eyelid, rev imp "sterling," maker's mark for Sam Kramer, 2-½" w × 1-½" . . . . **2,860 (A)**

Sterling, rock crystal, c. 1948, an open ovoid of flat wire with a superimposed V-shape of flat wire terminating in a bezel-set crystal cab at one end, a short round wire crossbar at the other, a flat plaque mounted in the center of the V, with two rows of sm perforations on one side, rev mkd "sterling," maker's mark for Margaret De Patta, San Francisco, Calif., 3-¼" w × 2" . . . . **1,840 (A)**

Sterling, rock crystal, c. 1950, a rounded elongated triangular plaque with a rounded triangular section cut out from one edge into the center, a circ crystal cab bezel-set between the opening edges, an appl cut-to-shape ster section with incised parallel lines on opposite side, a textured ster ovoid mounted and projecting from behind plaque, rev mkd "sterling," maker's mark for Margaret De Patta, 3" × 2" **3,500**

Sterling, c. 1950, a convex rect plaque with appl round wire around a central domed disk in a pinwheel design, rev mkd "Lewittes sterling" for Esther Lewittes, Los Angeles, Calif., 2-½" w × 1-½" **150**

Sterling, c. 1950, entitled "Intersection" (© 1949), a scrolled and looped tapered stylized leaf shape with a center strip mounted edgewise and extending past the wide scrolled end, rev sgd "Lobel" for Paul Lobel, New York, N.Y., 4" × 2" **275**

Sterling, c. 1950, a stylized horse's head, a plaque with cutout and appl design elements, eye, jaw, and mane, mkd "Lobel sterling" for Paul Lobel, New York, N.Y., 1-⅛" w × 1-½" **650**

Sterling, c. 1950, an irregular tapering sq wire horseshoe shape with an angled tapered textured bar at one end, enclosing a twisted volute of flat wire, sgd "P. Macchiarini" in engr script for Peter Macchiarini, San Francisco, Calif., 2-¼" w × 1-⅝" **300**

Sterling, c. 1950, cast freeform with textured

concave and raised surfaces, rev mkd "sterling," sgd "Rima ©," New York, N.Y., 2-½" w × 1-¾" **150**

Sterling, c. 1950, in the shape of a stylized penguin, lg oval and sm D-shaped plaques with raised edges forming body and head, a strip of flat wire mounted edgewise in an S-curve forming beak, wing and tail, rev sgd "Rosene," for Caroline Gleick Rosene, San Fransisco, Calif., mkd "sterling," 1-⅛" w × 3" **125**

Sterling, c. 1950, a stylized fish shape, an oxidized plaque with folded-over tapered segments of polished ster, polished rod eye, curved tapered tail, rev mkd "sterling," sgd "Tendler" for Bill Tendler, New York, N.Y., 2-⅛" w × ¾" **125**

Sterling, c. 1955, a slightly curved and tapered horizontal bar, with a cast sphere at the end of a short length of round wire mounted at a narrow angle surmounting the bar, imp "sterling, Cooke" for Betty Cooke, Baltimore, Md., 5" w .... **230 (A)**

Sterling, c. 1960, four cast textured curved bars, superimposed and intersecting at various angles, one upon another, rev mkd "sterling," sgd "Tendler" for Bill Tendler, New York, N.Y., 2-⅞" w × 3" **150**

Sterling, moonstones, variscite, c. 1950, a biomorphic triangular plaque with two circ moonstones and one circ variscite cab set in bezels mounted on posts above oxidized ground, enclosed within a frame set in from plaque edges, rev imp "Alex sterling" in block letters, 2-⅛" w × 1-½" **350**

Bar

Sterling, c. 1950, a flat bar with a half-tubular segment appl to upper left section, two folded-up parallel edges along bottom right side, rev mkd "sterling," maker's mark for Margaret De Patta, San Francisco, Calif., 2-⅛" w × ⅜" **300**

Earrings/Earclips

Sterling, c. 1950, irregular freeform (biomorphic) shaped plaques with irregular cutout sections and appl domed ovals, imp "sterling," maker's mark for Sam Kramer, 1-¼" w × 1-⅝" .... **990 (A)**

Sterling, c. 1950, a slightly twisted wide U-shaped plaque with appl forged crescent-shaped wire, one flattened end extending beyond plaque, oxidized surface around wire, unmkd, attributed to Art Smith, New York, N.Y., screwbacks, 1-¼" w × ⅞", pr **150**

Sterling, pearl, c. 1950, a concave rounded-corner triangle with oxidized surface set with a cultured pearl in one corner, rev mkd "sterling Lewittes" for Esther Lewittes, screwbacks, ⅝" × ⅝", pr **100**

Sterling, c. 1950, a circ disk with oxidized off-center circ depression, raised circ center rod with polished top surface, one earring rev imp "sterling," the other earring mkd "Levin," for Ed Levin, triangular clipbacks, ½" dia, pr **125**

Sterling, c. 1960, a concave disk with oxidized surface, a pearl mounted on a vertical wire in the center, rev mkd "sterling Levin," for Ed Levin, screwpost backs (for pierced ears), ⅝" dia, pr **50**

Sterling, c. 1950, a cutout boomerang-shaped plaque vertically bisected by a slightly curved oxidized strip of rect wire mounted edgewise, rev mkd "sterling," sgd "Steig" for Henry Steig, 1-¼" tl × ¾", pr **75**

Sterling, white stone, c. 1950, a rounded-corner rect plaque with a U-shaped strip mounted edgewise around sides and base, curv round wire piercing a round white stone bead mounted horizontally within U-shape, rev sgd "C. Pence" for Coralynn Pence, Seattle, Wash., screwbacks mkd "sterling," 1" × ¾", pr **85**

Pendent

Copper, enamel, c. 1950, a cutout angular abstract shape suspended from a semicirc surmount, orange enameled surface with an appl grid design of gilt enamel, rev sgd "Resnikoff" (engr script), screwbacks, 1-¾" tl × 1-¼", pr **150**

Copper, enamel, c. 1950, a cutout abstract vasiform shape with pierced center design of perpendicular lines and circles suspended from a sq surmount, vermilion enameled surface, rev sgd "Resnikoff" (engr script), screwbacks, 1-⅜" tl × ⅝", pr **100**

Sterling, c. 1960, a cutout tapered and elongated horseshoe-shaped drop surmounted by three uneven lengths of sq wire mounted horizontally and diagonally and extending past outer edges of drop, suspended from a cutout hole at the base of a rounded triangular surmount, post and clutch backs, unsgd, 2-¼" tl × 1", pr **175**

Sterling, c. 1950, a biomorphic four-lobed convex shape with a pierced design in each lobe: volute, asterisk, sperm, and undulating line, suspended from a two-lobed U-shaped surmount with a pierced U-shaped undulating line in the center, rev mkd "F. Miraglia N.Y. sterling," for Frank Miraglia, New York, N.Y., screwbacks, 2-½" tl × 1-⅛", pr **150**

Sterling, c. 1950, a textured trapezoidal plaque suspended within a bent strip forming a triangle suspended edgewise by round wire from an angled and looped strip surmount, plaque mkd "sterling," sgd "Steig" for Henry Steig, New York, N.Y., screwbacks, 2-¼" tl × ½", pr **150**

Sterling, c. 1960, an oxidized zigzag plaque

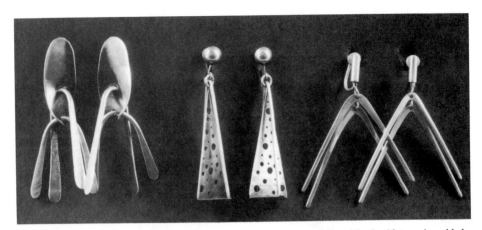

Pendent Earrings, sterling, c. 1950: L, a twisted vertical oval surmount, partially oxidized, with two pierced holes suspending two splayed U-shaped forged wire drops with flattened ends, hanging freely at right angles to one another, one surmount rev sgd, in script, "Art Smith," New York, N.Y., screwbacks mkd "sterling," 2" tl × 1-⅛", pr, $525; C, an elongated open pyramid shape formed with sq wire and a triangular plaque perforated with various sized circ holes, suspended from a domed surmount, base of pyramid mkd "sterling," sgd "I Bryner" for Irena Brynner, San Francisco/New York, screwback findings, 2" tl × ½", pr, $450; R, each constructed of two forged inverted V-shapes suspended free-swinging, one above the other, from a vertical tube-shaped surmount, mkd "sterling," sgd "renk" in lower-case script for Merry Renk, San Francisco, C.A., screwbacks, 2-¼" tl × 1-¾", pr, $250, *Courtesy of Before Antiques.*

surmounted by an appl sq wire of conforming shape, terminating in three round beads, suspended by a bead-tipped wire link from an inverted rounded triangular surmount with an appl undulating length of sq wire, post and handmade clutch backs, unsgd, attributed to Ed Wiener, 2" tl × ½", pr **250**

Sterling, c. 1960, biomorphic design, a forged L-shaped round wire hammered flat at the top, bent 90° with end mounted on an oxidized cutout tapered plaque, suspended from a rounded triangular surmount, hook earwire, rev imp "phyllis sterling" for Phyllis Maldonado, 2-¼" tl × ¾", pr **125**

Neckband
Sterling, c. 1965, forged rounded-end V-shape, flattened in front, tapering to curved ends in back, mkd "sterling," sgd "Pearson" for Ronald H. Pearson, 5-¼" w × 6-½" back to front, ¼" at center front **275**

Necklace
Bib
Sterling, rutilated quartz, c. 1950, five linked concave ovoid disks, each set with a quartz cab and each suspending another similar quartz-set disk, continuing to a flat oval and circ wire link chain, unmkd, 17-½" tl × 2" at center **800**

Chain
Sterling, c. 1950, heavy sand-cast oval and circ links and rods with crossbars in an alternating pattern of two and four per rod, split oval ring clasp, by Richard Gompf, San Francisco, Calif., 20-½" tl × ⅝" **800**

Choker
Sterling, gemstones, c. 1950, center section of nine stones, irregularly shaped, tumble-polished amethyst, peridot, and pink tourmaline, bezels formed around stones and mounted on cut-to-shape backplates linked with circ round wire jump rings, continuing to flat oval and circ round wire ster links, soldered plate mounted on rev mkd "sterling hand made H. Fred Skaggs," 14-½" tl × 1-½" **350**

Collar
Sterling, turquoise, garnet, c. 1950, six lg lobed, biomorphic freeform links, each suspending four matchstick-shaped drops of slightly varying lengths, a central freeform pendant suspended between two links, set with turquoise and garnet cabs, rev mkd "sterling," maker's mark for Sam Kramer, approx 20" tl, center approx 3-½" top to bottom .... **2,300 (A)**

Sterling, aventurine, pearls, c. 1950, openwork freeform bent and hammered ster wire forming an irregular inverted triangle terminating off-center in a peg-set aventurine bead, four smaller aventurine beads and four pearls peg-set in a random pattern throughout, continuing to two curved hammered wire segments, mkd "sterling Lewittes" for Esther Lewittes, hook and eye clasp, 17" tl, 3" center top to bottom **450**

Neckpiece

Sterling, bronze, c. 1960, narrow gauge hammered ster wire collar with hook-and-eye clasp, threaded through a semicirc ster band with a drilled hole suspending a rod terminating in a freeform bronze drop suspending a smaller freeform drop within a larger opposed curv ster band, mkd "sterling," sgd with a conjoined "FR" within a circle for Florence Resnikoff, neckring dia 5-¹/₂", pendant 3-¹/₂" tl × 2-¹/₈"w **350**

Pendant

Sterling, onyx, leather thong, c. 1950, abstract human figure, sand-cast ster with a disk of black onyx riveted to a backplate mounted within curved legs of figure, suspended from a leather thong, by Richard Gompf, pendant 3-¹/₄" tl × 1-¹/₂" **350**

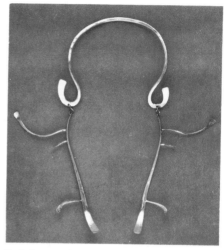

Neckpiece, sterling, c. 1953, an inverted U-shaped band of hammered (forged) ster rod with flattened ends forming C-scrolls, each end suspending a vertical hammered curved bar with flattened ends, wings of three horizontal hammered curv bars of varying lengths projecting outward, spaced at matched uneven intervals along one side of each vertical bar, worn suspended around the back of the neck, open in the front, mkd "© CF" (superimposed) for Claire Falkenstein, Venice, Calif., 11-¹/₂" w at widest point, 11-¹/₂" tl center back to tip of vertical, $1,500. *Courtesy of Before Antiques.*

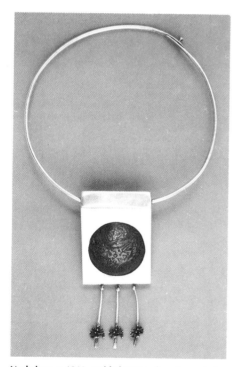

Neckpiece, c. 1960, entitled "Cosmology," a neck ring of round heavy-gauge sterling wire terminating in hammered ends with a notch and pin clasp, suspending a polished ster rect boxed plaque with cutout center fitted with a domed disk of repoussé and acid-etched copper, three cast-wire pendent drops with radiating biomorphic shapes suspended from base of rect, rev sgd "Florence Resnikoff" (engr script), Oakland, Calif., neck ring dia 5-¹/₂", pendant 2" w × 4-⁵/₈" tl, $600. *Courtesy of Before Antiques.*

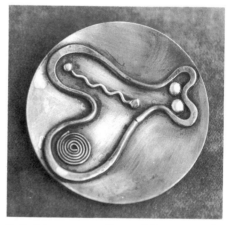

Pendant, brass, copper, silver, c. 1950, a concave circ brass disk with an appl central freeform design of undulating forged copper wire enclosing two silver beads, a silver wire volute, and an undulating length of wire with bead terminals, rev imp "Hand Wrought By ed wiener," New York, N.Y., 2-¹/₂" dia, $350. *Photo courtesy of Rochelle Mendle.*

Ring, sterling, smoky quartz, pearl, c. 1950, an open navette-shaped stylized eye design constructed of flat wire, a circ smoky quartz cab iris with a center concave depression set with a round pearl pupil, appl to a stepped and tapered shank, maker's mark for Margaret De Patta, San Francisco, Calif., ⁵/₈" w × 1-¹/₂", approx size 7, $2,200. *Terrance O'Halloran collection.*

Pendant and Chain, sterling, ebony, c. 1950, opposed lg and sm cutout ster crescents mounted on the ends of a waisted tablet-shaped plaque of ebony riveted to a ster backplate, surmounted by a sandcast textured domed ster disk, suspended from a handmade chain of lg and sm circ ster wire links, split-ring clasp, by Richard Gompf, San Francisco, Calif., 17" tl, pendant 2-¹/₂" tl × 1-³/₄", $350. *Courtesy of Before Antiques.*

Sterling, glass, c. 1950, an "Eye of God," a cast openwork design of concentric squares turned 45°, a series of radiating amorphous shapes around the outer four edges, the center set with a taxidermy glass eye, imp "sterling," maker's mark for Sam Kramer, 5-¹/₄" × 5-¹/₄" . . . . **690 (A)**

Ring
    835 silver, tourmalated quartz, c. 1960, a spherical movable quartz bead set in a crossed-ring silver cage, tapering to a narrow shank, mkd "835 EP" with a hammer in the center of a pentagonal reserve, bead ¹/₂" dia, ring ³/₄" **150**

    Sterling, c. 1955, a biomorphic abstract design with four projecting lobes, and a bent round wire mounted on the wide shank, curving to the front and terminating in a sphere which enters a circ perforation on front surface,

mkd "sterling," maker's mark for Sam Kramer, top approx ⁷/₈" × 1-¹/₄" . . . . . . **575 (A)**

Sterling, green stone, c. 1955, an irregular quadrangular plaque with a cutout rounded rectangle above a bezel-set circ green cab, flanked by the folded-over rounded tapered ends of a wide shank, mkd "sterling," maker's mark for Sam Kramer, top approx ³/₄" w × 1-³/₈" . . . . **1,955 (A)**

Sterling, jade, ebony, c. 1950, a sand-cast split (penannular) ring with a textured surface, one side a shaped triangle tapering to the shank, wrapping around to the other side with a flat circ top inlaid with concentric disks of jade and ebony, by Richard Gompf, approx size 6-¹/₂, 1-¹/₈" × ⁷/₈" **250**

Sterling, malachite, ivory, coral, ebony, c. 1950, an irreg rounded-corner oblong plaque, with a bezel mounted in from the edges, enclosing segmented sections set with a vertical row of flat rounded rect pcs of malachite, ivory, and coral on one side, and a narrow rounded baton-shaped section of ebony on the other, mounted on a tapered shank, unsgd, approx size 7, ³/₄" w × 1-¹/₄" **200**

Sterling, pearls, c. 1960, openwork freeform design enclosing a pinkish-white and a larger pinkish-grey baroque pearl, tapering to a narrow shank mkd "sterling," sgd "Lewittes" for Esther Lewittes, approx size 6, ⁵/₈" × ³/₄" **225**

Suite: Brooch and Earrings
    Sterling, c. 1950, stylized S-curved leaf shape with center strip mounted on edge perpen-

Suite: Brooch/Pin and Earrings, sterling, banded agate, c. 1950, a cutout angular stylized fish with cutout spiked and lobed center appl to oxidized ground, brooch with banded agate eye, matching all-ster earrings suspended by bead-tipped wire from sq surmounts, screwback findings, brooch, mkd "F. Miraglia N.Y. sterling," for Frank Miraglia, 2" w × 2-⅛", earrings, mkd "Miraglia" in script, "sterling modern," 1-¾" tl × 1-¼", suite, $300. *Author's collection.*

dicular to plaque, with pierced veins, oxidized along sides of strip, pr of matching earrings, screwbacks mkd "sterling," sgd "Tendler" for Bill Tendler, brooch 3-½" × ¾", earrings 1-¼" × ¼", suite **125**

Suite: Cuff Bracelet and Pendent Earrings
Copper, c. 1955, plain wide band with an oval cutout slightly off-center, a length of round

copper wire bent at angles across the opening and soldered at edges, sgd "Art Smith" in script, with a pr of copper wire earrings, each forming a tapering spiral enclosing a copper sphere suspended from a vertical wire surmount, post backs, unsgd, cuff approx 2-½" dia, 1" w, earrings approx 2-¼" tl × ¾", suite . . . . **575 (A)**

COSTUME JEWELRY C. 1935-1965
(DESIGNER/MANUFACTURER SIGNED)

Marcel Boucher   Eisenberg "E" mark   Trifari, Krussman & Fishel

History: A few years ago, no one would have believed that a brooch made of rhinestones and base metal could be worth more than one made of diamonds and platinum. Up until about 10 years ago, that same old rhinestone brooch probably would have been tossed in a drawer or thrown away. That was before costume jewelry collectors, and price guides, entered the picture.

Now, it seems that everyone knows and recognizes the name pieces—and knows their value, or at least knows better than to throw them away. Costume jewelry was elevated to an even higher level with the opening of an exhibition that toured museums in Europe and the United States, from 1991 to 1993, called "Jewels of Fantasy, Costume Jewelry of the 20th Century." The exhibit's accompanying catalog (see the references) has become an important reference resource.

A plethora of books has amply documented the history and products of the manufacturers and designers of signed and unsigned costume jewelry. The references following list some of them. While they are recommended for the examples, marks, and information they contain, readers should be aware that it is not uncommon to find conflicting information about the same makers in different sources. It is not likely, however, that the truth will ever be known: Most companies did not keep detailed records of their jewelry lines that, at the time they were produced, were thought to be as ephemeral and disposable as the fashions they were meant to complement. Much of the recent research on costume jewelry has of necessity been based on recollections of company executives, patent and trademark searches, advertising and articles in consumer and trade periodicals of the times. A listing of American costume jewelry manufacturers, including dates of operation if documented, can be found in the appendix.

Even though much has already been written by others, a few salient points should be made here, especially as they relate to the specific listings that follow. The bulk of the name jewelry that collectors seek was produced circa 1935 through the 1960s. The few manufacturers who were making costume jewelry before 1935—for example, Ciner, Coro, Miriam Haskell, Hobé, Napier, Trifari, and designer/couturiers Chanel, Hattie Carnegie, and Schiaparelli—did not consistently mark their pieces, if they signed them at all (the collector terminology for manufacturers' markings is "signed"). Their attributable circa 1920s designs are rare and usually expensive.

As mentioned previously, attribution of unsigned pieces and circa-dating of any piece should be backed up by printed evidence, or provenance. Because they assist in circa-dating, patent numbers found on the backs of pieces are given in the listings and captions, with the year they were issued in parentheses, which is the earliest year the piece could have been made. Other aspects of a piece, such as style and other elements, may date it later. For example, Coro patented the mechanism for the double clip brooch with Coro's tradename Duette in 1931, when the clips were flat-backed and the motifs were geometric, but figural motif Duettes with double-pronged hinged clips (often called fur clips) bearing this same patent number were made in the late 1930s and early 1940s.

Aside from novelty items, covered in the previous section on plastics, most costume, or fashion jewelry continued to follow fine jewelry trends until the late 1950s, when "fabulous fake" pieces became more exaggerated and glitzier than their fine jewelry counterparts. Hollywood had perhaps even more influence on nonprecious jewelry than precious. Joseff of Hollywood outfitted many stars with fabulous fakery for their roles in period films, and Marilyn Monroe's "diamonds are a girl's best friend" jewels were really rhinestones. It was also a profitable and common practice for manufacturers to produce costume jewels imitating the precious ones worn by the stars, so that even a woman of modest means could afford to emulate her favorite glamour queen. Mid to late 1930s and early 1940s Retro Modern costume pieces made of rhinestones and gold- or rhodium-plated white metal or sterling silver were often larger in scale than precious stone and metal equivalents, but many of the overall designs were quite similar. Some costume jewelry designers, such as Miram Haskell, also took inspiration from earlier styles, especially during the Victorian revival of the late 1930s and early 1940s.

During World War II, base metals were restricted for the war effort, as was platinum. Costume jewelry factories were called into service to make munitions and other military equipment. Jewelry production was diminished, but not curtailed. Sterling silver was used as a substitute for other metals. Fewer rhinestones were used because supplies from Czechoslovakia and Austria were cut off, as were simulated (faux) pearls from Japan. Manufacturers made do with existing stock and with stones made of Lucite and other plastics. Although base metal restrictions were lifted after the war, some manufacturers continued to use sterling for their higher-end lines until the mid-1950s.

Fashion jewelry forms also paralleled those of precious jewels. In the 1930s and 1940s, clips were just as stylish in rhinestones and white metal as they were in diamonds and platinum, moving to gold-plating and colored glass stones as fine jewelry changed to colored gold and gemstones. Gold-plated costume pieces of the late 1930s and early 1940s were often bicolored rose and yellow. As with fine jewelry, the late 1940s and 1950s saw the return of the parure, or suite of necklace, bracelet, earrings, and brooch, or two or three of these. (It should be noted that only one or two components of a suite may be marked with a manufacturer's name. If the pieces are separated, identification may prove difficult.) In the 1950s, the crafts movement influenced commercial production of modernist copper and enameled copper designs, notably by Rebajes of New York and Renoir/Matisse of California. Though mass-produced and inexpensive, this copper art jewelry was usually handmade or hand finished.

Although the majority of the jewelry in this section is American made, two of the genre's most important influences came from Europe—designers Gabrielle "Coco" Chanel (1883-1971) and Elsa Schiaparelli (1896-1973). While their influence was felt in the early years of costume jewelry manufacture (see "Costume Jewelry c. 1920-1935"), their early pieces, many of which are not signed, are rarely seen today.

Chanel closed her business in Paris in 1939 with the advent of World War II, and reopened in 1954, coming out of retirement at the age of 71 and working until her death. It is during this later period that the multicolored glass, faux pearl, and gold-plated metal necklaces, bracelets, brooches, and pendants most familiar to collectors were made. Chanel's company, under Karl Lagerfeld's supervision, continues producing costume jewelry designs today.

Elsa Schiaparelli's avant-garde and surrealistic touch is evident in her early 1930s jewelry designs (usually unsigned). She opened an office in New York in 1949 and licensed her name for mass production of costume jewelry and accessories. Her pieces were still bold and imaginative, but they lacked the off-the-wall look of her earlier work. Chunky suites set with molded iridescent glass stones (sometimes called "watermelon" or "oil-slick") and aurora borealis rhinestones (developed by Swarovski in 1955), or large faceted colored glass stones, were mid-1950s Schiaparelli trademarks, signed with her famous script signature. Schiaparelli retired in 1954, but American manufacturers continued producing her designs through the remainder of the decade.

Chanel and Schiaparelli also helped launch the careers of fine jewelry designers Verdura and Schlumberger, both of whom designed costume pieces for their respective employers in the 1930s (see the sections on fine jewelry).

Other currently sought-after designs include circa 1940s sterling vermeil (gold-plated) figural brooches and clips by Marcel Boucher, Coro (including sterling and white metal figural Duettes) and Corocraft, Eisenberg, Pennino, Reja, and Trifari, and well-made unsigned examples. Among these are the now-famous animal jelly bellies with clear Lucite centers (most signed Trifari, Coro, or unsigned). Vintage 1940s and 1950s Miriam Haskell necklaces, bracelets, and suites continue to have a following, particularly the designer's more elaborate creations. High quality real-looking rhinestone pieces by Boucher, Trifari, and others are also marketable.

Today, many collectors and dealers tend to focus on the name of the manufacturer or designer rather than on the jewelry itself. Novice dealers often price a piece high because it is signed, not because of its overall design and craftsmanship. It is true that certain manufacturers and designers have reputations for high-quality production and innovative design, and their names do make an upward difference in price compared to similar unsigned pieces. However, the same caveats apply to this genre of jewelry as to any other: A maker's mark is not a guarantee of quality. Be sure to evaluate a piece on its own merits before you turn it over to look for a mark.

Condition is an especially important factor in costume jewelry, because costume pieces are more easily damaged than fine jewelry and diffi-

cult to repair well. Major damage or major repairs lower value considerably. Replaced rhinestones and some wear are acceptable to most collectors, but replating, re-enameling, and soldering often are not. If badly done, the piece is ruined, and even if done well, it may end up not looking right. Proper restoration of a worn or broken piece is a job for a skilled professional who specializes in costume jewelry.

Note on prices in this section: This is one area of jewelry collecting that is comparable to other collectibles, e.g., dolls or glassware, because the pieces were mass-produced, and many of them are well-known, identifiable designs by recognized manufacturers and/or designers. A collector can say "Corocraft Josephine Baker" or "Trifari jelly belly frog," and another collector will know exactly what he or she is talking about. Some pieces are common and some are rare; rarity and demand drive this segment of the market in particular, as reflected by four-figure prices for the most sought-after rarities. However, prices are less stable than for collectibles like depression glass, for example. Regional differences affect prices, and trends are constantly changing in different parts of the country. In urban areas where the market is strong for particular designs by certain names, prices will undoubtedly be higher than those listed here. Outside of these markets, however, prices will be comparable or lower. Readers should keep in mind that the values given here are *average* retail. Most of the listings in this section are in the three-figure range or lower, reflecting the majority of readily available pieces on the market today. Pieces priced in the thousands of dollars assuredly do exist, but mostly in the collections of an elite few.

References: Lillian Baker, *Fifty Years of Collectible Fashion Jewelry, 1925-1975,* Collector Books, 1986, values updated 1992; Joann Dubbs Ball, *Costume Jewelers: The Golden Age of Design,* and *Jewelry of the Stars, Creations from Joseff of Hollywood,* Schiffer Publishing, 1990 and 1991; Vivienne Becker, *Fabulous Costume Jewelry,* Schiffer Publishing, 1993; Matthew Burkholz and Linda L. Kaplan, *Copper Art Jewelry, A Different Lustre,* Schiffer Publishing, 1992; Deanna Farneti Cera, ed., *Jewels of Fantasy,* Harry N. Abrams, 1992; Maryanne Dolan, *Collecting Rhinestone & Colored Jewelry,* 3rd ed., Books Americana, 1993; Lyngerda Kelley and Nancy Schiffer, *Costume Jewelry, The Great Pretenders,* Schiffer Publishing, 1987, values updated 1990; Roseann Ettinger, *Forties & Fifties Popular Jewelry,* Schiffer Publishing, 1994; Patrick Mauriès, *Jewelry By Chanel,* Bullfinch Press, Little, Brown & Co., 1993; Harrice Simons Miller, *Costume Jewelry Identification and Price Guide,* 2nd ed., Avon Books, 1994; Jane Mulvagh, *Costume Jewelry in Vogue,* Thames and Hudson, 1988; Nancy Schiffer, *Fun Jewelry,* Schiffer Publishing, 1991; Jody Shields, *All That Glitters, The*

Glory of Costume Jewelry, Rizzoli International, 1987

Periodical and Collectors' Club: *Vintage Fashion & Costume Jewelry Newsletter* and Club, P.O. Box 265, Glen Oaks, N.Y. 11004, published quarterly.

Museums: Glass and Costume Jewelry Museum, Jablonec nad Nisou, Czech Republic; Jewelers' Museum, Providence, R.I.; Schmuckmuseum, Pforzheim, Germany.

Reproduction Alert: Knockoffs of Eisenberg Originals, Trifari jelly bellies (the frog, turtle, stork, fish, and pig), and other big-name and pricey pieces have been infiltrating the market for the past several years. The most problematic are the ones that have been cast from the original pieces or molds, signatures intact. Some manufacturers, notably Cini, Eisenberg, Miriam Haskell, and Trifari, are reissuing their vintage designs now that they are so collectible. In some cases, only a side-by-side comparison of old with new will reveal subtle differences. Other reproductions are clearly marked, sometimes with dates. Many designers/manufacturers, such as Kenneth Jay Lane, never discontinue a line or design as long as it sells, which can be for many years. As usual, the best defenses are a buyer's knowledge and a seller's reputation.

Advisors: Charles Pinkham, Elayne Glotzer.

Bracelet
  Expandable
    Glass, rh pl wm, c. 1950, three rows of colorless faceted cylindrical glass beads attached with eyepins to wm tablet-shaped plaques with expanding and contracting hinge mechanisms, 1-1/4" w **45**
    Glass, gp wm, c. 1950, three rows of round translucent green glass beads attached with eyepins to wm tablet-shaped plaques with expanding and contracting hinge mechanisms 1-1/4" w **40**

Rhinestones, rh pl wm, c. 1950, a center row of marquise-cut colorless r.s. flanked by rows of circ r.s., prong-set, mounted on wm tablet-shaped plaques with expanding and contracting hinge mechanism, 5/8" w **25**
  Flexible
    Rhinestones, wm, c. 1935, a row of one lg pear-shaped colorless r.s. alternating with two lg oval colorless r.s., interspersed with groups of three sm r.s., tongue and box clasp, sgd "Eisenberg Original," 7-1/2" × 7/8" **185**
    Rhinestones, rh pl wm, c. 1950, two rows of citrine-colored circ and emerald-cut r.s. with appl curv wm strips pavé-set with sm circ colorless r.s., mounted in rh pl wm, mkd "Eisenberg Ice" in sm block letters, hook clasp, safety chain, 6-1/2" × 3/4" **125**
  Hinged bangle
    Glass, rhinestones, gp wm, enamel, Retro Modern, c. 1940, wide bangle with open center and appl floral and foliate motifs, flowerheads with red, green, and blue glass cab centers, pavé r.s. petals, painted green enamel leaves, appl plate on rev mkd "Corocraft," v-spring and box clasp, safety chain, 1-1/2" w 2-1/2" dia **450**
    Glass, rhinestones, rh pl wm, c. 1950, three lg rect-cut prong-set colorless r.s. encircled by lg and sm colorless faceted glass beads and black seed beads, appl to front half of a tapered bangle, continuing to a stamped relief scrolled cartouche on wm band, safety chain, 1-1/2" w tapered to 3/4", 2-3/8" dia **75**
  Link
    Copper, c.1950, wide rect links with oxidized centers joined with overlapping sq links turned 45°, a cutout strip wrapped around a raised bead in one corner of each

Bracelet, flexible, Retro Modern, gp wm, glass, rhinestones, c. 1940, a central convex cutout gp plaque with a floral and foliate motif of overlapping marquise-cut dk blue glass set *à jour* on the diagonal, sm pavé-set colorless r.s. accents, linked to looped double gp snake chain band, foldover clasp, unsgd, 6-3/4" × 2", $350. *Victoria Taylor collection.*

Bracelet, glass beads, rhinestones, gp brass, c. 1950, four strands of melon-cut lavender glass beads with an ornate front clasp of floral and foliate design in glass beads, molded glass leaves, and r.s. in purple, lavender, pink, and green, appl oval plaque on rev of clasp mkd "Miriam Haskell," 8" tl, clasp 1-1/2" w × 2-3/4", $395. *Kirsten Olson collection.*

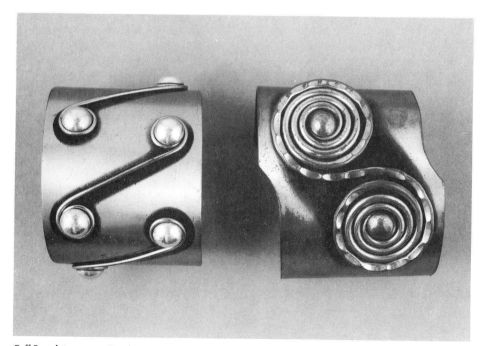

Cuff Bracelets, copper, Renoir, c. 1950: L, a smooth wide band with tapered ends, appl wire S-scrolls with riveted sterling domed disk terminals, oxidized ground behind each, outside end mkd "Handmade, Renoir of California," 2-1/4" dia × 2", $75; R, a wide stepped band with hammered copper wire S-scrolled volutes with riveted domed disk centers, appl diagonally on an oxidized ground, outside end mkd "Handmade, Renoir of California," 2-3/8" dia × 2-1/4", $50. *Author's collection.*

sq, mkd "Rebajes" on outside of link nearest v-spring, box clasp, safety chain, 7" × 1-⅝" **150**

Copper, enamel, c. 1955, open lozenge-shaped links with red enameled elliptical centers, foldover clasp mkd "© Matisse," 7-¼" × 1-⅛" **40**

Rhinestones, rh pl wm, c. 1935, tapered pierced articulated rect plaques alternating with sm sq plaques pavé-set with lg and sm circ colorless r.s., rev mkd with lg "T" flanked by sm "K" and "F" for Trifari, Krussman and Fishel, New York, N.Y., safety chain, v-spring and box clasp, 7" × ¾" **125**

Rhinestones, rh pl wm, c. 1935, stepped rect openwork plaques alternating with smaller open plaques pavé-set with colorless circ and baguette r.s. and joined with baguette links, rev mkd with lg "T" flanked by sm "K" and "F" for Trifari, Krussman and Fishel, foldover clasp, 7" × ¾" **125**

Sterling, c. 1950, oxidized brushed-finish sq plaques linked with raised domed disks within plaques with folded-up cusped corners forming squares turned 45°, mkd "Rebajes sterling" on outside of plaque nearest v-spring, box clasp, 7" × ⅞" **200**

Brooch/Pin

Faux pearls, rhinestones, gp ym, c. 1945, circ, with lg colorless r.s. center surrounded by ym flower petals, sm oval faux pearls, sm flat-backed r.s. and faux seed pearl border, stamped filigree backing mkd "Miriam Haskell" on appl horseshoe-shaped plaque, 1-½" dia **225**

Faux pearls, gp brass, c. 1950, numerous sm baroque faux pearls mounted with wire onto concentric layers of stamped gp foliate motifs, a lg round textured faux pearl prong-set in the center, appl oval plaque on rev mkd "Miriam Haskell," 2" dia **195**

Glass, ym, rhinestones, c. 1950, nine lg faceted green glass beads with fuchsia r.s. tips, encircling a concentric oval of green and fuchsia r.s. rondelles alternating with fuchsia faceted beads around a central large oval multicolored Venetian glass bead, ym stamped filigee back, sgd "Hattie Carnegie" in an appl oval plaque, 2-½" w × 1-½" **100**

Glass, gp brass, faux pearls, c. 1950, a wreath of green and pink glass seed beads accented with a sm gp and faux pearl floral spray, stamped gp filigree back, sgd "Miriam Haskell" in an oval plaque, 1-½" dia **70**

Gp wm, c. 1950, fluted scalloped-edge fan shape with scrolled end, smooth polished

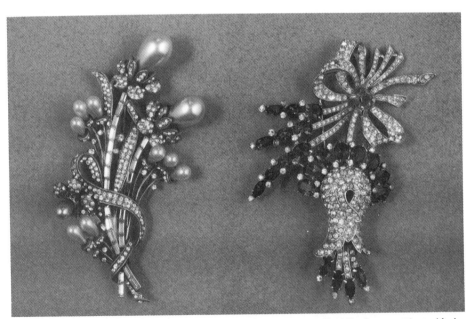

Brooches/Pins, Retro Modern, c. 1940: L, faux pearls, rhinestones, gp wm, a stylized floral spray pavé-set with circ and baguette colorless r.s., lg and sm pear-shaped faux pearls set in flower centers, appl plate on rev mkd "Eisenberg Original," 4-¼" × 2", $400; **R,** rhinestones, glass, rh pl wm, stylized floral spray with ribbon bow, pavé-set with colorless r.s. and grad oval-cut and marquise-cut dk blue glass, rev mkd "Coro," 4" × 3-¾", $275, *Victoria Taylor collection.*

finish, mkd "Trifari ©," 1-$^7/_8$" w × 1-$^5/_8$"
. . . . **50**

Gp wm, c. 1955, three fused strands of foxtail chain forming a bow with articulated ends, mkd "Napier ©," 1-$^7/_8$" w × 3" **40**

Gp wm, c. 1960, foliate design in an asymmetrical swirl, Florentine (brushed) finish, mkd "Monet ©," 2-$^3/_4$" w × 1-$^1/_2$". **35**

Gp wm, c. 1960, an equilateral cross with pinecone terminals and X-shaped center in Florentine finish and polished pierced reeded arms, rev mkd "Trifari ©," 2-$^3/_8$" × 2-$^3/_8$" **60**

Gp wm, c. 1965, cactus design with overlapping irregularly shaped disks of varying sizes, with a raised stippled pattern resembling cactus thorns, mkd "© Tortolani" in script on appl plate on rev, 2-$^1/_2$" w × 1-$^3/_4$" **75**

Gp wm, cultured pearl, c. 1950, gp chrysanthemum flower and stem with Florentine and bright-finished petals, a cultured pearl center, sgd "© Boucher," # 8374, string tag mkd "Genuine Cultured Pearls" and "Original by Marcel Boucher," 1-$^1/_2$" w × 2" . . . **95**

Gp wm, faux pearls, painted enamel, c. 1960, in the shape of a woman's wide brim hat, textured finish, crown encircled with faux pearls, bow in back accented with two red painted enamel flowers and green painted enamel leaves, mkd "Ciner," 1-$^3/_8$" dia . . . **65**

Gp wm, faux pearls, r.s., c. 1960, a crossover swirl of polished and Florentine finish goldtone tapered band with center section of pierced bars and two curv rows of faux pearls interspersed with sm colorless r.s., rev mkd "Trifari ©," 2-$^1/_4$" w × 1" **45**

Gp wm, faux pearls, rhinestones, c. 1960, a swirl of alternating polished and Florentine finish goldtone tapered bands in a center cluster of faux pearls and sm colorless r.s., rev mkd "Trifari ©," 2" w × 1-$^3/_8$" **45**

Gp wm, glass, Retro Modern, c. 1940, in the shape of an undulating gp double ribbon bow with a scrolled filigree center set with circ red and colorless and oval aqua faceted glass stones in millegrained bezels, rev mkd "Sandor," 2-$^3/_4$" w × 2-$^1/_2$" **125**

Gp wm, glass, c. 1960, inverted pear-shaped sunburst design with three grad serrated and reeded goldtone plaques layered concentrically, the second layer outlined in sm colorless r.s., surmounted by an inverted pear-shaped opaque lt blue glass cab prong-set in the center of the top layer, rev mkd "Jomaz," 1-$^1/_2$" w × 1-$^3/_4$" **85**

Gp wm, glass, rhinestones, Retro Modern, c. 1940, lily-of-the-valley shape with ruffled gp leaves, pavé r.s. stalk and scrolled tendrils, two rows of prong-set circ-cut open-backed colorless glass stones, rev mkd "Réja," 2-$^1/_4$" w × 4" **425**

Gp wm, glass, rhinestones, Retro Modern,

Brooch/Pin, sterling vermeil, painted enamel, rhinestones, c. 1940, depicting a horse and East Indian male rider with a parasol, black, yellow, red, green, white, blue, dk fleshtone, and brown painted enamel, pavé colorless r.s. on horse, red r.s. eye, rev mkd "Corocraft Sterling," 2-$^5/_8$" w × 2-$^1/_2$", $400. Kirsten Olson collection.

c. 1940, stylized feather plume, pierced gp center, encircled at one end by lg circ faceted colorless glass stones prong-set à jour, flanked by curv rows of sm pavé colorless r.s., mkd "Réja," 3-$^3/_4$" w × 2-$^1/_2$" **350**

Gp wm, glass, rhinestones, c. 1940, a fish with a lg pear-shaped purple faceted glass body prong-set à jour, gp head and tail with colorless r.s. accents, pavé r.s. fins, unmkd, 2-$^3/_8$" w × 2-$^1/_2$" **195**

Gp wm, glass, rhinestones, painted enamel, c. 1940, a rabbit (rear view) with lg faceted purple glass ears prong-set à jour, gp head and body, painted eye and mouth, pavé r.s.-set tail, unmkd, 1-$^1/_2$" w × 3" **250**

Gp wm, glass, rhinestones, Retro Modern, c. 1950, in the shape of of a stylized phoenix with outstretched wings, pavé-set with colorless and red r.s., translucent green and blue cabs in wings, red cab eye, rev Florentine finish of sp metal, mkd "© Boucher # 7759P," 2-$^7/_8$" w × 4-$^1/_4$" **350**

Gp wm, glass, rhinestones, c. 1955, upper torso of a turbaned genie holding a crystal ball (hollow glass), with a gp star shape inside, pavé r.s. around base and edge of his vest, red cab in front center of turban, sm brown r.s. around the turban's sides, mkd "HAR," 2" w × 2-$^1/_8$" **650**

Gp wm, rhinestones, c. 1935, a rect gp frame with concave chamfered corners, a central pierced geo plaque and corner-to-corner cross of sm circ pavé-set colorless r.s. and a horizontal center row of lg amber-colored

Brooches/Pins, Retro Modern, rhinestones, Pennino, c. 1940: L, sterling and sterling vermeil, a double flowerhead spray with gp petals, colorless baguettes and blue circ r.s. centers, pavé rhinestones stems and leaves, rev mkd "Pennino sterling," 2-1/2" w × 3", $450, *Kirsten Olson collection;* C, an open C-scroll formed of five rose gp ster flat wires, gathered at the top with a half-round tubular knot motif, terminating in sm flowerhead clusters of colorless r.s. with red r.s. centers, and two lg five-petal flowerheads, each set with five oval faceted purple glass stones around colorless and red r.s. centers, rev mkd "Pennino sterling," 2-1/4" w × 3", $500, *Author's collection;* R, rh pl wm, a flower spray prong-set with oval-cut aqua and orange-pink open-backed glass stones, lt and dk turq, pink, and colorless circ r.s., wm leaves and stems, rev mkd "Pennino," 2-1/8" w × 3-3/4", $325, *Kirsten Olson collection.*

emerald-cut r.s., an emerald-cut amber-colored r.s. in each corner, mkd "McClelland Barclay," 2" w × 1-7/8" **175**

Gp wm, rhinestones, Retro Modern, c. 1940, a lg gp metal double ribbon bow with center knot set with circ green and sm colorless r.s., rev mkd "Mazer" for Joseph Mazer, 3-3/4" w × 3" **250**

Gp wm, rhinestones, c. 1950, in the shape of the profiled head of a man wearing a turban with an articulated sash end, set throughout with red, green, and blue r.s., an articulated gp ring through his ear, pavé r.s. collar, rev Florentine finish gp metal, mkd "© Boucher" # 8381P, 1-1/4" w × 1-7/8" . . . **125**

Gp wm, rhinestones, c. 1950, a stylized bird with head and ridged gp wings set with oval amber-colored r.s., body with circ and baguette colorless r.s., scrolled ridged gp tail flanking long articulated tailfeathers prong-set with amber-colored rect-cut r.s., circ and pear-shaped colorless r.s., rev mkd "Mazer" for Joseph Mazer, New York, N.Y., 1-7/8" w × 3-5/8" **350**

Gp wm, rhinestones, c. 1950, sycamore leaf and seed pods design, pavé-set sm colorless r.s. on leaf and insides of pods, mkd "Jomaz," 2-1/4" × 2-1/4" **125**

Gp wm, rhinestones, c. 1955, central scrolled

goldtone ribbon, flanked by floral and foliate motifs set with circ colorless, lt green and yellow marquise-cut r.s., rev mkd "Hollycraft Copr. 195-" (last digit illegible), 2" w × 1-1/4" **45**

Gp wm, rhinestones, c. 1960, ribbed textured goldtone abstract design of three overlapping grad domed disks with cutout centers outlined in pavé colorless r.s., a larger circ r.s. prong-set in each center of two larger disks, a lg and sm stylized leaf form outlined in pavé r.s. projecting from top and bottom disks, rev mkd "Jomaz," 2-1/4" w × 1-1/4" **75**

Rhinestones, glass, rh pl wm, c. 1945, a swan with head tucked under its wing, pavé-set with colorless r.s., red r.s. eye, oval-cut aqua glass prong-set *à jour* in center of body, rh pl wm legs and feet, unmkd, attributed to Trifari, 2-1/4" w × 1-1/4" **450**

Rhinestones, glass, rh pl wm, c. 1945, a cockatoo pavé-set with colorless r.s., red r.s. eye, lg oval-cut red-orange glass stone prong-set *à jour* in center of body, rh pl wm legs, feet, and beak, unmkd, 3-1/2" w × 1-1/2" **300**

Rhinestones, glass, gp ym, c. 1950, comma-shaped design with aurora borealis red and blue circ r.s. and irid textured circ glass cabs,

Brooches/Pins, rhinestones, wm, Schreiner, c. 1950: L, a domed circle with diagonal rows of aqua, purple, and amber oval and marquise-cut r.s. and oval orange glass cabs, mkd "Schreiner New York," 2-⅜" dia, $375; **R,** Japanned metal (black lacquered) floral spray with flower buds *en tremblant,* set throughout with dk green, purple, blue, and brown circ and marquise-cut r.s., mkd "Schreiner New York," 2-¼" w × 2", $295, *Kirsten Olson collection.*

Brooch/Pin, glass, rhinestones, wm, c.1950, three lg faceted oval silvered black glass stones with imitation marcasite borders, surmounting two lg faceted pentagonal green glass stones flanking silvered black glass imitation marcasites in a pear shape below, encircled by six circ flat-cut black glass stones set in serrated bezels, and interspersed throughout with colorless circ r.s. and translucent green faceted truncated bicone beads tipped with sm colorless r.s. wired to a wm mount, suspending three lg faceted black glass drops, an appl oval plate on rev mkd "© Vendôme" (a division of Coro), 2-½" w × 3-½" tl, $200. *Author's collection.*

appl plate on rev mkd "Schiaparelli" in script, 2-⅛" w × 2-½" **140**

Rhinestones, gp wm, c.1950, a stylized stemmed flower with spiked petals pavé-set with red r.s., pierced and domed appl center petal section and stem pavé-set with colorless r.s., rev mkd "Trifari ©," 2-¼" w × 3" **125**

Rhinestones, rh pl wm, c. 1940, ribbon bow motif with pierced floral and foliate design, draped sash ends, pavé-set with sm colorless r.s., mkd "Trifari," 1-⅞" w × 3-¼" **300**

Rhinestones, rh pl wm, c. 1940, a pierced bow with cutout flowerheads, scroll and linear designs, pavé-set with colorless circ and baguette r.s., mkd "MB" under bird's head logo for Marcel Boucher, New York, N.Y., 3-⅞" w × 1-⅜" **175**

Rhinestones, rh pl wm, c. 1945, lg circ and oval colorless r.s., sm pavé r.s. in a tapered scrolled design, mkd "E" for Eisenberg, 1-¼" w × 2-⅛" **80**

Rhinestones, rh pl wm, c. 1950, lg and medium circ colorless r.s. in overlapping circles, topped with a cluster of circ and pear-shaped r.s. in a floral motif with looped and curved strips of sm pavé-set colorless r.s., mkd "Eisenberg Ice," 1-⅞" w × 2-¼" **85**

Rhinestones, rh pl wm, c. 1950, circ cluster of lg circ, emerald-cut, and marquise-cut r.s. with radiating ribbon-like strips of sm pavé-set circ r.s. on one side, mkd "Eisenberg" (block letters), 2" w × 2-½" **85**

Rhinestones, rh pl wm, c. 1950, a quatrefoil of circ domed clusters of sm circ dk blue and

Brooch/Pin, glass, rhinestones, gp wm, c. 1960, an equilateral (Moline) cross with a lg circ red glass cab prong-set in cutout center, pear-shaped faceted blue glass flanked by teardrop green glass cabs at terminals, pavé colorless r.s. ground, rev mkd "Trifari," from "Jewels of India" collection, 2-1/4" × 2-1/4", $250. *Victoria Taylor collection.*

purple r.s. with a medium and a lg pear-shaped purple r.s. set between each lobe, rev mkd "Warner," 2-1/2" × 2-1/2" **150**

Rhinestones, rh pl wm, faux pearl, c. 1955, spiral swirl design with lg center faux pearl, pavé circ and baguette colorless r.s., mkd "Kramer of New York," 1-5/8" w × 1-3/8" **60**

Rhinestones, white pot metal, c. 1940, curv pierced shield shape set with lg circ, pear, marquise, and emerald-cut colorless r.s., pavé circ colorless r.s. accents, mkd "Staret," 3" w × 3-1/2" **150**

Rhinestones, faux pearls, ym, c. 1950, a V-shape set with circ and marquise-cut lt to dk amber-colored r.s. and faux pearls, suspending a pear-shaped faux pearl drop with a cap of pavé r.s., mkd "Austria," 2" w × 2-3/4" **85**

Sterling, c. 1940, cast in the shape of a lizard, rev appl plaque mkd "sterling by Cini" for Guglielmo Cini, Boston, Mass., 3-3/4" × 2-1/2" **350**

Sterling, c. 1940, cutout stamped relief design of two lovebirds perched on a branch with leaves and berries forming an oval frame, unbacked, appl rect plate on rev mkd "Coro Craft sterling," 1-3/4" w × 2-1/2" **75**

Sterling, c. 1940, a cutout curv floral and foliate design in stamped relief within circ frame, unbacked, appl oval plate on rev mkd "Danecraft © sterling," 2-1/4" dia **65**

Sterling, glass, c. 1940, a foliate and floral

spray of ster buds and leaves, lg circ faceted aqua glass stones set in collets with open backs mounted on wires surmounted by a ribbon bow with rosebud center, appl plaqe on rev mkd "Hobé sterling," 2-1/2" w × 3" **300**

Sterling, rhinestones, c. 1940, a stylized bow of sq, oval, and marquise-cut r.s. prong-set within an open frame of sm circ r.s., one lg emerald-cut r.s. in the center, mkd "Eisenberg sterling," 3" × 2-1/4" **450**

Sterling vermeil, c. 1940, two lg flowers with curv leaves in stamped relief within circ frame, unbacked, rev mkd "Sterling Craft By Coro," 2" dia **60**

Sterling vermeil, glass, rhinestones, Retro Modern, c. 1940, lg sq-cut aqua-colored glass stone prong-set in a circ disk with cutout scrolled and twisted ster ribbon shapes and blue, green, pink, yellow, and purple prong-set r.s. on wires radiating out from center stone, rev mkd "sterling," 4-1/4" × 2" **45**

Sterling vermeil, glass, rhinestones, Retro Modern, c. 1940, lg rect-cut aqua-colored glass stone prong-set in the center of a cutout pierced and scrolled stylized leaf shape prong-set with aqua-colored r.s., rev mkd "sterling," 3-1/2" w × 2" **45**

Sterling vermeil, Lucite, rhinestones, c. 1940, fox jelly belly, Lucite center, pavé r.s. on ears, feet, and tail, green r.s. eye, mkd "sterling Corocraft" (with winged horse logo), 3" w × 1-1/2" **1,500**

Sterling vermeil, rhinestones, painted enamel, Retro Modern, c. 1940, sunflower motif, red and white painted enamel on petals, domed center of sm circ colorless pavé-set r.s., mkd "Nettie Rosenstein, sterling," 2-3/4" w × 2-7/8" **250**

Sterling vermeil, glass, rhinestones, c. 1940, peacock with pavé colorless r.s. body, red r.s. eye, tail of ster wires terminating in dk blue, burgundy, and dk aqua oval faceted glass prong-set *à jour* at the ends of pavé r.s.-set trefoils, flanked by scrolled ster wires, rev mkd "sterling," 4-1/2" w × 1-1/2" **250**

Sterling vermeil, glass, rhinestones, c. 1940, Mother Goose with amber-colored faceted pear-shaped glass prong-set *à jour* in the center of the body, pavé-set colorless r.s. tail, bonnet, and shawl, r.s. eye, gp umbrella, head, and shoes, rev mkd "sterling," 1-1/4" × 2-1/2" **225**

Sterling vermeil, glass, rhinestones, c. 1940, a fly with faceted pear-shaped dk blue-green glass body prong-set *à jour*, red r.s. eyes, colorless pavé r.s. thorax, gp wings and legs, rev mkd "Réja sterling," Réja, Inc., New York, N.Y., 1-1/8" × 1-1/2" **75**

Sterling vermeil, glass, rhinestones, c. 1940, an owl on a branch, lg faceted inverted pear-shaped red glass stone set *à jour* in center of body, pavé colorless r.s. tail, red r.s. eyes, rev mkd "Réja sterling," 1-3/4" w × 2-1/4" . . . **225**

Sterling vermeil, glass, rhinestones, c. 1940, crested bird with outstretched wings, fuchsia faceted oval glass center, green r.s. on wings, sm colorless pavé r.s. on head, wings, and tail, mkd "Trifari sterling," 3-1/4" w × 1-1/2" **450**

Sterling vermeil, rhinestones, c. 1940, a genie with semicirc red r.s. eyes, oval blue r.s. topknot, pavé and circ r.s. accents, colorless marquise-cut r.s. in center and on ears, mkd "Corocraft sterling," 1-5/8" w × 2-1/8" . . . **375**

Sterling vermeil, glass, rhinestones, Retro Modern, c. 1940, lg scrolled gp plume with center citrine-colored faceted oval prong-set glass stone, strips of pavé colorless r.s. in center and at sides of plume, rev mkd "sterling Nordic," 3" w × 2-3/8" **175**

Sterling vermeil, glass, rhinestones, c. 1945, a crown prong-set with two lg opalescent glass cabs, lt and dk blue, red, and pavé colorless r.s., mkd "Trifari sterling, des pat no 137542" (1944), 1-7/8" w × 1-3/4" **250**

Sterling vermeil, glass, rhinestones, c. 1945, stylized fish, green glass cab eye, lg oval dk pink glass center, lt pink, lt blue, and colorless r.s. accents, mkd "Trifari sterling des.pat.no.142661" (1945), 2-1/2" w × 2"

. . . . **625**

Wm, painted enamel, c. 1940, turbaned horseman on winged horse, with white painted enamel on wing, turban and shirt, red shoes and bridle, mkd "Thief of Bagdad, Korda," 2-1/2" w × 2" **125**

Wm, rhinestones, faux pearls, c. 1940, stamped filigree crescent shape set with dk blue marquise-cut r.s. and faux pearls, with central domed medallion set with marquise-cut and pear-shaped royal blue r.s. around center faux pearl, mkd "Thief of Bagdad, Korda," 3" w × 2-7/8" **175**

Brooches/Pins

Sterling, rhinestones, c. 1940, pr of peacock scatter pins, lg faceted oval dk blue r.s. prong-set in tails, pentagonal colorless r.s., sm green, red, and blue r.s. in bodies and heads, rev mkd "sterling," 1" w × 1-1/4", pr **75**

Gp wm, rhinestones, c. 1965, textured oxidized goldtone wm, one in the shape of a cartoonlike devil's head with red r.s. eyes, trident and spiked tail, the other an angel with blue r.s. eyes, colorless r.s. halo, each projecting at right angles to convex plaques with pinbacks mounted on rev, designed to be pinned on top of wearer's shoulders, mkd "© Tortolani," devil 1-1/4" w × 1", angel 1-3/8" w × 1-1/2", pr **65**

Trifari jelly bellies, sterling vermeil, Lucite, rhinestones, c.1945: L, Suite: Brooch/Pin and Earrings, flies, Lucite centers, red pavé r.s. accents, red cab r.s. eyes, mkd "Trifari, sterling, des pat no. 137200" (1944) on backs of wings, brooch 1-3/4" w × 2", clipback earrings 1-1/8" w × 1-1/4", suite, $850; R, Clip, owl, Lucite center, pavé r.s. accents, green glass cab eyes, double-pronged hinged clip on rev, mkd "Trifari" on clip hinge and "Trifari sterling" on back of tail, "des pat no. 135191" (1943) on side edge, 1-1/4" w × 2-3/8", $1,200, *Kirsten Olson collection.*

Clips, Retro Modern, Boucher, c. 1940: T, sterling vermeil, glass, rhinestones, scrolled circ stylized shell shapes outlined in rect-cut prong-set glass stones (one with green, one with red) and pavé colorless r.s., central prong-set D-shaped faceted glass stone, double-pronged hinged clip on rev, mkd "sterling," "MB" below bird's head logo for Marcel Boucher, New York, N.Y., 2" × 2", each, $150; BL, gp and rh pl wm, glass, rhinestones, a stylized curv ribbon bow and flower spray motif with pavé colorless r.s. and lg prong-set circ faceted red glass stones, double-pronged hinged clip on rev, mkd "MB" below bird's head logo for Marcel Boucher, 2" w × 3-½", $450, *Connie Parente collection;* BR, gp and rh pl wm, painted enamel, rhinestones, in the shape of a carnation with petals enameled in shades of pink and fuchsia, base of flower and petal edges pavé-set with colorless r.s., gp and green painted enamel stem, gp leaves, double-pronged hinged clip on rev, mkd "MB" below bird's head logo for Marcel Boucher, 2" w × 4", $400, *Author's collection.*

Clips, Retro Modern, rhinestones, double-pronged hinged clip backs, mkd "Eisenberg Original," c. 1940: L, white pot metal shield shape with openwork design set throughout with grad circ and lg sq-cut and cushion-cut colorless r.s., 2" w × 2-¾", $100; C, white pot metal, lg openwork cascading ribbon bow design with a central flowerhead of eight lg oval colorless prong-set r.s. encircling a lg circ center r.s., and set throughout with lg oval, marquise, and various sized circ colorless r.s., rev mkd "Eisenberg Original," double-pronged hinged clip, 2-¼" w × 4-½", $400; R, lead crystal, sterling, circ wreath design surmounted by curv pavé r.s.-set foliate motifs, with a lg lozenge-shaped faceted colorless crystal prong-set *à jour* at top center surmounting rect and grad circ colorless crystals concentrically prong-set *à jour*, mkd "sterling," 2-¼" dia, $400, *Victoria Taylor collection.*

Clip

Faux pearls, rh pl wm, rhinestones, Retro Modern, c. 1940, in the shape of a bunch of faux pearl grapes and pavé colorless r.s.-set leaves, double-pronged hinged clip on rev mkd "Coro" "E," 2-³/₈" × 3" **200**

Glass, rhinestones, gp and rh pl wm, Retro Modern, c. 1940, a stylized comet motif, lg red lozenge-cut unfoiled glass stones prong-set à jour in an open circle, a sm colorless r.s. between each stone, surmounting a pavé-set r.s.and gp scroll and rays, double-pronged hinged clip on rev, mkd "Réja," 2-¹/₂" w × 3" **350**

Gp wm, rhinestones, Retro Modern, c 1940, lg stylized gp flower with oval colorless r.s. cluster center and six lg oval r.s. buds around outer edges, double-pronged hinged clip on rev, mkd "Eisenberg Original," 4-¹/₂" w × 2-³/₄" **800**

Gp wm, rhinestones, Retro Modern, c. 1940, rose gp triple plume, prong-set with green and colorless r.s., double-pronged hinged clip on rev mkd "Trifari," 2-¹/₄" w × 3-¹/₂" **175**

Lucite, rhinestones, gp metal, c. 1940, stylized fish jelly belly with Lucite center, pavé r.s. on fins, red glass cab eye, double-pronged hinged clip on rev, mkd "Trifari, des pat no 129165" (1941), design attributed to Norman Bel Geddes, 2-¹/₄" w × 3-¹/₄" **1,800**

Rhinestones, glass, white pot metal, c. 1940, medium and lg oval faceted aqua-blue r.s., sm circ colorless pavé r.s. accents, stylized floral and foliate design, mkd "Eisenberg Original" on plate appl to rev center, double-pronged hinged clip, 2" w × 3-¹/₄" **250**

Rhinestones, gp, brass, c. 1940, twisted wire grid pattern with alternating amber-colored and colorless oval-cut r.s. in a patterned sq, double-pronged hinged clip back mounted diagonally, mkd "H.C." in a lozenge for Hattie Carnegie, 2-⁵/₈" w × 2-¹/₂" **75**

Sterling vermeil, glass, rhinestones, c. 1940, elongated oval with radiating star-shaped gp ster center set with an oval-cut colorless r.s., set throughout with emerald-cut, sq-cut, oval-cut and circ blue, red, yellow, dk green, pink, and aqua glass stones, and sm colorless r.s., double-pronged hinged clip on rev, mkd "Eisenberg sterling," 2" w × 3" **750**

Sterling vermeil, glass, Retro Modern, c. 1940, lg circ-cut aqua-colored glass stone prong-set in the center of a rose gp rev J-scroll with a cutout fringe along outside edge, double-pronged hinged clip on rev, mkd "Trifari sterling," 1-¹/₂" w × 2-¹/₂" **95**

Sterling vermeil, Retro Modern, c. 1940, a folded curv rose gp ribbon divided into three strips with scrolled ends, double-pronged hinged clip on rev mkd "Napier sterling," 1-¹/₂" w × 2-³/₄" **65**

Clips

Rh pl wm, painted enamel, rhinestones, c. 1940, a pr of clips in the shape of hydrangeas, stems tied with a bow, pink, blue, green, brown, and white painted enamel

Clips, Retro Modern, rhinestones, glass, painted enamel, rh pl wm, double-pronged hinged clip backs mkd "Trifari," c. 1940: L, an openwork scrolled foliate design pavé-set with colorless r.s., a vertical row of grad alternating faux moonstones and ruby-colored oval glass cabs prong-set à jour below a lg pierced leaf, one sm red cab above, dk red enamel accents on leaf tips, rev mkd "des pat no. 122097" (1940), 2-¹/₄" w × 2-¹/₂", $225; C, a floral spray of bluebells pavé-set with colorless r.s., painted enamel brown and green stems, red leaves, rev mkd "pat pend," 2" w × 3-¹/₄", $200, Victoria Taylor collection; R, in the shape of a pineapple with red painted enamel and r.s. center, green painted enamel leaves with colorless r.s. accents, 2" w × 2-³/₈", $250, Connie Parente collection.

with sm colorless r.s. centers and on bow and stem tips, double-pronged hinged clips on backs, mkd "Trifari," 2" w × 3-½", pr **250**

Cuff Links

Copper, brass, c. 1945, dumbbell type, the front of each a sq copper plaque surmounted by a lg and a sm rotating riveted brass gear, sgd "Rebajes," ⅝" × ¾", pr **50**

Copper, brass, c. 1950, dumbbell type, the front of each a palette shape with brass wire brushes, unsgd, ¾" × ⅞", pr **30**

Double Clip Brooch

Duette

Gp wm, rhinestones, c. 1945, a pair of clips in the shape of two winged cherubs, one holding a star mkd "July," the other holding a colorless heart-shaped r.s., pavé r.s. sashes on both, double-pronged hinged clips on rev, pinback mechanism for joining as a brooch, one angel mkd "Coro," 2-¼" w × 1-⅝" joined **250**

Rhinestones, rh pl wm, c. 1935, a pr of clips in curv ribbon-scroll design, each with a center row of four lg purple r.s., smaller pavé-set purple r.s. on outer ribbons, double-pronged hinged clips, with a detachable pinback mechanism for joining as a brooch, mkd "Coro Duette, Pat No.1798867" (1931), 2-¼" w × ⅞" joined **85**

Rh pl wm, painted enamel, rhinestones, c. 1940, a pair of clips in the shape of birds with red, green, and yellow painted enamel and pavé colorless r.s. heads, wings, and tails, double-pronged hinged clips on rev, with a detachable pinback mechanism for joining as a brooch, mkd "Coro Duette," "Pat No. 1798867" (1931), 2-½" w × 1-¾" joined **125**

Rh pl wm, rhinestones, painted enamel, c. 1940, a pair of clips in the shape of cockatoos with pavé r.s. heads and bodies, painted enamel crests, beaks, wings, and tails in pastel shades of blue and green, perched on a floral spray branch enameled in shades of pink, blue, and green, flowers with r.s. centers, double-pronged hinged clips on rev, with a detachable pinback mechanism for joining as a brooch, mkd "Coro Duette," "Pat No. 1798867" (1931), 2" w × 3-½" joined **150**

Sterling vermeil, Lucite, rhinestones, c. 1940, a pair of clips in the shape of fish jelly bellies, Lucite centers set with colorless r.s., blue marquise r.s. mouths, red cab eyes, gp fins bordered with colorless r.s., double-pronged hinged clips on rev, with a pinback mechanism for joining as a brooch, clips and pinback mkd "sterling," clips mkd "Coro," 2-½" w × 1-¾" joined **350**

Dress Clip

Rhinestones, white pot metal, c. 1935, elongated shield shape, openwork, foliate design, prong-set throughout with lg and medium oval-cut aqua and deep pink r.s., sm marquise and oval deep pink r.s., interspersed with various sized circ colorless r.s., flat-backed hinged clip on rev mkd "Eisenberg Original," 2" w × 4" **550**

Rhinestones, white pot metal, c. 1935, stylized leaf shape prong-set throughout with lg oval, pear, and circ colorless r.s., veins pavé-set with sm circ r.s., mkd "Eisenberg Original," engr flat-backed spring-hinged clip on rev, 2" w × 3-¾" **295**

Rhinestones, gp wm, c. 1935, inverted triangular shape, openwork scrolled and lobed design, a lg inverted pear-shaped colorless r.s. prong-set at top center, prong-set throughout with smaller rect, oval, sq, cushion, pear, marquise, and circ colorless r.s. and pavé-set with sm circ r.s., flat-backed hinged clip on rev mkd "Eisenberg Original," 3" w × 3-½" **225**

Dress Clips

Rhinestones, rh pl wm, c. 1935, flower-basket motif, pierced and pavé-set with colorless r.s., rev mkd with lg "T" flanked by sm "K" and "F" for Trifari, Krussman & Fishel, flat-backed hinged clips, 1-¼" × 1-¼", pr **125**

Earrings/Earclips

Glass, rhinestones, sterling, c. 1940, scrolled pavé-set r.s. crescents, each with three oval faceted purple glass stones prong-set à jour along one side flanked by grad pavé and collet-set colorless r.s., clipbacks mkd "sterling Pat Pend," ½" w × 1", pr **125**

Lucite, sterling vermeil, c. 1940, egg-shaped Lucite centers in ster frames with pavé r.s. accents, screwbacks mkd "sterling," ¾" × ½", pr **150**

Rhinestones, rh pl wm, c.1945, flowerhead cluster of pale green oval and pear-shaped r.s. with colorless r.s. center, flanked on one side by a pavé r.s.-set scrolled ribbon motif, clipbacks mkd "Pennino," ⅝" × 1-¼", pr **50**

Rhinestones, wm, c. 1950, one lavender and one blue marquise-cut r.s. prong-set diagonally within high-pronged frames, separated by a band of colorless r.s., clipbacks mkd "Carnegie" for Hattie Carnegie, ½" w × 1-¼", pr **45**

Rhinestones, rh pl wm, c. 1950, kite-shaped, open center set with a marquise-cut dk blue r.s. flanked by dk blue baguette r.s., pavé colorless r.s. in V-shape below center surmounted by a pavé domed disk, clipbacks mkd "Bogoff," ¾" w × 1-¼", pr **38**

Rhinestones, gp wm, c. 1950, flowerhead of marquise-cut lt and dk blue r.s. alternating with circ colorless r.s. around a lt blue circ

Earrings, c. 1940-50: TL, gp brass, rhinestones, c. 1945, floral and foliate clusters wired to stamped filigree backing and set throughout with colorless and olive green r.s., clipbacks, rev mkd "Miriam Haskell" on appl horseshoe-shaped plaque, ⁷⁄₈" w × 1-¹⁄₈", pr, $75, *Author's collection;* TR, gp brass, faux pearls, c. 1950, circ flowerheads with stamped gp petals, a lg baroque faux pearl in center of each, clipbacks mkd "Miriam Haskell," 1" dia, pr, $100; C, Pendent Earrings, faux pearls, brass, c. 1950, a lg baroque pearl drop surmounted by a brass collar encircled by faux seed pearls, suspended from cable-link chain, flowerhead surmount with sm baroque faux pearl wired to brass backing, combination screw/clipbacks mkd "Pat 2400513" (1946), rev surmount mkd "Miriam Haskell," 2-³⁄₄" tl × ¹⁄₂", pr, $175; BL, sterling, faux pearls, rhinestones, c. 1940, a lg round faux pearl mounted within a crescent-shaped collar of pavé-set colorless r.s., mkd "Eisenberg Original, sterling," screwbacks, 1" w × 1", pr, $95, *Victoria Taylor collection;* BR, rhinestones, faux pearls, glass, sp brass, c. 1950, floral and foliate clusters formed of faux pearls and colorless oval and circ r.s., sp leaves, surmounting a white glass disk and a stamped sp filigree backing, clipbacks mkd "Robért," 1" w × 1-¹⁄₄", pr, $45, *Author's collection.*

r.s. center, clipbacks mkd "Hobé," ⁷⁄₈" dia, pr
. . . . **40**
Rhinestones, gp wm, c. 1950, inverted comma shape, with a lg topaz-colored circ r.s. prong-set in center encircled by sm prong-set pavé colorless r.s. tapering upward to cusped tip, clipbacks with cylindrical vinyl lobe cushions at top, mkd "Hobé," 1" w × 1-¹⁄₂", pr **50**
Sterling vermeil, glass, c. 1940, owls of oval faceted yellow glass, prong-set *à jour* in center of bodies, rev mkd "sterling," screwback findings, ⁵⁄₈" w × 1" **65**
Sterling, c. 1945, face design, circ disk with raised features, rev mkd "Rebajes," New York, screwbacks mkd "sterling," 1" dia, pr
. . . . **100**
Sterling, c. 1950, pierced beaded and scrolled acanthus motif, lg sphere at center bottom, clipbacks, unmkd, attributed to Guglielmo Cini, 1" w × 1-¹⁄₄", pr **50**
Wm, marcasites, faux pearls, c. 1940, wm flowerheads pavé-set with marcasites, faux pearl centers, clipbacks, 1" × 1", pr **45**
Pendent
    Glass, rhinestones, gp wm, c. 1960, lg oval red glass cab flanked and surmounted by pear-shaped faceted blue glass stones and teardrop green glass cabs, outlined and

interspersed with pavé colorless r.s., suspended from red glass cab and r.s. surmount mkd "Trifari," from "Jewels of India" collection, clipbacks, 3-¹⁄₄" tl × 1-¹⁄₄", pr **200**
Rhinestones, rh pl wm, c 1955, alternating long and short four-strand fringe of articulated prong-set lt blue r.s., each strand terminating in a larger circ blue r.s., suspended from curv surmount prong-set with one lg marquise, lt blue r.s. and three rows of sm circ r.s., 3" tl × ⁵⁄₈", pr **25**
Rhinestones, rh pl wm, c. 1955, articulated triple-lobed drop outlined in sm colorless prong-set r.s. with lg r.s. centers, surmounted by a four-strand fringe of prong-set r.s., suspended from a V-shaped surmount with a lg circ r.s. in the center, clipbacks, 2-³⁄₄" tl × 1-¹⁄₂", pr **30**
Rhinestones, rh pl wm, c. 1955, double overlapping drops, each with three prong-set pear-shaped colorless r.s. forming trefoils, suspended *négligée* from articulated strands of rect and circ sm r.s., lg circ r.s. surmount, clipbacks, 2-³⁄₄" tl × 1", pr
. . . . **30**
Rhinestones, gp wm, c. 1960, a six-strand grad fringe of articulated prong-set aurora borealis r.s. terminating in larger mar-

quise-cut stones, suspended from a crescent-shaped surmount of grad circ aurora
borealis r.s. outlined in smaller r.s.,
clipbacks, 4-³/₄″ tl × ³/₄″ w, pr
.... **100**
Rhinestones, rh pl wm, c. 1960, a six strand
cascading grad fringe of articulated prong-
set colorless r.s. terminating in larger circ
r.s., suspended from a scrolled crescent-
shaped surmount, clipbacks, 4-³/₄″ tl × 1″,
pr **85**
Necklace
Copper, enamel, glass, c. 1950, nine linked
slightly curv rect plaques, each with a rect
center of translucent aqua glass fired onto a
white enameled ground, rev counter-enameled white, one plaque sgd "Denning" in
green, foldover clasp, 15-³/₄″ tl × ⁵/₈″, with
orig paper label, one side reading "Denning
originals handmade," rev reads "hand-
crafted jewelry made of stained glass or venetian glass enamelled on silver or copper."
.... **50**
Faux pearls, gp brass, c. 1945, a central triple
cluster of gp foliate motifs set with lg baroque
faux pearls tipped with gp rondelles and col-

**Necklace, gp metal, painted enamel, glass, rhinestones,
c. 1950, twisted gp mesh rope terminating in a cast-
metal two-part cobra motif, blue-green painted enamel
body set with irregularly shaped orange irid glass, circ
and marquise-cut amber aurora borealis r.s., front v-
spring and box clasp joins head and tail, unmkd, attributed to HAR, 19″ tl, 2-¹/₄″ top to bottom at center, $395.
Kirsten Olson collection.**

orless prong-set r.s. wired to a stamped filigree backing, continuing to a strand of faux
pearls joined to a double strand of flat coiled
link gp chain, terminating in a hook and faux
pearl chain closure, unmkd, attributed to
Miriam Haskell, 19″ tl × 1-¹/₂″ **350**
Faux pearls, rhinestones, gp brass, c. 1950, a
single strand of grad baroque faux pearls
with irid luster, colorless r.s. and gp rondelle
spacers, terminating in a hook clasp
surmounted by a faux pearl-set flowerhead,
rev mkd "Miriam Haskell," with faux pearl
and rondelle chain, 22-¹/₂″ tl, largest pearl ¹/₂″
dia (14 mm) **250**
Faux pearls, gp brass, c. 1950, a single strand of
textured baroque faux pearls with gp bead
spacers, hook and chain closure, strung on
fine chain, 17″ tl × ³/₈″ **85**
Faux pearls, gp brass, c. 1950, a single strand of
lg beige-tone textured baroque faux pearls
with gp seed bead spacers, hook and chain
closure, 17″ tl × ¹/₂″ **55**
Faux pearls, gp brass, c. 1950, a single strand of
alternating lg and sm baroque faux pearls
with sm rondelle gp brass spacers, terminating in double hook clasps with r.s. and faux
pearl flowerheads appl to tops of hooks, mkd
"Miriam Haskell," continuing to chains of
sm faux pearls joined with eyepins, 26-¹/₂″ tl
× ¹/₂″........................... **200**
Glass, rhinestones, wm, c. 1950, adjustable
choker with links prong-set with circ irid
pink glass cabs alternating with emerald-cut
and sm circ pink and aurora borealis r.s.,
hook and chain closure, attached metal tag
mkd "Vendôme," 17-¹/₂″ tl × ⁵/₈″ **150**
Rhinestones, gp wm, rh pl wm, painted
enamel, c. 1940, central foliate motif set
with red baguettes and pavé colorless r.s.
around two green enameled center leaves,
flanked by two gp and r.s. flowers with
baguette r.s. centers *en tremblant*, pavé r.s.
and green enameled leaves (some wear),
continuing to a circ pavé r.s. and red
baguette bar link chain, foldover clasp, rev
mkd "Corocraft, Reg.U.S.A. Pat.Off. D. Pat
110296" (1938), 17-³/₄″ tl, 2-³/₄″ center top to
bottom **250**
Rhinestones, gp wm, c. 1950, five linked
pierced and scrolled trefoils, each set with
three lg shield-shaped r.s., two dk amber-
colored and one smoky brown, and three sm
circ amber-colored r.s., continuing to a fancy
circ link chain, hook clasp, appl plaque on
rev of one trefoil mkd "Schiaparelli" in
script, 17″ tl, 1-¹/₂″ w **300**
Sp brass, c. 1940, linked stamped relief foliate
motifs, each with a central domed disk
surmounted by a round bead, suspending a
larger trefoil of similar design surmounted by
numerous round beads, oval plaque appl to
rev of one link mkd "Joseff Hollywood"

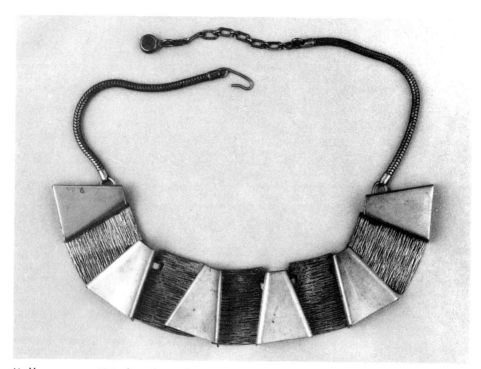

Necklace, copper, c. 1950, alternating overlapping textured flat and smooth trapezoidal plaques with folded sides, linked together, continuing to a snake chain, hook and chain-link closure terminating in a circ drop mkd "Rebajes," 17" tl × 1-⅛", $100. *Author's collection.*

Necklace, glass beads, faux pearls, wm, c. 1955, round fluted red and smooth green glass beads and faux pearls interwoven on a wm chain suspending a cluster of red and green glass beads with a lg baroque faux pearl center, faux pearl button on box clasp, mkd "Made in France" on rev, attributed to Chanel, 20" tl, center cluster 2" w × 1-½", $950. *Kathy Toledo collection.*

(block letters), 15-$\frac{1}{4}$" tl, center trefoil 2-$\frac{1}{2}$" w
× 2-$\frac{3}{4}$" **250**

Sterling vermeil, c. 1950, six prs of linked acorn and oak leaf motifs suspending a larger acorn and double oak leaves, appl plaque on rev mkd "sterling Nettie Rosenstein," hook and chain closure, 16" tl × 2-$\frac{1}{2}$" at center front **250**

Pendant and Chain

Gp wm, glass, rhinestones, c. 1940, an open-work inverted triangular pendant, gp S-scrolls with pavé r.s. accents surmounting a lg fluted oval red glass cab flanked by smaller fluted oval red cabs and sm inverted teardrop and circ blue glass cabs, interspersed with sm colorless r.s., suspended by circ and bar links from gp rope-twist chain, spring-ring clasp, pendant rev mkd "pat. pend Trifari" #19, 15" tl, pendant 2-$\frac{3}{4}$" w × 1-$\frac{1}{2}$" **90**

Suite: Bracelet and Earrings

Sterling vermeil, faux pearls, rhinestones, Retro Modern, c. 1940, bracelet of sq links, right-angle frames on two sides, lg faux pearl centers, colorless pavé r.s. spacers, safety chain, 6-$\frac{3}{4}$" tl × $\frac{3}{4}$", pr of matching clip earrings, $\frac{3}{4}$" × $\frac{3}{4}$", all pcs mkd "R. De Rosa sterling," suite **525**

Suite: Brooch/Pin and Earrings

Enamel, glass, rhinestones gp wm, c. 1960, scrolled quatrefoil brooch prong-set with center cobalt blue circ glass cab and four oval cabs each with clusters of three sm colorless r.s. within cobalt blue enameled C-scrolls, rev mkd "Trifari ©," matching earrings, each a single tapered enameled scroll set with a lg oval blue glass cab flanked by sm colorless r.s., clipbacks mkd "Trifari ©," brooch 1-$\frac{3}{4}$" w × 1-$\frac{7}{8}$", earrings $\frac{1}{2}$" w × 1", suite **95**

Enamel, faux pearls, rhinestones, rh pl wm, c. 1955, brooch a stylized pansy, the entire surface covered in gold-flecked yellow enamel, a center cluster of sm colorless r.s., petals dotted with seven faux pearls, rev mkd "Trifari," matching enameled earrings, circ domed disks, each interspersed with three faux pearls and sm colorless r.s., clipbacks mkd "Trifari," brooch 1-$\frac{1}{2}$" w × 2", earrings $\frac{3}{4}$" dia, suite **125**

Faux pearls, rhinestones, gp brass, c. 1950, a circ wreath brooch with gp leaves, set throughout with lg and sm baroque faux pearls and circ colorless r.s. mounted with wire onto a stamped filigree plaque, pr of clipback earrings of similar floral and foliate design, brooch unmkd, 1-$\frac{3}{4}$" dia, earrings mkd "Robért," $\frac{7}{8}$" w × 1", suite **50**

Glass, rhinestones, gp ym, c.1950, hexagonal brooch with amber-colored circ r.s. set in a center cluster and surrounding circle, six lg circ amber-colored glass cabs prong-set around outer edge, ym foliate accents throughout, mkd "Schiaparelli" in script,

Suites, Schiaparelli, c. 1950: L, Link Bracelet and Brooch/Pin, sp wm, glass, a five-link bracelet, each link a pr of wm leaves surrounding one lg oval black faceted glass stone, foldover clasp mkd "Schiaparelli," safety chain, 7-$\frac{1}{2}$" tl, each link 1-$\frac{1}{2}$" × 1-$\frac{1}{8}$", matching brooch a cluster of three glass stones and wm leaves, 2-$\frac{1}{2}$" × 2-$\frac{1}{4}$", suite, $400; R, Link Bracelet and Earrings, oxidized wm, glass, each link of bracelet a textured high-relief disk with fancy prong-set watermelon glass stone (irid blue, green, pink, yellow), safety chain, foldover clasp mkd "Schiaparelli," 7-$\frac{1}{2}$" tl, each link 1-$\frac{1}{8}$" dia, pr of matching button clip earrings, 1" dia, suite, $275, Charles Pinkham collection.

2-$\frac{1}{2}$" × 2-$\frac{1}{2}$", matching pr of pendent earrings with a lg amber-colored glass cab drop and surmount, r.s. and ym foliate accents, clipbacks, 2" tl × 1-$\frac{1}{4}$", suite **350**

Glass, gp wm, rhinestones, c. 1960, lg stylized flowerhead with a lg circ dk red faceted glass center encircled by six oval dk red faceted glass stones prong-set at the ends of textured gp petals separated by colorless pavé r.s tapered ribbons, circ clip earrings, each prong-set with a lg circ red glass stone in a fluted gp frame, all pcs mkd "Trifari ©," brooch 2-$\frac{7}{8}$" dia, clipback earrings, 1-$\frac{1}{8}$" dia **195**

Rhinestones, faux pearls, gp wm, c. 1955, oval brooch with a lg faceted oval green r.s. prong-set in the center, encircled by faux seed pearls within convex bands of sm green r.s. and faux seed pearls set diagonally around an open framework, matching circ earrings with five seed pearl and green r.s. rosettes around lg circ green r.s., clipbacks,

Suite: Necklace and Pendent Earrings, glass, gp brass, c. 1950, articulated collar of linked gp foliate motifs and faceted black glass beads forming seven rosettes suspending seven clusters of faceted black glass beads, four with gp caps above and below each cluster, continuing to links of gp foliate motifs and black glass beads, v-spring and box clasp with circ gp surmount prong-set with faceted black glass, 16" tl × 4" top to bottom at center, matching pendent earrings with black glass cab surmounts, rev mkd "Made in France, *Deposé*," open wire clipbacks, 2-¹/₂" tl × 1", suite, $800. *Kirsten Olson collection.*

all pcs mkd "Hollycraft Copr. 1954," brooch 2" w × 1-¹/₂", earrings 1" dia, suite **55**
Sterling, c. 1940, cast brooch in the shape of cherries on a branch with blossoms and leaves, clip earrings, each a pr of leaves, rev plaque on brooch mkd "sterling by Cini" for Guglielmo Cini, Boston, Mass., brooch 2-¹/₂" w × 3-¹/₂", earrings ³/₄" w × 1", suite . . . **195**
Sterling, glass, rhinestones, c. 1940, brooch in the shape of a bird with a pear-shaped faceted pink glass stone set *à jour* in a millegrained bezel on each wing tip, suspending a pierced ribbon bow with rosebud center set with a circ green r.s., chain tassel drop, rev mkd "Hobé sterling design pat.," 1-¹/₂" w × 3-¹/₄" tl, and a pr of rosebud earrings with green r.s. centers, screwbacks mkd "sterling," ⁷/₈" dia, suite **300**
Sterling, rhinestones, c. 1940, an openwork wreath brooch with red r.s. center, surmounted by a pierced ribbon bow with a central fuchsia r.s. millegrain-set in an open-backed collet flanked by six flower buds, a flowerhead at the base of wreath set with green r.s., suspending a flowerhead drop, and a pr of foliate flowerhead earrings with green r.s. centers, screwbacks mkd "ster-

ling," ⁷/₈" dia, brooch rev mkd "Hobé sterling design pat'd," 1-³/₄" w × 2-¹/₂", suite . . . **225**
Sterling, moonstones, citrines, amethysts, syn stones, c. 1940, a floral spray brooch, flowerheads bezel-set with circ citrine and amethyst centers, moonstone-set leaf, additional flowerheads and leaves set with circ and marquise-cut natural and synthetic stones, sgd "Parenti," 11.9 dwt, 3-⁵/₈" w × 1-³/₈", earrings of foliate design, each with an oval moonstone cab and five circ and one sq natural and syn stones, double screwbacks, sgd "Parenti," 9.1 dwt, 1-¹/₂" w × 1", suite . . . . **302 (A)**
Sterling vermeil, rhinestones, glass, Retro Modern, c. 1940, in the shapes of stylized fish with ruffled gp fins and tails, each with a faceted oval aqua glass center, brooch with pavé colorless r.s. above center stone, screwback earrings mkd "sterling," "MB" below bird's head logo for Marcel Boucher, New York, N.Y., 1-¹/₈" w × 1", mark illegible on brooch, 3" w × 1-³/₄", suite **200**
Suite: Clip and Earrings
Sterling vermeil, faux pearls, glass, rhinestones, c. 1940, an oval plaque with a center oval

Suite: Necklace and Pendent Earrings, faux pearls, gp wm, rhinestones, c. 1970, triple strand necklace of lg round faux pearls, hand-knotted, terminating in a fancy oval gp and pavé r.s. clasp, pr of matching pendent earrings, each with a lg pear-shaped faux pearl drop, gp and pavé r.s. surmount, clip backs, with original tags mkd "Kenneth J. Lane, Laguna" (Royal Craftsmen, Inc., N.Y., mfr), necklace approx 29" tl × 1-³/₄", earrings 2-¹/₄" tl × ³/₄", suite, $300. *Charles Pinkham collection.*

faceted pink glass stone encircled by eight colorless r.s., concentric rings of faux pearls, r.s., and an outer ring of lg faux pearls alternating with sm turq glass beads within rose gp ster, beaded frame, double-pronged hinged clip mounted on rev mkd "sterling," appl plaque imp "Nettie Rosenstein," matching clipback oval earrings unmkd, clip 1-5/8" w × 2", earrings 3/4" w × 1", suite **100**

Suite: Necklace, Bracelet, and Earrings

Plastic, gp wm, rhinestones, c. 1950, link bracelet and necklace of scrolled floral and foliate design, set with oval cabs and concave pear shapes of coral-colored plastic and lg and sm colorless r.s., bracelet with foldover clasp, necklace continuing to a chain with hook closure, matching clipback earrings, all mkd "Trifari," necklace 16" tl × 5/8", bracelet 7-1/4" × 5/8", earrings 1-1/8" × 3/4", suite **65**

Rhinestones, ym, c. 1950, necklace of flexible snake chain suspending a lg pear-shaped plaque of clustered prong-set pink, fuchsia, aqua, and green circ and oval-cut r.s., continuing to sm leaves of twisted ym wire flanked by sm oval plaques set with two r.s. each, bracelet a similar lg oval center plaque and four sm ovals joined with three rows of snake chain, unmkd, attributed to Hollycraft, necklace 15" tl, center 1-5/8" × 1-3/8", bracelet 6-7/8" tl, center 1-1/4" × 1", pr of matching oval clip earrings, 1" w × 7/8", suite **195**

Rhinestones, gp wm., c. 1950, clusters of lg prong-set circ lt blue and yellow r.s. and smaller colorless r.s. mounted on gp chain, necklace continuing to textured and cable link gp chain, hook and glass bead closure, bracelet terminating in a foldover clasp, pr of earrings, each with one yellow r.s. and one blue r.s. encircled by colorless r.s., clipbacks sgd "Hobé," necklace 17" tl × 1-1/8", bracelet 6-3/4" × 1-1/4", earrings 1" w × 1-1/2", suite **325**

Sp wm, c. 1965, articulated necklace, hinged bangle bracelet, and pr of clip earrings, a stylized cactus design with overlapping irregularly shaped disks in varying sizes, with a raised stippled pattern resembling cactus thorns, all pcs mkd "© Tortolani" in script on appl plates on rev, necklace 18" tl × 1", bracelet 2" inside dia, 1-3/8" w, earrings 7/8" w × 1-1/4", suite **225**

Suite: Necklace and Earrings

Glass, ym, c. 1950, three strands of grad tiered black glass beads, faceted rect with rounded corners, blue, green, and purple irid coating on one side, adjustable hook and chain closure, necklace unmkd, 16" tl × 1-1/2", pr of matching round button clip earrings mkd "Vogue," 3/4" dia, suite **100**

Rhinestones, gp wm, c. 1955, adjustable choker with links set with baguette and circ multi-colored pastel r.s., hook and chain clasp, mkd "Hollycraft Copr 1955," 17-1/2" tl × 3/8", floral and foliate design drop earrings,

Sweater Guard, rhinestones, rh pl wm, c. 1950, two clips with circ wm mesh frames, centers prong-set with one lg dk blue r.s. encircled by smaller dk blue r.s., linked by r.s.-set chain, on orig card mkd "Sweater Guard," logo for Weiss Co., orig tags for Weiss Co. and "The Fair Chicago," alligator-type clips on rev mkd with illegible pat number, 7-1/2" tl, clips 1-1/8" dia, $35. *Victoria Taylor collection.*

screwbacks mkd "Hollycraft," 1-$\frac{1}{2}$" × $\frac{5}{8}$", suite **125**

Suite: Necklace and Flexible Bracelet

Rhinestones, rh pl wm, c. 1950, articulated prong-set colorless r.s. necklace with triangular center cluster of lg circ r.s. surmounted by four appl wm tapered C-scrolls pavé-set with sm r.s., bracelet with two rows of lg and sm circ r.s. with appl wm tapered pavé-set sections, pavé foldover clasp, safety chain, necklace mkd "Weiss" on open rect notched clasp, 16-$\frac{3}{4}$" tl × 1-$\frac{1}{8}$" at center, bracelet unmkd, 7-$\frac{1}{4}$" × $\frac{5}{8}$", suite **150**

Suite: Necklace and Pendent Earrings

Bakelite, glass, bronzed metal, c. 1955, bead necklace strung with alternating round faceted yellow aurora borealis glass beads, and opaque amber-colored sq and grad round Bakelite beads, larger Bakelite cubes wrapped with four strips of amber-colored prong-set r.s. flanked by bronzed metal seed beads, terminating in a gp filigree fishhook clasp, unmkd, matching pendent earrings, clipback findings mkd "Vendôme," (a division of Coro, N.Y.), earrings 1-$\frac{3}{4}$" tl × $\frac{5}{8}$", necklace 28" tl × $\frac{5}{8}$", suite **450**

PART IV

Special Collectible Jewelry

INTRODUCTION

Certain types of jewelry do not fall neatly into period or style categories. While space does not permit exploring all of these special types of jewelry, the references following direct readers to other categories that could not be included here, for example, folk and ethnic jewelry and beads.

The three special collectible categories in this section, Native American, Mexican, and Scandinavian, are based on country of origin. While jewelry-making traditions date back to earlier periods in all three countries, availability and collector interest are concentrated in the twentieth century; most examples are from the 1920s or later. It is interesting to note that the three categories have certain features in common: the metal most often used is silver, the work is most often done by hand, and there was a certain amount of cross-cultural exchange of ideas and techniques among them. During the 1940s and 1950s, all three enjoyed a period of popularity in the United States, brought about in part by World War II.

References (for other categories not included in this section): Janet Coles and Robert Budwig, *The Book of Beads,* Simon and Schuster, 1990; Lois Sher Dubin, *The History of Beads, from 30,000 B.C. to the Present,* Harry N. Abrams, 1987; Peter Francis, Jr., *Beads of the World,* Schiffer Publishing, 1994; James J. Kellner, *Siam Sterling Nielloware,* self-published by the author, 1993; Robert O. Kinsey, *Ojime: Magical Jewels of Japan,* Harry N. Abrams, 1991; John Mack, ed., *Ethnic Jewelry,* Harry N. Abrams, 1988; Dona Z. Meilach, *Ethnic Jewelry, Design & Inspiration for Collectors and Craftsmen,* Crown Publishers, 1981 (out of print); Susan Stronge, Nima Smith, and J.C. Harle, *A Golden Treasury, Jewellery from the Indian Subcontinent* (Victoria and Albert Museum Indian Art Series), Rizzoli, 1988; Oppi Untracht, *Jewelry Concepts and Technology,* Doubleday, 1985.

NATIVE AMERICAN (INDIAN) JEWELRY

History: In the late 1960s and early 1970s, the booming popularity of Southwestern American Indian jewelry was at its peak. The volume of poor quality machine-made knockoffs, imported fakes, and "white man's work" had become so great that potential collector interest soured; most people were afraid to buy for fear a piece was not authentic. As a result, over the past 20 years, the market for Indian jewelry, both old and new, has changed considerably. Today, there are two kinds of collectors: those who collect only traditional old pieces, preferably dating before World War II, and those who buy the traditional and contemporary work of recognized artists. The first type of collector makes a distinction between jewelry made for tribal wear and jewelry made for the tourist trade, although old examples of both are considered collectible. The second type is primarily concerned with quality of workmanship and originality of design. Because this book is about antique and period jewelry, the following section concentrates on older, traditional Native American pieces. For readers interested in the work of today's Native American artists, Dexter Cirillo's *Southwestern Indian Jewelry* (see references following), which also includes a substantial amount of historical background, is recommended. As there are many caveats to be aware of, and much study required to fully understand the differences between old and new, authentic and imitation, readers are directed to a number of other reliable resources on traditional and old Indian jewelry.

Although other tribes in other parts of the United States made jewelry, the work of the silversmiths and lapidaries of the Southwest—the

Navajo, Santo Domingo, Zuni, and Hopi Pueblo tribes—is the best known and most sought after. What follows here is a basic introductory summary of the history, materials, techniques, and identifiable characteristics of typical traditional jewelry made by the major Southwest Native American tribes.

Many people are surprised to learn that silversmithing is a relatively new development in Native American arts, first practiced by the Navajo during the last quarter of the nineteenth century. However, other jewelry forms and materials, such as beads made from stone or shell, date to prehistoric times. Today, most of the oldest pieces are in museum collections. Ancient jewelry and silver jewelry made before 1900 (the period 1868-1900 is known as "first phase") rarely comes up for sale and is usually priced at more than $10,000 when it does.

The earliest silver work was made strictly for tribal use as symbols of status and portable wealth and for ceremonial purposes. During lean times, the Indians would take some of their jewelry to the trading post and pawn it for credit. There are common misconceptions about the term "old pawn," one being that pawn jewelry is somehow more valuable because it has been pawned. In fact, the opposite is true. The Indians would pawn only expendable less-important pieces that they were willing to risk losing. The pawn system is still in use today, but only pieces made before 1900 are correctly called old pawn.

The influence of the trader and burgeoning tourism should not be underestimated. Traders mentored many a tribal silversmith and encouraged the development of distinctive styles, providing designs as well as an outlet for the selling of finished goods. In addition to tools, the traders also brought in otherwise unavailable materials.

The building of the railroad (the Atchison, Topeka & Santa Fe, which ran from Chicago to Southern California via Albuquerque, New Mexico, was completed in 1880) led to the appearance of Harvey Houses—restaurants and rest stops constructed along the rail routes during the late nineteenth century. The commercialization of American Indian jewelry began in 1899, when the Fred Harvey Company placed its first order for silver jewelry to be made for the general public and sold in Harvey House curio shops. The company provided the silversmiths with sheet silver, machine-drawn wire, and precut stones. To appeal to tourists, it required the jewelry to be lighter in weight and decorated with stampings of arrows and other symbols that it thought souvenir buyers would associate with American Indian culture. Many of these symbols had no actual meaning to the silversmiths themselves. One symbol, however, the swastika, was taken from Navajo sand paintings. Although this ancient sign, representing the sun and infinity, had nothing to do with Nazism, its use was discontinued

around 1930. Today, pieces stamped with swastikas are understandably a tough sell.

Turquoise is a gemstone that has been used since ancient times in Southwest Native American cultures because the mines are indigenous to the area. Highly prized turquoise is often labeled with the name of the mine from which it came, and turquoise from an identifiable mine raises the value of a piece set with it. Most of these mines are not active today: The cost of extracting the turquoise from some of them has become prohibitive, and others have been exhausted. High-quality turquoise has also been imported from Persia since the turn of the century and is now coming from China. Porous and soft low-grade turquoise is often subjected to one of several alterations to enhance its appearance. It can be stabilized with the injection of polymer resin (plastic) to increase hardness, treated with dyes to alter its color, or completely reconstituted and formed into stones shaped from turquoise powder and particles mixed with resin. Stabilized turquoise is considered acceptable if identified as such, but its value is not as high as natural turquoise. Other types of treated turquoise, along with synthetics and dyed substitutes such as howlite, are usually found in lesser quality jewelry, imitations, and foreign imports of low value.

Other than turquoise, materials used in Native American jewelry, such as coral and shell, have been obtained through traders and imported. Several varieties of shell, brought in from the Gulf of California and the Pacific, have been used since prehistoric times. Coral, called "red gold," was first brought to the Zuni by traders around 1938 and later used by the Santo Domingo and the Navajo. Silver was never mined by the tribes. U.S. coins were used until they were prohibited in 1890, but Mexican coins continued to be used until the 1920s. Sterling silver sheet and wire were then purchased from traders.

The Navajo were the first to use turquoise in combination with silver in the late nineteenth century. However, most of their early work was all silver, with the occasional addition of a stone or two. The Navajo traded with Mexican *plateros* (silversmiths), from whom they learned silversmithing beginning in the 1870s. In the first phase period, before commercialization, the Navajo forged their own ingots from coin silver, which they then hammered into sheets and rods and drew into wire. They preferred making heavy pieces of simple design for tribal wear and continued to do so after they began using preformed sheet silver and machine-drawn wire for commercial tourist production. Therefore, Navajo jewelry from the so-called transitional or second phase period, 1900-1930, is a mixture of first phase and early tourist pieces.

Certain forms and techniques are associated with Navajo silver jewelry. The squash blossom necklace with naja pendant is one of the most familiar forms. The squash blossom is actually a pomegranate motif taken from Spanish and Mexican clothing ornaments, and the crescent-shaped or penannular naja was a bridle ornament for horses copied from the Spanish, who copied it from a Moorish amulet. Early squash blossom necklaces are heavy and simple with little if any turquoise and entirely handmade from ingot coin silver. Squash blossoms from the 1960s and 1970s are larger and gaudier, often composed of machine-made elements and elaborately decorated with turquoise.

Concha belts are another early Navajo ornament. Simple circular disks with lozenge-shaped cutout centers, minimally decorated and threaded on leather straps, date from the first phase period. Later conchas are oval with more stamping and other decorative elements, including turquoise. Concha belts were also made by Zuni and Hopi silversmiths.

Some jewelry forms are relative newcomers to the Native American idiom. Brooches did not appear until the 1930s. Bola ties and slides (the correct word is bola, not bolo) were invented and popularized by an Anglo Arizonan, Vic Cedarstaff, in 1949, although Indian antecedents from the 1920s are known but rare. The Bola Tie Society of Phoenix was formed in 1966, and bolas became the official Arizona state neckwear in 1971.

Tufa casting is a Navajo technique used since the first phase period to make najas, ketohs (ornamental wrist bowguards), buckles, rings, and bracelets. Sometimes referred to as sand casting, the technique involves carving a pattern for a mold in tufa, a porous volcanic rock, and then pouring molten metal into the mold. The hardened piece is then shaped, decorated, and polished.

Early decoration techniques included rocker engraving with a short-bladed chisel and stamped designs similar to those used by Mexican leather workers using a hand-held punch. In general, the early pieces had simple decorations; pieces made for tourists were more elaborately stamped and embellished. The Navajo taught silversmithing to other tribes who copied their designs, so it is often difficult to determine tribal origins of earlier pieces.

The Pueblo tribes, particularly the Santo Domingo, are known for their bead, shell, and mosaic work. The disk-shaped shell beads strung on string known as "heishi" (alternately spelled "heishe") are a Santo Domingo specialty and a 1,500 year-old tradition. The shells are individually cut into squares, drilled, strung, and then rolled by hand or machine to make thin circular disks. The word "heishi" is also erroneously used to refer to a similar type of bead made of turquoise or other stone. The Santo Domingo are also known for their mosaics—patterns of stone, jet, coral, and shell applied to a shell, wood, or bone

base. During the 1930s and 1940s, the Great Depression and World War II forced artisans to use car battery casings and 78 rpm phonograph records for bases and as jet substitutes. Pieces of old plastic toothbrush handles were used as substitutes for coral and turquoise. Depression-era necklaces strung with tubular shell beads interspersed with tabs and suspending thunderbird motif pendants, battery-backed with mosaic overlay, are now collectible. Prices range from $200 to $1,000, depending on quality. The necklace is the most common form of jewelry made by the Santo Domingo, but they also produce pendants, earrings, rings, and bracelets. The ancient tradition of fetish carving—animals and birds carved from stone or shell—is still carried on by the Santo Domingo and the Zuni. Small fetishes are strung on necklaces, often in combination with shell heishi.

The Zuni are another Pueblo tribe known for their lapidary work, but early Zuni silver jewelry is difficult to distinguish from that of the Navajo. The Zuni began establishing their own style of jewelry making around 1915. They are noted for bezel-setting stones in clusters and patterns and channel inlay of stone into silver. Numerous small, narrow navette-shaped turquoise slivers set in patterns are called needlepoint; somewhat larger pear-shaped or oval stones are called petit point. Zuni cluster work evolved during the 1920s, and petit point and needlepoint were developed in the 1940s. Channel inlay is a technique that the Zuni began using just before World War II. All of these techniques were made possible by the introduction of more sophisticated tools and equipment supplied by traders.

The Hopi were the last tribe to develop their own identifiable style, beginning in the late 1930s. Until that time, the jewelry they made was copied from Navajo and Zuni designs. The all-silver layered technique that the Hopi are now noted for is called overlay; it was introduced by the founders of the Museum of Northern Arizona in 1938, using Hopi pottery and textile patterns. Abstract and/or figural designs are cut out from a piece of silver, which is then soldered to another piece. The background is oxidized and textured to bring out the design. The earliest Hopi overlay was not signed, but later silversmiths began using hallmarks, either symbols or their names. (In general, pre-World War II Native American jewelry is not signed; since the 1960s, many artists have been hallmarking their work.)

World War II was a turning point in the history of Native American jewelry making. For the first time, Native Americans were drafted into the armed forces and sent overseas. They were exposed to cultures other than their own and returned with a broader view of the world, cash in their pockets, and an opportunity to further their education through the G.I. Bill. Like many other American veterans, they attended classes in jewelry making, learning new techniques using modern equipment. They formed guilds that enabled them to market their own goods. For some Native Americans, making jewelry became more than a traditional tribal occupation. They became artist-jewelers. Today, Native American silversmiths' work, both traditional and contemporary, is sought after for its unique designs and superb quality. The best pieces are priced in the four- to five-figure range. Many artists exhibit and sell at the annual Indian Market, a tradition since 1922, held every August in Santa Fe, New Mexico.

References: John Adair, *The Navajo and Pueblo Silversmiths,* University of Oklahoma Press, 1944 (out of print); Dexter Cirillo, *Southwestern Indian Jewelry,* Abbeville Press, 1992; Kathleen Conroy, *What You Should Know about Authentic Indian Jewelry,* Gro-Pub, 1975 (out of print); Larry Frank and Millard J. Holbrook, *Indian Silver Jewelry of the Southwest, 1868-1930,* Schiffer Publishing, 1990; William A. and Sarah P. Turnbaugh, *Indian Jewelry of the American Southwest,* Schiffer Publishing, 1988; Barton Wright, *Hallmarks of the Southwest,* Schiffer Publishing, 1989; Margaret N. Wright, *Hopi Silver, the History and Hallmarks of Hopi Silversmithing,* fourth ed., Northland Publishing, 1989.

Periodical: *Arizona Highways,* issues with articles on Native American jewelry: July 1971, January 1974, August 1974, March 1975, August 1976, October 1976, and April 1979.

Museums: Museum of Northern Arizona, Flagstaff, Ariz.; The Heard Museum, Phoenix, Ariz.; Southwest Museum, Los Angeles, Calif.; Field Museum of Natural History, Chicago, Ill.; Wheelwright Museum of the American Indian, Santa Fe, N.M.; Millicent Rogers Museum, Taos, N.M.; National Museum of the American Indian, New York, N.Y.; Smithsonian Institution, Washington, D.C.

Reproduction Alert: Low-quality imitation Indian jewelry is mass produced in Taiwan and the Philippines. Some skilled Anglo craftspeople copy old techniques and designs well enough to fool the experts. Old pawn may be neither old nor pawn (fake pawn tickets can be easily attached to any piece). Treated turquoise and simulants may be difficult to identify. Caveat emptor: know your source and obtain written documentation.

Advisors: Dexter Cirillo, Harmer Johnson, and Steve Nelson.

Bola tie
    Silver, turq, leather, c. 1955, Zuni, a braided leather tie with a pierced slide depicting a knife-wing god, enclosed by semicirc turq cabs, 2-³/₈" dia . . . . **220 (A)**
Bracelet
    Cuff
        Silver, c. 1880-1930, Navajo, forged ingot cuff with rocker-stamped, cold chiseled, and filed ribbed bands through center and

Cuff Bracelets, silver, turquoise, Fred Harvey, c. 1930: T, sm green turq cab framed by coiled snakes, flanked by appl thunderbirds, arrow, and flower stamped design, 2-¹/₄" inside dia, 1-¹/₂" w, $85; C, scroll, bead, and rope-twist wire frame around a lg oval green turq cab, arrow and cloud motifs stamped decoration, 2-¹/₄" inside dia, ³/₄" w, $65; B, a central oval green turq cab flanked by three raised silver beads within ropetwist frames, three smaller raised silver beads at top and bottom, a cluster of three appl spear shapes on each side, crossed arrow stamps, 2-³/₈" inside dia, 1-¹/₄" w, $175, *Courtesy of Mountain Lion Trading Post.*

along each edge, rounded ends, 2-¹/₂" dia, 1-¹/₈" w **750**
Silver, turq, c. 1940, Navajo, narrow half-round cuff, flattened center set with three sm turq in saw-toothed bezels, flanked by circ and serrate stamps, tourist design, 2-¹/₄" inside dia, ¹/₄" w **40**
Silver, c. 1945, made by Navajo Arts and Crafts Guild for Fred Harvey tourist sale, wide flat band with stamped arrow and feather motifs, 2-¹/₄" inside dia, 1" w **155**
Silver, turq, c. 1950, Navajo, narrow rope-twist heavy gauge-wire cuff, a bezel-set sm oval turq in center, 2-¹/₄" inside dia, ¹/₄" w **60**
Silver, c. 1950-60, Navajo, unusual interwoven twisted wire rope design in the center of a plain band, 2-³/₈" inside dia, ³/₄" w **140**

Silver, c. 1960, Navajo, raised bead and rope-twist heavy gauge-wire within cutout flat band, 2-⅝" dia, ¾" w **125**

Silver, turq, c. 1960, Navajo, tufa-cast open-loop bow shape with central circ turq cab within rope twist frame, 2-⅜" inside dia, 1-½" w **145**

Silver, turq (treated), c. 1960, Navajo, cast lozenge-shaped open center with irregular oval turq set in sawtoothed bezel, flanked by open loops continuing to a narrow shank, 2-⅛" dia, ½" w **85**

Silver, turq, c. 1930-40, Zuni, three rows of sm turq cabs separated by lengths of rope-twist wire, beaded edges, stamped decoration on each end, 2-½" inside dia, 1" w **235**

Cuff Bracelet, silver, Hopi, c. 1960, wide band with a center strip of overlay in a Greek meander pattern, flanked by narrow bands of engr reeding, 2-¼" dia, 1-½" w, $160. Margaret Levine collection.

Cuff Bracelets, turquoise, silver, Navajo: T, c. 1930, forged ingot narrow row bracelet, 11 grad oval turquoise cabs set in plain bezels with two rows of stamped silver beads in between, tapered band with heart-shaped appl wire at each end of row, oval and bead stamped patterns, 2-½" dia, ⅝" w, $850; C, c. 1930-40, forged ingot five-stone row bracelet, grad oval green turquoise flat cabs set in plain bezels alternating with a row of four half-round beads along each edge, tapered band stamped with sun ray, chevron, and lozenge patterns, 2-½" dia, 1-¼" w, $850; B, c. 1950-60, lg oval turquoise cab flanked by two smaller oval cabs, each set in plain bezels with appl half-round silver beads flanking rope-twist frames, mounted on a tapered cuff of three heavy-gauge silver sq wires tapering to solid rounded ends, 2-½" dia, 1-¾" w, $250, Courtesy of Before Antiques.

Silver, turq, c. 1940, Zuni cluster bracelet with concentric row-work oval and circ turq cabs forming oval center flanked by two parallel rows of turq cabs, mounted on three narrow tapering bands, 2-½" inside dia, 2-⅜" w . . . . **275 (A)**

Silver, turq, c. 1940, Zuni, a flat, slightly tapered band set with three rows of needlepoint turq with bead decoration between each, 2-½" inside dia, 1" w . . . . . **220 (A)**

Brooch/Pin

Silver, turq, c. 1940, Navajo, thunderbird motif with center irregular oval turq cab, feather stamps, 1-⅞" × ¾" **135**

Silver, turq, c. 1940, Navajo, butterfly motif with oval turq cab body, sun and scallop stamps on wings, 1-½" w × 1-⅞" **165**

Silver, turq, c. 1940, Navajo, an oval fluted convex disk with a sm center oval turq cab, 1-⅞" × 1-¼" **70**

Silver, turq, jet, shell, c. 1940, Zuni, depicting a rainbow god, in characteristic bent-over posture, with hands raised and wearing stepped tableta, bordered with silver drops, inlaid with turq, shell, and jet, 2-½" w × 3-½" . . . . **575 (A)**

Turq, silver, c. 1940, Zuni, two concentric rings of sm turq cabs around an open center, rope-twist wire decoration, beaded edge, 1-½" dia **125**

Turq, silver, c. 1940, Zuni, open nine-pointed star shape with needlepoint turq cabs around sm circ center cab, clusters of three silver beads at ends of open points, a sm turq cab between each point, 1-¾" dia **115**

Bar

Silver, turq, c. 1940, Navajo, lozenge shape flanked by two smaller lozenge shapes, central oval green turq cab, decorated throughout with crossed-arrow, sun ray, and serrated stamps, 2" × ¾" **80**

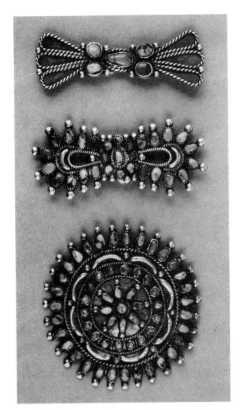

Brooch/Pin, Zuni, c. 1960, knife-wing god motif with turquoise, MOP, coral, and jet inlay bordered by silver feather design, interspersed with silver beads, 2-¼″ × 2-½″, $245. *Courtesy of Mountain Lion Trading Post.*

Brooches/Pins, turquoise, silver, Zuni, c. 1930-40: T, bow-shaped bar, with a central sm irreg turq cab flanked by two oval turq cabs on each side, oxidized ground and rope-twist wire loops, 3″ × ⅞″, $110; C, bow-shaped cluster with cutout center loops, set throughout with sm turq cabs, silver bead-tipped bezels, 3″ × 1-¼″, $225; B, a lg disk cluster, concentric rings of sm turq cabs, star-shaped cluster in the center, rope-twist and bead decoration, 3″ dia, $275, *Courtesy of Mountain Lion Trading Post.*

Turq, silver, c. 1940, Zuni, two rows of sm turq cabs with rope-twist wire center and a beaded border, 2-½″ w × ½″ **95**

Concha Belt

Silver, turq, leather, c. 1940, Navajo, a row of nine oval scalloped conchas on conforming leather pads threaded on a leather strap, each with a repoussé sunburst center, stamp-work perimeter and a center oval turq cab, terminating in a rect scalloped-edge buckle with stamped decoration, rect cutout center, set with four turq cabs at compass points, 43″ tl . . . . **1,610 (A)**

Silver, turq, leather, c. 1940, Navajo, five scalloped oval conchas alternating with four butterfly-shaped spacers, with repoussé centers radiating from sm oval turq cabs, stampwork perimeters, threaded on a narrow leather strap, terminating in a scalloped-edge rect buckle decorated with stamp-work and set with six sm turq cabs, 45″ tl . . . . . . **978 (A)**

Turq, silver, c. 1940, Zuni, seven circ scalloped silver conchas and a similar buckle, alternating with eight butterfly-shaped spacers, set throughout with clusters of ovoid and circ turq cabs in rope-twist, bead and crescent-shaped frames, linked together as a chain, 30″ tl . . . . **1,150 (A)**

Necklace

Bead

Silver, c. 1960, grad machine-stamped halves soldered together, strung on foxtail chain, 26″ tl, largest bead ⅝″ dia **175**

Turq, shell, c. 1900-20, Navajo, three strands of sm grey shell heishi interspersed with irregularly shaped natural turq nuggets, 28″ tl **475**

Squash blossom

Silver, c. 1920, Navajo, a tufa-cast double crescentic naja suspended from a strand of handmade round beads interspersed with 12 handmade squash blossoms, 28″ tl, *naja* 2-½″ × 3″ . . . . **2,588 (A)**

Silver, turq, c. 1950-60, Navajo, tufa-cast naja with cusped ends, surmounted by a cusped trefoil, cusped trefoil center drop bezel-set with pear-shaped turq, suspended from a double row of stamped silver beads alternating with stamped squash blossoms, continuing to a single row of silver beads, 24″ tl, *naja* 2-½″ w × 3-½″ **675**

Silver, c. 1972, antique Navajo style, with 14 squash blossoms attached to a double

Necklace, bone, shell, turquoise, jet, Santo Domingo, c. 1930, a strand of sm beige shell heishi suspending 21 grad tear-drop shaped bone plaques with encrustations of sm irregular pcs of turq covering top two-thirds of plaques, banded at lower end with rect strips of jet, 23" tl, largest plaque ⅝" w × 2", $400. *Courtesy of Before Antiques.*

Necklace, squash blossom, silver, turquoise, Navajo, c. 1900-20, heavy cast and forged ingot beads and 13 prs of squash blossoms suspending a tufa-cast pierced naja with a bezel-set oval green turquoise cab in open center, terminating in two sm turquoise disks set flush in bezels, strung on woven cloth cording, 26" tl, naja 1-⅞" w × 2-¼", $3,500. *Courtesy of Before Antiques.*

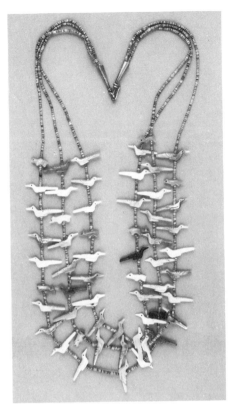

Necklace, turquoise, coral, serpentine, MOP, jet, and shell, Zuni, c. 1972, three strands of brown shell heishi, suspending 58 bird, weasel, and bear hand-carved stone and shell fetishes, 30″ tl, $275. *Sheryl Shatz collection.*

strand of round silver beads, suspending a lg naja, mkd with a conjoined "JK" for Joe Kieomyee, Hopi, 32″ tl, naja 3-¼″ × 2-½″ **550**

Turq, silver, c. 1960, Zuni, a double row of sm round silver beads supporting 14 squash blossoms, each set with an oval turq cab framed by tiny circ turq channel-work settings, suspending a scalloped-edge naja of similar design, continuing to a single row of sm silver beads, 24″ tl, naja 2-¾″ w × 2-½″ . . . . **1,870 (A)**

Pendant

Silver, c. 1950, Hopi, two-sided convex oval, a quail and bear paw overlay design on one side, a stylized floral and foliate overlay design on the other, ⅞″ w × 1-⅜″ tl **50**

Ring

Silver, turq, coral, c. 1960, Navajo, a rounded oblong plaque bezel-set with an oval coral cab and a slightly larger oval turq cab, a silver leaf shape extending out from one long side, mounted on a split tapered shank, approx size 5, ⅝″ w × 1-⅛″ **25**

Silver, c. 1960, Hopi, tapered wraparound with rounded ends, overlay crescent bar and bear paw design, maker's mark (star priest symbol) for Leroy Kewanyama (working 1955-87), approx size 6-½, ⅝″ w tapering to ¼″ **85**

Turq, silver, c. 1950, Navajo, lg irregular triangular spiderweb turq cab set in plain bezel with rope-twist wire frame, flat back, mounted on ¼″ half-round band, approx size 8, 1″ × 1″ **50**

Rings, turquoise and silver: L, Navajo, c. 1950, triangular turq cab set in plain bezel with rope-twist wire frame, flat back, mounted on split tapered shank, ¾″ w × ⅞″, $40, *Margaret Levine collection;* C, Zuni, c. 1940-50, sm cluster ring with center oval turquoise set flush in millegrained bezel with rope-twist wire frame encircled by pear-shaped turquoise in millegrained bezels, pierced tapered shank, 1″ w × 1-⅛″, $70; R, Navajo, c. 1930-40, oval green turquoise cab set in plain bezel, rope-twist wire shoulders, pierced tapered shank stamped with sun ray pattern, ⅞″ w × ⅝″, $80, *Courtesy of Before Antiques.*

MEXICAN JEWELRY (TAXCO SCHOOL) c. 1930-1970

Frederick Davis

William Spratling,
1931-1945

William Spratling,
c. 1949-1967

William Spratling,
c. 1949-1967

William Spratling,
"Silson" mark

Serafin Moctezuma

Antonio Pineda

Hector Aguilar

Hubert Harmon

Government assay
"spread eagle" marks

History: Metalsmithing is a centuries-old Mexican tradition. Mexican *plateros* had already been practicing their craft for generations when they taught silversmithing to the Navajo in the 1870s. There are those who collect the traditional, regional, religious and folk art jewelry of Mexico, which fall into the category of true ethnic jewelry, a subject covered in the first six chapters of Davis' and Pack's *Mexican Jewelry* (referenced below). The last chapter, and a primary source of information for many of today's Mexican jewelry collectors, however, is on the product of a unique, twentieth-century multicultural amalgam of Mexican, U.S., and European cultures, centered in the town of Taxco (pronounced TAHS-co). This is the place where one man and a serendipitous combination of events founded an industry in 1931.

The story really begins in the 1920s in Mexico City, where another man, an American named Frederick Davis, began designing jewelry and small objects as a sideline to his main occupation as manager of the Sonora News Company. His designs were based on ancient pre-Hispanic motifs, which he had made in silver, sometimes adding obsidian, a native volcanic glass, or amethyst quartz, a stone that is also indigenous to Mexico. Some of Davis' designs reflect the modernity of the period in smooth shaped plaques that were quite compatible with his use of the geometric motifs found in the clay stamps of pre-Conquest (before 1520) native Mexican tribes. During a time when most Mexican jewelry was based on

colonial, religious, or regional designs, and usually made of gold, Davis' work was unique, and seminal to later developments in Taxco. His simple, stylized obsidian face design, which he set into necklaces, bracelets, brooches, and clips, was the precursor to what would become the ubiquitous carved stone face jewelry sold to tourists in the 1940s and 1950s.

In 1933, Davis went to work for Sanborn's as the manager of the antiques and handcrafts shop housed in the restaurant and gift store in downtown Mexico City that still operates today in the historic House of Blue Tile. He continued designing jewelry, which was made and sold alongside Sanborn's own more conventional line of silver articles. Perhaps catering to the burgeoning tourist trade of the time, some Davis designs are of traditional Mexican motifs, like bullfighters and sombrero-clad *paisanos;* others are of then-popular floral sprays. Davis was not a prolific designer, so his pieces are relatively scarce and important to collectors because they were the first of their kind.

Earlier, in 1929, in a mining village in the mountains southwest of Mexico City, another American had arrived. As an architect from Tulane University in New Orleans, William Spratling had come to Taxco to study Spanish Colonial architecture. As a writer, he was to write a book about Mexico (*Little Mexico,* published in 1932). As an artist, he made sketches of the local scenery. But in fact it was as a designer and the proprietor of a little shop selling trinkets to tourists that this twentieth-century Renaissance man became most famous. Responding to a comment from a friend, U.S. Ambassador Dwight Morrow, Spratling conceived the idea of working the silver that had been mined in the area for centuries, along with other native materials, such as amethyst, obsidian, and rosewood. He created jewelry and objects that were a strikingly original synthesis of Mexican and cosmopolitan design.

When Spratling opened his shop, later called *Taller Las Delicias* (the Delights Workshop), in 1931, he had one master silversmith executing his ideas, and a few young local boys as apprentices. They made pieces entirely by hand with the crudest of implements. Spratling's earliest designs were necessarily simple: the plainest of button earrings, traditional buckles with incised decoration, and plaque brooches based on pre-Hispanic and *ranchero* motifs, all made of heavy-gauge, high-grade silver (early Spratling pieces are sometimes marked 980, containing only 2% alloy). These were offered for sale, along with other regional handcrafts such as textiles, tinware, and furniture, in the old abandoned customs house that became Taxco's first workshop.

In 1927, the road from Mexico City to the popular resort of Acapulco had reached Taxco, which was conveniently located halfway between the two cities. With the growth of auto travel and tourism, Spratling's timing was perfect. His shop became a favorite tourist stop, his pieces sold well, and his business grew. By 1940, he had more than 300 artisans working for him and had made Taxco a major tourist destination, famous for its silverwork. It became a single-industry town, with successive generations carrying on the work of their predecessors. Today, there are more than 10,000 silversmiths working in the area. While the artisanship of some of them is unquestionable, many continue to make the cheap tourist trinkets known as *chácharas,* or they merely copy the designs of others, a common practice since the 1940s. Only a few of the best and most original designers and workshops have survived the test of time. Their work, marks, and names have become well-known to collectors. Identification of marks is especially important with Mexican silver in determining values, which have escalated as interest has grown over the past few years. This is because copying of original designs was (and is) rampant. Spratling's work is understandably the most widely copied: He used a number of different marks, most of them incorporating a conjoined WS (one notorious copyist, Serafín Moctezuma, used his own conjoined initials, which look like WS upside down). He took his first mark from his ranch's brand for his horses.

Around 1940, Victor Silson, a businessman with whom Spratling has been in partnership, "appropriated" and patented some of his designs and manufactured them in the U.S., in pewter and

silverplate. He used Spratling's conjoined WS mark with "Silson, Inc." under it. These have limited collector interest and do not bring the high prices of Spratling originals.

During World War II, business in Taxco was booming. Spratling exported quantities of silver to U.S. stores cut off from European trade, including Neiman Marcus, Saks Fifth Avenue, Macy's, Lord & Taylor, and Montgomery Ward. Even Ward's catalogs pictured Spratling silver objects and jewelry with hefty price tags for the time. A 980 silver and carved amethyst Spratling cuff bracelet was originally priced at $45.95 in 1943.

Spratling changed his mark in 1949, after he had moved his shop to his ranch outside of town, where he lived and worked until his accidental death in 1967. The jewelry of Spratling's later period is more refined and stylized than his early work. He was influenced, as were many others, by abstract modernism and Scandinavian design. Some later pieces were also made in 18 karat gold.

Spratling established a hierarchical training system still in use today. As his apprentices moved through the ranks to become master silversmiths, some of them showed a talent for creativity as well as skill in executing Spratling's ideas. He encouraged them to open their own shops and produce their own designs. Many of them did; some were very successful at making names for themselves and establishing individual styles. They are recognized today as the innovators of the Taxco School begun and inspired by William Spratling.

The four brothers Castillo were among the first to go out on their own, opening their shop, Los Castillo, in 1939. The family business became one of the largest, expanding to stores in Mexico City as well as Taxco. They are still in operation today, with second and third generations turning out both old and new designs (of the brothers, only Antonio Castillo is still living). The Castillos' contributions include innovative metalworking techniques and many original designs. Their most famous design, *Perfil de Perico* (profile of parrot) incorporates the techniques of *metales casados* (married metals) and *mosaico azteca* (stone inlay), which are actually refinements of ancient Mexican Indian methods.

Antonio Pineda, another early Spratling apprentice, opened his shop in 1941. His mark, "Antonio Taxco" in the shape of a crown, is an important one to know, as his work is sought after and often copied. He is a favorite among modernists, because of the sleek simplicity and superior craftsmanship of his designs. He preferred to use high-grade (970) silver and often incorporated gemstones in his work, some not usually found in Mexican silver, such as moonstones, chrysocolla, and topaz. Antonio lives in Taxco today in semiretirement.

Equally sought after and unique is the work of

Héctor Aguilar, the manager of the Spratling shop until 1939, when he opened his own *Taller Borda* in the center of town. Aguilar was influenced by Spratling's early work with ranchero motifs. He usually used 940 silver without stones, but sometimes made belts and bracelets in leather with almost pure silver (990) decorative elements. In the 1960s, Aguilar moved to the resort town of Zihuatanejo, where he died in 1984.

Margot van Voorhies Carr Castillo, whose mark was "Margot de Taxco," was one of the few women who owned her own shop. She was married to Antonio Castillo and designed for Los Castillo before opening her shop in 1948. Margot was an artist and world traveler who is known for a wide variety of styles and motifs inspired by Art Deco, Egyptian, Arts and Crafts, Art Nouveau, and Mexican designs. She is most noted for the use of polychromatic champlevé and *basse-taille* enamels, which allowed the painterly expression of her love of color. Margot died in 1985.

Another woman whose work is unmistakably distinctive (and often copied) is Matilde Poulat. She began working in Mexico City in 1934 and opened a retail shop in 1950. Her pieces are typically repoussé silver set with amethysts, turquoise, or coral (or a combination). Her motifs are often figural—birds, fish, butterflies, or religious figures and crosses. Her larger items tend to be quite ornately decorated. Matilde (mark: "Matl") died in 1960, but her nephew, Ricardo Salas Poulat (mark: "Matl" over "Salas") continues to make jewelry in a similar style.

In the 1950s, the next generation of silversmiths began opening their own shops. They had trained under Spratling and also worked for his first protégés. Each of those whose jewelry and objects are collected today had a distinctive approach to design; the influence of 1950s modernism can be clearly seen throughout their work.

Enrique Ledesma was the first of this generation to have his own establishment, which he opened in 1950. Until then, he had worked for Spratling and Los Castillo. One of Ledesma's signature techniques was to inlay stone into silver and shape the two materials together as a unit. The units were then linked for bracelets and necklaces, or used singly for a brooch or an earring. Ledesma also used silver alone in shaped and oxidized hinged bangles and brooches. His mark is his last name with an elongated L underlining it. Ledesma died in 1979.

Another silversmith, Felipe Martínez, also opened a shop, called *Piedra y Plata* (stone and silver) in 1950. True to the name, most of Martínez' designs are combinations of silver and turquoise, azur-malachite, or other opaque stone inlaid in smooth geometric patterns, or bezel-set and joined to silver shapes.

Salvador Terán was a cousin of the Castillos, for whom he worked until the opening of his own shop in Mexico City in 1952 (he was also one of

Spratling's apprentices in the 1930s). Davis and Pack called him "original, inventive, and versatile" (*Mexican Jewelry*, p. 213), and indeed his imagination seemed to know no bounds. He designed some strikingly modern pieces and others that display a fanciful sense of humor. One of his trademarks was creating a three-dimensional effect with cutout motifs mounted on pegs above an oxidized surface. He signed his pieces "Salvador" in script. Salvador died in 1974.

The sole survivor of the 1950s generation of silversmiths is Sigi (pronounced SEE-hee), who opened his shop in Taxco in 1953, after working for Los Castillo and for Margot as her shop foreman. Sigi also studied silversmithing at International Silver in Connecticut and was a member of the American Craftsmen's Council. His designs reflect both American and Scandinavian modernist influence, yet they are identifiably his own. Sigi recently resumed designing and making new pieces, which are crafted with the same careful attention to detail and finishing as his earlier work. His signature is "Sigi Tasco" (the alternate spelling of Taxco).

Hubert Harmon was an eccentric American artist about whom little is known, except that he worked in Taxco during the 1940s. He designed out of the ordinary pieces which are scarce and highly collectible today. He had a bizarre sense of humor as well as an imaginative eye. Whimsical motifs were his specialty—including his mark, a pair of winged feet.

Many other Taxco designers and silversmiths have worked in relative obscurity. Only their output and their marks are known. Of the literally hundreds, and at present, thousands, who have worked or are working there, only a few, in addition to the ones mentioned above, have been identified and referenced in any book or catalog. These include: Ana Nuñez Brilanti (shop name and mark "Victoria"), Ysidro García (shop name and mark, "Maricela"), Bernice Goodspeed, Los Ballesteros, Emma Melendez and Miguel Melendez. Virtually no written documentation is available on those whose pieces surface repeatedly, which are well-made, with distinctive maker's marks, and whose initials are all that is known. In addition, there are many pieces of excellent quality with no identifying marks at all, other than "sterling, *Hecho en* or Made in Mexico" (or variations). Because of this lack of documentation, attribution, and name recognition, values are comparatively low. As with any jewelry, however, both signed pieces by known makers and unsigned or unknown work should be evaluated with the same criteria. Even some Spratling pieces are less than exemplary, and certainly there is a great quantity of Taxco silver made by unknowns who deserve to remain so.

References: Mary L. Davis and Greta Pack, *Mexican Jewelry*, University of Texas Press, 1963, reprinted 1982, 1991; Jorge Enciso, *Design Motifs*

of Ancient Mexico, Dover Publications, 1953; Christie Romero, "William Spratling and the Taxco School: Mexican Silver Jewelry, 1930-1970," in *Jewelers Circular-Keystone/Heritage,* March 1993; William Spratling, *File on Spratling* (autobiography), Little, Brown & Co., 1967; exhibition catalogs: Sandraline Cedarwall and Hal Riney with Barnaby Conrad, *Spratling Silver,* Chronicle Books, 1990; Centro Cultural/Arte Contemporaneo, *William Spratling/Plata* (Spanish text), Mexico City, 1987; Karen Davidov, *Mexican Silver Jewelry: The American School, 1930-1960,* Muriel Karasik Gallery, 1985; Penny Chittim Morrill, *Hecho en Mexico,* Carole A. Berk Ltd. gallery, 1990; Penny Chittim Morrill and Carole A. Berk, *Mexican Silver, 20th Century Handwrought Jewelry & Metalwork,* Schiffer Publishing, 1994. ·

Reproduction Alert: Between 1946 (or thereabouts) and 1979, the Mexican government required the stamping of a spread eagle assay mark on any piece that was made of 925 (sterling) silver or above. In 1979, the eagle mark was abandoned, and since then all workshops have been required to use individually assigned registry marks of two letters and two or three numbers, separated by a hyphen. Although some pieces escape marking, any item taken out or exported from Mexico should be marked. This is one way to differentiate new from old pieces by the same workshop. Since Spratling's death in 1967, his designs have been produced by the current owner of his estate. The recently made pieces bear the later WS maker's mark along with the registry number TS-24. Copies of Spratling designs, unsigned or signed by others, were also commonly made during Spratling's lifetime, as they continue to be today. Antonio Pineda and Margot de Taxco fakes regularly appear on the market. Unsigned Frederick Davis designs are common. Los Castillo and Héctor Aguilar designs are reproduced somewhat less frequently. Of the 1950s generation, Salvador and Ledesma are seldom copied, but Sigi's pieces often are.

Bracelet
  Cuff
    Sterling, amethysts, c. 1940, lg zigzag outline, cutout center bezel-set with a grad row of five circ amethyst cabs, flanked by incised lines parallel to the shape of the cuff, rev mkd "Spratling silver," pre-1945 maker's mark for William Spratling, 3" inside dia, 2-³/₄" w . . . . **1,320 (A)**
    Sterling (980), amethysts, c. 1943, a pierced and incised cuff with double-lobed terminals, depicting two opposed hands with cuffs and bows at the wrists, holding carved amethyst flowers, flanked by two circ amethyst cabs, each bezel-set in the center of a scroll, rev mkd "Spratling silver," pre-1945 maker's mark for William

Spratling (pictured in the 1943 Montgomery Ward catalog), 2-¹/₂" inside dia, 1-⁷/₈" w . . . . **660 (A)**
Sterling (980), rosewood, c. 1943, a central rounded sq ster plaque flanked by overlapping D-shaped plates, rosewood alternating with ster, riveted through the centers to a flat tapering cuff, pre-1945 maker's mark for William Spratling on rev, (pictured in the 1943 Montgomery Ward catalog), 2-¹/₂" inside dia, 1-¹/₄" w . . . ., . . . **950**

Cuff Bracelets, sterling, William Spratling, c. 1940: T, cutout and pierced band with incised geo pre-Hispanic design and repoussé scroll and fan elements soldered along edges on both sides, rev imp "Spratling Silver" and pre-1945 maker's mark for William Spratling, 2-¹/₄" inside dia, 1-³/₈" w, $1,250, *Courtesy of Before Antiques;* C, cutout and pierced heavy-gauge cuff with undulating edges and incised lines, three angled pairs of appl lg domed disks within incised circles and a center row of four sm disks with raised bead centers, scrolled and tapered ends, rev imp "Spratling Silver" and pre-1945 maker's mark, 2-¹/₄" inside dia, 1-³/₈" w, $850; B, a heavy-gauge band with an incised rope-twist design flanked by parallel incised lines, terminating in pierced and domed scrolls, rev imp "sterling," pre-1945 maker's mark, 2-¹/₂" inside dia, ⁵/₈" w at top, 1" w terminals, $650, *Author's collection.*

Cuff Bracelets, sterling (940), Héctor Aguilar, c. 1950: L & R, smooth wide flat band with rounded ends, incised lg scalloped design evenly spaced across width of band, rev imp with maker's mark (conjoined "HA") encircled by "made in Mexico sterling," 2-¼" dia, 1-½" w, pr, $900, *Courtesy of Before Antiques* ; C, braided twisted-wire center flanked by rope-twist borders, domed-disk terminals, rev mkd "940 Taxco" conjoined "HA," Mex govt eagle assay mark, 2-½" inside dia, 1" w, $450, *Kirsten Olson collection.*

Flexible link
    Sterling (980), brass, c. 1943, brickwork pattern of hinged hollow sq bars interspersed with spherical brass beads between each bar, appl plaque on rev imp "Spratling silver," second plaque imp with pre-1945 maker's mark for William Spratling, v-spring and box clasp, safety chain, (pictured in the 1943 Montgomery Ward catalog), 8" × ⅝" **800**
    Sterling, enamel, c. 1950, eight hinged rect plaques with cutout centers, *basse-taille*

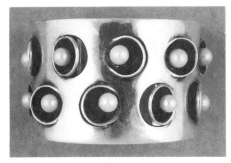

Cuff Bracelet, sterling (970), pearls, c. 1950, a wide band with two rows of partially cutout and raised oxidized concave disks, each set off-center with a round cultured pearl, rev imp "Hecho en Mexico ZZ 919," government eagle assay mark, "970" and maker's mark for Antonio Pineda (crown), 2-¼" inside dia, 1-⅝" w, $850. *Courtesy of Before Antiques.*

green, yellow, and orange stippled enamel over a raised stippled groundplate around central scroll and S-curve designs, three black enameled cutout tabs radiating from both ends of each plaque, rev imp "Hecho en Mexico 925," government eagle assay mark, "Margot de Taxco" # 5404, v-spring and box clasp, safety chain, 7" × 2-⅛" w **500**
    Obsidian, sterling, c. 1980, a series of paired overlapping hinged crescents of bezel-set obsidian, copy of a c. 1960 design by Antonio Pineda, mkd with fancy "L B" encircled by "Talleres de Los Ballesteros, Taxco, Gro" "925," "MM-34" (post-1979 registry mark), safety chain, 6-¾" × 1-⅝" **450**
    Sterling (980), copper, c. 1943, convex rounded rect plaques, each with a slightly curved diagonal band of copper through the center, joined to hinged vertical rows of three silver spheres each, hingepin closure, safety chain, rev imp "sterling," pre-1945 maker's mark for William Spratling (pictured in the 1943 Montgomery Ward catalog), 8-½" × 1" **1,050**
Hinged bangle
    Sterling (940), c. 1940, overlay design of a row of five four-lobed circles, each enclosing a Japanese *kamon* (family crest) motif, on a recessed oxidized ground, rev imp with conjoined HA for Héctor Aguilar, "Taxco 940," hingepin closure, safety chain, 2-⅜" inside dia, 1-¼" w **700**

Bracelets, sterling, Salvador Terán, c. 1955: T, hinged bangle, a rounded sq shadowbox with an open raised frame enclosing a cutout stylized man-in-the-moon and a star, each mounted above an oxidized ground, hinged on rev to convex tapered side pieces, hinged box clasp and v-spring, rev imp "Salvador, sterling Mexico," # 125, government assay mark, safety chain, 2-1/4" inside dia, 1-5/8" w, $550, *Author's collection;* B, a central rounded and convex rect plaque linked to two tapered and curved convex plaques each with an appl pierced and cutout abstract bird motif mounted above an oxidized ground, v-spring and box clasp with similar appl motif, rev center imp "Salvador, sterling Mexico" # 162, safety chain, 7-3/4" × 1-1/8" w, $500, *Courtesy of Before Antiques.*

Brooch/Pin, sterling, glass, c. 1940, repoussé design of a hand holding a bouquet of lilies with faceted cone-shaped purple glass centers, rev imp "Los Castllo Taxco sterling Mexico," # 196, 2-1/4" w × 4", $750. *Kirsten Olson collection.*

Sterling, obsidian, c. 1955, bypass design, hinged at sides, two shaped and tapered curved sections on one side, one on the other, each terminating in a six-sided cusped obsidian "crystal," crossing in front, mkd "Sigi Tasco, Made in Mexico, Sterling," # 261, government assay mark, v-spring and box clasp in back, safety chain, 2-3/8" inside dia, 1-1/2" w at center front **450**

Brooch/Pendant
   Malachite, sterling, c. 1950, a lg oval malachite cab bezel-set within a polished ster quatrefoil and bead frame, rev imp "Piedra y Plata, sterling Taxco," government eagle assay mark, # 175, "Martínez" (Felipe), 1-3/8" w × 1-1/2" **160**

Brooch/Pin
   Silver, c. 1930, circ disk with cutout and incised design of a man wearing a sombrero with a cactus beside him, rev imp with con-

joined "FD" for Frederick Davis, 1-1/4" dia **125**
Sterling, amethysts, c. 1940, in the shape of a chambered nautilus shell with three lg carved amethyst flowers set in ster calyxes projecting from open wide end of the shell, rev mkd "Spratling silver," pre-1945 maker's mark for William Spratling, 2-3/8" × 2-3/8" . . . . **880 (A)**
Sterling, amethysts, c. 1940, in the shape of a fancy bulbous vase flanked by voluted sq wire tendrils, surmounted by three lg carved amethyst flowers set in shaped ster calyxes, rev mkd "Spratling silver," pre-1945 maker's mark for William Spratling, 2-1/2" w × 2-1/4" . . . . **431 (A)**
Sterling (980), amethyst, c. 1943, a lg stylized bow with a row of raised beading across loops and at sash ends, a lg circ amethyst bezel-set in a beaded frame suspended from center bow knot, rev imp with pre-1945 maker's mark for William Spratling (pictured in the 1943 Montgomery Ward catalog), 4-3/8" w × 1-1/2" . . . . **633 (A)**
Sterling (980), amethysts, c. 1943, in the shape of a stylized owl with incised and stippled

Brooches/Pins, sterling, Los Castillo, stylized musician designs, c. 1950: T, the head and arms of a maracas player, with a twisted curv strip for arms, cutout oval for head, rev mkd "Los Castillo Taxco, made in Mexico 925" # 102, government eagle assay mark, 2-⅛" w × 1-¾", $275, *Courtesy of Before Antiques;* B, the head and arms of a singing man playing a guitar, rev imp "Los Castllo Taxco" encircling spread eagle assay mark, "925, made in Mexico," # 101, 2-½" w × 2-¼", $575, *Kirsten Olson collection.*

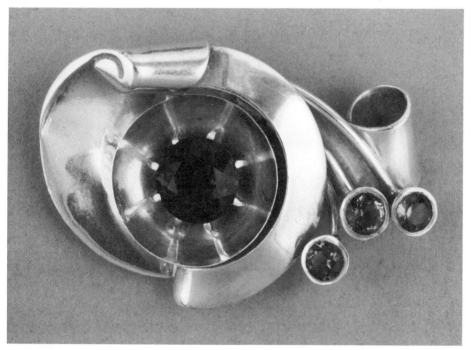

Brooch/Pin, sterling, syn alexandrite, c.1960, circ scrolled design with a concave center disk prong-set with a lg circ-cut syn alexandrite, three sm collet-set syn alexandrites mounted on wires flanking one side, surmounting a scrolled ster ribbon, rev imp "Antonio Taxco" in a crown shape, for Antonio Pineda, government spread eagle assay mk, # 17, 2-¼" w × 1-½", $400. *Kirsten Olson collection.*

Brooches/Pins, sterling, Hubert Harmon, c. 1940: L, repoussé stylized sea anemone design, flat backing, appl plate on rev imp with maker's mark, a pr of winged feet, and "sterling Hubert Harmon, made in Mexico," 2-1/4" w × 1-1/2", $225, *Kirsten Olson collection;* C, an equilateral cross of reeded trefoils, center and terminals bezel-set with lg circ cabs of green turquoise in brown matrix, rev mkd "sterling Hubert Harmon Made in Mexico," maker's mark, 2-5/8" × 2-5/8", $350; R, repoussé design of the head of a Nubian woman wearing an earring bezel-set with a pear-shaped amethyst cab, flat backing on rev mkd "sterling Hubert Harmon Made in Mexico," maker's mark, 1" × 2", $250, *Author's collection.*

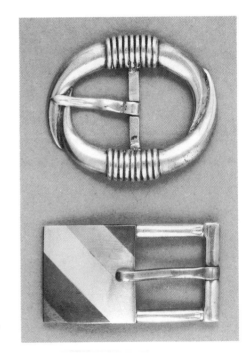

Buckles, sterling, c. 1950: T, annular oval with two raised and incised sections resembling wrapped cord at top and bottom, shaped overlapping side sections, center bar and hasp, rev imp with maker's mark for William Spratling after 1949, "925," 2" w × 1-3/4", $350; B, sterling, brass, copper, rect with a sq plaque of diagonal sections of married metals (*metales casados*) on one half, laminated to a ster backing, the other half an open ster frame with hasp, rev imp "Los Castillo Taxco sterling Mexico" # 95, 2-1/8" w × 1-1/8", $100, *Courtesy of Before Antiques.*

details, lg cab amethyst eyes, rev mkd "Spratling silver," pre-1945 maker's mark for William Spratling (pictured in the 1943 Montgomery Ward catalog), 1-7/8" w × 2-3/8" .... **385 (A)**

Sterling, obsidian, c. 1950, a rounded triangle formed by a shaped obsidian plaque enclosed on two sides by a boomerang-shaped ster bezel, rev imp "Ledesma" for Enrique Ledesma, "Hecho en Mexico Taxco 925," # 280, government assay mark, 2-3/4" w × 1-1/8" **125**

Sterling, c. 1950, an irregularly shaped concave plaque with undulating outline, a lg slightly domed circ disk appl to center of oxidized ground, rev imp "Ledesma" for Enrique Ledesma, "Taxco Hecho en Mexico 925," government assay mark, 2-1/2" w × 1-1/2" **65**

Sterling, enamel, c. 1960, an irregularly shaped, tapered, and ridged plaque pierced with various sizes of oval perforations, the entire surface enameled in turquoise flecked with purple *basse-taille* enamel over textured ground, rev imp "Ledesma 925," government assay mark, 2-1/4" w × 1-1/2" **85**

Sterling, crushed stone, c. 1950, stylized bird design with crushed green stone inlay, rev imp "B" encircled by "sterling Taxco" within a circle for Bernice Goodspeed, government assay mark, 1-1/2" w × 1-3/4" **60**

Sterling, c. 1950, circ disk with appl eagle motif, head projecting perpendicular to the surface with incised details on both sides, Spanish word "SITA" in raised letters around top edge of disk, imp mark for Bernice Goodspeed on rev, government assay mark, 1-1/4" dia **50**

Buckle

Sterling (980), c. 1935, sq outline, cutout rect section with hasp, rope-twist and parallel incised line decoration, rev imp "Taxco 980," conjoined WS for William Spratling (earliest mark), 2-1/8" × 2-1/8" **450**

Sp brass, enamel, c. 1960, based on a c. 1940 design, two-pc, cutout design of opposed jaguars with black enameled features, C-shaped and sm circ spots, rev mkd "plateado" (plated), "Los Castillo Taxco," hook and bar clasp, appl bars for belt attachment, 6-3/4" w × 2-5/8" **500**

Cuff Links

Sterling, c. 1940, a pr of chased and repoussé fish linked to shaped pyramidal backs, sgd "Hubert Harmon," 1-1/4" × 1/2", pr .... **248 (A)**

Sterling, bone, c. 1955, sq box plaque with inset carved and partially tinted bone in the shape of a parrot's head with ster bead eye, rev sgd "Salvador" in script for Salvador Terán, mkd "sterling Mexico" # 522, 7/8" sq swivel link backs, pr **100**

Sterling, c. 1955, rounded irregular quadrangular plaque and frame enclosing cutout and appl abstract face design, grad horizontal tubes behind mouth, raised above oxidized ground, rev sgd "Salvador," for Salvador Terán, mkd "sterling Mexico" # 151, 7/8" w × 1-1/8" **85**

Sterling (970), hawk's eye (grey tiger's eye), c. 1950, irregularly shaped, slightly concave textured plaques, each set with a tumble-polished hawk's eye, recessed in rev bezel, swivel link backs imp with hmk for Antonio Pineda, (crown), and "970," government assay mark, 1-1/4" × 3/4", pr **75**

Dress Clip

Sterling, obsidian, c. 1935, rounded triangular obsidian, shaped and cut as a stylized face, bezel-set in the center of a rect plaque with raised and engr columnar design, a flatback hinged clip with serrated strips on underside and on rev of plaque, imp "925," conjoined "FD" for Frederick Davis, 1-1/4" w × 1-3/8" **250**

Earrings

Sterling, glass, coral, c. 1950, modified twisted boomerang shape with a folded-over pierced and tapered strip encircling the center and returning with tip through center perforation, prong-set with sm irregular pcs of coral and green glass, three cutout sections, one rev imp "Chato Castillo 925" # 5, the other with maker's mark, "Taxco Mexico," screwbacks, 1-1/4" × 1", pr **185**

Sterling, brass, copper, stone, c. 1955, rounded sq plaques, *Perfil de Perico* (profile of parrot) design, prize-winning design at 1953 Taxco silver fair, in married metals and crushed malachite and onyx inlay, rev mkd "Metales Castillo" # 63, govrnment assay mark, screwbacks, 3/4" sq, pr **50**

Sterling, copper, c. 1940, copper repoussé sun and ster crescent moon faces on overlapping disks soldered to flat backing imp with pre-1945 maker's mark for William Spratling, screwbacks, 1-1/4" w × 7/8", pr **300**

Sterling, c. 1955, pierced and cutout profile of a stylized face with oxidized convex backing and overlay creating a three-dimensional effect, rev imp "sterling Salvador" for Salvador Terán, # 132, screwbacks, 1" w × 1-1/8", pr **100**

Pendent

Sterling, c. 1950, flared double-layered plaques with curv base, central cutout design of a stylized figure on upper plaque, oxidized surface on lower plaque, suspended from a domed disk surmount, screwback findings, rev mkd "Los Castillo Taxco," # 110, 2" tl × 3/4" w, pr **125**

Sterling, c. 1950, a cutout spiral with three bands tapering out and in to the center enclosed by a ster bead, then tapering out

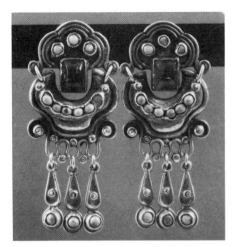

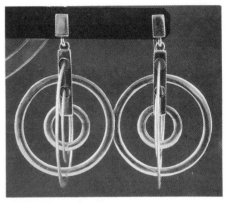

Pendent Earrings, sterling, amethysts, turq, coral, c. 1940, a lobed and incised repoussé surmount set with three sm coral beads, suspending a similar articulated center section bezel-set with a lg rect amethyst cab and a curved row of sm round turquoise (one missing), surmounting an undulating scrolled and beaded wire section suspending three teardrop-shaped drops, each terminating in a sm round bezel-set turquoise, rev sgd "Matl" in script for Matilde Poulat, screwbacks, 2" tl × 1" w, pr, $200. *Courtesy of Before Antiques.*

Pendent Earrings, 970 sterling, c. 1955, four concentric flat hoops suspended at right angles to one another from pierced holes in a vertical hollow sq bar, rect box surmount, rev mkd "Antonio Taxco" in a crown logo for Antonio Pineda, Mexican government assay mark, "970," screwbacks, 2-5/8" tl × 2", pr, $300. *Courtesy of Before Antiques.*

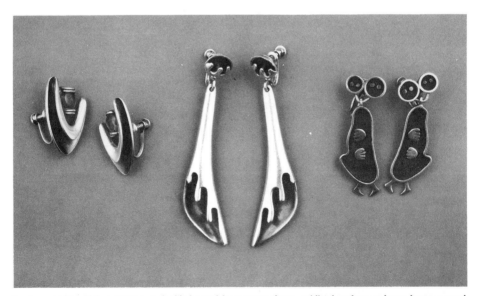

Earrings, sterling, Sigi, c. 1955: L, a double-layered boomerang shape, oxidized surface on lower layer, an oval amethyst cab mounted on inner curve, held by scrolled wire at top and bottom, one rev mkd "Sigi Tasco" and government assay mk, the other "sterling made in Mexico," # 34, screwbacks, 5/8" w × 1-1/8", pr, $75; C, pendent, an elongated tapered-out tubular form, a deeply undulating pattern cutout on the lower edge of the top layer, revealing oxidized lower surface, suspended from a circ surmount of similar design, rev imp "sterling made in Mexico, Sigi Tasco," # 29, 3/4" w × 2-7/8" tl, pr, $125; R, pendent, entitled "Ghosts," a biomorphic oxidized plaque with raised edge, central overlay of two cutout hands, two cutout feet at lower edge, suspended from a surmount of two oxidized disks with raised edges, a pr of appl round wire eyes in each, combination clip/screwbacks, one mkd "Sigi Tasco," 5/8" w × 1-7/8" tl, pr, $100, *Author's collection.*

and in to terminate in a pear-shaped ster drop, suspended from a half-bead surmount, one screwback mkd "Victoria Taxco Mexico" with government assay mark, the other # 278, "sterling," 2" tl × 1-1/4" w, pr **50**

Sterling, c. 1950, a circ disk surmount with overlay of two concentric rings, oxidized recessed areas, with a soldered loop in the center suspending a triangular plaque with triangular overlay, a round bead in the recessed oxidized center, incised and serrated base terminating in three round beads, one screwback mkd "Victoria Taxco Mexico," government assay mark, the other # 2, "sterling," 1-1/2" tl × 3/4", pr **50**

Necklace

Silver, obsidian, c. 1930, rounded triangular obsidian, shaped and cut as a stylized face, bezel-set, flanked by six slightly convex grad shaped silver plaques joined with reeded links, continuing to an open rect and reeded link chain, hook closure, rev imp "made in Mexico, silver," conjoined FD for Frederick Davis, 18" tl, 1-1/4" w at center **1,100**

Sterling, amethysts, c. 1940, two opposed cutout, chased, and repoussé pre-Hispanic dog motifs linked to a central spear-shaped motif, terminating in two smaller spear shapes, set throughout with 17 circ amethyst cabs, continuing to a detachable chain of wide flat links alternating with circ wire links, sgd "Spratling silver," pre-1945 maker's mark for William Spratling, approx 20" tl, front 8" w × 3" top to bottom . . . . **4,025 (A)**

Sterling, c. 1940, a collar of linked plaques in the shapes of dancing bare-breasted women with headdresses and loin cloths, hook closure, rev imp "Los Castillo Taxco sterling made in Mexico" # 519, approx 20" tl × 1-3/4" **800**

Sterling, enamel, c. 1950, in the shape of a snake with articulated scale links enameled in predominantly green polychrome champlevé, head with black enameled eyes attached to the tail with a spade-shaped tip at front center, v-spring and box clasp in back, rev imp "Margot de Taxco" # 5554, approx 15" tl, head 7/8" w . . . . **460 (A)**

Sterling (970), obsidian, c. 1950, 12 comma-shaped links with concave centers, each with a bezel-set circ obsidian disk set within the tapered curve, hook and jump-ring closure, rev imp with maker's mark for Antonio Pineda, "970," government assay mark, 17-1/8" tl, each link 1-1/8" × 5/8" . . . . . **805 (A)**

Sterling, obsidian, c. 1955, a strand of spherical ster beads, the front section interspersed with nine grad irregular rounded triangular plaques inlaid with obsidian of conforming shape, v-spring and box clasp mkd "Sigi

Tasco 925," government assay mark, 17-1/2" tl, center 1-7/8" top to bottom **275**

Pendant and Chain

Sterling, tortoiseshell, c. 1950, a lg pendant of two overlapping and opposed cutout hands, one inlaid with tortoiseshell, a Chinese yinyang symbol in the center of ster hand, one half inlaid with tortoiseshell, suspended from a flat elongated oval and circ round wire link chain attached to a lg ster ring, rev imp with post-1949 maker's mark for William Spratling, in original sgd pouch, pendant 5" w × 2-3/4", chain 15" tl . . . . **1,610 (A)**

Suite: Bracelet and Earrings

Sterling, amethyst, c. 1940, four carved amethyst frog links alternating with four ster frog links, each set with two circ amethyst cabs, v-spring and box clasp, handmade safety chain, pre-1945 maker's mark for William Spratling on rev, pr of matching earrings,

Pendant/Brooch and Chain, sterling, enamel, c. 1950, *champlevé* and *basse-taille* enameled pendant/brooch in shades of yellow, aqua, orange, black, and red, depicting the profile of a woman wearing a bird headress with three lengths of fine ster chain suspended in front of the ear, suspended from an enameled chain with lotus-shaped links in black, aqua, and orange, terminating in a box clasp, hook for pendant and pinback on rev, imp "Margot de Taxco, Hecho en Mexico 925," government assay mark (spread eagle) # 5242, pendant/ brooch 2-1/4" × 3", chain 21" tl × 3/8", $1,250. *Kirsten Olson collection.*

Suite: Necklace and Bracelet, sterling, amethysts, c. 1935, linked circ disks, each with a repoussé ridged fan-shaped design surmounted by a bezel-set amethyst cab, box clasps and v-springs, mkd "silver Mexico," conjoined "FD" for Frederick Davis, necklace 15″ tl × ⅝″, bracelet 7-¼″ × ⅝″, suite, $1,500. *Courtesy of Before Antiques.*

each a carved amethyst frog, screwbacks, bracelet 7-½″ × ⅝, earrings ⅝″ w × ¾″, suite . . . . **920 (A)**

Suite: Necklace and Bracelet

Sterling, c. 1940, lg repoussé openwork scroll, foliate and bead design, necklace of two opposed tapered linked plaques continuing to overlapping hand-riveted links of beaded volutes, hook and eye clasp, rev hand-engr "Los Castillo Taxco sterling made in Mexico # 396," matching wraparound hinged bangle with same mks and design number, imp instead of engr, necklace 16″ tl, 2″ at center top to bottom, bracelet 2-¼″ inside dia, 3-¼″ w at top center, suite **750**

Suite: Necklace, Bracelet, and Earrings

Sterling, copper, c. 1950, necklace and bracelet of linked copper-plated domed disks with repoussé silver scrollwork encasing one side,

hook closures, matching earrings, each a single domed disk, screwback findings, necklace and earrings imp with hmk for Los Ballesteros, Taxco, necklace 16″ tl × 1″, bracelet 7-⅛″ × ⅞″, earrings ⅞″ × 1″, suite **400**

Sterling (970), obsidian, c. 1960, a collar of intersecting arcs of heavy gauge sq wire with tapered ends, a pear-shaped obsidian double cab set in a hinged bezel within each of seven intersections, v-spring and box clasp, matching bracelet, pr of earrings, each a pear-shaped double cab surmounted by curved X-shaped sq wire, screwbacks, assay mks and maker's mark for Antonio Pineda, "970 Taxco," collar approx 18″ tl × 1-½″, bracelet approx 8″ × 1-¾″, earrings ⅞″ w × 1-½″, suite . . . . **978 (A)**

SCANDINAVIAN JEWELRY

| Georg Jensen, 1920s | Georg Jensen, 1930s | Georg Jensen, 1933-1944 | Georg Jensen, post-1945 | David-Anderson |

History: Scandinavians have approached design in a way that differs from all other European countries, perhaps because of a culture that is rooted in a separate and unique Nordic tradition. Before the turn of the century, when historicism was popular everywhere, jewelry designs were derived from direct copies of ancient pieces from the Bronze, Iron, and Viking Ages. Each of the four Scandinavian countries—Denmark, Finland, Norway, and Sweden—have also produced regional folk jewelry that has remained virtually unchanged in appearance and technique for several centuries. During the nineteenth century, too, Danish fine jewelry often had a British-influenced Victorian look, no doubt because the Princess of Wales, Alexandra, was a Dane. The art of hair jewelry making, another Victorian tradition, is said to have originated in Denmark and Sweden.

Scandinavians are noted for their metalwork, and silversmithing in particular has given expression to original design, most fully realized by twentieth-century Scandinavian designers and manufacturers. Many of these designers applied their talents to more than jewelry. Some, like George Jensen (1866-1935) of Denmark, began as sculptors, transferring the three-dimensional art form to silver hollowware, flatware, and jewelry. Others, like Tapio Wirkkala (1915-1985) of Finland, were multimedia artists: they designed glass, porcelain, and wood decorative objects as well as silver.

At the turn of the century, the Arts and Crafts movement found its way to Denmark, where it was called *skønwirke*, or, literally translated, "aesthetic activities." (There is little published documentation in English about jewelry of this period from other Scandinavian countries, but evidence exists of similar work being done in Norway.) Though similar in form and inspiration to other European Arts and Crafts work, one of the unique qualities of *skønwirke* jewelry is its sculptural three-dimensionality, achieved with repoussé and chasing. Silver was the most often-used material, sometimes set with cabochon gemstones such as amber, chrysoprase (or dyed green chalcedony), lapis, or moonstones. *Skønwirke* jewelry enjoyed widespread appreciation in Denmark, thanks in part to large-scale production by several manufacturing silversmithies, such as Bernhard Hertz. Like Liberty in Britain and Fahrner in Germany (see section on Arts & Crafts), Danish manufacturers commissioned designs from independent artists and also made their own versions of others' work.

It was during this period that Georg Jensen began making jewelry instead of sculpture. In 1901-1902, he worked in the shop of Mogens Ballin (1871-1914), one of the pioneers of the *skønwirke* style. In 1904, Jensen opened his own silversmithy and began designing and making the jewelry and silverware the company is now famous for. Today, Georg Jensen is the most recognized and collected name in Scandinavian silver. Over the past 90 years, a number of noted designers have created jewelry designs for the Jensen firm, many of which are familiar to today's collectors, including those by Torun Bülow-Hübe (b. 1927), Bent Gabrielsen (b. 1928), Henning Koppel (1918-1981), Arno Malinowski (1899-1976), and Harald Nielsen (1892-1977). A designer's initials are sometimes added to the company marks on a piece, which can raise its value. Many early designs are still produced today, although production methods have changed, in some cases, from die-stamping to casting. Shop hallmarks have changed as well. The mark currently in use, "Georg Jensen" inside a dotted oval, has been the same since 1945, but a number of different marks were used before that date. The earliest Jensen pieces, c. 1904 to 1914, are made of 826 silver. The grade of silver in pieces dating from c. 1915 through the 1920s is 830 or 925; after 1933, the company went to the sterling standard of 925 exclusively. It should be noted that some jewelry designs were also made in 18 karat gold.

In spite of a long tradition in its native countries, Scandinavian design was not well known in the United States until Frederik Lunning opened a shop and agency for Georg Jensen in New York in 1925. The shop helped to popularize Scandinavian design in general, and Jensen designs in particular. Lunning was an important figure in promoting awareness and appreciation of Nordic decorative and applied arts. From 1951 to 1970, he funded the Lunning Prize, awarded each year to two outstanding Scandinavian designers working in various media. Among the prizewinners were jewelry and silverware designers and metalsmiths Grete Prytz-Kittelsen (b. 1917), Norway; Henning Koppel, Denmark; Nanna (b. 1923) and Jørgen (1921-1961) Ditzel, Denmark; Torun

Bülow-Hübe, Sweden; Bertel Gardberg (b. 1916), Finland; Börje Rajalin (b. 1933), Finland; Bent Gabrielsen, Denmark; Björn Weckström (b. 1935), Finland; and Helga (b. 1939) and Bent (b. 1932) Exner, Denmark. Tapio Wirkkala was one of the first two prizewinners in 1951. All of these designers are well known in their own countries; some have achieved worldwide recognition. A number of them maintained their own studios and workshops. Most of them also designed for large manufacturing firms: in Denmark, Koppel, Bülow-Hübe, and Gardberg for Georg Jensen, Gabrielsen for Hans Hansen and Jensen, and the Ditzels for Jensen and A. Michelsen; in Norway, Prytz-Kittelsen for J. Tostrup; in Finland, Gardberg and Wirkkala for Kultakeskus, Rajalin for Kalevala Koru, and Weckström for Lapponia.

During World War II, the Nordic countries suffered shortages of both workers and materials, along with the anxiety of invasion and occupation. Remarkably, the arts communities in each country sustained themselves through the hard times. Gold and silver were restricted to mostly settings and inlays. Silversmiths and jewelers began adding other more readily available materials, like glass and ceramics, and substituting other metals, such as iron and bronze.

The postwar years gave Nordic artists the opportunity to display their talents as never before. For the first time, Scandinavian design was setting the pace for others to follow. Their work was highly influential in Europe and North America. Simplicity of line, adventurous abstract form, and flawlessness of execution were trademarks of Nordic products. For those used to seeing repetitious, derivative traditional styles, these designs were an exciting revelation.

The designers at Georg Jensen did not merely keep up with changing times, they were at the forefront of innovation. Collectors of modernist jewelry seek out their work, particularly that of Henning Koppel and the Ditzels. But they were not alone. Others, too, produced sleek and bold pieces that were the epitome of what came to be known as Scandinavian Modern. Although Jensen is the most well known in the United States, several other Danish manufacturers are just as well known in their own country, including A. Michelsen, A. Dragsted, and Hans Hansen. Hans Hansen's silversmithy has manufactured the work of several highly regarded modernist designers, among them Bent Gabrielsen, Karl Gustav Hansen (b. 1914), the founder's son, and Anni (b. 1926) and Bent (b. 1924) Knudsen. The company's mark is their name in script, or a superimposed double H. Individual designers are not identified on their pieces.

A company about which little is known, N.E. From, must have exported a quantity of jewelry to the United States, as modernist sterling pieces bearing the name turn up frequently on the secon-

dary market. Another familiar name, one that confuses dealers and collectors, is Jørgen Jensen, found on modern-looking Danish pewter pieces. The mark is a script signature, totally different from but often mistaken for Georg Jensen, who appears to be no relation, although Georg had a son Jørgen who worked for the company (both Jørgen and Jensen are common names in Denmark).

Midcentury Finnish silversmiths and jewelers were particularly adept at creating new, fresh concepts in both form and function. Although the Finns' silversmithing legacy goes back to the fourteenth century, Finnish jewelry design is a twentieth-century development. Shortage of silver during World War II led to the making of jewelry instead of larger objects from what little reclaimed metal was available. But forms remained traditional. A nationalistic revival of the ancient Iron Age epic, the Kalevala (c. 500-1100 A.D.), during the war yielded replicas of ornaments from ancient tombs, made and sold in a display of national solidarity. The company that made it, Kalevala Koru, went on to become one of the largest jewelry manufacturers in the country. After the war, the search for new ideas began in earnest, and it was then that talented artists began to emerge. But the Finns were slow to accept avant-garde design. Not until 1958, at an exhibtion at the Galerie Artek in Helsinki, were the works of a quartet of designers—Bertel Gardberg, Elis Kauppi, Börje Rajalin, and Eero Rislakki—finally appreciated. By this time, Finnish manufacturers and designers were beginning to venture into promoting Finnish products abroad. The Milan Triennale in 1951 was the first postwar international exhibition to display Finnish (as well as Danish and Swedish) decorative art. The modern designs found a receptive audience in Europe and the United States soon after. Triennales of 1954, 1957, and 1960 were likewise successful. Finland began exporting in volume. The Finnish hallmark for local manufacture is a crown inside a heart; they use assay marks, date letters, and manufacturers' marks in a manner similar to the British.

In Norway, the biggest and most well-known silver manufacturer is David-Andersen, established in 1876. Long famous for its hollowware and flatware enameled in jewel-toned *basse-taille*, the company also makes jewelry, although this is a more recent endeavor. Although David-Andersen is still in business and has been quite prolific, relatively little information about its production, especially its jewelry, has been recorded. Two of its recognized designers are Harry Sørby and Bjørn Sigurd Østern, both of whom designed objects and jewelry. Sørby worked for the company from 1946-1970; Østern began in 1961 (end date unknown). The latter often used the *basse-taille* enamel the company is famous for in his smoothly cast and sleekly simple modern pendants and brooches. Both designers also set stones such as amazonite and rhodochrosite in their pieces. Hallmarks usually include their initials after abbreviation "INV," meaning designer.

Basse-taille enamel is also predominant in the David-Andersen sterling vermeil production pieces most often seen today: long slender curved leaves made into suites of necklace, bracelet, brooch, and earrings, die-stamped figural pins in a wide assortment of animals, birds, and fish, and Viking revival scenes. The leaves are usually enameled in a single color, while the other pieces may be in subtle shades of a single color or multicolored. Circa 1950s abstract modern plaques and 1960s lost-wax cast biomorphic shapes are also enameled sterling vermeil. Marks are varied, sometimes with "David-Andersen" written out, sometimes "D-A" with the company logo, a pair of scales.

Sigurd Persson (b. 1914) is the most well-known Swedish metalsmith and jeweler of the midtwentieth century. His widely lauded designs are noted for their strength, simplicity, and innovative concepts. Several of his pieces are pictured in Oppi Untracht's book, cited below. Very little other Swedish jewelry has crossed the Atlantic, judging by its scarcity in the secondary market. There is also a paucity of information about it in print. The few pieces that turn up are as well-made and designed as other Scandinavian work.

Midcentury Scandinavian jewelry, other than Georg Jensen's, has only recently gained the attention of a small coterie of collectors. It is still obtainable and affordable. Until there is greater documentation and dissemination of information to the general collecting public, the market will undoubtedly remain small, and prices relatively low, despite the high quality of craftsmanship and design.

References: John Haycraft, *Finnish Jewelry and Silverware,* Otava, 1962 (out of print); Graham Hughes, *Modern Jewelry, An International Survey, 1890-1967,* Crown Publishers, 1968 (out of print); Jørgen E. R. Møller, *Georg Jensen The Danish Silversmith,* Georg Jensen & Wendel A/S, 1984; Tuula Poutasuo, ed., Michael Wynne-Ellis, English text, *Finnish Silver,* Teema Oy, 1989; Jacob Thage, *Danske Smykker/Danish Jewelry* (Danish and English text), Komma & Clausen, 1990; Tardy, *International Hallmarks on Silver* (translated from the French), Paris, 1985; Oppi Untracht, *Jewelry Concepts and Technology,* Doubleday, 1985 (contains many photographs of work by Scandinavian designers, especially Finns); exhibition catalogs: Martin Eidelberg, ed., *Design 1935-1965, What Modern Was,* Harry N. Abrams, 1991 (multinational, multimedia); *Georg Jensen Silversmithy, 77 Artists, 75 Years,* Renwick Gallery, Smithsonian Institution Press, 1980; *The Lunning Prize* (multilingual text), Nationalmuseet, Stockholm, 1986; *Scan-*dinavian Modern Design 1880-1980, Cooper-Hewitt Museum, 1983 (an all-media exhibition, including some jewelry).

Museums: The Georg Jensen Museum and The Museum of Decorative Art, Copenhagen, Denmark; Museum of Applied Arts, Helsinki, Finland; The Nationalmuseum, Stockholm, Sweden; The Oslo Museum of Applied Art, Oslo, Norway.

Reproduction Alert: Die-stamped copies of Georg Jensen and Jensen-inspired designs were made by Coro, Danecraft, and other American companies in the 1940s, but they are usually marked and easily identified because they are not backed with a flat plate as Jensen pieces are. Trade names like "Vikingcraft" and "Norseland" were used to evoke association with Scandinavian design. Pieces marked "Georg Jensen U.S.A." were first made and marketed by Frederik Lunning during World War II when sterling was in short supply in Denmark and trade routes were cut off. Lunning turned to American manufacturers and produced the Jensen line on his own, hence the U.S.A. mark. Values tend to be lower for these items. According to Jensen dealer Caryl Unger of Imagination Unltd in Miami, Fla., an Israeli firm was making knockoffs of Jensen jewelry about 10 years ago, taking molds of original pieces and leaving the marks intact. When purchasing on the secondary market, it's advisable to know your Jensen or know your sources.

Advisors: Caryl Unger (Georg Jensen), Ginger Moro.

Bracelet
  Bangle
    Sterling, c. 1950, a cast, shaped penannular bangle, tapering in, then out to rounded triangular terminals, sgd "Hans Hansen" in script, "925S Denmark," 2-1/4" inside

Bangle Bracelet, 830 silver, citrine, date letter for 1965, a tapered flat band with a front spring-hook closure, a lg collet-set circ-cut citrine mounted at the end of a sq rod, extending perpendicular to the bangle, Finnish hmk (crown within a heart), Turku assay mark, "813H" (830 silver), date letter M7, mfr's mark (anvil) for Kupitaan Kulta, designed by Elis Kauppi, 2-1/4" inside dia, 1-1/4" at front, top to bottom, $200. *Author's collection.*

Bracelet, link, 830 silver, lapis lazuli, c. 1920, alternating linked double foliate and flowerhead motifs bezel-set with oval and circ lapis cabs, sgd "Georg Jensen 830" # 3, 7" × ½", $1,045 (A). *Photo courtesy of Grogan & Co., Boston (9/22/93).*

dia, ½" w at front, 1-⅛" w at each end
.... 250
Sterling, rutilated quartz, c. 1970, a lg oval bezel-set quartz cab with a lg hook on each side attaching a narrow shaped bangle, designed by Torun Bülow-Hübe, sgd "Georg Jensen," # 203, center 1-¼" w × 1-¾", bangle 2-⅜" inside dia, approx ⅜" w
.... 303 (A)
Link
765 yg, pearls, c. 1925, repoussé design of open rect foliate links with circ flowerhead centers, each set with a half-pearl, alternating with five-petal flowerhead links, sgd "GI" for Georg Jensen, 6-½" × ⅝"
.... 1,870 (A)
Sterling, c. 1940, links of quatrefoils with raised bead and foliate centers, alternating with double domed ovals flanked by fluted fan shapes with raised bead centers, flat backings, joined with oval jump rings, rev imp "GJ" for Georg Jensen (a J enclosing a G within a square, mark in use 1933-1944) "sterling Denmark," # 27, v-spring and box clasp, safety clasp, 7-⅜" w × 1-⅛"
.... 1,100
Sterling, c. 1950, seven linked stylized leaf shapes, cast flat, circ disks, each with a slightly raised center ridge, tapering to form a link through a perforation in the base of the next disk, hook closure, rev imp "Hans Hansen" in script, "925S Denmark," 7-½" × ⅞" 175
Sterling vermeil, enamel, c. 1950, six linked sq plaques, white *basse-taille* enamel over stamped designs depicting two mythological scenes, a lady feeding a sea serpent alternating with a warrior on horseback with shield and sword, rev mkd with mfr's logo (scales), "D-A" for David-Andersen, "925S Norway sterling," 7-½" × 1" 225
Sterling, date letter for 1957, nine open-backed box-shaped links with concave tops, joined with triangular wire loops, hook closure, imp on outer side of two links with Swedish hmks, mfr's initials "HE," date letter G9, "sterling Sweden," designer name and hmk (illegible), 8" × ½" 75

Brooch/Pendant
Sterling vermeil, enamel, pearl, c. 1960, cast openwork convex circ abstract design resembling webbing, irregular depressions filled with bright green and green with orange translucent enamel, pearl center, rev mkd with mfr's logo (scales), "D-A" for David-Andersen (Norway), "925S sterling," designer name (illegible), 2-¼" w × 2-⅛"
.... 175
Brooch/Pin
830 silver, amber, c. 1900, Danish *skønvirke,* hammered & repoussé lozenge shape with scrolled border, a lg oval opaque butterscotch amber cab in the center, bezel-set within a rope-twist frame, rev mkd "830S," C-catch, tube hinge, 1-⅝" × 1-½" 145
830 silver, moonstone, c. 1920, a flowerhead set with a circ moonstone within a naturalistic quatrefoil in the center of an open oval frame with reeded vine, floral and foliate motifs, sgd "Georg Jensen," 1-½" w × 1-¼"
.... 330 (A)
Sterling, c. 1930, rect foliate and bead frame enclosing a dove, mkd "Georg Jensen" within dotted oval, "925 sterling Denmark," "GI" within dotted oval, (1930s mark), # 209, tube hinge, 1-¾" w × 1-¼" 225
Sterling, c. 1930, rect raised foliate and bead motif, die-stamped, flat backing, mkd "925 sterling Denmark GI," (1930s mark), # 215, 1-⅛" w × ¾" 145
Sterling, c. 1930, depicting a dove within a foliate wreath, die-stamped, flat backing, mkd "925 sterling Denmark GI," (1930s Georg Jensen mark), # 165, 1-⅝" dia
.... 275 (A)
Sterling, c. 1930, open oval curv grapes and leaves motif, stamped relief, flat backing, mkd "925 sterling Denmark GI," (1930s mark), # 177B, safety catch, tube hinge, 2" w × 1-¼" 375
Sterling, c. 1935, pierced oval plaque with raised asymmetrical fruit and foliate design, mkd "925 sterling Denmark," flanked by "GI & Georg Jensen," in dotted ovals, # 65, safety catch, 1-⅞" × 1-½" 475
Sterling, c. 1940, stamped relief depicting a bird eating berries suspended from a foliate branch, rev imp "GJ" for Georg Jensen, (a J

Brooches/Pins, silver, gemstones, Danish *skønvirke*, c. 1900-10: L, a mushroom-shaped pierced repoussé plaque with lg curv foliate motifs flanking an oval green chalcedony cab bezel-set within a quatrefoil surmounting an orchid motif, suspending a pendent drop from an elongated link, rev mkd "830S BH" for Bernhard Hertz, Denmark, C-catch, tube hinge, extended pinstem, 3-1/4" tl × 2-1/2", $525, *Gail Gerretsen collection;* C, three flowerheads with chrysoprase centers within a repoussé mushroom-shaped plaque, surmounting an oval cab amethyst in the center of a curv vine design, a hammered flat link suspending a pear-shaped drop of similar design, one flowerhead with chrysoprase center surmounted by an oval cab amethyst, C-catch, tube hinge, extended pin stem, mkd "830S, Wm F.," 3-3/4" tl × 2-1/4", $750, *Kirsten Olson collection;* R, a pierced, lobed, scrolled foliate motif repoussé plaque, an oval green chalcedony cab bezel-set in the center within a grad raised beaded border, suspending a foliate pendent drop from elongated oval links, terminating in an oval green chalcedony cab, rev mkd with dragonfly hmk, "826S B H" for Bernhard Hertz, Denmark, C-catch, tube hinge, extended pinstem, 3-1/8" tl × 2-1/4", $450, *Gail Gerretsen collection.*

Brooch/Pin, sterling, Georg Jensen, c. 1930, lg oval die-stamped relief of a winged deer with foliate bg, mkd "925 sterling Denmark GJ" (1930s mark), # 81, trombone catch, tube hinge, 2-1/8" w × 1-7/8", $650. *Private collection.*

enclosing a G within a square, mark in use 1933-1944), "sterling Denmark," # 175, 1-3/4" dia **275**

Sterling, c. 1940, a circ domed disk with a die-stamped relief center of four fan-shaped leaves forming a square around two sm raised beads, encircled by curved overlapping dumbbell shapes, rev imp "GJ" for Georg Jensen, (a J enclosing a G within a square, mark in use 1933-1944), "sterling Denmark," # 16, trombone catch, 1-3/4" dia **300**

Sterling, c. 1940, a cutout stylized sparrow in flight, engr details, designed by Arno Malinowski, sgd "Georg Jensen," # 320, 1-3/4" w × 1" . . . . **385 (A)**

Sterling, c. 1940, circ fish design, die-stamped, flat backing, rev imp "GJ" (a J enclosing a G within a square, mark in use 1933-1944), "sterling Denmark," # 10, trombone catch, tube hinge, 1-1/8" dia **185**

Sterling, post-1945 mark, open ridged oval with asymmetrical fruit and foliate design, mkd "Georg Jensen" in dotted oval, "sterling Denmark," # 18, 1-3/4" × 1-3/8" **325**

Brooches/Pins, sterling, Georg Jensen, designed by Arno Malinowski, post-1945 marks: L, a heron in flight within an open oval, cast, imp "Georg Jensen" in a dotted oval, "sterling Denmark," # 238, 1-³/₄" w × 1-¹/₄", $225; R, a stylized sparrow with spread wings in the center of two foliate branches within an open heart-shaped frame, designed by Arno Malinowski, imp "Georg Jensen" in a dotted oval, "sterling Denmark," # 239, 1-³/₄" w × 1-⁵/₈", $250, *Private collection.*

Sterling, post-1945 mark, dove within branches and berries (1915 design), brushed surface, mkd "Georg Jensen, sterling Denmark," # 134, 1-¹/₈" dia **225**

Sterling, post-1945 mark, stamped relief depicting a bird eating berries suspended from a foliate branch, flat backing, imp "Georg Jensen" in a dotted oval, "sterling Denmark," # 53, 2-¹/₄" dia **400**

Sterling, post-1945 mark, four tulips radiating from a raised bead center, petals continuing to four loops forming an open oval quatrefoil in die-stamped relief, flat backing, rev imp "Georg Jensen," in a dotted oval, "sterling Denmark," # 305, 1-³/₄" w × 1-¹/₈" **165**

Sterling, post-1945 mark, an articulated drop of a bunch of grapes suspended from a cluster of grape leaves, designed by Harald Nielsen, imp "Georg Jensen" in a dotted oval, "sterling Denmark," # 217, 1-¹/₂" w × 2-¹/₂" tl . . . . **385 (A)**

Sterling, post-1945 mark, two opposed scrolled and cusped leaves, raised bead center, surmounting a circ leaf shape, imp "Georg Jensen" in a dotted oval, "sterling Denmark," # 107, 1-³/₈" w × 1" **185**

Sterling, post-1945 mark, die-stamped relief in the shape of a pansy, flat backing, rev imp "Georg Jensen" in a dotted oval, "sterling Denmark," # 113, 1-¹/₂" w × 1-⁵/₈" **130**

Sterling, post-1945 mark, open oval formed by two curv floral and foliate motifs flanking a raised bead center, stamped relief, imp "Georg Jensen" in a dotted oval, "sterling Denmark," # 77, 1-³/₈" w × 1" **180**

Sterling, post-1945 mark, open oval with feather and flower motif, cast, imp "Georg Jensen" in a dotted oval, "sterling Denmark," # 227, ⁷/₈" w × 1-¹/₈" **135**

Sterling, moonstones, post-1945 mark, a central oval dome flanked by two flowerheads within an open scrolled and beaded lobed rect wire frame bezel-set with a circ moonstone at top and bottom, sgd "Georg Jensen, sterling Denmark" # 236B, approx 1-³/₄" × 1-¹/₂" . . . . **385 (A)**

Sterling, carnelian, c. 1950, a tapered cylindrical bar capped by a spherical bead at the wide end, surmounted by a crescent-shaped plaque with a cutout bombé curve on one side, bezel-set with a circ carnelian cab and perforated with sm holes, a length of forged wire following the curve and terminating at the narrow end of the bar, sgd "F. Hingelberg Denmark," 3-³/₄" w × 2-¹/₂" **650**

Sterling, enamel, c. 1950, rect shape made up of lengths of flat wire joined at right angles forming lg and sm rect boxes, some filled with enamel in shades of dk, medium, or lt green, rev mkd "Georg Jensen (post 1945 mark) sterling Denmark" # 331B, 1-³/₄" w × ⁷/₈" **400**

Sterling vermeil, enamel, c. 1950, rect plaque with abstract *basse-taille* and cloisonné enamel design in shades of blue-green, lt green, yellow, and lt and dk brown, rev mkd with mfr's logo (scales), "D-A" for David-Andersen "925S Norway sterling," 2-³/₈" w × 1-³/₈" **175**

Sterling, enamel, c. 1950, rounded shield-shaped plaque with a stylized clown face, features in red, green, white and black

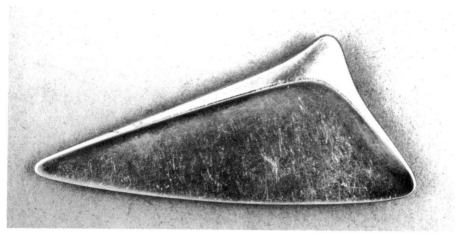

Brooch/Pin, sterling, post-1945 mark, a shaped rounded-corner triangle with a raised tapering edge on two sides, cast, imp "Georg Jensen" in a dotted oval, "sterling Denmark," # 324, 2-⅛" w × 1-⅛", $285. *Private collection.*

enamel on polished ster ground, sgd "Erik Magnussen, Denmark, 925S," 1-½" w × 1-¾" . . . . **385 (A)**

Sterling, enamel, c. 1950, biomorphic convex freeform with a blue enamel center conforming to brooch outline, flat backing, sgd "Georg Jensen" in dotted oval, "HK" for Henning Koppel, designer, "sterling Denmark," # 306, 2" w × 1-¾" . . . . . . **330 (A)**

Sterling, rhodochrosite, c. 1950, open asymmetrical abstract scrolled design with a rhodochrosite cab bezel-set in the center, rev mkd with mfr's logo (scales), "D-A" for David-Andersen, "Inv. H.S." for designer Harry Sørby, "925S Norway sterling," 2" w × 1-¼" **125**

Sterling vermeil, enamel, c. 1950, stamped in the shape of an egret with spread wings, *basse-taille* enameled in shades of lt to medium blue, mkd "David-Andersen Norway sterling 925S," 2-¼" w × 2" **95**

Sterling vermeil, enamel, c. 1950, David-Andersen, a rounded-corner rect plaque with a primitive figures design, white *basse-taille* enameled ground with design in shades of ochre-yellow, rev mkd "rock-carving from Norway 1000-500 B.C., D-A Norway sterling 925S Nora G," 2-½" w × 1-¼" **75**

Sterling, enamel, c. 1960, lozenge-shaped plaque elongated at one end with an oval black enamel eye and matte black enamel center, rev sgd "Poul Warmind Denmark," 2-½" w × 1-¾" **225**

Cuff Links

Sterling, 14k rose and yg, post-1945 mark, each link a ster disk with a central bicolor gold nautilus motif, mounted on a curved bar joining a hinged oval back, sgd "Georg Jensen, sterling Denmark" # 52, disks ¾" dia, pr . . . . **316 (A)**

Earrings/Earclips

Sterling, post-1945 mark, plain, slightly concave disks with recessed edges, screwbacks, mkd "Georg Jensen, sterling Denmark," ⅝" dia, pr **75**

Sterling, post-1945 mark, stylized scallop shells with engr fluting, screwbacks, mkd "Georg Jensen, sterling Denmark," ⅞" × ¾", pr **85**

Sterling, post-1945 mark, stamped relief double tulips, screwbacks, mkd "Georg Jensen, sterling Denmark," ⅞" × ¾", pr **125**

Sterling vermeil, enamel, c. 1950, rounded corner rectangles with white, teal, green, gray-blue, and yellow *basse-taille* and cloisonné enameled abstract design, mkd "D-A" for David-Andersen, "Norway sterling 925S," ½" w × ⅞", pr **50**

Pendant

Pewter, glass, c. 1950, a horizontal rounded rect plaque with a foil-backed navette-shaped amber-colored glass cab center, a sq rod mounted perpendicular to the plaque, terminating in a pendant ring, rev imp "pewter, Jørgen Jensen [script], Denmark" # 230 A, 1-⅝" w × 2-¼" **25**

Sterling, amethyst, c. 1950, 10 concentric faceted wire rings with a circ amethyst cab bezel-set in the center, held in place by a elongated tapered bar extending upward to form pendant bail, mkd "Georg Jensen," # 143, designed by Bent Gabrielsen, 2-¼" dia, 3-½" tl . . . . **825 (A)**

Pendant and Chain

18k yg, pearl, c. 1910, scroll form design with a button pearl in the center, suspended from

Necklace, link, 830 silver, lapis lazuli, Georg Jensen, c. 1920, alternating linked double foliate and flowerhead motifs bezel-set with oval and circ lapis cabs, mkd "GI, 830," 16-1/2" tl × 1/2", $2,090 (A). *Photo courtesy of Grogan & Co., Boston (9/22/93).*

an open link chain, 16-1/2" tl, maker's mark for Georg Jensen . . . . **660 (A)**
Patinated bronze, c. 1965, a highly stylized owl, with textured vertical bars in open stepped rows, terminating in an articulated section of bars and open-centered beads, suspended from a cable link chain, 26" tl, rev mkd "P. Sarpaneva" for Pentti Sarpaneva (1925-1978, Finland), pendant 1-3/4" w × 4-3/8" tl **95**
Sterling, amber, c.1960, a circ amber cab set within a ring of silver suspended from a sq rod, curved rod and link chain, mkd "N. E.

Pendant and Chain, 830 silver, labradorite, Georg Jensen, c. 1920, a lg oval labradorite cab bezel-set within a flower calyx and beaded frame, suspended from a circ stylized foliate surmount and an oval and circ link chain, 24" tl, pendant sgd "Georg Jensen 830," # 54, approx 1" w × 2" tl, $2,200 (A). *Photo courtesy of Grogan & Co., Boston (9/22/93).*

Pendant, sterling, amazonite, c. 1965, a cast, pierced stylized Viking ship design, an oval amazonite cab in the center of concentric annular ovals, a flattened and tapered outer penannular ring, and crossbars, the vertical bar tapering out at the top to form the pendant bail, rev imp "D-A, 925S," mfr's mark for David-Andersen (scales), "Norway sterling, Inv. B.S.Ø." for Bjørn Sigurd Østern, designer, 1-3/4" w × 2", $125. *Author's collection.*

From, sterling, Denmark 925S," 19" tl, pendant 1-1/4" dia **150**
Ring
830 silver, lapis lazuli, c. 1920, a vertical row of three lapis beads in the center of a rect foliate mount with lobed and beaded corners, sgd "Georg Jensen," 1/2" w × 3/4" . . . . **385 (A)**
Sterling, amethyst, c.1960, a stylized flowerhead design, a high-domed bezel-set amethyst cab, encircled by seven concave

Ring, sterling, lapis lazuli, date letter for 1974, six round lapis beads mounted three to a side on grad horizontal posts appl to a sq ring with rounded corners, mkd on outside surfaces with mfr's mk for Auran Kultaseppä, Finnish hmk (crown within a heart), "925," Turku assay mark, date letter V7, "PP" for designer Pekka Piekäinen, "Finland," ³⁄₄" w × ⁷⁄₈", $250. _Author's collection._

open hemispheres with oxidized interiors, mounted on a plain wide shank, mkd "925," mfr's mark (anvil) for Kupitaan Kulta, Finland, design attributed to Elis Kauppi, 1" dia, approx ring size 6 . . . . **125**

Sterling, rock crystal, c. 1950, a lg circ-cut rock crystal bezel-set in the center of three stepped concentric annular flat wire bands, mounted on a plain wide shank, outside of shank mkd "From 925S" (Denmark), ⁷⁄₈" dia, approx ring size 6 . . . . **75**

Sterling, date letter for 1966, four open-ended cubes, forming a sq box, with top surface showing two solid and two open sides, mounted at 45° on a narrow shank, Swedish hmks, mfr's initials GK, date letter Q9, ⁵⁄₈" × ⁵⁄₈" × ¹⁄₄" deep, approx ring size 6-¹⁄₂ **60**

Suite: Bangle Bracelet and Ring

Sterling, rose quartz, c. 1960, shaped bangle with front spring-hook clasp attached to a concave hammered central disk with appl beadwork and a bezel-set rose quartz cab, mkd "N. E. From, Denmark," 2-¹⁄₄" inside dia, central disk 1-¹⁄₂" dia, matching ring, top ⁷⁄₈" dia **180**

Suite: Brooch/Pin, Necklace, and Earrings, sterling vermeil, enamel, c. 1950, waterlilies and lilypads motif, necklace composed of six linked lilypads enameled in kelly green _basse-taille_ enamel, alternating with seven sm white enameled flowers, continuing to a gp ster cable-link chain, spring-ring clasp, matching clipback earrings and larger brooch with C-catch, each a single lilypad and flower, all pcs mkd with mfr's mark (scales) and "D-A" for David-Andersen, "925S Norway sterling," designer's mark (W in a circle), necklace 15-³⁄₄" tl × ⁷⁄₈", earrings ³⁄₄" w × ⁷⁄₈", brooch 2" w × 1-³⁄₄", suite, $250. _Terrance O'Halloran collection._

Georg Jensen, sterling, c. 1940-50: L, Suite: Brooch/Pin and Cuff Links, brooch a sm rect with chamfered corners, swan motif in die-stamped relief, flat backing, rev imp with a J enclosing a G within a square, mark in use 1933-1944, "sterling Denmark" # 213B, trombone catch, tube hinge, 1" w × 5/8", pr of cuff links each with two rounded rect plaques joined with a hinged curved bar, 1933-44 mark, # 55, 5/8" w × 1/2", suite, $400; TR, Earrings, grape leaf motif, screwbacks, mkd "Georg Jensen Silversmiths Ltd., sterling Denmark," # 50A, 1/2" w × 1", pr, $175; BR, Brooch/Pin, post-1945 mark, an articulated drop depicting a bunch of grapes suspended from two grapeleaves, designed by Harald Nielsen, imp "Georg Jensen" in a dotted oval, "sterling Denmark," # 217A, 1-1/8" w × 1-3/4", $250, *Private collection.*

Suite: Bracelet, Brooch/Pin, and Earrings
    Sterling vermeil, enamel, c. 1950, link bracelet
    of paired red *basse-taille* enameled leaves,
    v-spring and box clasp, rev mkd with mfr's
    logo (scales), "D-A" for David-Andersen,
    "925S Norway sterling," designer's mark W
    in a circle, spring ring clasp, 7" × 1/2", match-
    ing pr of clip earrings, 1/2" w × 5/8", brooch a
    single leaf, C-catch, 2-5/8" × 5/8", suite
    . . . . **175**
Suite: Brooch/Pin and Earrings
    Sterling, post-1945 mark, twin dolphin motifs,
    designed by Arno Malinowski, mkd "Georg
    Jensen, sterling Denmark," brooch 1-5/8" ×
    7/8", earrings 5/8" w × 1-1/8" **215**
    Sterling, c. 1930, die-stamped oval pierced
    curv floral and foliate design, flat backing,
    mkd "Georg Jensen" within dotted oval,
    "925 sterling Denmark," "GI" within dotted

oval, (1930s mark), # 13, 2" w × 1-1/2",
    matching earrings with post-1945 mark,
    clipbacks, imp "Georg Jensen" in a dotted
    oval, "sterling Denmark," # 84, 1/2" w × 1/8",
    suite **600**
Suite: Brooches/Pins and Earrings
    Sterling, c. 1930, each piece depicting a dove
    within a foliate wreath, flat backing, mkd
    "Georg Jensen," lg brooch 1-3/4" dia, sm
    brooch and screwback earrings 7/8" dia
    . . . . **495 (A)**
Suite: Pendant and Earrings
    830 silver, tiger's eye, date letter for 1971, ab-
    stract design, disk-shaped stone in upper left,
    seated figure within a C, hmkd, mfr's mark
    for Kultateollisuus KY, Turku, Finland, pen-
    dant 1-1/4" w × 2-3/4" tl, earwires 1-7/8" tl × 5/8"
    w, suite **200**

APPENDIX

TWENTIETH CENTURY AMERICAN COSTUME JEWELRY
MANUFACTURERS/DESIGNERS

Accessocraft, c.1930-present
Art, c.1950-?
McClelland Barclay, c.1930-1940
Beau (sterling), 1947-present
Bergère, 1947-c.1965
Les Bernard, 1962-present
Bogoff, 1946-?
Boucher, 1937-1971
Nadja Buckley, c.1940-1950
Calvaire, 1935-c.1960
Hattie Carnegie, 1918-1970
Castlecliff, c.1945-1970
Alice Caviness, c.1940-1965
Chanel, 1914-1939, 1954-present (most
    early, some later pieces unmarked)
Ciner, 1892-present
Cini (sterling), 1922-c.1970, 1993-present
Coro, 1919-1979
    Corocraft (some sterling), 1933-1979
    Vendome, 1944-1979
    (Coro, Inc. Canada, to present)
Sarah Coventry, 1949-present
Danecraft (sterling), 1939-present
Wm de Lillo, 1967-1978
DeMario, 1945-1960
R. (Ralph) De Rosa, 1935-1970
Di Nicola, c.1960-1970
Christian Dior, 1955-present
Eisenberg Original, c.1935-1945 (sterling
    1941-1945)
    E. (script mark), 1942-1945
    EISENBERG / ICE (block letters), 1945-
    1958
    Eisenberg Ice (script), 1970-present (no
    mark 1958-1970)
Eugene, c.1950-1960
Florenza, 1956-c.1965
Givenchy, 1952-present
Leo Glass, 1943-1957

Stanley Hagler, 1953-present
Miriam Haskell, 1924-present (most pieces
    not mkd. 1924-c.1948)
Hobé, 1903-present
Hollycraft, 1948-c.1965
Joseff of Hollywood, 1938-present
Kramer, 1943-c.1980
Krementz, 1884-present
KJL/Kenneth Jay Lane, 1963-present
Laguna, 1944-?
Lang (sterling), 1946-?
Ledo, 1949-60 / Polcini, 1960-present
    (DBA Leading Jewelry 1911-1949)
Lisner, 1938-present
Marvella, 1911-present (1982-present, a
    division of Trifari, now a subsidiary of
    Crystal Brands Jewelry Group)
Mazer Bros., 1926-1951
Jomaz/Joseph Mazer, 1946-80
Monet, 1937-present (1989-present, a sub-
    sidiary of Crystal Brands Jewelry
    Group)
Napier, 1922-present
Original by Robert, 1942-1979 (Fash-
    ioncraft Jewelry Co.)
Panetta, 1945-present
Pell, 1941-present
Pennino, 1930-1961
Rebajes, 1932-1960
Regency, 1948-present
Réja, 1940-1954
Renoir, 1946-1964/ Matisse, 1952-1964/
    Sauteur, 1958-1963
Nettie Rosenstein, c.1935-1975
Sandor, c.1940-1970
Schiaparelli, 1931-1960 (most pre-1949
    unmarked)
Schreiner N.Y., 1944-1977
Staret, c.1941-1947

Yves St. Laurent, 1966-present
Tortolani, c.1960-1975
Trifari, 1924-present (1975-1988: subsidiary of Hallmark, 1988-present: Crystal Brands)

TKF (Trifari, Krussman & Fishel) 1924-38
Vogue, 1915-c.1975
Weiss, 1942-1971
Whiting-Davis, 1876-present

OTHER AMERICAN MANUFACTURERS:
DATES OF OPERATION UNKNOWN

The following list contains names of manufacturers which you may find on jewelry. No further information concerning dates of operation or location is available.

BSK
D'Orlan
HAR
Ramé
Reinad
Van S Authentics
Warner
Wiesner

References: Joann Dubbs Ball, *Costume Jewelers, The Golden Age of Design*, Schiffer Publishing, 1990; Deanna Farnetti Cera, ed., *Jewels of Fantasy*, Harry N. Abrams, 1992; Maryanne Dolan, *Collecting Rhinestone & Colored Jewelry*, 3rd ed., Books Americana, 1993; Barbara Ellman, *The World of Fashion Jewelry,* Aunt Louise Imports (published by the author), 1986; Harrice Simons Miller, *Costume Jewelry Identification and Price Guide*, 2nd ed., Avon Books, 1994; Dorothy Rainwater, *American Jewelry Manufacturers*, Schiffer Publishing, 1988.

GLOSSARY

(Boldface words are defined elsewhere in the Glossary)

À Jour—an open setting which allows light to pass through.

Alloy—mixture of two or more metals.

Alpaca—yellowish-silver metal composed of copper, zinc, nickel, and 2% silver.

Amber—fossilized resin from extinct trees; lightweight and warm to the touch; can be translucent to opaque, imitated in plastics.

Amphora—ancient Greco-Roman two-handled jar or urn with a tapered base, popular mid-Victorian revivalist motif.

Annular—ring-shaped.

Articulated—having segments connected by flexible joints or jump rings.

Assay—analytical test to determine metal content.

Attributed—not **signed,** but considered likely to have been made by a particular person or firm.

Aurora Borealis—an iridescent coating applied to faceted glass beads or rhinestones, developed by Swarovski Corp. in 1955.

Baguette—narrow rectangular faceted stone.

Bail—pendant loop **finding** through which a chain or cord passes.

Bakelite—trade name for thermosetting phenol formaldehyde resin, the first entirely synthesized plastic, patented in 1909 by Leo H. Baekeland.

Balustered—swelled section.

Bandeau—ornamental band worn around the head.

Bangle—rigid circular or oval bracelet.

Baroque—in reference to pearls, having an irregular shape.

Base Metal—a nonprecious metal.

Basse-Taille—enamelling technique: translucent or transparent **enamel** applied over a decorated (engraved, chased, stamped) metal **groundplate,** similar to **champlevé,** but with a pattern or design visible through the enamel. When the groundplate has an engine-turned pattern, it is known as guilloché enamel.

Baton—narrow, stick-shaped.

Bead Set—setting in which stones are held in place by beads raised from the surrounding metal.

Beauty Pin—small brooch/pin, also called handy pin, lace pin.

Bezel—metal band with top edges burnished over to hold a stone in place.

Biomorphic—amoebalike, organic shape.

Blackamoor—depiction of an African man or woman.

Bog Oak—fossilized peat, found mainly in nineteenth-century Irish jewelry.

Bola—string tie of braided leather with a decorative slide and ornamental tips, usually silver.

Bombé—having swelled or bulging sides.

Bookchain—chain necklace with folded-over square or rectangular links, often engraved or stamped, popular mid to late nineteenth century.

Bouquet Pin—brooch with bowed-out center and a spike mounted on reverse, designed to hold a small flower bouquet.

Box Clasp—fastener for bracelets and necklaces, a slotted box into which a **v-spring** catch is inserted.

Brilliant—circular gemstone cut, especially for diamonds, with fifty-eight facets. The modern brilliant is a mathematically designed cut developed by Marcel Tolkowsky in 1919, also called the American or ideal cut (see also **old mine cut** and **old european cut**).

Briolette—gemstone cut, a three-dimensional faceted pear-shaped drop with small triangular facets.

Buff Top—gemstone cut, low cabochon top with a faceted pavilion (portion below the **girdle**).

Bulla—ancient neck ornament made of two hinged convex plates, usually circular, suspended from a cord or chain; revived in the mid-Victorian period.

Bypass—a bracelet or ring with open ends crossing parallel in front.

Cable-Link Chain—oval links formed of round wire.

Cabochon—an unfaceted, domed cut for stones or glass, with a flat base (a double cabochon has a convex base).

Calibré—small faceted gemstones, usually four-sided, cut to fit a setting, often in rows or groups.

Cameo—a design carved in relief, often (but not always) from stone or shell with layers of more than one color forming background and foreground; a cameo carved within a concave depression of a gemstone, with the highest part of the design level with the edge of the stone, is called a *chevet* or *chevée*, curvette or cuvette.

Cameo Habillé—depicting the head or bust of a person wearing jewelry set with diamonds or other gemstones (literally, "dressed up").

Cannetille—a type of metal ornamentation using thin wires to make a filigree pattern, often in tightly coiled spirals or rosettes, used in the early nineteenth century.

Carat—unit of weight for gemstones.

Carbuncle—cabochon cut almandine garnet.

Carré Set—a circular stone set within a square, flat-topped setting.

Catch—closure **Finding** for brooch/pin that holds the pointed end of the pinstem. A *C-catch* is a simple C-shaped hook. See also safety catch.

C-catch

Celluloid—trade name for semisynthetic pyroxylin-camphor thermoplastic, invented by John Wesley Hyatt in 1869.

Celtic Knot—also known as *entrelac*, an intricate interlaced motif common in ancient Celtic ornamentation, revived by the British Arts and Crafts movement.

Chamfered—having cut or beveled corners.

Champlevé—enamelling technique: opaque or translucent **enamel** fills recesses or depressions that are stamped, etched, or engraved into a metal **groundplate.**

Channel Setting—a row of same-size square or rectangular stones fitted into a continuous metal channel or trough that holds the stones in place.

Chasing—technique of decorating metal from the front, usually by hand, without removing any metal, forming a relief design by raising and indenting.

Chatelaine—ornamental clip worn at the waist from which implements or trinkets are suspended by chains.

Choker—short necklace that fits snugly around the neck.

Circa—within 10 years before or after a given date; literally, "around."

Clip—a type of brooch with a hinged double-pronged mechanism for attaching to

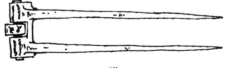

Clip

clothing, sometimes called a fur clip to differentiate from a **dress clip.**

Clipback—earring **finding** for unpierced ear with a hinged clip for clamping earring to ear.

Cloisonné—enamelling technique: a design or pattern is formed of wire soldered on to a **groundplate,** creating cells or cloisons that are filled with **enamel.**

Collet—a short tubular band or collar of metal enclosing a stone.

Compass Points—(North, South, East, West) to indicate position of stones or design elements: top, bottom, and two sides.

Costume Jewelry—made from nonprecious materials, especially since c. 1920.

Crystal—(see lead crystal, rock crystal)

Cuff Bracelet—a **penannular** rigid bracelet, usually wide with rounded ends.

Cultured Pearl—pearl produced by insertion of an irritant (small glass or mother-of-pearl bead) into a mollusk (a natural pearl is formed around a foreign particle that occurs in nature).

Curb Chain—twisted oval links forming a chain that lies flat.

Cushion Cut—rounded-corner, square-faceted stone.

Cusped—coming to a point; pointed end.

Cut-Down Collet or Setting—a method of setting gemstones in a collet or bezel with vertical ribs of metal holding the stone in place.

Cut Steel—small faceted steel studs, riveted closely together on a metal backing.

Demi-parure—two or three matched pieces of jewelry; a partial **suite.**

Déposé—registered (trademark or design), mark found on French items, and on items imported into or exported from France.

Die Stamping—method of mass production, a relief design produced from a flat sheet of metal with a two-part steel die forming the pattern under pressure.

Dog Collar—a wide ornamental choker necklace worn tightly around the neck.

Double Clip Brooch—a pair of clips joined with a detachable pinback mechansim.

Dress Clip—an ornament attached to clothing by means of a hinged clip with a flat back and small prongs on the underside.

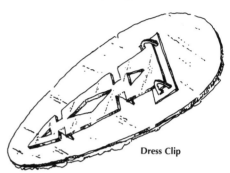

Dress Clip

Ebonite—(see Vulcanite).

Electroplating—electrolytic process of depositing a layer of metal over another metal.

Embossing—technique for creating a raised decoration on metal using punches and hammers on the reverse side; also known as **repoussé** work.

Emerald Cut—square or rectangular cut stone, square table, chamfered corners, step-cut sides.

Enamel—powdered pigmented glass fired onto a metal **groundplate** using a variety of techniques (see basse-taille, champlevé, cloisonné, Limoges, plique à Jour, taille d'épargne).

Engraving—creating a design or pattern on a metal surface with incised lines. It differs from **chasing** in that metal is removed with a tool called a graver, or a burin.

En Tremblant—a brooch or other ornament with a motif (often a flower) mounted on a wire or spring, that trembles with movement of the wearer.

Equilateral—all sides of equal length.

Estate Jewelry—previously owned; not necessarily antique, period, or vintage.

Essence D'orient (Pearl Essence)—coating used on glass or plastic to imitate pearls, made of fish scales.

Etching—process for creating a design on metal or glass using acids.

Etruscan Jewelry—ancient ornaments from central Italy (western Tuscany), usually of gold, reproduced in the nineteenth century.

Extended Pinstem—extends beyond the body of a brooch/pin; found on some nineteenth-century brooches with **C-catch** closures, used to secure the brooch by weaving back into the clothing.

Facet—plane-cut polished surface of a stone.

Faience—earthenware decorated with opaque colored glazes.

Faux—French: false or fake.

Faux Pearl—artificial or imitation pearl; a glass or plastic bead coated with *essence d'orient (pearl essence).*

Fibula—ancient style brooch, used to close garments, resembles a modern safety pin.

Filigree—metal decoration made of thin twisted wires.

Findings—the functional metal parts used in construction and wearing of jewelry: catches, clasps, clips, jump rings, spring rings, etc.

Fine Jewelry—made from **precious metal** and gemstones.

Flanged Hinge—brooch finding, a hinge (called a *joint* by jewelers) with projecting metal sides and a hingepin or internal posts to which pinstem is attached.

Flanged Hinge

Florentine Finish—textured, brushed surface created by engraving cross-hatched lines on metal.

Fob—a decorative ornament or seal suspended from a watch chain; a ribbon or metal band attached to a pocket watch.

Foiled Back—a thin sheet of metal backing a gemstone or paste, sometimes colored to enhance the appearance of the stone, used in closed-back settings; also, in reference to a **rhinestone** with painted-on metallic backing, as on a mirror, that can be set in an open setting.

Foliate, Foliated—any leaf or plant design.

French Jet—black glass.

Gadrooned, Gadrooning—decorative oval beading on a border or edge.

Gallery—a strip of metal with a pierced decorative pattern, used for settings.

Garter Motif—(Fr, *jarretière*) a strap with a buckle design.

German Silver—an alloy of nickel, copper, and zinc, also known as **nickel silver.**

Gilding—process by which a base metal is plated or coated with a thin layer of gold (called gilt metal).

Girandole—brooch or earring in which three pear-shaped drops are suspended from a center stone or motif.

Girdle—widest part of a stone, part usually grasped by the setting. In a **brilliant**-cut stone, the widest circumference where the crown (upper) and pavilion (lower) facets meet.

Gold Filled—a mechanical process using heat and pressure to join a layer of gold to a base metal; by law in the United States, the gold layer must be at least 1/20th of the total weight of metal.

Gold Plated—layer of gold of less than 1/20th of total weight, can be applied by any process, but often **electroplated.**

Gold Wash—a very thin coating of gold over base metal.

Graduated—arranged in ascending or descending order of size.

Granulation—ancient decorative technique of applying minute spheres of gold to a gold surface without visible solder, used in **Etruscan Jewelry,** a technique approximated by Victorian goldsmiths.

Groundplate—the metal base onto which enamels are fired; the method of decoration determines the name given to the technique (see enamel).

Gypsy Setting—a one-piece mount for a stone that is recessed into the metal, with the table (top facet) of the stone level with the metal surface; also called star setting when lines radiating from the stone are engraved in the metal.

Hair Jewelry—ornaments made of, decorated with, or containing human hair.

Hallmark—the mark(s) stamped on gold, silver, or platinum indicating fineness or karat; depending on country of origin, hallmarks can also include symbols for place of assay, date of assay (in the form of a letter or letter and number), maker's mark, and importation mark if applicable.

Handy Pin—(see beauty pin)

Intaglio—an engraved stone, opposite of a cameo, with a recessed design carved into the surface, common for signet rings and fob seals.

Invisible Setting—(*serti invisible*) a type of **channel setting** using specially cut square or rectangular colored gemstones (usually rubies or sapphires) that are notched to slide onto metal tracks and fit closely together in rows. No metal is visible from the front of the piece.

Jabot Pin—a pin with ornamental elements at both ends of a long pinstem that is invisible when worn at the collar (formerly worn on a jabot, a front ruffle on a shirt).

Japonaiserie—decorative motifs in the Japanese style.

Jarretière—(see garter motif)

Jet—a type of fossilized coal, used primarily for mourning jewelry in the nineteenth century.

Jump Ring—a round or oval **finding** for linking or attaching other parts, made of round wire.

Karat—one twenty-fourth of the total weight in a gold alloy, a measure of fineness (24 karats is pure gold).

Lace Pin—(see beauty pin)

Lavalier, Lavaliere, Lavallière—a neckchain suspending a gemstone or small pendant set with gemstones, popularly worn at the turn of the century.

Lead Crystal—colorless glass with a high percentage of lead added to enhance clarity and brilliance; resembles and is confused with **rock crystal.**

Limoges—enamelling technique: layers of finely ground colored **enamel** fired after each application, resulting in an image resembling a painting (without metal borders).

Locket—a two-part pendant or brooch with a hinge and cover, often containing a photo or lock of hair.

Longchain—a very long metal chain worn around the neck with the end attached to the bodice, forming a swag, often terminating in a **swivel** hook for suspending a watch or pendant.

Loupe—magnifying lens used by jewelers.

Lozenge—an equilateral, four-sided shape with corners at compass points; diamond-shaped (as in playing cards).

Lucite—Du Pont trade name for acrylic thermoplastic.

Mabé Pearl—a pearl with a flat bottom and rounded top.

Marcasite—iron pyrite with a silver luster, cut in small-faceted circular stones and often **pavé**-set in silver or other white metal.

Marquise Cut—a gemstone cut that is oval or elliptical with pointed ends; the shape is also called **navette.**

Marriage—a piece put together with two or more components from different sources; not as originally made.

Millegrain—a method of setting stones using a tool around the top edge of a **collet** to form minute beads of metal that hold the stone in place; also a decorative technique.

Mosaic—an object or jewel decorated with many small pieces of multicolored stone (called **pietra dura**) or glass (**tesserae**) inlaid flush into stone or glass to form a design, motif, or scene; often called micromosaic when the tessarae are very small.

Mother-of-Pearl—the iridescent inside lining of mollusks.

Mourning Jewelry—jewelry worn in memory of a deceased loved one, most often black, sometimes containing the hair of the deceased.

Naja—a horseshoe- or crescent-shaped silver pendant used in Navajo jewelry, often suspended from a **squash blossom** necklace, sometimes set with turquoise or coral.

Navette—(see marquise).

Neck Ring—a rigid, circular metal ornament worn around the neck.

Négligée—a pendant or necklace with two drops suspended unevenly.

Nickel Silver—(see german silver).

Niello—a metallic form of enamelling using a powdered mixture of silver, copper, and lead that is fused by heat into an engraved design in silver, or occasionally gold, creating a grayish-black contrast with the metal ground.

Old European Cut—brilliant cut for diamonds with a circular **girdle**, otherwise similar to **old mine cut.** The circular shape, developed c. 1860, was more easily produced with the invention of the power-driven bruting, or girdling, machine in 1891.

Old Mine Cut—old-style brilliant cut for diamonds, a cushion-shaped stone with a small **table,** high crown (top facets), and an open or large culet (the small flat facet at the base, virtually eliminated in a modern **brilliant**).

Open-Back Setting—setting that permits light to pass through a transparent or translucent stone (same as **à jour**).

Painted Enamel—enamel applied in liquid form and baked on at lower temperatures than required for firing powdered enamels; used on costume jewelry.

Parure—a complete set or **suite** of jewelry; matching pieces of three or more.

Paste—high-lead content glass that has been cut (faceted) to resemble a gemstone; also known as *strass.*

Patina—color change on the surface of metal, especially silver, copper, bronze, resulting from age and exposure to the atmosphere; a type of oxidation. Patina may be artificially applied using acids and/or liver of sulphur. Color is usually green, brown, or red on copper, brass, or bronze (called patinated), greyish-black on silver.

Pavé—method of setting many small stones very close together (literally, paved).

Pebble Jewelry—Scottish jewelry set with multicolored agates in silver or gold.

Penannular—open-ended ring shape.

Pendant (noun)—decorative element suspended from a necklace, chain, or cord.

Pendent (adjective)—hanging, suspended.

Pietra Dura—literally, "hard stone," a type of **mosaic** made of small pieces of stone that form a picture or scenic design, also known as Florentine mosaic.

Pinchbeck—alloy of copper and zinc, developed in 1720, used to imitate gold.

Piqué—the inlaying of gold or silver in patterns, usually into tortoiseshell.

Plique à Jour—enamelling process in which the **groundplate** is removed after firing. The end result resembles stained glass, the translucent enamel framed in metal.

Pot Metal—base white metal, tin and lead alloy, greyish in color, used in early twentieth-century costume jewelry.

Precious Metal—gold, platinum, or silver.

Prong Set—stones held in place by metal claws or prongs.

Provenance—the origin and history of a piece, including its former owners.

Quatrefoil—decorative element having four lobes.

Regard Ring—finger ring set with a variety of gemstones, the first letters of which spell "regard" (ruby, emerald, garnet, amethyst, ruby, diamond).

Relief—raised or standing out from the background.

Repoussé—a technique of hand-raising a design in metal, working with punches and hammer from the back of the piece.

Rhinestone—faceted colorless or colored glass, cut like a gemstone and usually with a fused metallic backing for light reflection (like silvering a mirror), used in costume jewelry.

Rivière—a necklace of **graduated** gemstones of the same kind (e.g., diamonds), each stone singly set and linked in a row without further decoration.

Rock Crystal—colorless quartz, occurring in nature as a six-sided (hexagonal) crystal.

Rolled Gold—a thin layer of gold fused over base metal.

Rondel, Rondelle—thin disk-shaped metal ornament, sometimes set with rhinestones, strung on a necklace between beads.

Rose-Cut—circular gemstone cut with triangular facets coming to a point at the top and a flat back.

Rose Gold—gold of a pinkish color (alloyed with copper).

Safety Chain—a chain attached to a piece of jewelry that prevents loss if clasp opens.

Safety Catch—brooch **finding** with a swiveling closure that prevents it from unintentionally opening.

St. Andrew's Cross—an X-shaped motif, Scottish national emblem.

Sautoir—very long necklace or strand of beads or pearls, often terminating in a tassel or pendant.

Scarab—Egyptian symbol of immortality, the *Scarabaeus* beetle, usually carved or molded in stone, clay, or glass.

Safety Catch

Scarf Pin, Stickpin, Tie Pin—decorative pin with a long pinstem and ornamental top, inserted into a scarf, cravat, or necktie.

Screwback—earring **finding** for unpierced ear with a screw mechanism for securing earring to ear.

Seed Pearl—a natural, cultured, or artificial pearl weighing less than one quarter of a grain.

Shank—the part of a ring that encircles the finger.

Shepherd's Hook, Fishhook, Kidney Wire—earring **findings** for pierced ears, primarily for pendent or drop earrings.

Shoulder—area of a finger ring where the **shank** and **bezel** or head (top) meet.

Signed—marked (engraved, stamped, impressed) with the name, initials, logo, or trademark of the maker, designer, or manufacturer.

Slave Bracelet—a link bracelet of glass and silver or brass, often enameled; also a bangle worn on the upper arm, popular in the 1920s.

Slide—movable decorative and functional element of a **longchain** that adjusts its opening. When longchains went out of fashion, collections of slides were strung together and made into bracelets.

Solder—metal alloy used to fuse pieces of metal together with the use of heat; hard solder requires high temperatures, is made of an alloy of the same metal being joined, and creates the strongest bond. Soft or lead solder fuses at a lower temperature; it is considered unsuitable (and damaging) for use on **precious metal.**

Solitaire—the mounting of a single stone, usually in a ring.

Spacer—decorative or functional element used to separate pearls or beads.

Spectacle Setting—a ring of metal around the girdle of a stone, like an eyeglass frame, often used for setting diamonds or other transparent stones linked at intervals on a chain.

Spring Ring—type of clasp **finding** used with a **Jump Ring** to connect one part to another.

Squash Blossom Necklace—Navajo, hollow silver beads interspersed with floral motifs resembling squash blossoms, sometimes set with turquoise, with a central *naja* pendant.

Sterling Silver—an **Alloy** that is 925 parts pure silver and 75 parts copper.

Stomacher—large, usually triangular, bodice ornament, also known as a corsage ornament or devant de corsage.

Strass—(see **Paste**).

Stud or Post and Clutch or Nut—earring **findings** for pierced ears.

Suite—several pieces of jewelry similarly designed to be worn together (see also **parure**).

Surmount—the decorative top part of an earring.

Swivel—a type of **finding,** a hook with a hinged spring closure joined to a swiveling base with a jump ring for attaching watches, **pendants,** or other items to chains.

Synthetic Gemstone—laboratory-created gemstone that is chemically, physically, and optically identical to its natural counterpart; in contrast to an imitation, which is only similar in appearance (e.g., purple glass imitating amethyst).

Table—the top facet or surface of a cut stone.

Taille D'épargne—enamelling technique: engraved design partially filled with opaque enamel, usually black (also known as *black enamel tracery*).

Tessarae—tiny colored glass pieces used in **mosaic** (sometimes called roman mosaic).

Tiffany Setting—a four- or six-prong elevated setting for a solitaire stone introduced by Tiffany & Co. in 1886.

Torsade—multistrand twisted short necklace, usually beads or pearls; cabled or twisted cord.

Trace Chain—chain with oval links of equal size.

Trefoil—decorative element having three lobes.

Trombone Catch—a two-part sliding tubular closure finding for brooches.

Tube Hinge—brooch **finding,** an elongated tubular hinge (called a joint by jewelers) to which the pinstem is attached.

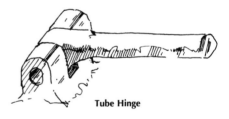

Tube Hinge

V-spring—part of a **box clasp** closure **finding** in which a wedge-shaped element fits into a metal box.

Vasiform—vase-shaped.

Vermeil—gold-plated silver, silver gilt.

Volute—spiral, snail-shell-shaped.

Vulcanite—vulcanized (hardened) rubber, used for mourning jewelry in the nineteenth century, also known as **ebonite.**

Watch Pin—a small brooch/pin with a hook at the base of the reverse with its open end up, for suspending a small watch; worn on women's bodices at the turn of the century.

White Gold—alloy of gold with nickel, palladium, or platinum (various formulas) that produces a silver-white color, approximating platinum, for which it is substituted.

Wirework—twisted wire decoration applied to metal ground.

Yellow Gold—alloy of gold with silver and copper; most common color of gold.

Ziggurat—stepped triangle or pyramid shape.

INDEX

(Page numbers in boldface indicate photos)